The fiscal crisis faced by the American federal government represents the end of a fiscal regime that began with the financing of World War II. In this volume, an interdisciplinary group of scholars explores the history of American taxation and public finance since 1941 in an attempt to understand the political, social, and economic forces that have shaped the current regime. Specifically, they examine the historical context of earlier tax programs and national crises; explore the ways post-1941 governments used taxation to finance war, social security, and economic stability; analyze the politics of post-1941 tax reform; and apply history to a consideration of the dynamics that are likely to characterize future tax regimes. The contributors recognize both the power of democratic forces outside the federal government and the influence of government institutions—the presidency, congressional leadership, professional experts within government, political partisanship, and constitutional strictures.

WOODROW WILSON CENTER SERIES

Funding the modern American state, 1941–1995

Other books in the series

Funding the modern American state, 1941–1995

The rise and fall of the era of easy finance

Edited by W. ELLIOT BROWNLEE

WOODROW WILSON CENTER PRESS

AND

CAMBRIDGE
UNIVERSITY PRESS

Published by the Woodrow Wilson Center Press and
the Press Syndicate of the University of Cambridge
The Pitt Building, Trumpington Street, Cambridge CB2 1RP
40 West 20th Street, New York, NY 10011-4211, USA
10 Stamford Road, Oakleigh, Melbourne 3166, Australia

© Woodrow Wilson International Center for Scholars 1996

First published 1996

Printed in the United States of America

Library of Congress Cataloging-in-Publication Data
Funding the modern American state, 1941–1995: the rise and fall of
the era of easy finance / edited by W. Elliot Brownlee.
p.   cm.—(Woodrow Wilson Center series)
Includes index.
ISBN 0-521-55240-0 (hardback)
1. Taxation—United States—History.   2. Finance, Public—United
States—History.   I. Brownlee, W. Elliot, 1941–   . II. Series.
HJ2381.F86   1996
336.2'00973—dc20   95-32770
                                       CIP

A catalog record for this book is available from the British Library.

ISBN 0-521-55240-0 hardback

WOODROW WILSON INTERNATIONAL CENTER FOR SCHOLARS

The Center is the living memorial of the United States of America to the nation's twenty-eighth president, Woodrow Wilson. Congress established the Woodrow Wilson Center in 1968 as an international institute for advanced study, "symbolizing and strengthening the fruitful relationship between the world of learning and the world of public affairs." The Center opened in 1970 under its own board of trustees, which includes citizens appointed by the president of the United States, federal government officials who serve ex officio, and an additional representative named by the president from within the federal government.

In all its activities the Woodrow Wilson Center is a nonprofit, nonpartisan organization, supported financially by annual appropriations from Congress and by the contributions of foundations, corporations, and individuals.

WOODROW WILSON CENTER PRESS

The Woodrow Wilson Center Press publishes books written in substantial part at the Center or otherwise prepared under its sponsorship by fellows, guest scholars, staff members, and other program participants. Conclusions or opinions expressed in Center publications and programs are those of the authors and speakers and do not necessarily reflect the views of the Center staff, fellows, trustees, advisory groups, or any individuals or organizations that provide financial support to the Center.

Woodrow Wilson Center Press
Editorial Offices
370 L'Enfant Promenade, S.W., Suite 704
Washington, D.C. 20024–2518
telephone: (202) 287–3000, ext. 218

Contents

Foreword

This volume is a result of a series of Woodrow Wilson Center workshops on the growth of the U.S. national government in the twentieth century. A collaborative scholarly effort, it is intended not only to advance our knowledge of the dynamics of the developments discussed but also to contribute new insights that may be helpful to all those who are involved in today's momentous debates over the size of the federal government and the proper scope of its duties. Here, the starting point for inquiry was the question of how the rise of the modern state had been paid for and justified within the context of the special constraints and opportunities inherent in the nation's traditions of political belief, an interest that led to a broad reexamination of the history of both the thought and the practice of American public finance. All who participated in the project hope that the chapters in this book will contribute something useful for marking out the current state of scholarly understanding on the basic issues involved.

A word of thanks is due not only to those whose work appears in the book but also to those former Woodrow Wilson Center fellows and advisers who helped set up the terms of reference for the workshop and get it under way: Hugh Heclo, Paul Offner, James T. Patterson, Thomas J. Reese, Stanford G. Ross, and Herbert Stein. A special acknowledgment is in order for W. Elliot Brownlee, the volume's editor and principal contributor. His patient leadership was the key throughout.

Michael J. Lacey, *Director*
Division of United States Studies
Woodrow Wilson International Center for Scholars

I

Methodological and historical introduction

1

Reflections on the history of taxation

W. ELLIOT BROWNLEE

THE PURPOSES AND ORGANIZATION OF THE BOOK

Toward the end of World War I, the Austrian sociologist Rudolf Goldscheid proposed a "fiscal sociology" as a new way to study the public
budget. He wanted to analyze the budget as "the skeleton of the state
stripped of all misleading ideologies."[1] Goldscheid explained, "Nowhere
[is] the entirety of any given order of society and economy . . . reflected
as clearly [as] in the public household, . . . the State cannot be very different from its financial system, [and] every single private household is
intimately connected with the State household."[2] Another Austrian
scholar, the economist Joseph Schumpeter, seconded Goldscheid's proposal and stressed that the fiscal sociology should have a historical basis.
In 1918 Schumpeter declared, "The spirit of a people, its cultural level,
its social structure, the deeds its policy may prepare—all this and more
is written in its fiscal history, stripped of all phrases. He who knows
how to listen to its message here discerns the thunder of world history
more clearly than anywhere else."[3]

The severe wartime fiscal crisis and attendant debates over the meaning of the modern state within the ruins of the Austro-Hungarian Empire

[1] Rudolf Goldscheid, *Staatssozialismus oder Staatskapitalismus* (Vienna, 1917), quoted by
Joseph A. Schumpeter, *Die Krise des Steuerstaats*, Zeitfragen aus dem Gebiete der Soziologie (Graz and Leipzig, 1918), translated as "The Crisis of the Tax State," in Alan
T. Peacock et al., *International Economic Papers: Translations Prepared for the International Economic Association*, no. 4 (London: Macmillan, 1954), 5–38.
[2] Rudolf Goldscheid, "Staat, offentlicher Haushalt und Gesellschaft, Wesen und Aufgaben
der Finanzwissenschaften vom Standpunkte der Soziologie," in *Handbuch der Finanzwis-
senschaft*, ed. W. Gerloff and F. Meisel, vol. 1 (Tubingen, 1925), translated as "A Sociological Approach to Problems of Public Finance," in Richard A. Musgrave and Alan T.
Peacock, *Classics in the Theory of Public Finance* (London: Macmillan, 1962), 202–13.
[3] Schumpeter, "The Crisis of the Tax State," 7.

stimulated Goldscheid and Schumpeter to develop their interest in fiscal sociology, fiscal history, and the history of taxation. In a similar fashion, the fiscal anguish of the American federal government during the 1980s and 1990s, and the related political discourse over the proper role and scope of the national government, prompted some American scholars to reconsider the history of public finance and especially of taxation. From a variety of political perspectives, they have begun to revive tax history in order to understand contemporary policy options and enrich our knowledge of American society and government.

Professional historians, however, have rarely shared Schumpeter's enthusiasm for the potential for understanding a society through the history of its taxation. They have contributed relatively little to broad-gauged scholarship on the history of American taxation, even during the recent revival of interest in tax history within other disciplines. To be sure, historians have provided some monographic research on specific aspects and periods of tax development and have occasionally commented on tax policy while writing on broader or related topics. But historians have left the overarching interpretations to policy scientists, primarily political scientists and economists.[4]

The primary goal of the contributors to this volume, and of the Woodrow Wilson International Center project that produced it, is to advance historical scholarship on taxation and public finance. They explore, in particular, the history of the nation's current fiscal condition. Their secondary goal is to contribute to public discourse on the fiscal condition of the nation. The scholars who contributed to this volume are convinced that a firmer historical understanding will help policymakers understand the possibilities and constraints that must be taken into account in evaluating, and possibly reforming, the ways in which the nation pays for government.

---

[4]No historian has ever authored an extended, comprehensive history of taxation in America. The most comprehensive book-length histories of American taxation have been written by Roy G. Blakey and Gladys C. Blakey (economists), Randolph E. Paul (an attorney), Sidney Ratner (an economist), Edwin R. A. Seligman (an economist), Frank W. Taussig (an economist), and John Witte (a political scientist). See Blakey and Blakey, *The Federal Income Tax* (London: Longmans, Green, 1940); Paul, *Taxation in the United States* (Boston: Little, Brown, 1954); Ratner, *American Taxation: Its History as a Social Force in Democracy* (New York: Norton, 1942) and *Taxation and Democracy in America* (New York: Wiley, 1967); Seligman, *The Income Tax: A Study of the History, Theory, and Practice of Income Taxation at Home and Abroad* (New York: Macmillan Company, 1914); Taussig, *The Tariff History of the United States* (New York: G. P. Putnam's Sons, 1931); and Witte, *The Politics and Development of the Federal Income Tax* (Madison: University of Wisconsin, 1985).

These two goals led the contributors to focus on the history of American taxation and public finance since 1941. Fresh scholarship is needed on virtually all aspects of the history of American public finance, but historical research on the period since World War II has been even thinner than for other periods. Moreover, historical understanding of the period is especially important for policy communities—and not just because of the chronological proximity of this period to the present. In this volume, the authors propose that the prolonged fiscal crisis faced by the federal government during the 1980s and 1990s represents the end of a fiscal regime—a system of taxation with its own characteristic tax bases, rate structures, and social intentions.

This tax regime began with World War II, which ushered in a long period of "easy finance" that has now run its course. Understanding the period and the regime as a whole, in the historical setting, is the only way to understand the political, social, and economic forces that have created, shaped, and undermined the regime. As Schumpeter put the matter, using public finance for an "investigation of society" achieves its "full fruitfulness" at the transitions between tax regimes—"at those turning points . . . during which existing forms begin to die off and to change into something new, and which always involve a crisis of the old fiscal methods."[5]

In this book, the authors divide their treatment of the post-1941 tax regime into four parts. In the first part, W. Elliot Brownlee, a historian, provides methodological and historical introductions to the analysis of the post-1941 tax regime. The present chapter is a discussion of the current state of the art in the scholarship that treats the central intellectual issues associated with the history of American taxation and public finance. The second chapter is a synoptic overview of the history of the national experience with tax politics and policy, in the broad context of economic, social, political, and intellectual change, from the Civil War through the present impasse in dealing with the nation's budget.

The second part contains three essays that explore the relations between the development of post-1941 taxation and the most important objectives of the federal government's tax policies—financing war, financing social security, and promoting economic stability. Carolyn C. Jones, a legal scholar, discusses the financing of World War II, the introduction of mass-based income taxation, and the creation of the tax-

[5]Schumpeter, "The Crisis of the Tax State," 7.

paying culture that served as the foundation for the mass-based tax. The historian Edward D. Berkowitz examines the development of the financing of social security from its origins in 1935, through its dramatic expansion in 1950–52, to the current fiscal crisis. And Herbert Stein, an economist, brings up to date his classic survey of the history of fiscal policy, *The Fiscal Revolution in America.*[6]

The third part analyzes the politics of post-1941 tax reform. Julian E. Zelizer, a historian, focuses on congressional politics. He takes the career of Wilbur Mills, a longtime chairman of the House Ways and Means Committee (1958–75), and considers Mills's relations to the development of a fiscal community that shaped tax policy in the late 1950s and early 1960s. The political scientist Cathie Jo Martin focuses on the presidency. She explores the dynamic relations among business interests, the ideas of the business community, and presidential leadership since World War II.

Finally, in the fourth part, C. Eugene Steuerle, an economist, applies history to the forecasting of what is likely to be the next tax regime. He does this in the context of looking closely at how economic change can both constrain and create opportunities for new tax regimes. He concludes that the nation must now do more than adopt new taxes or shift to a new tax regime in order to fund programs to meet new social needs. Economic as well as political conditions dictate, he argues, that the United States adopt a new fiscal regime—one that pays for changing priorities, at least in part, by reallocation of resources from existing government programs.

A DEMOCRATIC-INSTITUTIONALIST APPROACH TO TAX HISTORY

The authors of this volume approach the history of taxation and public finance since 1941 from diverse disciplinary perspectives. They have paid close attention to the important efforts scholars representing a wide variety of disciplines have made, within recent years, to consider the role of the government as a historical agent. But, in this volume, the contributors do not offer a comprehensive accounting of the influential literatures that have sought to "bring the state back" into social history. They do, however, want to associate their interpretations explicitly with

[6]Herbert Stein, *The Fiscal Revolution in America* (Chicago: University of Chicago Press, 1969).

the leading insights of a group of scholars who have recently explored the historical relationship between the rise of the modern state and the growth of knowledge in the United States and Great Britain.[7]

These scholars have gone far to establish that a process of "social learning" was at the core of the flowering of the "new liberalism" between the mid-nineteenth and mid-twentieth centuries and that the state was a central force in providing that process coherence in both direction and form. More generally, they have provided new ways to study the complex relationship between the intellectual and the institutional changes that have been bound up in the growth of modern government. The contributors to the present volume find that social learning has also characterized the process of creating the nation's tax regimes and that policy entrepreneurs and experts within the state often played a decisive role in shaping those regimes as they struggled to understand the relationship between fiscal policy, the growth of government, and underlying social and economic transformations.

At the same time that the contributors to the present volume have applied and elaborated this emerging social-learning approach to understanding the growth of government, they have come to describe the approach or interpretation as "democratic-institutionalist." In its "democratic" dimension, this approach recognizes the power of democratic forces outside the federal government. These were forces that contributed to the progressively redistributional cast of the twentieth-century tax regimes. At the same time, the interpretation stresses the potency of ideas—concepts of progressive equity, often expressed as the criterion of the "ability to pay" taxes—as independent creative forces. Such ideas shaped and gave intention to democratic pressures.

The "institutionalist" dimension of this interpretation accents the influence of governmental institutions—particularly the presidency and congressional leadership, professional experts within government, political partisanship, and constitutional structures—in shaping policy. Within these governmental institutions, ideas figure centrally in a process

---

[7]These scholars include, among others, the historians Robert M. Collins, Robert D. Cuff, Mary O. Furner, Michael J. Lacey, and Barry Supple, the economist William J. Barber, and the political scientists Hugh Heclo and Jack L. Walker. For representative samples of the work of many of them, see Mary O. Furner and Barry E. Supple, eds., *The State and Economic Knowledge: The American and British Experience* (Cambridge: Cambridge University Press and Woodrow Wilson International Center for Scholars, 1990), and Michael J. Lacey and Mary O. Furner, eds., *The State and Social Investigation in Britain and the United States* (Cambridge: Cambridge University Press and Woodrow Wilson Center Press, 1993).

of social learning. Presidents and other policy entrepreneurs, including professional experts, use ideas to understand social change. Moreover, they use those ideas to form alliances beyond the formal boundaries of government. Building those alliances, in turn, often encouraged the development of supportive policy communities.

The scholars who have contributed to this volume expand in two major ways on earlier democratic-institutionalist frameworks by drawing on insights from the field of economic history. First, they attempt to identify how economic development shaped the organizational options available to the creators of the "new liberalism." In the context of fiscal history, they try to assess how, over time, the changing condition of economic structure and organization has defined the institutional possibilities for the expression of democratic ideals. Brownlee notes, for example, that the federal government could not embody the ideal of "ability to pay" in its modern form until economic development created the administrative underpinnings for an effective income tax.

Second, the contributors set intellectual and institutional change in the context of historical contingency. Most important, the contributors suggest that national emergencies have heavily influenced the specific ways in which ideas, democratic forces, and policy networks have interacted to shape important changes in fiscal institutions. In each of the great wars, presidents employed tax reforms and invoked democratic ideals of taxation to mobilize the economy, to win support for their administrations, and to unify the nation behind the war effort. The contributors also stress the idea that the transitions between regimes have been heavily "path-dependent." In other words, the tax regime imposed in each emergency changed economic, political, and intellectual conditions in ways that made it difficult or even impossible for the federal government to return to the tax regime in force before the emergency. Consequently, today's tax system has a stratified quality. Each layer of tax institutions, almost like a layer of the earth's crust, represents the legacy of an earlier epoch, or fiscal regime.

RECENT TAX HISTORY AND
THE ANALYSIS OF SOCIETY AND STATE

The democratic-institutionalist history of taxation must take into account the very substantial, recent accomplishments of the political scientists and economists who have explored the history of the federal tax system. Their central focus has been to identify "who or whose interest it is that sets the machine of the state in motion and speaks through it," to use Schumpeter's words yet again. This section surveys the scholarly results—a rich menu of descriptions of the configuration of the "interests" shaping tax policy.[8]

All of the new approaches to understanding the role of social interests in tax politics have dramatically challenged the "progressive history" that was presented fifty years ago by Sidney Ratner. He was the last scholar to attempt a comprehensive narrative of the development of American taxation. He argued that the main theme of public finance and tax history during the twentieth century was the struggle between "the thrust for social justice and the counter-thrust for private gain." When Ratner wrote in 1942, the New Deal seemed to have established a clear victory for social justice by having secured progressive income taxation, which Ratner described "as preeminently fit for achieving and preserving the economic objectives of a democracy." Moreover, the adoption and expansion of income taxation seemed to have established the basis for a well-funded welfare state and for a federal government that could defend the cause of democracy around the world. Ratner's interpretation of tax history was an expression of a larger progressive view of the history of government and reform during the twentieth century. That view regarded the reform movements that culminated in the New Deal as an expression of social democracy and as a stream of victories for working people—farmers and factory laborers.[9]

Scholars who have challenged a progressive interpretation of social interests include, among others, neoconservative economists searching for historical foundations for the "Reagan revolution" and its attack on government. They have presented the history of taxation in the twentieth century not as a victory for principled forces of democracy but as the capture of "the state" by narrowly self-interested groups of "tax-eaters." Central to this neoconservative story is the adoption and expansion of the federal income tax. Ben Baack and Edward J. Ray, for example, argue that "the current issue of the impact of special-interest politics on our national well-being has its roots in the bias of discretionary federal spending at the turn of the century" and in the enactment of the federal

[8]Schumpeter, "The Crisis of the Tax State," 19 n. 19.
[9]Ratner's book was first published in 1942. It appeared in an expanded edition in 1967 with a new title but with no shift in interpretation. See Ratner, *American Taxation* and *Taxation and Democracy in America*. See pp. 14 and 16 in both editions.

income tax. They claim that the passage of the Sixteenth Amendment, which authorized income taxation, was intended to raise significant new revenues and was a result of special-interest groups that sought greatly expanded funding for military and social-welfare programs.[10]

The progressive and the neoconservative interpretations, despite their differences in identifying and characterizing socially powerful interests, agree that the federal income tax significantly enhanced the power of the state. But most recent scholars of tax history, when tracking group and class influence, have started from quite a different point. Rather than seeking to explain the rise of Leviathan, they have emphasized and tried to understand the weaknesses of the modern federal government.

In so doing, the analysts of weakness have begun by noting three seemingly interrelated fiscal characteristics. The first is the relatively small size of American tax revenues as a percentage of national income, when compared with tax revenues in Western Europe over much of the post-1941 tax regime. The second is the Swiss-cheese quality of the progressive income tax, a characteristic created by preferential rates of taxation and by "tax expenditures," or special benefits written into the income-tax code as deductions, exemptions, and credits. The third characteristic is the federal government's huge budget deficit, which has grown in absolute size in most years since 1980 and which many scholars regard as a reflection of both a weak tax-state and a national civic decline. These scholars who explore government weakness have developed two very different approaches, but both are based on the analysis of what Schumpeter called "social power relations."[11]

[10]Ben Baack and Edward J. Ray, "The Political Economy of the Origin and Development of the Federal Income Tax," in *Emergence of the Modern Political Economy: Research in Economic History, Supplement 4*, ed. Robert Higgs (Greenwich, Conn.: JAI Press, 1985), 121–38. The most comprehensive statement of a neoconservative interpretation of the expansion of the public sector is that of the economist and economic historian Robert Higgs. See his *Crisis and Leviathan: Critical Episodes in the Growth of American Government* (New York: Oxford University Press, 1987), esp. 112–13, 121. Higgs sees the passage of the Sixteenth Amendment as the "entering wedge" for interest groups to use government to redistribute income in their direction, largely by funding their favorite programs.

[11]Much might be gained in the future from closely argued, comparative histories of the international development of institutions of public finance in the twentieth century. For a useful beginning that includes the United States, see Sven Steinmo, *Taxation and Democracy: Swedish, British, and American Approaches to Financing the Modern State* (New Haven: Yale University Press, 1993). Steinmo has little to say about the role of historical contingency and path dependency, but he suggests important points of comparison among three tax systems. See also Carolyn Webber and Aaron Wildavsky, *A History of Taxation and Expenditure in the Western World* (New York: Simon and Schuster, 1986). The best international histories are for Europe, from the early modern

The first group of scholars who focus on governmental weakness works within a tradition of fiscal analysis that extends back to Rudolf Goldscheid. His central conclusion was that class politics had impoverished the state. Capitalism, he argued, had emasculated feudal states, which he believed had often possessed great fiscal power because of the assets they owned. "The rising bourgeois classes," Goldscheid argued, "wanted a poor State, a State depending for its revenue on their good graces, because these classes knew their own power to depend upon what the State did or did not have money for." So the capitalists "conquered the State by stripping it of its wealth" and created a "tax State," which was dependent on taxing or begging from the very capitalists who controlled the state. The capitalists used its fiscal instruments only when necessary "to enhance their profits and extend their power."[12]

Modern "capitalist-state" theorists follow the general thrust of Goldscheid's interpretation as they attempt to understand what they regard as the failures of the American state to adopt significant programs of social investment or progressive wealth redistribution. These scholars, primarily political scientists, accent the influence of the leadership of the corporate sector and argue that in the nineteenth century, the corporations and the wealthiest Americans captured federal fiscal policy in order to protect the investment system and protect their own power. As a consequence, these scholars argue, the federal government abstained from redistributing wealth in a progressive fashion and, instead, reinforced the process of capital accumulation. In so doing, the capitalist-state theorists argue, American government had to wrestle with an inherent dilemma created by democratic political institutions: How could it respond to democratic pressures for redistributional equity while maximizing capital accumulation?

Prominent among the capitalist-state theorists who focus on fiscal history is the historian and political scientist Robert Stanley, who describes the early history of the federal income tax, from the Civil War through

era through the industrial revolution. See, for example, Gabriel Ardant, "Financial Policy and Economic Infrastructure of Modern States and Nations," in *The Formation of National States in Western Europe,* ed. Charles Tilly (Princeton: Princeton University Press, 1975), 164–242, and D. E. Schremmer, "Taxation and Public Finance: Britain, France, and Germany," in *The Cambridge Economic History of Europe, Volume VIII, The Industrial Economies: The Development of Economic and Social Policies,* ed. Peter Mathias and Sidney Pollard (Cambridge: Cambridge University Press, 1989), 315–494.

[12]Goldscheid, "A Sociological Approach to Problems of Public Finance," 203, 205, 209, 211.

1913. He sees the passage of the Civil War law, the enactment of the Sixteenth Amendment, and the reenactment of a federal income tax in 1913 as an expression of capitalist desire "to preserve imbalances in the structure of wealth and opportunity, rather than to ameliorate or abolish them, by strengthening the status quo against the more radical attacks on that structure by the political left and right."[13] Consistent with Stanley's history of the income tax is a history of New Deal tax reform by the historian Mark Leff, who argues that Franklin D. Roosevelt looked only for symbolic victories in tax reform and was never willing to take on capitalist power by undertaking a serious program of income and wealth redistribution or by significantly expanding taxation of the incomes of upper-middle-class Americans. Thus, Stanley and Leff regard income-tax initiatives before World War II as hollow, primarily symbolic efforts to appease the forces of democracy.[14]

The political scientist Ronald King has also advanced an elaborate expression of the capitalist-state approach to fiscal history, and he carries the story told by Stanley and Leff into the post–World War II era in which income tax revenues came mainly from wages and salaries rather than profits, dividends, and rents, as had been the case earlier. He puts less emphasis on the symbolic use of the language of progressive redistribution to appease democratic forces. Instead, he stresses the role of a "hegemonic tax logic," based on the needs of American capitalism, which first appeared during the 1920s but prevailed only after World War II. This logic, King argues, called for the federal government to adopt tax policies that promoted capital accumulation but at the same time to trumpet them as measures that increased productivity, average wages, and jobs. He argues that all of the presidents after World War II invoked this logic in devising their tax programs. But he finds the administration of John F. Kennedy to have been the most creative in mobilizing investment tax-subsidies to accommodate the potentially conflicting interests of business and labor. Kennedy's was, therefore, according to King, "the quintessential presidency of the post-war American regime." Thus, in King's formulation, the loopholes in the federal tax code become more than "random loopholes drilled primarily to satisfy the demands of selfish factions." King argues that the

[13]Robert Stanley, *Dimensions of Law in the Service of Order: Origins of the Federal Income Tax, 1861–1913* (New York: Oxford University Press, 1993), viii–ix.
[14]Mark H. Leff, *The Limits of Symbolic Reform: The New Deal and Taxation, 1933–1939* (Cambridge: Cambridge University Press, 1984).

loopholes "reflect a more conscious intention consistent with systematic policy purpose."[15]

The second approach used to explain the fiscal weakness of the modern American state is that of scholars who have described themselves, in various ways, as "pluralists" because they emphasize the multiplicity of contending groups shaping tax policy and because they detail the ways in which the American political system encourages fragmentation of the polity into local and special interests. Whereas the capitalist-state theorists tend to consider tax policy as rationally advancing the interests of capitalists, the pluralists who have written at length about fiscal history stress the economically dysfunctional character of federal tax policy, especially the complex webs of special tax rates and tax expenditures. In this pluralist view, the federal tax code often distorts economic decisions and weakens the federal government by undermining the income-tax base. The political scientist John Witte, who has written the most comprehensive pluralist history of the income tax, describes the tax system as one of "enormous complexity, which may have reached the limits of legitimacy, the capacity to meet revenue demands, and the capability of reform."[16]

The pluralist analysis of "social power relations" also contrasts sharply with that of the capitalist-state theorists. Pluralists emphasize the extent to which a broad range of middle-class groups has prevailed in the political process. Thus, the political scientists Carolyn Webber and Aaron Wildavsky wrote, "As Pogo might have put it, we—the broad middle and lower classes—have met the special interests, and 'they is us.' " The outcome, in the words of John Witte, is a system that "essentially exempts the poor, taxes the broad middle class at a very stable

---

[15]Ronald F. King, *Money, Time, and Politics: Investment Tax Subsidies and American Democracy* (New Haven: Yale University Press, 1993), 37, 316. See also Ronald F. King, "From Redistributive to Hegemonic Logic: The Transformation of American Tax Politics, 1894–1963," *Politics and Society* 12, no. 1 (1983): 1–52.

[16]Witte, *Development of the Federal Income Tax,* 23. For the sake of clarity, it should be emphasized that this essay discusses only those pluralist scholars who have written extensive fiscal histories. Like Witte, virtually all of these scholars have rendered rather negative judgments of the political processes they characterize as pluralist. There are many other scholars—also pluralists—who have described politics in a similar fashion but have rendered much more favorable judgments. Robert A. Dahl and Samuel P. Hays are two of the most obvious examples of more optimistic pluralists. See Dahl, *Democracy and Its Critics* (New Haven: Yale University Press, 1969), and Hays, *The Response to Industrialism, 1885–1914* (Chicago: University of Chicago Press, 1957). But virtually none of the pluralists with more favorable normative evaluations have made substantial contributions to fiscal history.

rate, and taxes the rich at varying rates depending on political and ideological shifts."[17]

The pluralist history of the tax-state as weakened by the pluralist grinding of middle-class interest groups has, in turn, influenced public discourse through "declinists" like the historian Paul Kennedy and the political scientist David Calleo. They have blamed massive federal budget deficits on the failure to raise sufficient tax revenues and, in turn, on middle-class preferences for lower taxes, especially taxes that subsidize middle-class consumption patterns over public social investment. Calleo diagnosed America's economic troubles as in large part the price paid for democratic tax politics. He implied that significant reform of the public sector can come only if the process of tax politics is first reformed—by insulating the tax system from democratic politics.[18]

Thus, political scientists and economists have dramatically reinterpreted the forces of democracy lauded by Sidney Ratner. Within the new tax history, democracy has been subverted by narrowly selfish tax-eaters (the neoconservative interpretation) or captured by capitalists or their agents (the capitalist-state view) or transmogrified by the excessive grind of competitive interest groups (the pluralist analysis).

AN EMPHASIS ON FISCAL ACCOMPLISHMENTS AND THE FORCE OF IDEAS

In contrast with prevailing tax histories, each of which has its own dismal view of the condition of the polity, the contributors to this volume begin from a substantially more positive assessment of the accomplishments of American fiscal policy. They believe that "postprogressive" scholarship has lost sight of important aspects of these accomplishments. Moreover, they find that those accomplishments depended heavily on

[17]Webber and Wildavsky, *A History of Taxation,* 531; Witte, *Development of the Federal Income Tax,* 21. Influential political scientists who have analyzed the history of America's social security system, including its financing, have reached similar conclusions about the distribution of power. See, in particular, Martha Derthick, *Policymaking for Social Security* (Washington, D.C.: Brookings Institution, 1979), and Carolyn L. Weaver, *The Crisis in Social Security: Economic and Political Origins* (Durham, N.C.: Duke University Press, 1982).

[18]Paul Kennedy, *The Rise and Fall of the Great Powers: Economic and Military Conflict from 1500 to 2000* (New York: Random House, 1987), esp. 434, 527, 534–35; David Calleo, *Beyond American Hegemony: The Future of the Western Alliance* (New York: Basic Books, 1987), esp. 109–13, 126, and *The Bankrupting of America: How the Federal Budget Is Impoverishing the Nation* (New York: Morrow, 1992).

the success of the architects of the major tax regimes in embracing democratic ideals that called for taxation according to "ability to pay."

The contributors are in closest agreement with the pluralists on the point that the federal tax code became far more complex in the decades after World War II. Jones describes in detail the introduction of two of the income-tax loopholes—the joint return and the acceptance of community-property status—adopted in the early years of the mass-based income tax.[19] Both Zelizer and Martin regard the complexity of the tax code as a product of the pressure of private interests, just as the pluralists have suggested.[20] Brownlee stresses the fact that the highly progressive taxation enacted during World War I created enormous economic incentives for classes of taxpayers to seek special treatment.[21]

Nonetheless, in contrast with the pluralists, the contributors point out, as well, that at times the federal government, even after World War II, undertook reforms that significantly enhanced the coherence of the tax code. Zelizer claims that the Revenue Act of 1962 contained important base-broadening reforms, such as restrictions on foreign tax havens, on benefits for cooperatives, and on travel and entertainment deductions. Steuerle argues that the Tax Reform Act of 1986 implemented base-broadening measures to an unprecedented degree and that the measures have remained largely intact.[22] Strikingly, the pluralists failed to anticipate the magnitude of the 1986 tax reforms. For example, John Witte, writing shortly before the adoption of the Tax Reform Act of 1986, discovered the risks of using history for political forecasts.[23] But the contributors would not go so far as to agree with political scientists who argue that a "politics of reform" has replaced interest-group pluralism and who invoke the Tax Reform Act of 1986 to buttress their argument.[24]

---

[19]Chapter 3, this volume.
[20]Chapters 6 and 7, this volume.
[21]Chapter 2, this volume.
[22]See C. Eugene Steuerle, *The Tax Decade: How Taxes Came to Dominate the Public Agenda* (Washington, D.C.: Urban Institute Press, 1992), 121ff.; and Steuerle, chapter 8, this volume.
[23]More specifically, Witte forecast "some curtailing of tax expenditures (although elimination of very few), a reduction in the number of brackets (which simplifies nothing and will reduce progressivity), and then, in the years ahead a return to the more natural political impulses of conferring both broad and specialized benefits through the tax system." See Witte, *Development of the Federal Income Tax*, 386. For a summary of the actual provisions of the act, see W. Elliot Brownlee, chapter 2, this volume.
[24]The leading proponent of a "politics of reform" is James Q. Wilson. See Wilson, *The Politics of Regulation* (New York: Basic Books, 1980). For the application of this ar-

The contributors to this volume also concur with the pluralists in stressing the historic multiplicity of the purposes of taxation. Various regulatory and distributional objectives have made federal taxation far more than a revenue-raising instrument. But the pluralists, in their preoccupation with the complexities and inefficiencies of the tax code, have paid too little attention to the use of fiscal policy to manage the business cycle (through manipulation of aggregate demand for goods and services) and to stimulate productivity gains. Like the capitalist-state theorists, the contributors to this volume appreciate the interest of groups, both inside and outside of the state, in these functions. Martin, for example, discusses the shifting growth strategies of the postwar presidents and the effects of those strategies on the taxation of corporations. She finds intention, rather than chaos, in these strategies but regards them as more complicated than does Ronald King.

Of the contributors to this volume, Stein is probably closest to the pluralist approach in his description of the outcome of fiscal politics since 1964.[25] In an essay that continues his career-long interest in the evaluation of fiscal policy, Stein describes how the federal government, beginning as early as 1965, abandoned a coherent "aggregate rule" for setting countercyclical fiscal policy, including taxes. For example, Richard Nixon's 1971 commitment to balancing the full-employment budget could not withstand several competing economic and political objectives. Stein has concluded that in 1969 he was premature, at best, when he declared, in *The Fiscal Revolution in America,* that "domesticated Keynesianism" had triumphed in 1962–64. In fact, Stein now finds that during the last thirty years, not one of the major approaches to budget-balancing has prevailed. During the last thirty years, Stein argues, policymakers have been unwilling "to subordinate their desires for specific tax and expenditure programs to any aggregate goal." The simple obstacle to coherent fiscal policy, he suggests, is that "people—politicians and private citizens—cared about the ingredients of the budget for other reasons in addition to their cyclical consequences" and that "almost all were opposed to raising taxes most of the time."

But the pathbreaking *Fiscal Revolution in America* stands as the leading description of how, under the presidential leadership of Herbert

gument to the politics of the Tax Reform Act of 1986, see Timothy J. Conlan, Margaret T. Wrightson, and David R. Beam, *Taxing Choices: The Politics of Tax Reform* (Washington, D.C.: Congressional Quarterly Press, 1990).
[25]Chapter 5, this volume.

Hoover and Franklin Roosevelt, the Great Depression emergency and World War II shifted fiscal policy, albeit haltingly and incompletely, toward the intentional countercyclical management of the business cycle. And although Stein is reluctant to evaluate the economic results of that fiscal policy, he has not recanted his earlier praise for the post–World War II management of fiscal policy, which, for the first time following a major war, helped the nation avoid a serious deflationary crisis.[26]

In contrast with both the pluralists and the capitalist-state theorists, the contributors dwell more on the successes of the programs funded by tax regimes and on the contribution of the particular constructions of tax regimes to those successes. For example, Brownlee's essay, which seeks to set the World War II tax regime in historical context, points out that during each of the nation's major wars, the federal government undertook major reforms of its tax system and that these reforms were instrumental in acquiring the revenues required for the victory of the Union in the Civil War and the Allied victories in the two world wars. Part of the reason for the fiscal success of the two wartime tax regimes of the twentieth century was the fact that the architects of tax reform intended to do far more than finance the war. They sought to make the nation's tax system significantly more progressive, and the nation's economy more democratic, after the war as well as during it. Thus, the wartime tax regimes succeeded politically, in part, because they symbolized the democratic ideals at the heart of the American war efforts. In other words, in contrast with both the pluralists and the capitalist-state theorists, Brownlee finds that redistributional impulses, as much as the revenue requirements of wartime mobilization, shaped the tax regimes of the twentieth century. Moreover, these wartime tax regimes assisted in expanding the social programs of the federal government after the war. The expanded, and more progressive, tax capacity of federal government during wartime conditioned the American public to accept higher rates of taxation in the postwar era and helped mobilize interest groups to use the new tax regimes to advance social programs.

[26]Stein's scholarly interest in the history of fiscal policy began before World War II when he published *Government Price Policy in the United States during the World War* (Williamstown, Mass.: Williams College, 1939). He closely tracked the development of countercyclical fiscal policy in his years with the Committee for Economic Development (1945–67) before publishing his now classic historical study, *The Fiscal Revolution in America*. He served on the President's Council of Economic Advisers between 1969 and 1974 and was its chair from 1972 to 1974.

Some of the contributors find social merit even in the less progressive taxes that were central to federal taxation. Following the work of Theda Skocpol and others, Brownlee points out that the regressive post–Civil War tariff funded a substantial system of social benefits, which were distributed progressively among Union veterans and their families. Skocpol pointed out that the percentage of the American population covered by Civil War pensions, especially in northern states, compared well with the levels provided by German and Danish old-age systems, although it fell short of the level provided by British old-age pensions. Moreover, the Americans who were in the Civil War benefit system enjoyed terms of coverage, such as eligibility for benefits, that were "quite generous" when compared with those offered by European social programs.[27] Berkowitz regards the funding of the social security system through an earmarked payroll tax as a critical element in its political success—including its adoption in 1935 and the major increases in both benefits and tax levels that Congress enacted, beginning in 1950.[28] The champions of social security, he argues, "knew that they had managed to sustain what was probably the closest thing to a popular tax in America by emphasizing the close connection between payments and benefits." And Berkowitz makes clear that from its very outset, the benefit formula had a welfare or progressive element, which "permitted poorer people a greater return on their taxes or 'investments' than richer people."

The evaluations of fiscal policy by the contributors are consistent with their descriptions of the social interests that have shaped it. Thus, the authors of these essays tend to see the configuration of interests shaping tax policy, even in the period since World War II, as volatile and complicated, just as policy outcomes have been. They regard political conflict over control of the public sector and the instruments of taxation as more intense than do the pluralists and capital-state theorists who have revised the progressive interpretation. Brownlee argues that lower-income groups as well as corporations have played significant roles in the political plots and suggests that the intensity of the conflict lent tax politics an unstable, unpredictable quality. Berkowitz describes the passage of the Social Security Act in 1935 as "a near thing." Martin and Zelizer both find significant political differences, along sectoral lines, within the

[27]See Theda Skocpol, *Protecting Soldiers and Mothers: The Political Origins of Social Policy in the United States* (Cambridge, Mass.: Harvard University Press, 1992), 130–35, for international comparisons.
[28]Chapter 4, this volume.

American business community and find that these lines of differences were highly unstable.[29]

The contributors tend to see ideas—defined robustly to include values—as more powerful than class in shaping the definition of social interests, often shaping alignments that behavioral characteristics alone could not predict. Brownlee, for example, suggests that the idea of taxing according to "ability to pay" has had great force, with its appeal often reaching across class lines. Zelizer contends that a fiscal community—containing elements both inside and outside of government—coalesced in the late 1950s and early 1960s around "a shared political language" with a distinctive vocabulary and a concept of a "political economy" and that this fiscal community exerted a powerful influence on the development of public finance. The ideas promoted by Keynesians within this community contributed to the Kennedy-Johnson tax cuts of 1964. And another set of ideas, which followers of Henry Simons promoted within the community, advanced the ideals of horizontal equity and economic efficiency in income taxation. The latter movement, which the economist Thomas S. Adams had actually begun in the 1920s, found influential champions in the tax attorney Stanley Surrey and the economist Joseph Pechman and finally culminated in the Tax Reform Act of 1986. Martin argues that ideas regarding national growth strategy played a significant role even outside the state, shaping the way in which the business community defined its interests in approaching tax policy in the early 1960s and again during the 1980s, when supply-side and then market-efficiency ideas proved powerful.

Stein, however, entertains serious doubts, to say the least, about the extent to which coherent ideas have shaped a central aspect of fiscal policy since the Kennedy administration: countercyclical management of the business cycle. For example, based on a remarkable firsthand inventory, made in 1974, of the ideas of President Gerald Ford's economic advisers, Stein reports that no one "had a credible theory of fiscal policy at that time." Growing demands for tax relief came to fruition during the Reagan administration in part because decisions to increase deficits faced no intellectual resistance; few in power believed, in Stein's words,

[29]Elsewhere Cathie Martin has described the business community that was interested in federal tax reform as sharply divided into three sectors: finance and housing; capital-intensive manufacturing; and small business. See Cathie J. Martin, *Shifting the Burden: The Struggle over Growth and Corporate Taxation* (Chicago: University of Chicago Press, 1991).

"that there was some precise, knowable size of deficit that was consistent with the stability of the economy." But Stein does believe in the *potential* power of economic ideas. In *The Fiscal Revolution in America,* he delineated their considerable influence on policy, through their advocacy by economists within government, during the years between World War II and 1964. And he believes that if there had been a high-level " 'expert' consensus" on deficits in the late 1970s and early 1980s, it would have decreased the freedom of politicians to cut taxes. Moreover, Stein acknowledges that an important factor in 1981 was Ronald Reagan's personal belief in the "Laffer curve." The disarray of the experts left "a vacuum . . . for Reaganism to fill." Stein, of course, focuses on the role of ideas and experts in shaping aggregate fiscal policy at the presidential level, where their reputation certainly has waned since 1964. But their influence may well have been significant on other aspects of fiscal policy, through the further development of fiscal communities such as the ones described by Zelizer and Berkowitz.

AN EMPHASIS ON CONTINGENCY AND CRISIS

In contrast with other postprogressive scholars of tax history, the contributors believe that ideas configure fiscal policy in a highly contingent fashion. In other words, the intentionality that has given tax policy its shape has done so in the context of historical contingency and, more specifically, great national emergencies. The vagaries of international events—political conflict, economic competition, and business-cycle swings—have been especially important in the emergence of modern public finance. Thus, the contributors tend to see policy outcomes as less determined—that is, less certain or predictable—than do other postprogressive scholars. In particular, they believe that because new fiscal regimes materialized through contingent chains of events—chains embedded in significant national emergencies—the prediction of the components of new regimes lies well beyond the reach of behavioral models.

Some tax pluralists have recognized the importance of national emergencies in shaping fiscal institutions. John Witte, for example, cites national crises, especially the great wars, as "the single most important influence on the formation and structure of the tax code."[30] But Witte

---

[30]Witte, *Development of the Federal Income Tax,* 79.

refers only to the formal structure of contemporary taxation. He, as well as the other pluralists, regards the postwar periods as more important for establishing the substance of taxation. In contrast, the contributors to this volume view postemergency changes in the tax code as less significant than the changes enacted during the emergency itself and than the conditions that shaped those changes.

Brownlee proposes that the three total wars (the Civil War and the two world wars), with their unprecedented need for capital, and a depression, whose depth and length was without precedent, have been the major precipitating events in the formation of American fiscal regimes. Thus, the timing of those national emergencies—their chronological placement in the political, social, and economic development of the nation—played a critical role in determining the shape of American public finance.

Taking account of historical contingencies and path-dependent development assists in explaining much of the supposed "American exceptionalism" in taxation—the institutional elements that distinguish taxation in the United States from that in other industrial democracies. For example, the facts that two great war mobilizations were the occasions for adopting modern income taxation in America, and that Democratic administrations happened to manage the military mobilizations, go a long way to explain the adoption of tax regimes that relied unusually heavily on progressive personal income taxes and on corporate taxation and unusually lightly on general sales taxes. In turn, in a path-dependent fashion, the sharp progressivity of the income-tax system that emerged from World War I contributed to the unusual complexity of the American tax system by creating powerful incentives for groups to carve out "tax expenditures." Also, federal abstention from general sales taxes during World War I and the 1920s left the way open for the states to develop a powerful attachment to them and a growing hostility to their use by the federal government.

A more recent example of the compelling power of initial conditions is the program of tax cuts and deficits embarked upon by the Reagan administration in 1981—what Stein describes as the "Big Budget Bang." It may not have initiated a new fiscal regime, but as Stein suggests, it has dominated fiscal policy ever since. Moreover, it helps account for the federal government's heavy reliance on debt financing.

Compounding the neglect of historical contingency by the pluralist history of public finance is its limited historical perspective. Regardless of the formal chronologies of the pluralist historians, they focus their analysis on the development of federal policy between 1964 and the administration of Ronald Reagan. But during this period, political divisions resulting from the war in Vietnam and the Watergate crisis seriously weakened national political leadership. If, instead, we look at the period from 1941 as a whole, and set that period in the context of the larger history of American tax regimes, we can more accurately gauge the significance of tax reform episodes and identify those moments when historical contingencies made significant reform possible, as they did in 1950 (the year of major social security amendments), 1964, 1986, and most dramatically, the points of transition to new tax regimes.

AN EMPHASIS ON STATE AUTONOMY AND THE ROLE OF EXPERTS

At the center of the nexus of ideas, crisis, and contingency that shaped long-term fiscal development has been "the state." In particular, during crises, the state has played a central role in the mobilization of economic ideas to bring about changes in fiscal policy. Nonetheless, in the last analysis, each of the major interpretations of American tax history— progressive as well as postprogressive—is "society-centered" rather than "state-centered." That is to say, in explaining the development of the federal government and its fiscal policies, each attaches greater importance to the influence of interests outside the government than to the role of interests within it.

At the same time, however, the neoconservative, capitalist-state, and pluralist interpretations all pay close attention methodologically to the role of the state. Even the pluralist interpretation, which dwells on the weakness of the state, attempts to consider theoretically the role of the state. And both the neoconservative and the capitalist-state arguments accord a degree of autonomy to institutions and actors within the government.

The neoconservative fiscal story offers little detailed analysis of the institutions of the federal government, but in the story, the federal government acquired considerable autonomy during the course of the twentieth century. In particular, neoconservative scholars highlight the success of the federal government in manipulating politics to undermine traditional American resistance to taxpaying, particularly during the New Deal and World War I. Neoconservative scholars highlight agents

of the state who gain control of the instruments of national communication, manipulate federal power to discourage or suppress grass-roots
challenges to the state, and cultivate a class of experts capable of de-
signing taxes whose effects are difficult to detect. The historian David
Beito, for example, emphasizes the power of a tax-resistant culture that,
he claims, dates back to John C. Calhoun. He argues that it was vital
at the state and local levels as late as the 1930s and claims that the New
Deal played a crucial role in breaking its back.

The result, the neoconservatives argue, is government growth that im-
pairs productivity, growth fueled both by interest-group politics and by
self-interested, relatively autonomous agents of the state. In a sense, they
echo one of Schumpeter's warnings about the growth of social programs:
"If the finances have created and partly formed the modern state, so
now the state on its part forms them and enlarges them—deep into the
flesh of the private economy." Neoconservative scholars emphasize the
need to limit state autonomy in order to restore the health of the republic, and they offer historical evidence to support political movements
designed to impose new constitutional restraints, such as balanced-
budget amendments and Proposition 13–style limits on tax rates.[31]

For their part, capitalist-state theorists of fiscal policy have moved
beyond simplistic models of state capture to express an appreciation for
the complexity of the relationship between political leaders and capitalists and for the extent to which the former can acquire autonomy and
exercise initiative in establishing policy. Robert Stanley, for example,
argues that "political officials" were far more than tools of the capitalists. They acted "as relatively autonomous trustees . . . through the use
of multiple dimensions of the law." Thus, Stanley sets the history of
early income taxation in what he calls an "omnipresent legal environment" and explores "the full network of lawmaking agencies in their
symbiosis with other dimensions of the social structure." Legislatures
and courts were aware of the "crucial rhetorical consequences" and the
distributional implications of tax law and used their autonomy, through
the law, Stanley proposes, to shape popular values and beliefs. He attributes overwhelming responsibility for the enactment of income taxes
during the Civil War, in 1894, and again in 1913 to the initiative of the
capitalists' "trustees," who he believes acted to preempt the adoption of

---

[31]David Beito, *Tax Payers in Revolt: Tax Resistance during the Great Depression* (Chapel
Hill: University of North Carolina Press, 1989); Schumpeter, "The Crisis of the Tax
State," 19.

more radical measures. And he views the fight over the constitutionality of income taxation not as a confrontation between classes but as an argument within the state for control over "centrist" mechanisms of allocation. Thus, Stanley interprets *Pollock v. Farmers' Loan and Trust Co.* (1895), which invalidated the 1894 income tax, as a Jacksonian attack by the Supreme Court on the dominant role of Congress in "statist capitalism" rather than as an assault on income taxation.[32]

Ronald King also finds considerable state autonomy, based on the responsibility of political leaders to reconcile the interests of contending groups and classes. It was by working effectively under this responsibility, King argues, that the architects of the post–World War II tax regime took into account the interests of labor—as well as their own fundamental devotion to capital accumulation—and replaced the "zero-sum redistribution game" with "the politics of non-zero-sum productivity" and a tax policy of economic "growthmanship." By manipulating both tax policy and tax symbolism, state managers induced labor to reduce its pressure for short-run economic and fiscal gains in favor of long-run gains "within overall capitalist hegemony."[33]

In contrast, the federal government portrayed in the pluralist histories of public finance is one of pathetic weakness. Pluralists complement their stress on the power of middle-class interests with a view of the American state as so fragmented that it cannot stand up to the grinding of interest-group competition. The weak political structures cited by the pluralist scholars of tax history include fragmented political parties, a decline of partisanship after World War II, a system of federalism that reinforces local interests, a bureaucracy paralyzed by multiple decision points, and a federal government constitutionally fractured along the legislative-executive fault line. The pluralists argue that these structural weaknesses, combined with a high degree of democratic access to government and with a tax system that encompasses virtually all households and businesses, will necessarily produce an inefficient tax policy that is an incoherent jumble of complexity and that fails to raise adequate revenue. And because of these structural weaknesses, those who would reform public finance are condemned to a frustrating process of slow and incremental change.

A political scientist recently made an important effort to strengthen

[32]Stanley, *Dimensions of Law in the Service of Order*, esp. vi–x, 3–14, 136–75.
[33]See King, *Money, Time, and Politics*, 47–85, for the core of his theoretical argument.

the pluralist understanding of the development of American taxation by paying close attention to the role of institutions. But he did not significantly alter the pluralist diagnosis. Sven Steinmo concluded that a "fragmentation of political authority"—checks and balances and the localism encouraged by American federalism—strengthens special-interest groups at the expense of political parties and frustrates tax reformers who would broaden the income-tax base or adopt national consumption taxes in order to expand social programs. The fragmentation encourages groups to be exceptionally hostile to any increase in their tax burdens.[34]

The contributors to this volume all acknowledge the existence of the structural difficulties emphasized by the pluralists. But they place less stress on them and emphasize instead certain characteristics of modern government that have lowered, in varying degrees over time, barriers to making coherent policy. In general, the contributors pay more attention to how political leaders develop opportunities to exercise power.

Brownlee, for example, suggests that during the formation of the great tax regimes of the twentieth century, presidents and congressional leaders discovered how pluralism itself created possibilities, through brokering the competing demands of interest groups, for increasing their power over tax policy. Berkowitz credits Franklin Roosevelt's leadership, including his reinforcement of the influence of social-insurance experts, with the victory for old-age insurance and its funding through payroll taxes.

Berkowitz also shows how earmarking tax revenues helped defeat pluralist hostility to increasing taxes during peacetime. Jones tells how, during World War II, the federal government used a dramatic and well-organized set of campaigns to create a taxpaying culture and introduce the contemporary tax regime. The campaigns included propaganda initiatives—that is, campaigns in the mass media—undertaken by the executive branch to advertise the mass-based income tax and "sweeteners," such as withholding, designed in part to make the new tax code more palatable.

One might take Jones's argument one step further and suggest that the wartime conditions under which the federal government introduced

---

[34]See Steinmo, *Taxation and Democracy*. Steinmo is among those political scientists attempting to embrace the full range of institutional factors in full-bodied models of public sector development. For a general description of this approach, see James G. March and Johan P. Olsen, *Rediscovering Institutions: The Organizational Basis of Politics* (New York: Free Press, 1989).

mass-based income taxation had much to do, in a path-dependent manner, with the shaping of postwar administrative practice. Scholars often describe this practice—a heavy reliance on voluntarism through self-reporting—as another example of American exceptionalism in taxation.[35]

Berkowitz's and Jones's interpretation squares with Brownlee's emphasis on the ways in which national emergencies tend to create opportunities for public-finance reforms that have clear social intent and display organizational coherence. Prompted by the threat to the nation's security, the Roosevelt administration decisively influenced the enactment of payroll and income taxation and then exercised initiative in using the media to persuade the American middle class to accept the taxes. These were examples of decisive presidential leadership but not of coercive government. The Roosevelt administration persuaded rather than coerced. During World War II, as well as during World War I and even the Civil War, a liberal democratic state demonstrated the fiscal power that a trusting (and wealthy) public can mobilize. That trust, nurtured by the federal government, permitted and encouraged the adoption of income taxation, which is, along with property taxation, the most coercive and statist means of revenue-raising. Perhaps only the liberal-democratic states can impose coercive taxation in a sustained fashion— and still survive. The weaknesses of those states have proved to be largely superficial, at least during national emergencies.

Jones, Martin, and Zelizer find signs of considerable state autonomy even during the post–World War II era, which provided the evidence that has fueled the pluralist weak-state interpretation. Jones points out that after World War II the federal government shifted its efforts from moralizing about the virtues of sacrifice to the standardization of taxation. It adopted measures, such as the income-splitting joint tax return for husbands and wives, and propaganda (more campaigning in the media) that coerced the public with threats of uniform and effective enforcement of the law. With such provisions, the federal government sought to bring payment of income taxes more directly under the control of tax officials in the Bureau of Internal Revenue. Martin argues that Presidents Kennedy and Reagan used the power of ideas to shape the interests of powerful groups outside the state and, thereby, to expedite

---

[35]For useful international comparisons of income-tax administration, see Arnold J. Heidenheimer, Hugh Heclo, and Carolyn T. Adams, *Comparative Public Policy: The Politics of Social Choice in Europe and America* (New York: St. Martin's, 1975), 235–42.

changes in corporate taxation. President Kennedy, she argues, actively sought help from private interests in support of Keynesian policies so that he could overcome the limitations of divided government. In the process, Kennedy transformed the way in which business groups defined their interests. Business was powerful, to be sure, but was more divided and less enthusiastic about the investment tax credit than capitalist-state theorists suggest.

Zelizer claims that even Wilbur Mills, whom pluralist scholars have treated as a whipping boy in their saga of the perils of divided government and localism, played an important role as a policy entrepreneur in leading the public-finance initiatives undertaken during the Kennedy administration. Mills, Zelizer argues, significantly contributed to the movement within the fiscal-policy community for base-building reform of the income tax. The centerpiece of Zelizer's interpretation of Mills's entrepreneurial role in the political process is his argument that Mills learned how to manage and lead bipartisan consensus-building within Congress. Mills drew on his own considerable skills, and the power of the tax-writing committees, to rise above the conservative constraints imposed by his southern district. He acted as a broker between fiscal experts and the larger political world, he became a fiscal expert in his own right, and he used the mass media to advance his reform interests. In so doing, Zelizer suggests, Mills participated in the creation of a political culture within the complex administrative state created by the New Deal and World War II and thus helped lend a surprising coherence to the making of policy. More specifically, Mills, through an extended process of political learning, helped create and nurture a tax-policy community that drew various issue networks together and became forceful in shaping fiscal policy during the post–World War II era. Berkowitz would point out that Mills's reach extended to the bureaucrats in the Social Security Administration, with whom he developed a collaboration that became "practiced and smooth."[36]

The power of tax-policy communities and cultures of reform rests on their ability to mobilize and deploy knowledge focused on the intentional solution of social problems. The contributors find that crisis con-

[36]The contributors to this volume do not agree on every important point, of course, and an example of this is the diversity of the opinions regarding Wilbur Mills's approach to tax reform. For more conventional views of Mills and the Ways and Means Committee as impediments to modern tax and fiscal policy, see Cathie Jo Martin, chapter 7, this volume, and Herbert Stein, chapter 5, this volume.

ditions often enhance the demand for the services of "experts" and provide opportunities for them to increase their influence over policy from within the state. All of the contributors to this volume find that experts within government—including economists, lawyers, accountants, actuaries, statisticians, social workers, public relations specialists, pollsters, and professional bureaucrats—exercised considerable influence over policy by defining social issues, proposing legal and administrative measures, guiding the administration of policy, and estimating future trends. Some experts, such as the public relations experts discussed by Jones, even shaped popular culture through the media with the goal of promoting acceptance of new policies.

The contributors extensively discuss the expert roles of economists and lawyers within government. Stein details the influence of economists at the highest level by detailing the fiscal-policy relationship between the Council of Economic Advisers and the rest of the executive branch, especially during the administrations of Nixon and Ford. Zelizer inventories the membership of the various issue networks of economists and suggests that Wilbur Mills was to a large extent responsible for their influence by helping to knit the networks into a fiscal community. Zelizer and Stein, in *The Fiscal Revolution in America,* demonstrate how the Great Depression emergency, and the desire to avoid a return to depression conditions after World War II, brought economists and policy entrepreneurs like Mills, who valued economic advice, to an unprecedented level of influence on countercyclical policy during the early 1960s.

Berkowitz, along a line of inquiry that parallels Zelizer's, describes the development of a social security network that formed around experts in government. He details how a professionally diverse set of experts in the Social Security Administration not only made substantial intellectual contributions to social security but also acted as policy entrepreneurs to create a network of allies elsewhere in the government and within the public at large. During the 1930s and 1940s they formed a "social security crowd"; they defended the system against political threats, including ones launched by Keynesian economists during the 1930s and 1940s; they advanced programs incrementally; they engineered a major expansion of program coverage and payroll taxation in 1950; and they won strong bipartisan and congressional support during the 1950s.

Steuerle emphasizes the role of expert Treasury lawyers and economists (of which he was one) in influencing base-broadening reform in

1986. It is true, of course, that they could not have succeeded without presidential leadership that provided shelter for the principled approach of the Treasury; the Reagan administration shielded the experts at the Treasury from the tax-writing committees and the special-interest lobbyists until the Treasury had formulated a reasonably comprehensive approach to reform. But the experts had a coherent vision of reform, derived from the intellectual legacy left by their predecessors within the Treasury.[37]

Steuerle flags as well the increasingly important role that professional estimators, who were located within the government, played in shaping fiscal policy during the 1970s and 1980s. Berkowitz provides a graphic example of this point. He describes the work of the actuaries within the Social Security Board. Their estimates contributed to the chronic windfalls that helped expand social security programs.

More generally, the contributors suggest that at critical junctures in the development of American tax regimes, systematic knowledge and social theory shaped the adoption and implementation of policy. Information produced within the federal government, or stimulated by the federal government, was especially important to policy entrepreneurs who were also within government. With the power of ideas and information, these political leaders shaped the composition and culture, the dynamics, and the impact of fiscal networks.

AN EMPHASIS ON ECONOMIC DEVELOPMENT AND FISCAL OPTIONS

The architects of the new tax regimes that accompanied national emergencies faced constraints and opportunities created not only by the path-dependent character of historical change but also by economic development. The essays by Stein, Brownlee, and especially Steuerle suggest that economic history can help illuminate the shifting pattern of

---

[37]On the principled approach of the Treasury to tax reform during the 1980s, see Steuerle, *The Tax Decade*, esp. 99–120. He bases his conclusions in part on his experience as deputy assistant secretary for tax policy during the Reagan administration, when he had responsibility for coordinating the Treasury's 1984 version of comprehensive reform. Strong support for Steuerle's analysis is found in Conlan, Wrightson, and Beam, *Taxing Choices*, esp. 230–64. In addition to the roles of the president, Treasury experts, and their ideas in 1986, these political scientists identify the role of congressional entrepreneurs, such as Senator Bill Bradley,'who acted as brokers between professional experts and the larger political arena, and the role of the media, which enabled the "policy entrepreneurs" to build public support for reform.

options available to the makers of tax policy. In contrast, other post-progressive scholarship pays scant attention to the role of economic development in providing context for fiscal change.

These authors suggest, in particular, that long-run economic change constrains tax reformers, and sometimes creates opportunities for them, by influencing administrative costs and the size of potential tax bases. If we know the relationship between economic development and the taxing potential of the state, we can better understand how policymakers assessed the options before them.

To approach the matter somewhat differently, it should be remembered that legislating a tax rate is just one element in determining the revenue outcome of tax policy—the revenue produced by tax policy. How effective a given tax rate will be in producing revenue will depend on how effectively government can administer the rate and on the size of the tax base to which the rate is applied. Economic development affects these two elements—administrative capacity and the size of the tax base—in a direct fashion. Thus, economic development, defined to include the emergence and refinement of modern technology and organizational structures as well as economic growth, shapes the public-finance options available to policymakers.[38]

For two centuries, steady and often dramatic economic growth—defined as growth in productivity—has provided a resource base for enhancing the fiscal capacity of the federal government. The constitutional limitation on property taxation by the federal government and the lack of large corporations to help administer income or payroll taxes restricted the effectiveness of direct taxation by the federal government until the twentieth century. Nonetheless, as Brownlee points out, economic growth (expressed through per capita increases in demand for imported goods), coupled with reliance on ocean commerce channeled largely though major ports, provided the basis for well-administered, highly productive tariffs.

Then, during the twentieth century, as the Brownlee and Steuerle essays suggest, the proliferation of modern corporations and their ad-

---

[38]The public-finance economist Richard Musgrave has led his profession in thinking about the relationship between structural economic change and the development of fiscal regimes. He has proposed an even stronger view of the relationship than the one Brownlee and Steuerle suggest. He argues that structural change in highly developed economies has, in fact, driven dramatic changes in tax structure, which would have occurred even without major wars. See Richard A. Musgrave, *Fiscal Systems* (New Haven: Yale University Press, 1969), 125–206.

ministrative structures, coupled with shifts in popular culture—what Steuerle calls the "broad public acceptance of a rule of law" or what Jones describes as a "mass taxpaying culture"—enabled the federal government to exploit effectively the taxation of incomes, both corporate and personal, and payrolls. In more general terms, a strong economy, as well as strong political institutions, is vital to the fiscal capacity of the state. Thus, the robustness of American economic institutions has compensated to a significant degree for the weakening of fiscal capacity by pluralism, localism, and divided government.

Steuerle stresses the influence of economic change on revenue production, and thus on tax policy. He emphasizes that between World War II and the 1970s, both economic growth and long-term inflation created the fundamental conditions that enabled the federal government to garner increasing revenues and, as a consequence, to reduce corporate taxes and excise taxes and to avoid the politically damaging process of increasing tax rates. In other words, both economic growth and inflation helped to extend the life of the World War II tax regime. Berkowitz finds the same economic processes working to generate easy revenues for social security financing, including, at first, the funding of Medicare. Then, during the 1980s, the decline of inflation, along with the weakening productivity that had ensued during the 1970s, undermined the "easy financing" period of the post-1941 fiscal regime and pushed the makers of fiscal policy toward reliance on deficit financing and toward reduction of tax expenditures (as in the Tax Reform Act of 1986). Even without the historically contingent tax cuts of the first Reagan administration, cuts that helped to eliminate what Steuerle calls "fiscal slack," the changing economic circumstances would have ended the period of easy finance.

TOWARD THE NEXT CENTURY

Of the essays in this volume, Steuerle's looks most squarely at the tax and fiscal-policy issues that the nation must face during the next generation. He pays close attention to how analysis of long-term economic forces can help identify future possibilities. As he puts it, understanding historic economic trends can provide clues as to "what the nation must do—or do differently than in the past," even though the clues may be "vague about the specifics of how this will be achieved." Thus, he turns his historical analysis in a prospective direction and abstains from trying to predict highly contingent events.

Specifically, Steuerle suggests that the nation will have to enter a new fiscal regime if it is to reduce significantly the federal budget deficit while at the same time funding programs that respond to the newer needs of society. Most fundamentally, economic conditions remain unfavorable for an expansive fiscal regime. But even if inflation or productivity increases, the existing income tax will not be as productive in the future. For one thing, the federal government indexed the income tax for inflation in years after 1984. For another, the "peace dividends," which have always been important to funding new domestic programs after major military endeavors, will soon be exhausted. Tax policy could change, of course; the federal government could restore indexing, further reduce tax expenditures to broaden the income-tax base, or adopt new taxes. But Steuerle argues that new tax revenues would be unlikely to be large enough to both reduce the deficit and throw off what he calls the "yoke of prior commitments"—the cost of the many programs, including tax-expenditure programs, that automatically grow more rapidly than does the economy and that relentlessly narrow the discretion available to legislators.

Thus, Steuerle argues, if the federal government wants to create new domestic programs or to meet new international challenges, it will have to rely, to an unprecedented extent, on reallocating funds from established domestic programs. But acquiring significant new resources through such reallocations would normally require the same kind of identification of losers that has constrained the politics of raising taxes. So, Steuerle suggests that the federal government may have to adopt a new set of budget procedures or rules. Such rules would require policymakers to look comprehensively at expenditures and taxation and take into account the total effect on the economy. If effective, the kind of procedural changes he proposes would be of sufficient scope and influence to define a new fiscal regime. In effect, Steuerle is responding to Stein's call, sounded as early as 1970, for the federal government to consider and determine federal fiscal policy with reference not only to budgetary effects—an approach that Stein deems an intellectual failure—but also to the effects on the size and distribution of the nation's economic product.[39]

---

[39]On Stein's 1970 position, see chapter 5, this volume. For his more recent elaboration, see Herbert Stein, *Governing the $5 Trillion Economy* (New York: Oxford University Press, 1989).

But it may be that a new fiscal regime is already in place—one very different from the regime of "deficit neutrality" and deficit reduction that Steuerle .would prescribe for the nation's economic health. Perhaps we have already experienced a regime shift with the enormous increase in federal deficits during the 1980s—an intentional shift in the social contract to impose on future generations a substantially larger share of the costs of domestic programs. In the absence of inflation, deficits now will require higher taxes in the future. Stein describes the "Big Budget Bang" in 1981 as just such a policy choice, initiating a new fiscal regime.

A national fiscal regime heavily dependent on deficits would be without precedent in the United States. Its emergence, however, would be understandable historically. As Brownlee and Steuerle point out, each of the nation's previous fiscal regimes was based primarily on tax increases, and a process of social learning that accompanied the increases, during national emergencies. But fifty years have elapsed since the last one. Until the 1980s, massive reliance on deficit spending was limited to the funding of wars. Thus, until the 1980s, taxes—rather than borrowings—lent fiscal regimes their distinctive character. Until then, consequently, the terms "fiscal regime" and "tax regime" could be used interchangeably.

Nonetheless, Steuerle sees in recent policy shifts a basis for believing that the nation might embrace a new fiscal regime, one that could include breaking the yoke of prior commitments, base-broadening to deal with the tax-entitlement portion of that problem, and, possibly, restructuring taxes themselves. He suggests that the deficit-reduction measures enacted by Gramm-Rudman-Hollings (GRH) and subsequent legislation, the social security reforms of 1983, and the Tax Reform Act of 1986 (which accepted the principle that tax reductions be offset by tax increases) all reflect the kind of political leadership and discipline that would be required, on a larger scale, to usher in the new regime. Stein, however, points out that even in 1994, the makers of fiscal policy still lacked an understanding of the economic consequences of deficits—an understanding that might contribute to fiscal discipline.

The other essays in this volume do not render judgments on the accomplishments of the 1980s, but they do suggest lessons from earlier, transforming episodes of reform—lessons that may be valuable for would-be architects of a new tax regime. Perhaps most obviously, the history of America's fiscal crises suggests that if the nation does fabricate a new, more elastic fiscal regime, a prerequisite will be a restoration of public trust in the federal government—the kind of trust that enabled the mass-based income tax to finance World War II. Americans must believe that the federal government is working effectively to solve the nation's structural problems before they will be willing to support significant tax increases or reductions in the benefits they receive from the federal government.

Until trust returns, political slogans like "Read my lips: No new taxes!" (George Bush in 1988)—and the betrayal of such slogans (Bush in 1990)—will continue to motivate not only the affluent but also the middle- and low-income families who are alienated from politics and government. During the 1980s these people came to agree with the pronouncement of the hotel magnate and convicted tax-evader Leona Helmsley: "We don't pay taxes. Only the little people pay taxes."[40] Many middle-class families may have understood, for example, that escalating social security tax rates effectively canceled out any benefits they received from the income-tax rate cuts that took place during the Carter and Reagan administrations, and that the changes in the tax code between 1980 and 1991, taken as a whole, produced virtually no net change in the effective tax rates for any income group.[41]

The history of tax regimes outlined in the Brownlee, Jones, and Berkowitz essays suggests that reestablishing a trusted fiscal regime may require a deliberate restructuring of tax policy to provide some combination of (1) enhanced progressivity in rate structure, (2) allocation of revenues raised by regressive taxes to programs whose benefits are distributed progressively, and (3) regulation widely regarded as improving national well-being. The Civil War tax regime, based on high tariffs, incorporated the second (for Civil War pensions) and the third elements. The World War I regime was swept in not only on an ethos of national sacrifice but also on the conviction that government should tax away or deter the accumulation of ill-gotten or socially dangerous assets (e.g., excess profits and incomes, large estates, undistributed profits) and punish "sinful" behavior. The New Deal tax regime encompassed all three elements, and the regime introduced during World War II justified mass-based income taxation in terms of not only sacrifice for national survival but also progressive social justice. Although the Tax Reform Act of 1986 did not necessarily signal a new tax regime, it was the most important change in tax policy since World War II, and to a significant extent it did represent an effort both to promote horizontal equity and to enhance economic productivity.

---

[40]*New York Times*, July 12, 1989.
[41]Kevin Phillips, *The Politics of Rich and Poor* (New York: Random House, 1990). For a summary of the changes in net tax rates, see Steuerle, *The Tax Decade*, 194–96.

In addition to offering suggestions on the substance of tax policy, the history of the great transformations of American taxation may provide the architects of future tax reform with some lessons regarding the process of reform. On the one hand, the history of taxation in America has been turbulent, ridden with conflict involving the interests of both the state and the modern corporation, heavily constrained by constitutional rules, institutional habits, and technology. It has always been uncertain in its outcome, and today the future of taxation in America may still be very much "up for grabs." On the other hand, the history of national fiscal crises suggests that the federal government, in league with other powerful interests, has the capacity to produce dramatic, strategic changes, including those that significantly enhance tax revenues.

The history of national crises suggests that the cause of tax reform must have effective presidential leadership. As party loyalties, and party discipline, have waned in significance during the twentieth century, presidential leadership has become more important. Whatever the national objectives might be—promotion of domestic savings (public and private), increase in economic productivity, advance of distributional equity, or growth in jobs—they must be stated with coherence, with a clear sense of internal priorities, and with drama. If taxes are to be increased, the specific purposes of those increases must be identified with clarity and cogent justification, linked to the general purposes of government, and developed through a process of consensus-building with outreach to contending groups in civil society. This consensus-building will offer the greatest potential for success if any increases are embedded in a reform program that is comprehensive in scope—one that involves a systematic integration of all the modes of federal taxation and expenditure.

Presidents not only must articulate and dramatize goals but also must lend coherence to the process of legislation. The exigencies of major wars and depressions forced, or enabled, presidents to approach tax reform with a sense of mission and a degree of procedural coherence rarely possible under the American constitutional order. But recent experience suggests that a national emergency is not a necessary condition for coherent reform. Despite the absence of an emergency, the Reagan administration approached tax reform in 1986 with an appreciation of this kind of coherence.

The history of tax policy during periods of national crises suggests as well that reformers must be alert for the moments in which key players may be willing to change their minds. Tax reformers would do well to

listen to the advice of Thomas S. Adams, the most important economist
in the Treasury between 1917 and 1933. Although he viewed taxation
as heavily shaped by class politics, he found that on some tax issues, "a
majority of legislators and voters are unaffected and disinterested; they
may cast their votes as a more or less disinterested jury." And, "in the
adoption of tax legislation there come zero hours, when the zeal of the
narrowly selfish flags." The challenge that Adams saw was for experts,
and for politicians, to take advantage of such openings. "There are thus
many important tax problems," he declared, "which may be settled on
the broad basis of equity and sound public policy, if one is wise and
ingenious enough to find the right solution."[42]

The most dramatic changes in American tax regimes have occurred
when administrations have been able to take advantage of the opportunities, identified by Adams, for what political scientists have called
"social learning." For dramatic change, administrations must approach
tax reform in a comprehensive fashion, articulate the goals of reform in
ways that rise above the interests of particular groups, and organize the
process of reform to insulate experts from political pressure. In the politics of tax reform, conflict has always been severe and the outcome
uncertain. But in this turbulence, the most significant transformations of
tax policy have been managed by politicians and experts who, despite
their immersion in a grinding political process, proved able to define a
transcendent public interest.

[42]Thomas Sewell Adams, "Ideals and Idealism in Taxation" (presidential address delivered
at the Fortieth Annual Meeting of the American Economic Association, December 27,
1927), published in *American Economic Review* 18 (March 1928): 1–7.

2

Tax regimes, national crisis, and state-building
in America

W. ELLIOT BROWNLEE

AN OVERVIEW

The enormous growth of the federal government in the United States
has depended heavily on great national crises or national emergencies:
three major wars and the Great Depression. During each emergency, the
federal government crafted a distinct tax regime. These tax regimes
proved to be crucial in financing not only the wartime mobilizations,
which were unprecedented in scale, but also the subsequent peacetime
expansions of the federal government. Understanding the growth of
government, and the nation's current fiscal condition, requires understanding the development of these tax regimes, as well as the historic
connections between them. Understanding those tax regimes can, in
turn, reveal much about the social underpinnings of fiscal policy.

The need of the federal government for vast new revenues to meet
national emergencies invariably forced its leadership to reexamine thoroughly the nation's financial options. In so doing, leaders faced issues
that went far beyond the financial problem of meeting demands to increase government spending. Each crisis stimulated debate over national
values and intensified ideological and distributional divisions within
American society. Because wars required the sacrifice of lives as well as
treasure, they were potentially powerful stimulants of social division.
The resulting political conflicts often centered on issues of taxation; tax
politics was always an important vehicle for the expression of the underlying social and ideological conflicts that national emergencies intensified.

Within the economic and social turbulence of each national crisis,

37

political leaders in the executive and legislative branches of government struggled to establish coherent tax policies. On the whole, crisis conditions strengthened the power of these leaders, and the tax systems they implemented further enhanced their influence. They mobilized party government and administrative technique, including professional expertise, to expand the capacity and productivity of the federal tax system. To be sure, there was always tension between executive and legislative leaders over tax policy, and both the president and Congress had to address the demands of local interests. But during the Civil War and World War I, the common partisan loyalties and shared social values of the nation's political leaders largely overcame the pressures that tended to fragment American government. Consequently, during those two emergencies, the nation's political leadership created tax regimes with a high degree of coherence and intention.

Tension between the executive and the legislative branches, and the pressure of local interests, intensified during the 1920s and again during the late 1930s. Consequently, the administration of Franklin D. Roosevelt found it more difficult to influence the new tax regimes demanded by national emergencies than had the administrations of Abraham Lincoln and Woodrow Wilson. But appeals to party loyalty worked to Roosevelt's advantage, and he proved resilient in forging coalitions both inside and outside the federal government. As a result, the two tax regimes produced by the New Deal and World War II bore the imprint of his administration more than of Congress, and of a national interest more than of local interests.

Within the conflicted politics of each of the emergencies, the leaders of the federal government worked to persuade Americans to accept new taxes. During wartime, the architects of national mobilization made taxation part of larger strategies of persuading Americans to accept sacrifice. In the Civil War and each of the two world wars, they crafted new tax programs designed both to implement sacrifice and to convince the mass of taxpayers that their sacrifices were fair.

To help make the case for fairness, the nation's political leaders experimented with progressive income taxes in the Civil War and then introduced them on a grand scale during the two world wars. The adoption of progressive taxes during those two wars took into account and exploited powerful impulses, stimulated by the forces of democracy and industrialization, for a restructuring of American society. As a consequence, both wars produced major advances in the cause of progressive taxation at the same time that they broadened the social and financial base for funding warfare and other purposes of the federal government.

During World War I, progressive impulses were so strong that the framers of tax policy launched major initiatives designed to democratize production and finance. The most radical initiatives did not survive the postwar reaction of the 1920s, but they continued to influence tax policy until World War II, when the fear of postwar depression and the requirements of unprecedented mobilization led the framers of progressive tax measures to focus on the taxation of salaries and wages rather than of rents, interest, and profits.

The tax regimes of the two world wars did not produce a social revolution, but they did establish tax policy that was far more progressively redistributional than it had been before World War I. The social tensions—tensions of class and section—created by industrialization might have led the nation eventually to adopt progressive income taxation even in the absence of war. But historical contingency played a powerful role. The wartime mobilizations and the fact that both mobilizations were managed by the leadership of the Democratic Party, which was more strongly committed to progressive income taxes and more opposed to regressive general sales taxes than the Republican Party, accelerated the process. In addition, by contributing to the resolution of wartime social crises, the emergency-driven tax policies acquired a legitimacy and cultural force that helped keep them in place well after the emergency was over.

The opportunity to establish new taxes provided the policy architects with openings to modernize the tax system, in the sense of adapting it to new economic and organizational conditions and thereby making it a more efficient producer of revenue. No process of "modernization" dictated the selection of options. But, in each crisis, policymakers discovered that the organizational maturing of industrial society had created a new menu of feasible options. Exploiting the new tax options during emergencies provided a structure and an administrative apparatus that allowed the federal government to capitalize effectively on postcrisis economic expansion.

By creating systems of taxation that had acquired an independent legitimacy and were administratively more robust, each crisis opened up new opportunities for proponents of expanded government programs to advance their interests after the emergency was over. They were able to forge new expenditure programs—both direct and indirect—without in-

W. Elliot Brownlee

curring the political costs associated with raising taxes or introducing new ones. The popularity of the expenditure programs, in turn, reinforced the popularity of the tax system behind the programs. Thus, the crisis-born enhancement of tax capability contributed to the much-discussed "upward ratchet" effect that emergencies had on government spending.[1]

Each new tax regime drew political strength from the fact that it not only increased the size of the federal government but also increased the centralization of government. The relative growth of federal taxing was most rapid during the four national emergencies. To some extent, the expansion of federal taxing undercut the tax base of state government. But the federal government offset this, and won state and local support for its tax regimes, by assuming part of the burden of financing public services after the crisis and by finding ways to expedite the levying and collecting of state and local taxes.

The indirect expenditure programs were particularly important to the political survival of new tax regimes after national emergencies. The indirect programs, which are now known as "tax expenditures," were networks of privileges within the tax code and constituted responses to the resurgence of local interests after the emergencies. These programs reduced tax bases and often made rate structures less progressive. But they left intact the fundamental intent of the emergency tax regimes. In fact, they provided significant political protection to the new regime.

The survival of each emergency-born tax system in the postcrisis era lent the nation's tax system an increasingly layered, or diversified, quality. Each new regime preserved important elements of its predecessor—elements that had survived earlier postcrisis political tests. Thus, the World War II system contained not only the features that lent it distinction but also features that it inherited from the Civil War, World War I, and Great Depression regimes.

In the absence of a new national emergency, the Civil War, World War I, and New Deal systems might have survived much longer. Each of them produced revenues adequate for funding expansive postcrisis programs. Each of the systems faced substantial criticism, but in each instance political leaders developed successful strategies, including com-

---

[1]The first work of historical scholarship to focus attention on the upward-ratchet effect that wars had on public expenditures in industrial democracies was Alan T. Peacock and Jack Wiseman, *The Growth of Public Expenditure in the United Kingdom* (Princeton: Princeton University Press, 1961).

promises in tax policy, for preserving the regime. Nonetheless, each tax system proved inadequate—both politically and economically—to meet the fiscal demands of a subsequent national emergency, and each gave way to a new system.

In the absence of a new national emergency, the World War II tax regime remains in place today, although its fiscal force and political legitimacy have become badly eroded. During the 1980s, the federal government, for the first time, embarked on comprehensive tax reform without facing a national emergency. It remains to be seen whether the reformed tax system can meet the economic challenges facing the nation during the 1990s without further, even more dramatic reform.

THE EARLY REPUBLIC

The period of the American Revolution and the formation of the U.S. Constitution reveals much about the ideology and culture underlying American taxation. Eighteenth-century Americans preferred direct taxation—primarily the taxation of property—in part because they wanted taxation to hurt and thus retard the growth of government.[2] Some of this resistance to taxation grew out of traditional liberal thought. This line of thinking emphasized individualism, celebrated the pursuit of private self-interest and financial gain, and regarded with suspicion governmental initiatives that might impede the search for individual gain. More generally, the era of the early republic provides much evidence to support the view that America was, and remains, a society of profit-maximizing tax resisters. Then, as now, in large numbers, Americans cheated, evaded taxes, exploited the loopholes in the tax codes, migrated to low-tax havens, and sought political groups and representatives committed to reducing taxes.

But the nation has other sides to its ideological history, sides often rooted in the same formative era. Even then, traditional liberalism did not hold sway, unopposed or unqualified. Historians now agree that the central language of the Revolution contained not only a Lockean liberalism, with its emphasis on private rights, but also a classical republi-

[2]Excellent surveys of taxation during these formative years are Robert A. Becker, *Revolution, Reform, and the Politics of American Taxation, 1763–1783* (Baton Rouge: Louisiana State University Press, 1980), and Roger H. Brown, *Redeeming the Republic: Federalists, Taxation, and the Origins of the Constitution* (Baltimore: Johns Hopkins University Press, 1993).

canism, or a civic humanism, that stressed communal responsibilities. These ideas focused on the threat of corruption to public order, the dangers of commercialism, and the need to foster public virtue. The Founding Fathers (and even Adam Smith) held these ideas of classical republicanism in tension with those of liberalism.[3]

Commitments to civic humanism could create pressure for higher, rather than lower, taxes. For example, the ideal of a harmonious republic of citizens equal before the law created demands for taxes to destroy islands of privilege by taxing the privileged more heavily. That ideal also embraced the notion that taxpaying was one of the normal obligations of a citizenry bound together in a republic by ties of affection and respect. This communal thinking went further, emphasizing the direct relationship between wealth and the responsibility to support government and public order. It embraced enlightened self-interest and included "ability to pay" as a criterion in determining patterns of taxation. In his first canon of taxation, Adam Smith (in *Wealth of Nations*) declared, "The subjects of every state ought to contribute towards the support of the government, as nearly as possible, in proportion to their respective abilities." In an era when most wealth was in the form of real estate, the property tax seemed to offer the greatest potential for taxing according to "ability to pay."

The founders of the republic, however, through Article 1, Section 9, of the Constitution, severely limited federal taxation of property by specifying, "No capitation or other direct tax shall be laid, unless in proportion to the census." But this limitation on the national government was not a victory for liberalism so much as for civic humanism. The limitation reflected the fact that the framers of the Constitution thought about taxation in the context of the corruption of the British Parliament and the monarchy and sought to prevent similar abuse by the new federal government. They believed that local control was necessary for the equitable operation of the property tax. The federal government, they feared, might abuse the tax to attack certain categories of property (such

---

[3]A useful introduction to the modern intellectual history of the Revolutionary era is found in the essays in Jack P. Greene, ed., *The American Revolution: Its Character and Limits* (New York: New York University Press, 1987). For important suggestions as to the long-run influence of civic humanism, see Dorothy Ross, "The Liberal Tradition Revisited and the Republican Tradition Addressed," in *New Directions in American Intellectual History*, ed. John Higham and Paul K. Conkin (Baltimore: Johns Hopkins University Press, 1979), 116–31. On Adam Smith, see Donald Winch, *Adam Smith's Politics: An Essay in Historiographic Revision* (Cambridge: Cambridge University Press, 1978).

as slaves), to favor town dwellers over farmers, or to punish a particular section of the country.

The constitutional limitation also reflected the fear of factionalism that James Madison, a civic humanist, expressed in *Federalist No. 10*. He predicted that "the most common and durable source of factions" would be "the various and unequal distribution of property." He concluded that the issue of taxation, more than any other, created an opportunity and temptation for "a predominant party to trample on the rules of justice." Moreover, the intent of the constitutional limitation was not to deny the new republic the resources it needed. Indeed, a central hope of Madison, Alexander Hamilton, and the other supporters of the Constitution was that the new central government, in contrast with the government of the Articles of Confederation, would have the taxing power that was required for a strong and meaningful nation.

Thus, even with the limitation, the Constitution left the way open for the new federal government to raise the tax revenues it needed, through indirect taxes such as tariffs.[4] Such taxes worked, both politically and financially. When tariff rates were low, they won popularity. Low tariffs were productive of revenue in periods of expanding foreign trade; they were inexpensive to collect; they were widely diffused; they seemed to tax extravagant living; and they were useful in economic diplomacy. Low and moderate tariffs allowed the leaders of the early republic to limit the political divisiveness of taxation. In their effort to create a unified and just republic, the early American leaders used relatively low tariffs to prevent tax issues from arousing the disruptive forces of factionalism.

Had it not been for the Civil War, changes in the tax system of the early republic might well have been minimal during the rest of the nineteenth century. Low tariffs, joined with the borrowing power that Secretary of the Treasury Alexander Hamilton's financial program had helped establish and with the enormous landed resources of the federal government, would probably have been adequate to meet the needs of

---

[4]Excise taxes were also possible, but they seemed to unfairly single out particular classes of producers. President Washington's and Secretary Hamilton's excise tax on whiskey touched off the Whiskey Rebellion of 1794. Washington had to raise fifteen thousand troops to discourage the Pennsylvania farmers who had protested by waving banners denouncing tyranny and proclaiming "Liberty, Equality, and Fraternity." Subsequently, the Federalists abandoned efforts to raise excise taxes, and the Jefferson administration abolished all of them. See Thomas P. Slaughter, *The Whiskey Rebellion: Frontier Epilogue to the American Revolution* (New York: Oxford University Press, 1986).

the federal government if a great national emergency had not intervened.

THE CIVIL WAR SYSTEM

The Civil War was the first emergency that transformed government and its revenue systems. It was the nation's first modern war in the sense of creating enormous requirements for capital, and those requirements evoked a program of emergency taxation that was unprecedented in its scale and scope. Broad electoral support within the North enabled the newly dominant Republican Party to meld its interests with those of the federal government and achieve a great deal of latitude in setting national tax policy. Despite the dramatic break with the modest liberal state of the past, Republican leaders did not face significant resistance to the huge new taxes or need to rely on coercion for their collection. The Republicans were able to persuade the American public to accept the massive broadening of the fiscal foundation of the federal government.

The Republicans introduced a tax system composed primarily of high tariffs and excise taxes, which had been so unpopular during the early republic. These new taxes funded about 20 percent of wartime expenditures. Republican Congresses increased tariffs every year during the war, and the tariff act of 1864 imposed duties that were almost half the total value of all dutiable imports.[5] They also imposed excise taxes on virtually all consumer goods. To administer these taxes, in 1862 Republicans created the office of the commissioner of Internal Revenue. The first commissioner, George S. Boutwell, described the office as "the largest Government department ever organized."[6] During and after the war this system of consumption taxation became the centerpiece, in turn, for the Republicans' ambitious new program of nation-building and national economic policy.[7]

The Republican consumption taxes were regressive, taxing people

---

[5]The standard history of tariff legislation remains Frank W. Taussig, *The Tariff History of the United States* (New York: G. P. Putnam's Sons, 1931).

[6]George S. Boutwell, *Reminiscences of Sixty Years in Public Affairs,* vol. 1 (New York: Greenwood Press, 1968), 313.

[7]On the ways in which the Republicans powerfully fused the interests of the party, the state, and the nation during the Civil War, see Richard F. Bensel, *Yankee Leviathan: The Origins of Central State Authority in America, 1859–1877* (Cambridge: Cambridge University Press, 1990), 1–237.

with lower incomes at higher rates than those with higher incomes. Republican leaders generally preferred such taxes, but they also recognized that regressive taxes might undermine confidence in the Republican Party and the war effort, particularly in western and border states. Consequently, they looked for a supplementary tax that bore a closer relationship to "ability to pay" than did the tariffs and excises. The twin goals would be to raise additional tax revenue, thus easing inflationary pressures, and to convince taxpayers that the wartime fiscal system was fair.

The leadership had few options. The rudimentary accounting methods followed by homes, farms, and businesses meant that the most practical method to raise huge amounts of revenue quickly was the one they had already chosen: taxing goods at the point of importation or sale. Even this approach required the swift development of a large administrative apparatus for the collection of excises. Less practical, but perhaps feasible, was adapting the administrative systems that state and local governments had developed for property taxation. Secretary of the Treasury Salmon P. Chase and Thaddeus Stevens, chairman of the House Ways and Means Committee, favored this approach at first, and they proposed an emergency property tax modeled after one adopted during the War of 1812. But virtually everyone regarded a property tax as a "direct" tax, and Article 1, Section 8, of the Constitution required the federal government to allocate a direct tax among the states on the basis of population rather than property values. Members of Congress from western states (including some from the Old Northwest), border states, and poorer northeastern states protested that this would mean a higher rate of taxation on property in their states. They also complained that the tax as written would not reach the personal property held as real estate improvements and as "intangibles" such as stocks, bonds, mortgages, and cash. Congressman Schuyler Colfax of Indiana declared, "I cannot go home and tell my constituents that I voted for a bill that would allow a man, a millionaire, who has put his entire property into stock, to be exempt from taxation, while a farmer who lives by his side must pay a tax." In response to the complaints, the leadership took note of how the British Liberals had used income taxation in financing the Crimean War as a substitute for heavier taxation of property. Justin S. Morrill of Vermont, who chaired the Ways and Means Subcommittee on Taxation and was a staunch proponent of high tariffs, introduced a proposal for a new and very different tax—the first federal income tax.

Congressional leaders viewed the tax as an indirect tax because it did not directly tax property values.[8]

The first income tax was ungraduated, imposing a basic rate of 3 percent on incomes above a personal exemption of $800. Amendments in subsequent war years reduced the exemption and introduced mild graduation. In 1865, the tax imposed a 5 percent rate on incomes between $600 and $5,000 and 10 percent on incomes over $5,000. The rates seem low by twentieth-century standards, but they imposed higher taxes than the wealthy of the mid-nineteenth century were used to paying under the general property tax.[9] The tax reached well into the affluent upper middle classes of the nation's commercial and industrial centers. The administrative machinery created by the commissioner of internal revenue relied heavily on the cooperation of taxpayers, but compliance was high, promoted by patriotic support for the war effort and by the partial enactment of British "stoppage-at-the-source." The law required agencies of the federal government to collect taxes on salaries and required corporations (railroads, banks, and insurance companies, primarily) to collect taxes on dividends and interest.

By the end of the war, more than 10 percent of all Union households were paying an income tax, and the rate of taxpaying probably reached 15 percent in the northeastern states, where the federal government collected three-fourths of its income-tax revenues. These households probably constituted roughly the slice of society that economic historians have estimated as owning 70 percent or more of the nation's wealth in 1860. The income base for taxation was so substantial that in 1865 the tax, even with its low rate, produced nearly $61 million—21 percent of the federal tax revenues for that year. (The various excises accounted

---

[8]The most informative scholarship detailing the development of income-tax legislation between the Civil War and World War I remains Roy G. Blakey and Gladys C. Blakey, *The Federal Income Tax* (London: Longmans, Green, 1940), 1–103; Sidney Ratner, *American Taxation: Its History as a Social Force in Democracy* (New York: Norton, 1942), 13–340; and Edwin R. A. Seligman, *The Income Tax: A Study of the History, Theory, and Practice of Income Taxation at Home and Abroad* (New York: Macmillan Company, 1914). Robert Stanley has revised this scholarship, emphasizing the conservative forces behind the development of the federal income tax through 1913. In explaining the adoption of the first federal income tax, he emphasizes the Republican desire to provide political protection for the consumption-based tax regime. See Robert Stanley, *Dimensions of Law in the Service of Order: Origins of the Federal Income Tax, 1861–1913* (New York: Oxford University Press, 1993).

[9]On the point that propertied New Yorkers paid substantially higher income taxes than property taxes, see Seligman, *The Income Tax*, 473–75.

for 50 percent and the tariffs the remaining 29 percent.) With the end of hostilities and the resumption of full-scale foreign trade, customs revenues more than doubled in 1866, but income-tax revenues still accounted for 15 percent of all tax revenues. (The share of custom duties rose to 37 percent while the share of excises fell slightly, to 48 percent.)[10]

During the late 1860s and early 1870s, Republican Congresses phased out most of the excise taxes, which the general public resented in peacetime and blamed for postwar increases in the cost of living. Abolishing the excise taxes made it easier for the Republican leadership to phase out the income tax as well. Congressional Republicans generally wanted to respond to the demands of the extremely affluent citizens, who had accepted the income tax only as an emergency measure and now lobbied vigorously to ensure first the reduction of the tax and then its discontinuance at its sunset date of 1870. Little organized support emerged for permanent income taxation, and only a minority of the party's congressional leadership thought about the tax as a valuable rhetorical shield to protect regressive tariffs. Fewer still actually liked the distributional effects of the tax. Consequently, beginning in 1867, the Republican leadership increased the exemptions and lowered the rates. In 1870, Congress mistakenly feared a deficit and extended the tax but then allowed it to expire in 1872.

Republicans, however, maintained the consumption basis of the federal tax system by keeping two elements of the Civil War tax system. First, they retained the high tariffs. Frequent revisions of the tariff schedules left intact the fundamental structure of the tariff system. Until the Underwood-Simmons Tariff Act of 1913 significantly reduced the Civil War rates, the ratio between duties and the value of dutiable goods rarely dropped below 40 percent and was frequently close to 50 percent. The highest rates were imposed on manufactured goods, particularly metals and metal products and including the iron and steel industry, on cotton textiles, and on certain woolen goods. On many such items the

[10]These estimates are based on the well-known taxpayer data developed by the commissioner of internal revenue for 1866. In contrast with my emphasis, Robert Stanley, citing a figure of only 1.3 percent of the American people paying income taxes, claims that the tax did not reach the middle class. Stanley arrives at a lower number, and a serious underestimate of the social reach of the income tax, by including the Confederate population and by not estimating taxpaying households. See Stanley, *Dimensions of Law in the Service of Order*, 39–40, 263–64. On estimates regarding the distribution of income and wealth from 1790 to 1860, see W. Elliot Brownlee, *Dynamics of Ascent: A History of the American Economy* (New York: Alfred A. Knopf, 1979), 134–36.

rate of taxation reached 100 percent. By 1872 tariff duties dominated federal revenues and did so until 1911 except in a few years of severe depression and during the financing of the Spanish-American War.

Second, Republicans left in place the taxes on alcohol and tobacco products and a few taxes on luxury items such as perfumes and cosmetics. Buoyant, price-inelastic demand for alcohol and tobacco products meant that taxes on them yielded substantial revenues, even after the federal government reduced the tax rates. In the years before World War I, revenues from levies on alcohol and tobacco always produced at least one-third of all federal tax revenues, and by the mid-1890s they averaged close to one-half. During 1911–13, alcohol and tobacco taxes produced even more revenue than did the tariffs.

The Republican taxes worked politically and survived, despite their regressivity, partly because, like consumption taxes in general, they escaped the notice of many taxpayers. More important, however, the taxes actually won public acceptance, for a variety of reasons. Most critically, the new tax regime had acquired political momentum by helping to finance a war that redefined the meaning of the American nation. For most of northern society, the Union victory had enhanced the legitimacy of Republican tax measures and, more generally, its program of nationalist state-building and promotion of economic development.

Important as well to the acceptance of the taxes was the popularity of the programs they funded. After the Civil War the consumption-tax regime financed other popular military operations, including the early phases of Reconstruction in the South, the continuing warfare with Native American tribes, and the initiation of a modern navy. Most of the tax revenues that financed the Spanish-American War came from a doubling of the taxes on tobacco and alcohol products.

Broadly popular new programs of public works and transfer payments were also all visibly financed by consumption taxes. These federal programs rewarded loyalty to the Union cause and to the Republican Party. Community leaders throughout the North became accustomed to feeding from what became known as the "pork barrel"—the annual rivers and harbors bill that the consumption-tax revenues funded. Republican governments also used consumption taxes to fund the nation's first major system of social insurance: an ambitious program of pensions and disability benefits for Union veterans and their dependents. As the pensions grew decidedly generous during the 1880s and 1890s, they became a central element in the strength of the Republican Party and continued to be important politically and economically into the twentieth century. Disbursements for disability and old-age benefits, all funded from consumption taxes, soared after the 1879 Arrears Act and the 1890 Dependent Pension Act liberalized benefits, and the benefit spending remained at a high level until World War I. During the late 1890s, the pensions required about 45 percent of all federal receipts. The taxes that funded the transfer payments were regressive, but the distribution of benefits was progressive, at least within the states of the victorious Union.[11]

Leaders of state and local governments, particularly when under the control of Republicans, welcomed the government centralization that the new social programs created. State and local leaders appreciated the way in which the programs satisfied demands for public works and welfare that they would otherwise have had to meet. During the 1880s and the first decade of the twentieth century, urbanization accelerated significantly, requiring cities to invest more in parks, schools, hospitals, transit systems, waterworks, and sewers. State governments increased their investments in higher education and began to aid localities in the financing of schools and roads.

The federal programs were especially welcome because they indirectly relieved the beleaguered system of property taxation that state and local governments employed. Industrialization and economic instability after the Civil War undermined the egalitarian promise of the general property tax to tax all wealth at the same rate. The self-assessment procedures commonly used were inadequate to expose and determine the value of cash, credits, notes, stocks, bonds, and mortgages, especially in the nation's largest cities. The insensitivity of assessment procedures to changes in price level increased the inequities during the economic crises of the late nineteenth century. State and local governments began to develop the modern property tax, with its standardized assessment practices and its focus on real estate.[12]

The consumption-tax system was popular as well because of its reg-

[11]See William H. Glasson, *Federal Military Pensions in the United States* (New York: Oxford University Press, 1918), and Theda Skocpol, *Protecting Soldiers and Mothers: The Political Origins of Social Policy in the United States* (Cambridge, Mass.: Harvard University Press, 1992), 102–51.

[12]On the complex difficulties with the general property tax, see Clifton K. Yearley, *The Money Machines: The Breakdown and Reform of Governmental and Party Finance in*

ulatory dimensions. The enactment of the system represented a stunning victory for economic protectionism and, more generally, for government regulation through taxation. The Republican consumption-tax system made tax incentives (and disincentives) and tax subsidies important, popular, and permanent elements in the federal revenue structure.

The high taxes on alcohol and tobacco appealed to much of the middle-class population as discouragements to, and punishments for, the consumption of commodities thought to be sinful and threatening to a virtuous republican social order. At the same time, the distilling and brewing industries valued the taxes because they provided legitimacy and meant tacit support from the federal government in the struggle against prohibitionist forces.

American business leaders lauded the regulatory effects of the tariff system. Manufacturers welcomed the protection they believed the tariffs afforded them against foreign competitors, and they praised the tendency of a favorable trade balance with Europe to encourage capital formation in America. Beginning in the 1870s and 1880s, manufacturers were especially enthusiastic about the high-tariff system because it allowed them to build national marketing organizations free of worries about disruptions caused by European competitors. The high tariffs provided benefits not so much to the infant industries favored by Adam Smith as to the giant American corporations that were integrating vertically and gaining a long-term advantage over European competitors, who were restricted to smaller markets.

Bankers and members of the financial community generally favored less emphasis on protection, more attention to the stimulation of international trade, and reductions in spending on lighthouses and pensions, coupled with further tax reductions. Nonetheless, they liked the way in which substantial taxes on consumption forced increases in the nation's rate of savings and facilitated the repayment of the wartime debt. By using consumption taxes to finance the war debt and interest payments (the latter rendered in the gold collected by customs duties), the Republican leadership transferred significant amounts of capital from consumers to holders of federal debt (Europeans as well as Americans), who tended to be wealthier than the average consumer and more likely to invest. And creditors, especially the holders of the federal debt, appre-

the North, 1860–1920 (Albany: State University of New York Press, 1970), 3–95, 137–65.

ciated the way in which the Republican taxes tended to produce budget surpluses in the 1870s, reduced the debt, helped to contract the money supply, and eased the return to the domestic gold standard in 1879.[13]

High tariffs also seemed to benefit workers, who commonly feared competition from lower-wage labor in Europe, Latin America, and Asia and favored tax policies that advanced the prosperity of their industries. Labor support for the high-tariff position of the Republican Party had much to do with its smashing victory in the "critical election" of 1896 and its strong electoral displays, which continued until the Great Depression.

Finally, the high-tariff system received vigorous support from congressional leaders for purely political reasons. They discovered that the tariff system created significant opportunities for them to reinforce or enhance their power. By making adjustments within the complex and poorly understood web of tax subsidies, congressional politicians could offer benefits to narrowly defined groups or threaten these groups with penalties, without fear of fatal reprisal from larger publics.

The Republican architects of the tax regime, however, had to face significant partisan resistance to their tax policy, especially after the resumption of serious two-party competition. During the 1870s and 1880s, the Democratic Party challenged Republican power with a biting critique of a central element of the consumption-tax system—the tariff. To some extent, sectional interests drove the Democratic challenge. It was an appeal to the southerners who received neither the regulatory nor the programmatic benefits, like the Civil War pensions, of the tariffs and excises they paid. But the critique was a more general attack on special privilege, monopoly power, and public corruption—one that harkened back to the ideals of the American Revolution and the early republic. The Democrats described the tariff as the "mother of trusts" and, more generally, as the primary engine of a Republican program of subsidizing giant corporations. The Democrats framed their message to appeal to southerners, to be sure, but also to farmers, middle-class consumers, and owners of small businesses throughout the nation.

In fact, during the 1880s and 1890s, the two competing political par-

---

[13]According to one estimate, debt retirement and interest payments accounted for as much as one-half of the rise in the share of national economic product devoted to capital formation between the 1850s and the 1870s. See Jeffrey G. Williamson, "Watersheds and Turning Points: Conjectures on the Long-Term Impact of Civil War Financing," *Journal of Economic History* 34 (September 1974): 636–61.

ties came to base their appeals on sharply conflicting ideological views of the tariff and of taxation in general. In a kind of path-dependent politics initiated by the Civil War crisis, those identities would have a major influence on revenue policy until World War II. The Republicans' invocation of high tariffs and the Democrats' response had sharply polarized the parties on issues of taxation. These tax issues would exacerbate class conflict for nearly a century.[14]

Criticism of the tariff intensified during the depression of the mid-1890s. Economic distress stimulated Populists in the West and the South, and champions of Henry George's "single-tax" scattered throughout urban America to promote social justice through tax reform. These two movements converged in their efforts to find ways to use the tax system to punish and discourage monopoly power. The Populists championed a progressive tax on the profits of corporations and the incomes of the wealthy, and "single-taxers" often supported it at the federal level while they sought radical reform of the property tax at the state and local levels.[15]

The new grass-roots pressure began to change the politics of federal taxation. During the Civil War, the Republican leaders had exercised a great deal of discretion in crafting the income tax. To be sure, they had developed the tax in anticipation of sectional and class resistance to a federal property tax. But they had designed the tax without any group's insistence that they do so. And, after the war, they set their own timetable for its demise. In contrast, when Congress began to seriously reconsider income taxation during the early 1890s, it did so primarily in response to popular pressure. Moreover, Congress then faced numerous proposals for a high degree of progression, and the arguments of the proposers had a sharp, radical edge.

Central to the appeal of a highly progressive income tax during the 1890s was the claim that the tax would both reallocate fiscal burdens according to "ability to pay" and help restore a virtuous republic free of concentrations of economic power. The rhetoric was, in a sense, con-

---

[14]On the partisan and ideological nature of the tariff debates, see Tom E. Terrill, *The Tariff, Politics, and American Foreign Policy, 1874–1901* (Westport, Conn.: Greenwood Press, 1973), esp. 210–17.

[15]The traditional "progressive" scholarship placed a great deal of emphasis on the importance of such grass-roots pressure by farmers in shaping the inception of the federal income tax. See, for example, Elmer Ellis, "Public Opinion and the Income Tax, 1860–1900," *Mississippi Valley Historical Review* 27 (September 1940): 225–42, and Ratner, *American Taxation.*

servative; it directed attention to the values of the early republic. What was potentially radical about the movement for progressive income taxation was its content: the goal of raising the government's revenues primarily or even entirely from the largest incomes and corporate profits. The radical advocates for income taxation argued that their tax would not touch the wages and salaries of ordinary people but would, instead, attack unearned profits and monopoly power. The tax would, its proponents claimed, redress the wealth and power maldistribution that was responsible for the evils of industrialization. Those who believed they had faced expropriation would now do the expropriating.

Thus, support for a radical progressive income tax had far more to do with the search for social justice in an industrializing nation than with the quest for an elastic source of revenue. The tax became an integral part of democratic statism—a radical program of invoking instruments of government power to create a more democratic social order. This redistributional aspect of democratic statism was a major theme uniting some of the important legislative initiatives undertaken by the federal government before World War II. It was, in part, a new kind of liberalism, a realignment of classic nineteenth-century liberalism and the commonwealth tradition of early republicanism, which included a distrust of commerce. Democratic statists like the Populists and the single-taxers regarded themselves as applying the ideals of the American Revolution to the new conditions of industrial society. Although the strategy remained one of liberating individual energies by providing a social order of abundant opportunity, the tactics had changed. To these new liberals, the state had become a necessary instrument and ally, not an enemy. They designed their tax program to restructure the market-driven machinery for distributing income and wealth.[16]

During the severe economic depression of the mid-1890s, the pressures for progressive tax reform from western and southern Populists became

[16]For a discussion of the meaning of democratic statism and its relationship to progressive income taxation, see W. Elliot Brownlee, "Economists and the Formation of the Modern Tax System in the United States: The World War I Crisis," in *The State and Economic Knowledge: The American and British Experience*, ed. Mary O. Furner and Barry E. Supple (Cambridge: Cambridge University Press and the Woodrow Wilson International Center for Scholars, 1990), 401–35. Democratic statism also had an expression in the regulatory taxation of individual and corporate behavior. In this regard, after the turn of the century, reformers built on the precedents of alcohol and tobacco taxation and used the federal taxing power to regulate grain and cotton futures, the production of white phosphorous matches, the consumption of narcotics, and even the employment of child labor. See R. Alton Lee, *A History of Regulatory Taxation* (Lexington: University Press of Kentucky, 1973).

strong enough to begin to shift the position of the leadership of the Democratic Party. A contributing factor also was the decline of foreign trade and tariff revenues during the depression. This enabled the Democrats to embrace a proposal for a new tax while still calling for the shrinkage of swollen Republican programs. Democrats took control of both houses of Congress in 1893, and its leaders in the House from the South and the West, including Benton McMillin of Tennessee, who chaired the Ways and Means Subcommittee on Internal Revenue, led in enacting an income tax in 1894 as part of the Wilson-Gorman Tariff. They sensed an opportunity to use tax issues for a major realignment of the two political parties along sectional and class lines, and they debated the income tax with unprecedented agrarian ferocity.[17]

Hostility from northeastern Democrats, as well as the opposition from most Republicans (including leaders, like Senator John Sherman of Ohio and Senator Morrill, who had supported the Civil War income tax), limited the progressivity of the tax. Within both parties, leaders recalled how effective the Civil War income tax had been in reaching the incomes of the nation's wealthy families. Congress reproduced many of the technical features of the Civil War income tax but established a much higher personal exemption ($4,000) and a somewhat lower rate on incomes and profits (2 percent). In any event, the 1894 tax was short-lived because in 1895 the Supreme Court, in *Pollock v. Farmers' Loan and Trust Co.*, declared that the income tax of the Wilson-Gorman Tariff was unconstitutional.[18]

The *Pollock* decision raised a significant institutional barrier to pro-

[17]For suggestions of this kind, see Charles V. Stewart, "The Federal Income Tax and the Realignment of the 1890s," in *Realignment in American Politics: Toward a Theory*, ed. Bruce A. Campbell and Richard J. Trilling (Austin: University of Texas Press, 1980), 263–87. Stewart also describes the way in which political parties, in building consensus, moderated the content and rhetorical tone of income-tax proposals after 1896. See Charles V. Stewart, "The Formation of Tax Policy in America, 1893–1913" (Ph.D. diss., University of North Carolina at Chapel Hill, 1974).

[18]Modern scholarship has modified an older "progressive" interpretation of the *Pollock* decision as a conspiratorial act of judicial fiat. For that view, see Robert G. McCloskey, *The American Supreme Court* (Chicago: University of Chicago Press, 1960), 140–41, and Sidney Ratner, *Taxation and Democracy in America* (New York: Wiley, 1967), 193–214, among others. The best current discussion of the role of the Court is Stanley, *Dimensions of Law in the Service of Order*, 136–75. Stanley argues that the Court was engaged in a kind of Jacksonian attack on the dominant role of Congress in "statist capitalism." Consistent with his interpretation is Morton Horwitz's argument that the *Pollock* decision was a logical culmination of a process that established an "anti-redistributive principle" as "part of the very essence of the constitutional law of a neutral state." See Morton J. Horwitz, *The Transformation of American Law, 1870–1960: The Crisis of Legal Orthodoxy* (New York: Oxford University Press, 1992), 19–27.

gressive taxation, but it also stimulated some support for income taxation. The Populists and the Democrats from the South and the West now attacked the Court and found that their audiences responded enthusiastically. In response, Democrats began to introduce constitutional amendments that would permit income taxation, and in 1896 the Democratic Party formally endorsed income taxation. This was the first time a major party had done so.

But the Democrats went down to a decisive defeat in 1896, and the Republican Party's leaders believed the results proved that they need not feel any urgency in confronting pressure for progressive tax reform. When Republicans faced the problem of financing the Spanish-American War in 1898, they had recovered the power to neutralize the Democratic thrust for income taxation, and they did so with confidence.[19]

During the next fifteen years, however, support for income taxation grew gradually. The gains were most marked across rural America but especially in the Midwest and the West. There, Republican leaders like Robert M. La Follette of Wisconsin discovered that income taxation was one of those reform issues that attracted and held voters to the alignment the party had crafted in 1896. Both Presidents Theodore Roosevelt and William Howard Taft recognized this support and made vague gestures of support for a graduated income tax (in 1906 and 1908, respectively). But support for income taxation grew too in the urban Northeast as both Republican and Democratic leaders found that the tax had begun to appeal to their constituents.

Important to the new support for federal income taxation was the formation of an urban-rural alignment of middle-class citizens who supported state and local tax reform. The economic depression of the 1890s, followed by accelerating demands for services from state and local governments, accentuated the flaws in general property taxation. Both farmers and middle-class property owners in towns and cities resented how their tax burdens grew as a consequence of the inability of local and state governments to use general property taxation to reach intangible

[19]For suggestions of the influence of what political scientists call "critical elections" on tax policy, see Susan B. Hansen, *The Politics of Taxation: Revenue without Representation* (New York: Praeger, 1983). Hansen rests heavily on these elections, which produced long-term realignments of party loyalty, for explaining the timing of major shifts in tax policy, but the fit is very loose. Among the critical elections, only the 1860 (and possibly the 1980) election was followed by an immediate shift in tax regimes; the 1896 election confirmed the existing regime rather than ushering in a new one; and the introduction of the World War I regime was not associated with a critical election.

personal property. And these groups became interested in the adoption of new taxes—such as income, inheritance, and corporate taxes—as replacements for state property taxes.[20] Small property owners, both rural and urban, increasingly believed that income taxes would help restore the progressivity lost in the administrative collapse of the Jacksonian general property tax under industrial conditions.[21]

But states were very slow to adopt the new, alternative taxes, and industrial states were especially slow in adopting income taxes. Administrative difficulties and fears of damaging industry and jobs discouraged them. Nonetheless, the debates promoted widespread interest in any approach, including adoption of income taxes, that might rebalance the equity of the tax system. In addition, the sluggish progress of income taxation at the state level increasingly convinced middle-class citizens that it would be desirable to enact the tax at the federal level.[22]

During the ferment over tax issues at the state and local levels, some defenders of the wealthiest property owners joined in support of federal income taxation. They concluded that the tax might help take the wind

---

[20]For an example of early advocacy for replacing personal property taxation with state income taxation, see Richard T. Ely, *Taxation in American States and Cities* (New York: Thomas Y. Crowell, 1888), 287–311.

[21]The impetus for reform of state taxes in Wisconsin was predominantly rural, but David P. Thelen presents persuasive evidence that in the late 1890s urban tax issues transformed Wisconsin mugwumps, many of whom were "conservative businessmen," into "crusaders against corporate arrogance." See Thelen, *The New Citizenship: Origins of Progressivism in Wisconsin, 1885–1900* (Columbia: University of Missouri Press, 1972), 202–22. Clifton K. Yearley offers a similar interpretation in an overview of urban fiscal reform before World War I. See Yearley, *The Money Machines: The Breakdown and Reform of Governmental and Party Finance in the North, 1860–1920*, 193–250. In contrast, John D. Buenker finds strong support for urban tax reform among Democratic "representatives of the urban new stock working class." Buenker is not clear as to the possible overlap between "working class" and the "urban middle class." See Buenker, *Urban Liberalism and Progressive Reform* (New York: W. W. Norton, 1973), esp. 103–17. Morton Keller concludes that "a welter of conflicting goals and interests determined tax policy and practice" in cities and states during this period. See Keller, *Regulating a New Economy: Public Policy and Economic Change in America, 1900–1933* (Cambridge, Mass.: Harvard University Press, 1990), 208–15.

[22]In 1911, Wisconsin adopted the first modern income tax. The state finessed the administrative problems by collecting most of the revenues from corporations, which faced a stringently administered 6 percent tax on their profits. Manufacturers accounted for about two-thirds of the corporate burden. Massachusetts and New York did not adopt income taxes until they faced the fiscal problems imposed by World War I and until they were confident that they could build the administrative machinery required to assess and collect a tax based primarily on individual incomes rather than corporate profits. Most industrial states did not enact income taxes until the revenue crisis created by the Great Depression. For the history of the Wisconsin income tax, see W. Elliot Brownlee, *Progressivism and Economic Growth: The Wisconsin Income Tax, 1911–1929* (Port Washington, N.Y.: Kennikat Press, 1974).

out of the sails of more radical tax measures at the state and local levels. The most influential among these conservatives was a group of urban economists and attorneys who were tax experts. Edwin R. A. Seligman of Columbia University and Charles J. Bullock of Harvard University led them in promoting income taxation, on the one hand, and in moderating the rhetoric used to justify the tax, on the other. As early as 1894 Seligman had argued that the point of the tax was to "round out the existing tax system in the direction of greater justice."[23] Such language helped shift the discourse over taxation from a focus on the salvation of industrial America to an emphasis on a moderate redistribution of the tax burden.

Conservative support for moderate income taxation might be described as expressing a kind of "corporate liberalism," or "progressive capitalism." More generally, this vision, developing in tension with democratic statism, influenced not only the development of income taxation but also the ideas of the so-called progressive movement. Reformers of this more conservative persuasion wanted to bring a greater degree of order to industrial society and to strengthen national institutions, just as did the democratic statists. But, in contrast with democratic statists, "progressive capitalists" or "corporate liberals" looked with admiration on the efficiency of the modern corporation. Government regulation, including taxation, was desirable only if it served to protect the investment system.[24]

By 1909, there were enough insurgent Republicans in Congress who supported a graduated income tax to force action. A diverse group of representatives and senators from both parties supported the immediate enactment of such a tax. Congressman Cordell Hull, a first-term Democrat who represented the same Tennessee district as had Benton McMillin, noted changes in the composition of the Supreme Court and found it "inconceivable" that the country had "a Constitution that would shelter the chief portion of the wealth of the country from the only effective method of reaching it for its fair share of taxes."[25] A bipartisan group hammered out a proposal, but they had to limit the pro-

---

[23]Edwin R. A. Seligman, "The Income Tax," *Political Science Quarterly* (1894), 610.
[24]Exemplary discussions of corporate liberalism are Mary Furner, "Knowing Capitalism: Public Investigation and the Labor Question in the Long Progressive Era," in Furner and Supple, *The State and Economic Knowledge*, 241–86, and Martin J. Sklar, *The Corporate Reconstruction of American Capitalism, 1890–1916* (Cambridge: Cambridge University Press, 1988).
[25]Cordell Hull, *The Memoirs of Cordell Hull*, vol. 1 (New York: Macmillan, 1948), 49.

gressivity of the tax in order to generate enough support. Senator Nelson Aldrich, the chair of the Senate Finance Committee, proved resourceful in both preserving Republican Party union and blunting the thrust toward income taxation. He worked closely with President Taft to persuade the insurgents to accept a modest corporate income tax, described as "a special excise tax," and the submission of the Sixteenth Amendment, legalizing a federal income tax, to the states for ratification. Aldrich and the northeastern Republicans recognized the growing popular support for income taxation but hoped that the measure would fail.

Ratification prevailed in 1913, much to the surprise and consternation of standpat conservatives.[26] The process of ratification succeeded in part because of two other campaigns. One was a revival of the single-tax movement. Beginning in 1909, the soap magnate Joseph Fels, who had converted to Henry George's faith, began to finance campaigns for constitutional reforms permitting classification of property for the purpose of taxation (and thus high rates of taxation on the "site value" of land) and for local option in taxation. Although the campaigns won no significant electoral victories except in Oregon in 1910, they awakened the interest of the urban middle class in using the income tax to redistribute wealth.[27] The campaigns also convinced more wealthy property owners that they needed moderate reform as a defensive measure, and their support was important to the crucial victory of ratification in New York in 1911. The other set of campaigns was the presidential election of 1912. As a consequence of the campaigns of Woodrow Wilson, Theodore Roosevelt, and Eugene Debs, popular enthusiasm for federal policies designed to attack monopoly power reached an all-time high.

In 1913, bipartisan support for income taxation was broad, and the Democrats controlled Congress. Nonetheless, the income-tax measure they enacted was only modest. To some extent this was because the leaders of both parties were cautious and wanted to maximize support for income taxation within the Northeast, where they feared the tax would be unpopular, and thus maintain party unity. To a greater extent it was because the nation's political leaders, as well as the general public,

[26]The standard source on the ratification movement is John D. Buenker, *The Income Tax and the Progressive Era* (New York: Garland, 1985).
[27]On Joseph Fels's campaigns, see Arthur P. Dudden, *Joseph Fels and the Single-Tax Movement* (Philadelphia: Temple University Press, 1971), 199–245, and Arthur N. Young, *The Single Tax Movement in the United States* (Princeton: Princeton University Press, 1916), 163–83.

were unsure of how much redistribution they wanted the new tax instrument to accomplish. Woodrow Wilson urged caution on Furnifold M. Simmons, chair of the Senate Finance Committee. "Individual judgments will naturally differ," Wilson wrote, "with regard to the burden it is fair to lay upon incomes which run above the usual levels."[28] Moreover, the supporters of income taxation were themselves uncertain how income ought to be defined or how the income tax would work administratively.

Finally, virtually no proponent of the tax within the government believed that the income tax would become a major, let alone the dominant, permanent source of revenue within the consumption-based federal tax system. Certainly the advocates of income taxation who were hostile to the protective tariff hoped that the tax would succeed and expedite reduction of tariffs. But they doubted that the new revenues would be substantial. And the idea that the tax would enable the federal government to grow significantly was far from the minds of the drafters of the 1913 legislation. To be sure, Congressman Hull, who was the primary drafter of the 1913 legislation, wanted to make certain that the federal government would have access to the income tax in wartime; he believed that the federal government could make the tax, as an emergency measure, even more productive than it had been during the Civil War. But for Hull, as well as the other income-tax enthusiasts, the revenue goals of the tax were far less important than the desire to use the tax to advance economic justice.[29]

[28]Woodrow Wilson to Furnifold M. Simmons, September 4, 1913, in Arthur S. Link, ed., *The Papers of Woodrow Wilson*, vol. 28 (Princeton: Princeton University, 1978), 254.

[29]Jordan A. Schwartz has cited Cordell Hull's emergency-revenue argument in stating, "Anticipation of war made the income tax a war tax." See Schwartz, *The New Dealers: Power Politics in the Age of Roosevelt* (New York: Alfred A. Knopf, 1993), 14. There is no evidence, however, that Hull expected war in 1910, when he made the cited comment, and there is much evidence that Hull was then primarily interested in a redistribution of the tax burden. For Hull's own description of his important role in federal tax reform before World War I, see Hull, *Memoirs* 1:45–74. Between 1894 and 1913, when champions of income taxation referred to the possible need to levy it in wartime, they were usually buttressing their legal arguments for the constitutionality of the federal tax. See, for example, the dissenting opinion of Justice John Marshall Harlan in *Pollock v. Farmers' Loan and Trust Company*, 158 U.S. 601, 15 S.Ct. 673, 39 L.Ed. 1108 (1895), and Seligman, "The Proposed Sixteenth Amendment to the Constitution," *The Income Tax*, 627–28. (Seligman first published this part of the essay in 1910.) Historians have only rarely claimed that the architects of the Sixteenth Amendment or the 1913 legislation expected the tax to produce major additions to federal revenue. The leading examples are Ben Baack and Edward J. Ray, who claim that the passage of the 1913 income tax "signaled voters that the federal government had the wherewithal to provide

Consequently, the Underwood-Simmons Tariff Act of 1913 was less progressive and less ambitious in its revenue goals than the Civil War legislation or even the legislation of 1894. The new tax established the "normal" rate of 1 percent on both individual and corporate incomes, with a high exemption ($3,000 for single taxpayers) that excused virtually all middle-class Americans from the tax. The tax also established a graduated surtax up to 6 percent, but this did not come into play for incomes under $20,000. In the first several years of the income tax, only about 2 percent of American households paid taxes. Meanwhile, the tariff and the taxation of tobacco and alcohol remained the most productive sources of revenue. The tariff, in fact, became even more productive because the 1913 reduction of tariff rates by the Wilson administration stimulated trade and increased revenues. If it had not been for World War I mobilization, the major consequence of the passage of the income tax in 1913 might have been the protection of the regime of consumption taxation inherited from the Civil War.

THE WORLD WAR I SYSTEM

The financial demands of World War I, set in the context of redistributional politics, accelerated tax reform far beyond the leisurely pace that corporate liberals would have preferred. In fact, the wartime crisis produced a brand-new tax regime—one that was close to the ideals of democratic statists. This new tax system, the most significant domestic initiative to emerge from the war, probably would not have taken the form it did had the United States not entered the war.[30]

something for everybody." See Baack and Ray, "The Political Economy of the Origin and Development of the Federal Income Tax," in *Emergence of the Modern Political Economy: Research in Economic History, Supplement 4,* ed. Robert Higgs (Greenwich, Conn.: JAI Press, 1985), 121–38.

[30]On the financing of World War I, see the following: W. Elliot Brownlee, "Wilson and Financing the Modern State: The Revenue Act of 1916," *Proceedings of the American Philosophical Society* 129 (1985): 173–210; Brownlee, "Economists and the Formation of the Modern Tax System"; and W. Elliot Brownlee, "Social Investigation and Political Learning in the Financing of World War I," in Michael J. Lacey and Mary O. Furner, eds., *The State and Social Investigation in Britain and the United States* (Cambridge: Cambridge University Press and Washington, D.C.: Woodrow Wilson Center Press, 1993), 323–64. Another study that appreciates the role of political contingencies, and the radical thrusts of Congress between 1916 and 1921, is Jerold L. Waltman, *Political Origins of the U.S. Income Tax* (Jackson: University Press of Mississippi, 1985). For a different interpretation of World War I finance, see Charles Gilbert, *American Financing of World War I* (Westport, Conn.: Greenwood, 1970). Gilbert, an economist, was interested in World War I finance as an example of how democracies tend to abstain from

The tax-reform process began in 1916 when President Wilson and Secretary of the Treasury William G. McAdoo made the single most important financial decision of the war. They chose to cooperate with a group of insurgent Democrats in arranging wartime financing on the basis of highly progressive taxation. Led by Congressman Claude Kitchin of North Carolina, who chaired the House Ways and Means Committee, the insurgent Democrats attacked concentrations of wealth, special privilege, and public corruption. Kitchin exploited the influence of the Ways and Means Committee. The Democratic insurgents could insist that if preparedness and later the war effort were to move forward, they would do so only on the insurgents' financial terms. They embraced taxation as an important means to achieve social justice according to the humanistic ideals of the early republic. Redistributional taxation then became a major part of the Wilson administration's program for steering between socialism and unmediated capitalism.[31]

The war provided an opportunity for Democratic progressives to focus the debate over taxation on one of the most fundamental and sensitive economic issues in modern America: what stake does society have in corporate profits? More specifically, the question became one of whether the modern corporation was the central engine of productivity, which tax policy should reinforce, or whether it was an economic predator,

the kind of taxation that would promote strategic mobilization with the least inflation and disruption of productive capacity: taxation transferring purchasing power from consumers to the government. "War finance," Gilbert wrote, "is and always has been a victory of expediency over economics" (236). Gilbert's characterizations of tax institutions are similar to those of the political scientists described as pluralists. Herbert Stein offered a more positive view of McAdoo's Treasury but offered one similar criticism of its approach to taxation. Stein suggested that the Treasury was unwilling to pay the political costs of devising a tax program focused on discouraging "nonessential production." See Herbert Stein, *Government Price Policy in the United States during the World War* (Williamstown, Mass.: Williams College, 1939), 78–84, 124.

[31]Southern sectionalism reinforced the class-based populism of Claude Kitchin. Some political science scholarship has stressed the crippling effect of post–Civil War southern sectionalism, and the associated hostility toward the federal government, on the development of a modern state. But this scholarship does not discuss progressive federal income taxation, which, if anything, this sectionalism, expressed in the careers of Claude Kitchin and Cordell Hull, promoted during World War I. See Richard Bensel, *Sectionalism and American Political Development, 1880–1980* (Wisconsin: University of Wisconsin Press, 1984); Bensel, *Yankee Leviathan;* and Jill Quadrango, *The Transformation of Old Age Security: Class and Politics in the American Welfare State* (Chicago: University of Chicago Press, 1988). Historians are well aware of the general significance of the southerners who were in Wilson's administration or among his supporters in Congress, but no one has systematically examined their ideas on government. The best analyses are Arthur S. Link, "The South and the 'New Freedom': An Interpretation," *American Scholar* 20 (1950–51): 314–24, and George B. Tindall, *The Emergence of the New South, 1913–1945* (Baton Rouge: Louisiana State University Press, 1967), 1–60.

which tax policy could and should tame. The outcome of the debate was that the nation embraced a new tax system: "soak-the-rich" income taxation.[32]

Thus, during the period of crisis, one in which the pressure of fighting a modern war coincided with powerful demands to break the hold of corporate privilege, Wilson and the Democratic Party turned Republican fiscal policy on its head. The Democrats embraced a tax policy that they claimed, just as the Republicans had for their tariff system, would sustain a powerful state and economic prosperity. But the new tax policy of the Democrats was one that assaulted, rather than protected, the privileges associated with corporate wealth.

The Democratic tax program, implemented in the wartime Revenue Acts, transformed the experimental, rather tentative income tax into the foremost instrument of federal taxation. Their program introduced federal estate taxation. It imposed the first significant taxation of corporate profits and personal incomes but rejected moving toward a more broadly based income tax—one falling most heavily on wages and salaries. Last but far from least, it adopted the concept of taxing corporate "excess profits." Alone among all the World War I belligerents, America placed excess-profits taxation—a graduated tax on all business profits above a "normal" rate of return—at the center of wartime finance. Excess-profits taxation turned out to be responsible for most of the tax revenues raised by the federal government during the war. Taxes accounted for a larger share of total revenues in the United States than in any of the other belligerent nations, despite the fact that by the end of 1918 the daily average of war expenditures in the United States was almost double that in Great Britain and far greater than that in any other belligerent nation.[33]

---

[32]A contrasting view of the importance of redistributional impulses is John Witte's. In explaining the crucial Revenue Act of 1916, he stresses the "dictates of war" and asserts, "There is little evidence of an independent interest in redistributing income through the tax system." See John Witte, *The Politics and Development of the Federal Income Tax* (Madison: University of Wisconsin Press, 1985), 81–82.

[33]A comprehensive explanation of differences among the belligerents in their reliance on taxation would have to incorporate economic constraints as well as political culture. The explanation would have to recognize, for example, that whereas Great Britain financed somewhat less of its war costs through taxation (roughly 29 percent, compared with 37 percent for the United States), the war costs of Britain were about 21 percent larger than those of the United States. Gerd Hardach provides limited international comparisons regarding war finance. See Hardach, *The First World War, 1914–1918* (Berkeley: University of California Press, 1977), 150–55. The source behind most of Hardach's figures is Harvey E. Fisk, *The Inter-Ally Debts: An Analysis of War and Post-War Public Fi-*

The income tax with excess-profits taxation at its core outraged business leaders. Redistributional taxation, along with the wartime strengthening of the Treasury (including the Bureau of Internal Revenue, the forerunner to the Internal Revenue Service) posed a long-term strategic threat to the nation's corporations. Those most severely threatened were the largest corporations, which believed their financial autonomy to be in jeopardy. In addition, the new tax system empowered the federal government, as never before, to implement egalitarian ideals. No other single issue aroused as much corporate hostility to the Wilson administration as did the financing of the war. Wilson's longtime supporters within the business community, like Bernard Baruch, Jacob Schiff, and Clarence Dodge, bitterly attacked his tax program within the administration and often quietly supported Republican critics. The conflict between advocates of democratic-statist, soak-the-rich taxation, on the one hand, and business leaders, on the other hand, would rage on for more than two decades.

Despite the damage to business confidence, the Wilson administration and congressional Democratic leaders moved forward with excess-profits taxation with almost no attention to the complaints of Baruch and other business critics. The Democratic leaders did so in part because they shared Kitchin's ideal of using taxation to restructure the economy according to nineteenth-century liberal ideals. They presumed that the largest corporations exercised inordinate control over wealth and that a "money trust" dominated the allocation of capital. For Wilson and McAdoo, the tax program, with its promise to tax monopoly power and break monopoly's hold on America's entrepreneurial energy, seemed to constitute an attractive new dimension to Wilson's "New Freedom" approach to the "emancipation of business." Thus, wartime public finance was based on the taxation of assets that democratic statists regarded as ill-gotten and socially hurtful, comparable to the rents from the land monopolies that Henry George and his followers had wanted to tax. In fact, both Wilson and McAdoo entertained explicit single-tax ideas as they developed their tax-reform program.[34]

nance, *1914–1923* (New York: Bankers Trust Company, 1924). The most careful accounting of American war costs remains Edwin R. A. Seligman, *Essays in Taxation* (New York: Macmillan, 1921), 748–82.

[34] Wilson, however, had far greater suspicion of the administrative state than did McAdoo. In 1916, because of that suspicion, Wilson may well have been attracted to using taxation, rather than administrative regulation, to tackle "the monopoly problem." As the war wore on, and as he was unable to resist the growing influence of business within

Party government also played a crucial role in the decision of the Wilson administration. Wilson and McAdoo knew they could have easily engineered passage of a much less progressive tax system—one relying more heavily on consumption taxes and taxation of middle-class incomes—in cooperation with Republicans and a minority of conservative Democrats. They were confident in their ability to administer such broad-based taxes effectively. But they regarded mass-based taxation as a betrayal of the principles of their party. After all, the Democratic Party had strong traditions of representation of the disadvantaged, of hostility to a strong central government as the instrument of special privilege, of opposition to the taxation of consumption, and of support for policies designed to widen access to economic opportunity. A failure to adopt a highly progressive and "reconstructive" tax program would have had serious consequences for Wilson and McAdoo. They would have bitterly divided their party. They would have spoiled their opportunities for attracting Republican progressives to their party. And they would have destroyed their strong partnership with congressional Democrats—a partnership that both leaders regarded as necessary for the effective advancement of national administration.[35]

Closely related to the Wilson administration's tax program was its sale of war bonds to middle-class Americans. Rather than tax middle-class Americans at high levels, the Wilson administration employed a voluntary program to mobilize their savings, a strategy that McAdoo called "capitalizing patriotism." He attempted to persuade Americans to change their economic behavior: to reduce consumption, increase savings, and become creditors of the state. He hoped that after the conclusion of the war, the middle-class bondholders would be repaid by tax dollars raised from corporations and the wealthiest Americans.

Selling the high-priced bonds directly to average Americans on a multibillion-dollar scale required marketing campaigns far greater in scope

the wartime bureaucracy, Wilson became even more attracted to the antimonopoly potential of excess-profits taxation. But no scholar has fully explored the linkages between Wilson's approach to the taxation of business and his overall relations with business. Consequently, the issue of whether or not Wilson's ideas and policies, considered comprehensively, represent democratic statism or corporate liberalism lies beyond the scope of this essay. The best study of Wilson and business during the war is Robert D. Cuff, *The War Industries Board: Business-Government Relations during World War I* (Baltimore: Johns Hopkins University Press, 1973).

[35]For a discussion of the sustained hostility toward special privilege within the Democratic Party, see Robert E. Kelley, *The Transatlantic Persuasion: The Liberal-Democratic Mind in the Age of Gladstone* (New York: Alfred A. Knopf, 1969).

than those used anywhere else in the world. Largely through trial and error, the Wilson administration pioneered a vast array of state-controlled national marketing techniques, including the sophisticated analysis of national income and savings. Financing by the new Federal Reserve system, which McAdoo turned into an arm of the Treasury, was important, but not as much as McAdoo's efforts to shift private savings into bonds. In the course of managing and promoting four "Liberty Loans," Secretary McAdoo and the Treasury expanded the federal government's and the nation's knowledge of the social basis of capital markets. The Treasury team used information gathered by its own systematic investigations; it armed itself with modern techniques of mass communication; and it placed its loans deep in the middle class—far deeper than it had during the Civil War or than European governments did in World War I. In the Third Liberty Loan campaign (conducted in April 1918), at least one-half of all American families subscribed. Thus, the new public-finance regime installed by the Wilson administration encompassed a revolution in borrowing strategy as well as tax policy.

The new tax regime had broad and significant administrative implications. The complex and ambitious program of taxing and borrowing required a vast expansion of the Treasury's administrative capacity. A major arm of the Treasury was the Bureau of Internal Revenue (BIR), whose personnel increased from 4,000 to 15,800 between 1913 and 1920 and which underwent a reorganization along multifunctional lines, with clear specifications of responsibilities and chains of command. One of the most demanding chores of the bureau was the administration of the excess-profits tax. In the process of interpreting, selling, explaining, and assessing the new business tax, the Treasury made great strides in the creation of a modern staff of experts—accountants, lawyers, and economists. Much of this new bureaucracy also implemented the new individual income tax by processing the huge volume of information on individual taxpayers. This flow of information resulted from an "information at the source" provision in the Revenue Act of 1916, which required corporations to report on salaries, dividends, and interest payments. In short, the Treasury built a class of mediators—defining themselves as experts—whose task was to reconcile the goals of the corporation and affluent individuals with the needs of the state. But under McAdoo's leadership, the Treasury undertook far more than a "broker-state" balancing of contesting interest groups; it enhanced the power of the state to advance economic justice and the war.

Running the Treasury was an exceptionally capable team assembled by McAdoo. It employed "businesslike" methods and demonstrated intellectual flexibility and entrepreneurship. Lacking an adequate civil service, McAdoo fashioned within the Treasury the kind of organization one political scientist has called an "informal political technocracy," or a "loose grouping of people where the lines of policy, politics, and administration merge in a complex jumble of bodies." This was an early example of what would become a typical expression of America's unique form of a "higher civil service."[36]

The Treasury group did far more than administer new taxing and borrowing programs. It served as the Wilson administration's primary instrument for learning about financial policy and its social implications, for shaping the definition of financial issues and administration programs, and for mobilizing support for those programs. The group developed a significant degree of autonomy. It became the means for McAdoo to form and dominate networks linking together competing centers of power within the federal government and linking the government with civil society. Because McAdoo had formed such a group, he was able to design and implement a financial policy with clear social objectives. Under his leadership, the Treasury avoided falling under the control of competing centers of power within the government and of other groups outside. The Treasury escaped the disarray that befell much of the Wilson administration's mobilization effort.

Wilsonian democratic statism finally succumbed to a business counterattack. In 1918, corporate leaders and Republicans found an opening when President Wilson tried to make a case for doubling taxes. Using vigorous antitax, antigovernment campaigns throughout the nation, and antisouthern campaigns in the West, Republicans gained control of Congress. Then, in 1920, they rode to a presidential victory during the postwar economic depression. The Democratic Party of Woodrow Wilson had failed to do what the Republican Party of Abraham Lincoln had done—establish long-term control of the federal government and create a new party system.

Although defeated politically, the Wilson administration had proved that the American state, despite its weakness, was capable of fighting a sustained, capital-intensive war. The key was popular support. Critically important both to building popular support and to mobilizing resources

---

[36]See Hugh Heclo, "The State and America's Higher Civil Service" (paper delivered at the Woodrow Wilson International Center Conference on the Role of the State in Recent American History, October 23–24, 1982).

on a vast scale was the method of finance: progressive taxation and the sale of "the war for democracy" to the American people through the bond drives. Both proved to be critical steps in increasing political authority for the federal government—in increasing its ability, through democratic politics, to acquire resources for national defense and the waging of war. The shaping influence of democratic values on mobilization explained the federal government's success in adopting coercive and statist means for financing the war.

The freewheeling debate over federal tax options continued during the postwar period. Because the federal government had now acquired substantial experience with a modern income-tax system, and because tax experts had become more influential within the federal government, the scope of the debate widened. It encompassed not only the reform of income taxation but also the adoption of a variety of new taxes: sophisticated general sales taxes (including a value-added tax), expenditure taxation, undistributed profits taxation, and federal regulatory taxes.

The Republicans who assumed control of both the presidency and Congress in 1921 approached tax reform as a means to roll back Wilsonian democratic statism. The three Republican administrations, under the financial leadership of Secretary of the Treasury Andrew Mellon, adopted the strategy of protecting capital markets by reducing taxation. But the Republican administrations did not simply roll back expenditures and wartime tax programs. They reduced taxes according to two potentially contradictory goals—responding positively to the demands of powerful new segments of the economy and mediating class conflict.

In reducing taxes, the Republicans enlarged the attack on the most redistributional parts of the wartime tax system. In the process, they granted substantial tax reductions to corporations and the wealthiest individuals. In 1921 they abolished the excess-profits tax, dashing Claude Kitchin's hopes that the tax would become permanent, and made the nominal rate structure of the income tax less progressive. Also in 1921, in response to intense lobbying, they began to install a wide range of special exemptions and deductions, which the highly progressive rate structure of the income tax had made extremely valuable. The Revenue Acts during the 1920s introduced the preferential taxation of capital gains and a variety of deductions that favored particular industries, deductions such as expanded oil- and gas-depletion allowances.[37]

[37] A capitalist-state theorist, Ronald King, has stressed the importance, and sincerity, of the progrowth arguments of the Republicans who introduced these measures. King argues that Mellon invoked a "hegemonic tax logic" that was finally victorious in the Kennedy-

Along with the new tax structure came enhanced power for the tax-writing committees of Congress. They discovered how much influence they wielded through the incremental, relatively invisible consideration of valuable loopholes. Although they did not use the term, the legislators had discovered the political appeal of "tax expenditures." They were able to promote what amounted to new expenditure programs by creating pockets of privileges within the tax code. In turn they won or maintained the support of powerful groups and individuals while avoiding the political costs associated with raising taxes.

To exert and reinforce their new power, the committees won approval in the Revenue Act of 1926 for creating the Joint Committee on Internal Revenue Taxation (JCIRT), which would become the Joint Committee on Taxation (JCT) in 1976. Congress originally charged the JCIRT with investigating avenues to simplify the law and with improving its administration, and the professional staff of the JCIRT did increase the technical capabilities of the tax-writing committees. But the JCIRT immediately became primarily a vehicle for enhancing the influence of the senior members of the tax-writing committees.[38]

Secretary Mellon made his greatest impact on the reformed tax system by leading a struggle within the Republican Party to protect income taxation from those who wanted to replace it with a national sales tax. Mellon helped persuade corporations and the wealthiest individuals to accept *some* progressive income taxation and the principle of "ability to pay." This approach would, Mellon told them, demonstrate their civic responsibility and defuse radical attacks on capital. Thus, while shrinking the state, the Republican leadership took care to preserve the progressive income tax, including the corporation income tax, and thus maintain a revenue system that seemed to promote social justice as well as finance both normal expenditures and tax expenditures. Mellon went so far as to advocate providing a greater reduction in taxes on "earned" than on "unearned" incomes, and the Revenue Act of 1924 included

Johnson tax cuts of 1964. See Ronald F. King, "From Redistributive to Hegemonic Logic: The Transformation of American Tax Politics, 1894–1963," *Politics and Society* 12, no. 1 (1983): 1–52. Also on the 1920s, see King's *Money, Time, and Politics: Investment Tax Subsidies and American Democracy* (New Haven: Yale University Press, 1993), 104–11.

[38]On the formation of the JCIRT, see Blakey and Blakey, *The Federal Income Tax*, 542–43, 546–48. See also Donald R. Kennon and Rebecca M. Rogers, *The Committee on Ways and Means: A Bicentennial History, 1789–1989* (Washington, D.C.: Government Printing Office, 1989), 330–33, and Thomas J. Reese, *The Politics of Taxation* (Westport, Conn.: Quorum Books, 1980), 61–88.

such a provision. "The fairness of taxing more lightly incomes from wages, salaries or from investments is beyond question," Mellon asserted. He explained, "In the first case, the income is uncertain and limited in duration; sickness or death destroys it and old age diminishes it; in the other, the source of income continues; the income may be disposed of during a man's life and it descends to his heirs."[39] Mellon's strategy was what might be described as the pursuit of enlightened self-interest— as corporate liberalism, in contrast with Wilson's democratic statism. Mellon received crucial support for his approach from the tax-writing committees of Congress, which wanted to preserve the influence they found they could exert under a progressive system of income taxation.

The new program consolidated the flow of income-tax revenues into the Treasury. The portion of general revenues provided to the federal government by indirect taxes (largely the tariff) fell from almost 75 percent in 1902 to about 25 percent in the 1920s; meanwhile, income-tax revenues increased, accounting for nearly 50 percent of the general revenues of the federal government. As in World War I, the income-tax revenues proved to be more abundant than the Treasury experts had forecast, and the Republican administrations incurred substantial, growing budget surpluses until the onset of the Great Depression.

The large revenues from income taxation provided the basis for the expansion of federal domestic programs and for the political reinforcement of the World War I tax system. During the 1920s, the federal government expanded its programs of grants-in-aid, which it had begun in 1914 with the support of the Smith-Lever Act for agricultural extension. This system provided federal funding that included matching requirements, formulas for distribution among the states, and monitoring of states' expenditure plans. Highway programs were the major beneficiaries; as early as 1921, roughly 40 percent of all highway funding came from the federal government, based on the Federal Aid Road Act of 1916.

As had been the case after the Civil War, state and local governments welcomed this new federal funding. The federal revenues helped state and local governments satisfy demands for public services, especially schools and roads, and relieve pressure on their tax systems. State governments became the most swiftly growing level of government during

---

[39]Andrew W. Mellon, *Taxation: The People's Business* (New York: Macmillan, 1924), 56–57.

the 1920s, and they replaced their crumbling systems of state property taxation with new arrays of sales taxes (such as gasoline taxes), user charges (such as motor vehicle fees), and special taxes on corporations and incomes. In 1902, states were getting about 53 percent of their tax revenues from property taxation; by 1927, they raised only about 23 percent from that source. Of the new taxes, those on sales, especially on gasoline, were the most dynamic. Sales taxes increased as a share of state tax revenues from 18 percent in 1902 and 1913 to 27 percent in 1927 and to 38 percent in 1932.

Mellon also strengthened the World War I tax system by protecting and rationalizing the influence of the Treasury. Most important, Mellon promoted the passage of the Budget and Accounting Act of 1921, which drew on the 1911 reports of the Taft Commission to create the first national budget system. The act established presidential responsibility for preparing a comprehensive budget rather than simply assembling and transmitting departmental requests. It created two important agencies: the Bureau of the Budget (located inside the Treasury) to assist in budget preparation, and the General Accounting Office (as an arm of Congress) to conduct independent audits of the federal government.[40]

Mellon also attempted to strengthen the Treasury by transforming it into a "nonpartisan" agency. In his book of 1924, *Taxation: The People's Business* (written largely by his expert assistant secretaries), Mellon explained, "Tax revision should never be made the football either of partisan or class politics but should be worked out by those who have made a careful study of the subject in its larger aspects and are prepared to recommend the course which, in the end, will prove for the country's best interest."[41]

Mellon was interested in more than scientific policy-making. His main goal was to insulate the Treasury from pressure from Democratic Congresses. He wanted to ensure that the Treasury worked within conservative assumptions about the state and corporate power and within a political framework that advanced the Republican Party. Consequently, when he approached tax cutting during the postwar reconver-

---

[40]On the movement to establish a national budget system, see Charles Stewart III, *Budget Reform Politics: The Design of the Appropriations Process in the House of Representatives, 1865–1921* (Cambridge: Cambridge University Press, 1989), esp. 172–215. On the implementation of the system, see Annette E. Meyer, *Evolution of United States Budgeting: Changing Fiscal and Financial Concepts* (New York: Greenwood Press, 1989).

[41]Mellon, *Taxation*, 10–11.

sion and downsizing of government, he rejected the advice of Thomas S. Adams, a Yale University economist and his primary tax adviser. If the federal government was to dismantle its wartime system of taxation, Adams believed, it should take the opportunity to replace the system with an economically efficient income tax or a progressive "spendings" tax, one that would tax "unnecessary or surplus consumption." Adams began to despair of income taxation, concluding that it contained "incurable inequalities and inconsistencies" and had "reached a condition of inequality the gravity of which could scarcely be exaggerated." He advocated eliminating the excess-profits tax and reducing the rate of progression, but he urged avoiding the kind of special deductions introduced by Mellon. In addition, Adams favored the integration of corporate and individual income taxation. Instead, however, Mellon chose to recommend tax cutting that created privileged groups and industries while providing protection to Republican administrations and Congresses against the charge that they favored the abolition of progressive taxation.[42]

The Republican administrations and Congresses of the 1920s had shifted ground within the World War I tax regime. Soak-the-rich remained, but only at reduced rates containing major loopholes and with its sharp anticorporate edge dulled. As a consequence of the path-dependent nature of the development of the tax regime initiated by American involvement in World War I, the income tax conveyed very mixed messages about the nature of wealth and civic responsibility in America. Without the wartime crisis, the growth of the federal government almost certainly would have been slower and reliant on some combination of tariff revenues, sales taxes, and low-rate taxation of personal and corporate incomes or spending. That system might have been as riddled with inconsistencies, departures from horizontal equity, and theoretical confusion as the highly progressive tax system that emerged during and after the World War I crisis. But, in contrast with the system that probably would have emerged from a more incremental process, the system for financing World War I involved a substantial raising of the stakes of conflict over tax policy. Along with highly progressive taxation came opportunities both for undertaking massive assaults on wealth and corporate power and for carving out lucrative enclaves of

[42]For discussion of Adams's analysis, see Brownlee, "Economists and the Formation of the Modern Tax System," 430–31.

special privilege within the tax code. These high stakes helped keep taxation at the center stage of politics through World War II.

The Great Depression—the nation's worst economic collapse—produced yet another tax regime. Until 1935, however, depression-driven changes in tax policy were ad hoc quests for short-term economic stimulation and revenue growth rather than efforts to seek comprehensive tax reform. Until then, both the Republican administration of Herbert Hoover and the Democratic administration of Franklin Roosevelt put economic recovery and budgetary considerations ahead of any others. Both stressed the need for tax policies that would maintain the confidence of the business community.

In the first phase of its fiscal policy, the Hoover administration, working with Congress, extended the scope of corporate liberalism to include fiscal activism. Judged by the standards of the day, Hoover was an activist in the manipulation of tax rates to stimulate investment and reduce unemployment. Hoover began his innovative program soon after the stock market crash in 1929. He managed to cut taxes payable in 1930, called on state and local governments (and public utilities as well) to increase capital outlays, and during 1930 and the first half of 1931, pushed up the federal public works budget, financing projects such as the building of Boulder Dam (begun in 1928 and completed in 1936). As a result of Hoover's policy and supportive congressional action, federal fiscal policy took a distinctly expansive turn between 1929 and 1931. Even if the economy had been in full employment in 1931, and thus had retained a large base for income taxation, the budgetary surplus of $1 billion in 1929 would still have become a large deficit—roughly $3 billion, by 1931. Not until 1936 was the full-employment deficit as large, and not until World War II was the rate of change in the deficit as substantial in an expansionary direction.

In October 1931, however, the Federal Reserve system produced a monetary contraction that severely limited the ability of the nation's banking system to meet domestic demands for currency and credit. Hoover feared that continued deficit spending would increase competition between government and private borrowers, produce an increase in the long-term interest rates, and inhibit private investment. He also believed that wavering confidence in the dollar within foreign quarters stemmed in part from the persistent deficits of his administration. Reducing the deficits, he was convinced, would diminish the gold flow and thus relieve international pressure on the Federal Reserve Board to tighten the monetary screws. Consequently, in December 1931, Hoover invoked a new phase of his fiscal policy—the phase that has tended to predominate in the public's memory. He asked Congress for tax increases that promised to raise revenues by one-third, and he and his new secretary of the Treasury, Ogden Mills, suggested enacting a general sales tax.[43]

The severity of the depression and the unpopularity of deficits led many congressional Democrats, including Speaker of the House John Nance Garner and all but one of the members of the Ways and Means Committee, to support a general sales tax. But a group of Democratic insurgents in the House, led by Robert L. Doughton of North Carolina, the only member of the Ways and Means Committee to oppose the sales tax, and Fiorello La Guardia of New York, challenged the leadership. Doughton described the tax as a violation of "ability to pay" and as a measure that would undercut the plans of some state governments, including that of North Carolina, to enact general sales taxes. He and the insurgents worried that the general sales tax might replace the income tax as the centerpiece of the federal tax system, just as Garner's patron, the publisher William Randolph Hearst, intended. The insurgents won the support of most House Democrats and blocked the tax. Doughton privately described the victory as "the greatest victory . . . achieved for the common people since the days of Woodrow Wilson."[44]

In the end, the Revenue Act of 1932, enacted with bipartisan support, did impose some new federal sales taxes (on gasoline, electricity, refrigerators, and telephone messages, for example) but increased revenues mainly by raising personal and corporate income-tax rates across the board and by reducing income-tax exemptions. The act imposed the largest peacetime tax increases in the nation's history.

[43]The best description of the development of Hoover's fiscal policy is Herbert Stein, *The Fiscal Revolution in America* (Chicago: University of Chicago Press, 1969), 6–38. See also William J. Barber, *From New Era to New Deal: Herbert Hoover, the Economists, and American Economic Policy, 1921–1933* (Cambridge: Cambridge University Press, 1985). Both scholars pay close attention to the role of ideas and actors inside the federal government in shaping tax policy.
[44]For the quotations from Robert Doughton, and for an excellent description of the congressional consideration of the Revenue Act of 1932, see Walter Kraft Lambert, "New Deal Revenue Acts: The Politics of Taxation" (Ph.D. diss., University of Texas, 1970), 1–103. See also Jordan A. Schwarz, "John Nance Garner and the Sales Tax Rebellion of 1932," *Journal of Southern History* 30 (May 1964).

Taxation was not a central issue in the critical election of 1932, but the politics of the Revenue Act of 1932 may have advanced the career of Franklin D. Roosevelt. Garner's support of the general sales tax damaged his candidacy for the Democratic presidential nomination, and almost all of the congressional insurgents backed Roosevelt's candidacy. And voters upset over the large tax increases may well have blamed them on Hoover and the Republicans.

In the first hundred days of his administration, Franklin Roosevelt moved beyond the corporate liberalism of Herbert Hoover to apply the coercive power of government to the tasks of relief and economic recovery. It may have been a high-water mark for democratic statism but not for the implementation of tax principles in the democratic-statist tradition. This was true despite the fact that, like Woodrow Wilson before him, Roosevelt was personally devoted to *both* balanced budgets and redistributional taxation. In the 1932 campaign, Roosevelt pledged to balance the federal budget, which for three years the administration of Herbert Hoover had been unable to do. In 1933, Roosevelt warned Congress, "Too often in recent history liberal governments have been wrecked on the rocks of loose fiscal policy." Also, Roosevelt personally opposed general sales taxes, which he regarded as "the last word in foolishness," and favored soak-the-rich taxation— shifting the tax burden to the wealthiest individuals and corporations according to "ability to pay."[45] Moreover, he recognized the large constituency the depression had created for the kind of redistributional and anticorporate tax reform undertaken by the Wilson administration. Nonetheless, in contrast with the early phase of Wilson's financing of World War I, Roosevelt's early New Deal brought no progressive fiscal innovations.[46]

[45]In 1932, after his election, Roosevelt outlined his views on sales taxation through a letter from Felix Frankfurter to Walter Lippmann. See Max Freedman, ed., *Roosevelt and Frankfurter: Their Correspondence, 1928–1945* (Boston: Little, Brown, 1967), 68. On Roosevelt's opposition to sales taxation in 1932–33, also see Frank Freidel, *Franklin D. Roosevelt: Launching the New Deal* (Boston: Little, Brown, 1973), 53.

[46]A very different view of Roosevelt and his program can be found in the work of the historian Mark Leff, who argues that Franklin D. Roosevelt looked only for symbolic victories in tax reform. See Mark H. Leff, *The Limits of Symbolic Reform: The New Deal and Taxation, 1933–1939* (Cambridge: Cambridge University Press, 1984). Walter K. Lambert found no evidence that Roosevelt favored a radical distribution of tax burdens, but he did find a deep ethical commitment to the principle of "ability to pay." See Lambert, "New Deal Revenue Acts." See also W. Elliot Brownlee, "Taxation as an X-ray," *Reviews in American History* 14 (March 1986): 121–26.

Depression conditions posed massive problems for Roosevelt, problems that Wilson had not faced in the expansive years of 1916 and 1917. The fact that the Great Depression had shrunk the tax base meant that a serious effort at pay-as-you-go financing of expensive New Deal programs would have required massive increases in tax rates or the introduction of substantial new taxes. The problems with doing this were political and economic. Both Roosevelt and Congress disliked having to pick the losers in the political game of increasing taxes. Both feared, in particular, that a democratic-statist tax policy would arouse business opposition to innovative New Deal programs and pave the way for a conservative counterattack on the New Deal if economic recovery failed. On this score they had learned from Wilson's experience. Roosevelt, the Democratic candidate for vice-president in 1920, remembered all too well the success of the Republican backlash against Wilsonian taxation during the economic troubles of 1918–20. Worrisome too, although of lesser consequence to Roosevelt and Congress, were the possible economic consequences of democratic-statist taxation. They acknowledged that if they raised income and corporate taxes sufficiently to balance the budget in the short run, they might run the risk of worsening the economic depression by undermining business confidence and investment.

Finally, Roosevelt faced an important institutional barrier to a democratic-statist tax policy. Twelve years of Republican leadership had built a Treasury staff that was unenthusiastic about undertaking the work of devising new progressive taxes. Roosevelt's long-term secretary of the Treasury, Henry Morgenthau, Jr., did not take office until January 1934, and his immediate deputies needed several years to rebuild a capability within the department for advancing democratic-statist reform. Meanwhile, Roosevelt instructed him to leave the proposal of new taxes to Congress and, in particular, to the Ways and Means Committee, now under the leadership of North Carolina's Robert Doughton.

During the first two years of the New Deal, the combination of Roosevelt's hostility to sales taxation and progressive initiatives on the part of Congress produced the adoption of modest increases in income taxes and loophole-closing reforms. The National Industrial Recovery Act imposed a 5 percent tax on dividends and a small excess-profits tax and tightened provisions for deducting business and capital losses. The Agricultural Adjustment Act added a tax on food processing. In addition, other acts restored the earned income credit, slightly increased progressivity of income-tax rates, and raised capital gains taxes.[47]

During the early years of the New Deal, Congress and the Roosevelt administration relied far more heavily on automatic revenue increases that resulted from the interaction of existing taxes (enhanced by the Hoover administration's Revenue Act of 1932) and from the economic recovery that began in 1933. The repeal of Prohibition was especially fortuitous. Liquor taxes were still on the books and were far more popular among Democratic voters than general sales taxes or other excises. Between 1933 and 1936, revenues from alcohol taxes increased by almost $500 million. In 1936, special excise taxes, led by the increases in liquor taxes and levies on tobacco and gasoline consumption, produced about $1.5 billion, which was more than 40 percent of federal tax collections and larger than the $1.4 billion raised by income taxes in that year. (In 1936 only about two million American households—out of a total of thirty-two million—owed any federal income tax; the personal income tax accounted for less than half of income-tax collections.) In addition, Roosevelt and Congress allowed federal deficits to grow—from $2.6 billion in 1933 to $4.4 billion in 1936, over 40 percent of federal expenditures. During his first term, in every annual budget message, Roosevelt asserted that the deficits would disappear along with the depression.[48]

In 1935 Roosevelt decided that political and economic conditions favored a resumption of a democratic-statist tax policy. Most important, the growing "Thunder on the Left," particularly Huey Long's "Share Our Wealth" movement, opened the way for vigorous redistributional taxation designed to remedy flaws in the nation's economic structure. Moreover, he had gained confidence in the prospects for economic recovery and was less worried about a business backlash. And Morgenthau had finally established the required infrastructure of professional expertise within the Treasury.[49]

[47]On the importance of the sales tax issue during the first year of the New Deal, see Freidel, *Franklin D. Roosevelt*, 51–59, 446–51.

[48]For analysis of the trends of the various federal revenue sources during the Great Depression, see John M. Firestone, *Federal Receipts and Expenditures during Business Cycles, 1879–1958* (Princeton: Princeton University Press, 1960), 36–54.

[49]The following account of the making of tax policy within the Roosevelt administration through World War II draws on the following works by John Morton Blum: *From the Morgenthau Diaries: Years of Crisis, 1928–1938* (Boston: Houghton Mifflin, 1959), 297–337, 439–51; *From the Morgenthau Diaries: Years of Urgency, 1938–1941* (Boston: Houghton Mifflin, 1965), 22–30, 278–318; and *From the Morgenthau Diaries: Years of*

Morgenthau's staff contained a group of law professors, including General Counsel Herman Oliphant and Roswell Magill. Magill, a tax expert from Columbia University, directed a comprehensive survey of the federal tax system in preparation for a reform initiative. The monetary economist Jacob Viner also advised Morgenthau on tax issues, and Carl S. Shoup, Roy Blough, and Lawrence H. Seltzer—all economists who specialized in public finance—worked closely with Magill. Central to their efforts was an intensified effort to study the distributional effects of taxation at all levels of government.[50]

At the end of the summer of 1934 Magill and his colleagues in the Treasury had presented Morgenthau with recommendations that were designed to raise new revenues and attack concentrations of wealth, and in December Morgenthau had forwarded the proposals to the White House. In developing a tax proposal for Congress, Roosevelt drew assistance from Felix Frankfurter, who, from the outset of the New Deal, had been urging the president to use the taxing power to attack bigness in business. Roosevelt and Frankfurter drew on the Treasury recommendations to craft an ambitious program of radical tax reform, which Roosevelt presented to Congress in June. He told Secretary of the Interior Harold Ickes that the speech was "the best thing he had done as President."[51]

Roosevelt proposed a graduated tax on corporations to check the growth of monopoly, a tax on the dividends that holding companies received from corporations they controlled, surtaxes to raise the maxi-

---

War, 1941–1945 (Boston: Houghton Mifflin, 1967), 33–78. Blum's work still stands as the best general treatment of this subject. Also valuable is Randolph E. Paul, *Taxation in the United States* (Boston: Little, Brown, 1954), 168–406. See as well Lambert, "New Deal Revenue Acts," for excellent details on the relations between the Roosevelt administration and Congress.

[50]The most important 1930s study of tax incidence was the unpublished analysis of the economist Louis Shere. See "The Burden of Taxation," memorandum, Division of Research and Taxation, U.S. Department of the Treasury, Washington, D.C. For an excellent survey of the modern measurement of the tax burden in the United States, see B. K. Atrostic and James R. Nunns, "Measuring Tax Burden: A Historical Perspective," in *Fifty Years of Economic Measurement: The Jubilee of the Conference on Research in Income and Wealth*, National Bureau of Economic Research Studies in Income and Wealth, vol. 54, ed. Ernest R. Berndt and Jack E. Triplett (Chicago: University of Chicago Press, 1990), 343–408.

[51]On the significance of Frankfurter's interest in this tax legislation, see Ellis Hawley, *The New Deal and the Problem of Monopoly: Study in Economic Ambivalence* (Princeton: Princeton University Press, 1966), 344–59. Hawley, however, concludes that the revenue acts of 1935 and 1936 were "relatively innocuous" (359). Harold Ickes's discussion of the 1935 tax measure is in the June 19, 1935, entry in Harold Ickes Diaries, Harold L. Ickes Papers, Library of Congress, Washington, D.C.

mum income-tax rate on individuals from 63 to 79 percent, and an inheritance tax, to be imposed in addition to federal estate taxation. In his message to Congress, Roosevelt explained that accumulations of wealth meant "great and undesirable concentration of control in relatively few individuals over the employment and welfare of many, many others." Moreover, "whether it be wealth achieved through the cooperation of the entire community or riches gained by speculation—in either case the ownership of such wealth or riches represents a great public interest and a great ability to pay." But Roosevelt's goal was not a simplistic redistribution of wealth and power. Later that year, he explained to a newspaper publisher that his purpose was "not to destroy wealth, but to create a broader range of opportunity, to restrain the growth of unwholesome and sterile accumulations and to lay the burdens of Government where they can best be carried." Thus, he justified his tax-reform program in terms of both its inherent equity and its ability to liberate the energies of individuals and small corporations, thereby advancing recovery.[52]

In the Revenue Act of 1935, Congress gave Roosevelt much of the tax reform he wanted. In 1935, and throughout the peacetime New Deal, Roosevelt was able to count on the support of Doughton, who chaired the House Ways and Means Committee from 1933 until 1947. (Counting a second term, from 1949 to 1953, he was the longest-serving chair of the committee in its history.) Doughton's support was often decisive in Congress, where Senator Pat Harrison of Mississippi, chair of the Senate Finance Committee, and other conservative southern Democrats often opposed New Deal tax reform. Doughton at times had his doubts about the more sophisticated New Deal tax proposals and resisted large tax increases of any kind. He privately complained in 1935, "We have had too many theories in key places under this administration." But he believed in the justice of shifting the distribution of taxes away from the "poor, weak, and humble," who—he was certain—paid a higher percentage of their incomes in taxes than did the wealthy. And, ever since he had begun his service in Congress in 1911, he had put party loyalty and the need to establish a record of Democratic leadership first.[53]

---

[52]For the Roosevelt quotations, see Arthur M. Schlesinger, Jr., *The Age of Roosevelt: The Politics of Upheaval* (Boston: Houghton Mifflin, 1960), 328, and Lambert, "New Deal Revenue Acts," 259–60.

[53]For suggestions as to the significance of the early New Deal of Doughton in particular and of southern members of Congress in general, see Tindall, *Emergence of the New South*, 607–13. Pat Harrison was less energetic and effective than Doughton, but he was

Offsetting the progressivity of Roosevelt's income-tax reforms was the regressivity of the payroll taxes that were enacted in 1935 as a central part of the social security system.[54] The incongruity might suggest that Roosevelt was little more than a cynical manipulator of the powerful symbolism of taxation. But Roosevelt conceived of social security as an insurance system. He thought of the taxes paid by middle-class people as premiums that established investments. Thus, in his mind, taxpayers received the benefits for which they had paid. In addition, he realized that the insurance principle worked to protect the system from conservative counterattack. Roosevelt believed, "With those taxes in there, no damn politician can ever scrap my social security program." He succeeded, probably beyond his wildest expectations, in protecting social security. In addition, the benefit formula of even the initial social security program had a progressive dimension. In 1939, Roosevelt and Congress firmly established a progressive benefit formula and introduced pay-as-you-go financing.[55]

Roosevelt believed that the passage of the Revenue Act of 1935 meant that he would not have to request any further new taxes until after the presidential election of 1936. But in early 1936, the Supreme Court invalidated the processing tax of the Agricultural Adjustment Act, and Congress overrode Roosevelt's veto of a bonus bill for World War I veterans. Both events threatened a substantial increase in the federal deficit.

In response, Morgenthau again recommended an undistributed profits tax, a revenue-raising measure that Roosevelt had previously ignored. The proposal was to eliminate the existing taxes on corporate income, capital stock, and excess profits and replace them with a tax on retained

able to kill Roosevelt's proposal for the taxation of inheritances in 1935. The Doughton quotations are from Lambert, "New Deal Revenue Acts," 297, 226.

[54]For histories of the adoption of social security, as told from the perspectives of experts within the Roosevelt administration, see Edwin E. Witte, *The Development of the Social Security Act: A Memorandum on the History of the Committee on Economic Security and Drafting and Legislative History of the Social Security Act* (Madison: University of Wisconsin Press, 1962), and Arthur J. Altmeyer, *The Formative Years of Social Security: A Chronicle of Social Security Legislation and Administration, 1934–1954* (Madison: University of Wisconsin Press, 1968). See also Theron F. Schlabach, *Edwin E. Witte: Cautious Reformer* (Madison: University of Wisconsin Press, 1969).

[55]One historian of the origins of social security describes the 1939 changes as designed to "speed up the creation of vested interests in the program, create coalitions of beneficiaries whose interests were coincidental with those of the bureaucracy, and eliminate the potential discipline of a funded system." See Carolyn L. Weaver, *The Crisis in Social Security: Economic and Political Origins* (Durham, N.C.: Duke University Press, 1982), 112.

earnings—the profits that corporations did not distribute to their stock-holders. The tax would be graduated according to the proportion of the profits that were undistributed. Magill's team of experts had discovered this idea when digging into the Treasury archives for inspiration. They had found Thomas S. Adams's 1919 proposal for an undistributed prof-its tax, which he had favored then as a replacement for excess-profits taxation.[56]

Morgenthau and his Treasury staff believed that the measure would fight both tax avoidance and the concentration of corporate power. Cor-porations, they were convinced, deliberately retained profits to avoid the taxation of dividends under the individual income tax. Further, they believed that the largest corporations had the power to retain shares of surpluses greater than those retained by small companies. The surpluses, they were certain, gave large corporations an unfair competitive advan-tage by reducing the need to borrow new capital. Moreover, the Trea-sury believed that the tax would promote recovery. Oliphant and Morgenthau believed that large corporations saved excessively or rein-vested their surpluses unwisely. The undistributed-profits tax would pro-vide a powerful incentive for such corporations to distribute their profits to their shareholders. Those shareholders, in turn, as Oliphant and Mar-riner Eccles, the chairman of the Federal Reserve Board, stressed, would spend some portion of their dividends and thus stimulate the economy.

Roosevelt endorsed the undistributed-profits tax in a message to Con-gress in March and received support, in principle, from the Ways and Means Committee. But the administration faced the hostility of the Sen-ate Finance Committee and its staffs, which feared revenue loss and preferred retaining the existing corporate income taxes while adding a small, flat tax on undistributed earnings. In June 1936 Congress passed a graduated tax on undistributed profits, despite heavy business lobbying against Roosevelt's proposal and intense wrangling over widely diver-gent revenue estimates. Morgenthau intervened in the negotiations be-tween the House and Senate and had much to do with the outcome. Because of Senate objections, the graduation was less severe than the Treasury had proposed, but Congress retained the corporate income tax.

The new corporate tax posed the greatest threat to the autonomy of corporate finance since the passage of the excess-profits tax during

---

[56]For evidence of Adams's influence, see Louis Shere, assistant secretary of the Treasury, to Robert M. Haig, March 6, 1936, Robert Murray Haig Papers, Butler Library, Colum-bia University, New York City.

World War I. In July Secretary of the Interior Ickes talked privately with Harry F. Guggenheim and concluded, "The fundamental policy issue today is taxation." The increases in the higher brackets, "taxing surpluses in corporation treasuries, and fear of further increases," Ickes concluded, had made "a bitter enemy out of practically everyone" among the "very rich."[57]

Throughout Morgenthau's service as secretary of the Treasury, he sought, with Roosevelt's support, the prosecution of tax evaders and the closing of loopholes used by tax avoiders. Most spectacularly, in 1934 the Treasury promoted the prosecution of its former secretary, Andrew Mellon, for tax evasion. The Treasury claimed Mellon owed more than $3 million in back taxes and penalties. Morgenthau told the government prosecutor, "I consider that Mr. Mellon is not on trial but Democracy and the privileged rich and I want to see who will win." Mellon won in court but lost the public relations battle. A grand jury refused to indict, and in 1937 the Board of Tax Appeals found him innocent of tax evasion. But the board also said he had made errors that happened to be in his favor and added that he owed $400,000 in back taxes. The board used the Mellon case to publicize the loopholes in the tax code. The commissioner pointed out that as secretary of the Treasury, Mellon had solicited from the Bureau of Internal Revenue "a memorandum setting forth the various ways by which an individual may legally avoid tax." It turned out that Mellon had used five of the ten methods detailed in the memorandum, as well as some others that he had devised on his own.

In spring 1937, the outcome of the Mellon case, coupled with a $600 million shortfall in tax revenues, a deficit that Treasury analysts blamed on tax avoidance, led Morgenthau and Roosevelt to seek remedial legislation. At the same time that the Treasury systematically investigated tax avoidance, Roosevelt won the support of the chairs of the tax-writing committees for creating the Joint Committee on Tax Evasion and Avoidance, with powers to acquire the names of tax avoiders from the Treasury. With staff assistance from Thurman Arnold, whom the Treasury borrowed from the Department of Justice, Treasury witnesses inventoried loopholes and identified sixty-seven "large, wealthy taxpayers" who used the device of incorporation to reduce taxes. The press zeroed in on Alfred P. Sloan, the president of General Motors,

[57]See July 27, 1936, entry in the Harold Ickes Diaries, Ickes Papers.

who had incorporated his yacht. Sloan explained, "While no one should desire to avoid payment of his share [of taxes] neither should anyone be expected to pay more than is lawfully required."[58]

The evidence mobilized by the Joint Committee persuaded Congress to pass, unanimously, the Revenue Act of 1937. The measure increased taxation of personal holding companies, limited deductions for corporate yachts and country estates, restricted deductions for losses from sales or exchanges of property, reduced incentives for the creation of multiple trusts, and eliminated favors for nonresident taxpayers. These increases, coupled with those undertaken the year before, raised tax rates high enough to create a full-employment surplus—the surplus of revenue that would have been attained had the economy been operating at full employment.[59]

Encouraged by the economic recovery, which had cut the rate of unemployment in half by 1937, Roosevelt intended to intensify his reform program in 1938. He planned to increase the undistributed-profits tax, to establish a graduated tax on capital gains, and to tax the income from federal, state, and local bonds.

These plans, more than any other dimension of the New Deal, aroused fear and hostility on the part of large corporations. They correctly viewed Roosevelt's tax program as a threat to their control over capital and their latitude for financial planning. There is no evidence that capital went "on strike," as many New Dealers charged, citing a lag in business investment. But business leaders searched for a political opening. Unfortunately for Roosevelt's tax program, he made major tactical errors: reinforcing the recession of 1937–38 and opening the disastrous court fight in 1937. These provided the opening. Conservative Democrats, led by Bernard Baruch and Joseph P. Kennedy, broke with the president and argued that tax cuts were necessary to restore business confidence. They agreed with Senator Pat Harrison who declared, in December 1937, that Roosevelt's tax program had "retarded progress and contributed to the unemployment situation."[60]

In 1938, a coalition of Republicans and conservative Democrats, working through the tax-writing committees, took advantage of Roose-

[58]Blum, *From the Morgenthau Diaries,* 335.
[59]This was the only year in which New Deal fiscal policy created a full-employment surplus and not a deficit. For the full-employment surplus (deficit) data, see E. Cary Brown, "Fiscal Policy in the Thirties: A Reappraisal," *American Economic Review* 46 (December 1956): 857–79.
[60]For the Harrison quotation, see Lambert, "New Deal Revenue Acts," 422.

velt's mistakes and tried to block any more New Deal tax reform. Roosevelt fought back, denouncing—at a Jackson Day dinner—the businesspeople who would "fight to the last ditch to retain [their] autocratic control over the industry and finances of the country." But conservative Democrats had gathered enough strength to push through Congress, over the opposition of Ways and Means Chair Doughton, a measure that gutted the tax on undistributed profits and discarded the graduated corporate income tax. Roosevelt, respecting the strength of the opposition, decided not to veto the bill. Instead, he allowed the Revenue Act of 1938 to become law without his signature and denounced it as the "abandonment of an important principle of American taxation"—taxation according to "ability to pay." In 1939 Congress wiped out the undistributed-profits tax and formally eradicated the brief regime of New Deal tax reform.

Roosevelt's defeats in 1938 and 1939 also signaled a reassertion of congressional power over the shape of revenue legislation. From that time until the end of World War II, the tax-writing committees of Congress carefully maintained their control over the initiation of tax policy. The influence of Morgenthau and his Treasury advisers had waned; they were able to influence Congress decisively only when Roosevelt was able to mobilize public opinion.

The New Deal program of tax reform ended in the late 1930s, but Roosevelt and Congress had already ushered in a new tax regime, composed of a strengthened soak-the-rich component, an expanded taxation of consumption, and the new social security taxes. The Roosevelt administration did not redistribute income through taxation in any significant fashion, but in net, the tax system had become somewhat more progressive in its incidence. And Roosevelt's program of reform of income taxation had conditioned Americans to expect that significant tax increases would take place through increasing taxes on the wealthy and on corporations. Whatever its redistributional limitations, the new system dramatically enhanced the revenue capacity of the federal government. Despite the fact that in 1941 (fiscal year) economic recovery had not yet restored full employment, federal tax collections—led by social security taxes, consumption taxes, and corporate income taxes—had more than doubled; collections had increased from $2.9 billion in 1929 to $7.4 billion in 1941.

The expansion of this federal tax capacity found a welcome audience in state and local governments, just as it had during the post–Civil War era and the 1920s. The early 1930s had been especially traumatic for state and local leaders, and they generally applauded the reduced pressure on their tax systems. Local governments had faced sharply increased relief obligations but suffered declining property tax revenues, soaring rates of default, and even popular revolts, including a tax strike in Chicago. States had provided growing subventions by increasing sales taxes and reducing spending on highways and schools. State constitutions, however, limited deficit finance, and new state and municipal bonds were extremely difficult to market. As the depression worsened in 1931 and 1932, state and local governments found it impossible to conduct business as usual and still balance their budgets. They adopted more drastic economies, scaled back total expenditures in 1931, and sharply contracted spending in 1933 and 1934. State and local governments had pushed up tax rates every year between 1929 and 1933, and they maintained those high levels until 1936, when they raised rates even further.

State governments also increased the scope and rates of their sales taxes until, in 1940, they were raising most of their funds through such levies. By 1940, consumer taxes—on gasoline, tobacco, liquor, soft drinks, and oleomargarine—produced $1.1 billion, and the new general retail sales taxes, which thirty-three states adopted between 1932 and 1937, produced $500 million. Meanwhile, local governments increased their effective rates of property taxation.

In its latter stages, the New Deal did much to strengthen state and local revenue systems through a massive, complex system of intergovernmental transfers, which accounted for over 10 percent of state and local revenues by the end of the New Deal, and through the promotion of taxpaying. A key example of such promotion was the work of the Home Owners' Loan Corporation (HOLC), which required borrowers to pay off back taxes as a condition for receiving subsidized mortgage loans.[61]

The demise of New Deal tax reform was part of the larger collapse of any political effort to develop a comprehensive, democratic-statist program. The New Deal had thrust the federal government into new

[61]The economist John J. Wallis argues that New Deal programs "explain" the relative decline of local governments and the sustained growth of state governments during the 1930s. See Wallis, "The Birth of Old Federalism: Financing the New Deal, 1932–1940," *Journal of Economic History* 44 (March 1984): 139–59. David Beito argues that tactics such as those of the HOLC were part of a larger strategy to undermine traditional, virtuous resistance to taxpaying. See his *Tax Payers in Revolt: Tax Resistance during the Great Depression* (Chapel Hill: University of North Carolina Press, 1989).

zones, but the American public had not embraced a coherent theory that would justify the greatly expanded state. Instead, the various groups that the New Deal had served tended, on the one hand, to embrace the capitalist order and, on the other, to appreciate the particular benefits they had received. These groups wanted the rewards of capitalism but expected the federal government to protect them against substantial risks in the marketplace and, when social discord became too severe, to broker agreements with rival entities. Those agreements might involve, for example, favored treatment in the tax code, through special exemptions or deductions, for particular groups. But the agreements did not encompass far-reaching tax reform that produced broad shifts in the distribution of taxation.

The Roosevelt administration's innovation of the broker state was associated with an assumption of a greater responsibility for promoting economic recovery through fiscal mechanisms such as cutting taxes, increasing expenditures, or expanding deficits. But this assumption of responsibility was slow, erratic, and by the time of American entry into World War II, highly incomplete.[62]

It is true that, judging by *actual* deficits, the Roosevelt administration's fiscal policy might be interpreted as one of consistent, and increasingly more vigorous, promotion of economic recovery through deficit spending. However, the deficits were often unintentional results of a depressed tax base and were always unwelcome to Roosevelt. In fact, only about half of the Roosevelt deficits resulted from deliberate policy decisions. Roosevelt and Morgenthau never intended the deficits to be a permanent feature of the nation's system of public finance.[63]

In Roosevelt's first term, the president and Congress adopted an expansionary fiscal policy in 1933 and 1935. But the stimulus was only modest. Because of the persistent efforts of Roosevelt and Morgenthau to balance the budget, his first-term fiscal policy was no more expansive than that of Hoover between 1929 and 1931. In fact, Roosevelt's policy was more conservative than Hoover's. In contrast with Hoover, Roo-

---

[62]The following account of the development of Roosevelt's fiscal policy draws from the sources cited above and from Stein, *Fiscal Revolution in America*, 39–196, which remains the best general treatment of the subject.

[63]The stimulus of the deficits pales even further in the light of state and local fiscal policy. State and local governments enacted such large tax increases between 1933 and 1939 that they would have had huge budget surpluses if the economy had been at full employment. The state and local full-employment surpluses were large enough to offset the expansive effects of federal deficits in all but two of those seven years.

sevelt had succeeded in liberating monetary policy from Federal Reserve control and in creating an expansive money supply. Consequently, he did not face Hoover's problem: that increased deficits were likely to drive up interest rates to the point of discouraging investment. Roosevelt certainly had not chosen to seek salvation in the prescriptions of John Maynard Keynes, who, in *The Means to Prosperity,* had urged depression governments to stimulate private investment through the vigorous use of deficits. Recalling a visit with Roosevelt in 1934, Keynes remarked that he had "supposed the President was more literate, economically speaking." Roosevelt remembered that Keynes "left a whole rigmarole of figures." Roosevelt added, "He must be a mathematician rather than a political economist."

In 1938, after both tax reform and economic recovery had faltered, Roosevelt did adopt a more reformist fiscal policy—moving it toward a Keynesian position. Near the end of the recession of 1937–38, Roosevelt launched an energetic new spending program that was unaccompanied by significant tax increases. Consequently, the full-employment surplus became a full-employment deficit, and it surged upward in 1938 and 1939.

But the influence of Keynesian ideas on Roosevelt's fiscal policy was still only indirect; Roosevelt had not become a convert. He had shifted policy largely because he decided to abandon tax reform. He recognized that conservative opposition to the New Deal had grown too strong for him to seek significant tax increases or to pursue economic recovery through his preferred means of redistributional tax reform. Moreover, Roosevelt could not ignore the strong indications that restrictive fiscal policy had contributed to the sharp downturn in 1937–38. Consequently, he listened more closely to a group of government officials, scattered across the WPA, the Department of Agriculture, and the Federal Reserve, who had become more partial to deficits and had begun to discover, in the work of Keynes, a rationale for their political position. There is no evidence that Harry Hopkins, Henry Wallace, or Marriner Eccles ever convinced Roosevelt of their view that permanent deficits would be necessary to achieve and maintain full employment. However, Roosevelt did adopt a Keynesian argument to justify his shift in tax policy. In 1938 he explained to Congress that his large increases in expenditures, unaccompanied by tax increases, would add "to the purchasing power of the Nation."

During the years of economic recovery immediately before Pearl

Harbor, economists within the federal government intensified the advancement of Keynesian ideas. Some, like Alvin Hansen, were senior economists who learned Keynes's concepts late in their careers but used his ideas to order their long-standing beliefs that economic stagnation was inevitable without permanent deficits or drastic income redistribution. Others were weaned on *The General Theory,* which appeared in 1936. These economists staffed agencies such as the Division of Industrial Economics within the Department of Commerce, the Bureau of the Budget (including the Office of Statistical Standards, created in 1939), and the National Resources Planning Board. Within the Treasury, the economists Harry Dexter White and Lawrence H. Seltzer, chief economist in the Research Division, began to promote and apply Keynesian ideas. All these economists, and their colleagues outside government, had a significant effect on expert advisers throughout the Roosevelt administration. These experts included many of the lawyers who advised Morgenthau within the Treasury. As early as 1937 Magill argued for budget-balancing over a number of years. He explained, "The effects of borrowing will be stimulating to the national economy." Oliphant was even more explicitly Keynesian. And the assistant New York tax lawyer Randolph Paul, who took over the Tax Division in late 1941 and became general counsel in mid-1942, was the most vigorous in pressing Keynesian ideas upon Morgenthau.

But the success of Keynesian ideas was limited at the time of American entry into World War II. Within the Treasury, Morgenthau never abandoned his desire to balance budgets on an annual basis, although he encouraged argument over this point among his expert advisers. Within the administration at large, Keynesian advocates had succeeded in establishing a consensus on only two vague propositions. The first was that the federal government should avoid adopting restrictive fiscal policies (such as the Hoover administration's tax increase of 1932 and Roosevelt's expenditure cuts of 1937) during recession or depression conditions. The second was that the federal government should expand spending programs during economic reversals. But the Roosevelt administration had not translated these ideas into a clearly defined strategy of spending and deficits. The administration had created no federal agency with the responsibility or the capability for specifying reliable techniques and magnitudes.

The Roosevelt administration had, however, taken important steps toward the centralization of budgetary authority. In 1939 the Reorganization Act created the Executive Office of the President (EOP), transferred to it the Bureau of the Budget (from Treasury) and the National Resources Planning Board (from Interior), and established within the EOP the Office of Emergency Management. For public consumption, Congress emphasized the goal of reducing expenditures through coordination and elimination of overlapping agencies, but the primary purpose was to enhance presidential control over a greatly expanded executive branch. Thus, at the same time that the Roosevelt administration edged toward the embrace of deficit spending as a positive good, it moved toward a more self-conscious use of the federal budget as an instrument of national policy.

THE WORLD WAR II SYSTEM

World War II presented Roosevelt with another opportunity to resuscitate progressive tax reform. The scale of the war effort and the resources it required meant that there had to be a new tax regime. Energized by Pearl Harbor, government spending soared and continued to increase through 1945. The wartime expenditures represented a more massive shift of resources from peacetime endeavors than had been the case during World War I. The average level of federal expenditures from 1942 through 1945 amounted to roughly half the national product, more than twice the average ratio during World War I. In addition, the shift of resources was faster and more prolonged.

The widely shared goals of mobilizing on an unprecedented scale and at the same time controlling inflation shaped wartime tax policy. Meeting both goals seemed to dictate placing heavier reliance on taxation than had been the case during World War I and heavier reliance on taxation that prevented consumers from bidding up prices in competition with the government. Thus, the federal government hitched taxation more firmly to expenditure needs and dramatically broadened the tax base. In the process of broadening the base, Congress and Roosevelt deemphasized the redistributive taxation of corporations. Because of buoyant new tax revenues, the federal deficit, after increasing from $6.2 billion in 1941 to $57.4 billion in 1943, held at about the 1943 level for the remainder of the war.

The political process of adopting this new fiscal policy was not smooth or direct. Although a strong bipartisan consensus favored major tax increases, the specific taxes and the level of taxation employed were matters of severe contention.

Like Wilson and McAdoo in 1916–17, Roosevelt and Secretary of the Treasury Morgenthau set out to finance a large fraction of the costs of war with taxation and to use taxes that bore heavily on corporations and upper-income groups. The president worried first about the tax structure. He began to prepare for financing mobilization as early as 1939, when he talked widely about the need for excess-profits taxation. In the summer of 1940 he proposed such a tax, to be steeply graduated, on both individuals and corporations. Roosevelt, the Treasury, the Ways and Means Committee, and Senate liberals like Robert M. La Follette Jr. favored a World War I–style tax on profits above a minimum rate of return, but Pat Harrison and other conservative Democrats opposed this and prevailed. In the Second Revenue Act of 1940, passed in October, they established a graduated tax on excess profits, reaching a maximum of 50 percent, but provided a generous credit based on prewar profits. Secretary of the Interior Ickes complained that this was "abandoning advanced New Deal ground with a vengeance," but Roosevelt decided not to challenge the power of Congress by accusing it of having sold out to big business.[64]

In 1941, following the passage of the Lend-Lease Act, the Roosevelt administration faced growing inflationary pressures. In response to those pressures, as well as to the need for new revenues, Roosevelt and Morgenthau now supported lowering the exemptions from personal income. But they did not abandon reform. Morgenthau proposed taxing away all corporate profits above a 6 percent rate of return, as well as increasing surtaxes on personal income, increasing the base for gift and estate taxes, and increasing excise taxes on beer, tobacco, and gasoline. Roosevelt made it clear he favored a massive elimination of personal income-tax deductions by switching to the taxation of gross income. In the Revenue Act of 1941 Congress once again rejected most of the reform measures; its major provisions were for lower exemptions and higher tax rates on upper-middle-class families.

After Pearl Harbor, Morgenthau and Roosevelt continued their bid for public support of tax reform. "In time of this grave national danger, when all excess income should go to win the war," Roosevelt told a

---

[64]In June, Roosevelt had favored a graduated tax on all profits in excess of 4 percent. June 9, 1940, and August 10, 1940, entries, Harold Ickes Diaries, Ickes Papers.

joint session of Congress in 1942, "no American citizen ought to have a net income, after he has paid his taxes, of more than $25,000." But opposition to radical war-tax proposals grew even stronger in the face of the revenue requirements of full mobilization.

One source of opposition came from a diverse group of military planners, foreign-policy strategists, financial leaders, and economists. Throughout the turbulence of the 1920s and 1930s, these experts had marshaled the economic lessons of World War I and its aftermath. Now, this collection of experts wanted to mobilize even greater resources, to do so more smoothly and predictably, and to reduce inflationary pressures. They promoted a policy of mass-based taxation. They favored a general sales tax or an income tax that produced most of its revenue from wages and salaries—one that would build on the successful performance of social security taxation. One of the leading experts was Russell C. Leffingwell, who had been assistant secretary of the treasury during World War I and a partner in J. P. Morgan and Company since the early 1920s. He urged Morgenthau to avoid steep excess-profits taxation and to adopt, instead, "taxes widely spread on all the people." An income tax that not only was broad-based but also taxed people "to the very limit of endurance" was the core of successful war finance, he told Morgenthau.[65]

The second source of opposition to Roosevelt's and Morgenthau's radical wartime tax proposals came, in sharp contrast with Wilson's situation during World War I, from Democrats in both Congress and the administration itself. Many Democratic members of Congress, especially the leadership of the Senate Finance Committee, shared the verdict of *Time* magazine, which warned that the kind of plan that Morgenthau proposed would put corporations in a "weakened financial position to meet the slump and unemployment that [would] come with peace." This same concern led Federal Reserve Chairman Marriner Eccles, Budget Director Harold Smith, Office of Price Administration (OPA) Director Leon Henderson, and Vice-President Henry Wallace all to support the sales-tax approach to war finance. Morgenthau complained that his opponents had forgotten about the "people in the lower one-third." He noted, "I can get all my New Dealers in the bathtub now."[66]

---

[65]Leffingwell to Morgenthau, October 2, 1941, and June 11, 1942, Russell C. Leffingwell Papers, Yale University Library, New Haven, Connecticut. This was part of an extensive wartime correspondence between Leffingwell and Morgenthau.

[66]Blum, *From the Morgenthau Diaries*, 35.

In the summer of 1942 Morgenthau, on the recommendation of Randolph Paul and Roy Blough, tried to bridge the gap between the administration and Congress by proposing the adoption of a sharply graduated spendings tax designed to raise large revenues and restrain consumption while increasing progressivity. The tax-writing committees regarded this proposal as too radical economically and too threatening to the influence they enjoyed as gatekeepers for the complex exemptions and deductions in the income tax. Roosevelt recognized the power of the committees and regarded the spendings tax as a bargaining tool for defeating a general sales tax and for making the income tax more progressive. The president decided not to support Morgenthau, explaining to him, "I always have to have a couple of whipping boys."[67]

In October, Congress finally agreed to a few progressive concessions and settled on the income tax as the centerpiece of war finance. To be sure, the tax-writing committees demonstrated their power by refusing to adopt the World War I method of taxing corporate excess profits, although they did increase the rate of such taxation to 90 percent. The committees also protected major loopholes favoring the wealthy and provided less than half the revenues that Roosevelt had requested. But the Revenue Act of 1942 represented agreement between Congress and Roosevelt on what became the core of a new tax regime—a personal income tax that was both broadly based and progressive. The act made major reductions in personal exemptions, establishing the means for the federal government to acquire huge revenues from the taxation of middle-class wages and salaries. Just as important, the rates on individuals' incomes, rates that included a surtax graduated from 13 percent on the first $2,000 to 82 percent on taxable income over $200,000, made the personal income tax more progressive than at any other time in its history. Once again, Roosevelt had defeated a general sales tax, just as he had in 1933, the last time significant support for one had surfaced. A highly progressive income tax, coupled with the absence of general sales taxation, was the major payoff from Roosevelt's earlier tax-reform campaigns, which had established widespread public expectations that any significant new taxes would be progressive.

Roosevelt continued his fight to make the income tax even more progressive, to tax corporations more heavily, and to shift revenue raising from borrowing to taxation, but he suffered two major defeats in 1943. The first was over withholding. In 1943, to accelerate further the flow of tax revenues into the Treasury, and thus restrain inflation, the Treasury proposed adopting a system for withholding taxes through monthly payroll deductions or quarterly payments. The federal government had already employed such a system of "collection at the source" during the Civil War and, again, between 1913 and 1916, in an effort to replicate the administrative accomplishments of the British income tax.[68] More recently, the federal government had achieved great success with a similar administrative system in collecting social security taxes. By mid-1940 the Bureau of Old-Age Benefits had processed, without the benefit of electronic computers, over 312 million individual wage reports forwarded by the Bureau of Internal Revenue and had posted over 99 percent of them to over 50 million individual employee accounts.[69]

The proposed collection system would keep taxpayers current rather than allow them to pay the year after the taxes were incurred. In addition, it would expedite taxpaying by citizens, such as most industrial workers, who had no experience in filing income-tax returns. In effect, withholding would make it possible, for the first time, to vary income-tax rates and collections in an effective countercyclical fashion, and Keynesians within the Treasury had supported withholding at the source for that reason. Adoption of the plan meant, however, that during 1943, taxpayers would pay both their 1942 and their 1943 obligations.

One of the first to oppose the double payment was Beardsley Ruml, chairman of the New York Federal Reserve Bank and treasurer of R. H. Macy and Company. He launched a radio and press campaign to challenge the Treasury. He favored withholding but proposed the forgiveness of 1942 taxes to ease the pinch in 1943. Ruml's plan gained public support, but Roosevelt defended the Treasury, telling the chair of the Ways and Means Committee, "I cannot acquiesce in the elimination of a whole year's tax burden on the upper income groups during a war period when I must call for an increase in taxes . . . from the mass of people." After some modest concessions to Roosevelt, Congress adopted the Ruml plan in the Current Tax Payment Act of 1943.

The second Roosevelt defeat occurred in the Revenue Act of 1943. Led by the tax-writing committees, Congress rejected the Treasury's ad-

[68]The Wilson administration abandoned "collection at the source" in favor of "information at the source" in 1916 both in response to pressure from large corporations, which received no compensation for their administrative costs, and out of concern that corporations were undercollecting individual income taxes. See Brownlee, "Wilson and Financing the Modern State," 196–97.

[69]Altmeyer, *The Formative Years of Social Security*, 86–87.

vice and passed legislation providing for only modest tax increases ($2.3 billion versus the $10.5 billion requested by the Treasury) while creating a host of new tax favors for business, especially the mining, timber, and steel industries. Roosevelt denounced the bill as "not a tax bill but a tax relief bill, providing relief not for the needy but for the greedy." He vetoed the bill, but for the first time in history, Congress overrode a presidential veto of a revenue act. Alben Barkley, the Democratic majority leader in the Senate, described Roosevelt's veto message as a "calculated and deliberate assault upon the legislative integrity of every member of Congress." Ickes hoped that Roosevelt would go "to the people with his case against the Congress" for enacting "a vicious bill designed to protect the rich at the expense of the poor."[70] But the humiliating defeat convinced Roosevelt that he had to accept the structure of the income taxation without further complaint. His defeats in 1943 essentially ended the conflict, which had begun during World War I between business and progressive advocates, over soak-the-rich income taxation.

Under the new tax system, the number of individual taxpayers grew from 3.9 million in 1939 to 42.6 million in 1945, and federal income-tax collections over the period leaped from $2.2 billion to $35.1 billion. By the end of the war nearly 90 percent of the members of the labor force submitted income-tax returns, and about 60 percent of the labor force paid income taxes. Mass taxation had replaced class taxation. At the same time, the federal government came to dominate the nation's revenue system. In 1940, federal income tax had accounted for only 16 percent of the taxes collected by all levels of government; by 1950 the federal income tax produced over 51 percent of all collections. Installation of the new regime was the most dramatic shift in the nation's tax policies since 1916.

The structure of the new tax helped win middle-class support. General deductions (e.g., for interest on home mortgages and for payments of state and local taxes) sweetened the new tax system for the middle class. And the new method of collection, by payroll withholding and quarterly installment payments, took much of the sting out of taxpaying. Moreover, middle-class taxpayers preferred the mass-based income tax to a national sales tax, which many corporate leaders favored and promoted. Furthermore, fear of a renewed depression made the middle-class public

[70]February 26, 1944, entry, Harold Ickes Diaries, Ickes Papers.

more tolerant than it had been during World War I toward taxation that
was favorable to corporations and corporate privilege. This leniency may
have seemed naive to radical New Dealers, but it expressed a widely
shared commitment to the pursuit of enlightened self-interest. In the
same spirit, many New Deal legislators favored the mass-based income
tax during World War II as the best way to ensure a flow of revenues
to support federal programs of social justice.

The new regime of mass taxation succeeded too because of the popularity of the war effort. It was less necessary to leverage popular support and sacrifice for the war by enacting a highly redistributional tax
system. More so than in World War I, Americans concluded that their
nation's security was at stake and that victory required both personal
sacrifice through taxation and indulgence toward the corporate profits
that helped fuel the war machine.

Despite Roosevelt's and Morgenthau's reservations about the structure of the income tax, they used the extensive propaganda machinery
at their command to persuade the millions of new taxpayers to pay tax
obligations. The massive propaganda campaign of the Treasury, its Bureau of Internal Revenue, and the Office of War Information invoked
the same calls for civic responsibility and patriotic sacrifice that the Wilson administration had made so effectively during the bond campaigns
of World War I. A new message was that the average citizen would find
the new income taxes easy to pay. Although the effects of the propaganda campaign are difficult to determine, the campaign revealed that
the Roosevelt administration recognized that a tax regime relying on
mass-based income tax must rest heavily on voluntary cooperation and
compliance. Whatever the manipulation of patriotic symbols by the federal government, the success of the income tax during World War II
once again dramatically demonstrated the financial power of democratic
government.[71]

[71] On the income-tax advertising campaigns, see the following works by Carolyn C. Jones:
"Class Tax to Mass Tax: The Role of Propaganda in the Expansion of the Income Tax
during World War II," *Buffalo Law Review* 37 (1989): 685–737; "Taxes to Beat the
Axis: A Comparison of American and British Income Tax Publicity during World War
II" (paper presented at the Tenth International Economic History Congress, Leuven,
Belgium, June 12, 1990); and chapter 3, this volume. These campaigns ought to be set
in the context of all of the propaganda efforts by the Roosevelt administration. Mark
Leff has usefully suggested viewing such campaigns as part of the "politics of sacrifice."
However, as in his study of New Deal tax policy, Leff neglects the material, as opposed
to the symbolic, interest of Roosevelt and Morgenthau in increasing the sacrifice of cor-
porations and the wealthy. Mark Leff, "The Politics of Sacrifice on the American Home
Front in World War II," *Journal of American History* 77 (March 1991): 1296–1318.

The winning of World War II and the surge of economic prosperity following so closely on the heels of the Great Depression helped produce a popular, bipartisan consensus of support for sustaining the basic policy shifts undertaken during the Roosevelt administration. One expression of this consensus was the congressional passage of the Employment Act of 1946. This was the first formal commitment by the federal government to what was believed to have been the implicit fiscal policy of Franklin Roosevelt. The act captured three important elements in Roosevelt's fiscal policy. First, it declared the federal government's central responsibility for managing the level of employment. Second, by creating the Council of Economic Advisers and charging it with the development of an annual published report (*The Economic Report of the President*), the act established that the president and the public should have economic advice that was expert and independent. And third, it formally embodied a central objective of the New Deal: to embrace human values as the context for setting and evaluating fiscal policy. The institutional framework was in place for the proactive manipulation of the federal budget on behalf of economic stability.

Like Roosevelt's real fiscal policy, however, the act provided policy-makers with little guidance on the substance of fiscal policy. It failed to make a government guarantee of full employment; it restricted counter-cyclical actions to only those consistent with other economic objectives; and it avoided a specific definition of appropriate policy. Keynesian ideas had won a larger audience during World War II, but public finance experts significantly disagreed over the content of countercyclical policy. On the one hand, some regarded the conjunction of great deficits and dramatic economic expansion as proof that deficits not only had produced the economic expansion of World War II, ending the Great Depression, but also were required for sustained prosperity in peacetime. On the other hand, other experts, such as the leadership of the Committee for Economic Development (CED), which represented business-people interested in Keynesianism, had a more conservative view. In 1947 the CED issued a statement on fiscal policy, *Taxes and the Budget,* which accepted deficits during recessions but advocated budget surpluses during times of high employment and stable rates of taxation.[72]

In the realm of tax policy, the World War II emergency institutionalized a new tax regime—one that combined progressive but mass-based

[72]On the 1947 report of the CED, see Stein, *Fiscal Revolution in America,* 220–40.

income taxation for general revenues with a regressive payroll tax for social insurance. Although some important differences remained between the two major political parties, both insisted on maintaining the central characteristics of the World War II revenue system and eschewing both progressive assaults on corporate financial structures and the regressive taxation of consumption. For the first time since the early nineteenth century, the two parties agreed on the essential elements of the nation's fiscal policy.

The general decline of partisanship after World War II no doubt contributed to the convergence of the two parties on fiscal policy. The convergence on tax policy involved acceptance by the Republican Party of higher levels of taxation of corporate profits and large incomes, levels that the business community had regarded as unconscionable at the time World War II ended. But the convergence was more the product of a shift in direction by the Democratic Party. In the postwar era, Democrats largely abandoned taxation as an instrument to mobilize class interests. Although Presidents John F. Kennedy and Lyndon B. Johnson continued to support tax reforms, such as the taxation of capital gains at death, they also advocated a variety of tax cuts and did so by hawking the "supply-side" benefits in ways reminiscent of Andrew Mellon. In 1964, Congress responded to Johnson's call for a tax cut "to increase our national income and Federal revenues" by slashing taxes in the face of large deficits. The Council of Economic Advisers, also committed to "growthmanship," actively supported the 1964 cuts, which reduced capital gains taxes and allowed more generous depreciation allowances. Most liberals regarded the 1964 tax cuts as a victory for aggressive countercycle stimulation of demand while they also embraced a conservative supply-side rationale for the cuts.

Thus, Democrats assisted the Republican Party in finishing the job it had begun during the 1920s: taking both the partisan sting and the redistributional threat out of taxation. The shift in the tax policy favored by the Democratic Party was part of its more general shift—one begun after 1937, accelerated during World War II, and completed in the Kennedy-Johnson era—away from democratic statism and toward corporate liberalism, a line of thinking that had expanded its intellectual ambit, and its political potency, by incorporating Keynesian countercyclical policies.[73]

---

[73]The scholarly literature on the Kennedy-Johnson tax programs has become impressive

The bipartisan consensus ushered in an era of buoyant public finance that lasted until the 1980s. Usually well removed from the contested turf of partisan politics, the tax policies and political actions that produced the era were nearly invisible.

For example, with remarkably little public debate, and with bipartisan agreement, the federal government embraced a policy of steadily raising social security tax rates. The higher tax rates, as well as increases in the tax base, produced an increase in social security taxes from less than 1 percent of GNP in the late 1940s to over 7 percent by the late 1970s. With this funding, social security payments increased from $472 million in 1946 (less than 1 percent of GNP) to $105 billion in 1979 (about 4.3 percent of GNP).[74]

Even less visible was the role of persistent inflation, which peaked first in the late 1940s, then increased again during the late 1960s, and continued throughout the 1970s. Accelerating inflation reduced the value of outstanding debt and thereby played a role of unprecedented proportions in financing the federal government. Inflation also pushed increasing numbers of families into higher tax brackets faster than their real income increased. Thus, the structure of income-tax rates became substantially more progressive, especially at the higher levels of income. The same effect, coupled with a failure to increase the personal exemption as rapidly as prices rose, propelled many low-income families into the tax system. By the early 1980s the portion of the labor force paying taxes had increased to over 75 percent from the 60 percent level reached at the end of World War II.[75] Because of unanticipated inflation, the revenue system proved to be far more elastic after World War II than experts had predicted. Economists at the CED, for example, had believed that after the war, federal tax receipts as a share of gross domestic product would fall from the wartime peak of 22 percent to somewhere between 10 and 15 percent. In fact, the tax share of national product dipped below 15 percent only briefly, in 1950. By 1952 it was approach-

in depth and scope. See, for example, the following: King, *Money, Time, and Politics*, 151–319; Cathie J. Martin, *Shifting the Burden: The Struggle over Growth and Corporate Taxation* (Chicago: University of Chicago Press, 1991), and chapter 7, this volume; Stein, *The Fiscal Revolution in America*, 372–453; Witte, *Development of the Federal Income Tax*, 155–75; and Julian E. Zelizer, chapter 6, this volume.

[74] On the postwar expansion of the social security system, see Edward D. Berkowitz, chapter 4, this volume.

[75] For a summary of the operation of postwar individual income tax, including the trends in progressivity, see Jon Bakija and Eugene Steuerle, "Individual Income Taxation since 1948," *National Tax Journal* 44 (December 1991): 451–75.

ing 20 percent and ever since has remained close to, or slightly above, 20 percent.[76]

"Bracket creep" meant that the federal government could often respond positively to requests for new programs without enacting politically damaging tax increases. The highly elastic revenue system paid for the strategic defense programs of the cold war and, without any general or permanent increases in income taxation, for the mobilizations for the Korean and Vietnam wars as well. But the size of the defense budget relative to GNP tended to decline through the 1970s, except during the Korean and Vietnam wars. Thus, the increases in federal revenues went largely for the expansion of domestic programs—education, welfare, health services (including Medicare), urban redevelopment, and the channeling of federal revenues to state and local governments through indirect methods such as grants-in-aid and revenue sharing. The intergovernmental support expanded on the programs developed after the Civil War, after World War I, and during the New Deal. By 1974, more than 20 percent of state and local revenues came from federal aid, which amounted to a kind of tax relief to state and local governments. Following World War II, state and local tax receipts had increased even more rapidly than had federal taxes, and by the late 1970s, state and local governments became popular targets of general attacks on the growth of government.

The inflation-driven increases in revenues also permitted new "tax expenditures"—special preferences offered under the tax code in the form of exclusions, deductions, and credits. During the 1960s and 1970s, as had been the case in the 1920s, tax expenditures became increasingly popular, and both old and new ones grew relative to conventional expenditures. Politicians became attracted to them as a way to accomplish social goals—such as the promotion of homeownership embedded in the deduction of mortgage interest—without having to make large and politically difficult direct expenditures of funds. In other words, many Democratic and Republican members of Congress found self-serving political benefits in hiding tax programs from public scrutiny. Contributing to the movement as well were taxpaying groups that aggressively sought preferential treatment within the tax code in order to offset the effects of "bracket creep." In turn, the taxpayers and legislators who benefited

---

[76]Herbert Stein provided the information regarding the CED estimates at the end of World War II. Stein to Brownlee, June 20, 1994.

from the tax expenditures developed a vested interest in increasing the complexity of the process of tax legislation.[77]

Whereas the general public was slow to recognize the significance of tax expenditures, a collection of tax lawyers and economists struggled to expose the inequities resulting from increasing exemptions and deductions. Especially influential were the economist Joseph Pechman and the law professor Stanley Surrey. They drew on a line of analysis based on the arguments of the economists Thomas S. Adams, Robert Murray Haig, and Henry Simons, who, during the 1920s and 1930s, had suggested that the federal government ought to rationalize the personal income tax by basing it on a comprehensive, economic definition of income—one that measured, in Haig's words, "the money value of the net accretion of one's economic power between two points in time." Adopting Haig's definition for the purposes of income taxation would require the taxing of items such as net capital gains and the income-in-kind that an owner enjoys from an owner-occupied residence.[78]

Base-broadening won a wider audience during World War II when the CED commissioned Henry Simons to develop a reform program focused on broadening the income-tax base. In 1959, Congressman Wilbur Mills, chair of the House Ways and Means Committee, held hearings and published papers that put base-broadening reforms on the agenda of a new fiscal community that coalesced in the late 1950s and early 1960s.[79]

Beginning in 1967, Surrey, as assistant secretary of the Treasury (1961–69), further enhanced the visibility of base-broadening by intro-

[77]The leading analysis of the bureaucratic complexity of making tax policy, especially within Congress, during the 1960s and 1970s is Reese, *The Politics of Taxation.*

[78]Robert M. Haig, "The Concept of Income," *The Federal Income Tax* (New York: Columbia University Press, 1921), 7.

[79]For a summary of the base-broadening movement, see Joseph A. Pechman, "Tax Reform: Theory and Practice," *Journal of Economic Perspectives* 1 (Summer 1987): 11–28. The CED published Simons's program in 1944 as Committee for Economic Development, *A Post-war Federal Tax Plan for High Employment* (New York: CED, 1944). Simons later published an elaborate version of his plan. See Henry C. Simons, *Federal Tax Reform* (Chicago: University of Chicago Press, 1950). For an assessment of Simons's contributions to tax theory, see Harold Groves, *Tax Philosophers: Two Hundred Years of Thought in Great Britain and the United States*, ed. Donald J. Curran (Madison: University of Wisconsin Press, 1974), 74–85. For the influential hearings sponsored by Wilbur Mills, see U.S. House of Representatives, Committee on Ways and Means, *Tax Revision Compendium: Compendium of Papers on Broadening the Tax Base*, 2 vols. (Washington, D.C.: Government Printing Office, 1959). On Mills's interest in base-broadening reform, see Julian Zelizer, chapter 6, this volume. It should be noted that Pechman lent support to Zelizer's interpretation of Mills by crediting Mills with boosting the cause of comprehensive personal income taxation. See Pechman, "Tax Reform," 12.

ducing the organizing concept of tax expenditures.[80] He led in articulating the Treasury's position that the government should pursue social goals openly, through direct expenditures. Surrey, economists within the Treasury, and a string of Treasury assistant secretaries and commissioners of internal revenue who favored base-broadening worked in ways that would have pleased Thomas S. Adams. From within the Treasury they highlighted the massive size of tax expenditures and underscored the kind of economic inefficiencies, distortions, and unfairness that the tax expenditures created. In 1974, the Congressional Budget Act acknowledged the importance of the concept and advanced the debate by requiring the annual publication of a "tax expenditure budget." Subsequently the Congressional Budget Office estimated that in 1967, tax expenditures cost the federal government nearly $37 billion (equal to 21 percent of federal expenditures) and that the total cost had soared to $327 billion by 1984 (equal to 35 percent of federal expenditures).[81]

In 1976, presidential candidate Jimmy Carter responded to the growing awareness of the incoherence of federal income taxation by calling the American tax system "a disgrace." He promised to make the federal income tax more progressive, to broaden its base, and to avoid "a piecemeal approach to change." But during his first two years in office, Carter found himself embroiled in piecemeal change and frustrated in his efforts to reduce the taxes of lower-income families. Congress insisted on avoiding tax cuts that might stimulate consumption and inflation and concentrated instead on seeking ways of stimulating business investment to discourage inflation and encourage productivity growth, which had slowed during the 1970s. Congress prevailed, and President Carter reluctantly signed the Revenue Act of 1978, which provided only minimal

[80]For a discussion of Surrey's views, including his 1967 proposal of a "tax expenditure budget," see Stanley S. Surrey, *Pathways to Tax Reform: The Concept of Tax Expenditures* (Cambridge, Mass.: Harvard University Press, 1973).

[81]Such expenditures ought to be incorporated into any systematic analysis of the long-term relationship between tax and expenditure policies. Just as tax expenditures mask the social effects of tax policy from the polity at large, they may make it difficult for social scientists to identify the "sandbox" effects of tax policy. (In 1981 Secretary of the Treasury Donald Regan commented, "My favorite part of the tax bill is the indexing provision—it takes the sand out of Congress's sandbox.") The growing significance of "tax expenditures" during the 1970s may help account, institutionally, for the disappearance of the "causal" association between taxation and expenditures as noted by Hoover and Sheffrin during that decade. See Kevin D. Hoover and Steven Sheffrin, "Causation, Spending, and Taxes: Sand in the Sandbox or Tax Collector for the Welfare State?" *American Economic Review* 82 (March 1992): 225–48.

tax relief and simplification for individuals while it offered generous cuts in capital gains and business taxes.

THE REAGAN "REVOLUTION"

The era of buoyant revenues for domestic programs came to a quick end during the 1980s. Some signs of its impending demise had been apparent in the late 1970s. Most important, the Federal Reserve had begun to attack inflation, pushing interest rates well above the rate of inflation. But the major changes were also the result of a shift in tax policy: the sharp reduction of taxes associated with the Reagan "revolution" and the antigovernmental movement symbolized by the "Proposition 13" revolt of taxpayers in California in 1978.

The Reagan administration undertook the reduction of taxes through the passage of the Economic Recovery Tax Act of 1981 (ERTA), which may well have been the most powerful part of the Reagan revolution. Its impact was international as well as domestic; along with Margaret Thatcher's tax reforms in Great Britain, it inspired a rate-lowering movement of income-tax reform that swept through Europe and Japan during the 1980s. The political basis for ERTA was Republican control of the Senate, conservative domination of the House, and growing popular enthusiasm for tax cutting—an enthusiasm reinforced by the president's rationalization of the tax cutting as supply-side stimulation of economic expansion, productivity, and even tax revenues.

ERTA's key provisions—indexing of rates for inflation and severe slashing of personal and business taxes—helped ensure the end of dynamic federal tax revenues. ERTA reduced the role of the income tax in the nation's revenue system for the first time since the Great Depression. By 1990, indexing alone had reduced federal revenues by about $180 billion a year, and the ERTA rate reductions cost the Treasury an additional $80 billion annually. Meanwhile, income-tax revenues as a share of all federal taxes declined from 63 percent in 1980 to 57 percent in 1990. During the early 1980s, largely as a consequence of ERTA, relatively invisible, politically low-cost means of increasing tax revenues had vanished. For the moment, the Reagan revolution seemed to have succeeded in breaking the "upward ratchet" of federal taxation.[82]

---

[82]But at least one of the Reagan administration's central participants in the passage of the

Meanwhile, increased budget deficits (roughly the size of the ERTA reductions in revenue) and interest payments began to restrain domestic spending. In response to the deficits, Congress took extraordinary action, passing the Gramm-Rudman-Hollings Act in 1985, which imposed automatic spending reductions (*but not tax increases*) whenever the deficit exceeded prescribed levels. "Gramm-Rudman" also placed "off-budget" expenditures, mainly expenditures for the social security and other federal trust funds, in a unified federal budget. These expenditures had expanded since World War I and had escalated during the 1970s and 1980s. By 1985, they had reached almost one-quarter of all federal outlays. Gramm-Rudman had some disciplinary effect, but deficits continued to increase into the 1990s.

During 1984 and 1985, while the deficit crisis mounted, both the Reagan administration and congressional Democrats, supported by Treasury staff, edged into a competitive scramble to occupy the high ground of tax reform. The consequence of this process was the passage of tax legislation even more consequential than ERTA—the Tax Reform Act of 1986. This act amounted to the most dramatic transformation of federal tax policy since World War II.

Like ERTA and the tax reforms of the 1920s, the 1986 measure was initiated by Republicans seeking to reduce the taxes on wealth. But the reform process was different in 1986. First, the Republican administration had new goals; it was more interested in improving economic incentives for enterprise capitalism than in protecting corporate bureaucracies or the real estate industry.[83] Second, the writing of the 1986 act included substantial Democratic participation. Senator Bill Bradley, who had studied the role of Stanley Surrey within the Treasury, played a particularly crucial, creative part in the drama. Third, these political entrepreneurs successfully championed a position never previously as-

---

1981 legislation denies that the tax cut was a deliberate effort to create deficits. See David A. Stockman, *The Triumph of Politics: How the Reagan Revolution Failed* (New York: Harper and Row, 1986), esp. 229–68. Stockman's interpretation, reinforced by recent memoirs and well-researched journalism, is that the deficits were simply the result of the president's stubborn refusal to lend serious support to the cutting of expenditures. The recent memoirs are Donald T. Regan, *For the Record: From Wall Street to Washington* (San Diego: Harcourt, 1988), and Martin Anderson, *Revolution* (San Diego: Harcourt, 1988); the journalism is Lou Cannon, *President Reagan: The Role of a Lifetime* (New York: Simon and Schuster, 1991), 253–60.

[83] Assistant Secretary of the Treasury Richard Darman described this as "tax populism." See Darman, "Populist Force behind Tax Reform Suggests Future Culture Shifts," *Financier* 10 (December 1986): 23–32, and "Beyond Tax Populism," *Society* 24 (September–October 1987): 35–38.

sociated with either of the two major parties: focusing reform of the income tax on broadening its income base and creating a more uniform—a more "horizontally" equitable—tax, even at the expense of sacrificing its progressive rate structure.

The fiscal environment was vastly different as well. Massive deficits, ERTA, and Gramm-Rudman meant that Congress could no longer enact "reform" bills—ones providing tax reductions to particular groups—that reduced the overall level of taxation. Nor could Congress any longer rely on inflation-driven tax increases to finance tax reductions. Every reduction in tax rates and every increase in tax loopholes had to be paid for by identifying losers—through a reduction in another loophole elsewhere in the tax code.[84]

The passage of the Tax Reform Act of 1986 came as a great surprise to tax experts, especially to the political scientists who believed in the powerful sway of grinding interest-group pluralism. But taxes were "up for grabs" more than "pluralist" scholars had realized. The act left significant losers as well as winners in its wake. The 1986 act eliminated some important tax expenditures favoring the middle class—those subsidizing consumer interest payments and payments for state and local taxes. It also repealed the investment tax credit for corporations and the preferential taxation of long-term capital gains. And it provided important benefits for both lower- and upper-income groups. Sharp increases in the personal exemption and the standard deduction favored taxpayers in the lowest income brackets. Reductions in the rates on the top brackets, and the cut in the top corporate rate from 48 percent to 34 percent, favored the wealthiest taxpayers. By attacking special deductions and credits, the act moved toward eliminating tax-based privilege and reaffirming the duties of citizenship. It preserved progressivity and "ability to pay" while promoting efficiency and uniformity.[85]

Thus, the 1980s reforms created major changes in federal taxation, changes that disrupted the post–World War II policy equilibrium. The income tax was in more flux than at any other time since the 1940s,

[84]For discussions of the influence of changed fiscal circumstances, see C. Eugene Steuerle, *The Tax Decade: How Taxes Came to Dominate the Public Agenda* (Washington, D.C.: Urban Institute Press, 1992) and chapter 8, this volume.

[85]The best detailed accounts of the passage of the Tax Reform Act of 1986 are the following: Jeffrey H. Birnbaum and Alan S. Murray, *Showdown at Gucci Gulch: Lawmakers, Lobbyists, and the Unlikely Triumph of Tax Reform* (New York: Random House, 1987); Timothy J. Conlan, Margaret T. Wrightson, and David R. Beam, *Taxing Choices: The Politics of Tax Reform* (Washington, D.C.: Congressional Quarterly Press, 1990); and Steuerle, *The Tax Decade*, 71–162.

and from the turmoil emerged a relatively diminished role for income taxation (while income-tax revenues continued to grow in absolute terms) and a somewhat more broadly based income tax.

Broadening the base of income taxation may have helped build a foundation for a future tax regime that would once again expand the role of income taxation. In assessing the 1986 reform act, Joseph Pechman emphasized how it significantly strengthened the base for income taxation. In 1989 he estimated that as a consequence of eliminating tax shelters, the adoption of a very modest increase in rates, as little as three percentage points across the board, could raise as much as $100 billion a year.[86]

Between 1986 and 1995, however, the federal government moved no farther along the lines of reform pioneered in 1986. That was largely because of the continued growth of popular hostility to government, and the way the nation's political leaders, including Presidents George Bush and Bill Clinton, responded: drifting back to bidding for support by offering favors such as cuts in capital-gains taxes or middle-class tax breaks.

Widespread concern over the federal deficit prevented significant erosion in the elements of the Tax Reform Act of 1986. In fact, during 1995, deficit worries prompted leaders in both parties to respond to hostility to taxes by deemphasizing tax cutting in favor of tax reform. They proposed reforms to protect revenues, stimulate investment, promote horizontal equity, and simplify taxes. Their ideas included a national sales tax or an expenditures tax to replace the income tax, a "flat tax" that would tax individuals only on their wages and salaries, and income tax reform that would both broaden the base radically and increase progressivity. In mid-1995, tax reform seemed likely to be a major issue in the 1996 elections.

For the moment, however, the essentials of the tax system introduced during World War II remain in place, although changing economic circumstances and policy shifts in the 1980s have largely eliminated its revenue elasticity. As the twenty-first century nears, it is still uncertain whether the nation can, for the first time, devise a fiscal regime capable of meeting new social problems without first enduring a new national emergency.

[86]Joseph Pechman, "More Tax Reform," Wilson Quarterly 13 (Summer 1989): 141–42.

II

Taxation for war, social security, and
economic stability

3

Mass-based income taxation:
Creating a taxpaying culture, 1940–1952

CAROLYN C. JONES

On March 9, 1943, Secretary of the Treasury Henry Morgenthau, Jr., received a call from George Gallup. The pollster was quite concerned about recent polling data suggesting that one-half to one-third of the interviewees were unclear about their obligation to file a federal income-tax report.[1] Some people believed a proposed withholding system negated the duty to file a return, while others thought that buying war bonds canceled the obligation. Gallup suggested that Morgenthau "might possibly want to fire all the 16-inch guns" he had before the March 15 due date.[2]

The next morning, Morgenthau convened a meeting in his office. Those present discussed their response. Radio announcements were the first device chosen. Before long, the conversation focused on the newness of income-tax obligations to many Americans. One participant asked, "Do you feel that the majority of the people in the country recognize the tax day as something that they have to live up to?" Secretary Morgenthau placed the situation in the framework of wartime psychology. "After all, this is the one place, I suppose, where the United States Government hits more people face to face than any other front. It is a ques-

---

[1] Telephone conversation from George Gallup to Henry Morgenthau, Jr. (4:10 P.M., March 9, 1943), and Atlanta Speech Meeting (9:29 A.M., March 10, 1943), both in Morgenthau Diaries 615:96, 131, Franklin D. Roosevelt Library, Hyde Park, New York; George H. Gallup, *The Gallup Poll: Public Opinion, 1935–1971*, vol. 1 (New York: Random House, 1972), 373. ("Findings indicate that unless last minute efforts to acquaint people with the provisions of the new tax law and the penalty for not filing are effective, the number of persons who file a return may fall below the 40 million mark.")

[2] Telephone conversation from George Gallup to Henry Morgenthau, Jr., Morgenthau Diaries 615:96.

tion of domestic morale." He suggested that union leaders be enlisted to survey members quickly to see if they had filed. Morgenthau's assistant noted, "It would be very good propaganda to have union people going around asking others, 'Have you paid your taxes?' It would be the best kind of propaganda."[3]

In the event of massive noncompliance, Morgenthau was considering a filing deadline extension for new taxpayers or for those making less than $3,000. Morgenthau asked, "Suppose we have to go out and try to arrest five million people?" The idea of an extension troubled some. It was feared that a postponement would "soften up the tax-paying day." One participant commented that the situation could produce "public relations fireworks."[4]

Morgenthau and his assistants were creating a new culture of taxpaying. If they were to be successful, the legal rules that created a mass federal income tax required the creation of new customs and a radical change in the social realities surrounding income taxpaying. During the World War II years, federal budget expenditures were twelve times greater in 1945 than they were in 1940, the number of taxpayers on the income-tax rolls increased sixfold, from seven million taxpayers in 1940 to more than forty-two million taxpayers in 1945.[5]

In a 1943 *Michigan Law Review* article, the legal scholar Alexander H. Pekelis wrote of two types of legal rules: "rules which are a simple restatement of existing custom, and rules which are enacted with the very purpose of reversing existing customs and which should be read as we read the negative of a snapshot: white for black and black for white."[6] The changes in federal income-tax law during the 1940s markedly changed the profile of the average taxpayer. If such changes were to be effective, a new culture of taxpaying needed to be created. Society needed to be shaped so that the snapshot negative would eventually become a snapshot of taxpaying in the United States.

The tax-filing incident in March 1943 brought together important elements of the government's challenge and its solutions. Public relations concerns were central. As noted, one strategy suggested was the

---

[3]Taxes Meeting (11:05 A.M., March 10, 1943), Morgenthau Diaries 615:144, 145–46, 150.
[4]Ibid., 149.
[5]U.S. Commerce Department, Bureau of the Census, *Historical Statistics of America* (Washington, D.C.: Government Printing Office, 1975), Ser. Y 605–37, 1123–24, Ser. Y 402–11, 1110.
[6]Alexander H. Pekelis, "Legal Techniques and Political Ideologies: A Comparative Study," *Michigan Law Review* 41 (1943): 665–92.

use of union officials to ask members if they had filed returns. This type of technique was used frequently during the World War II years and involved the government's appropriation of voices in the effort to justify the radical expansion of the federal income tax to ordinary taxpayers. It was developed with considerable attention at the highest levels of the Treasury Department in late 1941 through 1943 and continued in operation with less involvement by high-level officials until the end of the war. The appropriation strategy apparently lost favor after the war as more hierarchical official messages from government officials replaced protax media messages from Roy Rogers, Donald Duck, and others.

The March 1943 "crisis" was prompted by the recent congressional consideration of the withholding system for wages and salaries. This was one of two major structural changes implemented in the 1940s to make the mass income-tax system workable. Such structural change was part of a second strategy, identified in this chapter as standardization, which was used throughout the 1940s. Standardization sought to move various aspects of income-tax payment more clearly into the control of tax officials. Two major structural innovations from the 1940s represent the standardization strategy: withholding and the income-splitting joint tax return for husbands and wives. Wage-earning taxpayers were not free to decide when to save to meet tax obligations or how to finance tax payments. Taxes were withheld by employers from paychecks. Until 1948, some states sought federal income-tax savings for their citizens by adopting community property regimes. Taxpayers in other states attempted to reduce their tax burdens by reconfiguring patterns of property and business ownership. The adoption of the income-splitting joint return made such state and individual decisions either irrelevant or far less significant. Structural changes were combined with increasing technological and administrative capacity in the hope of minimizing dissonance between the law as written in statutes and the behavior of taxpayers. Hierarchical government-sponsored or government-assisted messages in the media were also used, particularly after the war, to suggest massive, effective, and standard enforcement of the law. The March 1943 incident demonstrated that such structural changes and their enforcement had a public relations component. Public relations efforts by the government undergirded the creation of a mass taxpaying culture.

It is not the aim of this chapter to evaluate definitively the effectiveness of the appropriation and standardization strategies. Even if the efficacy of the efforts of tax policymakers is difficult to gauge, the consideration of these two strategies provides valuable insight into the decisions made by those charged with conversion to mass income taxation.[7]

APPROPRIATION

Social scientists and legal scholars interested in legal processes have noted how the law as written in statutes, regulations, and court decisions (official legal pronouncements) differs from legal reality in various contexts and localities. These scholars have often viewed this incongruence as the result of local or contextual interpretation of official documents.[8] This model assumes that official lawmakers can communicate only through statutes, court decisions, and regulations. The adoption of the mass federal income tax illustrates that lawmakers and administrators also attempt to shape "social reality" through other means. During World War II, tax administrators, using public relations techniques, wrapped official messages in popular culture. As Treasury Secretary Morgenthau stated in 1941, "If we can get people to pay taxes with that God-awful Mickey Mouse, we will have arrived socially."[9]

The Roosevelt administration's use of publicity did not begin with the selling of the mass federal income tax. In his first term, Roosevelt substantially expanded the government publicity system to get the

[7]This evaluation is hampered to some extent by the variability of source materials within the period studied. It appears that in recent years, the Internal Revenue Service has not been particularly careful in retaining and making available documents that may have had some impact on this study. For the World War II years, however, the Office of War Information records and the voluminous Morgenthau Diaries, Morgenthau Papers, and Peter Odegard Papers fortunately provide an ample data base. For the postwar years, the record is more scanty, and it is not possible to make sweeping quantitative judgments.

[8]This is a point made by Barbara Yngvesson when she criticizes interpretative literature in anthropology. According to some anthropologists, "Legal culture not only differs in different contexts, but law is 'invented,' 'negotiated,' or 'made' in local settings." Barbara Yngvesson, "Inventing Law in Local Settings: Rethinking Popular Legal Culture," *Yale Law Journal* 98 (1989): 1689, 1690. She believes that this account does not provide sufficient weight to "the centrality of power in the meaning-making process."

[9]Group Meeting (9:45 A.M., December 15, 1941), Morgenthau Diaries 473:28. A more extensive treatment of this campaign and, particularly, of the themes used in the World War II income-tax campaign is presented in Carolyn C. Jones, "Class Tax to Mass Tax: The Role of Propaganda in the Expansion of the Income Tax during World War II," *Buffalo Law Review* 37 (1989): 685–737.

message of the New Deal to the public through the press, radio, and film.[10] There were even Roosevelt administration precedents in the area of government finance. In the 1936 election, for example, social security came under attack from conservative Republicans. In response, the Social Security Board released a movie entitled *We the People and Social Security* and printed a circular, "Social Security in Your Old-Age."[11] Roosevelt's Treasury Department had previous experience in the public relations of public finance. In 1935 Secretary of the Treasury Morgenthau initiated "baby bonds," which were aimed at people of average means. The baby bond campaign included a newsreel of Roosevelt purchasing bonds for himself and his grandchildren. In 1937, Morgenthau employed an advertising agency, Sloan and Bryan, to promote bond sales.[12]

Beginning in the spring of 1941, the Treasury Department launched its Defense Savings Bond Campaign. For a dime, average Americans could purchase savings stamps, which could be collected in an album until they could be exchanged for a bond. Morgenthau built on his experience with baby bonds in helping to fashion the promotional campaign for defense bonds. He advocated newspaper coverage of purchases by political leaders. He broadcast promotional addresses on the radio and asked other cabinet officials to do the same. Bond sales were also promoted on the *Treasury Hour,* a weekly radio broadcast that began in July 1941.[13]

The methods used to sell mass income taxation built on these previous efforts. Secretary of the Treasury Morgenthau continued to be actively involved in several public relations efforts. Often, people involved in the bond campaigns worked on income-tax publicity as well. For example, Peter Odegard, a political science professor from Amherst College and the author of *The American Public Mind,* served as a consultant to the Treasury on public relations matters, particularly on defense and war bond sales. The Treasury Department was primar-

[10]For a detailed discussion of earlier propaganda efforts, see Richard W. Steele, *Propaganda in an Open Society: The Roosevelt Administration and the Media, 1933–1941* (Westport, Conn.: Greenwood Press, 1985).

[11]Carolyn L. Weaver, *The Crisis in Social Security: Economic and Political Origins* (Durham, N.C.: Duke University Press, 1982), 107.

[12]John Morton Blum, *From the Morgenthau Diaries: Years of Crisis, 1928–1938* (Boston: Houghton Mifflin, 1959), 340–41.

[13]John Morton Blum, *From the Morgenthau Diaries: Years of Urgency, 1938–1941* (Boston: Houghton Mifflin, 1965), 300–304.

ily responsible for public relations regarding the income tax. Strategies
were developed in part by Department of the Treasury staff and private sector consultants.[14] Early in his tenure as Treasury secretary,
Morgenthau directed those in the department to submit all press statements or other news releases to Herbert Gaston, assistant to the secretary.[15] Throughout his years as secretary, Morgenthau continued to
express concern about public relations efforts.[16] Not only did the
Treasury Department have its own public relations men doing traditional press releases,[17] but the Bureau of Internal Revenue within the
Treasury had public relations people as well.[18] A pamphlet may have
needed approval by the commissioner of internal revenue, several assistant secretaries of the Treasury, the Treasury's director of public relations, and Secretary Morgenthau.[19]

Overall coordination of government public relations proved to be
difficult. After various domestic propaganda agencies were created
during the early 1940s and failed, Roosevelt in 1942 created the Office of War Information (OWI) to coordinate informational activities
of all federal agencies. The OWI, however, had no authority to com-
pel other departments to follow its lead. In its dealings with the Treasury Department, the OWI was relegated to implementation rather
than formulation of strategy. Its work ranged from coordinating radio
announcements, contacting particular segments of the press (for example, black press, labor press, women's editors),[20] distributing post-

[14]Letter from Fred Smith to Secretary Morgenthau (May 3, 1943), Morgenthau Diaries
    631:90; John Morton Blum, *V Was for Victory: Politics and American Culture during
    World War II* (New York: Harcourt Brace Jovanovich, 1976), 17.
[15]Blum, *Years of Crisis*, 80.
[16]Marginalia on memorandum to Ferdinand Kuhn from Secretary Morgenthau (March 16,
    1941), Morgenthau Diaries 508:292 ("I am *very* disappointed that we have got no where
    on our tax publicity program"); Group Meeting (9:15 A.M., March 16, 1942), Morgen-
    thau Diaries 508:8–15.
[17]Harold N. Graves, "Memorandum for the Secretary, Regarding the Public Relations
    Division" (February 13, 1941), Morgenthau Diaries 372:104.
[18]Taxes Meeting (3:00 P.M.), Morgenthau Diaries 652:189–90; Group Meeting (9:00 A.M.,
    July 29, 1943), Morgenthau Diaries 652:158–60; Group Meeting (8:45 A.M., August 11,
    1943), Morgenthau Diaries 655:105–11.
[19]For example, the folder "Your New Income Tax," created in 1942, was prepared in
    collaboration with the Treasury's director of public relations, Chick Schwarz, the Bureau
    of Internal Revenue, and the Division of Tax Research. It was read and approved by
    Norman Cann, for the Bureau of Internal Revenue, Assistant Secretaries of the Treasury
    Bell and Herbert Gaston, and Ferdinand Kuhn and George Buffington. Finally, the doc-
    ument was submitted to Secretary Morgenthau for his approval. Memorandum from
    Sullivan to Morgenthau (November 19, 1942), Morgenthau Diaries 596:233.
[20]This market segmentation was utilized in other ways during World War II. For example,
    in the defense bond program, the "special areas" were identified as "the Schools, Women,

ers, producing newsreels,[21] and providing occasional advice about a public relations crisis.[22]

The importance and undeveloped state of public relations strategy regarding taxation was recognized within the Roosevelt administration. A memorandum in Odegard's papers noted: "Public relations in the field of taxation has made little progress. But with increased demands for social services of all kinds from government and the resulting need for greater revenues some attention is being given to this most important problem."[23] Fred Smith, an advertising executive who worked in the Treasury Department, said that despite the fact that Morgenthau "couldn't lay out an advertisement if his entire apple crop depended on it," he was "the number two advertising man in Washington," exceeded only by Roosevelt. "Perhaps the most important advertising decision he ever made was the decision to use *bonds* to sell the *war,* rather than vice versa." In 1942, Roosevelt and Morgenthau saw the massive sales campaign for bonds as a means of making the "country war-minded." The voluntary nature of war bond purchase was seen as "democratic."[24]

The involuntary feature of tax payments created somewhat different problems for those charged with selling the mass income tax. The problem was particularly difficult because in the 1930s, income taxation was

Farmers, Workers, Negroes, groups of Foreign Origin, and so forth." Letter from Peter H. Odegard to the secretary (April 8, 1944), Morgenthau Diaries 719:53; Tentative Outline (n.d.), Morgenthau Diaries 719:59; Defense Savings Staff, "Field Organization News Letter" (December 13, 1941), Morgenthau Diaries 472:353.

[21]Memorandum from Simon O. Lesser, program manager, to J. D. Nunan, Jr., George J. Schoeneman, Charles Schaeffer, Irving Perlmeter, Norman Cann, Charles P. Suman, Harvey Goddard (March 24 1945), in Taxes—Radio, Records of Simon Lesser, Program Guides and Publicity Materials for the Economic Stabilization Campaign, Records of the Office of War Information, RG 208, National Records Center, Suitland, Maryland (hereafter cited as Taxes—Radio); Simon O. Lesser, program manager, to J. D. Nunan, Jr., George Schoeneman, Charles Schaeffer, Irving Perlmeter, Norman Cann, Charles Suman, Harvey Goddard (April 26, 1945), in Taxes—Radio; Memorandum to Station Relations Regional Chiefs from Willett Kempton (February 19, 1945), in Taxes—Radio; Advance Bulletin of New Posters (February 1944), in Taxes—Radio; Memorandum to Bureau Chiefs from Gardner Cowles, Jr. (February 5, 1943), and Memorandum from James R. Brackett to Fred Smith (August 4, 1943), both in Treasury/Correspondence, General Records of Assistant Directors James Rogers and William Lewis, January to July 1943, Records of the Office of War Information, RG 208, National Records Center, Suitland, Maryland (hereafter cited as General Records of Assistant Directors).

[22]Treasury Conference Report (March 10, 1943), in Conference Reports (Treas.), General Records of Assistant Directors.

[23]Public Relations and Taxation (n.d.), Tax, General Correspondence: S-Z, Peter H. Odegard Papers, Franklin D. Roosevelt Library, Hyde Park, New York.

[24]John Morton Blum, *From the Morgenthau Diaries: Years of War, 1941–45* (Boston: Houghton Mifflin, 1967), 16–22.

directed at the wealthiest Americans, and taxable returns covered no more than 5 percent of the population. The tax was justified during the first two Roosevelt terms as a means of combating an "unjust concentration of wealth and economic power."[25]

With average Americans becoming subject to the income tax for the first time, punitive class-based justifications that built on redistribution of wealth were no longer apt. The Roosevelt administration used the war as the fundamental reason for the adoption of the mass income tax. In fact, in the pamphlet "Battle Stations for All," issued in February 1943, an accented box headlined "Non-war Expenditures Reduced" sought to defuse accusations that increased taxation would benefit the New Deal social agenda.[26] During early phases of the war, the OWI and Treasury spokesmen attempted to suggest that Americans should blame "the real authors of our tax burden . . . in Berlin and Tokio."[27] Other propaganda messages throughout the war used a theme of comparative sacrifice. This idea was exemplified in one radio plug in which the announcer said: "Well, nobody says filling out these forms is fun. But it's more fun than sitting down in a foxhole, and it's more fun than being shot down in a plane. And it's more fun than waiting for a torpedo to hit."[28] Particularly during 1943 and into 1944, there was an attempt to sell taxes as a means of controlling wartime inflation. Public relations advisers expressed deep reservations about the average citizen's capacity to understand this last approach.[29]

The most common theme, however, was "Taxes to Beat the Axis." Radio plugs featured American citizens choosing to be taxed by a "democratic" tax system. The choice theme was consistent with capitalism and economic notions of choice. Roy Rogers and many others reminded audiences, "Your income tax money pays for Victory."[30] Rational Amer-

---

[25]Mark H. Leff, *The Limits of Symbolic Reform: The New Deal and Taxation, 1933–1939* (Cambridge: Cambridge University Press, 1984), 102–19.

[26]Office of War Information, "Battle Stations for All" (February 1943), in Pamphlets, 1942–43, Records of the Office of War Information, RG 208.

[27]Dorothy Ducas, "Wartime Taxes" (December 7, 1942), in Occasional Publications, 1942–43, Miscellaneous Publications on War Subjects, 1942–43, Records of the Office of War Information, RG 208.

[28]Broadway Matinee (February 21, 1944), in Taxes—Radio.

[29]"Public Appreciation of the Problem of Inflation," Memorandum 62 (August 12, 1943), Printed Matter, Odegard Papers; "Public Appreciation of the Problem of Inflation," Memorandum 66 (October 27, 1943), Printed Matter, Odegard Papers; James G. Rogers, Jr. to James Allen (March 10, 1943), in Allen, James, General Records of Assistant Directors.

[30]"Roy Rogers Show" (February 6), in Taxes—Radio.

icans, as economic actors, could make a wise consumer decision by buying victory with their tax dollars. The legitimacy of taxpaying obligations was approached as "a question of domestic morale" in time of war.[31]

In getting these ideas to the public, straightforward messages from government officials were sometimes used. For example, speeches by Treasury officials were sometimes broadcast.[32] Collectors, the local representatives of the Bureau of Internal Revenue, were provided scripts for speeches before local groups or on the radio.[33] The straightforward approaches sometimes attempted to make use of governmental and private hierarchies in distributing Treasury Department messages. One example of this variation can be found in the Treasury pamphlet "Your New Income Tax," developed at the end of 1942. The pamphlet was a small folded page with a brief message from Secretary Morgenthau and explanations of aspects of the income tax. Such circulars were reminiscent of "Social Security in Your Old-Age." The 1936 circular had been distributed to AFL unions. By 1942, however,[34] an elaborate distribution scheme was developed to get the 1942 income-tax pamphlet to the public through state and local government officials and employers.[35] A similar local strategy can be seen in the dissemination by the Treasury and the OWI of booklets and pamphlets to women's clubs.[36]

---

[31]Taxes Meeting (11:05 A.M., March 10, 1943), Morgenthau Diaries 615:145–46.

[32]Address by Assistant Secretary of the Treasury, John L. Sullivan, over the Mutual Network (10:15 P.M., January 2, 1943), Morgenthau Diaries 601:109.

[33]"Summary of Publicity Schedule," September 15 declaration (undated, cover letter dated August 4, 1943), in Taxes—Radio; Memorandum from Guy Helvering to Secretary Morgenthau (December 15, 1942), Morgenthau Diaries 596:274.

[34]Weaver, *Crisis in Social Security*, 107.

[35]Memorandum from Sullivan to Birgfield (November 26, 1942), Morgenthau Diaries 596: 246 (with regard to letters to mayors, town clerks, chief executives of counties); Memorandum from Sullivan to Cann (November 24, 1942), Morgenthau Diaries 596:235 (discussing deliveries of the pamphlets to collectors of the Internal Revenue, federal reserve banks, state governors, departments and agencies of the federal government, state and local school boards and the U.S. Treasury's Chief Clerk's Office); Memorandum from Sullivan to Cann (November 24, 1942), Morgenthau Diaries 596:236. Pamphlets mailed to the collectors of the Internal Revenue were to be sent to employers of eight or more and to city and county employees. Memorandum from Sullivan to Secretary Morgenthau (November 19, 1942), Morgenthau Diaries 596:233.

[36]Naomi L. Engelsman to Simon O. Lesser (February 1, 1944), in Taxes—Radio. ("I am enclosing a list of organizations to which your tax pamphlet went yesterday. I think we picked out a pretty good cross-section of our best and most interested women's clubs.") Memorandum from George Buffington to Secretary Morgenthau (December 5, 1941), Morgenthau Diaries 469:64. Buffington discusses the distribution of the 1941 pamphlet, "Know Your Taxes," and suggests, "It may also be advisable to ask the various Women's Clubs to arrange for a series of talks by treasury people to members regarding taxes."

The depiction of direct contact between tax official and the populace was another means of displaying a responsive and democratic tax system. A round-table discussion carried over the Columbia radio network discussed tax deadlines and obligations. Assistant Treasury Secretary John Sullivan was said to be conversing with a woman war worker, a farmer, and a small businessman.[37] In the round table, Mrs. Charles Anderson, who was "employed in a war industry," expressed enthusiasm when Sullivan explained that withholding would satisfy her income-tax obligation: "Say, September 15th is going to be a red letter day for us. Before this my husband used to have a quarterly payment to make; but this time . . . September 15th will be just another day in our family."[38] These direct messages from government officials to members of the public were an effort to influence popular conceptions of the income tax and taxpayers' obligations under it.

The use of the comments of "Mrs. Anderson" is emblematic of a more indirect strategy favored by the Treasury. Many of the tax messages were conveyed in voices of nongovernmental speakers. These were official messages intended to be seen as products of popular culture—more particularly, a popular culture in complete support of the official tax law.

At the local level, it was hoped that respected citizens would convince their neighbors of the government's need for income taxation on a broader scale. Odegard viewed these local efforts as important. In a 1942 speech at Princeton University entitled "Public Opinion and Propaganda in Wartime America," Odegard surveyed "local" channels of information—"systems of communication with their own local organizations—labor bodies, farmers, manufacturers, bankers, business and professional men, women's clubs, churches, fraternal bodies of all kinds, patriotic societies." The means of communication these groups employed included newspapers, magazines, letters, conventions, and according to Odegard, "most important of all, regular meetings of small groups in thousands of cities, towns, and hamlets in every corner of the country." Odegard asserted that information received through citizens' voluntary organizations was more likely to be persuasive than propaganda from outside sources. He regarded face-to-face communications at regular lo-

[37]Treasury Department Press Service, Press Release (June 11, 1943), in Taxes—Radio. Columbia Network aired the Treasury roundtable on the September 15 declaration (August 26, 1943): see Taxes—Radio.
[38]Treasury roundtable on the September 15 declaration (August 26, 1943): see Taxes—Radio.

cal meetings as particularly valuable to public opinion makers. "The tens of thousands of such meetings shared throughout the United States may be regarded as ready-made classrooms where the story of the war and what it means can be told by word-of-mouth in face to face contact, the most effective of all forms of communication."[39]

Some Treasury Department strategies, particularly at the end of 1942, took the classroom idea quite seriously. Some citizens were expected to educate others about the mechanics of income-tax compliance. Union leaders were expected to assist their members with unfamiliar tax forms.[40] Secretary Morgenthau seemed particularly interested in having schoolteachers instruct others in the community on how to fill in their income-tax forms.[41] After it was pointed out that schoolteachers were one of the worst groups at filing their own returns, it was eventually decided that schoolteachers could teach their own students about income-tax forms but that a more general community effort was not advisable.[42]

Another effort to reach local groups in 1942–43 was the OWI-sponsored Victory Speakers program. Choosing among topics in a government bulletin subtitled "Ideas for Original Speeches," the creative toastmaster could address taxes. An approach to the issue was suggested. "The new income taxes will call for many sacrifices, especially by people of low income who have never paid income tax before. But these sacrifices, difficult though they may be, are small compared with the sacrifices of those whose breadwinners have been drafted or who are serving in the armed forces."[43]

[39]"Public Opinion and Propaganda in Wartime America" (May 5, 1942), 23, Speeches and Articles, Odegard Papers.

[40]Office of War Information, Treasury Department Press Release (n.d.), Income Tax Treasury, General Records of Assistant Directors.

[41]Income Taxes Meeting (11:40 A.M., December 9, 1942), Morgenthau Diaries 595:288. See the memorandum from Odegard to Secretary Morgenthau proposing such a program (December 15, 1942), Morgenthau Diaries 596:175; Howard E. Wilson and Forrest Long, "Memorandum Concerning School Services on the Reporting of Income Taxes in 1943" (n.d.), Morgenthau Diaries 596:278.

[42]Income Taxes Meeting (11:40 A.M., December 9, 1942), Morgenthau Diaries 595:288; Income Taxes Meeting (10:10 A.M., December 15, 1942), Morgenthau Diaries 596:173; Memorandum from Odegard to Secretary Morgenthau (December 11, 1942), Morgenthau Diaries 595:288; Income Taxes Meeting (11:20 A.M., December 16, 1942), Morgenthau Diaries 597:4–17; Memorandum to the secretary from Messrs. Gaston, Helvering, Cann, Odegard, Mager, Lemmon, and Sullivan (December 15, 1942), Morgenthau Diaries 596:273.

[43]Special bulletin addressed to victory speakers: "Ideas For Original Speeches" (n.d.), in Pamphlets, 1942–43, Records of the Office of War Information, RG 208; see also memorandum from Herbert Little to Charles Schwarz (February 17, 1943), in Income Tax—

The OWI also hoped to stimulate and direct local discussion of tax policy with the issuance of two 1943 pamphlets that provoked tremendous controversy. In the first, "Battle Stations for All," OWI pamphleteers put forth Roosevelt administration arguments for income taxes on the middle and lower classes, current taxation, and elimination of such tax loopholes as the exemption of interest on state and local bonds.[44] These specific proposals in the February 1943 pamphlet were particularly noteworthy because the administration, in its January 1943 budget message, had chosen only to set a revenue target and deliberately did not specify the taxes that would be utilized in reaching the target. "How to Raise $16 Billion," a discussion guide issued by the OWI, told the story of a tax bill in terms laudatory of the Treasury and featured questions that verged on the rhetorical. For example, after a section condemning federal sales-tax proposals, the following question was presented for local discussion: "6. Ought the people who receive less than $500 a year to be taxed, in view of the fact they have less than enough money to buy their fair share of goods and services?"[45]

The use of public funds to produce pamphlets like "How to Raise $16 Billion" demonstrated administration attempts to shape debate about the structure of the revenue system. The political situation was made more complex by disagreements within the administration in 1942 and early 1943 about the advisability of a federal sales tax. Some Roosevelt advisers—Vice-President Henry Wallace, Secretary of Agriculture Claude Wickard, Budget Director Harold Smith, Marriner Eccles, and Leon Henderson—supported the creation of a committee that recommended a sales tax as a part of an anti-inflation program in April 1942. The Treasury Department opposed the imposition of a sales tax, suggesting instead a program that included the closing of various income-tax loopholes. Roosevelt opted in large part for the Treasury plan and did not advocate a sales tax. The adoption of a sales tax remained a

---

Treasury, General Records of Assistant Directors. The theme of sacrifice in World War II propaganda has been explored in Mark Leff, "The Politics of Sacrifice on the American Home Front in World War II," *Journal of American History* 77 (March 1991): 1296–1318.

[44] Office of War Information, "Battle Stations for All" (February 1943), in Pamphlets, 1942–43, Records of the Office of War Information, RG 208.

[45] Office of War Information, "How to Raise $16 Billion" (1943), 4, in Gardner Cowles, Jr., General Records of Assistant Directors. Although the points made may have been persuasive, asking them as questions with obvious answers tended to undermine genuine or serious discussion of the issues.

threat in 1942 and 1943.[46] During that period, Randolph Paul, general counsel of the treasury, spoke to groups such as the Iowa Bankers Association, Cornell University Law School, and the Economic Club of Detroit, Michigan.[47] These were organizations in the category Fred Smith, Morgenthau's public opinion aide, called "the leader group, the upper crust in the formation of public opinion, the group which tends to lead the general public."[48] In some of his 1942 speeches, Paul opposed adoption of a sales tax—an effort both to influence local groups and to shape the content of the debate.[49] Although his speeches were direct government messages, it was hoped that the opinion leaders to whom he spoke would convey the Treasury's anti–sales tax message to others, that their voices would become the Treasury's vehicle.

In addition to local spokesmen and discussion groups, tax publicists sought to cover overtly governmental messages by using the mass media—newspapers, magazines, radio, and film. The government provided material to editors and producers, encouraging the development of supportive messages credited to editors, writers, and producers outside the government.

While the Bureau of Internal Revenue prepared releases for the daily and financial press,[50] the OWI attempted to reach specialized segments of the press,[51] contacted news commentators, and provided fillers for

[46]Blum, *Years of War*, 34–58.
[47]The following addresses are in Income Tax—Treasury, Treasury-WPB, General Records of Assistant Directors: Address by Randolph Paul before the Annual Convention of the Iowa Bankers Association, Des Moines, Iowa (October 27, 1942); Address by Randolph Paul before the Cornell University Law School (December 11, 1942); Address by Randolph Paul before the Economic Club of Detroit, Michigan (March 1, 1943); and "Taxation in War Time," address by Randolph E. Paul before the National Lawyers' Guild (September 26, 1942).
[48]James R. Brackett to Fred Smith (August 4, 1943), in Treasury/Correspondence, General Records of Assistant Directors.
[49]"Taxation in War Time," address by Randolph E. Paul before the National Lawyers' Guild (September 26, 1942), and address by Randolph Paul before the Cornell University Law School (December 11, 1942), both in Income Tax—Treasury, Treasury-WPB, General Records of Assistant Directors.
[50]Memorandum from Simon O. Lesser, program manager, to J. D. Nunan, Jr., George J. Schoeneman, Charles Schaeffer, Irving Perlmeter, Norman Cann, Charles P. Suman, Harvey Goddard (March 24, 1945), in Taxes—Radio.
[51]Ibid.; Memorandum from Simon O. Lesser, program manager, to Joseph D. Nunan, Jr. (April 18, 1944), in Taxes—Radio; Memorandum from Herbert Little to Charles Schwartz (February 17, 1943), in Income Tax—Treasury, General Records of Assistant Directors. Regarding the women's pages of newspapers, see the following in Taxes—Radio: "Fortnightly Budget for Wartime Editors of Women's Pages" (March 4, 1944); Simon O. Lesser, program manager, to Joseph D. Nunan, Jr. (April 18, 1944); "OWI Fortnightly Budget for Wartime Editors of Women's Pages" (February 5, 1944); and "OWI Fortnightly Budget for Wartime Editors of Women's Pages" (January 22, 1944).

newspaper editors.[52] The Treasury provided newspapers with short articles during the income-tax filing period.[53] Similarly, cartoons promoting income-tax compliance were provided by the OWI.[54]

Government assistance even extended to the editorial page. By January 1942, the Writers' War Board was organized. There is some evidence that the Treasury was instrumental in the establishment of this group, although credit for organizing the group is usually given to the mystery writer Rex Stout. The group was subsidized in part by the OWI and the Office of Civil Defense.[55] In February 1945 the board sent six hundred editors a pro–income tax editorial entitled "Sure as Death and High Taxes."[56]

Income-tax messages reached magazine editors primarily through the OWI and its bimonthly publication, *Magazine War Guide*.[57] The *Guide* suggested story ideas, giving a three-month lead time before the desired publication date. For example, carpooling to conserve rubber could provide a romantic situation for a story by a wartime magazine fiction writer.[58] Taxation perhaps did not lend itself to such narrative treatment, and the *Guide* tended to provide Treasury statements or reminders of tax deadlines.[59] On one occasion, for example, the *Guide* sought the

[52]"Your Federal Income Tax" (1941), Morgenthau Diaries 501:396.
[53]Guy Helvering to Secretary Morgenthau (December 15, 1942), Morgenthau Diaries 596: 274.
[54]Bo Brown Cartoon (n.d.), Corka Cartoon (n.d.), Bo Brown Cartoon (January 29, 1945), and Colin Allen cartoon (January 29, 1945), all in Tax Program, Program Guides and Publicity Materials for the Economic Stabilization Campaign, Records of the Office of War Information, RG 208.
[55]J. Street, "High Lights of My Work with Writers and Artists for the Treasury Department, Nov. 1, 1941 to Jan. 31, 1946," 15, Odegard Papers; Maureen Honey, *Creating Rosie the Riveter: Class, Gender, and Propaganda during World War II* (Amherst: University of Massachusetts Press, 1984), 45, 46.
[56]Memorandum from Simon O. Lesser, program manager, to J. D. Nunan, Jr., George J. Schoeneman, Charles Schaeffer, Irving Perlmeter, Norman Cann, Charles P. Suman, Harvey Goddard (April 26, 1945), and Writers' War Board, "Sure as Death and High Taxes" (n.d.), both in Taxes—Radio.
[57]Memorandum from Simon O. Lesser, program manager, to Joseph D. Nunan, Jr. (April 18, 1944), 2, in Taxes—Radio. Lesser notes that the OWI Magazine Bureau arranged a meeting of magazine editors at which David Frederick gave a presentation of "the March 15 informational problem." Simon O. Lesser, program manager, to J. D. Nunan, Jr., George J. Schoeneman, Charles Schaeffer, Irving Perlmeter, Norman Cann, Charles P. Suman, Harvey Goddard (March 24, 1945), 3, in Taxes—Radio.
[58]Honey, *Creating Rosie the Riveter*, 37, 46.
[59]*Magazine War Guide*: February 1945, 5; January 1945, 4; October–November 1943; Supplement 25, March 1945, 1–11; February–March 1944, 3–4; all in Magazine War Guide and Supplement, 1942–45, Records of the Office of War Information, RG 208. And see Ducas, "Wartime Taxes" (December 7, 1942), in Occasional Publications, 1942–

support of action magazine editors in urging tax compliance. "The action magazines can help these new taxpayers understand why they are called upon for these payments out of what are small earnings."[60] The OWI's Magazine Bureau dutifully kept track of magazine editorials, articles, and fiction stories based on government suggestions. Magazines such as *American Hairdresser, Ladies' Home Journal, Radio Mirror, House Beautiful, True Detective, Kiwanis,* and *Personal Romances* were listed as providing income-tax messages.[61]

During World War II, radio reached over 90 percent of the population.[62] Thus it is no surprise that tax officials sought to use radio to influence popular perceptions of the new mass income tax. An early effort to use radio involved the apparent commissioning of a song from Irving Berlin to support taxpaying.[63] Previously, Morgenthau had requested a special song from Berlin to promote bond sales. Berlin's effort then had been "Any Bonds Today?" It was the theme song for the *Treasury Hour,* which began in July 1941.[64] In late 1941 Berlin submitted, to Treasury Secretary Morgenthau, a song entitled "I Paid My Income Tax Today." The first verse and chorus expressed the pride a lower-income taxpayer felt in paying income taxes to assist the war effort:

43, Miscellaneous Publications on War Subjects, 1942–43, Records of the Office of War Information, RG 208.

[60]*War Guide Supplement 4 for Action Magazines* (December 10, 1942), Magazine War Guide and Supplement, 1942–45, Records of the Office of War Information, RG 208.

[61]"Magazine Editorials, Articles, and Fiction Stories on Programs Which Are Being Promoted by OWI," March 1943, January 1944, February 1944, March 1944, April 1944, May 1944, September 1944, October 1944, November 1944, December 1944, January 1945, February 1945, March 1945, April 1945, May 1945, June 1945, July 1945, August 1945, in Reports on Magazine Articles on War Programs, 1943–45, Records of the Office of War Information, RG 208. Magazines in which articles, editorials, or stories on taxation appeared included *The Woman, This Week, Pic, Mademoiselle, Look, Liberty, Ladies' Home Journal, Front Page Detective, Radio Mirror, Inside Detective, Army and Navy Women, Women's Home Companion, House Beautiful, Successful Farming, True Detective, Extension Service Review, Barron's, Saturday Evening Post, Nation's Business, Air Force, Farm Journal, U.S. News, Capper's Farmer, Charm, True Confessions,* and *Foreign Service.*

[62]"Plans for the Coordination of the Government's Wartime Use of Radio, 1941–42," Odegard Papers; U.S. Commerce Department, *Historical Statistics of America,* Ser. R 93–105, Ser. A 288–319, 796.

[63]Letter from Henry Morgenthau, Jr., to Irving Berlin (December 30, 1941), Morgenthau Diaries 480:82. Berlin transferred the song to Morgenthau, as secretary of the Treasury. The royalties from the song were to go to the Army Ordinance Association. Letter from Henry Morgenthau, Jr., to Irving Berlin (January 1, 1942), Morgenthau Diaries 484:285; Letter from Henry Morgenthau, Jr., to Lt. Col. L. A. Codd (January 28, 1942), Morgenthau Diaries 489: 285.

[64]Blum, *Years of Urgency,* 303.

I said to my Uncle Sam
"Old Man Taxes here I am"
And he—was glad to see me
Lower brackets that's my speed
Mr. Small Fry yes indeed
But gee—I'm proud as can be.

I paid my income tax today
I'm only one of millions more
Whose income never was taxed before
A tax I'm very glad to pay
I'm squared up with the U.S.A.
You see those bombers in the sky
Rockefeller helped to build them
    so did I
I paid my income tax today.[65]

In early 1942 the Treasury Department sent a recording of "I Paid My Income Tax Today" to 872 radio stations, with a letter asking for frequent air time. Four days later, the Danny Kaye recording of the same song was sent out as well. Sheet music was sent to sponsors of musical programs, and the networks were asked to play the song as often as possible until the March 15 deadline.[66]

The Treasury had its own variety show, *Treasury Star Parade,* often featuring the musical talents of David Broekman and the Treasury Orchestra and Chorus as a backdrop for appearances by such luminaries as Yehudi Menuhin or the Broadway cast of *Rosalinda.*[67] The purpose of *Star Parade* was the promotion of the sale of war bonds, but taxes were discussed. Morgenthau was concerned about the effect that income-tax withholding would have on purchases of war bonds.[68] When the pay-as-you-go system was enacted in 1943, the Treasury attempted to counter this concern on its variety show. The announcer at the end of one sketch said: "And, friends—I'll bet you'll find you *can* buy more

[65]I. Berlin, "I Paid My Income Tax Today" (December 21, 1941), Morgenthau Diaries 480:83.
[66]Letter from Mr. Sullivan to the secretary (March 11, 1942), Morgenthau Diaries 507: 14; Treasury Conference Report (March 13, 1942), in Conference Reports (Treasury), General Records of Assistant Directors; Callahan to Graves (January 22, 1942), Morgenthau Diaries 487:410. "Mr. Kaye has expressed the desire to tour New York night clubs after his show closes and sing 'I Paid My Taxes Today' without charge. Arrangements are being made for this at the present time."
[67]*Treasury Star Parade:* June 9, 1943; June 21, 1943; To Be Recorded, June 2, 1943; To Be Recorded, June 15, 1943; all in Treasury Star Parade, May–June 1943, Odegard Papers. See also Blum, *V Was for Victory,* 17.
[68]Blum, *Years of War,* 43.

War Bonds, now that the pay-as-you-go tax plan has been put into effect. . . . You know exactly what you have to live on, so it's easier to figure out how much *more* you can *save* in War Bonds."[69]

The more pervasive form of radio tax propaganda was the short advertisement, or "plug," presented during entertainment programming. The Bureau of Internal Revenue prepared "Income Tax Brevities" and spot announcements for use on the radio.[70]

During the course of the war, the OWI developed a plan, the Network Allocation Plan, under which each network program received an allocation of government messages on a regular schedule. Standard announcements were not written for programs. Rather, the writers and producers for the network programs were asked to prepare the messages themselves but were guided by important points in a fact sheet provided by the OWI.[71] The OWI decided which messages would be placed on the network plan for a particular week. For the week beginning February 21, 1944, for example, the war messages featured were "Top Legal Prices," "Join the WAC," and "Pay Your Taxes."[72] On at least one occasion, the government got more than a short plug. In March 1943, when the popular radio show *The Great Gildersleeve* devoted its complete script to the subject of the income tax, government publicists saw the network radio show as a vehicle for reaching millions.[73]

The writer of the network tax messages sometimes attempted to tie propaganda to the show. An introductory spot for *Burns and Allen* in

[69]*Treasury Star Parade*, To Be Recorded, June 23, 1943, in Treasury Star Parade, May–June 1943, Odegard Papers.

[70]Guy Helvering to Secretary Morgenthau (December 15, 1942), Morgenthau Diaries 596: 274.

[71]Apparently, the Network Allocation Plan was first implemented by the Office of Facts and Figures in April 1942. See "Plans for the Coordination of the Government's Wartime Use of Radio, 1941–42," 2–3, Odegard Papers; "Summary of Radio Campaign for Bureau of Internal Revenue, December 30, 1944, to January 14, 1945, February 5, 1945, to March 11, 1945," in Taxes—Radio; Memorandum from James G. Rogers, Jr., to Herbert Gaston (March 13, 1943), in Income Tax—Treasury, General Records of Assistant Directors.

[72]"Allocation Schedule for War Information Messages, Week Beginning February 21, 1944 (final)," in Radio Bureau Allocations, Records of the Deputy Director, Records of the Office of War Information, RG 208.

[73]Memorandum from James G. Rogers, Jr., to Herbert Gaston (March 15, 1943), and memorandum from James G. Rogers, Jr., to Charles Schwarz (March 15, 1943), in Income Tax—Treasury, General Records of Assistant Directors. "You know enough about the programs on the list to know that several draw enormous audiences. Programs like Maxwell House, One Man's Family, Chase and Sanborn, and the Great Gildersleeve will each get one-fifth to one-third of the total number of sets in the country. It would seem to me that we could estimate that probably 65% of the sets in the country got the tax message in the last four days . . . several of them more than once."

1945 was given by Harry Von Zell. After mentioning the show's sponsor and introducing the orchestra, the announcer continued: "Say, here's a very important message. Uncle Sam is asking us to file our regular March fifteenth income tax returns early this year. The money is needed for victory. If you have made more than five hundred dollars during 1944 you must file a return—regardless of withholding tax. . . . For complete information and to secure the proper form, see your local collector. But do it early—like George Burns. In fact, we find George working on his return right now—as we meet the people who live in the Burns house—George and Gracie! (Applause.)"[74]

Radio programs like *Perry Mason, Breakfast at Sardi's, Abbott and Costello, Snow Village, Stella Dallas, Young Doctor Malone, The Adventures of the Thin Man,* and *Confidentially Yours* carried income-tax messages during the war.[75] To ensure the quality of these spots, members of the Domestic Radio Bureau of the OWI were asked to monitor and evaluate messages under the Network Allocation Plan.[76] The following is a sample of comments made on two 1945 radio shows:

The Roy Rogers Show: "One of the best jobs I have ever heard. Roy started off, then announcer gave straight message after which Roy followed up by urging listeners to file promptly as 'Taxes paid for victory.' A difficult job well done."

Andrews Sisters: "Straight, formal message by Patty Andrews. Preceded earlier in script by a forty-five second gag routine on taxes which was effective. For instance, one remark during the routine was to the effect that 'taxes spelled backwards spells Alcatraz.' "

The monitors gathered statistics on where the message was placed in the program (opening, middle, closing, or within script) and on the technique of presentation (announcement, dramatized, or other) and awarded quality ratings.[77]

Tax messages were also included in the *Women's Radio War Program*

[74]*Burns and Allen* (first spot—revised) (February 5, 1945), and "Summary of Radio Campaign for Bureau of Internal Revenue, December 30, 1944, to January 14, 1945, February 5, 1945, to March 11, 1945," 5, both in Taxes—Radio.
[75]See in Taxes—Radio: *Perry Mason* (OWI announcement) (February 1945); "Summary of Radio Campaign for Bureau of Internal Revenue, December 30, 1944, to January 14, 1945, February 5, 1945, to March 11, 1945"; *Snow Village* (closing commercial) (August 23, 1943); *Stella Dallas,* (income tax estimate conclusion), (September 3, 1943); *Young Doctor Malone* (August 31, 1943); *The Adventures of the Thin Man* (government message) (August 27, 1943); and *Confidentially Yours* (August 31, 1943).
[76]"Summary of Radio Campaign for Bureau of Internal Revenue, December 30, 1944, to January 14, 1945, February 5, 1945, to March 11, 1945," 5, in Taxes—Radio.
[77]Ibid.

Guide.[78] This monthly OWI publication was similar in concept to the *Magazine War Guide* and contained suggestions for women's radio programmers on the encouragement of early filing. "Impress your listeners with the necessity for early return filing of tax returns. Tell homemakers that even if they personally are not going to fill out the tax return this year, they should urge their husbands to do so early. Tell them it is more complex than usual and the earlier they tackle their returns the easier it will be to get help if they need it. Also, they will find out sooner where they stand on payments or refunds."[79]

It is estimated that while radio reached 90 percent of Americans, each week 80 million Americans—two-thirds of the population—saw at least one movie.[80] The movies provided another popular culture vehicle for government tax messages. Movie efforts included direct government speeches, as in the newsreels. In 1945, for example, Commissioner of Internal Revenue Joseph Nunan made an announcement. This was, according to an OWI official, "made a part of all five major reels," and another announcement was prepared for the All-American reel, which was released "to some 400 theaters catering to Negroes."[81]

The most notable tax effort was *The New Spirit,* a Disney animated short commissioned by the Treasury in 1942 and starring Donald Duck.[82] In the film, the radio informs Donald, "[It is] your privilege, not just your duty, but your privilege to help your government by paying your tax and paying it promptly." Donald collects a bottle of aspi-

---

[78]*Women's Radio War Program Guide,* February 1944 and March 1944, in Taxes—Radio.
[79]Ibid., February 1944, 21.
[80]Clayton R. Koppes and Gregory D. Black, *Hollywood Goes to War: How Politics, Profits, and Propaganda Shaped World War II Movies* (New York: Free Press, 1987), 1.
[81]Memorandum from Dave Frederick, director of war programs, to all deputies and program manager, October 21, 1944, in Motion Pictures, Records of the Deputy Director, Records of the Office of War Information, RG 208; Simon O. Lesser, program manager, to J. D. Nunan, Jr., George J. Schoeneman, Charles Schaeffer, Irving Perlmeter, Norman Cann, Charles P. Suman, Harvey Goddard (March 24, 1945), in Taxes—Radio.
[82]*The New Spirit* (Disney, 1942), in U.S. Government Film Collection, Motion Picture Collection FAA 188, Library of Congress, Washington, D.C. The first apparent mention of the film in the Morgenthau Diaries emerges at a group meeting on December 15, 1941:

SULLIVAN: We have been doing some work on this idea of putting across tax returns through movies. We are pretty much in agreement that it can't be done in the ordinary way, but George Buffington has an awfully good idea, I think, and that is that what John Barrymore can't do, maybe Mickey Mouse could, and we would like to get Disney on here and talk it over with him.
H.M., JR.: Is that the result of seeing "Fantasia"?
Group Meeting (9:45 A.M., December 15, 1941), Morgenthau Diaries 473:28.

rin and other supplies, but with the help of an animated ink bottle and pen, he finds the job easier than he had anticipated. As an actor with an income of $2,501, Donald used exemptions and dependent credits for Huey, Dewey, and Louie and found that his taxes came to $13.[83] After Donald races from Hollywood to Washington, the film shows how tax revenues are transformed into guns, planes, and ships. Taxes were needed to beat the Axis. At the end, when the American flag is formed by clouds around a setting sun, the narrator intones, "Taxes will keep democracy on the march." *The New Spirit* was seen by over thirty-two million people, in twelve thousand theaters, in early 1942.[84] Of those polled by Gallup, 37 percent felt the film had affected their willingness to pay taxes.[85] In 1943 a new tax film, *The Spirit of '43*, was commissioned. It consisted largely of clips from the earlier short subject.[86] The government also sought to insert wartime messages into movies that were largely for entertainment. The OWI's *Government Information Manual for the Motion Picture Industry* suggested that movies show uncomplaining taxpayers. David O. Selznick's *Since You Went Away* implemented this suggestion by showing a

[83]Richard Shale, *Donald Duck Joins Up: The Walt Disney Studio during World War II* (Ann Arbor, Mich.: UMI Research Press, 1982), 28.
[84]Group Meeting (9:15 A.M., March 16, 1942), Morgenthau Diaries 508:18; George Buffington to Secretary Morgenthau (March 20, 1942), Morgenthau Diaries 509:289; Louis Patz to Herman Robbins (February 7, 1942), Morgenthau Diaries 495:391–93. Members of the projectionists' union were strongly urged in a union publication to be supportive of *The New Spirit*: "Its running time is approximately eight minutes and its exhibition is a 'must.' Consequently, as a matter of patriotic duty our members are enjoined to cooperate in every manner at their disposal so that its purposeful objective may be achieved. Since we have been designated as disciples to project the gospel of 'The New Spirit,' it would hardly seem proper that we confine ourselves to its mechanical projection. Instead let us all conscientiously carry out its precepts to the letter and not wait until tomorrow or next week to file our returns, but do it now!" General Offices of International Alliance of Theatrical Stage Employees and Moving Picture Operators of the United States and Canada, *General Bulletin #312* (January 1, 1942), Morgenthau Diaries 492:138. The union's assistance was not, apparently, always spontaneously offered. Morgenthau suggested that the union's support be elicited. George Buffington to Secretary Morgenthau (February 4, 1942), Morgenthau Diaries 492:137. In the *Motion Picture Herald*, a letter from Secretary Morgenthau urged motion picture exhibitors to show the picture without delay and to send it along to the next exhibitor. Letter from Henry Morgenthau to the Motion Picture Exhibitor Addressed (January 28, 1942), *Motion Picture Herald*, January 31, 1942, Morgenthau Diaries 491:201. See also letter from Henry Morgenthau, Jr., to the Moving Picture Exhibitor Addressed (January 22, 1942), Morgenthau Diaries 487:256.
[85]Shale, *Donald Duck*, 32.
[86]*The Spirit of '43* (Disney, 1943), in U.S. Government Film Collection, Motion Picture Collection FAA 256, Library of Congress, Washington, D.C.

wealthy man claiming, "[It] suits me if they tax me 100 percent!"[87] Assurance that the wealthy were willing to pay their fair share apparently was intended to make income-tax payments by the less well-to-do more palatable.

Peter Odegard's 1942 Princeton speech recognized the importance of advertisers, copywriters, and professional entertainers and their contributions to mass media messages. Odegard suggested "intelligent centralized planning, not regimentation, of the communications industries." He argued, "We need to have dramatically brought home to us how this war came, how we were involved in it from the beginning, what it is all about . . . how defeat or victory will affect us, what we can do not only to avoid defeat but to bring victory."[88]

Through media from local clubs and speakers to the printed word in pamphlets, newspapers, and magazines and finally to radio and the movies, government tax propagandists sought to convey their message about the new mass income tax. Although at times this was done directly by a government spokesman, often during World War II the speaker was a local person, the Great Gildersleeve, George Burns, Roy Rogers, or Donald Duck. The conscious shaping of popular culture, particularly by using the popular culture voices, was a most significant feature of the selling of the mass federal income tax.

After the war, however, it appears that such massive efforts centered on popular culture ended. Tax messages remaining from the postwar years appear, largely, to consist of identifiable government officials speaking about tax issues. At least two possibilities emerge for why this was so. First, it may have been that the income tax efforts were dependent on the existence of a very large government public relations effort. Without the OWI to mobilize and coordinate radio programming for the war effort as a whole, for example, it may have been difficult for the Treasury alone to secure sufficient mass media interest. Second, it may also have been that such "selling of the income tax" became less essential as average Americans became accustomed to their status as income taxpayers. In part, such acclimation could be seen as the result of a second strategy, standardization, employed by tax policymakers.

[87]Koppes and Black, *Hollywood Goes to War*, 68, 157–58.
[88]"Public Opinion and Propaganda in Wartime America" (May 5, 1942), 34, Speeches and Articles, Odegard Papers.

STANDARDIZATION

Whereas the appropriation strategy sought to gain compliance with the new mass federal income tax by using local spokespeople and mass media, tax administrators and policymakers did not place total reliance on propaganda in implementing the tax.

In the 1940s, Congress created two fundamental structural features of the federal income tax to better adapt it as a mass tax. Both the withholding on wages and salaries and the income-splitting joint return, though addressing different concerns, sought to standardize citizens' payment of taxes. Withholding attempted to ensure tax payment, often by a third party, at the earliest point in time. The income-splitting joint return sought to achieve more uniformity in the ways that married couples were treated for tax purposes, regardless of differences in spouses' legal rights to income under state law. Such structural change was the first element of the standardization strategy.

A second part of the strategy involved increased technological and administrative capacity for enforcement in the postwar years. Because actual enforcement could not be completely effective, however, revenue authorities returned to reliance on a mass media to suggest the inevitability of apprehension for tax evasion. Tax administrators continued to find public relations an essential instrument in creating a mass income tax even after structural changes and administrative improvements.

Standardization through structural change. Mass income taxation was vulnerable to mass culture because at the beginning of the 1940s, it was not collected at the source and it was not collected currently but rather was paid in quarterly installments in the following year.[89] Tax policymakers, including General Counsel of the Treasury Randolph Paul, viewed these features as "poorly adapted to the budgets and flow of income of 44 million taxpayers."[90] At a group meeting on December 4, 1941, a Treasury aide described a conversation with a man who employed three thousand workers and who had found that few of the employees were prepared to make their income-tax payments in March. The employer arranged guaranteed loans for his employees at the local banks, but the employer was reportedly "quite disturbed" about it.[91]

[89]Randolph E. Paul, *Taxation in the United States* (Boston: Little Brown, 1954), 328–32.
[90]Ibid., 333–34.
[91]Group Meeting (9:30 A.M., December 4, 1941) Morgenthau Diaries 468:229.

Beardsley Ruml, treasurer of R. H. Macy and Company and chairman of the board of the Federal Reserve Bank of New York, was an outspoken advocate of current taxation. Ruml professed concern for retirees who experienced declining incomes yet were expected to pay income taxes for a previous year out of more meager incomes. The solution was for the federal government to require income-tax payments currently, but the problem was in creating a transition to current payment. Under the tax system at the beginning of World War II, Year 1's tax liability was paid in Year 2. If tax payments were to be made current, a taxpayer would be required to pay two years' taxes in one year. This was seen as an unacceptable situation. Ruml proposed to forgive the Year 1 tax liability to enable a transition to current payment. For Ruml, this was the "daylight savings" approach to government finance—a proposal under which the Treasury would lose only when "the books would finally be closed [on Judgment Day]."[92]

The Treasury opposed the Ruml plan for two reasons. First, the plan initially did not provide for collection at the source—a revision that tax administrators viewed as crucial to the burgeoning income-tax system and to the fight against inflation. Second, the Ruml plan was seen as inequitable by top Treasury officials because the forgiveness of the Year 1 tax liability would benefit higher-bracket taxpayers more than those in lower brackets.[93] Secretary Morgenthau advised President Franklin Roosevelt, "The plan presented about $64,000 to an individual with a net income of $100,000, . . . for a man who had earned $2,000 only $140."[94] He added, "Increases would probably fall largely on lower income groups since earlier increases had impinged primarily on the wealthier."[95] Congress, in the Current Tax Payment Act of 1943, compromised in favor of what was essentially a 75 percent forgiveness of the lower of the 1942 or the 1943 tax liability. Unforgiven tax liabilities could be paid over the next two years.[96]

The act also established the now-familiar withholding system of tax collection. Income over the family status withholding exemption was withheld at a rate of 20 percent.[97] The new collection system caused considerable confusion. Some citizens thought it was a new tax, while

[92]Paul, *Taxation*, 328–29, 335.
[93]Ibid., 329, 334.
[94]Blum, *Years of War*, 59.
[95]Paul, *Taxation*, 334.
[96]Current Tax Payment Act of 1943, Pub. L. No. 78–68, § 6, 57 Stat. 126, 145–49 (1943).
[97]Ibid., §2, 128.

others thought that withholding definitively established the amount of tax liability.[98] The withholding system revolutionized the income tax. Elimination of delay in payments made the income tax more responsive to wartime revenue expansion. As wage earners became used to periodic deductions from their paychecks for the income tax as well as for Social Security, the income tax became somewhat more hidden—an acceptable routine of American life. The advent of withholding ensured the status of the income tax as a major and massive revenue source.[99]

After almost thirty years of operation under the modern federal income tax, the withholding system was perceived as imperative at the time lower-income groups joined the taxpayer ranks. The withholding system, as finally enacted, was directed to wage and salary income, which would constitute almost all of the income of the new income taxpayers.[100] Although Secretary Morgenthau also suggested withholding on bond interest and dividends, these receipts, which are more characteristic of upper-income groups, escaped collection at the source.[101]

The "crisis" meeting held by Secretary Morgenthau on March 10, 1943, illustrated the importance of public relations, especially as withholding was being considered. When it appeared that one-third to one-half of Gallup's interviewees were uncertain about whether they were obligated to file income-tax returns, the immediate response was to step up radio announcements urging compliance. Many income-tax messages during World War II were exhortations for compliance with income-tax deadlines. One of the most frequently mentioned themes was "file early."[102] It was hoped that such messages would make the March 15 deadline for tax returns a very routine part of the average citizen's existence.

The withholding system continued to be seen, into the Truman administration, as crucial to the enforcement of the mass income tax. Treasury officials monitored evidence of nonadherence to the withholding law. Two incidents received considerable publicity in the early 1950s. Tax administrators feared that these examples of noncompli-

---

[98]One confusion was that withholding would take 20 percent of pay. The Treasury tried to assure the American public that this was not the case. *Treasury Star Parade,* To Be Recorded, June 23, 1943, Treasury Star Parade, May–June 1943, Odegard Papers.
[99]Ibid.
[100]Current Tax Payment Act of 1943, Pub. L. No. 18–68, § 6, 57 Stat. 126 (1943).
[101]Paul, *Taxation,* 330.
[102]*Burns and Allen* (first spot—revised) (February 5, 1945); Bo Brown Cartoon (January 29, 1945); Colin Allen Cartoon (January 29, 1945); Bo Brown Cartoon (n.d.); "Advance Bulletin of New Posters" (February 1944); all in Taxes—Radio.

ance, magnified by the mass media, would inspire others to disobey the law. In 1951, some household employers in Marshall, Texas, refused to pay withholding tax for their employees. The bureau requested that collectors advise it of any additional lack of compliance attributable to the Marshall, Texas, tax protestors. Of the collectors, 25 percent responded that the attention given the Marshall protest had, perhaps, increased awareness of the household employer's obligation and, therefore, compliance.[103] The secretary of the Treasury's monthly report for January 1952 also noted Vivien Kellems, another prominent withholding tax protestor. Kellems had been of interest to tax authorities as early as 1944. In that year, she had been named as a leading businesswoman by the National Association of Manufacturers and had been highlighted in the *Saturday Evening Post*. She had contracts with the U.S. Navy and a rather substantial outstanding tax liability. Kellems's relationship with Count Frederick Charles Zedlitz, a German living in Argentina and a suspected German agent, was the subject of investigation by Treasury agents. Kellems's antitax actions continued to receive extensive coverage in the *New York Times* and are described from her viewpoint in her 1952 book *Toil, Taxes, and Trouble*.[104] The report to the secretary contained the reassuring news that Kellems had paid the withholding tax since the last quarter of 1950.[105]

By collecting taxes at the source, a feature viewed by tax administrators as more important than current collection, and by punishing employers who refused to withhold taxes, the government sought to minimize the impact of individual choice and financial management. Tax administrators realized, however, that choices still remained with em-

---

[103]"Confidential Narrative Report for the Secretary on Treasury Activities during the Month of August, 1951," 1, and "Confidential Narrative Report for the Secretary on Treasury Activities during the Month of September, 1951," 1, both in Monthly Reports 1951, John W. Snyder Papers, Harry S Truman Library, Independence, Missouri.

[104]Vivien Kellems, *Toil, Taxes, and Trouble* (New York: E. P. Dutton and Co., 1952).

[105]"Confidential Narrative Report for the Secretary on Treasury Activities during the Month of January 1952," 2, in Monthly Reports 1952, Snyder Papers. Letter from Dominic A. Ierardi to chief coordinator, Treasury Enforcement Agencies, January 29, 1944, "Confidential Reports about People—1944," in Correspondence and Papers: 1933–45, Henry Morgenthau, Jr., Papers, Franklin D. Roosevelt Library. This report was forwarded to Morgenthau. Memorandum from Sullivan to the secretary, February 3, 1944, "Confidential Reports about People—1944," in Correspondence and Papers: 1933–45, Morgenthau Papers. United States of America National Censorship from Vivien Kellems to Sr. F. C. Zedlitz, "Confidential Reports about People—1944," in Correspondence and Papers: 1933–45, Morgenthau Papers.

ployers and that resistant employers, like those in Marshall and like Vivien Kellems, posed a threat.

A second major structural change intended in part to standardize the habits of American taxpayers was the adoption of the income-splitting joint return. Before 1948, the twentieth-century federal income tax was assessed on an individual basis.[106] The progressive rate structure of the income tax meant that a couple would pay the least tax if their income was divided equally between them.[107] The implementation of a mass income tax and particularly the use of marginal rates of tax exceeding 90 percent occasioned a greater visibility for a variety of income-splitting techniques, from holding property in joint tenancy to adopting community property regimes to using family partnerships. Those benefiting most from income splitting were often those who were relatively well-to-do. The tax savings from income splitting ranged from $38, or 4.8 percent for those with a net income before exemption of $5,000, to

---

[106]Boris Bittker, "Federal Income Taxation of the Family," *Stanford Law Review* 27 (1975): 1389, 1400. Married couples could file joint returns, but the same rate schedule applied to both individual and joint returns, making the joint return a more expensive option in most cases. If one spouse had a joint income less than the personal exemption amount, filing a joint return would avoid wasting that spouse's personal exemption.

[107]Marvin Chirelstein, *Federal Income Taxation,* 4th ed. (Mineola, N.Y.: Foundation Press, 1985), 157; William Vickrey, *Agenda for Progressive Taxation* (New York: Ronald Press: 1947), 276.

A simple example of how the choice of tax unit could affect the amount of tax liability in relation to a progressive rate structure will illustrate the point. Suppose the tax system is proportional, imposing a 10 percent rate on all income. There are four taxpayers: A, B, C, and D. A and B are married to each other, as are C and D. A and B each make $10,000 this year, C makes nothing, and D earns $20,000. The tax liabilities for each, under an individually assessed system, would be as follows:

	Income tax	Liability
A	$10,000	$1,000
B	$10,000	$1,000
C	$ –0–	$ –0–
D	$20,000	$2,000

As couples, A-B and C-D have $20,000 of income and $2,000 of tax liability whether the individual or the couple is the tax unit. The choice of tax unit, then, does not affect the amount of tax due under a proportional tax system.

If the tax system is altered so that it is progressive—one in which the *rate* of tax increases as the amount of income increases, then the choice of tax unit does make a difference. Suppose that instead of imposing a flat 10 percent tax on all income, the tax was 10 percent on all income above $10,000; income $10,000 and below would not be subject to tax. This is a progressive tax because the rate of tax increases from 0 percent to 10 percent as income increases. A, B, and C would pay no tax if the tax unit was the individual. D would owe $1,000. As couples, A-B would pay no tax, and C-D would pay $1,000 even though both couples have equal incomes.

$2,622, or 28.9 percent for those with a net income before exemption of $25,000. For those with a net income of $1,000,000, the amount saved by income splitting was $23,921, or 2.8 percent.[108]

The adoption of the income-splitting joint return can be related to perceptions of gender roles in the postwar period. During World War II, many women took on unconventional roles as a result of the war. Successful income splitting for tax purposes before 1948 could result from residence in a community property state. That property system expanded during the 1940s but was not regarded as typical and was seen by some as conferring too much power on women. In non–community property states, husbands and wives could reallocate property between themselves to equalize income, or women could become partners in businesses by contributing their own capital or making managerial or creative business decisions. Success in splitting income in these cases seemed to correlate with departures from stereotypical gender roles. As the war ended, "Rosie the Riveter" was often forced out of the factory gate. When the income-splitting joint return was adopted, Stanley Surrey said, "Wives need not continue to master the details of the retail drug business, electrical equipment business, or construction business, but may turn from their partnership 'duties' to the pursuit of homemaking."[109] The lack of standard treatment of husbands and wives before 1948 and the awareness of this problem in the popular media became a problem for those responsible for the new mass income tax.

Beginning in 1939 and ending abruptly with the adoption of the income-splitting joint return in 1948, five states and the territory of Hawaii abandoned their common-law marital property systems and adopted community property regimes. These states were motivated by the recognition of community property as an income-splitting device. The U.S. Supreme Court, in the 1930 case *Poe v. Seaborn,* held that each spouse in a community property state should be taxed on one-half of the community income, whether that income arose from labor or from capital.[110] The upshot of this recognition of community property for tax purposes was a geographical disparity in the tax treatment of married

[108]U.S. Treasury Department, "The Tax Treatment of Family Income," reprinted in "Revenue Revisions, 1947–48," *Hearings before the House Committee on Ways and Means,* 80th Cong., 1st sess., 1947, 849.
[109]In Carolyn C. Jones, "Split Income and Separate Spheres: Tax Law and Gender Roles in the 1940s," *Law and History Review* 6 (1988): 259.
[110]*Poe v. Seaborn,* 282 U.S. 101, 111–12 (1930) (Washington); *Goodell v. Koch,* 282

couples. If a couple lived in a community property state and only one of them produced taxable income, federal recognition of that state's law allowed an equal division of income between the husband and the wife. This income-splitting opportunity meant that the aggregate community income was often subjected to lower marginal rates than if that income had been earned by an unmarried taxpayer in a community property state or by one spouse in a common-law state. The certainty of favorable tax treatment in community property states, plus the mixed success of such devices as family partnerships and family trusts for income-splitting taxpayers in common-law states, led some of the latter states to conversion to or consideration of a community property regime. The pressure toward community property became greater as tax rates and incomes began to increase at the end of the 1930s.[111]

There seems to have been a general awareness of the favored tax status of couples in states with this system and an underlying tone of resentment in accounts written about it. For example, George Werning of Newhall, Iowa, wrote to his senator, Bourke B. Hickenlooper: "I wish you would do all you can to inact [*sic*] a law, so that husband and wife can split their income and thereby reducing their income tax. It isn't right that some states are able to do so and others are not. For instance Calif. has that law. I have a brother-in-law there that has much larger net income than I have and yet we have to pay more income taxes than they do."[112] Magazines such as *American Magazine, Business Week, Collier's, Fortune, Nation's Business, Newsweek, Saturday Evening Post, Time,* and *U.S. News and World Report* carried articles explaining the tax benefits of a community property system and emphasizing the point with illustrations and maps.[113] To the extent that the disparity

U.S. 118 (1930) (Arizona); *Hopkins v. Bacon,* 282 U.S. 122 (1930) (Texas); *Bender v. Pfaff,* 282 U.S. 127 (1930) (Louisiana).
[111]Editorial, *New York Times,* May 31, 1947, 12.
[112]Letter from George Werning to Bourke B. Hickenlooper (January 6, 1948), in "Tax Income, 1948," Bourke B. Hickenlooper Papers, Herbert Hoover Presidential Library, West Branch, Iowa. Senator Hickenlooper received other letters on the subject of community property as well. Out of fifty-three letters in his "Tax, General 1948" topical file, five related to community property. These letters included the following: Letter from A. L. Killian to Bourke B. Hickenlooper (February 21, 1948); Letter from E. B. Oyaas to Bourke B.Hickenlooper (January 22, 1948); Letter from Geo. H. Jones to Bourke B. Hickenlooper (January 23, 1948).
[113]See John L. McClellan, "Where You Pay Less" and "Treasury Loses," *Business Week,* December 11, 1943, 32–33; "Tax Detour Lost," *Business Week,* December 2, 1944, 20; "Joint Property Act," *Business Week,* May 5, 1945, 79–80; "Tax Saving Due," *Business Week,* January 5, 1946, 27–28; "Income Tax Detour," *Business Week,* December 21, 1946, 34–35; "Trend Toward Income-Splitting Tax Laws," *Business Week,* December

between community property and common-law states was seen as inequitable, it could be a threat to mass income taxation. Earlier, Peter Odegard had seen "an equitable distribution of the tax burden" as necessary to the war effort.[114] Concerns about perceived inequities and the impact on mass federal income taxation continued into the postwar period.

In states that did not convert to community property, other income-splitting techniques came to the fore. Joint owners of property could split the income from that property. Empirical evidence suggests that the frequency of joint tenancies increased dramatically in the 1940s.[115] By far the greatest attention in common-law states was given to the proliferation of husband-wife partnerships. The number of partnership returns increased from 244,670 in 1930 to 673,771 in 1945.[116] Estimates in one state indicated that 57.2 percent of those returns in 1945 were family partnerships.[117]

27, 1947, 22–24; "His Taxes and Hers," *Collier's,* August 17, 1946, 82; "The Worth of a Wife," *Fortune,* September 1948, 122; Bernard B. Smith, "Divorce Is Cheaper Than Marriage," *Harper's,* September 1947, 232–33; Junius B. Wood, "Share Bed, Board, and Taxes," *Nation's Business,* June 1947, 54; "Oregon Tax Balm" and "Community Dilemma," *Newsweek,* October 13, 1947, 64–65; "Mr. Whiskers Breathes Easier," Robert M. Yoder, "How Nine States Beat the Income Tax," *Saturday Evening Post,* May 24, 1947, 23; and "Family Split," *Time,* November 3, 1947, 20; "Split Tax to Aid Families?" *U.S. News and World Report,* May 16, 1947, 14; "New Support for Tax Splitting," *U.S. News and World Report,* June 27, 1947, 45; "Spread of Income Splitting," *U.S. News and World Report,* September 12, 1947, 44; "Community-Property Tangles," *U.S. News and World Report,* October 17, 1947, 40; "States' Troubles over Income Split," *U.S. News and World Report,* December 5, 1947, 51; "How Income Splitting Works," *U.S. News and World Report,* January 9, 1948, 43.

[114]"Public Opinion and Propaganda in Wartime America" (May 5, 1942), Speeches and Articles, Odegard Papers.

[115]William Hines, "Real Property Joint Tenancies: Law, Fact, and Fancy," *Iowa Law Review* 51 (1966): 582, 586.

[116]The following tabulation shows the increase in number of partnership returns filed for the income years 1930 through 1945:

1930—244,670	1938—273,361
1931—230,407	1939—290,876
1932—216,712	1940—372,796
1933—214,881	1941—453,911
1934—221,740	1942—490,320
1935—222,293	1943—491,544
1936—237,367	1944—577,295
1937—261,470	1945—673,771

Letter from commissioner of Internal Revenue to Bourke B. Hickenlooper (May 10, 1947), 1–2, in "Legislative File, Sponsored, Taxation, 1947, HR 1, Partnerships," Hickenlooper Papers.

[117]"In the case of the state of Iowa, the records indicate that for the tax year 1945 there was a total of approximately 26,500 partnership returns filed, or about 3.9 percent of

Generally, individual partners, in computing their incomes on their own returns, included their distributive shares of capital gains and losses and partnership income or ordinary net loss of the partnership. As long as there was an arm's-length agreement among the partners, their decisions as to profit percentages and forms were recognized. Contributions and control in partnerships varied widely. Some concentrated management in one partner. Sometimes partners contributed only capital, sometimes only labor.[118] As long as the parties were dealing at arm's length, it was assumed that they had reached a mutually acceptable and self-interested arrangement for profit distribution that would, theoretically, reflect their contributions to the partnership.

The presumed absence of arm's-length bargaining in the context of family partnerships caused the courts and the Bureau of Internal Revenue to apply different rules to such arrangements. In two 1946 cases, *Commissioner v. Tower* and *Lusthaus v. Commissioner,* the husband-wife partnerships were not given the desired tax effect.[119] Justice Hugo Black's majority opinion included a passage that came to be seen by the lower courts as the test for tax recognition of husband-wife partnerships: "If she either invests capital originating with her or substantially contributes to the control and management of the business, or . . . performs vital additional services . . . she may be a partner under the federal tax laws." Justice Black clearly stated that if "the end result . . . is that income produced by the husband's efforts continues to be used for the same business and family purposes as before the partnership, failure to tax it as the husband's income would frustrate [the tax laws]."[120] In Income Tax Division ruling (I.T.) 3845, issued in 1947 (after the *Tower* and *Lusthaus* cases), the Bureau of Internal Revenue built on the Supreme Court's factors for determining whether a partnership should be recognized for income-tax purposes and added a proportionality test. That test inquired into "the reasonableness of the relation between the proportionate share of the profits granted to any member of the family by the agreement and the proportion of the earnings which is fairly

the total for the country as a whole. Of the 26,500 partnership returns filed in Iowa, 15,160 have been estimated on the basis of the names shown as members of the partnership to be partnerships where there was a family connection between its members." Ibid.

[118]J. Mertens, *The Law of Federal Income Taxation,* rev. ed. (Chicago: Callaghan, 1948), 157, 158, 118 n. 87, 114 n. 58, 115 nn. 62–64; 14 nn. 60–61.

[119]*Commissioner v. Tower,* 327 U.S. 280 (1946); *Lusthaus v. Commissioner,* 327 U.S. 293 (1946).

[120]*Commissioner v. Tower,* 327 U.S. 290–91 (1946) (citations omitted).

attributable to the services rendered by, or the contributed capital originating with, said member."[121]

The skepticism in the cases and administrative rulings is clear. The existence of a valid state-law partnership was insufficient to guarantee income splitting for federal income-tax purposes.[122] This judicial and administrative skepticism did not seem justified to a number of taxpayers and members of Congress who objected to administrative and judicial refusal to view validity under state law as the sole test of tax recognition for partnerships. For example, Jack Shepard of Cedar Rapids, Iowa, wrote to Senator Hickenlooper in 1945: "Dear Hick: . . . In 1941 I constituted my business as a husband and wife partnership. . . . Now the Department says that they elect not to recognize this partnership. They say that we may have all the partnership we wish but so far as tax is concerned they choose not to recognize it! It is odd that they do recognize it in some seven states where by State Law the income of husband and wife is a partnership income for the purpose of tax, whereas according to Law, they feel they have the authority to waive this aside."[123]

Senator Hickenlooper and others in Congress agreed with this position and introduced Internal Revenue Code amendments generally designed to achieve this result.[124] These amendments were not enacted, and it was the joint return that emerged in 1948 as the remedy to the "inequality" caused by community property and to the administrative hostility to husband-wife partnerships. The income-splitting joint return allowed couples throughout the United States to divide their joint income between them equally, even if there was no underlying legal obligation to make such a division, as there arguably had been under community property statutes, joint ownership, or a family partnership agreement.

---

[121]I. T. 3845, 1947–1 C. B. 66–67. There is some suggestion in the Internal Revenue "Field Procedure Memorandum No. 408" that the four criteria may predate *Tower* and *Lusthaus*. "Field Procedure Memorandum No. 408," from Deputy Commissioner E. I. McLarney to Internal Revenue agents in charge of field divisions (February 10, 1947), in "Legislative File, Sponsored, Taxation, 1947, HR 1, Partnerships," Hickenlooper Papers.

[122]Ibid., 66.

[123]Letter from Jack Shepard to Bourke B. Hickenlooper (September 5, 1945), in "Legislative File, General, Taxation Partnerships 1945," Hickenlooper Papers. "Topical File, Tax, Income, 1948," Hickenlooper Papers, contains other letters expressing this opinion: Letter from G. A. Kent to Bourke B. Hickenlooper (May 26, 1948); Letter from F. H. Schierbrock to Bourke B. Hickenlooper (May 25, 1948); Letter from W. H. Nicholas to Bourke B. Hickenlooper (January 23, 1948).

[124]John D. Morris, "Senate Aides Back July 1 for Tax Cuts," *New York Times*, May 8, 1947, 17.

The adoption of the joint return had a variety of dimensions. It served as a tax-reduction device and as a way of preserving more traditional patterns of business and property ownership. The Senate Finance Committee report summarized its reasons for adopting the joint return: a desire for geographic equalization; "forestalling" the "impetuous enactment of community property legislation by States that have long used the common law"; reducing incentives to create trusts, joint tenancies, and family partnerships; and lessening administrative difficulties resulting from income splitting.[125] Concerns about the management of the tax system became more pressing during the 1940s with the emergence of the income tax as a mass tax. Yet income-splitting measures in existence before 1948 were not all administratively burdensome. The recognition of community property as an income-splitting device produced relatively few administrative difficulties. Senators from community property states did not hesitate to point out that the "inequities" could be remedied if those in common-law states would be willing to accord wives more legal rights by adopting a community property system. The joint return made tax obligations seem more uniform by removing the impact of some of the elements of state and taxpayer choice.[126] Taxpayers' decisions to create husband-wife partnerships were rendered much less significant, and the possibility of resistance was reduced, by limiting the advantages of the community property or family partnership system.

Standardization through increased technological and administrative capacity. During much of World War II, there was relatively little propaganda about tax evasion, avoidance, or penalties. The Andrews Sisters' joke about Alcatraz seemed to refer to the results of failure to pay, but

---

[125]*S. Rep. No. 1013*, 80th Cong., 2d sess., 1948, 26.

[126]Of course, income splitting still had some attraction if income could be split among family members. The Supreme Court spoke on nonspousal family partnerships in *Commissioner v. Culbertson*, decided June 27, 1949. Chief Justice Frederick Vinson criticized the Tax Court's use of "vital services" or "original capital" as decisive factors rather than as "circumstances [to be taken] into consideration" in deciding family partnership cases. Vinson went on to state what the real test for partnerships was to be: "Whether, considering the facts—the agreement, the conduct of the parties of execution of its provisions, their statements, the testimony of disinterested persons, the relationship of the parties, respective abilities and capital contributions, the actual control of income and the purposes for which it is used, and any other facts throwing light on their true intent—the parties in good faith and acting with a business purpose intended to join together in the present conduct of the enterprise." *Culbertson*, then, was a directive to explore subjective intent of the partners. The case established no clear criteria to guide the lower courts. It therefore did nothing to enable easier resolution of family partnership cases.

this was not a commonly invoked theme during the war. This fact is particularly interesting because public pronouncements about the more narrowly based income tax of the 1930s had been focused to a considerable degree on tax evasion. Hearings for the Revenue Act of 1937 drew attention to personal holding companies, hobby losses, incorporated yachts, country estates, and other tax-minimization devices used by the wealthy.[127] Part of the reason for silence on this theme during the war years was, no doubt, the inability of the Bureau of Internal Revenue to investigate many instances of evasion.

Tax administrators were well aware of the degree to which the new mass income tax was stretching scarce and irreplaceable resources. In the March 1943 "crisis" Morgenthau had asked, "Suppose we have to go out and try to arrest five million people?" In fact, the commissioner of Internal Revenue doubted that a withholding system could be implemented because of shortages of adding machines and office supplies. More Internal Revenue agents were always needed.[128] With inadequate administrative capacity, the public's willing self-assessment was essential.

With the end of World War II and the disappearance of that reason to pay taxes, one would expect to see a return to harsh or punitive propaganda directed at tax evaders. This does seem to have been the case during the postwar period. In part, this resulted from the increased availability of enforcement personnel after the war.[129] Even after the Korean War began, war seems not to have been as integral a part of the tax message as it had been during World War II.[130] The extent and nature of the tax-evasion propaganda that was used is somewhat striking in its emphasis. Instead of returning to the popular theme of evasion by the rich and famous, the Treasury seemed to have adopted two emphases

---

[127]*Revenue Act of 1937: Hearing before the House Committee on Ways and Means,* 75th Cong., 1st sess., 1937.

[128]Paul to the secretary (May 19, 1942), Morgenthau Diaries 529:262; Cann to the secretary (July 28, 1942), Morgenthau Diaries 554:285; Memorandum to Assistant Secretary Sullivan from Acting Commissioner Cann (July 29, 1942), Morgenthau Diaries 555:64; Sullivan to the secretary (July 30, 1942), Morgenthau Diaries 555:220.

[129]The Treasury recruited and trained additional personnel from the armed forces. By 1946 there was a net increase of 8,175 people in the investigative force. *Annual Report of the Commissioner of Internal Revenue* (1946), 5.

[130]See John Snyder, "Report to Taxpayers" (September 10, 1952), Snyder Papers (no mention of the Korean War). A radio, newsreel, and television script in the Snyder Papers do invoke the Korean War as a reason for citizens to pay taxes. "Radio Statement by Secretary Snyder, Sunoco 3-Star Extra Program" (July 25, 1950), Snyder Papers; "Recording for Mutual Newsreel, 2:30 p.m., Tuesday, June 26, 1951," Snyder Papers; "Television Program 'Battle Report,' NBC—WNBW, Sunday, December 3, 1950, 3:00–3:30 p.m.," Snyder Papers.

in its postwar campaigns directed at tax evaders. Initial targets were people who had made their wealth in black market transactions or who had otherwise profiteered during the war.[131] One reason for this focus on black market wealth may have been legal strategy. The statute of limitations under the Emergency Price Control Act was ordinarily one year. By using the tax laws, the statute of limitations was three years and an unlimited time if fraud was involved.[132] In March 1945, Secretary of the Treasury Morgenthau ordered a crackdown on such "free spenders" in the Miami area with an extension of the drive to "New York City, Philadelphia, Chicago, San Francisco, Seattle and 'all big pleasure and spending centers.' " In a news conference, Morgenthau claimed that his department was "interested in the fellow with the suite of big rooms and the lush boys."[133]

The day after announcing the Miami campaign, Morgenthau was concerned about possible overpublicity in that investigation. "I read those Miami stories and don't see that they have served any purpose other than to scare people to cover. . . . It seems to me that heretofore we had investigators go out and once they had a case that is finished and we got something to talk about, then we can blow our horn, but this idea of beating around the bush through a newspaper and thinking we are going to get a case, I just don't understand."[134] Morgenthau seemed to

[131]"Some Results of the Federal Tax Drive," address by Thomas C. Atkeson before the National Tax Association Conference, Chicago, Illinois (June 3, 1946), 10–15, in Tax Evasion and Avoidance, Papers of Roy Blough, Harry S Truman Library. "Part I Narrative Report, December, 1946," 4, in Monthly Report of the Secretary of Treasury, November–December 1946, Snyder Papers. This drive against tax evaders was highlighted in Paul D. Green, "Free-Lance Informer," *Nation's Business*, July 1945, 42. This article emphasized the role of the tipster. "No sum is too small to ignore, if the case is good and, often enough, the tipsters' net snares social outcasts—racketeers, gamblers, black marketers and grafting politicians." The article also highlighted the participation of Elmer Irey in the 1945 drive against tax cheats. Irey was the revenue official credited with sending Al Capone to the federal penitentiary.

[132]"OPA Turns In 3,000 for Tax Inquiries," *New York Times*, May 14, 1945, 24.

[133]" 'Free Spenders' Are Trailed in Drive against Tax Evasion," *New York Times*, March 23, 1945, 1, 12. President Truman publicly supported this drive. Statement by the president (June 1, 1945), in Official file (1945), Harry S. Truman Library. Truman seemed to endorse this antiwealth aspect of the tax campaign: "We are not fighting this war to make millionaires." Truman's statement was reported in the press. "Truman Supports War on Tax Cheats," *New York Times*, June 2, 1945, 17. Morgenthau was kept abreast of the tax drive. Memorandum to Secretary Morgenthau from Joseph J. O'Connell, Jr. (April 3, 1945), and attached memoranda, Morgenthau Diaries 834:110–32. Memorandum to Secretary Morgenthau from acting general counsel (April 10, 1945) and attached memoranda, Morgenthau Diaries 835:201–18, 227.

[134]Internal Revenue Meeting (March 24, 1945), Morgenthau Diaries 832:23, 27. Earlier Gaston, a Treasury aide, had touted the Miami investigation and "the play" the story

value the public relations surrounding enforcement actions, though he understood that ill-timed public relations could prove to be counterproductive.

Whereas earlier rhetoric had urged the breakup of established fortunes, postwar tax administrators turned their attention to the nouveau riche. A Bureau of Internal Revenue official noted that taxpayers' "inability . . . to satisfactorily account for the funds used for the purchase of stocks and bonds, houses, fur coats, expensive jewelry and other evidence of sudden wealth" would make them bureau targets. Further, he noted that the files were "bulging" with such cases.[135]

Later in Harry Truman's presidency, the "public enemy" type of tax evader would be targeted again in publicity surrounding a drive against racketeers. This effort, however, appears to have been largely defensive and not a result of imaginative strategic thinking. In the fall of 1950, the California Commission on Organized Crime issued a report linking the underworld and "certain officials of the Federal Bureau of Internal Revenue."[136] Shortly thereafter, the Special Senate Committee to Investigate Organized Crime in Interstate Commerce (the Kefauver Committee) began to hold hearings in San Francisco. In those and later hearings, the Kefauver Committee and, in 1952, the King Subcommittee of the House Ways and Means Committee investigated allegations of bribery, "fixing" of cases, and embezzlement in the San Francisco office of the Bureau of Internal Revenue and in other offices.[137]

The focus on racketeers and corrupt officials, people with whom the average American probably did not identify, as targets of Internal Revenue investigations was consistent with the recent past of the income tax. It appears that there may have been some shift in the treatment of the wealthy, with tax investigations now aimed at those who had gained their wealth by illegal means or profited unduly from the war. Another notable shift in emphasis from World War II federal income-tax propaganda was the postwar public relations effort that threatened punishment for average Americans who failed to pay their taxes.[138] Not only

would get that would "have a good effect." Memorandum to Secretary Morgenthau from Gaston (March 2, 1945), Morgenthau Diaries 824:227.
[135]"Some Results of the Federal Tax Drive," address by Thomas C. Atkeson before the National Tax Association Conference, Chicago, Illinois (June 3, 1946), 15, in Tax Evasion and Avoidance, Papers of Roy Blough, Harry S Truman Library.
[136]James Hill Shelton, "The Tax Scandals of the 1950's" (Ph.D. diss., American University, 1971), 130.
[137]Ibid., 132–62.
[138]A precedent for this type of campaign could be found in the "Pay Your Taxes" campaign

in the selection of target but also in the portrayal of the government's role in the tax-collection process, one can discern a change in course from the propaganda strategies of Morgenthau's Treasury Department during World War II.

In World War II income-tax propaganda, ordinary citizens were portrayed as making enthusiastic choices for taxpaying when presented with a rationale for such payment. Of course, World War II and the related inflationary situation provided fundamental reasons for ordinary citizens to be taxed. Once given these reasons, entertainers or "ordinary citizens" endorsed the notion of income taxation in accordance with the Treasury's appropriation strategy. During the Truman administration, however, a new form of public relations effort appeared in weekly magazines favored by the middle class. In articles by Commissioner of Internal Revenue George J. Schoeneman and by Undersecretary of the Treasury A. L. M. Wiggins, readers were regaled with stories of tax evasion by and capture of ordinary citizens. In a *Collier's* article entitled "They Can't Fool the Revenue Man," Wiggins told of a friend's challenge to him. "Oh, yes, I know you get most of the big boys. But how about the little fellows? There must be thousands of them who get away with murder every year." Wiggins went on: "Well, my friend was wrong. Take the case of the man who ran a filling station and lunch counter on the outskirts of a sizeable city. . . . He figured that he could chisel a few hundred dollars in income taxes without running any risk. He operated on a cash basis; how could anyone know how much he took in? So what finally happened? . . . I estimated that it cost this man about $1,000 to try to evade $300 in taxes."[139]

Commissioner Schoeneman in "Tax Cheaters Beware!" wrote of a delicatessen owner who fed his family from the store shelves and failed to include the price of the food in his gross income. Schoeneman's article even addressed evasion issues that could arise for a boy with a paper route.[140] Even the American farmer could come under scrutiny by the Bureau of Internal Revenue. One hundred twenty-eight revenue agents were sent to a farming community in Minnesota to examine bank accounts, store accounts, government payments, yields per acre,

---

during the depression. David T. Beito, *Tax Payers in Revolt: Tax Resistance during the Great Depression* (Chapel Hill: University of North Carolina Press, 1989).

[139] A. L. M. Wiggins, "They Can't Fool the Internal Revenue Man," *Collier's*, September 20, 1947.

[140] George Schoeneman, "Tax Cheaters Beware!" *American Magazine*, February 1949, 24, 128, 127.

and the record of grain and cattle buyers. Over $5 million in additional taxes and penalties was collected from the farmers in the community.[141]

Evasion by the less-than-well-to-do was perceived as a threat to the Treasury. Commissioner Schoeneman noted a change in the profile of the tax evader. In the past, tax crimes had been "done mostly by criminals of the 'public enemy' type." The commissioner added, "In recent years, the problems of scarcities, inflation, war-swollen tax rates, and unprecedented profits have tempted a tragic group of otherwise respectable individuals to dodge their tax responsibilities."[142] Because such a large portion of federal income-tax revenues was collected from average citizens, widespread petty "tax chiseling" could pose a significant threat. In January 1947, the Bureau of Internal Revenue announced that income-tax evasion had reached a peak, costing the Treasury about $3 billion a year.[143] In March 1950, the bureau estimated that $750 million was lost due to taxpayer "mistakes."[144]

As a counterpoint to messages about massive evasion, a series of government messages sought to make threats of apprehension and punishment effective by convincing would-be tax evaders that they would be caught. Tax administrators, in their "threat genre" articles, sought to paint the Bureau of Internal Revenue as an almost omniscient agency, ever clever in its techniques of ferreting out evasion. Commissioner Schoeneman assured the readers of *American Magazine*, "You see, it's almost impossible to deceive our investigators, because most of them are generally familiar with every type of dodge ever attempted, and if they run across what appears to be a new one, they can look into the files and find it's been tried before."[145] In a *Life* article that was exceedingly complimentary to the Bureau of Internal Revenue, this wealth of agent experience was described more concretely.[146] One agent was said to have computed the earnings of a

[141]Wiggins, "They Can't Fool."
[142]Schoeneman, "Tax Cheaters," 129.
[143]"Tax Evasion Total Held Record Peak," *New York Times*, January 19, 1947, 16.
[144]Ernest Havemann, "Moral for March 15: You Can't Win," *Life*, March 6, 1950, 112, 118. It is unclear what relation the "mistake" figure has to the earlier computation of income-tax evasion losses.
[145]Schoeneman, "Tax Cheaters," 126.
[146]"The collector is such a relentless and efficient fellow—in his quiet and unobtrusive way—that he has made the U.S. income tax one of the modern wonders of the world." Havemann, "Moral for March 15," 112. It is reasonable to infer, based on the information in the article, that the Bureau of Internal Revenue assisted in the preparation of Havemann's article.

house of prostitution by checking the weight of the laundry sent out, estimating the number of towels (allowing one per customer), and multiplying the number of towels by price charged per customer. "The income figure he arrived at was so accurate that one madam, when confronted with it, looked as if she had seen a ghost and was barely able to mutter, 'How did you know?' "[147] All sorts of sources were said to provide the grist for Internal Revenue investigations. Tax evaders could be tripped up by "disgruntled or underpaid employees," "unusual currency transactions," "sudden displays of wealth," "hatcheck receipts, tips to waiters," an "estranged and angry wife," even success stories in newspapers and magazines. Tax officials sought to create the impression that a lone tax evader would inevitably be caught by the government's observation of his or her daily life or by its elucidation of information from those in the tax evader's circle.[148]

The mass-media descriptions of the inevitable apprehension of small-time tax evaders and avoiders are interesting artifacts. If, in fact, the Bureau of Internal Revenue was truly as effective as it claimed, average citizens would be aware of neighbors who had been caught in the tax dragnet. The use of mass-media messages using anecdotes about people like the Minnesota farmers was an interesting attempt to influence or construct popular culture understandings of how the tax system worked. Absolute effectiveness would, theoretically, not require the assistance of mass media. Short of that, media messages may have served to exaggerate bureau effectiveness.

This is not to suggest that no progress was made in tax administration during the Truman years. In Secretary of the Treasury John W. Snyder's papers is a document entitled "Objectives of Mr. Snyder's Treasury Department—Reorganize the Treasury from a World War controlled operation to a peacetime enterprise financial function."[149] Snyder's regard for businesslike efficiency was consistent with his boss's expression of one of his primary purposes as president. Truman had identified this goal as "organizing the machinery of government to meet the new needs and responsibilities that had arisen."[150] Snyder was responsible for a

[147]Ibid., 114.
[148]Wiggins, "You Can't Fool"; Havemann, "Moral for March 15," 114. Actually, it appears that tax informing was a relatively rare event. Fewer than one hundred tipsters were paid in one year. "Tax Informing Slackens: Pay $1,000,000 to Government, $55,000 to Tipsters in Year," *New York Times,* August 14, 1946, 27.
[149]"Objective of Mr. Snyder's Treasury Department" (n.d.), Snyder Papers.
[150]*Harry S. Truman: Year of Decisions,* vol. 1 of *Memoirs of Harry S. Truman* (1955), quoted in William E. Pemberton, *Bureaucratic Politics: Executive Reorganization during the Truman Administration* (Columbia: University of Missouri Press, 1979), 1.

critical component of the machinery of government: revenue collection and enforcement of revenue laws. During Snyder's years as secretary of the Treasury, the importance of "efficiency" and "management techniques" was reflected in the narrative monthly reports to the secretary of the treasury. In October 1946 Snyder launched the Management Improvement Program. In his 1952 "Report to Taxpayers," Snyder characterized the program: "In every day terms, it meant cutting red tape, speeding up operations, cutting down overhead, streamlining administration, replacing obsolete methods with modern ones, getting more done with the same manpower and money, making both tax paying and tax collecting simpler." Outside consultants were employed to make a comprehensive study of organization and procedures in the field offices and within the bureau.[151] Snyder was kept abreast of experiments like the one in Cleveland in 1948 using IBM punch-card equipment.[152]

This stress on efficiency within the Treasury Department did not receive much attention, at least not in the *New York Times*. President Truman saluted the management efforts at the Bureau of Internal Revenue in his budget messages in 1949 and 1950. These compliments were, however, buried within lengthy messages that escaped the notice or attention of many citizens.[153] During the war, according to Snyder, taxpayers waited a year or more for refunds.[154] By early in Snyder's administration, the situation had improved markedly.[155] Although the *New York Times,* in covering the progress of tax refunds in 1949, noted improvement over the statistics of the previous year, articles like "Refunds on U.S. Tax Slowed by Volume" hardly conveyed a sense of progress.[156]

Snyder's concern with efficiency and the difficulty in conveying the improvements made suggest an additional function served by the "threat to ordinary citizens" type of public relations. Commissioner Schoeneman in his 1949 article "Tax Cheaters Beware!" discussed the bureau's new

[151]*Annual Report of the Commissioner of Internal Revenue* (1952), 8, 10.
[152]Parsons, letter to Secretary Snyder (March 2, 1948), in Taxes—General, 1946–52, Snyder Papers.
[153]"Text of President Truman's Budget Outlining Government's Spending Proposals," *New York Times,* January 11, 1949, 19, 22; "Text of President Truman's Message to Congress Outlining the National Budget," *New York Times,* January 10, 1950, 23.
[154]Snyder, "Report to Taxpayers" (September 10, 1952), 7, Snyder Papers.
[155]Snyder, letter to Joseph D. Nunan, Jr. (August 15, 1946), in Taxes—General, 1946–52, Snyder Papers (expressing delight on Commissioner Nunan's announcement of the completion of the payment of refunds to individual taxpayers on their 1945 income-tax returns).
[156]"$1,535,222,925 Rebated in Income Taxes So Far," *New York Times,* April 28, 1949, 26; "Refunds on U.S. Tax Slowed by Volume," *New York Times,* April 15, 1949, 26.

Auditing Control Program. "Previously only those returns which seemed to contain surface discrepancies—or those about which we had received outside information—were investigated thoroughly. From now on a small percentage—in addition to those normally selected—will be investigated in each income, occupational, and geographical group." The chief tax collector then went on to illustrate the effectiveness of the program in examining the return of a Minneapolis grocer.[157] The efficiency theme also emerges in the *Life* article noted earlier. The author portrayed the deplorable state of the bureau during the war, then praised the managerial efficiency of the bureau. "[It] deserves great credit and has certainly qualified as one of the most competent of all government agencies. Since 1938 the number of personal-tax returns that the bureau receives has increased by 800%; at the same time its own personnel, including secretaries, typists and phone operators, has increased by only 150%."[158]

Through explicit praise of government efforts and through the portrayal of the government's revenue agents as resourceful and ubiquitous, the message of efficiency was being conveyed. Although tax-auditing efforts against average citizens may have suggested an intrusive state and although these messages were departures from the World War II messages, the ability to communicate the Treasury's efforts at efficiency and, perhaps, Truman's emphasis on management may have been worth the cost. By possibly improving the administration of the income tax and, perhaps more important, by using the mass media to claim efficiency improvements, the Treasury and the Bureau of Internal Revenue sought to suggest uniform enforcement of the law. The information on evasion suggests something less than completely effective enforcement. Failing that, the assertion of effectiveness in popular magazines was an attempt to minimize evasion.

CONCLUSION

In the Treasury Department's "Report on Postwar Taxation," there was no doubt as to the intent to retain the income tax as a mass tax after the war. The report asserted, "The individual income tax . . . must be kept a mass tax, because after the war very large amounts of revenue will still need to be raised for many generations to come." The mass

---

[157]Schoeneman, "Tax Cheaters," 25.
[158]Havemann, "Moral for March 15," 113.

federal income tax was seen as "the most important" and flexible revenue source available to the federal government. The report urged variation in rates rather than exemptions. "It would be bad for tax morale to drop millions of taxpayers from the tax rolls one year and in another year to bring them again under the income tax, only to drop them again as revenue requirements change."[159] The Treasury's report is evidence of the continuing significance of the creation of a taxpaying culture and of the maintenance of "tax morale." In essence, these were the very issues faced by Secretary Morgenthau and his advisers during the war.

The report reflects a conscious concern about popular perceptions of the income tax and compliance with its official rules. In shaping public opinion and compliance, tax administrators in the Roosevelt and Truman administrations relied on public relations techniques. The establishment of the mass income tax can be attributed in part to the World War II advertisement of the tax in the voices of popular culture figures. Even more plausibly, a structural change like withholding sharply limited taxpayer choice about payment of income taxes on wages and salaries. In addition, by further standardizing the tax treatment of spouses, the federal government parried state and individual efforts to selectively reduce taxes by splitting income between spouses. By adopting the income-splitting joint return, federal tax policymakers supported some popular perceptions about property ownership and gender roles. Finally, it appears that administrative improvements were made in the postwar period or, at least, that more resources were applied to income-tax enforcement. In the postwar period, tax administrators once again turned to the mass media to sell an aspect of income taxation to the public. This time the product was effective enforcement. As the 1940s economy rebounded from the depression and as an active consumer culture took hold, one product being sold was the mass federal income tax.

[159]Department of Treasury, "Report on Postwar Taxation" (n.d.), 37–38, Blough Papers. Legislative developments from this era are discussed in Paul, *Taxation*.

4

•━━━•━━━•━━━•━━━•━━━•━━━•━━━•━━━•━━━•━━━•━━━•━━━•━━━•

Social security and the financing of
the American state

EDWARD D. BERKOWITZ

As a source of tax revenues, social security has proved a conspicuous success. During the war years between 1941 and 1945, social insurance accounted for 6 percent of all federal tax collections; in the period between 1976 and 1980, social insurance represented 31 percent of all federal tax collections.[1] By 1990, one authority estimated that nearly three-quarters of those who contributed to social security paid more in social security taxes than in income taxes.[2] In a discussion of the financing of the American state, therefore, social security deserves prominent mention. In this essay I attempt to account for the growth of the program over time and the apparent willingness of Congress to support increases in social security taxes. As a means of discovering why the program no longer enjoys the strong support that characterized the years between 1950 and 1972, I also look at some economists' objections to the program. What follows is primarily a political narrative, with particular attention paid to the politics of social security taxes.

SOCIAL SECURITY AND ITS CRITICS

If one wanted an indication of the appeal of social security, one might follow the career of Wilbur J. Cohen, who arrived in Washington in 1934 to work as a research assistant on the Social Security Act and who

[1]Mark H. Leff, *The Limits of Symbolic Reform: The New Deal and Taxation, 1933–1939* (Cambridge: Cambridge University Press, 1984), 6.
[2]See Edward Berkowitz, *America's Welfare State: From Roosevelt to Reagan* (Baltimore: Johns Hopkins University Press, 1991), 83.

remained to become Lyndon Johnson's secretary of health, education, and welfare (HEW). Early in 1968, at a particularly bad moment for the Johnson administration, Cohen, then under secretary of health, education, and welfare, tried to interest the president in a new social-insurance program.[3] Cohen saw such a program as an antidote to the considerable criticism the president had been receiving for his handling of the Vietnam War and as a means of reasserting the primacy of the "Great Society" over foreign affairs as the administration's major focus. Cohen proposed extending health coverage similar to that of Medicare to children in their first year of life.

Presenting his program, Cohen told the president that any plan should follow basic social insurance principles. These began with universality of protection. Cohen said that everyone should be covered, with no exclusions. "This appeals to the egalitarian nature of the majority of the Americans and it thus includes all of the poorest people who otherwise are not effectively covered. To cover all the poor you cover the rich as well," Cohen argued. As he explained, "a plan limited to the poor may be desirable from the point of view of cost-effectiveness but it does not appeal to the 50% of the people who consider themselves middle-class, self-supporting, respectable, independent." Furthermore, the benefits should be contributory, with part of the cost borne by a payroll tax or an *earmarked* income tax. According to Cohen, "This gives beneficiaries the psychological feeling that they have helped to pay for *their* protection. It is the reason why social security has been so popular and well-accepted. People do not want something that is called a hand-out or welfare."[4]

In this view of things, people supported social security taxes because they felt that they were getting something in return. Unlike many social

[3] Social insurance and social security are related but not interchangeable. Examples of American social insurance programs include workers' compensation, unemployment compensation, and social security (or old-age, survivors, disability, and hospital insurance). Of these three, social security is the only one financed at the federal level. Hence, federal social insurance and social security expenditures are nearly identical, although the federal government also supports a railroad retirement program and collects some of the money for the administration of unemployment compensation.

[4] Wilbur Cohen to Joseph Califano (January 19, 1968), Wilbur Cohen Papers, Wisconsin State Historical Society, Madison. Here and throughout, I draw on the research for and the contents of Edward Berkowitz, *Mr. Social Security: The Life of Wilbur J. Cohen* (Lawrence: University Press of Kansas, 1995). Where possible, I specify box numbers for the Cohen Papers. As this is being written, however, the collection is just being put in final order. For researchers who need to find a specific document, I would recommend checking with the archivists.

welfare programs, social security did not restrict its benefits to the poor. Although it contained a benefit formula that permitted poorer people a greater return on their taxes, or "investments," than richer people, it nonetheless linked contributions to benefits. Only those who belonged to families in which one of the members had paid social security taxes received benefits, yet the program came the closest of all social welfare programs to universal protection. Cohen believed that social insurance was how the government operated effectively in a culture that distrusted government.[5] In particular, social insurance was not welfare, in that it took little or no money from the government's general revenues. As the Princeton economist and social security defender Douglas Brown observed in the 1970s, welfare—defined as a "wholesale distribution of funds to the needy poor"—was "costly, inefficient, and degrading over time." According to Brown, contributory social insurance, in contrast with welfare, both prevented people from becoming dependent and preserved incentive.[6]

Yet, for all of that, social security was a tax and a transfer program that lacked what economists have called target efficiency. It did not concentrate its benefits on the people who needed them the most, raising doubts about its efficiency as an antipoverty program. For that reason and many others, the program, almost from its inception, drew criticism from members of the economic profession. In the 1940s, with the growth of the economy and the failure of the social security program to keep pace with inflation or to expand its coverage, these criticisms tended to be muted. In the 1960s, economists intensified their criticism of social security, at a time when the program was enjoying its greatest success and the economists were at the height of their influence over public policy.

Economists attacked social security as an income-redistribution program pretending to be a form of insurance and as a program that complicated efforts to control fiscal policy. In 1971, to cite an example, Milton Friedman argued that neither the taxes nor the benefits of social security would be popular in themselves. He noted: "Yet the two combined have become a sacred cow. What a triumph of imaginative pack-

---

[5]On the origins and meaning of social insurance, see Ann Shola Orloff, *The Politics of Pensions: A Comparative Analysis of Britain, Canada, and the United States* (Madison: University of Wisconsin Press, 1993), 9.
[6]Brown to Wilbur Cohen (June 1, 1972), Cohen Papers. I develop this point further in Berkowitz, *America's Welfare State*.

aging and Madison Avenue advertising."[7] In 1986, Michael Boskin, who later headed President George Bush's Council of Economic Advisers, noted that because social security and Medicare constituted the largest federal government expenditures and because social security taxes were the second-largest source of federal revenues, social security played a key role in fiscal policy. In common with a long line of economists that went back to Alvin Hansen and other early Keynesians in the 1930s, Boskin noted that the program, with its inflexible tax rate, often had adverse consequences on the economy. In addition, drawing on work by Martin Feldstein and others, Boskin argued that the system created many disincentives to continue working and to engage in private savings, "resulting in uneconomic decisions with regard to retirement and saving."[8]

Social security supporters, such as Cohen, contended that the economists missed the point. As Cohen noted, both Congress and the people favored social security. The statistics on the growth of the program certainly appeared to support this view. The sheer volume and the growth of the program were impressive. In 1940, the program had about seventy-seven thousand beneficiaries; in 1970, it had more than 16 million beneficiaries. The importance of the program as a source of retirement income increased over time. In 1940, less than 1 percent of the aged population received social security benefits; in 1970, the percentage of the aged population receiving social security benefits was 85.5. In 1940, the money collected for social security amounted to $0.6 billion in federal receipts; in 1970, the money collected through payroll taxes to pay for social security and the hospital insurance part of Medicare was $39.7 billion. And the real growth of the program lay ahead. Between 1970 and 1975, federal receipts for social security and the hospital insurance part of Medicare reached $75.6 billion.[9]

EARLY YEARS OF SOCIAL SECURITY, 1935–1950

The growth of the program becomes all the more remarkable when one considers the insignificance of the program between 1935 and 1950. As a percentage of personal income, for example, its expenditures were

[7]Wilbur J. Cohen and Milton Friedman, *Social Security: Universal or Selective* (Washington, D.C.: American Enterprise Institute, 1972), 26.
[8]Michael J. Boskin, *Too Many Promises: The Uncertain Future of Social Security—a Twentieth Century Fund Report* (Homewood, Ill.: Dow Jones–Irwin, 1986), 10.
[9]Data from Alicia H. Munnell, *The Future of Social Security* (Washington: Brookings Institution, 1977), 6, 10, 85, 87.

less than 0.05 percent between 1937 and 1940 and no more than 0.4 percent in 1950. In 1970, by contrast, its benefits as a percentage of personal income reached 4.7 percent; they are close to 8 percent today.[10] Although the program eventually became large and consequential, it cannot be considered an inevitable success. Instead, it struggled for its very existence until 1950. By that time, a remarkable group of administrators and political proponents in Congress and in the labor movement had developed a convincing rationale for social security, enabling the program to grow into an entity that, in Senator Robert Dole's words, overwhelmed all other domestic priorities.[11]

Like many other landmark pieces of legislation, passage of the Social Security Act in August 1935 was a near thing. President Franklin D. Roosevelt slipped it through a window of political opportunity that opened in the middle of the depression and closed very soon afterward. In the most immediate sense, the Social Security Act was the product of a report from the Committee on Economic Security. Created by President Roosevelt in the early summer of 1934, the committee was chaired by Secretary of Labor Frances Perkins. Social insurance experts staffed the committee from top to bottom, practically guaranteeing that it would recommend the creation of a social insurance program to cover the risks of old age and unemployment.[12]

In 1934, social insurance, to which the committee staff was intellectually predisposed, also met pragmatic political needs. It depended on the taxing power of the federal government, a power that was explicitly sanctioned by the Constitution. It relied on payroll taxes. These supplied a source of revenue independent of income and other taxes. If the framers of social security had relied on income taxes, they would have found it necessary to lower income-tax exemptions or, in simpler terms,

---

[10]Social Security Administration, *Annual Statistical Supplement, 1992* (Washington, D.C.: Government Printing Office, 1993), 147. This source contains a wealth of statistical data about the social security program, and I have relied on it extensively. Unless otherwise noted, statistics cited in this chapter come from this source.

[11]For Dole's remark and other comments on the immense size and significance of social security, see Eric Kingson and Edward Berkowitz, *Social Security and Medicare: A Policy Primer* (Westport, Conn.: Auburn House, 1993), chapter 1.

[12]For an overview of the passage of the Social Security Act, see Kingson and Berkowitz, *Social Security and Medicare*, chapter 3, Edwin E. Witte, *The Development of the Social Security Act: A Memorandum on the History of the Committee on Economic Security and Drafting and Legislative History of the Social Security Act* (Madison: University of Wisconsin Press, 1962), and Arthur J. Altmeyer, *The Formative Years of Social Security: A Chronicle of Social Security Legislation and Administration, 1934–1954* (Madison: University of Wisconsin Press, 1968).

broaden the income tax so that more people paid it. Otherwise, there simply would not have been enough money generated; this was, after all, an era in which 95 percent of Americans paid no income taxes.[13] Important, also, was the fact that not everyone would be covered by social security. Thus, if sales or income taxes were used, some people would pay taxes that supported social security but would receive nothing in return. It made more sense to tie tax collections and benefit receipts together through the use of a payroll tax. In this way, not only would enough money be collected but taxpayers would also hold a financial stake in the program. Broadening the income tax or imposing a new sales tax would have been a much harder political sell.

As matters turned out, the exact structure of the social security tax plan became an object of considerable controversy among the president's advisers. These advisers had no trouble accepting tax policy as an important form of social policy. Edwin Witte, the Wisconsin professor and former Wisconsin state employee who headed the committee staff, was a student and protégé of John R. Commons. From Commons, Witte had learned about taxation as a means of inducing employers to engage in socially productive behavior.[14] The social security tax was a form of forced savings that would require employers and employees to fund the employees' retirement. It would facilitate the transition between a living wage during an employee's working lifetime and an adequate income during an employee's retirement.

What was less clear was how to schedule the taxes over time and to blend payroll taxes and general revenues. The staff working on the problem decided to recommend a gradually rising tax rate that would accommodate the growing number of people who would retire in the future. The tax would begin in 1937 at a rate of 2 percent, split evenly between the employer and the employee, and would rise every two years until it reached 5 percent in 1957. According to the staff calculations,

---

[13]Leff, *The Limits of Symbolic Reform,* 46.
[14]On Commons, see John R. Commons, *Myself: The Autobiography of John R. Commons* (Madison: University of Wisconsin Press, 1963), first published in 1934, and Lafayette G. Harter, Jr., *John R. Commons: His Assault on Laissez-Faire* (Corvallis: Oregon State University Press, 1962). The best source on Witte is Theron F. Schlabach, *Edwin E. Witte: Cautious Reformer* (Madison: State Historical Society of Wisconsin, 1969). For other biographical details on Witte, see the introduction by Robert J. Lampman to Edwin Witte, *Social Security Perspectives: Essays by Edwin E. Witte* (Madison: University of Wisconsin Press, 1962), and see Wilbur Cohen, "Edwin E. Witte," in *Biographical Dictionary of Social Welfare in America,* ed. Walter I. Trattner (Westport, Conn.: Greenwood Press, 1986), 785–87.

which were subject to the vagaries of trying to predict population, wage levels, and unemployment rates into the future, the system would develop a deficit by about 1967. At that time, should such a deficit develop, the government could remedy it by adding general revenues. Roosevelt objected to this formulation, however, and insisted that the tax rates be redrawn so as not to allow a deficit. He did not like the idea of burdening future generations because of an action taken in 1934. Accordingly, the committee staff substituted a plan in which the combined employer and employee tax rate reached 6 percent by 1949. Employers and employees would pay taxes on the first $3,000 of the employee's income.[15]

Subject only to the command that the tax rates be reworked, Roosevelt passed the committee's recommendations along to Congress in the beginning of 1935. Congress reacted politely, as it might have to any administration proposal that followed the Democratic landslide in the congressional elections of 1934. At the same time, no groundswell developed in support of social insurance programs because they did not affect the major problems of relieving the victims of the depression. The work of the Committee on Economic Security bore little relationship to the urgent business of coping with the consequences of massive unemployment or the poverty of old age. To aid people in immediate distress, states continued to depend on their old poor laws, supplemented by federal emergency public works programs.[16]

Despite this problem, President Roosevelt persevered. At several points, Congress threatened to drop old-age insurance from the omnibus economic security bill, which also included welfare, unemployment compensation, vocational rehabilitation, child welfare, and public health components.[17] The president insisted that the various parts of the legislation be kept together. As a consequence, Congress passed a federally administered old-age insurance program for industrial and commercial workers, funded by payroll taxes that initially amounted to 2 percent of the employee's first $3,000 in wages. Then, as now, employers and employees split the tax. The deduction from an employee's paycheck was 1 percent, and 1 percent was paid by the employer. Then, as now, the

[15]See Berkowitz, *America's Welfare State*, 21–24.
[16]See Edward Berkowitz and Kim McQuaid, "Social Security and the American Welfare State," in *Research in Economic History*, Supplement 6 (Greenwich, Conn.: JAI Press, 1991), 169–90.
[17]See Witte, *Development of the Social Security Act*.

Internal Revenue Service collected the payroll taxes from employers. This program eventually became known as social security.

The formulation of the legislation and its presentation to Congress had important implications for the future of social security policy. Because the bill rested on the government's power to tax, it went to the tax committees in Congress. By 1939, provisions were worked out in which the money collected for social security was automatically placed in a trust fund. That meant that the social security program bypassed the appropriations process and became the exclusive preserve of the Ways and Means Committee and the Finance Committee in Congress. That, in turn, provided the program with a source of continuity and support that other social welfare programs, which had constantly to fight for appropriations, lacked.[18]

Despite this advantage, the social security program initially had far more liabilities than assets. The problems had several dimensions. One concerned the relationship of contributions to benefits. Social insurance, by definition, depended on what I have described as the "pay to play rule." Someone who contributed nothing received nothing from the program. That meant that someone already old in 1935 could not expect a pension, undermining the relevance of the program as a tool of social policy. Those nearing retirement age who contributed only a little to the program could expect little back from the program. That, in turn, necessitated considerations related to having minimum pensions that were more than mere pittances. If the program adopted minimum pensions (rather than totally "earned" pensions), as it did, then younger workers necessarily subsidized the pensions of older workers, complicating the financing plans.[19]

Another dimension of the problem was that the program would show up as a payroll tax before it began to pay benefits. This situation created political vulnerabilities that faced any program that relied on a tax, and

---

[18]Martha Derthick, *Policymaking for Social Security* (Washington, D.C.: Brookings Institution, 1979), 39–43.

[19]See Berkowitz, *America's Welfare State,* 24–25. The initial formula applied to "cumulative creditable wages" and featured a higher return on initial contributions than on later contributions, thus favoring the relatively old and the relatively poor. The formal terms of the formula, which lasted only until 1939, were as follows: one-half of 1 percent of first $3,000 plus one-twelfth of 1 percent of next $42,000 plus one–twenty-fourth of 1 percent of next $84,000. See *Social Security Bulletin, Annual Statistical Supplement, 1984–1985* (Washington, D.C.: Government Printing Office, 1985), 5. In commemoration of the fiftieth anniversary of social security, this issue of the bulletin contained longer runs of historical data than most other issues.

it raised questions related to the role that the tax would play in macroeconomic policy. A final dimension of the problem was inherent in the long-run financing of the program, if it was to be self-supporting from payroll taxes. At first, the costs of the program would be low. Over time, as more people who had contributed to the system retired, these costs would rise. The question was whether the system might prefund its liabilities. If it was not to use general revenues, then payroll taxes would have to be set so as to yield early surpluses that could then be used to pay later expenses. The alternative was for early program participants to pay very low taxes and for later program participants to pay much higher taxes.

Each of these problems posed early stumbling blocks to the expansion of the system, obstacles that were not resolved until 1950. The fact that so few people initially benefited from the program meant that welfare programs for the elderly became more popular than social security. State welfare programs for the elderly, known as public assistance programs, were subsidized by the federal government through general revenues. Under the terms of the Social Security Act, the federal government agreed to match the first fifteen dollars that the state contributed toward the pension of an elderly person. These state-administered pensions were gratuities, not entitlements. The states awarded them only to people who could prove they were poor, and the states reserved the right to rescind the pensions for such things as immoral behavior. Still, old-age assistance (welfare) reached far more people and paid much higher benefits than did old-age insurance (social insurance or social security) in the period between 1935 and 1950. Over one-fifth of the elderly population received old-age assistance payments by the end of the 1940s; in a few states, such as Colorado and Louisiana, the percentage was over half. Not only did more of the elderly receive old-age assistance than old-age insurance, but the welfare benefits were also, on average, 70 percent higher than the social insurance benefits.[20]

In this situation, many people questioned the purpose of social security taxes. The program appeared to lack social relevance, and the taxes

[20]Mark Leff, "Speculating in Social Security Futures," in *Social Security: The First Half-Century,* ed. Gerald Nash, Noel Pugach, and Richard F. Tomasson (Albuquerque: University of New Mexico Press, 1988), 268; Carole Haber and Brian Gratton, *Old Age and the Search for Security* (Bloomington: University of Indiana Press, 1994); W. Andrew Achenbaum, *Social Security: Visions and Revisions* (New York: Cambridge University Press, 1986).

created macroeconomic difficulties. Congress reacted to this situation by simply abandoning the plans to raise social security taxes every three years. In 1939, before the tax rise scheduled for 1940, Congress opted instead to maintain the current tax rate and, simultaneously, to expand the benefits offered to include pensions for survivors of workers who reached retirement age and larger pensions for married workers than for single workers. Each time a scheduled benefit increase approached in 1943, 1946, and 1949, Congress voted to freeze the tax rate at its 1937 level. In 1947, the Republican Congress took the further step of reducing *future* payroll tax raises, dropping the future maximums from 3 to 2 percent. Neither the tax rate nor the "taxable wage base" rose until 1950.[21]

Part of the reason for abandoning plans to raise taxes was a fear that, contrary to the president's desires in 1935, the liabilities of the program could not be prefunded by building up a large reserve. The "reserve fund" became an object of ridicule from both the Left and the Right. Conservatives, such as the presidential candidate Alfred Landon, branded the plans for a social security fund as a "cruel hoax." Liberals, such as those associated with the Congress of Industrial Organizations (CIO), could not see the point of building up a large reserve when current economic conditions were so bleak and the needs of the elderly so pressing.[22]

As that critique implied, social security taxes were far from popular when they were initiated in 1937. Indeed, the first overt conflicts between social security administrators and economists arose in that year. This conflict would become a continuing feature of the bureaucratic politics of social security. At issue was how social security was to be judged: as a tax and transfer program that, at any given time, helped or hindered the economy, or as an enduring institution whose integrity depended on orderly financing patterns. Almost from the beginning, Arthur Altmeyer, who served as the director of the program from 1937 to 1953, received considerable criticism from a group of economists who questioned the point of an old-age insurance program that impounded money, in the form of compulsory payroll taxes, as the economy slipped into a recession. "Every time we face a tendency toward recession," wrote the Har-

[21]Leff, "Speculating in Social Security Futures." For a good chronology of congressional action, see Derthick, *Policymaking for Social Security*, 429–32.
[22]Berkowitz, "The First Social Security Crisis," *Prologue* (Fall 1983), 132–49.

vard economist Hansen to Altmeyer in 1937, "the impounding of this Old Age Reserve Account will plague us and add to our difficulties in overcoming a recession."[23]

In 1939, when Altmeyer testified before the Finance Committee, Lauchlin Currie and Harry Dexter White, of the Treasury Department, planted questions with Wisconsin Senator Robert M. La Follette on the adverse economic effects of social security taxes. Currie and White favored a plan that simply paid old-age benefits to people out of general revenues, a modified version of a plan proposed by the physician Francis Townsend. In fact, none of the many alternatives to social security discussed in the 1930s involved the use of payroll taxes. Townsend would have financed his plan through sales taxes. Louisiana Senator Huey Long, before he died in 1935, offered a plan that utilized massive increases in the income tax. Currie and White represented a far more respectable segment of public opinion, and in an effort to mollify them, Altmeyer invited them to his house, along with New Deal insider Benjamin Cohen, to discuss the importance of contributory taxes to funding social security. Asked by Altmeyer if there was value in relating social security contributions and benefits to wages, the economists replied, "That's just a lot of ———."[24]

The program remained in precarious condition through the 1940s. The whipsawing of the economy from depression to prosperity failed, at least initially, to increase the popularity of what was then known as old-age and survivors insurance. The administrators tried to position themselves for a postwar recession and, for a time, earned the approval of the Keynesian economists in the Treasury Department. In 1941, for example, Altmeyer, the chairman of the Social Security Board, and his young assistant Wilbur Cohen turned the tables on the Keynesians by linking the social security program and the government's efforts to manage the wartime economy. According to Altmeyer's wisdom, the social security program could tax workers' wages in a time of prosperity and become a vehicle for social spending in a time of depression. The immediate proposal was for a greatly expanded federal social insurance program that would contain old-age, survivors, disability, unemployment, and health insurance benefits. The new program would cover

[23]Alvin Hansen to Arthur Altmeyer (November 8, 1937), and Altmeyer to Hansen (December 7, 1939), File 025, RG 47, Records of the Social Security Administration, National Archives, Washington, D.C.

[24]Altmeyer, *The Formative Years of Social Security*, 108–10.

more of the labor force and pay substantially higher benefits than the existing social security program.

If Congress had adopted all of Altmeyer's suggestions, the newly expanded social security program would have run a substantial surplus and made an estimated $1.7 billion available for the Treasury to spend on defense.[25] Then, after the war, the new social program would have supplied a sustained purchasing power of at least $6 billion per year, if a depression of the magnitude of the one following 1929 occurred. When the next depression hit, for example, the federal government would have been able to pay twenty-six weeks of unemployment benefits.[26] The Treasury Department, long opposed to the Social Security Board's plans, agreed with the analysis behind the plan, calling it a "happy coincidence that the improvement of the insurance plan harmonizes almost perfectly with fiscal considerations."[27]

Unfortunately for the proponents of social security expansion, the plan harmonized with little else, particularly in the chaotic days after Pearl Harbor. Concerned with pursuing a war and contending with a conservative Congress, President Roosevelt hesitated to put the social security proposals at the top of his agenda. Social security officials pushed him hard but achieved little in the way of substantive results. When the postwar depression failed to materialize, their plans were thrown into further disarray. Social security appeared to have lost its urgency in the war and immediate postwar eras. The welfare program appeared more than able to take up the slack. As Congress refused to countenance increases in the social security tax rate, it twice took the time to raise the level of federal contributions to the welfare program.[28]

THE FORMATION OF THE SOCIAL SECURITY APPARATUS, AND THE 1950 AMENDMENTS

For all of that, the 1940s were not entirely a lost decade for the proponents of social security. During this period, the individuals who would lead the program in the period between 1950 and 1972 found one another. In the 1940s, they worked together on the ambitious efforts to

[25]"An Expanded Social Security Program" (August 13, 1941) and Cohen to Byron Mitchell, chief budget examiner (June 6, 1941), both in Box 26, Cohen Papers.
[26]"An Expanded Social Security Program," Box 26, Cohen Papers.
[27]"Comments on the Social Security Board's Legislative Proposals" (September 30, 1941), Box 26, Cohen Papers.
[28]See Berkowitz, *Mr. Social Security,* chapter 3.

create a federal unemployment, health, and disability program. In the 1950s, the group collaborated, with considerably more success, on the incremental expansion of the social security program.

Elizabeth Wickenden acted as a convener of the social security crowd that included, among others, Wilbur Cohen and Robert Ball, of the Social Security Administration, and Nelson Cruikshank, of the American Federation of Labor (AFL). One of her chief contributions was to bring together representatives of a splintered labor movement, divided between the industrial approach of the CIO and the craft approach of the AFL, and unite them in support of social security.

Elizabeth Wickenden, born in 1909, graduated from Vassar in 1931. After college, she went abroad for a year and then took a job with the Emergency Exchange Association, which was organized to provide barter and exchange among the unemployed. Moving from New York to Washington in 1933, she slipped into the life of the New Deal, serving as acting director of the Transient Program of the Federal Emergency Relief Administration and later becoming part of a social crowd that also included Abe Fortas and Lyndon Johnson. Eventually, she served as an assistant to Aubrey Williams, the deputy administrator of the WPA, and worked for the National Youth Administration. In 1940, as the character of the New Deal public works programs began to shift from social work to defense preparedness, she quit the government, did odd jobs, and emerged as a half-time Washington representative for the American Public Welfare Association in Washington.[29] In 1945 she put together, for the association, a statement of public welfare objectives that advocated the "need for public assistance [to] be reduced to a minimum through strengthening the social insurance programs."[30] In other words, she put the association on record as favoring precisely the opposite of what Congress was doing, which was restraining the growth of social security and encouraging the growth of public assistance.

Nelson Cruikshank, another key member of the group that came together in the 1940s, had started his career as a Methodist minister and a labor organizer. During the 1930s he worked for the WPA and then for the Farm Security Administration before moving, during the war

[29] I draw this account almost entirely from an oral interview with Elizabeth Wickenden, October 16, 1991, Haverford, Pennsylvania.
[30] Wickenden Interview; Public Welfare Association, "Objectives for Public Welfare Legislation, 1947," *Public Welfare*, April 1947, reprinted in William Haber and Wilbur Cohen, eds., *Readings in Social Security* (New York: Prentice-Hall, 1948), 520–31, quotation on 531.

years, to the War Manpower Commission. In 1944 he came to the AFL—innocent, as the political scientist Martha Derthick puts it, "of experience with social insurance or acquaintance with the SSA's staff." He soon remedied that, becoming a true social security insider. As much as anyone else, Cruikshank helped to persuade union leaders to support social security, despite the long tradition of union indifference or hostility to social benefits managed by the government. Furthermore, Cruikshank helped union leaders from the AFL and the CIO negotiate a common position on social security.[31]

Like Wickenden and Cruikshank, Robert Ball became an important part of the liberal apparatus in the postwar era. He, along with Wilbur Cohen, was the key contact between the bureaucracy and the supporters of social security in the unions and in Congress. Ball, born in 1914, studied at Wesleyan, where he received an undergraduate degree in English (1935) and a graduate degree in economics (1936). In college he experienced the ferment of the depression years, at one point rounding up a group of his classmates and going off to Hartford and picketing at the Colt Fire Arms plant.

The son of a Methodist minister, Ball came from solidly American stock. Standing more than six feet tall and wearing black-rimmed glasses, he projected a very serious image, as though he were a business executive rather than a social reformer. Despite his air of gravity, he managed always to be affable, quick to smile at other people's jokes. He seldom fumbled in his social interactions, being endowed with what a later generation would call interpersonal skills. He appeared always to be prepared, to know what he wanted from a situation, and yet he seldom gave the impression of dictating to others.[32]

Like Cohen, Ball had the talent to rise rapidly through the social security ranks. After a brief stint as a minor financial functionary at a

---

[31]On Cruikshank, see Alice M. Hoffman and Howard S. Hoffman, *The Cruikshank Chronicles: Anecdotes, Stories, and Memoirs of a New Deal Liberal* (Hampden, Conn.: Archon Books, 1989); see also Edward Berkowitz, "How to Think about the Welfare State," *Labor History* 32, no. 4 (Fall 1991): 489–502. Both of the quotations come from Derthick, *Policymaking for Social Security*, 126. For AFL support of social security and collaboration with Cohen, see Cohen to Altmeyer (January 11, 1949), Box 28, Cohen Papers.

[32]Theodore R. Marmor, with the assistance of Philip Fellman, "Entrepreneurship in Public Management: Wilbur Cohen and Robert Ball," in *Leadership and Innovation: A Biographical Perspective on Entrepreneurs in Government*, ed. Jameson W. Doig and Erwin C. Hargrove (Baltimore: Johns Hopkins University Press, 1987), 246–81; Robert Ball, oral interview with David McComb, November 5, 1968, LBJ Library Oral History Collection, Washington, D.C.

New York department store, Ball accepted a job with the Social Security Board in 1939. He entered the agency not in the central administration, as Cohen did, but rather as a field representative in Newark, New Jersey. He worked in a variety of field positions, all in the northern New Jersey area, before eventually settling in the central training office, where he instructed new employees on the principles of social insurance. Ball's calm manner and extraordinarily agile mind made him an exceptional teacher.

In 1945, Ball decided to leave government employment and to join a new venture, housed in the American Council on Education, called the University Government Center on Social Security. In this job, Ball met many of the leaders in the field, who would come to the center to lecture on topics related to social security. Two years later, Ball accepted an assignment from Senator Eugene Milliken, of the Senate Finance Committee, to serve as staff director of a Social Security Advisory Council. The senator wanted an expert on social security, one who was not an employee of the Social Security Administration and who would not be dominated by Arthur Altmeyer. Douglas Brown, the Princeton economist on the board of the center, suggested Ball.[33]

The work of the advisory council that met in 1947 and 1948 was crucial to the future of social security. The members of the informal apparatus that had been created in the 1940s all played a part. Ball, the staff director, relied on Cohen, the assistant to Altmeyer, for information and advice. Cruikshank was a member of the advisory council, and Wickenden followed its activities with intense interest. The reports of this council formed the basis for amendments to the Social Security Act, amendments that Congress, coached in large part by Cohen, passed in 1950.[34]

The advisory council, relying heavily on data generated by the Social Security Administration and on Ball's ability to tutor the members on the fundamentals of social security without appearing to dictate to them, issued a series of reports between April and December 1948. The key report on old-age and survivors insurance arrived in April. The council, no doubt with Ball's urging, accepted the Social Security Administration's policy formulation that equated preventing dependency and reducing the need for public assistance. The best way to lower the public

[33]Much of the material on Robert Ball derives from my interview with him in Washington, D.C., on May 20, 1992.
[34]Cohen to J. Douglas Brown (October 1, 1947), Cohen Papers.

assistance rate, according to the council, was to extend social insurance. In this manner, the council came to recommend a major expansion of the social security program.[35]

On August 28, 1950, after considerable congressional scrutiny and debate, the recommendations of the advisory council became law. Through this law, the proponents of social security gained much of what they wanted—a greatly expanded social security program that paid substantially higher benefits. The increase in benefits was 77 percent. Further, the impasse over social security taxes was broken. Congress agreed to raise the tax level to 3 percent and to raise the taxable wage base from $3,000 to $3,600. Once again Congress, reaffirming the principle that the system should never have to depend on general revenues, included a schedule of future tax increases in the measure, with a maximum rate of 6.5 percent to be reached in 1970. These congressional actions paved the way for the first increase in social security taxes to take place in 1951. The 1950 law also added a new feature to the tax. Self-employed persons received social security coverage, at a tax rate of 2.25 percent of taxable payroll. This change meant that the program no longer was limited to commercial and industrial employees. Instead, the self-employed could pay social security taxes through their income-tax returns. Altmeyer, who remained in charge of the program throughout the Roosevelt and Truman years, later termed the 1950 law "crucial" to the survival of social security. It meant that social security had finally attained parity with welfare.[36]

Despite the importance of these amendments, they have become invisible to subsequent observers and have not received much attention from historians who write about postwar America. Instead of the climax of the battle between welfare and social security, the historians often transform the amendments into another failed skirmish in the battle for national health insurance.[37] In addition, the fact that the amendments became law at the very beginning of the Korean War distracted the nation's attention from their importance. As a result, the 1950 amend-

[35]The report is reprinted in Haber and Cohen, *Readings in Social Security* (see, in particular, 255).
[36]Achenbaum, *Social Security*, 43; Altmeyer, *The Formative Years of Social Security*, 169.
[37]In this regard they may take their cues from President Truman. See his statement on signing the bill, cited in Wilbur J. Cohen and Robert J. Myers, "Social Security Act Amendments of 1950: A Summary and Legislative History," *Social Security Bulletin,* October 1950, 1. This source also contains a complete list of committee reports and other documents associated with the amendments, as well as a useful overview of the contents of the act and the legislative maneuvers involved in its passage.

ments, like so many aspects of the history of taxation, simply do not appear in the history texts, even though they are arguably the most important piece of social welfare legislation in the entire postwar period.

What produced these amendments? One explanation hinges on the fact that unions, particularly those in the coal, steel, and automobile industries, had recently secured more adequate retirement pensions from employers. These collectively bargained agreements provided for pensions that included social security benefits. In agreeing to this provision, the unions gave the employers an incentive to favor higher social security benefits. Social security, the argument went, was cheaper for employers than private pensions. Among other things, employees contributed to social security pensions, and the program contained special benefits for low-income workers. So, when the time came to testify on the 1950 social security amendments, the union leaders did so enthusiastically, and the business leaders did not oppose higher social security benefits. This coalition made higher benefits possible. "It appears," wrote Cohen at the time, "that employers may take a greater interest in social security than ever before." Where once employers regarded social security as an added cost, "they may look upon social security as a way of reducing costs."[38]

For Cohen and Altmeyer and the other social security supporters, the 1950 amendments became a source of almost instant satisfaction. In an article that appeared early in 1952, Cohen described 1951 as a milestone year. He noted that in February 1951, for the first time in the nation's history, more people received old-age insurance than received old-age assistance. In August 1951, also for the first time in the nation's history, the total amount of insurance payments exceeded the amount of old-age assistance payments.[39]

EXPANDING SOCIAL SECURITY IN 1952

After 1950, the incremental engine of social security expansion kicked into high gear. Compared with the sedate, even moribund, pace of the

[38]Cohen and Myers, "Social Security Act Amendments of 1950"; Cohen to Representative Herman P. Eberharter (September 19, 1952), Cohen Papers; Wilbur Cohen, "Aspects of Legislative History of the Social Security Amendments of 1950," *Industrial and Labor Relations Review* 4 (January 1951): 198. It is interesting that Cohen's interpretation has since been adopted by the few historians and historical sociologists who have studied the 1950 amendments. See Jill Quadagno, *The Transformation of Old Age Security* (Chicago: University of Chicago Press, 1988).
[39]Cohen, "Income Maintenance for the Aged," *Annals of the American Academy of Political and Social Science*, January 1952, 154.

1940s, Congress began to amend the program with a startling frequency in the 1950s, as exemplified by major benefit increases in 1952, 1954, 1956, and 1958. The 1952 amendments were perhaps the most surprising. If past experience served as a guide, the Korean War should have made the passage of social security legislation almost impossible. Since Congress had devoted so much time and energy to social security in 1949 and 1950, and since the country was fighting a war, one might have expected another long hibernation period of the sort that had prevailed between 1939 and 1950. But that proved not to be the case.

Congress expanded the social security program in 1952 in part because the social security bureaucrats and the members of the social security apparatus understood the importance of being ready. In 1952, Cohen and Ball, the latter now back in government as a high-ranking official at the Social Security Administration, helped to prepare a bill that, they hoped, would receive the backing of the Truman administration and of the House Ways and Means Committee. Among other things, the bill called for an average increase of five dollars in monthly social security benefits and a rise in the level of federal grants for public assistance.[40]

The recommendation for a rise in the level of federal grants for public assistance was a bow to the inevitable. In 1950, Congress had decided not to raise welfare benefits for the elderly because the outbreak of the Korean War had made legislators careful about increasing current government expenditures. But between August 1950 and July 1951, prices increased somewhere between 6 and 7 percent. Social security administrators realized that eventually rising prices and the political appeal of helping the elderly would make a public assistance increase irresistible. Indeed, in June 1951 Senator Ernest McFarland (D-AZ) had introduced an amendment to a minor revenue bill that would have raised welfare benefits by five dollars a month to the aged, blind, and disabled and by three dollars a month to dependent children. Although the Senate had hastened to back the majority leader, the House Ways and Means Committee refused to consider the bill, and it died. Nonetheless, the sentiment in favor of an increase in public assistance remained strong.[41]

Cohen, Ball, and the other bureaucratic leaders believed that social

[40]Cohen to Arthur Altmeyer (April 14, 1952), Cohen Papers.
[41]See Wilbur J. Cohen, "Should Old-Age Assistance Again Outpace Old-Age Insurance?" *American Economic Security*, July–August 1951, reprint available in Cohen Papers; Wilbur J. Cohen, "The Legislative History of the Social Security Amendments of 1952," mimeo, June 1954, Division of Research and Statistics, Social Security Administration, Baltimore, Maryland.

security benefits should be increased for reasons related to the actuarial traditions of the Social Security Administration and the state of the economy. From the beginning, the Social Security Board contained an Office of the Actuary. After the establishment of a federal old-age and survivors trust fund in 1939, the actuarial function became increasingly important to the organization, since the actuary's office prepared an annual report on the status of the trust fund. These figures carried great authority with Congress and with academic experts who commented on social security. In making long-run estimates of the program costs, the actuaries established a number of conventions. One crucial assumption was to base cost estimates on a level average annual wage. In the postwar era, this assumption flew in the face of reality. "No economist today would maintain that the trend in wages which has been so clearly upward will suddenly become level for the next 50 years," noted two exasperated economists in 1951. The actuaries, in their defense, argued that it would be inappropriate to show a rising wage rate in combination with a static benefit formula. That would seriously understate the costs of the program. Instead, the actuaries chose to overstate the costs by, in effect, consistently underestimating the increased revenues that would come from rising wage levels.[42]

That meant that the program regularly received windfalls. In the 1940s, when total receipts increased from $368 million to nearly $3 billion, these increases in revenue failed to motivate Congress to raise benefit levels or expand the range of benefits. There was little demand, other than from the Social Security Administration, that it do so. In 1939, only 43 percent of the labor force was covered by social security; by 1949, this percentage increased to only 54. Little of the money collected in the 1940s went for benefit payments. In 1944, for example, the trust fund received $1.4 billion, and the program spent only $238 million on benefits, occasioning a large net growth in the trust fund.[43] In 1944, of course, the government needed the revenue collected for social security to finance the war effort. Although this money was in a trust fund, the government could borrow from that trust fund to pay for current expenditures. After the war, the Republican Congress halted any

[42]Charles C. Killingsworth and Gertrude Schroeder, "Long-Range Cost Estimates for Old-Age Insurance," *Quarterly Journal of Economics*, May 1951, 199–213.
[43]For the labor force data, see *Social Security Bulletin, Annual Statistical Supplement, 1984–85*, 66; for the data on receipts and expenditures, see *Annual Statistical Supplement, 1992*, 144–45.

plans to expand social security. For these and other reasons, legislators reacted to the windfall by freezing the tax rate.

Social security supporters hoped that the 1950s would be different and that part of the social security surplus created by rising wage rates would be spent on increased benefits. The fact that more people were insured by social security (the percentage of insured workers went up to 78 percent by 1960) because of the 1950 amendments provided one source of encouragement. More members of Congress had a stake in social security benefit increases in the 1950s than in the 1940s. The 1950 increase in benefit levels also made social security more attractive in the 1950s than in the 1940s, as did the newfound union and management support for the program. So, social security advocates hoped that rising wages after 1950 might occasion a benefit increase in 1952.

The irresistible aspect was that, because of rising wages, benefits could be increased without raising the tax rates already specified in the 1950 law. Cohen referred to this phenomenon as a "miracle," which made it possible to change the system "without changing the contributions of the program or impairing the actuarial soundness of the system." Hence social security became a relatively popular tax in the 1950s because the public could see tangible returns in the form of benefits that reached members of many American families. Although the Ways and Means Committee tended to favor at least a nominal increase in the rates each time there was a benefit increase, the tax seemed less burdensome as the country prospered.[44]

Members of the Ways and Means Committee, some of whom had acquired expertise in social security while working on the 1950 amendments, understood the opportunity they had in 1952 to raise benefits without any sort of tax increase. Chairman Robert Doughton (D-N.C.), who had shown little interest in social security up to this point and had made a point of blocking expansion of the program to cover farmers, decided to introduce a comprehensive social security bill. He did so largely on his initiative, although the measure was written by Ball and Cohen. This bill moved quickly through the Ways and Means Committee. Whereas it had taken a year and a half for Congress to consider the 1950 amendments, in this instance the Ways and Means Committee decided to skip hearings altogether and reported the 1952 bill out in

[44]Cohen, "Legislative History of the Social Security Amendments of 1952," 11; Cohen, "Should Old-Age Assistance Again Outpace Old-Age Insurance?"

four days. Under a suspension of the rules that allowed social security supporters to bypass lengthy proceedings in the Rules Committee, the House voted on the bill on May 19. The bill failed to pass by the necessary two-thirds margin, and most people thought that would end the matter. The very next day, however, Representative Daniel Reed, the ranking Republican on the committee, introduced another social security bill that included an increase in social security benefits. For the first time, the Republicans and the Democrats agreed on the political desirability of an increase in social security benefits, and both parties thought that such an increase would be helpful to them in an election year. Four weeks after the introduction of Reed's bill, the House voted to pass Doughton's original bill. In less than a week, the Senate Finance Committee, racing to conclude the matter before Congress adjourned for the political season, reported out a bill. On June 26, 1952, the Senate passed its version of the bill by a voice vote.[45]

In the conference committee, a snag developed. The issue concerned not the increase in social security benefits but rather the provision for a program, known as a disability freeze, that would provide a modest beginning of a social security disability program.[46] Conservatives like Senator Robert Taft (R-Ohio) accepted the fact that social security benefits could be increased without raising tax rates. They remained skeptical, however, of the desirability of extending the social security system into new realms. In time, Cohen worked out a compromise on disability. Both houses accepted this compromise on July 5, and the bill, complete with a 12.5 percent rise in benefit levels, became law on July 18, 1952.[47]

Cohen, for one, gloated over a big victory. "I believe that very few people thought we would get any legislation in 1952," he told Wickenden. "But we exploited our advantages," he continued, including "the ability to increase OASI without any tax increase." According to Cohen, "[The legislation] gets us away from the idea that OASI is a depression phenomenon and that it will be another 10 years before benefits can be increased."[48] Cohen astutely grasped the fact that the 1952 amendments were different—that they were the first of what would be a steady stream

---

[45]See Berkowitz, *Mr. Social Security*, chapter 4.
[46]See Edward D. Berkowitz, *Disabled Policy: America's Program for the Handicapped* (Cambridge: Cambridge University Press, 1987).
[47]Berkowitz, interview with Wilbur Cohen, Austin, Texas; Cohen, "Legislative History of the Social Security Amendments of 1952"; Berkowitz, *Disabled Policy*.
[48]Wilbur Cohen to Elizabeth Wickenden (August 1952), Elizabeth Wickenden Papers, Wisconsin State Historical Society.

of incremental expansions of social security, the first bipartisan endorsement of the program, the first real manifestation of the political popularity of social security. In 1952, unlike in 1939 or 1950, the bureaucrats did not need to push the politicians; instead, Congress pushed the Social Security Administration.

MEETING THE EISENHOWER CHALLENGE, 1953–1954

In 1952, with the program finally in high gear, another snag developed: Dwight D. Eisenhower's election. As matters turned out, however, even a change in political regime in both the presidency and Congress failed to halt the expansion of social security. When President Eisenhower delivered his State of the Union message on February 2, 1953, he recommended that the "old-age and survivors insurance law should promptly be extended to cover millions of citizens who have been left out of the social security system."[49] Despite this presidential rhetoric, conservatives hoped to create an alternative that would expand coverage, create a new type of social security system, and be acceptable to the president.

The main conservative proposal came from Albert Linton, an actuary who was the head of the Provident Mutual Life Insurance Company. Linton was something of a social security insider, having served on the advisory councils of 1934, 1938, and 1948. Like other conservatives, Linton objected to the tendency to expand social security benefits without making adequate provision for their long-term financing. Vague promises to raise taxes in the future would, he feared, never be realized, since Congress enjoyed spending short-term surpluses and avoided raising tax levels. The 1950 legislation, for example, called for taxes to rise in 1954, 1960, 1965, and 1970, yet Linton had little confidence that such rises would occur. Spending short-term surpluses that were the results of expanding coverage, rising wages, and the relative youth of the social security system itself, Congress would expand the system far into the future and leave future generations to face the consequences.[50]

Linton came up with a clever plan, which he offered to the Eisenhower administration and for which he even helped to create a political demand. The key to the plan was to expose all the costs of old-age pensions

[49]Eisenhower statement quoted in Wilbur J. Cohen, Robert M. Ball, and Robert J. Myers, "Social Security Act Amendments of 1954: A Summary and Legislative History," *Social Security Bulletin*, September 1954, 16.
[50]See Derthick, *Policymaking for Social Security*, 144–57.

in the present rather than in the future. That involved two major steps.
One was to collapse state welfare programs for the elderly and the federal old-age insurance program into one unit. The other was to make
coverage under the new plan universal, both for present workers and
for present retirees. All retirees would receive something, regardless of
whether they had contributed to social security or whether they were
poor. Linton chose payroll taxes as a means of financing his scheme.
First, the country would spend the surplus in the social security trust
fund. After the fund was exhausted, tax rates would be set to bring in
enough to pay for current benefits but not enough to fund a surplus. If
the tax rates were set on a year-by-year basis, there would be fewer
unanticipated revenue windfalls. If Congress wanted to expand benefits,
payroll tax rates would have to increase. According to Linton, the plan
marked an effective way to eliminate the inherent tendency toward expansion in the social security program. It was, he believed, a responsible
conservative response.[51]

Linton and others in the insurance industry sought a national referendum for their idea and found it in the form of a policy declaration
from the U.S. Chamber of Commerce. Beginning on November 15,
1952, the chamber polled its members in referendum 93 on "Social Security for the Aged." The actual proposal followed the terms of Linton's
idea. Every old person, regardless of whether he or she had ever paid
social security taxes, would be covered under social security at a minimum pension of twenty-five dollars a month, and there would be an
adjustment of payroll taxes to make current receipts and current payments equal one another. In this manner, as the publication accompa-
nying the referendum explained, the chamber hoped to institute "more
checks and balances" into the program and inhibit its growth. Whether
or not the members of the U.S. Chamber of Commerce understood the
meaning of this proposal is not clear. What is clear is that the referendum carried overwhelmingly, by a margin of 16 to 1 and with the highest vote total of all referendums in the chamber's history.[52]

[51]See M. Albert Linton to Robert L. Hogg, executive vice-president of American Life Convention (December 17, 1952), Box 26, Oveta Culp Hobby Papers, Dwight D. Eisenhower
Library, Abilene, Kansas.
[52]Elizabeth Wickenden, "Comments on Proposed Revised Policy Declaration by the United
States Chamber of Commerce on Social Security for the Aged" (December 9, 1952), Box
51, Cohen Papers; Altmeyer, *The Formative Years of Social Security*, 206; *Improving
Social Security: An Analysis of the Present Federal Security Program for the Aged and*

Like other proposals in the field, the chamber plan worked better as a general approach than as a specific guide to political action. As a practical matter, the guaranteed benefit had to be high for the package to be appealing, and as the authority Eveline Burns pointed out, the twenty-five-dollar level in the chamber plan was below the average old-age assistance payments in all but five states. Nor did the chamber plan go into detail on how benefits above the minimum level would be determined. If the entire package depended on payroll taxes, the elderly would be supported by highly regressive payroll taxes rather than by broad-based general revenues. Not only would the working population support people who had never worked, but poorer workers would bear a far greater burden than richer workers. Someone earning $100,000 would pay the same amount as someone making $3,600.[53]

Ball, Cohen, Cruikshank, and Wickenden viewed the chamber plan with particular alarm. It came at the exact moment of political transition from the Democrats to the Republicans. Like any universal pension plan, it had its inherent appeal. Just as the social security advocates had fought the Townsend plan in the 1930s, so they now found it necessary to mobilize against the Chamber of Commerce plan in the 1950s. In one case, the challenge had come from the Left, and in the other the threat derived from the Right. Yet the plans were strikingly similar calls for flat benefits, without the elaborate features of social security designed to link contributions to benefits.

Early in the administration, Federal Security Administrator Oveta Culp Hobby, whom Cohen described "as a very smart lady" and "difficult to influence," sought advice on the Chamber of Commerce plan from some outside experts.[54] This group became known as the "Hobby lobby." It was to function something like an advisory council of the sort that had met in 1938 and 1948, except that this group contained no

the *Proposal of the Chamber of Commerce of the United States* (Washington, D.C.: Chamber of Commerce, 1953), 128.
[53]Eveline M. Burns, "Comments on the Chamber of Commerce Social Security Proposals" (n.d.), Box 51, Cohen Papers; Cohen to Wickenden (August 1952), Wickenden Papers; Arthur Altmeyer, "Social Security, the Republican Party, and Eisenhower," draft manuscript for *Progressive Magazine* (n.d.), Cohen Papers.
[54]Cohen to Wickenden (February 2, 1953) and Cohen to Wickenden (March 12, 1953), both in Elizabeth Wickenden Personal Papers (in her possession). Hobby became the first secretary of health, education, and welfare as the result of the reorganization, prepared by Nelson Rockefeller and approved by President Dwight Eisenhower, at this time.

labor leaders or others who might have been sympathetic to social security. Instead, the five-person group consisted of three people associated with the insurance industry and the Chamber of Commerce (including Linton), one person from New Hampshire who was apparently selected by the presidential assistant Sherman Adams, and only one academic expert.

When Cohen and the other social security officials heard of the existence of the Hobby group early in March 1953, they were frightened and worried. The administration appeared to be taking the Chamber of Commerce plan seriously and might interpret the president's mandate to expand the system to mean that the Chamber of Commerce plan should be adopted. That was what Linton would advise. "You can see how fast the CofC boys will work," Cohen advised Wickenden in a letter that he deliberately wrote at home rather than at the office.[55]

Although Altmeyer remained in office when the Hobby lobby was appointed, he and Cohen decided that they should stay away from the initial meeting. They agreed that the best representative would be Ball. As Cohen noted, Ball already knew many members of the Hobby lobby from his work serving as staff director of the 1948 council and from his earlier work arranging seminars in social security at the American Council on Education. Ball was astute, patient, and conciliatory, and his job as a deputy director within the Bureau of Old-Age and Survivors Insurance was not in immediate danger of being made into a presidential appointment.[56]

When the Hobby lobby met on March 5, Ball quickly established himself as a de facto staff director. Before the meeting, he and Altmeyer and Cohen prepared a kit of materials and held extensive strategy sessions.[57]

Cohen and Wickenden, meanwhile, did all they could to sabotage the Hobby lobby. When Wickenden asked if she should leak the story about the limited range of the group's membership to the press, Cohen told her to wait until the group had more meetings. "Then it can really be exploited," he said. He noted that Hobby had already turned down a chance to meet with the CIO Social Security Committee. "If she also refuses the AFL, then it will make a terrific story, don't you think? My

[55] Cohen to "My dear Wicky" (March 12, 1953), Wickenden Personal Papers.
[56] Cohen to Wicky (March 1, 1953), Wickenden Personal Papers.
[57] "Report to the New York headquarters," Cohen to Wickenden, (March 7, 1953), Wickenden Personal Papers.

idea is that they will use enough rope to hang themselves."[58] Within a few days, Cohen decided that the time had come to expose the Hobby lobby in the press. He urged Wickenden to publicize the fact that Hobby had chosen not to meet with representatives of organized labor and other liberal groups.[59] Within two more days, Cohen told Wickenden that he had begun to get phone calls about the Hobby lobby.[60] In another ten days, he informed her that the criticism of the Hobby lobby had yielded definite results. By now labor leaders like Walter Reuther had sent telegrams to their senators. Under congressional pressure, Hobby announced that she would meet with labor and farm groups. In the end, Hobby extended an offer to the AFL and the CIO to join her group.[61]

When the augmented group met on April 1, 1953, it resembled nothing so much as a conventional social security advisory council, right down to the fact that Ball served as the staff director. The group soon agreed to limit its discussions to the extension of coverage. As Martha Derthick has written in her magisterial and authoritative account of social security policy: "The broadening of representation narrowed the potential range of discussion and inhibited conservative innovation. Extending coverage was the one measure on which the forces contending over social security policy could agree."[62]

On June 24, a report appeared that, far from attacking social security, simply laid out ways of extending coverage to new groups of current workers such as farm operators (rather than the groups of retired people that the chamber plan would cover). Astute readers of the report could detect Ball's hand in its composition. Once again, he had transformed a major threat to social security into an affirmation of the program. As he modestly recalled, the Hobby lobby "proved very helpful in shaping the attitude of the Eisenhower Administration . . . and bringing it toward a much more favorable attitude toward the program. This group ended up by recommending very good improvements in social security."[63] So it did, but only because of the behind-the-scenes maneuvering of Cohen,

[58]Cohen to Wickenden (March 7, 1953), Wickenden Personal Papers.
[59]Cohen to Wickenden (March 12, 1953), Wickenden Personal Papers.
[60]Cohen to Wicky (March 14, 1953), Wickenden Personal Papers.
[61]Cohen to Wickenden (March 25, 1953), Wickenden Personal Papers.
[62]Derthick, *Policymaking for Social Security*, 149.
[63]Robert Ball, oral interview with David McComb. See also Altmeyer, *The Formative Years of Social Security*, 215, and Consultants on Social Security, *A Report to the Secretary of Health, Education, and Welfare on Extension of Old-Age and Survivors Insurance to Additional Groups of Current Workers* (Washington, D.C.: Government Printing Office, 1953).

Wickenden, and Cruikshank, in addition to Ball's own diligent staff work.

As the battle over the Hobby lobby occurred, Cohen, who might be described in this period as the Social Security Administration's chief lobbyist, continued to pursue his agency's, rather than the president's, agenda in Congress. When Cohen went to see Jere Cooper, the ranking Democrat on the Ways and Means Committee, he outlined the Chamber of Commerce proposal in a way that highlighted its potential shortcomings. Cohen urged Cooper to, as he put it, "take the initiative," and he wrote a modest bill for Cooper to introduce. He noted in one of his many letters to Wickenden, "Leo Irwin (the Ways and Means Committee minority staff director) and I feel overjoyed in getting him off dead center and his agreeing to take some initiative." Cohen began to write other bills for Cooper and provided suggestions for what he called a "constructive program," which, among other things, included higher social security benefits, a $6,000 wage base, and disability insurance benefits. Although Cohen did not know how many of these suggestions Cooper would take, he resolved to continue talking with Cooper, patiently modifying the proposal until he had something Cooper would accept.[64] The striking fact about this process was that the Eisenhower administration had not officially accepted any of the items on the list, yet Cohen pushed them anyway.

Cohen also led a tortured and complicated fight in 1953 to discredit the work of the Curtis Social Security Subcommittee. At first, Cohen had hoped that there would be no Curtis Subcommittee. He hoped that if the Committee on Ways and Means decided to appoint a special subcommittee to investigate social security, Robert Kean (R-N.J.), with whom he was in close contact, would be chosen to head it.[65] Instead, Chairman Dan Reed chose Carl Curtis of Nebraska, an extremely conservative congressman who was not sympathetic to contributory, wage-related social insurance and who wanted Eisenhower to replace the Democratic holdovers at the Social Security Administration.[66]

The subcommittee and its staff followed a line that had been devel-

---

[64]Cohen to Wickenden (March 7, 1953), Wickenden Personal Papers.

[65]Cohen diary entry (February 23, 1953), Cohen Papers.

[66]Cohen, oral interview with Maclyn L. Burg, March 31, 1976, Eisenhower Library; Harold B. Hinton, "House Unit Balks President on Plea to Widen Pensions," *New York Times*, February 21, 1953, 1.

oped in a 1950 Brookings monograph on social security. Indeed, Karl Schlotterbeck, the subcommittee staff director, had written the Brookings book, which argued that social security, contrary to the claims of its supporters, was not really insurance and that the public would be better served by a plan similar to the Chamber of Commerce plan.[67]

Setting the tone for the hearings, Curtis brought a beleaguered census official to the stand on day one and made him speak from a chart headed "What We Don't Know about the U.S. Population." The exercise exposed the fact that the 1935 population projections, on which the Social Security Act was based, understated the 1950 population by ten million people.[68] The subtext of the exercise implied that expert planning, much praised by social security officials, added little to the efficient conduct of the program. A group that could not even get population trends right deserved little of the public's trust. As Curtis later charged, in a story that appeared in the *New York Times,* "The Social Security System had been seriously affected by bad guessing about the nation's growth in population."[69] It made as much sense to convert the program to a simpler, pay-as-you-go proposition as to maintain the present costly and deceptive social security program.

At the end of 1953, Congressman Curtis sent Chairman Reed a report that his staff had prepared on the subcommittee's findings. This report made the case that social security was not insurance and that the right to its assistance was "a conditional, statutory right—subject always to legislative change." After sixteen years of social security coverage, 60 percent of the aged remained without social security benefits. Those who did receive benefits would get back more than 50 times the amount they had paid into the system. The line between insurance benefits and no insurance benefits was "often a seemingly whimsical one for an insur-

[67]See Carl Curtis to Daniel Reed (December 22, 1953), Curtis Files, Cohen Papers; Lewis Meriam, Karl Schlotterbeck, and Mildred Maroney, *The Cost and Financing of Social Security* (Washington, D.C.: Brookings Institution, 1950). Schlotterbeck was the subcommittee staff director.

[68]Statement of Honorable Carl T. Curtis, Chairman, Social Security Subcommittee, Committee on Ways and Means (July 24, 1953), and Arthur E. Hess to Robert M. Ball (July 30, 1953), both in Curtis Files, Cohen Papers.

[69]See Curtis Files, Cohen Papers: U.S. House of Representatives, Committee on Ways and Means, Social Security Subcommittee, "Congressman Curtis Asks Why Facts on Social Security Are Withheld," Press Release No. 3 (August 25, 1953), and "Bad Guess Charged in Social Security," *New York Times,* October 10, 1953 (from an AP wire), which follows "Population Trends and Social Security," Press Release No. 4 (October 9, 1953).

ance program," Curtis noted, yet the public had "been misled into believing" that social security was insurance.[70]

Early in 1954, when Curtis introduced his own social security bill, he found little support for it. He proposed that federal welfare grants to dependent children and the elderly be ended in favor of a minimum grant of forty-five dollars to the aged and thirty dollars each to a widow and her child. Above this minimum, there would be wage-related benefits, funded by a 4 percent payroll tax and a new 2 percent tax on all unearned income. The plan contained some gaping political liabilities. For example, it entirely eliminated federal grants to poor families in which the father had deserted the mother. Even conservatives in the administration opposed it.[71]

In the fall of 1953, things once again fell into place for the expansion of social security. Although Altmeyer had left the government, Cohen and Ball remained. Congressman Curtis was in retreat. The Hobby lobby had endorsed the program in July, and the administration tentatively proposed the extension of coverage, along the lines of the Hobby report, in August. In September the administration agreed to the appointment of John Tramburg as commissioner of social security. The director of public welfare in Wisconsin, Tramburg, although a certified Republican, was sympathetic to social security.

The administration conducted an intensive internal review that fall to prepare a comprehensive social security bill that would be ready in January. By this time, as Cohen noted in his diary, "Mrs. H. and N. Rockefeller [the under secretary of health, education, and welfare and the future governor of New York] seemed particularly opposed to the CC plan."[72] In November Cohen reported to Altmeyer: "After much travail I think the recommendations will be on the constructive side. We have shed a lot of blood in the process but we are eating lots of red blood to make up for our loss."[73] As these comments implied, the administration decided to follow the incremental path established by the 1952 amendments. It opted for extending coverage to farm operators and other groups, for raising the average level of social security benefits by 13 percent, and for raising the tax base from $3,600 to $4,200. In addition,

[70]"Staff Memorandum: Some Major Findings" (December 23, 1953) and Curtis to Reed (December 22, 1953), both in Curtis Files, Cohen Papers.
[71]Roswell B. Perkins to the secretary (November 24, 1953), Cohen Papers.
[72]Cohen Diary entry (October 7, 1953), Cohen Papers.
[73]Cohen to Altmeyer (November 3, 1953), Cohen Papers.

the administration acquiesced in the scheduled tax increase from 3 percent to 4 percent of covered payroll.

Due in large part to the tutelage of Cohen and Ball, who were working from within the state as agents of its expansion, the administration rejected the Chamber of Commerce plan as one that would destroy the social security system. As President Eisenhower expressed the decision in a letter to the stockbroker E. F. Hutton, "It would appear logical to build upon the system that has been in effect for almost twenty years rather than embark upon the radical course of turning it completely upside down and running the very real danger that we would end up with no system at all."[74]

INTERLUDE: THE FIGHT FOR DISABILITY INSURANCE, 1954–1956

After 1954, with the principle of social security expansion firmly established, the political issue shifted to the question of establishing a disability insurance program as part of the social security system. To be sure, the issue was not new. It had figured in the social security proposals in the 1940s, in the recommendations of the 1948 advisory council, and even in the social security amendments of 1952 and 1954. The Social Security Administration and the AFL strongly supported the establishment of disability insurance as a means of providing pensions to people forced to drop out of the labor force due to a physical impairment. The Ways and Means Committee tended to support this position; never, however, had disability insurance made it through the Senate. Opposition from insurers and organized medicine prevented passage.[75]

Within the Social Security Administration, disability insurance became a real source of tension between program administrators such as Robert Ball and agency actuaries such as Robert J. Myers, who joined the agency in 1935 and who became the chief actuary in 1947. The trouble was that the actuaries, taking their cues from actuaries who worked for private insurance companies, regarded disability insurance as extremely problematic, as a difficult program in which to contain costs and predict future expenditures. Disability was more difficult to define than old age, and the actuaries tended to fear that it was an elastic concept that would

---

[74]Eisenhower to Edward F. Hutton (October 7, 1953), File 156-C, Central Files, Box 848, Eisenhower Library.
[75]Berkowitz, *Disabled Policy*, chapter 2.

respond to such factors as unemployment. Administering a disability program required federal administrators to decide just who was capable of working and who deserved a ticket out of the labor force. These problems created a sense of caution in the same actuaries, such as Myers, who enthusiastically supported the old-age and survivors insurance program. When the matter was first discussed in 1938, W. Rulon Williamson, then the agency's chief actuary, said that he could not possibly give one estimate of the cost of disability insurance and "maintain his professional dignity."[76] In 1941, Myers argued that the cost figures for old-age and survivors insurance, which possessed "a much higher degree of accuracy" than those for disability, deserved to be called estimates and that "those for disability should more properly be termed illustrations."[77]

Despite this internal friction, social security advocates pushed for the enactment of disability insurance in 1955. The efforts paid off in 1956 when Congress initiated a program of disability protection that applied to people aged fifty or older. Because of the age restriction and because the program did not provide benefits for the dependents of disabled beneficiaries (that would not come until 1960), the taxes required were relatively modest. According to the plans made in 1956, disability insurance would cost only 0.5 percent of covered payroll through 1975. In common with the rest of the program, subsequent liberalizations were funded through unexpected revenue increases, so that the rate for disability insurance remained at 0.5 percent until 1966. Beginning in that year, the volatility that the actuaries had predicted—in particular, a disturbing correlation between applications for disability insurance and a rise in the unemployment rate—began to manifest itself; as a result, the tax rate increased from 0.7 percent in 1966 to 1.5 percent in 1979.[78]

THE 1958 AMENDMENTS:
EXPANSION IN THE FACE OF MILD ADVERSITY

In the 1950s, the problems with disability insurance, problems that would occasion major political battles in the late 1970s and early 1980s, lay far in the future. The social security program continued on its course

---

[76]Wilbur J. Cohen to Arthur Altmeyer (October 13, 1938), File 025, Box 10, RG 47, Records of the Social Security Administration.

[77]Robert J. Meyers to D. C. Bronson (December 10, 1941), File 056.11, Box 20, Accession 56–533, RG 47, Washington National Records Center, Suitland, Maryland.

[78]*Social Security Bulletin, Annual Statistical Supplement, 1984–85,* 24–25.

of expansion without major interruption. In 1958 the program gained even more support with the arrival of Wilbur Mills as chairman of the House Ways and Means Committee, although social security supporters reacted warily to him at first. Cohen, at the time on a brief hiatus as a professor of public welfare administration at the University of Michigan, compared Mills with the previous Ways and Means Committee chairman and told Altmeyer, "We are likely to have more problems with Wilbur Mills."[79] Mills, a small-town lawyer from Arkansas who had been in Congress since 1942, was regarded by social security supporters as both conservative and cautious. In 1956, during the crucial legislative fight over disability insurance, for example, Altmeyer had bluntly written Cohen that he had "no confidence in Mills."[80] In 1958, with the administration taking a passive role, Mills became the single most powerful influence over social security. Whatever their true preferences, social security supporters would have to work with Wilbur Mills.[81]

Late in December 1957, Cohen advised Mills that the Eisenhower administration would not sponsor any changes in social security and that this would leave "a vacuum" that the Democrats could "step into if they want[ed] to do so."[82] In dealing with Mills, Cohen always outlined his arguments in actuarial, rather than in personal, terms. He seldom spoke about people in need. Instead, he talked about such concepts as the taxable wage base and the percentage of payrolls on a level premium basis. Mills was a tax man, the head of the congressional tax committee, and Cohen and his fellow social security advocates counseled him about tax revenues and expenditures.

Even though 1958 was a recession year without the usual large increases in the wage rate, Cohen still advised Mills that changes could be made in social security "without increasing the tax rate!" The idea was not to increase the tax rate but rather to increase the tax base, by raising the amount of a person's income on which he or she paid social security taxes. Representative Kean, the liberal Republican on the Ways and Means Committee, wanted to raise this taxable wage base from the present $4,200 to $4,800. Another technical adjustment involved changing the interest rate on the money in the social security trust fund. Taken

[79]Cohen to Arthur Altmeyer (December 27, 1957), Cohen Papers.
[80]Altmeyer to Cohen (May 17, 1956), Cohen Papers.
[81]For Cohen's views on Mills, see Cohen, oral interview with David McComb, December 8, 1968, 5, Tape 2, LBJ Library Oral History Collection, Washington, D.C.
[82]Cohen to Wilbur Mills (January 8, 1958), Cohen Papers.

together, these changes would yield, in the jargon that Mills favored, one-half of 1 percent of taxable payrolls. Mills kept his own counsel.[83]

The Ways and Means Committee held hearings on social security in June.[84] When HEW Secretary Marion Folsom testified before Mills, he said that the administration would not oppose an increase in the earnings base to $4,800. Then he proposed his own type of benefit increase. It would be temporary rather than permanent. Someone who retired before 1955 would get a raise of 8 percent; someone who retired before 1957 would get 5; someone who retired in 1957 or 1958 would get 3. Folsom promised nothing to those who would retire after 1958.

On the surface, this proposal did not appear to be bad politics. First and foremost, it could be accomplished without raising the tax rate. Folsom's proposal raised social security benefits but did not create a permanent liability for the social security trust fund. The temporary liability would disappear after those who retired in 1958 or before (and their spouses and other associated beneficiaries) died. Further, Folsom's proposal did not offend those still working, since it kept taxes low and left open the possibility that retirement benefits might someday be raised for them too.

At first Mills rather liked the idea of what came to be called a temporary increase in benefits.[85] He worried, however, that it might create dissatisfaction among those who retired between 1956 and 1958 and received less than their slightly older friends. The administration countered that the proposal was equitable, since it gave more to those who retired at a time when their wage rates were relatively low. The more recent a person's retirement, the more time the person had to work at recent, higher wage rates and, consequently, the higher the worker's so-

---

[83]Cohen to Mills (January 8, 1958) and Mills to Cohen (January 17, 1958), both in Cohen Papers.

[84]Wilbur Cohen, "Outline of Social Security Proposals for 1958" (February 9, 1958), Appendix D of Wilbur Cohen, "Materials for the Study of Factors Influencing the Social Security Amendments of 1958" (September 10, 1958), Social Work 353, Social Welfare Policy. This remarkable document, prepared for Cohen's students, gives an intimate view of the passage of the 1958 amendment and highlights Cohen's role in the process. I base my account largely on this source. A fuller and more comprehensive view is Wilbur J. Cohen, "The Social Security Amendments of 1958: Another Important Step Forward" (October 17, 1958), Subcommittee on Income Maintenance and Social Security of the Coordinating Committee on Social Welfare Research, School of Social Work, University of Michigan, and Wilbur J. Cohen and Fedele F. Fauri, "The Social Security Amendments of 1958: Another Significant Step Forward," *Public Welfare*. All are in Cohen Papers.

[85]This was called "temporary" even though the increase was permanent for those who received it.

cial security benefits, based on average wages, would be. Mills soon learned that the AFL could support a "temporary" increase of 10 percent through 1960, with no tax increase.

In time Mills changed his mind and opted for both a permanent (not a temporary) benefit increase and a tax increase. As usual, the tax increase was rather subtle in its effect. As matters stood, taxes were scheduled to rise from 4.5 percent to 5.5 percent of payroll in 1960. Mills's revision called for a rise to 6 percent in 1960. In addition, the annual maximum taxable earnings would rise from $4,200 to $4,600. In return for this change, the average monthly amount of a benefit went from $74 to $81 a month.[86]

Mills had changed his mind about the nature and financing of the 1958 social security amendments at the urging of Cohen. On July 7, Cohen talked with Mills and Staff Director Leo Irwin by phone. He told them that, contrary to the feelings of the AFL, he was not in favor of a temporary benefit increase. Cohen explained that a temporary benefit increase violated the bureaucratic axiom that the long-term costs of benefit increases must be fully financed, if necessary by writing future tax increases into the law. Dean Fedele Fauri of the University of Michigan School of Social Work, a frequent consultant to the Senate Finance Committee, had told Cohen that Senator Harry Byrd, its chairman, would never accept a benefit increase unless it was soundly financed. Cohen, for his part, emphasized what he described as "the financial integrity of the system." One reason for his insistence on putting slightly increased taxes in the law was to keep the system solvent so as to do nothing to undermine support for Medicare, which was the next major project in the extension of social security. Cohen's instincts, reinforced by the advice of his friends, told him that he could best protect his long-range interests if he argued against the temporary benefit increase and in favor of a tax increase.

Cohen talked to Mills on July 10, but Mills seemed unconvinced by his arguments. Cohen concluded his visit by walking with Mills to the Ways and Means committee room. As Cohen turned to leave, Mills said: "You know more about this than I do. You may be right. See if you can work it out." Cohen, like a salesman given a last-minute reprieve, assured Mills that he would work out the details and get back to the congressman that afternoon. Cohen, who thrived on this sort of dead-

[86]*Social Security Bulletin, Annual Statistical Supplement, 1984–1985,* 24–25, 99.

line, quickly produced a memorandum that contained much of what was subsequently enacted.

Cohen went back to see Mills. They talked in a relaxed and informal manner, and then Cohen gave Mills the memo he had prepared. According to Cohen, "[Mills] seemed impressed with my point that he shouldn't get tainted by newspaper men with the mantle of 'fiscal irresponsibility.' " He seemed on his way to accepting Cohen's notion of a tax increase. Cohen flew home, and Mills led his committee into executive session. He told them that the board of trustees, in charge of overseeing the trust fund, reported a long-range deficit in the fund. Mills, like Cohen, stressed to the members of his committee the importance of fiscal responsibility, which he defined as paying off the deficit and funding any benefit increases. These were both highly abstract concepts. As for the supposed deficit, there was enough money on hand to pay social security benefits in the short run, even though current outgo slightly exceeded current income. As even Cohen admitted, "Whether there will be an actuarial imbalance or not . . . cannot now be ascertained." As for funding benefit increases, that depended on Congress honoring its commitment to raise taxes in the future.[87]

Still, Mills believed that the appearance of fiscal propriety mattered. He wanted to retain his identity as a hard-line tax man and add to it a new identity as a defender of social security. The social security tax rise accomplished those twin goals for him. Mills spoke so fervently on the subject that Representative John Byrnes, a conservative Republican, urged that taxes be increased in 1959, rather than in 1960, as Cohen and Mills had originally proposed. Mills, in fact, got bipartisan support for his bill, which passed on July 31 by an overwhelming majority.

The 1958 amendments continued the incremental growth of social security and showed how the program could expand even in mildly adverse economic and political circumstances. Over time, the collaboration between Mills and the bureaucrats in the Social Security Administration became practiced and smooth. Although there were things on which they disagreed, such as Medicare, they nonetheless worked together to produce social security benefit increases. After 1958, therefore, the program enjoyed true bipartisan backing in Congress and at least the tacit support of the White House. The issues that arose between 1958 and 1972

---

[87]Cohen, "The Social Security Amendments of 1958: Another Important Step Forward," 17.

tended to center on extensions of the program into new areas, such as health care, rather than on the desirability of expanding the basic old-age insurance program itself. Even in the controversial health and disability field, the social security proponents eventually gained much of what they wanted.

THE ECONOMISTS REDUX: MEDICARE IN THE 1960S

Economists, who had objected to the drag that social security taxes put on the economy in the 1930s, reemerged as important critics of the program in the 1960s. For the entire decade, the tax rate remained below 10 percent, and the taxable wage base stayed below $8,000. Furthermore, the rates were never stated in that manner; instead, program officials preferred to show how much employers and employees each paid, thus reducing the stated tax rates by half. Still, the criticisms of economists mounted as social welfare, broadly defined to include expenditures on the state and local levels for social insurance, welfare, health care, and education, grew to account for 14.7 percent of GNP by 1970. (It was only 8.2 percent of GNP in 1950 and 10.3 percent of GNP in 1960.)[88]

These criticisms mattered because, in the 1960s, economists had more influence over the formation of policy than ever before. Presidents John Kennedy and Lyndon Johnson, in particular, made strong use of their Council of Economic Advisers (CEA) as a source of policy guidance. Walter Heller, an economist and the chairman of the CEA, was a favorite of both presidents. The council functioned as part of the president's own bureaucracy and could be expected to offer advice with the interests of the president, rather than a program or external constituency, in mind. If the economists represented a constituency, it might have been the economics profession itself.

Cohen, who served in both the Kennedy and the Johnson administrations, certainly understood the importance of the CEA. "In many ways," Cohen told an interviewer, "the Budget Director and the Chairman of the CEA were many times more important than the Secretary [of HEW], and I kept this in mind. They had the ear of the President many times more intimately, more frequently, and more sensitively than the Secretary did." Medicare, which fell into Cohen's bailiwick, was a depart-

[88]*Social Security Bulletin, Annual Statistical Supplement, 1984–1985,* 64.

mental concern, but economic growth was a presidential concern. Heller undoubtedly spoke to Kennedy about economic growth many more times than Cohen did on Medicare.[89]

To be sure, liberal economists of the type close to Kennedy and Johnson found much to admire in the social security program. Paul Samuelson, the noted MIT economist, wrote a laudatory column in *Newsweek* early in 1967. He said that "the beauty about social insurance is that it is actuarially unsound. Everyone who reaches retirement age is given benefit privileges that far exceed anything he has paid in." According to Samuelson, there were always more young people than old people in a growing population, and the growth in real wages, which he expected to last indefinitely, meant that "the taxable base upon which benefits rest in any period are much greater than the taxes paid historically by the generation now retired."[90] In short, the system worked, and it worked well.

At the same time, economists and social security advocates became policy rivals in the 1960s. There was an irony at work here, since Ball had a master's degree in economics and Cohen had majored in economics at Wisconsin. By the 1960s, however, the institutional economics that these program executives had studied was almost completely out of fashion. Old-fashioned labor economists, for example, became modern human resource economists. In labor economics, every bit as much as in macroeconomics, econometrics, with its often elaborate models and its efforts to quantify economic variables, held sway. As a profession, economics was no longer devoted to what might be described as political economy as much as it was to the empirical testing of econometric models. In this sense, neither Ball nor Cohen qualified as an economist.

It was not a matter of the two sides opposing one another's goals so much as inadvertent conflicts over the primacy of the goals. Economists had definite plans to use tax policy as a means of promoting economic growth; social security supporters regarded it as crucial to maintain social security taxes and to expand them to cover new projects such as Medicare. Hence, marginal disagreements between the two sides arose over macroeconomic policy. It made little sense to stimulate the economy with a tax cut, as President Kennedy eventually proposed and President Johnson enacted, and then to put a damper on the stimulus through

[89]Cohen, oral interview with David McComb, May 10, 1969, 8, Tape 5.
[90]Paul Samuelson, *Newsweek* column of February 13, 1967, quoted in Robert J. Myers, *Social Security*, 3d ed. (Homewood, Ill.: Richard D. Irwin, 1985), 355–56.

social security taxes. Economists believed it was necessary to examine each social security bill and determine the relationship of income (tax collections) and outgo (benefits paid). Social security advocates put much more emphasis on the passage of Medicare, whatever the immediate effects of the program on the economy.

Another conflict concerned the very design of the social security program. Social security supporters, who had witnessed the growth of the program in the 1950s, placed great stock in political symbolism and in the development of congressional support. They knew that they had managed to sustain what was probably the closest thing to a popular tax in America by emphasizing the close connection between payments and benefits. Economists failed to see the need for the elaborate rituals that surrounded social security, yet to the social security supporters, these rituals concerning contributions and benefits were vital. As Cohen told Johnson in 1968, people's "psychological feeling" that they paid for their own protection was the very reason why social security had been "so popular and well-accepted." By way of contrast, Joseph Pechman, Henry Aaron, and Michael Taussig, three economists who analyzed the program for the Brookings Institution in 1968, said it was appropriate to think of social security as a tax-and-transfer program. As they put it, the idea of social security as a form of insurance had "widespread acceptance and appeal." But the differences were significant, and the program was better viewed "as a system of transfers which, like any other government program, must be financed by taxes."[91]

A good example of how the latent conflicts between economists and social security supporters played themselves out concerned the establishment of Medicare in 1965. The process, which began in earnest in 1957, took many twists and turns. The measure nearly passed the Senate in 1962, gained Senate but not House approval in 1964, and finally became a key part of the Great Society legislation passed in 1965.[92] Never did members of the Council of Economic Advisers suggest that social security was an inappropriate vehicle for funding medical care. Their expertise did not extend that far into the social policy realm. Still, economists shadowed the process and even induced some modifications in the final

[91]Joseph A. Pechman, Henry J. Aaron, and Michael K. Taussig, *Social Security: Perspectives for Reform* (Washington, D.C.: Brookings Institution, 1968), 4.

[92]For the political development of Medicare, see Berkowitz, *Mr. Social Security*, chapters 10–11, James L. Sundquist, *Politics and Policy: The Eisenhower, Kennedy, and Johnson Years* (Washington, D.C.: Brookings Institution, 1968), and Theodore Marmor, *The Politics of Medicare* (Chicago: Aldine Publishing Company, 1973).

proposal. At a critical moment in the spring of 1964, for example, President Johnson turned to Cohen on an Air Force One flight and asked him whether he had discussed the Medicare bill with the economist Walter Heller and Budget Director Kermit Gordon. Cohen said he would do so immediately. In particular, Johnson wondered if the Medicare bill would put additional costs on the budget for fiscal year 1965.[93]

Later in the process, in the summer of 1964, the economists once again raised practical objections to the legislation. At this point, the House had passed a social security bill with a large benefit increase but without Medicare. The leaders of the Johnson administration were contemplating how to handle the debate in the Senate. On August 21, 1964, Gordon told Cohen that the proposals Cohen favored would withdraw funds from the economy in 1965; the already passed House proposals would boost purchasing power. Gordon said he did not want to stop what Cohen described as the "unbroken advance of the economy." To Gordon, this advance meant more than the passage of Medicare.[94]

In 1965, as the administration made final preparations for Medicare legislation under far more favorable political circumstances, the economists once again raised objections to the social security proposals. Heller was gone from the scene, but the administration economists, including Gordon and Gardner Ackley, worried that the bill would take more money out of the economy than it put in and would create a "fiscal drag" on the economy's continued growth. On March 15, Cohen, Ball, and the actuary Robert Myers spent one and one-half hours talking with the Council of Economic Advisers and other administration economists. As a result of these discussions, they agreed to lower the tax rates in the bill and to reduce the reserve funds. Mills went along with the notion of reducing the excess of collections over disbursements in calendar 1966 below what he had originally proposed.[95]

Still later in the process, HEW Secretary Anthony Celebrezze grew concerned that press criticism of the bill as a drag on the economy was a sophisticated way of derailing the passage of Medicare. Celebrezze appealed to the president for help. Johnson typically saw the matter in

---

[93]Wilbur Cohen, "Plane Ride with President Johnson to Ann Arbor, May 22, 1964," privately held by Eloise Cohen; Cohen to the secretary, May 25, 1964, Chronological Files, Cohen Papers.

[94]Wilbur Cohen, "Meeting at the White House, Saturday, August 21, 1964," privately held by Eloise Cohen.

[95]Cohen to the secretary (March 16, 1965), Box 16, Accession 69A-1793, RG 235, Washington National Records Center.

political rather than economic terms. "Please ask Ackley and Fowler [the secretary of the Treasury] to ask their friends to pipe down," the president commanded. Meanwhile, Gordon, Ackley, and Henry Fowler met with Cohen and with White House officials to negotiate a means of reducing the predicted $2.4 billion drag on the economy in 1966. One way to accomplish this result was to raise the taxable wage base and reduce the tax rates written into the bill.[96] Myers later noted, with disapproval, that the final 1965 act reduced the old-age, survivors, and disability insurance (OASDI) tax by about 0.5 percent and that the reduction was made for "economic reasons." He wrote, "This was the beginning of the use of the OASDI and HI [Hospital Insurance] programs, as to their tax income, for overall national fiscal purposes."[97]

Of course Medicare, like the other postwar components of social security, was folded into the program with a minimum of fiscal disruption. As matters stood, the tax rate for old-age, survivors, and disability insurance was scheduled to be 8.25 percent of taxable payroll in 1966. The addition of Medicare (or more properly of hospital insurance) raised the rate only to 8.4 percent of taxable payroll, along with a rise in the taxable wage base from $4,800 to $6,600. The actual 1968 tax rate, including Medicare, was actually below the rate that had been legislated in 1961 for OASDI alone. Economic growth facilitated the growth of the program, as it had in the 1950s, and made it possible to fund Medicare without major new taxes.[98] In time, Medicare, like disability, would put a great strain on social security finance; at the time, however, it seemed a relatively easy matter to use the great tax-collecting power of social security to pay for the elderly's health care. The economists encouraged the use of low taxes in the process.

PROBLEMS OF THE MATURE PROGRAM, 1965–1983

As these bureaucratic skirmishes indicated, the level of funds involved in social security had become large enough to influence the behavior of

[96]Cohen to Lawrence O'Brien (March 17, 1965), Accession 69A-1793, RG 235, Washington National Records Center; Jack Valenti to the president (April 22, 1965) and Bill Moyers to the president (April 26, 1965), both in White House Central Files, LE/IS, Box 75, LBJ Library, Austin, Texas.

[97]Myers, *Social Security*, 257–58. It should be noted that the reduction in OASDI tax rates was offset by the introduction of taxes for hospital insurance.

[98]*Social Security Bulletin, Annual Statistical Supplement, 1984–85*, 24–25; *Annual Statistical Supplement, 1992*, 14.

the economy. Economists pushed to have the social security trust funds reflected in a "unified budget" for the federal government. As Martha Derthick has explained, "Whereas the rationalizers of income support policy could win no victories at the expense of social security in the late 1960s, rationalizers of the federal budget did." Derthick notes that the adoption of the unified budget was indicative of a process by which "rival experts within the executive branch were beginning more or less regularly to look over the shoulders of social security program executives."[99]

When the problems of economic management turned from stimulating the economy to reducing inflation, social security payroll taxes became coveted as a source of revenue. In 1967, for example, the administration toyed with the idea of using a $6 billion surplus in social security as a partial substitute for higher income taxes. Another idea that was discussed concerned raising taxes in 1968 but delaying the start of benefit increases by four months. Although social security remained overwhelmingly popular, liberals, such as Senator Vance Hartke (D-Ind.), did not hesitate to denounce the administration's social security tax proposals as a "cruel hoax" designed to finance the Vietnam War. The social security tax no longer looked quite so innocent.[100]

In the 1970s, the social security program had to cope with the much more fundamental problem that real wages, contrary to Samuelson's expectations in the 1960s, would not increase indefinitely. At the same time, proposals for a guaranteed or minimum income once again became fashionable. These ideas, like the Townsend plan of the 1930s and the Chamber of Commerce proposal in the 1950s, challenged the legitimacy of social security as the nation's major form of income maintenance.

A good example of the sort of infighting that developed between liberal economists and social security officials occurred in the presidential campaign of George McGovern. Unlike Kennedy, Johnson, and Hubert Humphrey, for example, McGovern did not appear predisposed to accept Cohen's advice on social security. At the end of August 1972, McGovern made a major speech on income maintenance. Earlier in the month, a member of McGovern's staff had talked with Senator Abraham

[99]Derthick, *Policymaking for Social Security,* 169.
[100]See, for example, Frank C. Porter, "Old-Age Tax Raised by Panel," *Washington Post,* November 3, 1967, 1; Cohen to Joseph Califano (October 26, 1967), Cohen to Califano (October 30, 1967), and Cohen to LBJ (November 3, 1967), all in Box 94, Cohen Papers.

Ribicoff about what McGovern should recommend. Ribicoff, in turn, asked for·Cohen's help. As a consequence, Cohen received an invitation to attend a meeting at Robert Kennedy's house in Virginia on Sunday, August 13. Cohen went to Hickory Hill and found McGovern, in a bathing suit, surrounded by a group that, according to Cohen, contained "lots of economists." The group discussed whether McGovern should repeat his proposal of a national income payment, or "demogrant," of $1,000 per person.[101]

Writing to his friend Douglas Brown in Princeton, Cohen said that he was troubled by the influence that economists such as James Tobin of Yale and Joseph Pechman of Brookings had over McGovern. "They are not only anti-welfare (which is understandable) but, in my opinion, they are also anti–social security." Cohen believed that the social security system was "under attack from Harvard-Yale-MIT-Brookings economists" who were "relatively uninterested in differential benefits" and who attacked "the financing of payroll taxes for the program." Cohen said that these sophisticated economists resembled earlier adherents of the Townsend program. What they really wanted was a uniform national benefit, something like the demogrant that McGovern had proposed.[102]

Cohen, repeating a line of argument that ran throughout the history of the social security program, believed that the economists did not understand social security. They analyzed it as though it were an ordinary tax. As a tax, social security constituted a dubious form of social policy. It was, for example, mildly regressive, placing a heavier burden on low- and mid-income wage earners than on upper-income wage earners (although the progressive benefit formula benefited those same wage earners). Cohen, by way of contrast, regarded social security "as much more than a tax system." He noted, "This is a point that is very difficult to get the tax economists to really understand." Cohen added that he was "deeply troubled by the role that the Macro-economists" were playing "with regard to the social security system."[103]

Cohen, like Brown, believed that social security was a carefully constructed institution that redistributed income in a manner that accorded

[101]Fragment—Discussions on McGovern Presidential Campaign, 1972, Box 478, Cohen Papers, LBJ Library; Cohen to William Gorham (August 31, 1972), Box 15, Cohen Papers, Bentley Historical Library, Ann Arbor, Michigan.

[102]Cohen to J. Douglas Brown (July 31, 1972), Cohen Papers.

[103]Cohen to J. Douglas Brown (August 31, 1972), Cohen Papers.

with American behavioral norms and the norms of American political behavior. Income redistribution was difficult to achieve in America. It was necessary to accomplish this goal in a manner that did not appear to undermine work incentive. The economists, by way of contrast, simply assumed the need to end poverty and sought the most rational way of accomplishing it. Hence, Cohen put stock in things that he believed Congress was predisposed to accept; the economists welcomed what Brown described as "clever inventions." Social security was an established institution that had the blessing of Congress. The negative income tax, an idea of the time, was a clever invention.

In time, many of the economists, such as James Tobin, several other "rational" program critics, such as Stanford Ross, who served as social security commissioner for President Jimmy Carter, and some influential academics from other social science fields, such as the Harvard sociologist Theda Skocpol, came to appreciate the wisdom of Cohen's approach.[104] Although they regarded many aspects of social security as open to discussion and debate—particularly in the areas of disability, Medicare, long-term financing, and gender equity—they accepted the fact that social security was America's major antipoverty program. For example, social security helped to reduce the elderly poverty rate, defined in 1988 as an income of $5,672 for a single individual over sixty-five, from 35.2 percent of this group in 1959 to 12.2 percent in 1987.[105] In part, this intellectual reorientation was the result of the failures of the negative income tax in Congress during the 1970s. In part, it stemmed from the arrival of Ronald Reagan and the realization of just how vulnerable liberal social programs were in a conservative political regime. In part too, it came from an observation of how Congress was willing to rescue the program from a financial shortfall in 1983.

As matters stood in the late 1970s, a combination of circumstances made social security vulnerable to a downturn in the economy. Partly as a response to the criticisms of economists and partly for reasons of partisan politics, Congress opted in 1972 to index future benefit increases to the rate of inflation, rather than continuing the system of ad hoc benefit increases of the sort that Mills had done so much to nego-

---

[104]Ross engaged in spirited debates with Ball and Cohen in the late 1970s; in the 1990s, he accepted a term as president of the National Academy of Social Insurance, which Ball had organized. See Theda Skocpol, *Protecting Soldiers and Mothers: The Political Origins of Social Policy in the United States* (Cambridge: Harvard University Press, 1992).

[105]Berkowitz, *America's Welfare State*, xix.

tiate. When prices rose faster than wages, as they did in the years of the Carter inflation, a crisis developed. In 1980, for example, the benefit increase, as determined by the automatic indexing formula, was 14.3 percent, but wages went up only 9.0 percent and employment remained sluggish.[106] The effect on social security was immediate and direct. From a high of $37.8 billion in 1974, the old-age and survivors trust fund declined to a low of $19.7 billion in 1983.[107] At one point in 1983, there was the possibility that the program would not be able to meet its obligations and send out checks to beneficiaries.

Working with program loyalists such as Ball and with Reagan administration officials, Congress improvised a solution to the problem. A key part of the compromise involved a six-month delay in the cost-of-living adjustment, a delay that amounted to a permanent reduction for social security beneficiaries. Because of the 1983 amendments, a 15.3 percent tax rate that went into effect in 1990, and the small size of the depression-age cohort that began to retire in the 1990s, the social security trust funds showed an impressive rate of recovery. The old-age and survivors trust fund, for example, stood at $267.8 billion in 1991.[108] The politics of the situation began to shift toward old fears about the meaning of a large social security surplus at a time of a substantial federal deficit.

By the 1990s, social security taxes were no longer invisible to the general public, nor was the link between contributions and benefits so direct as it had once been. A system that had once approached bankruptcy lost some of its political goodwill. People once again debated the advisability of maintaining such high social security taxes at a time when economic policymakers were trying to stimulate the economy and induce a greater rate of economic growth. Yet the fact remained that social security was an undeniably important form of American taxation, one that had weathered the stagflation era, the Reagan economic reforms, and the neoliberal experiments of President Bill Clinton and had managed to grow in the process. For all of the loss of innocence in the program, social security remained America's most important form of social policy. Little indicated that the situation would change soon.

---

[106]Eric R. Kingson, *What You Must Know about Social Security and Medicare* (New York: Pharos Books, 1987), 26.
[107]*Annual Statistical Supplement, 1992*, 144.
[108]Ibid. For more on the 1983 amendments and their aftermath, see Berkowitz, *America's Welfare State*, chapter 4.

CONCLUSION:
ROOTS OF SUCCESS AND CONTEMPORARY PROBLEMS

What are we to make of this long narrative? In the first place, social security, although a considerable success as a generator and distributor of federal tax dollars, was not an inevitable triumph. It did not begin as a successful or large program. Instead, a cohort of individuals, acting on a level far below that of the president and the secretary of HEW, actively worked to make social security a success in the late 1940s and 1950s. They used prosperity and rising wages in particular as a rationale for expanding social security. By the 1960s they had developed for the program a convincing rationale in which they argued, in effect, that social security should be the nation's income-maintenance program of choice because it enjoyed political acceptance. The key laws that marked the triumph of social security were passed in 1950, 1952, and 1954, even though the program itself began in 1935. The program was a creature of prosperity, not depression.

The very size and success of the program furthered its expansion. As a tolerated tax program and one whose scope and reach enabled it to generate large amounts of revenues as the economy grew, social security became an important vehicle through which to fund social projects, such as disability protection and Medicare for the elderly. Often, the creation of these new projects, which were very different from old-age insurance in terms of their design and means of operation, created overt conflicts within the organization and even among program supporters. Actuaries, trained to be wary of projects whose future costs could not be accurately predicted, expressed concern over disability insurance and Medicare. Wilbur Mills, a strong program supporter, nonetheless developed reservations about Medicare. Despite these conflicts, the popularity of the program allowed these new projects to be created with the same nominally low tax rates as the rest of social security.

At the same time, the size and success of the program eventually attracted the attention of those with an interest in tax policy, notably macroeconomists who worked in the Council of Economic Advisers. In the 1960s, these economists represented a new generation of rational policy analysts who failed to appreciate the many political compromises embedded in the program. Politicians like Lyndon Johnson hoped to use the expertise of the economists to maintain prosperity and to use the expertise of the social security advocates to create Medicare, one of the key projects of the Great Society. Even though the two groups were on the same side, working for the same boss, they often disagreed with one another over the primacy of expanding social security or maintaining prosperity.

By the 1980s, many of the rational policy analysts came to appreciate the political success of social security and the strong redistributional effects that were the result of its progressive benefit formula and its general tendency to redistribute money toward the elderly and the disabled. If these groups were not perfect proxies for the poor, they were nonetheless the best that the political system could provide.

Historians, who often lament the imperfect workings of social security, have done little to explore its history.[109] This chapter has highlighted the politics of social security in the 1950s in an effort to illustrate the events that led to the emergence of social security as America's largest social welfare program. If nothing else, this history suggests that Americans have historically tolerated taxes reflecting a shared social purpose but that even these taxes can reach a threshold that threatens to undermine the enterprise the tax supports. Whether the success of social security is an artifact of the postwar era and whether social security will now be viewed as just another tax are major questions that social policymakers will answer in the brief interlude before the retirement of the baby boom generation tests all of the resilience of the program. Whatever the interpretation that the historians ultimately apply, the development of social security stands out as an important story in the financing of the American state.

[109]Linda Gordon, an influential historian, has recently written, "Social Security was shaped by racist conspiracy." Gordon, "Welfare Reform," *Dissent,* Summer 1994, 325.

5

The fiscal revolution in America, part II: 1964–1994

HERBERT STEIN

My 1969 book, *The Fiscal Revolution in America,* is the story of the change in American fiscal policy between 1932 and 1962. The change was epitomized in the difference between Herbert Hoover's recommendation of a tax increase in 1932 during a serious recession and John F. Kennedy's recommendation of a tax reduction in 1962 when the budget was in deficit and the economy was in recession, or at least was weak. I interpreted this change as the triumph of what I then called "domesticated Keynesianism."

I use the word "triumph" to mean only that this policy had, I thought, become accepted national policy. I did not mean to suggest that the policy had in fact succeeded in overcoming the problems to which it was addressed. There were people at the time who did believe that the policy had triumphed in the sense that it had demonstrated its ability to achieve and maintain high employment, stability, and rapid economic growth. This belief was best reflected in the December 31, 1965, edition of *Time* magazine, which had a picture of John Maynard Keynes on its cover and celebrated the victory of Keynesianism.

In 1965–67, when I was writing the book, it was still too soon to judge whether the policy had triumphed in the sense of achieving its economic goals. Anyway, to make such an evaluation would have been beyond my capacities as an econometrician. In fact, it is fair to say that subsequent empirical studies have not revealed whether the fiscal policy of the Kennedy years did succeed or would have succeeded if continued. In what I am now writing here about the course of fiscal policy since the Kennedy years, I do not try to evaluate the success of the policy

194

actually followed; rather, I concentrate on discussing what changes came about and how. It may seem surprising, or even ironic, to say that one can explain the evolution of fiscal policy without reference to the effects of the policies pursued. But I believe that to be the case. Decisions about policy did not seem to emerge from evidence about what had worked or failed. In fact, we never knew very reliably what had worked or failed.

According to the "domesticated Keynesianism" that I thought had triumphed in 1962, tax rates would be set high enough to balance the budget (or yield a moderate surplus) when the economy was operating at high employment. If this was done, the budget would automatically go into deficit when the economy was below high employment and into surplus (or a larger surplus) when the economy was operating above high employment. The automatic variations in the surplus position would be accepted as helping to stabilize the economy, and there would be no attempt to offset these variations. At the same time there would be no attempt to supplement these automatic variations by discretionary changes of tax schedules or expenditure programs unless the departure from high employment was of great magnitude. The relevant budget for this purpose was the "cash-consolidated" budget, which included the receipts and expenditures of the trust accounts, mainly social security, along with the transactions of what was more conventionally called "the Government." A departure from the rule of keeping taxes high enough to balance the budget at high employment might be justified in the case of a large nonrecurring expenditure.[1]

This kind of policy had been most precisely articulated in 1947 in a statement, "Taxes and the Budget: A Program for Prosperity in a Free Economy," which I had drafted for the Research and Policy Committee of the Committee for Economic Development. This statement had been endorsed by the Douglas Subcommittee of the Joint Economic Committee of Congress in 1950. It was more or less explicitly adopted by the

---

[1]What I call "domesticated Keynesianism" is sometimes called "commercial Keynesianism." I think that is misleading. It is true that the most prominent articulation of the policy came from a group of businesspeople (the Committee for Economic Development), but they were businesspeople outside the mainstream of the business community. In fact, the more orthodox business organizations initially rejected the idea. The idea originated with economists, mainly connected with the University of Chicago, some of whom had espoused the idea of a stabilizing fiscal policy before John Maynard Keynes wrote his *General Theory of Employment, Interest, and Money* (1936) but who objected to what they considered the extreme, unrealistic, and shortsighted applications of the idea by Keynes's more enthusiastic American followers. I use the word "domesticated" to mean that the wilder aspects of Keynesianism were removed.

administration of Dwight Eisenhower. And when the Kennedy administration proposed a large tax cut in 1962, although the conventional budget was in deficit, it justified the move on the ground that the cash-consolidated budget would be in substantial surplus if the economy were operating at high employment. I took that as definitive evidence of the triumph of "domesticated Keynesianism."

Obviously, this interpretation of the history had a self-serving element in it for me. I identified myself with the new policy and was pleased to be able to report that it had "triumphed." It not only had triumphed over the traditional budget balancers but also had triumphed over the traditional Keynesians who believed in flexible management of the budget to achieve high employment with no inhibitions about balancing the budget and with no doubt of their ability to do the managing successfully. But the new policy had triumphed over these traditional views by preserving what seemed most important and practical in each and discarding what was not. That is where the word "domesticated" Keynesianism came in. The policy would synthesize what was possible in the use of the budget for short-run stabilization with what was useful, or at least strongly imbedded in popular attitudes, about balancing the budget.

In this chapter I propose to review the course of fiscal policy in the thirty years since the end of *The Fiscal Revolution in America*. I cannot tell the story with the amount of detail and documentation found in my earlier book. Essentially, I shall tell how the story looks to one who lived through those years as a participant and close observer and who had written the earlier book. I give a disproportionate amount of space to the administration of Richard Nixon, not because it was unique but because that is the period about which I may be able to contribute the most information.

Before I begin the chronological narrative, I will give a bird's-eye view of what I think has happened to fiscal policy in the past thirty years. This bird's-eye view will control the story I tell. I might as well admit this at the start so that the reader will be better able to follow where I am going.

The idea that domesticated Keynesianism had become the accepted national policy by 1964, when the Kennedy-Johnson tax cut was passed, was wrong and naive. From here, that action does not look like the end of an evolution toward "rationality" but merely looks like one episode in a history that was, and still is, far from completed. There were several reasons why the 1964 policy was not a stable resting place.

1. The Keynesians, who were important in the Kennedy-Johnson administration and who were to be important in and out of government for many years thereafter, did not really believe in the domesticated part of the policy. When the Committee for Economic Development (CED) came forth with its policy of balancing the budget at high employment, the "true" Keynesians—Walter Heller, for example—said that this was a pretty good idea for a group of businessmen but that it did not embody the real gospel. Later, in office with President Kennedy, they used the language of the high-employment budget, and pointed to the fact that the high-employment budget was in balance, to justify the tax cut to those who were assumed to care about balancing something. But they never accepted high-employment balance as a rule of policy, and they abandoned the recourse to it when it gave signals they did not want to follow.

2. The policy of balancing the budget at high employment left many questions open, even given the acceptance of the basic strategy:

a. Does "balancing the budget" mean literally zero surplus or, as the CED had said, a "moderate" surplus, and if the latter, what does that mean quantitatively?

b. How high is "high employment"?

c. Since the budget position depends not on the rate of employment but on the level of national income, "high employment" being only a stand-in for something like "potential" or "equilibrium" real national income, how is that level of national income to be calculated?

d. Since the budget position will be influenced by the price level and the rate of inflation, what is the price level or inflation rate at which the budget is to be balanced?

e. Which among several possible definitions of "the budget" is relevant for the purpose of this rule?

f. How is the "extraordinary" departure from high employment, justifying the extraordinary use of discretionary budget measures, to be identified?

g. What discretionary action, and how much, is to be taken in the extraordinary case?

h. If the budget is not initially at its desired position—for example, if there is a deficit in the budget when the economy is actually at high employment or above—on what path is the desired position to be achieved?

3. The standard compensatory Keynesian budget policy, which makes no reference to budget-balancing as a goal, avoids some of the foregoing problems but has many problems of its own. Outstanding among them is the reliance on continuous short-run forecasting that the high-employment budget-balance policy was designed to avoid.

4. In the mid-1970s the economy ran into a period of unusually high unemployment alongside unusually high inflation—a condition then called stagflation. This accentuated the problem, already noted, of defining the high-employment conditions at which the budget should be balanced. It further complicated the difficulty of carrying out a compensatory policy because even the direction in which policy should try to push the economy was unclear.

5. Until the latter part of the 1970s, stabilization of the economy at a level close to its potential, without inflation, was the dominant goal of fiscal policy in its macroeconomic sense—that is, having to do primarily with the size of the deficit or surplus. But concern then began to rise about the evident slowdown in the growth of productivity and its implications for the long-run growth of the economy. This created another goal—the acceleration of growth—that might conflict with and certainly complicated the devotion of fiscal policy to the stabilization goal. For one thing, policymakers needed to ensure that measures taken to affect the economy in the short run did not prejudice the later adherence to policies that would promote growth.

6. The high-employment budget-balance policy, as enunciated by the CED and others, assumed that there was a strong public attachment to the idea that balancing the budget was the normal and proper thing to do. Logically and pragmatically, the CED kind of policy did not require that the budget be balanced at high employment. It required only that the balance or deficit at high employment be constant. This constant was set at zero (or, in the specific CED case, a small surplus) partly to make the idea more acceptable to traditionalists and partly in the expectation that public sentiment was more likely to enforce adherence to that rule than to any other.

After the government had run several years of large deficits, beginning in 1982 in the administration of Ronald Reagan, the notion that a balanced budget was the normal condition became hard to sustain. And the notion that it was the proper condition also became hard to sustain when those deficits had been generated by allegedly the most conservative administration since that of Calvin Coolidge. Although the rhetoric of budget-balancing remained, the idea became less and less effective as an anchor for fiscal policy. There have been attempts to reestablish this anchor by enacting a constitutional amendment requiring a balanced budget, but at this writing the attempt has not succeeded.

7. Most important, all the "aggregate" strategies suffered from a failure to recognize the nature of the instruments by which they would have to be implemented. This was equally true of traditional budget-balancing, high-employment balance, and the policy of continuous adaptation of the budget surplus or deficit to achieve an aggregate economic target such as full employment. They all assumed that the decision about the size of the surplus or deficit was superior to other budget decisions and that these other budget decisions, or enough of them, could be made to conform. These other decisions were decisions about tax rates and expenditure programs. The aggregate policy assumed that these "lower-level" decisions, or enough of them, were neutral, value-free counters that could be freely put on the scales of the budget, or taken off, to achieve the desired aggregate budget position. But of course, that was not the case. These "lower-level" decisions were not value-free counters. They were pounds of flesh to taxpayers and beneficiaries of government programs and could not be put on the scales of the budget without shedding many drops of blood. Beyond the interests of particular taxpayers and beneficiaries, these specific tax and expenditure decisions had microeconomic effects of significance to the whole economy. Moreover, these counters, which were to be put on the scales or taken off for short-run effects, developed lives of their own— constituencies that counted on them—and they could not be readily removed. In the macroeconomic textbook, the desired balance in the budget is achieved by the management of variables called "T" and "X." But these are symbols for real things, not only taxes and expenditures but taxes on particular people and expenditures for particular people, things about which these people feel strongly—and with good reason. These variables resist manipulation for the sake of achieving the aggregate goals.

The story I told in *The Fiscal Revolution* was the story of the contest among three versions of budget-balancing: the traditional version, the high-employment version, and the thoroughly Keynesian version. The story of the past thirty years is dominated by the decline of all of those budget-balancing strategies and the resistance of the specific instruments of budget policy to any general rules. The deficits we ran in those years, especially in the Johnson years and the Reagan-Bush years, were not determined by any of the rules of budget-balancing—not even by the Keynesian one. They were determined by the unwillingness of policy-makers to subordinate their desires for specific tax and expenditure programs to any aggregate goal. All of these factors interacted. Concern with specific tax and expenditure programs was able to resist constraint by aggregate goals for the budget because the theories on which the aggregate goals rested had come to seem less valid and less relevant to changing national conditions and priorities than they had earlier.

I have previously described this story as the "disintegration" of fiscal policy.[2] From a certain point of view—the point of view of, say, 1965—it was disintegration. It could be described as resulting from the ignorance or shortsightedness or partisanship of policymakers. But that would be unfair. The considerations that stood in the way of budget-balancing were perfectly legitimate. If we are considering whether to reduce the budget deficit by, say, $50 billion, it is not only legitimate but logically necessary to ask whether reducing the deficit is more valuable than spending $50 billion on defense or spending $50 billion on aid to the poor or cutting tax rates by $50 billion. And it is entirely possible that a well-informed, farsighted answer would be that there is no possible budget action less valuable than reducing the budget deficit. I am not saying that this was the correct answer all the time during the past thirty years or that the answer resulted from an explicit process of cost-benefit analysis. I am saying only that failure to conform to any of the rules about budget-balancing is not necessarily evidence of the ignorance or irresponsibility of politicians. It is at least partly evidence that budget policy has more consequences and objectives than are taken into account by budget-balancing rules.

This tension between aggregate rules and the specific measures needed to implement them has always been present in some degree, and budget procedures of various kinds have been proposed or adopted to deal with it. Until recently these budget reforms have been aimed at forcing the specific tax and expenditure measures into conformity with some pre-

[2]Herbert Stein, "Budget Imperatives," *American Enterprise*, March–April 1993.

determined aggregate goal, either for the size of the deficit (traditionally zero) or for total expenditures and revenues. We still use the rhetoric of that approach. But that is not where we really are today. We have some loose and shifting notions about the acceptable size of deficits. But beyond that we are adapting the decision about the grand totals to the decisions about the specific measures. We recognize, although not very explicitly, that the decision about the size of the deficit, like any other decision about the budget, is a decision with its own costs and benefits and that it must be balanced with these other decisions. For example, when President Bill Clinton recommended a budget with a deficit of $200 billion for fiscal 1999, that was not because he had first determined that $200 billion was the proper deficit for that year. In fact, although he made many claims for the benefits of deficit reduction, he never explained why the proposed deficit for fiscal 1999 was $200 billion rather than $250 billion or $150 billion. It can be inferred that he chose this figure because, after he had looked at all the tax and expenditure decisions that would be required to make the deficit a different number, he had decided that a combination of tax and expenditure decisions that yielded a deficit of $200 billion was the best he could do.

In what follows I shall try to describe the main episodes in the history of the fiscal policy by which we got from the 1960s to the 1990s.

THE JOHNSON ADMINISTRATION

The policy of functional finance—of adjusting the aggregate stance of the budget to the estimated requirement for high employment and price stability—was tested by the Vietnam War. In 1965, before our engagement in the war became expensive, the administration of Lyndon Johnson was still basking in the success of the 1964 tax cut. The Council of Economic Advisers (CEA) described the experience as demonstrating the effectiveness and feasibility of flexible use of fiscal policy to achieve stability and growth. Output was rising, and unemployment was falling. Unemployment was still at about 5 percent, but that was attributed to the delay of Congress in not enacting the tax cut until early 1964. There was little doubt, in the thinking of the council, that the same policy could boost the economy up to its full-employment orbit. The budget was in deficit, but on a full-employment basis it was in surplus. So the president proposed a topping-off dose of fiscal stimulus to get the economy up to full employment. Excise taxes would be reduced and social security benefits raised. The administration would remain alert to the possible need for additional stimulus. Nothing was said about the possible need for less. The president and his economic advisers showed complete confidence in their ability to manage this fine-tuning.

There was little complaint about this attitude, as long as it implied only the use of some discretion in giving people tax cuts or benefit increases. But one warning is worth noting. It came from Senator William Proxmire (D-Wisc.), who was a member of the Joint Economic Committee. He appended these comments to the majority opinion of the committee in February 1965:

The less than 1 year that has elapsed since the Revenue Act of 1964 became effective represents an insufficient period for appraising that measure as "an outstanding success" as the majority reports.

The full fiscal effect will take years to measure. What happens to the price level and employment in 1966, and subsequently, will be a consequence of the Revenue Act of 1964 more important than what has happened to date.

. . . The report's assumption that the final case for the 1964 tax cut has now been established would seem to urge the Congress to a policy of deliberate, planned Federal deficits whenever unemployment is above 4 percent regardless of how well the economy is moving without such a stimulus.

If the philosophy espoused in this report takes hold we may kiss goodby to balanced budgets in our lifetime and say a big hello to national debts of astounding proportions and to a steady and increasing inflation.

. . . Few, if any, economists from government, business or academia seem interested in exploring the full implications of the tax cut which they now seem to feel is the sure, proven, economic elixir—the new economic miracle drug—that will guarantee employment for all, profits for almost all and, of course, elections for all incumbents who go along.

Within the past few weeks Republicans in Congress seem to have walked away from their traditional role as advocates of "fiscal soundness" and balanced budgets. They are now engaged in offering alternative spending plans to the administration's proposals that would cost far more: for medical care for the aged (without providing any pay-as-you-go financing basis); a school aid proposal destined to cost three times as much as the administration's proposal ($5 billion compared to $1.3 billion, according to the Wall Street Journal of March 9, 1965) and general resistance to such administration economy moves as the closing of veterans' hospitals and agricultural research stations.

But here's the main reason why the Federal spending boom is ticking toward explosion: almost all of the newly proposed education, housing, welfare programs will cost more and in some cases many times more a few years in the future.

Combine all this with the happy political medicine of regular, fat tax cuts.

Result: expanding future deficits will be rushing on us and with virtually no political or economic opposition to temper them in view.[3]

But there were not many such alarms sounded. On the contrary, this was a time of great confidence that under the guidance of a defunct economist, Keynes, we had discovered the prescription for permanent full employment and rapid economic growth. But behind the scenes, the difficulty of filling the prescription was beginning to appear.

In December 1965 the chairman of the Council of Economic Advisers, Gardner Ackley, raised the question with President Johnson of recommending a tax increase in the budget to be submitted the following month. The rising costs of the Vietnam War and the signs of some increase in inflation pointed in that direction. But the president resisted the suggestion. His resistance was not based on economic grounds, on the idea that a tax increase was unnecessary for economic stabilization. It was based on the president's belief that if he proposed a tax increase, Congress would take the opportunity to force him to accept a cut in expenditures as a price of agreement. Both the Vietnam War and his new social programs, especially the latter, had their enemies in Congress, who would have insisted on cuts there instead of or in addition to tax increases.

Johnson preferred to save the expenditure programs he wanted even if that meant departing from what seemed the optimum budget policy from the standpoint of economic stability. He did propose some acceleration of individual and corporate income-tax payments, without an increase of tax liabilities, and the temporary retention of some excise tax rates that had been scheduled for reduction. But no one thought that was enough to satisfy the requirements of a stabilizing budget policy.

In its January 1966 annual report, for the first time in five years, the CEA did not present a chart or an estimate of the full-employment budget. At the time the unemployment rate was 4.1 percent, very close to the 4 percent standard that had been used as a measure of full employment, and the rate was declining. There was no longer any cover for actual deficits to be obtained from referring to the full-employment deficit.

[3]"Supplementary views of Senator Proxmire" in *Report of the Joint Economic Committee, Congress of the United States, on the January 1965 Economic Report of the President with Minority and Additional Views* (Washington, D.C.: Government Printing Office, 1965), 47–48.

The report did say that both the actual budget and the full-employment budget would be approximately in balance in the fiscal year 1967. This raised an issue that I later explored further with Arthur Okun, a member of the CEA, in private correspondence. The issue was how to treat inflation in the calculation of the full-employment surplus. Suppose that 4 percent unemployment is the standard for full employment and that the budget would be in deficit at 4 percent unemployment and a given price level. If the price level then rises, and unemployment remains at 4 percent, the deficit will diminish and a budget surplus may emerge because receipts will rise more than expenditures. Even if tax rates are flat or completely indexed for inflation, receipts will rise as much as the price level, whereas expenditures will not. For example, interest on the debt will rise only after a long lag. But in the usual case, with a progressive tax rate system that is not indexed for inflation, receipts will rise even more than inflation, and the decline of the deficit or the rise of the surplus will be even larger. Should we say, in that situation, that no tax increase is required or even that a tax reduction is permitted? That would negate the force of the automatic reaction of the budget as a stabilizer against inflation. The anti-inflation argument would suggest that the rule should be to balance the budget at high employment and the price level as it was before the inflation occurred. But if inflation does occur and the price level remains elevated for some time, the attempt to balance the budget at a price level of a period some years earlier seems unrealistic. It would put downward pressure on output and employment. As a matter of policy, we seem to have accepted the fact that whereas we will try to reduce rates of inflation, we will not try to reduce the level of prices, once it has risen. This suggests that we should accept the new, higher price level as the basis for calculating the full-employment surplus.

In 1966 and 1967 I thought that the administration was deluding itself and us by claiming that its fiscal policy was adequate because the high-employment budget was in balance, even though the balance was being achieved by inflation. That was the burden of my correspondence with Okun at the time. The issue was not resolved then. When I was chairman of the CEA we wrestled with the issue again, in our annual report of 1974, to which I shall return later, but we did not resolve it then either.

But the decisions of 1966, 1967, and 1968 did not depend on such niceties. Although the administration economists did claim that the full-employment budget was in balance, that was for the benefit of the few people (like me, I suppose) who cared about balancing the full-employment budget. It was not their way of calculating the desired budget position. They were relying on a more pragmatic, ad hoc calculation of the budget policy that would yield the best short-run economic results. And President Johnson was not relying on, or following, these calculations either. He was debating whether he could get a tax increase without giving up some of his preferred expenditure programs, and he concluded that the answer was negative.

He was probably right in this conclusion. Discussion at the time showed both a common concern that the budget position might be inflationary and a certain willingness to do something about it. But it showed a sharp division about what to do. Many in Congress and in the intellectual community shared the president's belief that the increase of federal expenditures for social purposes was absolutely essential and should not be sacrificed to pay for the costs of the Vietnam War. The comments of the majority of the Joint Economic Committee in February 1966 reflect this view in language that could just as well have been written in 1994. Referring to the budgeted amounts for "Great Society" programs, their report said:

Against this very minimal increase is the need for vast public investment. Our educational system has been undernourished for a long time and requires substantial improvement at all levels. We neglect it at the risk of cheating the generations to come. In spite of our material wealth, 32 million Americans live below a minimal poverty line, and millions of people are lacking sufficient skills to work effectively in our economy. The massive physical restoration of our cities, our land, and our lakes and rivers will eventually require outlays of billions if the job is done properly. Of course, the job does not have to be done all at once, nor should it be financed only by Federal funds. Nevertheless, it is obvious that the present Federal expenditures are merely a first stage of a growing investment, both public and private, in the development of human resources and the improvement of our environment. It is the obvious direction that the course of investment must take if we are to achieve our own destiny.

In the circumstances, to speak of our proposed rate of progress in 1967, minimal as it is, as an inflationary threat or as a luxury in view of our involvement in Vietnam, is misleading and unrealistic. The committee believes that we can do no less than is proposed in dealing with our domestic deficiencies and that, in fact, we cannot delay doing more.[4]

[4]"Report on the January 1966 Economic Report of the President" in *Report of the Joint Economic Committee, Congress of the United States, on the January 1966 Economic Report of the President with Minority and Supplementary Views* (Washington, D.C.: Government Printing Office, 1966), 15.

So the majority on this committee, that is, the Democrats, were ready to raise taxes. Indeed, without a proposal from the president, they wanted Congress to enact a standby tax increase that would go into effect later, when approved by a congressional joint resolution and signed by the president. The Republicans, of course, were firmly opposed to all this. Recognizing the need for fiscal restraint, they wanted to cut or hold back expenditures—"low priority" or "nonessential" expenditures, meaning just the ones Johnson cared for most. In this attitude they were joined by the business and financial community, although the CED showed some willingness to prepare for the possible need to raise taxes.

But it was not the expected opposition of the Republicans and business that deterred Johnson. It was the opposition of a branch of the Democratic Party in Congress, led by Wilbur Mills, chairman of the House Ways and Means Committee. Mills had been a leader of the bloc that in 1963–64 had held up the Kennedy-Johnson tax bill until they got what they wanted, which was the elimination of most of the revenue-raising and tax-reform features of the bill and a lid on spending. Mills would be the key to congressional support for Johnson's budget policy.

In December 1965 or January 1966 Johnson met with Mills. Ackley later described this meeting:

I was at a meeting with Wilbur Mills—and I think only Wilbur from the Congress—in which LBJ put the question to Wilbur as to what he thought would be the desirability or the feasibility of a tax increase. I don't remember with absolute clarity what Wilbur said about the necessity or the appropriateness, but I do remember that he said absolutely it was a political impossibility, with no chance of getting a tax bill through the Ways and Means Committee. His answer was absolutely clear-cut: "A tax increase is out of the question."[5]

Johnson was especially reluctant to push the tax issue in 1966 because he still had the Democratic Congress that had come into office with him in 1964 and that he felt he could count on to support his social programs. He did not want to risk missing that opportunity by throwing the divisive issue of a tax increase on the table. After the 1966 election, he was more willing to consider a proposal to raise taxes. But by that time the economy was cooling off and his economists were less eager for a tax increase.

The economic situation gave Johnson an excuse to put off taking the

[5]Edwin C. Hargrove and Samuel A. Morley, eds., *The President and the Council of Economic Advisers* (Boulder, Colo.: Westview Press, 1984), 250–51.

medicine. In an exercise of fine-tuning that now looks naive, the president proposed a 6 percent tax surcharge on individual and corporate incomes, to take effect on July 1. The rationale was that the economy would be weak in the first half of the year and so could not stand a tax increase, but that it would be strong in the second half, and in 1968, and so would need a tax increase. As Okun later said, the administration economists were claiming an ability "to see around corners." But the proposal also assumed that the private sector could not see around corners. That is, private individuals and corporations would not curtail their investments and expenditures in the first half even though they could see a tax increase coming later in the year.

In fact, the economy did pick up in the second half of the year, but Johnson did not get the tax increase by July 1 or by December 31 either. The Ways and Means Committee, under Mills's leadership, did not begin hearings on the tax increase until September, and on October 3 it voted to suspend action on a tax increase until the president and Congress reached agreement on expenditure cuts.

Starting in November 1967 and continuing until May 1968, the administration and Mills engaged in bargaining about how much of an expenditure cut would be needed to get approval of a tax increase. Finally, in June 1968 a revenue act was passed and signed; it mandated a cut of $6 billion in expenditures below the budget for fiscal 1969. (That would be about 0.6 percent of GNP, or the equivalent of about $40 billion in the 1994 budget.)

The Johnson experience of 1967–68 is the story of a budget policy that conformed to all the aggregate standards but that had great difficulty in adoption anver did get adopted in the form the president proposed. A reduction of the deficit was called for by the old-fashioned standard of balancing the budget, by the standard of balancing the budget at high employment, and by the standard of ad hoc adjustment to the requirements of economic stabilization. Hardly anyone disagreed with that, although some were doubtful that these standards made the tax increase as imperative as the president maintained. There was some skepticism about the economic forecast on which the tax increase was justified. Also, some questioned whether a tax increase announced to be temporary would have the desired effect in holding down spending by consumers and businesses.[6]

---

[6] I discussed the case for the tax increase in an article in *The Reporter*, October 19, 1967.

The case for the tax increase on aggregate economic grounds was not so compelling as to require members of Congress to subordinate their own contrary interests. Passage of the tax increase was held up for a year and a half after the president asked for it and for two and a half years after his advisers thought it was appropriate. It was held up by disagreements over the specifics of the measures to achieve the aggregate results. There were three factions: Republicans and conservative Democrats who wanted to use the occasion to hold down the new social programs; liberals, mainly Democrats, who did not want to vote to finance the Vietnam War; and the president, with supporters in Congress, who did not want to give up either the war or the social programs.

The tax increase not only was delayed but also was supplemented by a ceiling on expenditures. The president's economists thought the combination was "overkill"—more fiscal restraint than the economy could bear. The Federal Reserve thought so also and moved to offset the deflationary effect of the budget package with a dose of monetary expansion.

The difficulty of implementing the administration's fiscal policy from 1965 to 1968 intensified the interest of economists and some others in the idea of a fiscal "magic bullet." This was a neutral, probably temporary tax change agreed upon in advance to be put into effect by some expedited procedure when circumstances justified it. The neutrality of the change, which might be an across-the-board change of income-tax rates, and the prior agreement were expected to eliminate the need for bargaining when the time came for implementing it and were expected to prevent the tax action from being encumbered by irrelevant and possibly counterproductive legislation. Suggestions to this end were made during this period by the Council of Economic Advisers, the Joint Economic Committee, the Committee for Economic Development, and several economists. I made such a proposal and explained the reasons for it in an essay in *Agenda for the Nation* published in 1968.[7] But these

---

[7]This essay, which had been written well before the 1968 election, was published after the election and after I had been named one of Nixon's economic advisers. Some journalists speculated that the idea would be an element of Nixon's policy. But in fact it was not, and my colleagues and I at the Council of Economic Advisers, being now more aware of the real political world, made no effort to promote it. The difficulty was not only the continuing one of the balance of power between the president and Congress. There was the added obstacle of the hostile relations between Nixon and the Democratic Congress, relations that made it quixotic to think that Congress would give him the power to change tax rates. Anyway, the effort to implement the immediately necessary budget policy left little room or energy for longer-run reforms. Herbert Stein, "Unemployment, Inflation,

ideas bore no fruit. Congress had no interest in giving up its ability to get concessions from a president when he wanted approval for a change of taxes.

By 1968 the New Fiscal Policy—the policy of Keynes, Kennedy, and Heller and the policy that had seemed so triumphant four years earlier— was clearly in decline. As I said at the time:

> My general thesis is that we now stand near the intersection of two trends. One is a trend of rising general acceptance of the modern textbook fiscal policy as the conventional wisdom of the times. . . . The other is a trend of declining confidence among students in the relevance and utility of the New Fiscal Policy and declining acceptance of its compelling force by policy-makers. . . . As a result, while the New Fiscal Policy has become the standard doctrine by which we rationalize fiscal decisions, we are passing through or away from that policy as a determinant of the decisions.[8]

The problem was that economists could not reliably calculate the unique best fiscal policy and that partly, but not only, for this reason, the decision-making politicians would not follow the advice of the economists. Their unwillingness to follow was not, or not only, the result of ignorance or greed. It was also due to the fact that the politicians had perfectly respectable objectives that were not the same as those the economists took into account.

The decline of the New Fiscal Policy did not mean the revival of traditional budget-balancing or adherence to the policy of balancing the budget at high employment. Most of the difficulties of the New Fiscal Policy were the difficulties of any aggregate rule of fiscal policy. So we were left at the end of the Johnson administration with no clear and generally accepted guidance for the management of total expenditures and revenues and of the relation between them.

THE NIXON ADMINISTRATION

Nixon came into office with a pragmatic attitude toward fiscal policy. He seemed to recognize, or believe, that the idea of balancing the budget had public appeal, but he was by no means dogmatically attached to

and Economic Stability," in *Agenda for the Nation*, ed. Kermit Gordon (Washington, D.C.: Brookings Institution, 1968), 277–300.

[8]Herbert Stein, "Where Stands the New Fiscal Policy?" *Journal of Money, Credit and Banking* 1 (1969): 465.

that idea himself. He regarded fiscal policy as an instrument to be used to achieve certain economic objectives, but balancing the budget was not in itself an objective. In the particular circumstances of 1968, when he was running for the presidency, he could criticize the Democrats for running big budget deficits—because, in the years 1966–68, the deficits had caused inflation and not because deficits were bad per se. Thus, while calling for a balanced budget, he sought to distinguish himself from the traditional Republican attachment to balanced budgets. (In this he was no different from earlier presidents, Republican and Democratic, back to and including Hoover. It was, after all, Eisenhower who had said that he did not make a "fetish" of balancing the budget.)

In the 1968 campaign Nixon said: "There are times when the Federal Government can and should use credit wisely to invest in the future. What we need is not a mechanically balanced budget but an intelligently balanced economy."[9]

The route by which the deficit led to inflation was through the money supply: "The accelerated rise in prices in recent years has resulted primarily from an excessively expanding money supply which in turn has been fed by the monetization of federal government deficits. The way to stop the inflation is to reverse the irresponsible fiscal policies which produce it."[10]

Another comment, on the "new economics," was characteristically Nixonian, although it surprised those who thought of him as a traditional "Neanderthal" Republican: "I do not believe it is fruitful to segregate our economic knowledge under specific labels such as the old or the new economics; we have much to learn from both. We should rather make full use of our experience in economic affairs in confronting the problems of the future."[11]

Not too much should be made of what a candidate says during a campaign, but these statements reflect attitudes that operated after Nixon became president. He was not himself much interested in how the budget looked but was very interested in how the economy looked— meaning inflation in those years but with an underlying concern about unemployment, a concern left over from his experience in losing the 1960 election. Still, he thought that the word "balance" had a good

[9]Nixon Speech, July 8, 1968, reprinted in *Nixon Speaks Out* (New York: Nixon-Agnew Campaign Committee, 1968), 99.
[10]*Nixon on the Issues* (New York: Nixon-Agnew Campaign Committee, 1968), 128.
[11]Ibid., 129.

resonance in the country, and he wanted to have it on his side. He had a great concern with and worry over monetary policy. He had no specific ideas about how to use fiscal policy to achieve a "balanced" economy other than not to disturb monetary policy.

A new CEA—with Paul McCracken as chairman and with myself and Hendrik Houthakker as members—came into office with Nixon. Shortly after we came into office, McCracken was asked by a reporter whether the new advisers were Friedmanites. He replied that we were not but that we were "Friedmanesque." The extent of agreement and reservation implied by McCracken's answer helps to explain the CEA's later positions.

Much of Milton Friedman's work had been devoted to demonstrating that, contrary to the views held by some economists who considered themselves Keynesians, the rate of change of the money supply was an important determinant of the rates of change of nominal income, of the price level, and at least in the short run, of real output and employment. The McCracken CEA agreed with that, and probably by 1969 most other economists did also. Friedman also argued that because of the economic and political difficulty of adapting the rate of growth of the money supply to the condition of the economy, the best policy for the long run was to keep money growing at a constant rate. Moreover, he believed that he knew what that constant rate should be. On these latter points, the McCracken CEA was less Friedmanite. The argument for the superiority of a constant rate, and especially for one that could be specified forever in 1969, seemed less compelling than the argument for the simpler proposition that money matters a great deal. Also, the CEA was not in the business of prescribing a policy that might be the best on the average over an infinite length of time. It was in the business of advising a president who, naturally and not unwisely, gave much more weight to what would happen between 1969 and 1973 than to what might happen on the average over the next century.

The McCracken CEA was also much impressed with the argument that Friedman had made in his address as president of the American Economic Association in December 1967.[12] (A similar argument had been made earlier by Edmund Phelps.[13]) Friedman rebutted the notion,

---

[12]Milton Friedman, "The Role of Monetary Policy," *American Economic Review* 58 (March 1968): 1–7.
[13]Edmund S. Phelps, "Money Wage Dynamics and Labor Market Equilibrium," *Journal of Political Economy*, July–August 1967, 687–711.

then common, that a lower persistent unemployment rate could be achieved by accepting a higher persistent inflation rate. He maintained, persuasively it seemed to many, including the new CEA, that there was a "natural" rate of unemployment that would prevail at any constant, expected inflation rate, including zero, and that lower unemployment could be achieved only temporarily while the inflation rate was rising and unexpected. The Friedman argument also implied that to get the inflation rate down from one expected level to another would require a transitional period in which unemployment would be above its "natural" rate. Though accepting all that, the CEA did not find the argument adequate for its purposes. Friedman did not tell, and no one really knew, what the natural rate was, how high the transitional unemployment would have to be, and how long the transition would last. This made forecasting the consequences of anti-inflation policy difficult. It also raised the possibility that if the transitional costs were great, reducing the rate of inflation might not be worthwhile. The Friedmanesque CEA would have to wrestle with these limitations of the Friedmanian map throughout its term in office.

The new CEA gave the first articulation of Nixon's fiscal policy in testimony to the Joint Economic Committee on February 17, 1969.[14] The council's statement was characterized by much modesty about what economists know and what government can do and by an emphasis on monetary policy as a partner with fiscal policy—even as the senior partner—in the pursuit of aggregate economic objectives.

Regarding fiscal policy, the key was stability. There was, however, no attempt to lay down a general definition of fiscal stability. Both McCracken and I had been steeped in the CED rule of balancing the budget at high employment. We relied on this concept in the February testimony. When we wanted to show the unfortunate consequences of past instability, we used the change in the high-employment surplus as an indicator of instability. And when we came to the immediate situation we said, "Our view of the outlook and goal for 1969 implies the need for continuation of a budget whose expenditures are at least matched by the revenues from the tax system (assuming reasonably full employment)." But that was a prescription for 1969, and the CEA did not advance it as a general rule.

---

[14]U.S. Congress, Joint Economic Committee, *Hearings on the Economic Report of the President*, February 1969, 284–332.

The prescription for 1969 was assumed to mean continuation of the status quo in the budget. The budget for that year was in balance; the budget has, incidentally, not been in balance in any year since, and no balance is in sight for the future. But it was in balance, with an inflation rate that seemed very high and with an unemployment rate that was below what was then considered "high employment," that is, 4 percent. The budget was not in balance at a 4 percent unemployment rate and a stable price level. Moreover, and even more perplexing, to get the inflation rate down would probably require an interval in which the unemployment rate would be above 4 percent, in order to break the expectations of large wage and price increases. The basic logic of the CED policy of 1947 had been that a 4 percent unemployment rate represented the desirable path of the economy and that keeping constant the budget surplus that would be realized in this condition would help to keep the economy on that path. But we had realized in 1966 and 1967 that the path had a price dimension as well as an employment dimension. By 1969, following Friedman's argument already mentioned, we were also realizing that the desirable path was not necessarily one of a constant unemployment rate. These problems would occupy a good deal of the time of the CEA in the years to come, but they did not surface in this original testimony.

The council was also circumspect about the notion that as a general matter, stability meant a stable *surplus:* "We believe that the conduct of anti-inflationary monetary policy is easier, and can be counted on more reliably, if the Federal government is not a continuous large borrower *during periods when restraint is needed*" (my emphasis). The implication is that in some environments, which might be the usual ones, a stable deficit might meet the requirements of sound fiscal policy.

The council was also eager to avoid the appearance of rigidity or dogmatism in its prescription:

Circumstances are possible when departures from the steady path for fiscal or monetary policy or both would be desirable. There may be fluctuations in the private economy too strong to be constrained within reasonable limits without extraordinary fiscal or monetary action. Moreover, once fiscal or monetary policy [has] strayed far from the reasonably steady path, measures of adjustment are needed to get back to it. Our point is that frequent adjustments of policy to correct dimly foreseen future departures from the desired path of the economy are on balance likely to be more unstabilizing than stabilizing.

Then followed a sentence that presages the theme and problem of the present essay: "To achieve a stabilizing fiscal policy, or at least avoid a destabilizing one, we need to learn how to separate decisions about the over-all position of the budget from decisions about particular expenditures and questions of the tax structure." From today's vantage point, that is like saying that we need to learn how to take a pound of flesh without spilling a drop of blood.

Although the council's description of the administration's fiscal policy was full of qualifications and uncertainties, no great difficulty appeared in determining what the administration should do in the spring of 1969. The budget for fiscal 1969 was in balance. The big economic problem was inflation. Surely there was no case for moving to a deficit for fiscal 1970. A case might have been made for trying to raise the surplus. That could have been justified as a way to get the inflation down. It could also have been justified as consistent with the principle of balancing the budget at high employment, since the existing balance had been achieved only with extra-low unemployment and extra-high inflation.

But raising the surplus was never in the picture. The FY1969 surplus was maintained with the assistance of a tax surcharge scheduled to expire on June 30, 1969. During the campaign, Nixon had indicated his desire to get rid of the surcharge as soon as possible and had claimed to disagree with his rival, Hubert Humphrey, on that point. The operative question was whether the new president could cut FY1970 expenditures enough to permit the preservation of the surplus while allowing the surcharge to lapse on June 30. The answer was that he could not cut expenditures that much—meaning that he found the cuts that would have been necessary to be unacceptable on political, economic, or other grounds. So he announced that he would ask for an extension of the surcharge for a year—until June 30, 1970.

One might think that there would have been no problem in getting the surcharge extended. The surcharge had been enacted in 1968 by a Democratic Congress, which was still in charge. And Johnson, in his final budget message before leaving office, had recommended that the surcharge be extended for one year. Nevertheless, a number of difficulties did appear in the form of prices Congress would exact from Nixon for approving his proposal to extend the surcharge—a proposal that he was not too happy about having to make.

The first obstacle was the one that had been encountered on the way to the Kennedy-Johnson tax cut of 1964 and the Johnson tax surcharge of 1968. That was Wilbur Mills, still chairman of the Ways and Means Committee.[15] As on the two previous occasions, he wanted assurance of a limitation on expenditures; as in 1968, he wanted a legislative ceiling on total spending. Nixon was reluctant about that, as any president would be. But the form of the ceiling enacted by Congress was so elastic that Nixon had no trouble signing it. The president had proposed expenditures of $192.9 billion for FY1970 (about 20 percent of GNP). Congress, to show that it was outdoing him, enacted a ceiling of $191.9 billion (a difference of about 0.1 percent of GNP). But it also provided that "uncontrollable" expenditures—interest, social security, etc.—could exceed estimates by a total of $2 billion without the ceiling being considered as broken. Moreover, the ceiling was to be automatically raised to the extent that congressional action on appropriations exceeded the budget estimates. In signing the bill containing the ceiling, the president stated that congressional action had already exceeded the ceiling by several billion dollars and that he would take executive action to hold the line at his figure of $192.9 billion.

A more serious problem arose on the revenue side of the budget. This first appeared in the form of the question of the investment tax credit (ITC). Many on the Democratic side regarded this as an unjustified boon to business, and they wanted it removed as payment for agreeing to continue the surcharge on ordinary individuals. Charls Walker, who was under secretary of the treasury and chief liaison with Congress on tax matters, told the president that he would gain one hundred votes in the House for extension of the surcharge if the president would give up the ITC.

The president asked the CEA for a memo on the effects of eliminating the ITC. Overnight the CEA produced a memo estimating what the effect of that action would be on the long-run rate of economic growth— to two decimal places—and the effect did not seem to be great. (In retrospect, its boldness in making such estimates seems foolish.) The memo also made the further argument that stimulating private invest-

---

[15]Zelizer's chapter in this volume examines Mills's thinking and methods, including his relations with "modern" economists. In the episodes of my history where he appears, his behavior can, I think, be rather simply explained. First, he wanted to assert the power of his position as chairman of the House Ways and Means Committee. Second, in demanding restraint of expenditures in 1964 and 1968, he was following the pattern of southern conservatives of his time. Third, in pushing through a large increase in social security benefits in 1972, he was acting like one who hopes to be nominated for the presidency.

ment in plant and equipment was not as high a priority as sharing revenue with the states, assisting the poor, and encouraging the housing industry—all of which would be made more feasible if the government had the revenue that would be gained by eliminating the ITC.[16]

The president commented favorably on this memo, but how much influence it had on his decision is unclear. In any case, he did announce that he would support the elimination of the ITC and that since this would increase the revenue, he would ask that the surcharge be extended at a rate of only 5 percent rather than 10 percent in the first six months of calendar 1970. The decision to eliminate the ITC did not, however, satisfy the Democrats in Congress, and the extension of the surcharge got tied up in further haggling over "tax reform." Before leaving office, Johnson's Treasury secretary, Joseph Barr, had released a report showing that many people with high incomes—millionaires—were paying no income tax.[17] That created a furor in the country and a demand for tax reform. Early in its term, the Nixon administration decided that it would submit a plan for tax reform. The plan would reduce the possibility for upper-income individuals to escape tax and at the same time would relieve millions of low-income individuals of any income-tax liability. The plan was intended to be revenue-neutral and, therefore, presumably without effect on the budget or the economy.[18]

President Nixon announced his tax reform proposal on April 21. But Congress was not buying it. A substantial group, led by Senator Al Gore, Sr. (D-Tenn.), father of the future vice-president, wanted further reduction of taxes, especially on low-income individuals, and they proposed to increase the personal exemption and to install a minimum standard deduction. These revenue-losing provisions would be phased in over several years so as not to upset the budget balance for FY1970.

---

[16]McCracken was out of town, and I wrote this memo as acting chairman. In discussions with the president, Arthur Burns took the position opposing mine, and when McCracken returned, it was clear that he also would have been on the side opposing elimination of the ITC, but he did not try to undercut my memo. Here and throughout the section on the Nixon Administration, I refer to unpublished internal memoranda and speeches that are in my possession.

[17]In fact, Barr's report understated the number of millionaires who paid no income tax; in counting only those people with over $1 million of income, it used an extremely narrow definition of income.

[18]Shortly after joining the CEA, I called the assistant secretary of the Treasury for tax policy, Edwin Cohen, to tell him that I was on the job and was prepared to cooperate in the consideration of tax proposals. I had spent twenty-two years at the CED writing many policy statements on taxes and thought I knew something about it. Cohen told me that the Treasury was working on tax reform and that if any economics came up he would call me. Later it became clear that some economics had come up, and the CEA became involved.

This plan was quite unacceptable to the administration. To get the revenue it wanted for FY1970, it would have to give up revenue it was counting on in its budget plans for later years. The CEA wrote the president several memos pointing out that the congressional plan would give up the revenue expected from the repeal of the ITC, revenue that had been expected to be available for revenue-sharing and other social purposes. The president made several public statements complaining about the congressional plan.

On August 4 Congress passed a bill extending the surcharge for the second half of calendar 1970, but the fate of the rest of the tax package—the extension of the surcharge for the first six months of 1970, the repeal of the ITC, the president's proposed reforms, and the revenue cuts proposed in Congress—remained uncertain until the last day of the year. On December 18 the president was asked whether he could sign a bill, just passed by the Senate, that included an increase of the personal exemption to $800 (from $600) and a 15 percent increase of social security benefits. His answer was "no."

After the president's statement, Congress revised the tax bill to reduce somewhat the revenue loss involved. The president was then very uncertain about whether to sign the bill. People in the administration were divided on the subject. McCracken sent the president a memo advising him to sign it. An internal CEA staff analysis of the economic consequences of the bill indicated that it would not make much difference for the performance of the economy in 1970 or 1971. On December 30 the president signed the bill while complaining about the revenue loss, which he said would make it more difficult to achieve a balanced budget in FY1971 and so would obstruct his anti-inflation policy. He added, "I am also concerned about the constraint this act imposes on government revenues in future years, limiting our ability to meet tomorrow's pressing needs."[19] (Less than two years later, on August 15, 1971, the president proposed to Congress that it accelerate the tax reductions contained in the 1969 Revenue Act, in order to stimulate the economy.)

For all its aversion to fine-tuning, the administration devoted much attention to trying to assess the short-term behavior of the economy and its implications for policy.[20] As the year 1969 progressed, the adminis-

---

[19]*Public Papers of the Presidents, Richard M. Nixon, 1969* (Washington, D.C.: Government Printing Office, 1970), 1045.

[20]In a speech on April 29, 1969, I said: "Of course, the Administration is constantly trying to assess the outlook for the economy. I am amazed at how much of this we do, and particularly amazed to find myself involved in it. But we are not asking ourselves every time we make a forecast what would be the optimum fiscal policy if we had a clean slate

tration's outlook gradually changed. At the beginning there was no question that the problem was the "overheating" of the economy and the need to cool the inflation. But as early as April, the worry that the economy might be cooling off too fast, even before inflation had been visibly reduced, began to surface. This concern never caused the administration to deflect from its pursuit of fiscal restraint and a balanced budget, however. Instead, the worry took the form of concern about possible excessive tightness of monetary policy. That was a matter on which the president was very sensitive.

At a meeting of the Cabinet Committee on Economic Policy (CCEP) on April 10, George Shultz, who had learned about monetary policy from Friedman, expressed his concern that the Federal Reserve, which had been loose for too long, was now getting too tight. Arthur Burns was also worried about hawkish anti-inflationary sentiment at the Fed. (Arthur Burns was counselor to the president; in 1970 he would become a member of the Federal Reserve.) Not everyone agreed, but the president urged his economic advisers to watch the Fed closely. He said: "I remember '58. We cooled off the economy and cooled off 15 Senators and 60 Congressmen at the same time. I recognize the danger of inflation—but there is no way to get a deficit faster than to bust the boom."[21]

At meetings a month later (May 16 and 28) many of the conflicts among the administration's economic objectives became clear. The inflation was continuing, but the real economy was slowing down. One

to write on. Rather we are asking whether there is so marked and certain a change from our expectations as to justify a change of policy given the costs of change and the advantages of stability. In this perspective we have not found the need for a change of policy."

[21]President Nixon established the Cabinet Committee on Economic Policy as a way of fulfilling his promise to various cabinet members—notably the secretary of commerce, Maurice Stans—that they would participate in the formation of economic policy. But the committee never made any decisions; it served only as a discussion group. Still, the record of those discussions reveals the thinking within the government at the time. At the end of 1969, the president turned the chairmanship of the committee over to the vice-president, and later in 1970 the committee expired. It was succeeded by other cabinet committees on economics, usually chaired by the secretary of the Treasury. With one exception these committees did not make decisions and rarely met. The exception was, for several months, the Cost of Living Council (CLC), established to manage the price and wage control system. The CLC dealt with a matter in which many departments had an interest but for which none had a claim to control. The only way the department secretaries could get into the action on the subject of greatest public attention was to attend the meetings of the CLC. Moreover, because of the intense public interest, for several weeks the television cameras attended the openings of the sessions of the CLC. That was an irresistible inducement for attendance by cabinet secretaries. But after a few months this attraction also faded, and the work of the CLC was left to a small core group.

possible strategy seemed to be to attack inflation first, knock it out, and then turn to reviving the real economy. The instrument would have been the continuation of tight money. But whether the turnaround could be accomplished before the 1970 election was doubtful. Moreover, tight money would depress housing construction, and the administration placed weight on achieving a goal of 1.8 million houses a year—a goal that was valued for the sake of the houses and not just for its contribution to aggregate output and employment. My report to the committee about the post-Vietnam planning exercise indicated that budgetary commitments already in existence for 1971 and beyond would exhaust the revenue available and leave no room for new initiatives the president favored. The president urged boldness in looking at ways to cut expenditures and raise revenues. But discussion of ways to cut expenditures or raise revenue to correct the budgetary situation for the out-years came to no conclusion, partly because the options were all unpleasant and partly because the existing, 1969–70 economic situation seemed too fragile.

By September the fact that the economy was slowing down while inflation showed little if any sign of abating was becoming painfully obvious. Even McCracken, who had heretofore been more supportive than Shultz or Burns of the Fed's policy, was suggesting that the time for easing might not be far away. The problem was that according to the CEA's forecasts, unemployment would rise and peak above 4 percent in the third quarter of 1970, which would be just before the congressional election. By McCracken's calculations, the lag between a turn of monetary policy and its effect on the economy might be twelve months, so the third quarter of 1969 was the crucial time.

The administration's entire focus was on the need for a turn of monetary policy in a more expansive direction and on the timing of such a turn, rather than on a possible turn in fiscal policy. The administration was then engaged in a struggle with Congress to hold down expenditures and preserve the revenues against the congressional desire for tax cuts. The administration wanted to be able to portray itself to the public as the defender of economy in government and a balanced budget. Moreover, it believed that expectations of inflation, especially the expectations of the financial and business community, were the main obstacle to achieving a more stable price level without high unemployment. It thought that these inflationary expectations reflected skepticism about the government's ability to follow a responsible fiscal course and that to dispel that skepticism, the Nixon administration would have to demonstrate its commitment to fiscal prudence. Also the administration looked forward to being able to introduce new Nixonian programs, like revenue-sharing, and did not want to foreclose that possibility by cutting taxes or increasing existing expenditure programs.

For all of these reasons, the administration was extremely reluctant to try to utilize an expansionary fiscal program to counter the slowdown in the economy. This reluctance continued until the end of 1971. As a result the administration found itself in continuing tension with the Federal Reserve, to which it looked for support. This reluctance was not based on rejection of the Keynesian notion that fiscal policy could stimulate the economy in the short run. Almost every week, the administration's economists made estimates of the effects that even small changes in taxes and expenditures would have on nominal and real GNP, on the price level, and on unemployment. The Nixon economic officials were probably more modest than their predecessors about the precise accuracy of such estimates, but they thought that they knew at least the direction of the effects and roughly the magnitudes. The reasons for reluctance to try to use the fiscal instrument in the standard Keynesian way were concern with the political effect in the short run and with the allocation effect in the longer run.

In January 1970 the president submitted a budget that would be balanced, but barely, in FY1970 and in FY1971. There would be a surplus of $1.5 billion in FY1970 and of $1.3 billion in FY1971, the latter to be achieved with the aid of $1.6 billion of additional revenue to be yielded by new legislation. (All of these numbers were around 1 percent of GNP.) "The surplus," the president said, "an estimated $1.3 billion, is essential both to stem persistent inflationary pressures and to relieve hard-pressed financial markets." The long-run goal was "obtaining budget surpluses in order to generate additional savings so housing and local construction can be financed without undue reliance on Federal aid."[22]

The tendency of the president and his political aides at this time was to make a big fuss about the difference between a tiny surplus and a tiny deficit, the tiny surplus being anti-inflationary and the tiny deficit being inflationary. This was not only analytically incorrect but also dan-

---

[22]*Public Papers of the Presidents, Richard M. Nixon, 1970* (Washington, D.C.: Government Printing Office, 1971), 49, 59.

gerous, because the budget could so easily slip from its tiny surplus to a tiny deficit and leave the president seeming to have abandoned his anti-inflation efforts.

The annual report of the CEA, submitted at the same time, was somewhat more sophisticated about the budget for 1970 and 1971 but not much more satisfactory as explanation. The administration was portrayed as fighting a two-front war, against inflation and against the slowdown of the economy. It would use the balanced budget as defense against inflation and would count on monetary policy to bring about economic expansion. The economy would slow down in the first half of 1970, knocking out inflation, after which it could safely expand. (The CEA was seeing around the corner again, in Okun's words.) But the report did not explain what combination of fiscal restraint and monetary expansion would move the economy along the desired path or indeed give any reason to believe that there was such a combination.

The implicit argument was that there was a normal moderate budget position, which was balance, and a normal moderate monetary position, unspecified, and that these combined would yield the desired results. Basically, the administration was committed to a balanced budget, for the reasons given above, and counted on the Federal Reserve, now in the hands of Nixon's friend Burns, to do what was necessary.[23]

In its report the Council did not rely on the standard that the budget should be balanced at high employment as an explanation of policy for 1970 and 1971. But when it came to describing optimum policy for the long run—beyond the responsibility of the immediate incumbents—it did refer to that standard. It did not complicate the brief reference to high-employment balance by questions about the rate of inflation at

---

[23]Burns and Nixon first knew each other in the first term of the Eisenhower administration, when Nixon was vice-president and Burns was chairman of the Council of Economic Advisers. In 1960 Burns, then a private citizen, had warned Nixon that the restrictive policy of the Federal Reserve was depressing the economy and endangering his prospects in the presidential election—a warning that apparently was justified. Nixon regarded Burns as a trusted friend and adviser. When Nixon became president, he named Burns counselor, as a holding place from which Burns could move to the chairmanship of the Federal Reserve when William McC. Martin's term expired at the end of 1969. As chairman, Burns acquired personal and institutional goals not always congruent with the president's. For one thing he did not want to have the residual responsibility for the performance of the economy, a role he might have been assigned by the monetarist ideas of the Nixon economists. Also, Burns acquired an independent source of power because of the respect accorded his utterances, especially in the financial community and Congress. The relationship between Burns and Nixon became more and more distant and wary as time wore on.

which the budget would be balanced or about the possibility that high employment did not describe the optimum path of the economy. These questions were, however, in the minds of the council members at the time.

The 1970 report of the council was noteworthy for its chapter proposing that federal fiscal policies, and other policies, should be considered and determined by reference to their effects on the allocation of the entire national output and not, as conventionally done, by reference to their effects on a smaller total called the federal budget. The chapter was an attempt to deal with the problem of having no adequate framework for thinking about how federal decisions affected the things the country was really interested in, including the level of personal consumption, housing construction, provision for defense, future growth, and so on. One implication of this approach was that the size of the surplus or deficit was not a decision separate from and prior to decisions about how much to spend for one thing or another but was to be decided along with these other decisions and balanced against them in terms of its effects, presumably on private investment.

There was some objection in the White House to the inclusion of this chapter in the economic report on the ground that it smacked of "economic planning." However, it was included in the CEA report and was also emphasized in the president's message. It seemed to satisfy the president's desire to be seen as getting outside the conventional way of looking at things, when he could safely do so. But this idea of budgeting the national output lay dormant for about twenty years until it again received a small amount of attention with the publication of my book *Governing the $5 Trillion Economy.*[24]

As 1970 wore on it became clear, and not only to the CEA, that the economy was off the track in several directions. It was off the budget-balancing track, off the inflation-reducing track, and possibly off the track to reviving growth of output and employment. This raised questions about how the administration would respond. A speech that I made on April 1 to the Downtown Economists' Club in New York was a good indication of the forces and ideas at work at the time:

On the fiscal side there has been no change in the overall objectives of policy or in the policy itself since the Budget was submitted at the beginning of February.

---

[24]Herbert Stein, *Governing the $5 Trillion Economy* (New York: Oxford University Press, 1989).

The Budget was a reflection of the difficulty of tailoring the thousands of decisions on taxes and expenditures to conform to an overall objective about the size of the surplus or deficit. The Administration would have preferred a larger surplus than it submitted, $1.3 billion, for fiscal 1971 in order to get interest rates down and stimulate residential construction. However, although it made a noble effort it could not squeeze a larger surplus out of the expenditure claims it had to deal with. Since the Budget was submitted the Administration has made or acquiesced in some small expenditure-raising decisions that were not individually consistent with the preferred overall budget posture. The early termination of the State and local construction cutback and the increase of certain veterans benefits are examples. Each of these cases has its own reasons. None should be interpreted as meaning that the Administration is now seeking to pump up the economy or is relaxed about the possibility that Congress would do so.

Since we started with a budget surplus projected for fiscal 1973 of $1.3 billion, it would not take many one hundred million dollar increase decisions to convert that to a deficit. I think it is important to emphasize that a change of $1.5 billion or $2 billion in the budget position is not a fact of enormous effect on the economic situation. It is not more important if the change in the budget position carried us across the line which separates surplus from deficit. To interpret the crossing of that line, if it should occur, as a sign of a basic change in the Administration's intentions would be a serious mistake.

To the president and some of the White House staff, crossing the line from surplus to deficit seemed a critical thing, or at least they liked to say so. I thought that was not only wrong but also dangerous, because we were going to cross the line and we were not going to fight hard to prevent it. On April 29 I wrote a memo to McCracken complaining about the way the president talked about the budget. "The important thing," I said, "is to get him off this terrible hook where red ink equals inflation equals bad."

Within a few weeks, the crossing of the line became obvious. On May 19 the administration published a revision of the budget estimates, now showing deficits for both FY1970 and FY1971, and getting off the hook became necessary. The president attributed the deficits to the tax cuts made by Congress and then said, "Despite this premature reduction by the Congress, our tax system would produce sufficient revenue to cover the present, restrained level of government spending if we had normal economic growth without inflation today."[25]

This was not quite saying that the budget should be balanced at high employment, but it was saying, for the first time, that the standard of policy was to balance the budget under hypothetical conditions that

[25] *Public Papers, 1970,* 442.

were not the same as the actual present or actually forecast conditions. On June 17 the president made his first major speech devoted entirely to the problems of the economy. The need for the speech was created by the continuation of inflation alongside rising unemployment and, most particularly, by the suggestion that "some kind of incomes policy" (meaning "voluntary" price and wage controls) could resolve the difficulty and permit the achievement of both price stability and high employment. This suggestion was common not only among "outsiders" but also, in varying degrees, among people within the president's circle, including Burns, who was by then the chairman of the Federal Reserve. The administration had to formulate its position and make it known. Production of the speech took about two months of effort to reconcile the different views within the administration (again including, for this purpose, Burns); the effort was led by William Safire, the president's speechwriter.

I will not try to describe the negotiations on the subject of incomes policy and the position finally taken in the June 17 speech. They would be part of a long story of its own. What is interesting from the standpoint of the present story is that in none of the drafts was there any commitment to the idea of balancing the budget, however that might be defined. In a suggestion for an early draft, I had included a sentence stating, "We are determined not to repeat the great mistake of 1965 to 1968 when the budget plunged from near balance to a $25 billion deficit." But even this limited commitment was absent from the speech as delivered. Near the end of the drafting process, the following reference was added: "In the decade of the sixties, Federal deficits totaled $57 billion." But there was no attempt to describe a Nixon position on balancing the budget or on the desirable size of the deficit.

Whereas this subject could be finessed for the purposes of the speech, it could not be finessed for the purposes of the administration's planning and decision-making. On June 26 the Cabinet Committee on Economic Policy held a full-scale discussion of budget policy and the economic outlook. By that time the president had turned over chairmanship of the CCEP to the vice-president, so he was not present at the meeting, but the sense of the meeting was reported to him by McCracken and probably by others.

I submitted a memorandum to the CCEP on behalf of its Subcommittee on Fiscal Policy Guidelines. In it I said that the economy was off the track in both dimensions. That is, the economy seemed to be falling short of the path that led back to the neighborhood of 4 percent unemployment by the third quarter of 1972—a fateful time. And the budget was on a path that would still leave a large deficit for fiscal 1972. With the existing budget programs, the economy might be brought up to the desired path by a more expansive monetary policy than the Fed was then following. The memorandum also suggested that the desired economic path could be achieved even with a tighter budget—that is, cutting expenditures—but that this would require even more monetary expansion. Moving the budget in the other direction, to increase spending, might contribute to economic expansion but would leave the budget with a larger deficit.

The memo leaned in the direction of cutting expenditures somewhat below the existing programs, mainly for the sake of the long-run availability of capital, but this implied relying on the Fed for more stimulus. However, the CCEP made no decisions but only expressed concern about being seen as on the side of increasing the deficit. As it turned out, actual expenditures for FY1971, and FY1972 expenditures as proposed in the budget for that year, were very close to the amounts assumed in this memo. Whatever may have been the intention, in fact no steps were taken to cut expenditures below the projections of that time. My memo also suggested that the administration should stop harping on the $57 billion deficit of the Kennedy-Johnson years, since we were about to have our own large deficits, and that advice was followed.

On July 18, a month after his major economic address, President Nixon made his first assertion of full-employment balance as the standard of budget policy. It was also, I believe, the first such assertion by any president. The Kennedy-Johnson administrations had made use of the fact that the budget was in full-employment balance, when true, but that was more to reassure those people who were still so puritanical as to be interested in a balanced budget than it was to express any commitment of the administrations. Nixon said: "In raising the issue of budget deficits, I am not suggesting that the Federal government should necessarily adhere to a strict pattern of a balanced budget every year. At times the economic situation permits—even calls for—a budget deficit. There is one basic guideline for the budget, however, which we should never violate: Except in emergency conditions, expenditures should never be allowed to outrun the revenues that the tax system would produce at reasonably full employment."[26]

[26]In a news conference two days later the president said: "As you know, our budget for the year 1970 will not be in balance; and our budget for the year 1971 will not be in balance. We announced that in February" (Ibid., 603). But the budget message in Feb-

The president did not get this formulation from the Council of Economic Advisers, despite the long connection that I, and to a lesser extent McCracken, had with the idea of high-employment balance. By this time I was thinking in more complicated terms, about balancing the budget on the optimum feasible path of the economy and about the rate at which one should get into the desired position. The president was introduced to the full-employment balance notion by Shultz, who had become the director of the Office of Management and Budget (OMB). (Shultz had been dean of the University of Chicago Business School when the school published my book *The Fiscal Revolution in America,* and he had written the introduction to it; this was, I believe, his first writing on fiscal policy.) Nixon's statement was not accompanied by any estimate of the budget position on a full-employment basis, however. That would not come until the budget message in January 1971.

The idea of balancing the budget at high employment had the advantage of avoiding the embarrassment of showing a budget deficit on the president's watch. It also appealed to Nixon's desire to appear as an innovator but without breaking one of his party's taboos. The president, or at least his speech-writers, had a magical notion of the power of the policy of balancing the budget at high employment. They thought that doing so would get the economy to high employment and that failing to do so would cause inflation. The policy did not really promise this at all, as its original developers understood. It promised only a certain contribution to moderating fluctuations of the economy and the avoidance of the destabilizing effects of either traditional budget-balancing or ad hoc Keynesian intervention. The president's speech-writers liked to describe the policy as a "self-fulfilling prophecy," a phrase that I could not keep out of the January 1971 budget message.[27]

There was some ambiguity in the way the administration described the policy of full-employment balance. In the July 18 statement just quoted, the policy seemed to mean that at every moment the expendi-

---

ruary had predicted small surpluses for both of those years. The discrepancy is a mystery to me.

[27] The difference between the way the president and the speechwriters described the policy and the way the CEA described it did not imply any difference between their ideas of what the policy should be at that time, nor did it imply any desire to conceal what the policy was. The difference mainly resulted from the effort of the president and the speechwriters to explain the policy in terms that they understood and that they thought the public would understand. Conceivably, in other circumstances these differences of interpretation could have led to different views of what policy should be, but this never happened.

tures should not exceed the revenues that would be obtained at that moment if the economy was at high employment. Two days later, on July 20, the president said, "Our goal in a period when the economy will be working at full employment, which is a goal we think we can achieve during fiscal 1972, is, of course, to operate with a balanced budget." This is a different idea. It describes where the actual budget should be when the economy is actually at full employment, but it does not say where the budget should be when the economy is not at full employment. That is, the hypothetical full-employment budget might be in deficit while the economy is not at full employment, as long as there are plans to bring the budget into balance when full employment is actually achieved.

McCracken's statement on the same day, July 20, in testimony to the Joint Economic Committee, seemed to be using the second definition. "The transition to the desired full employment balance or surplus should be made smoothly as the economy rises to its potential." This implied that the economy might not be in full-employment balance but that it should gradually get there, arriving when full employment was achieved.

Later, on December 3, I gave still another version of the policy: "In a period when tax rates on balance are unchanged Federal expenditures should rise at about the same percentage rate as GNP. That would approximately keep the full-employment budget position constant." This says nothing at all about balancing the budget except in the marginal sense that the increase of expenditures should equal the increase in full-employment revenues. The word "approximately" in the second sentence presumably was used to recognize the fact that full-employment revenues, with constant tax rates, would rise faster than full-employment GNP.

These fine distinctions were of no practical importance in 1970. Policy was not being precisely led by any of these formulations. I cite them only to illustrate that the full-employment-balance rule is itself fairly elastic. Once a formulation had been found that permitted the administration to rationalize approximately the existing fiscal position, policy consisted mainly of minor skirmishes with Congress to show that the president was on the side of economy in government.

Two main economic policy problems remained. One was to fend off demands, coming in part from within the administration, for "some kind of incomes policy." The other was to nudge the Federal Reserve toward a more expansive monetary policy to help get the economy on what the administration considered "the optimum feasible path." This effort was unsuccessful. The economy was recovering, but not at the desired rate. Moreover, in the fourth quarter a strike at General Motors depressed aggregate output considerably. This raised questions about whether the economy was really expanding and left policy-making for 1971 exceptionally uncertain.

January 1971 was the high-water mark of the idea of balancing the full-employment budget as the standard of fiscal policy—meaning that it began to recede shortly thereafter. In his New Year's Day press conference on television (January 4) the president said: "What we are going to do first is to have an expansionary budget. It will be a budget in deficit, as will be the budget in 1971. It will not be an inflationary budget because it will not exceed the full employment revenues."[28]

The president had been saying things like that for about six months, but this time it got more attention than it had previously. Perhaps this was because the new budget was about to be announced. More probably it was because, after the interview, Nixon said to one of the reporters, Howard K. Smith, "Now I am a Keynesian in economics." The use of the "K" word by Nixon rang alarm bells in the minds of many of his conservative friends.[29]

A week later the president announced that the administration would make changes in the treatment of depreciation for tax purposes. This was intended to stimulate the economy, but he explained that the revenue loss would not be so large as to disrupt the balance in the full-employment budget. He also went on to say that there would be a "feed-back" effect from the tax change, through the increase in the tax base expected to occur. "As a result, Federal tax collections in the long run will increase." (The supply-side idea did not originate with Arthur Laffer and Ronald Reagan. Indeed, it antedated Nixon.)

A more formal espousal of the full-employment-balance standard came with the State of the Union message on January 22. There the president set forth six goals. One was to achieve "full prosperity in peacetime." The main policy he proposed for achieving that was the full-employment budget. "By spending as if we were *at* full employment, we

---

[28]*Public Papers of the Presidents, Richard M. Nixon, 1971* (Washington, D.C.: Government Printing Office, 1972), 8.

[29]Nixon is regularly misquoted as having said, "We are all Keynesians now." Friedman said that in December 1965. The statement to Howard K. Smith was reported in the *New York Times*, January 7, 1971.

Table 5.1 *Receipts minus expenditures (billions of dollars)*

	Actual	Full employment
FY1970, actual	−2.8	2.6
FY1971, est.	−18.6	1.4
FY1972, est.	−11.6	0.1

Note: GNP was at approximately $1,000 billion, so these figures range from an actual deficit of about 1.9 percent of GNP in fiscal 1971 to a high-employment surplus of about 0.26 percent of GNP in fiscal 1970.

will help to *bring about* full employment." But he warned against spending beyond the full-employment revenues, which would "reignite the fires of inflation."[30]

The idea was further developed a week later in the budget message. There the "self-fulfilling prophecy" view became more explicit. The message said, in italics: *"The full employment budget idea is in the nature of a self-fulfilling prophecy: By operating as if we were at full employment, we will help to bring about full employment."* The budget program submitted would be in balance at full employment, barely. (See Table 5.1.)[31]

The 1971 annual report of the Council of Economic Advisers (February 1) devoted an appendix of five pages to explaining how the full-employment budget was measured and what its significance was. The claims made there for the full-employment budget were more modest than the claims in the president's statements. The report said:

It has been found of interest to ask how the surplus or deficit would change if the economy moved along a specific path. Conceptually, any number of growth paths could be selected for this purpose; it is the change in the budget position along the assumed path that will indicate whether the budget policy has been or will be restrictive relative to that path—that is, whether the budget is tending to push the economy above or below the assumed path.

[30]*Public Papers, 1971,* 52.
[31]These full-employment budget estimates assumed that 4 percent unemployment was full employment. Later estimates by the Congressional Budget Office, estimates based on calculations of the unemployment rate consistent with stable inflation, used an unemployment rate closer to 6 percent and showed the budget to be in full-employment deficit in all of those years. These estimates did not, however, significantly alter the picture of the year-to-year changes in the full-employment deficit.

In order to give the concept more relevance it is common to select a growth path that has some normative significance. The full employment growth path has been used most frequently since the concept of a full employment budget was developed and publicized by the Committee for Economic Development in 1947.

The absolute level of the full employment surplus or deficit is of limited significance for indicating how much restraint or stimulus the budget would exert on the economy if it followed the full employment path, or indeed for indicating which of these directions the influence would take. Changes in the full employment surplus from period to period are much more important indicators of how much fiscal policy is moving toward contraction or expansion. The fact that the full employment budget has a surplus does not imply that the budget is not having an expansionary impact on the economy; the effects may be expansionary if the surplus is declining. Similarly, a budget with a deficit may be restrictive if the deficit is declining.

What is significant here, in contrast with the president's formulation, is the focus on the change in the budget position rather than its level and on the resulting change in the economic position rather than its level. Thus, the council was not saying that balance in the full-employment budget would help achieve full employment but only that a reduction in the full-employment surplus or an increase in the deficit would help to lift the economy relative to full employment—that is, toward or beyond full employment.

The council made another qualification, which was to become significant in August, after the radical change of policy. It stated:

Although changes in the full employment budget balance provide a convenient summary measure of changes in fiscal policy, they do not tell the whole story. A given change in the balance may exert a different force, depending on whether the change stems from a change in transfer payments, purchase of goods and services, corporate taxes, personal taxes, or other instruments of fiscal policy. Results vary because different policy changes affect economic behavior differently, even though the same amounts of money are involved.

If, as the council said, it was the change in the full-employment balance that mattered and if the budget proposals called for the full-employment surplus to be essentially constant, the council could not expect the fiscal policy to achieve full employment or even to move the economy toward it. In fact, the administration did not expect full employment to be achieved in fiscal 1971 and 1972 on the average. This could be seen from the fact that the actual deficits would be substantial in both years, whereas there would be full-employment surpluses, even though tiny ones.

The administration's goal and forecast was that the economy would be rising with inflation declining and with unemployment falling to approximately full employment by the end of fiscal 1972—that is, a few months before the presidential election.[32] There was some disagreement within the administration, especially between the OMB and the CEA, about how the economy was to be moved along that path. Given the commitment to a constant, small full-employment surplus, fiscal policy could not be the primary instrument. That meant reliance on monetary policy. The view of the OMB, based on a study by Arthur Laffer, who was then on the OMB staff, was that the desired path of the economy would be achieved if the money supply (M1) rose by 6 percent a year, about what was believed to be the path the Federal Reserve was then on. The CEA looked at several studies indicating that a more rapid growth of money would be required. Probably more important, the CEA believed that no one could tell in advance precisely what combination of policies would yield the desired path for the economy in the particular conditions of 1971. All that the econometric studies could reveal was what the relationship between policy measures and outcomes had been on the average in the past.

The administration embraced the target path for the economy without a commitment to a precise set of policies but believing that policies could be flexibly adapted. As the CEA explained in its report:

The reasons for a new stability in fiscal and monetary policy are weighty. But the need to press forward to reduce unemployment and inflation is also great.

---

[32]This goal and forecast was quantified in the forecast that nominal GNP in calendar 1971 would be $1,065 billion. That is probably the most famous forecast the government ever made. It exceeded by about $20 billion the forecasts being made by private experts and was commonly regarded as having been made only for a political purpose. In fact, the logic of the forecast was strong, though usually misunderstood. The administration believed, on what seemed objective evidence, that $1,065 billion lay along the optimum feasible path. That is, given the existing interactions between unemployment and inflation, this figure was consistent with declines in both, and it was a path that could be achieved by some combination of fiscal and monetary measures. Therefore, $1,065 billion was a proper and achievable goal for the government, and the government could not forecast that it would not take the necessary combination of measures to achieve that. Outsiders could forecast the failure of government, and they could be right, but government could not forecast its own failure. As it turned out, making that forecast, however sophisticated the argument for it, was a political mistake. The administration would probably have been better off politically to have made a less ambitious forecast so that the subsequent shortfall would have been smaller, giving the opposition less ground for attack. Shortly after the $1,065 billion forecast, and the public complaint that followed, the Reverend Billy Graham came to the White House to visit the president, and the staff was invited to meet him. I asked Graham to pray for $1,065 billion, but he gave no sign that he knew what I was talking about, and I saw no sign thereafter that he had responded to my request.

After the economic instability we have experienced in the past 5 years the param-
eters of the system cannot be located with precision and may well be in flux. It
would be unwise to try to freeze a course of policy which is expected to carry
us through the difficult months ahead without change. A course of flexibility
and determination, with cooperation and division of labor among the several
instruments of economic policy, will be needed, and if followed will lead to the
goals we all seek.

This, of course, left open the question of the evidence that would
justify a change of policy. It was clear when this was written, and it
became clear in public within a few months, that the CEA was more
receptive to the idea of change, more willing to be "flexible," than the
OMB.

The president's espousal of the idea of balancing the budget at full
employment, especially coupled with his identification of himself as a
Keynesian, did not win him many plaudits. The leading Democratic politicians and the economists associated with them did not welcome him
into the Keynesian ranks. They were not interested in budgetary standards that gave much weight to balancing the budget, however that
might be defined. They wanted a more expansionist fiscal policy, as they
had for most of the previous twenty years and would for most of the
next twenty years. The economist Robert Solow said about Nixon's
budget message, "It is one small step forward for Richard Nixon and
one giant leap backward for mankind."[33]

On the other hand, traditional conservatives were not mollified by the
claim that the requirement to balance the budget at high employment
would be a discipline against extravagant spending and wild fine-tuning.
They jeered at the notion of balancing the budget with revenues that did
not exist. As the person who had the most connection with the origins
of the idea, I tried to explain that high-employment balance was really
a "conservative" idea, but I had no success. In numerous letters to outraged Republicans, I tried to explain that being a "Keynesian" in Nixon's sense was not the same as being a Red atheist. But despite
conservative scorn of the idea of balancing a "hypothetical" budget,
there was no conservative push to balance the "real" budget.

Nevertheless, Nixon liked the idea and found it useful. The self-
fulfilling prophecy became his mantra for many months. Whenever he
felt it necessary to say something about his economic policy, he ex-

---

[33]*New York Times,* February 7, 1971.

plained that balancing the budget at full employment would tend to achieve full employment but would not be inflationary.

But in fact the mantra was not working. Early in the year the economy rose strongly, to an uncertain degree the result of a natural rebound after the General Motors strike in the fourth quarter of 1970. But it soon became clear that the economy was not moving along the desired path. The failure of unemployment to decline was especially worrisome, because the administration's strategy depended on a gradual decline of the unemployment rate to a significantly lower level—in the "neighborhood" of 4 percent—before the 1972 election. Moreover, the platform of the opposition, so far as economics was concerned, consisted mainly of complaint about the persistence of unemployment in the range of 6 percent and the promise to do better.

During the first quarter the money supply (M1, which is what everyone looked at then) seemed to be growing slowly, by less than 6 percent a year. Some in the administration, notably in the CEA, thought this was a reason to try to nudge the Federal Reserve into a more expansive policy. But Chairman Burns made it clear that he would not be nudged. He intended to keep money growth to no more than 6 percent a year, arguing that the sluggishness of the economy was due to lack of confidence rather than to lack of money.

But by the end of the quarter it was revealed that the estimates of the growth of the money supply were incorrect; M1 was actually growing faster than had been thought. Moreover, the growth of the money supply was accelerating. As it turned out, the rise of M1 in the first half of the year was at an annual rate of about 10 percent, despite Chairman Burns's insistence that he did not intend to exceed 6 percent.

In this situation, with money growing at a rapid pace and little hope of getting Chairman Burns to provide more, attention turned to the budget as a possible way to get the economy moving faster. The administration was divided on this. The CEA was increasingly on the side of some fiscal stimulus, specifically through tax reduction. The OMB was continuously opposed.[34] This difference became known and raised some speculation in the press on what the administration would do.

[34]Shultz, director of the OMB, wrote a speech in April with the title "Steady as She Goes," arguing against any change of policy. He sent it to me for comment before he delivered it. I replied to him that "Steady as She Goes" could have two different meanings. One was to keep the policy constant. The other was to keep the goal constant and adapt the policy when that seemed necessary to achieve the fixed goal. He was unpersuaded.

The president was not dogmatic on the subject. When asked at a press conference on May 1 about the possibility of a tax cut to stimulate the economy, he said: "This is an activist Administration. When I think that action can be taken to stimulate the economy, we are going to take it. And if I find, as we look at the April figures and the May figures and the June figures, that this economy is not moving as fast as it should move to deal with the unemployment problem, then we will act. We will act on the tax front and on other fronts."[35]

The division and uncertainty about policy continued until the president summoned his chief economic officials to a meeting at Camp David on June 28. McCracken argued for a tax cut. Burns argued for a wage-price review board. Shultz argued for a "steady as you go" policy—that is, for no change. The position of John Connally, secretary of the treasury, is unclear.

The outcome of the discussion was a decision for no change. The president, intending to stop the appearance of division within the administration, designated Connally as his "chief economic spokesman."[36] Connally then issued what were to become known as "The Four Nos": No tax cut, No expenditure increase, No controls on prices and wages, and No devaluation.

Since this is the first time disagreements among the economic officials appear in this narrative, it may be appropriate to describe the organizational structure within which fiscal decisions were made. Beginning at least in the time of Kennedy and Heller, there was a group responsible for analyzing the economic situation and recommending fiscal policy to the president. The group, called the Troika, consisted of the secretary of the treasury, the director of the budget, and the chairman of the CEA. It had a subordinate level, T-II, consisting of a member of the CEA, an assistant secretary of the treasury, and an associate director of the

---

[35]*Public Papers, 1971,* 608.

[36]This move seemed to be aimed mainly at the CEA and intended mainly to placate Connally. The president called the three CEA members to a meeting with Connally in the cabinet room and told them that they could write him any memos they liked, for the sake of their memoirs, but that they were to keep quiet in public. Although Connally was obviously the strongest person in the cabinet and the closest adviser to the president on political matters, he seemed always to be worried that he wasn't getting enough respect. In his diaries, Robert Haldeman reported about Connally: "He feels there's clearly a conspiracy or at least a series of actions against him by the White House staff, and he named K [Kissinger] with some meeting he had on Chile; E [Ehrlichman], Shultz, Stein especially, Flanigan, and that there's just too much participation by other people." *The Haldeman Diaries* (New York: G. P. Putnam's Sons, 1994), 439. Anyone who knows me and knew Connally will recognize this as an extreme manifestation of paranoia.

budget, and a further level, T-III, consisting of staff members of the three agencies.

By tradition the secretary of the treasury was the leader of the Troika, and the member of the CEA was the leader of T-II. When the Nixon team came into office in 1969 Paul McCracken, the chairman of the CEA, was the member of the Troika with the most experience in White House decision-making, derived from his earlier experience in the Eisenhower administration. He therefore fell into, rather than asserted, the leadership role. This fact was symbolized by the custom of holding meetings of the Troika at breakfast at the Cosmos Club, where McCracken was a member.

The arrival of John Connally as secretary of the treasury in December 1970 restored the Treasury to leadership, symbolized then by the practice of meeting for lunch in the secretary's dining room at the Treasury. This condition of leadership, and this venue, continued after George Shultz became secretary in May 1972. Leadership in this context was a procedural matter; it did not imply dominance in decision-making. The Troika reached agreement by free and equal discussion. The case I have just described, culminating in the Camp David meeting of June 28, 1970, was the only one in which the president was called on to resolve differences within the Troika. It is significant that on this occasion, the president designated Connally as the chief "spokesman," not as the chief adviser or decision-maker on economic policy.

Such differences as there were among the members of the Troika did not, in general, reflect special interests of their institutions. The disagreements between William Simon and Roy Ash in 1974, which I report later, were probably an exception. Shultz in 1970 was more committed to "steady as you go" than McCracken not because he was director of the OMB but because he was a devotee of Friedman and was fresh from the University of Chicago. Connally did not take the positions he did because he was secretary of the treasury. He took them because he was one of the president's closest *political* advisers and also because he wanted to be *seen* as in charge, whatever the policy was.

Neither was there any important difference within the Nixon "team" between economists and noneconomists, presumably "politicians," regarding fiscal policy. Except for Connally and the president, all the important players were economists, and that included the people in the Treasury on whom Connally relied. Connally did not have strong views about fiscal policy, and the president depended on his team as far as

fiscal policy was concerned.[37] Of course, the distinction between economists in the administration and politicians is unrealistic. The economists are operating in a political milieu, they have a responsibility to the
president, and they know the dates of elections. Their advice is not di-
vorced from politics. (Neither is the advice of economists who are not
in the administration.)

The June 28 decision served for a time to remove the appearance of
division within the administration. But it did not halt the division, and
it solved no economic or political problems. In fact, there would be a
radical change of economic policy within about six weeks, and at least
the president and Connally knew that this was a distinct possibility,
although it was not yet certain and the timing was unsettled.

After this meeting the president stopped referring to the full-
employment budget as a self-fulfilling prophecy. In a speech on July 6
in which he talked a good deal about the economy, he did not mention
the full-employment budget. In testimony to the Joint Economic Committee on July 9 McCracken acknowledged that the full-employment
budget was not in balance, and he used this as evidence, in response
to demands from the committee for more stimulus, that the budget was
already more stimulative than originally planned. He also recognized
that the goal of a $1,065 billion GNP for calendar 1971 would not be
met.

As is often the case with administrations, the Nixon administration
was then saying that it had a deficit but that its deficit was "just right"—
big enough to stimulate the economy by a desired amount but not big
enough to be inflationary. In its January 1972 economic report, the CEA
described the situation thus:

It seemed in the summer of 1971 that there would be a significant shift from a
full-employment surplus in fiscal 1971 to a full-employment deficit in fiscal
1972. The Administration considered this development appropriate in view of
the sluggishness of the economy. At the same time the Administration was averse
to making decisions [emphasis added] that would add substantially to expenditure commitments for the future. Even within the limits of fiscal 1972, while

---

[37] I am not here telling the story of the price and wage controls, which were the most
dramatic aspect of the Nixon economic policy. Connally was much more dominant in
this area than he was in fiscal policy because the decision to impose the controls was
more clearly determined by political argument than was the case with fiscal policy, which
relied heavily on economic argument. But even in the case of wage and price controls,
where Connally was the leader because he was chairman of the Cost of Living Council,
he did not intervene much in substantive matters except when there was great political
sensitivity.

more fiscal stimulus was desired, there was danger of excessive expansion in the prevailing inflationary atmosphere.[38]

The administration was then in a stage of what might be called passive fine-tuning. It would not recommend tax cuts or expenditure increases intended to pump up the economy if they violated the full-employment-balance rule. But given the weak state of the economy, it was willing to accept expenditure increases that originated elsewhere or that seemed to have their own justifications, even if they did unbalance the full-employment budget. Thus, the president accepted, with minimum protest, a large increase in social security benefits, one that had originated in Congress, and he signed an Emergency Employment Act with no reference to its budget consequences.

Before I come to the dramatic events of August 15, 1971, I should remind the reader of the general context. The economy was not the main focus of attention at the time—at least not in the political and media world. Attention was on the Vietnam War. When the president held a press conference, the great bulk of the questions were about Vietnam. The condition of the economy was not disastrous, by the standards of later performance. The unemployment rate was about 6 percent; it would be lower than that in only three of the eighteen years from 1975 to 1993. Consumer prices were rising by about 4.5 percent a year, compared with an average of 5.5 percent a year from 1975 to 1993.

But even when the economy was the object of attention, the focus was not on fiscal policy. The big debate concerned incomes policy or price and wage control. This is a separate subject, which I have treated to some extent elsewhere.[39] But it is worth pointing out that the price-control debate interacted with the argument about fiscal and monetary policy. Many of the people who wanted a more expansive fiscal and monetary policy—usually emphasizing the fiscal element—also wanted "some kind" of incomes policy. They could protect themselves against the charge that their fiscal and monetary proposals were inflationary by pointing to incomes policy as a defense. In a peculiar way the argument worked in reverse with Arthur Burns. He maintained that the problem

[38]*The Annual Report of the Council of Economic Advisers* (Washington, D.C.: Government Printing Office, 1973), 65.
[39]Herbert Stein, *Presidential Economics: The Making of Economic Policy from Roosevelt to Clinton*, 3d rev. ed. (Washington, D.C.: American Enterprise Institute for Public Policy Research, 1994), esp. 176–87; Herbert Stein, "Price-Fixing as Seen by a Price-Fixer, Part II," in *Contemporary Economic Problems: 1978,* ed. William Fellner (Washington, D.C.: American Enterprise Institute for Public Policy Research, 1978), 113–35.

was not inadequate fiscal and monetary stimulus but was instead a lack of confidence, which he attributed to the wage-price situation and particularly to the upward pressure of wages on business. Thus he believed that with a "wage-price review board" to strengthen business confidence, the economy would recover without fiscal-monetary stimulus, and that without the wage-price review board, fiscal-monetary measures would do no good.

By the middle of August the administration was ready for the big change of economic policy. The economic situation was not deteriorating. By some measurements the inflation rate seemed to be abating. But unemployment seemed stuck at 6 percent. The time remaining for showing significant improvement was getting shorter. The clamor for some kind of direct restraint on wages and prices was getting louder, from both the Republican and the Democratic sides of Congress and from the national media. Leaders of business were also asking for help from the government to restrain wage increases, and to do that without also imposing restraint on price increases was inconceivable. The U.S. balance-of-payments deficit was rising, and there was a threat that some country would demand conversion into gold for the dollars it was acquiring. The actual date of the decision to change economic policy was probably determined by the fear of a demand for gold. Whether policy would have been changed without that is uncertain, but probably it would have, given the demand for controls from so many sources, including many of the president's natural allies, and the approach of the 1972 elections.

The new policy decided on at a Camp David meeting from August 13 to 15 and announced to the public by the president in a television address on August 15 called for wage and price controls, suspension of the U.S. government's commitment to converting dollars held by foreign governments into gold, and a new budget package. I confine myself here to the budget package.

The decision made at Camp David about the budget had two elements. First, quick expansion of the economy was to be stimulated, and second, the administration would not recommend an increase of the deficit. At this point the statement in the CEA's report earlier in the year becomes relevant. Different kinds of budgetary changes have different effects per dollar on the economy, so that equal dollar changes of revenues and expenditures are not necessarily neutral in their effects. Therefore the Camp David package had to consist of equal tax reductions and expenditure reductions, but the tax reductions had to be more stimulative per dollar than the expenditure cuts were repressive so that the net effect of the equal total revenue cuts and expenditure cuts would be stimulative.

In fact, the package went a little further than was necessary to meet these two requirements; the proposed expenditure reductions exceeded the revenue reductions, but still it could be reasonably argued that the net effect was stimulative. The revenue side of the package included one revenue *increase,* the imposition of a surcharge on imports, which was expected to increase demand for U.S. product. The elimination of the excise tax on automobiles was expected to encourage a big increase in car sales. But the major stimulus in the package was the restoration of the investment tax credit with the unusual feature that a 10 percent credit would be given for investment in the first year of the program and 5 percent thereafter. That, the administration believed, would tend to push the inauguration of investment projects into the first year of the program. About 40 percent of the proposed expenditure cuts, on the other hand, consisted simply of the recognition that some new expenditure programs were not about to be enacted by Congress as early as had been proposed in the budget.[40]

Another aspect of the administration's thinking about how this "balanced" combination of tax cuts and expenditure cuts would be stimu-

---

[40]A table in the 1972 economic report of the Council of Economic Advisers summarized the budget changes in the August 15 program:

Type of change	Billions of dollars
Revenue reductions	5.8
Job development credit	2.7
Accelerated increase of personal exemptions	.9
Elimination of auto excises	2.2
Revenue increase	2.0
Import surcharge[a]	2.0
Revenue reductions, net	3.8
Expenditure reductions	4.9
Freeze of Federal pay increase	1.3
Deferral of general revenue sharing	1.1
Reduction of Federal employment	.8
Deferrals of some special revenue sharing	.5
Deferral of welfare reform	.6
Other	.6
Excess of expenditure reductions over net revenue reductions	1.1

[a]It was arbitrarily assumed that the surcharge would continue until June 30, 1972.
Source: Department of the United States Treasury.

lating was not announced at the time. The president believed that if he proposed a cut of individual income taxes of a certain size, Congress would enact a bigger one. In this he turned out to be correct. Congress did not, however, enact the investment tax credit quite as the president had proposed. Instead of a 10 percent rate for the first year and a 5 percent rate thereafter, Congress enacted a constant 7 percent rate.

The new economic policy announced by the president on August 15, 1971, was the most popular thing he ever did in the field of economic policy and probably in all fields. Attention naturally concentrated on the most dramatic aspect of the program, namely, the wage and price controls. The fiscal package received little notice and little complaint. The only significant argument came from Democratic politicians and their economists who argued that a program in which expenditure cuts exceeded revenue cuts could not be stimulative. Sophisticated economists, including Paul Samuelson, a future winner of the Nobel Award in Economics, made their argument on the basis of a simple-minded proposition from the elementary economics textbook, a proposition better known for its curiosity than for its relevance. The proposition is the balanced-budget multiplier theorem, which states that an equal increase of revenues and expenditures is expansionary. The theorem depends on certain limitations on the nature of the expenditures and the revenues. The expenditures must all be for the purchase of goods and services. The only effect of the revenues must be to change consumers' disposable income and thereby change consumption expenditures by a fraction-less-than-one of the revenue change. Neither of these limitations applied to the August 1971 budget package, as has been explained above.

At this point the administration had taken two steps in carrying out a fine-tuning, expansionary fiscal policy while seeming to adhere to a stable, neutral policy of balancing the budget at high employment. First, it had accepted expenditure increases that violated the high-employment balance rule if it could attribute the violation to Congress. Second, it had just shown how an expansionary policy could be accommodated within the limits of a budget-balancing policy by the appropriate choice of specific tax and expenditure measures.

The third step would come in December 1971. The inflation rate had come down nicely, as a result of the price and wage controls, but the unemployment rate was still not showing the desired response. The administration decided to inject another dose of fiscal stimulus into the economy. It did not, however, want to lose its budget-balancing credentials. The method chosen was to increase spending as rapidly as possible during the remainder of the current fiscal year (the fiscal year then ended on June 30) but show a budget for the next year, fiscal 1973, that would be balanced on the full-employment basis. Fiscal 1972 would be regarded as water over the dam, and public attention would focus on fiscal 1973 as indication of the administration's policy. (This strategy had been followed by Franklin D. Roosevelt and probably other presidents before and since.)

Accordingly the president called a meeting of the cabinet in December. He told the members that, peculiar as it might seem coming from him, on the advice of his economists he was asking them to spend as much as they could out of existing appropriations before June 30, 1972. In the upshot, this instruction did not have much effect on the rate of expenditures except in the case of the Department of Defense, which managed to increase its outlays by a few billion dollars above its previous plans.

In the first part of 1972 the administration continued to describe its budget policy as "just right." The president's budget message (January 24) was explicit about that. "If we were to spend less, we would be 'too little and too late' to stimulate greater business activity and create more jobs; if we were to spend more, we would be spending 'too much, too soon' and thereby invite a renewal of inflation. Instead, we must spend 'enough and on time' to keep the economy on a steadily upward peacetime course while providing jobs for all who want them and meeting the urgent needs of the American people."[41]

This was, of course, fine-tuning worthy of Heller or Okun. But the administration promised that after this dalliance with fine-tuning, it would return to the straight-and-narrow path of budget-balancing, at least in the sense of balance at full employment. Thus, the full-employment budget would be in deficit by $8.1 billion in fiscal 1972 but would have a surplus of $0.7 billion in fiscal 1973. In this way the president staked out his claim to being the champion of sound and conservative fiscal policy while also the champion of economic recovery and high employment. In a further assertion of this claim he asked, or challenged, Congress to enact a ceiling of $246 billion on expenditures for FY1973.

---

[41]*Public Papers of the Presidents, Richard M. Nixon, 1972* (Washington, D.C.: Government Printing Office, 1973), 78.

The CEA, in its January 1972 report, was as usual more modest in its claim for the "just right" fiscal policy, although it did list the shift from full-employment-budget surplus to full-employment-budget deficit between 1971 and 1972 as one of the reasons to expect the economy to expand in 1972.

In a discussion of fiscal policy for the longer run, the CEA made the standard argument for full-employment-budget balance as the desirable rule of fiscal policy:

Adherence to the principle of keeping expenditures that would be made at full employment within the level of the receipts that would be yielded by the existing tax system under conditions of full employment would contribute to the avoidance of inflationary surges of demand. Certainly the shift of the budget position from approximate balance at full employment in fiscal 1965 to a large full-employment deficit in fiscal 1968 was a major cause of the current inflation. There are rare circumstances in which a deficit or surplus at full employment may be unavoidable or even appropriate economic policy. But in general more reliable results will be achieved from minimizing such departures than from following any of the alternative courses—trying to balance the actual budget continuously, disregarding budget balance, or making annual ad hoc decisions about the proper size of the deficit or surplus.

This statement differs from earlier CEA formulations of the full-employment-balance idea in several respects, which need not be parsed out here. What is interesting is the reference to the "rare circumstances" in which a deficit (or surplus?) at full employment may be appropriate. There is no explanation of what the rare circumstance was that made a full-employment deficit appropriate in 1972. The original CED formulation had recognized that there might be recessions of such extraordinary depth or duration that they would justify departure from the full-employment-balance rule. But the CED had never found such a situation to exist, even during the 1957–58 recession. The 1971–72 recession, in which unemployment did not exceed 6 percent, does not seem such a rare circumstance. This is especially so because by 1972 there was considerable opinion among economists that "full employment" was not 4 percent unemployment but was more probably 5 percent or more. In fact, the administration was considering a public statement to the effect that it had raised its definition of full employment. It decided not to do so because it thought, correctly, that it would be charged with moving the goalposts in order to claim victory in the effort to achieve full employment. If the administration had raised the amount of unemployment to be considered full employment, the budget for FY1973 would not have been in full-employment balance. Moreover, the expected gap between actual and full employment would have been small, and it would have been harder to find the rare circumstance that would have justified the deficit.

These fine points of doctrine received no attention at the time. By spring, discussion of fiscal policy changed significantly. The exact date of this change can be identified. It was the last meeting of the Troika before Connally left as secretary of the treasury and Shultz took his place. The decision was then made to switch from an emphasis on the Keynesian, stimulative aspect of the budget, with concentration on the size of the deficit, to an emphasis on the level of expenditures per se and on the level of taxation per se. This was not abandonment of concern with the stabilization implications of the budget entirely, and the administration would continue to talk about inflationary consequences of fiscal policy, but that would no longer be in the forefront.

The emphasis on the levels of expenditure and taxation, essentially on the size of government, was not new. I called it "The Old Time Religion," which suggested its age. But it had not been in the forefront of talk about the budget, especially from the executive branch, for a long time—probably since the time of Coolidge.

The reasons for the administration's shift were both economic and political. The economy was performing well. Output was rising strongly, and with the controls in effect the rate of inflation was low. (In July, after the economic statistics for the second quarter were released, I held a press conference at which I claimed that these represented "the best combination of economic numbers to be released on one day in all of history, or at least in the Christian Era.") The administration economic officials were worried about how they were going to get out from under the controls without a resurgence of inflation.[42] They no longer talked about a "just right" fiscal policy—just stimulative enough and not inflationary. Their attention was concentrated on the inflation danger. But since they were taking credit for the low rate of inflation, they could not get the public alarmed about inflation. There was, however, something more durable in the new attitude. There was a feeling of having strayed too easily from the fiscal rule, and there was a determination to stick to

---

[42]There was a parallel here to the problem of trying to pump an economy out of recession with temporary tax reductions or concessions. How are these temporary measures to be ended without a downward shock to the economy?

it more faithfully in the future, a determination that would be tested in 1974 when the economy weakened.

At the same time, the Democrats were behaving in a way that gave the Republican administration a good opportunity to exploit the antispending, antitax issue. This was particularly true after George McGovern became the Democratic candidate for the presidency and began to expound his "Demogrant" plan, which would have had most of the American people paying higher taxes in order to make a cash grant to a minority of the American people. Since the economy was rising so smartly, an administration position against more government spending could not be credibly criticized as neglect of the unemployment problem and could be viewed purely as defense of the taxpayer. Moreover, the administration was sincerely surprised and shocked by the level to which federal spending had risen. As Shultz, then secretary of the Treasury, said, "There must be a lot of people out there who say to themselves, 'Those guys ought to be able to get along on a quarter of a trillion dollars.' "[43]

So the administration began an all-court press against the Democrats and Congress on the subject of government spending, with the threat of higher taxes in the background. The president repeated his request for Congress to enact a ceiling on expenditures. He vetoed many appropriation bills. He faced a difficult decision about a bill, sponsored by Congressman Wilbur Mills, the great opponent of government spending, that would raise social security benefits by 20 percent. That was too popular a proposal for even Nixon to veto, and moreover it was part of legislation raising the debt ceiling, which was necessary if the government was to continue. He signed it on July 1 with a complaint that the increase of benefits was not matched by an increase in social security contributions and warned: "As a result of this failure, it would add an additional $3.7 billion to the more than $3 billion by which earlier actions and inactions by the Congress have thrown the full employment budget for the fiscal year 1973 into deficit—thus threatening dangerously to escalate the rate of inflation at a time when the Administration's economic policies are succeeding in turning it back."[44]

[43]*National Journal* 4 (1972): 1314.
[44]*Public Papers, 1972,* 723.

He promised to cut other spending to compensate. In addition to vetoing many appropriation bills, the president impounded—that is, withheld from expenditure—many billions of dollars of appropriations that had been passed. Moreover, he criticized Congress in general for failing to follow any procedure that would enable it to decide how much to spend in total and to make disciplined choices among possible expenditures.

The administration's defense of its antispending program ran along two lines. One, already noted in the president's response to the social security benefit increase, raised the danger of inflation. The other raised the danger of higher taxes.

In a speech on June 17, I said that the tax reform desired by "the great majority of people" was "relief from the specter of high taxes and a reasonable prospect of tax reduction." I continued: "A good deal of the current debate revolves around two assertions. First is the assertion that Federal expenditures will, should, and must rise at a rate which requires a tax increase. The second proposition is that the necessary additional revenue can be obtained from the very rich and from corporations, that is from a small segment of the population, without imposing additional burdens upon the vast remainder."

One response to the administration's new austerity about the budget was widespread skepticism about the president's determination to hold the line on spending. Congressman George H. Mahon, chairman of the House Appropriations Committee, predicted that the FY1973 deficit could be much larger than the $25 billion shown in the budget message. In fact, expenditures were held to the $246 billion proposed by the president, and the deficit turned out to be $14 billion.

The response of the Democratic economists to the president's strategy was predictable. Summarizing testimony before the Joint Economic Committee, the *National Journal* said, "Now, Democratic economists claim, Stein is advising a policy that will stop the emerging recovery in its tracks and that ignores the unemployment problem." Heller told the committee, "The major policy prescription has to be a negative one: don't prematurely cut off the monetary and fiscal life blood of the expansion." And Samuelson added: "The Republicans can stand everything but success. In the summer of our health advance, they look forward to the winter of our excess. Already official and unofficial witnesses are appearing before you . . . warning that strong growth is too much of a good thing."[45]

But despite the administration's budget austerity, unemployment in calendar 1973 averaged 4.9 percent, about what economists then commonly considered full employment. Total output in 1973 was 10 percent higher than in 1971. Despite the controls, inflation accelerated again in 1973, and although that was due in part to poor world harvests and the oil embargo, after-the-fact judgment is probably that fiscal policy and monetary policy, especially the latter, were too expansionist in 1972. The money supply, whether narrowly or broadly defined, rose exceptionally fast in that year.

A more serious response came from many members of Congress who regarded Nixon's policy both as an embarrassment to them about their inability to make responsible budget decisions and as a usurpation of their role in determining how much to spend for what. They especially resented the president's impoundment of funds they had appropriated, something his predecessors had also done but not on so large a scale. It was not only that he cut expenditures but that he cut them selectively, according to his priorities and not theirs.

The president's right to impound funds was being contested in the courts.[46] However, there were those in Congress who believed that they would have to defend themselves by legislation and that, moreover, if they were to reassert their authority, they needed to establish means to exercise it more responsibly. This was the origin of what became the Budget Reform Act of 1974, which enters Congress more directly into the process of making fiscal policy and about which more will be said later.

The administration's emphasis on the antitax issue was a forerunner of Reaganism and Bushism. There was, however, a difference. The Nixon administration started with expenditure restraint as the necessary condition for tax restraint. Reagan, particularly, was not so fastidious. And the Nixon administration did not claim that tax reduction would increase the revenue. Indeed it did not claim any direct economic benefits

---

[45]John F. Burby, "Economic Report: No Letup for President's Economic Advisers Despite Good Second Quarter," *National Journal* 4 (1972): 1283.

[46]In connection with this litigation, I wrote an affidavit saying that presidential impoundment of funds was legitimated by the Employment Act of 1946, which instructed the president to use all his powers to achieve high employment and purchasing power. The president lost this suit, and I never learned that my affidavit made any difference.

from tax restraint. It based its position on the idea that taxpayers did not like to pay taxes and were entitled to do as little of that as possible.

The Nixon team clung to the Old Time Religion for the rest of its time. It was against spending, against taxes, and against deficits. And although it continued to make the stabilization argument—that is, that fiscal conservatism was necessary to prevent inflation—it increasingly emphasized aversion to government spending and, especially, to taxes, as such. In his January 28, 1973, radio address explaining his new budget, the president pointed to the trend of increasing federal expenditures since 1952 and warned that if the trend continued, the budget would exceed one trillion dollars by the 1990s. (Ah, wilderness!) He then said:

We must resist this trend for several reasons. The first involves your taxes.

Since 1950, the share of personal income taken by taxes for all levels of government has doubled—to more than 20 percent of your family budget.[47] This growing burden works to dull individual incentive and to discourage responsibility. As government takes more from people, people can do less for themselves. The only way to restrain taxes is to restrain spending.

In the campaign last fall, I promised I would not propose any new tax increases. By keeping a tight lid on spending, my new budget keeps that promise.[48]

The CEA report of the same month as usual put deficits and stability at the forefront of its discussion of fiscal policy. But in sounding the concern about spending, it used more fundamentalist terms than it had formerly. After presenting a table showing federal, state, and local expenditures, in total and for various purposes, as a percent of full-employment GNP for selected years starting with 1955, the council said:

The rise in the share of Federal civilian spending in the United States has accelerated since the mid-1960s along with the large increase in the number and scope of social programs. Many of these were introduced without any firm estimate of how effective they would be in solving the problems to which they were addressed or how much they would cost in the long run. At the same time there has emerged the need for new social programs, especially in the field of pollution abatement.

[47]These figures are puzzling. These results can be approximately obtained, however, if social security contributions, which are deducted from personal income and excluded from personal taxes in the standard national income accounts, are included in both.

[48]*Public Papers of the Presidents, Richard M. Nixon, 1973* (Washington, D.C.: Government Printing Office, 1974), 30.

The continued existence of large social problems alongside a greatly expanded volume of government expenditures designed to correct these problems is not a strong argument for devoting a still-larger share of the national output to similar government programs. On the contrary, it is an argument for close scrutiny of these programs to see whether they can be justified by their results. Such a scrutiny, carried out by the Administration, has led to decisions to cut back many programs, even though total Federal spending, after the cuts, will still be rising by about $20 billion a year.[49]

The administration's definition of a balanced budget tightened as 1973 and 1974 went on. It retained the notion of balancing the budget at high employment in its lexicon, but from time to time it indicated a desire for more. In a statement of July 18, 1973, announcing Phase IV of the price-wage control program, the president said that in the existing inflationary environment, the country could not "afford to live by that minimum standard" of balancing the budget at high employment. He added, "We must take as our goal the more ambitious one of balancing the actual budget."[50]

In one sense the goal of balancing the actual budget was not more ambitious. The unexpectedly large inflation had raised forecast revenues for fiscal 1974 to a level at which they equaled budgeted expenditures, so the actual budget would be in balance if expenditures could be kept from exceeding the budget. At the same time, since actual unemployment had not fallen to the magic figure of 4 percent, balancing the actual budget implied a surplus in the full-employment budget. This surplus would have been achieved with the aid of an undesirably high rate of inflation, a condition that seemed not to worry anyone outside the CEA. The president's move to balancing the actual budget as a standard may have served to avoid the argument that since there was a surplus in the full-employment budget, there was room for more spending. It also served to get him more in tune with the more traditional advocacy of balanced budgets. Thus, the call for balancing the actual budget met the president's political needs and was consistent with the CEA's view of an appropriate fiscal period for the time.

Debate about the president's budget policy was muted during 1973. Real output was rising and unemployment was declining, while inflation was again reaching an alarming rate, despite the continued price and

[49]*The Annual Report of the Council of Economic Advisers* (Washington, D.C.: Government Printing Office, 1974), 77–78.
[50]*Public Papers, 1973*, 652.

wage controls. This was not a condition in which the usual Democratic-liberal-Keynesian call for a more expansive fiscal policy would have had much plausibility. At the same time, the president had occupied the restrictionist position, and no one seemed more interested in proposing a tighter budget than he did. Moreover, national attention on economic policy, such as there was, concentrated on the controls, which were going on a roller-coaster ride from relaxation in Phase III to tightening in Phase IV to relaxation and preparation for abandonment in Phase V. Anyway, Watergate was absorbing the nation's attention to the exclusion of everything else. It is significant that in all of President Nixon's press conferences during 1973, there was not one question about the budget.

By the time of the budget of January 1974, the "problem" of the full-employment surplus had become more awkward. Partly because of unforeseen increases connected with health and income-security programs, expenditures had risen, so that despite the increased receipts resulting from inflation, the actual budget was in deficit for fiscal 1974 and was expected to be in deficit for fiscal 1975. But the full-employment budget was projected to be in surplus in both years. And at that time, because of the slowdown in the economy, there was a rising demand for fiscal stimulus, mainly in the form of a tax cut. The administration was at pains to explain why the full-employment surplus did not justify such a move.

In his budget message, after saying that his proposals would yield a full-employment surplus of $4 billion in FY1974 and $8 billion in FY1975 (about 0.25 and 0.5 percent of expected GNP respectively), the president explained:

In large part, the estimated increase in the full-employment surplus is the result of the high inflation rate experienced in calendar year 1973 and expected to continue for the first half of 1974. In the short run inflation increases receipts more than it increases outlays. Thus, it increases for a time the surplus that would be achieved at high employment. This means that the budget has the effect of restraining inflation. The rising full-employment surpluses estimated here are largely the product of an inflation that is proceeding too rapidly. To use the size of these surpluses as an invitation or an excuse for more spending would only make the inflation worse.

A 4% unemployment rate is used in calculating full-employment receipts and outlays as a conventional standard which approximately removes the effects on the budget estimates of year-to-year changes in the level of economic activity. To serve this purpose the unemployment rate used for the calculations must be reasonably stable from year to year. However, this does not mean that the feasible and proper target for unemployment is always represented by the same figure. In fact, as a result of changes in the composition of the labor force, a 4% unemployment rate today would mean much tighter conditions in labor markets than would have been true ten or twenty years ago.[51]

In its annual report issued a few days after the budget, the Council of Economic Advisers attempted to estimate the size of the qualifications expressed there about the implications of "full-employment balance." In the process it revealed the estimates and discretionary decisions that are involved in the use of a full-employment-balance rule. The report presented a table estimating the size of the year-to-year change in the full-employment surplus on three bases: (1) 4 percent unemployment and the actual or forecast inflation rate, (2) 4 percent unemployment and constant inflation rate from year to year, and (3) unemployment "standardized" for changes in the age-sex composition of the labor force, with the actual or forecast inflation rate. (See Table 5.2.)[52]

In addition to these assumptions, the calculations also required a decision to use the national income accounts budget, rather than the unified budget, to assume the normal growth rate of real GNP to be 4 percent per annum rather than the 4.3 percent previously assumed, to treat the $9 billion of overwithholding of individual tax payments in 1972 as private saving rather than government taxation, and to exclude from expenditures the expected transfer of $2.1 billion worth of rupees to the Indian government in 1974. Also, at one point the report showed a calculation of the full-employment budget for federal, state, and local governments combined, suggesting that the combined figure might be a better measure of fiscal impact than the federal figure alone.

The net of all this was not to suggest that the full-employment budget was inferior to the conventional "actual" budget as an explanation of past economic behavior or as a guide to policy. But it did show that the implications and guidance of the full-employment budget were not unequivocal.

In fact, however, the budget debates of 1974, which were active, did not revolve around the measurement or implications of the full-employment budget. Especially after the departure of Shultz as secretary of the Treasury, to be succeeded by William Simon, even in the administration no one cared about the full-employment budget except the

[51]The Budget Message of the President, February 4, 1974, 7.
[52]*Annual Report* (1973), 31.

Table 5.2 *Federal budget surplus or deficit under alternative*
assumptions, national income accounts basis, calendar years
1969–1974 (billions of dollars)

		Full-employment budget surplus or deficit $(-)$ under alternative assumptions[1]		
Calendar year	Actual budget surplus or deficit $(-)$	4 percent unemployment	4 percent unemployment standardized inflation rate[2]	Variable unemployment rate[3]
Level:				
1969	8.1	8.8	—	4.9
1970	−11.9	4.0	—	.3
1971	−22.1	−2.1	—	−5.0
1972	−15.9	−7.7	—	−10.4
1973	.6	5.8	—	3.1
1974	−4.6	6.0	—	2.1
Change from previous year:				
1970	−20.0	−4.8	−4.8	−4.6
1971	−10.2	−6.1	−5.3	−5.3
1972	6.2	−5.6	−5.6	−5.4
1973	16.5	13.5	10.2	13.5
1974[4]	−5.2	.2	.3	−1.0

[1]$9 billion in overwithholding excluded from 1972 receipts.
[2]Change in surplus or deficit between two succeeding years assumes that inflation rate is constant at rate of first year.
[3]Assumes that unemployment rates of the civilian labor force are constant at their 1956 levels in each of four sex-age categories: males and females 16–24 years and males and females 25 years and over. Instead of staying at 4 percent, the overall unemployment rate used to represent a constant rate of utilization of the labor force in this estimate rises to about 4.6 percent by 1973 because the labor force was increasingly composed of groups (females, youths) characteristically having higher unemployment rates than older males.
[4]Excludes transfer of $2.1 billion worth of rupees to the Indian government expected in the first half of 1974.
Sources: Department of Commerce (Bureau of Economic Analysis), Office of Management and Budget, and Council of Economic Advisers.

CEA. And even the CEA did not regard the full-employment budget as the last word in fiscal policy.

The main issue was how to interpret the current economic situation and what to do about it. After the oil embargo and the big increase in the price of imported oil, the economy was obviously slowing down. Real GNP rose at an annual rate of only 1.3 percent in the fourth quarter of 1973 and actually declined in the first quarter of 1974. At the same time the inflation rate was rising to alarming heights. This was partly a direct reflection of rising oil prices. But it also reflected other factors: rising food prices, the disintegration and then the termination of the price controls, and the general pressure of demand. One can hardly think of any earlier period when so much inflation corresponded with so sharp a decline of output.

The reaction of the economists to whom expansive fiscal policy was the never-failing remedy was to prescribe more of that remedy. They were supported in this position by a certain number of politicians, especially those on the Joint Economic Committee of Congress. They argued that the American consumer was being subjected to an oil-import tax, namely the additional amount the consumer had to pay to buy imported oil. This tax was reducing the income available to purchase American products, thus depressing domestic demand. The proposed remedy was a cut in federal taxes.

The administration response to this had several parts, but the main one was that inflation remained the overwhelming problem. Even without the oil crisis the inflation rate, as represented in the actual and the expected behavior of wage rates, was worrisome. To regain a liveable rate of inflation would entail a period of slowdown—a message repeated from 1969 but now in more urgent circumstances. Beyond the slowdown involved in restraining inflation, the economy was slowing down because of the oil shortage, which directly affected production in some industries and especially reduced demand for automobiles and tourism. To try to correct that part of the slowdown by general fiscal expansion would not succeed but would only make the inflation worse. That is, the administration—even the CEA—did not rely simply on the general rule that the budget should be balanced at high employment. It maintained that in this particular economic situation, the proposed fiscal policy was appropriate. Moreover, as it had always done, the CEA continuously reviewed its forecast of the economic situation to see whether the outlook had changed sufficiently to justify a change of policy.

The administration's forecast at the beginning of the year, and indeed through the first half of the year, was that the effect of the oil crisis would dissipate and the economy would turn up in the second half— looking around the corner again. The exceptional unpredictability of the economic situation was recognized. As a safeguard against the possibility that unemployment would increase, the administration recommended a strengthening of the unemployment compensation system. Moreover, the president promised that there would be no recession and that if the necessity arose, he would take fiscal measures to prevent a recession.

Within the administration, attitudes differed somewhat. Arthur Burns, if he may be considered an "honorary member" of the administration, was most apocalyptic in his alarms about inflation.[53] Moreover, he didn't like government spending per se and was prepared to recommend a cut of spending at every opportunity. Simon, the new secretary of the Treasury, was scornful of the idea of the full-employment budget and had a hankering for "Balancing the budget, period!" He was in a contest with Roy Ash, director of the OMB, for the leadership of the administration's economic team and had staked out expenditure cuts as the program on which he would campaign for that position. Ash could not match him in proposing expenditure cuts because, as director of the OMB, he would have the responsibility for finding whatever amount of cuts was agreed on, a responsibility Simon would not share. But Ash also presented himself as the champion of whatever expenditure cuts could realistically be made.

The debate about how much to cut expenditures for FY1975—whether by $10 billion or $5 billion (a difference of about 0.3 percent of GNP) or by some smaller amount—dominated talk about fiscal policy during the remainder of the Nixon term. The debate was, however, largely symbolic. The CEA tried to estimate the possible effect of such cuts on the inflation rate and the unemployment rate and always concluded that the results were minimal. Cutting expenditures by $5 billion might reduce the inflation rate by 0.1 percentage point and raise the unemployment rate by the same amount. Estimates by private economists yielded similar results, which was not surprising since they used similar models of the economy. But to say that the effects were largely symbolic does not mean that they were unimportant. The administration considered the economy to be at a crucial point, where expectations for inflation might solidify at the existing very high rate or where the view might be accepted that after bulging in 1974, for transitory reasons, the inflation rate would subside to an acceptable level. The administration's logic was that a demonstration of firmness about the budget would increase the chance for the more favorable outcome. Moreover, the ad-

---

[53]After one of Burns's jeremiads about the danger of inflation, a reporter asked me if the administration shared his view. I said that we did but that we didn't all talk in the voice of an Old Testament prophet.

ministration thought it was good politics for it to stick to its posture as the enemy of both government spending and inflation.

The discussion within the administration about how much to cut the budget is of interest as an indication of what people thought, but it was of no practical importance for policy. The revisions of the national income data that came out in July gave a gloomier picture of the economy than had previously been apparent. The slowdown of output had been larger than expected, and the accumulation of inventories in the first half of the year was a bad sign for the future. The continuing high inflation was driving up the full-employment-budget surplus, and although that might be tending to restrain inflation, its initial impact was to depress output. Similarly, because of the inflation the *real* increase of the money supply was less than it appeared to be.

As a result of this revised appraisal of the economy, the CEA, and economists in other agencies, concluded that a push for tighter budget policy was no longer appropriate. It was, however, too late for the Nixon administration to shift gears. In a major address on the economy, in Los Angeles on July 28, the president called for a cut of $5 billion in FY1975 expenditures. But eleven days later he would be out of office, and the budget problem would be left to a new president.

It may be appropriate at this point to summarize the state of American fiscal policy at the end of the Nixon administration. Probably the most general thing to say is that fiscal policy would be an elastic response to a combination of factors whose outcome could not be precisely determined from any objective data.

1. The idea that the budget should be balanced retained some appeal in the country. Yet this appeal did not force the government to balance the budget. Since 1960 the budget had been balanced only once, in 1969, and at this writing, 1994, it has not been balanced again. But politicians felt obliged to show deference to the idea. Moreover, mainly because of fear of public reaction but also because of their own fears, they did not like to get "too far" away from the balanced budget. How high was "too high" was unclear, but it was probably a matter of what the country had become accustomed to. Between the end of World War II and 1974, the annual deficit averaged about 0.4 percent of GDP. It reached 3 percent in only one year—1968—during the Vietnam War, and that was regarded as shocking enough to force the tax increase and expenditure ceiling that gave us the lonely balanced budget of 1969. In

FY1974 the deficit was 0.4 percent of GDP. In *The Fiscal Revolution in America* I said that the balanced budget was a flag that was more often saluted than followed. A more accurate description might have been that it was a flag that was followed—but at a distance that was not fixed but would change with experience.

2. The idea that the budget should be unbalanced in recessions was accepted. But the idea that the full-employment budget should be balanced—which would have determined the *size* of the actual deficit in a recession—had only a shadowy influence. It could be used to rationalize recession deficits for people presumed to care about balancing the budget, but it would not serve as a precise guide to policy. This was partly because the full-employment deficit could not be uniquely and objectively measured. The full-employment concept would survive as a way for economists to think and talk about fiscal policy.

3. Within the elastic limits set by these notions of balance, fiscal policy would be set by two considerations. One was a rough, ad hoc response to the cyclical situation. This meant expansive measures, usually expenditure increases, in recessions and the reverse in conditions of inflation. This countercyclical policy did not, however, precisely determine the policy that would be followed. The interpretation of the economic situation and the choice of the prescription for it were always uncertain and disputed. The 1974 situation, in which we did not know whether the main problem was inflation or recession, was only the most extreme example.

4. But even when the economic situation, and the appropriate countercyclical remedy, seemed clear, the prescription might not be followed closely because of another consideration. People—politicians and private citizens—cared about the ingredients of the budget for other reasons in addition to cyclical consequences. Some were devoted to particular expenditures and would resist cutting them for the sake of a countercyclical effect. Some were opposed to particular expenditures and would persist in the effort to cut them without regard to the cyclical situation. Almost all were opposed to raising taxes most of the time.

By one of nature's marvelous harmonies, those who were most resistant to cutting expenditures were most likely to interpret the economic situation as requiring stimulus and thus requiring more spending. Those who were most reluctant to see expenditures increase were most likely to interpret the economic situation as requiring fiscal restraint. Thus, most people did not feel any conflict between their ideas of what was necessary for economic stability and what was appropriate budget policy for other reasons. The two camps did, however, have to be reconciled, and this resulted in compromises that did not exactly suit anyone.

5. Most of the time it was the president who took responsibility for the aggregate state of the budget and especially for restraining deficits. The president did not have complete control, being limited by past commitments and contemporary Congresses. But still he had much more control than anyone else. Presidents felt this responsibility and also felt that the public would hold them responsible. So it was presidents who resisted tax cuts, who pressed for tax increases on the rare occasions when that happened, and who vetoed appropriations and impounded funds. This situation would change to some degree when Congress attempted to assert control through the 1974 Budget Reform Act, which Nixon signed a few days before leaving office. It would also change further when Ronald Reagan came into office, with a different view of presidential responsibility.

THE FORD AND CARTER YEARS

On the afternoon of August 9, immediately after being sworn in as president of the United States, Gerald Ford held a meeting in the cabinet room with his economic advisers. With one exception these were all left over from the Nixon administration—Ash, Burns, Rush, Simon, and myself. The exception was Alan Greenspan, who had been named by Nixon to succeed me but who would not take office until September 1.

No one was well prepared, and the meeting was unproductive. I suggested that each of the participants should be asked to write a two- or three-page statement of his views; these could be the basis of another meeting within a few days. The president agreed. These submissions, with a summary and analysis written by me, were distributed in advance of a meeting on August 15. Since I was about to leave to take up a professorship at the University of Virginia, I asked the president whether I could take the papers to use in classes as evidence of what economic advisers and policymakers think about. The president gave his consent, and thus we have an unusually concise picture of the economic problem as viewed by the administration at the beginning of the Ford term.

1. Everyone agreed that inflation was the great problem. In the second quarter the GNP deflator had risen at an annual rate of 8.8 percent. Simon thought it was unlikely to be very far below 10 percent by mid-

1975. I was more optimistic and thought the rate would be around 7.5 percent in mid-1975 and 6.5 percent in mid-1976. (As it turned out, the actual inflation rate would be below even this forecast.) Others did not give quantitative estimates. My estimate was close to that of the major private forecasting services. I noted that even in the best view, these forecasts justified great stress on anti-inflation policy. "Nevertheless," I added, "the differences in the forecasts are of some significance in determining how rigorous the policy should be, since the policy entails costs and risks, which become more worthwhile the greater the inflationary danger seems."

2. Everyone recognized that unemployment would be rising above the 5.5 percent rate of the second quarter. But no one, neither in the government nor in the private forecasting agencies, foresaw a rate in excess of 6.2 percent for mid-1975. (It turned out to exceed 9 percent.)

3. Everyone wanted to cut expenditures for FY1975 below the $305 billion then planned. Ash and I did not want to cut below $300 billion (which was the figure in Nixon's July 28 speech) because we feared excessive restriction of the economy and did not think a larger cut could be made without excessive damage to the defense program. Rush suggested a $5 billion to $10 billion cut. Burns referred to $5 to $10 billion, "preferably" $10 billion. Simon wanted to balance the FY1975 budget, which implied a $10 billion cut. Greenspan wanted to cut FY1975 expenditures "as much as possible." (Expenditures for FY1975 turned out to be $332 billion and the deficit $53 billion.)

For 1976 Burns urged the president to pledge to submit a balanced budget. Rush wanted to aim for a small surplus in that year. I warned against promising to balance the budget, since the economy might be so sluggish as to make that practically unattainable. In general, remembering the experience of the past five years, I warned against any promises.

4. Burns and Simon, the two most eager to cut expenditures, recognized that this might be, or might seem to be, a policy that ignored the risk of rising unemployment. They both proposed a public-service employment program to go into effect if unemployment exceeded a moderate level (6 percent or so). Whether they included the costs of such a program in their targets for cutting the budget, or did not expect the program to take effect, was unclear. The others were skeptical of the whole idea.

Underlying most of these suggestions was an attempt to get out of a real economic dilemma—the simultaneous existence of high inflation and rising unemployment—by psychological means. The usual calculations of economists did not show that expenditure cuts of the size contemplated would have a significant effect on the rate of inflation. These same calculations also showed that a fiscal policy that would have a significant effect on inflation would also sharply depress employment.

The rationale of the suggestions made to the president in August was that cutting federal expenditures would show the administration's determination to fight inflation, which would in turn reduce expectations of inflation, lowering the actual inflation rate and making it consistent with lower unemployment. This was traveling in uncharted territory. As I said in the summarizing memo: "Much of the argument for cutting the FY1975 budget turns on the assumed psychological effect of showing determination to fight the inflation. But how much cut is required to show that determination is unclear, and may depend on what the Administration itself says. If many people in the Administration are pushing for a $10 billion cut, a $5 billion cut may be made to look like weakness rather than determination. Determination may be shown as much by the quality of the cuts as by their quantity. Cutting 'untouchables,' like social security, may count much more than cutting easy marks, like education."

It is of interest that no one, including myself, mentioned balancing the budget at high employment as a standard of fiscal policy. Simon talked about "Balancing the budget, period!" But that was bravado. No one seriously meant that the administration would balance the budget come what may. Everyone was trying to make an ad hoc judgment about the application of the budget to the particular economic situation without reference to any more lasting principles. But this effort to adapt the policy to the situation was devoid of any quantitative basis or any underlying model of the economy. And although everyone recognized that the situation was highly uncertain, no one had any plan for policy to be followed if the economy behaved differently than they hoped and expected. A reasonable summary of the state of mind was that no one wanted to make any strong move, and everyone wanted to do as little as was necessary to *show* a determination to resist inflation and to care for the unemployed.

This is not a criticism of the particular people who met with President Ford in August 1974. The fact is that no one in or out of the government had a credible theory of fiscal policy at that time. The situation was, of course, exceptionally difficult because of the simultaneous existence of high inflation and high unemployment. This was like the situation President Nixon had faced in 1971, except that the inflation in 1974 was much higher and hardly any one believed any longer that there was a way out of the dilemma through "some kind of incomes policy." But aside from the peculiarities of the 1974 situation, it was true that none of the old rules of fiscal policy commanded much respect any more.

The new member of the group advising President Ford at that time was Greenspan, who would become chairman of the CEA on September 1. Since he would be the chief theoretician and rationalizer of the administration's economic policy, his view is of importance. He later described his position as chairman as follows:

I believed that we should stop trying to engage in short-term fiscal fine-tuning, which, at best, we are poor at and, at worst, is counterproductive. We should try instead to focus on solving longer-term problems and in that process engage in as little policy as was both economically and politically possible. My view was that we had to slow down the pace of governmental policy actions, if we were to restore a level of risk in the system consistent with long-term noninflationary growth.[54]

But being against "fine-tuning" and for engaging "in as little policy as . . . possible" is not a guide to action without some other rule or principle. Without some other rule, it is impossible to tell whether one is "fine-tuning" or not. That is, one needs some definition of "not fine-tuning." The full-employment-balance rule was an attempt to define the absence of fine-tuning. So was the traditional balanced-budget rule. In a constantly changing environment, the government constantly needs to make decisions, including possibly a decision to do nothing, but if it intends to do nothing, it needs some rule by which to measure what doing nothing is. Thus, the originators of the full-employment-balance rule argued that the traditional balanced-budget rule was a "fine-tuning" rule, requiring that tax rates and expenditure programs be constantly adapted to cyclical changes in the economy.

In fact, by the beginning of the Ford administration no one had a rule of fiscal policy that he was willing to live by. I shall not try to give a blow-by-blow account of fiscal policy in the Ford and Carter years. The main thing to say is that fiscal policy exemplified a continuation and even an intensification of the disintegration of all the fiscal rules that have been noted already.

[54]Quoted in Hargrove and Morley, *The President and the Council,* 418.

The years 1974 to 1981 were a period of extreme, even frantic, fine-tuning, of a ceaseless attempt to keep up with economic conditions that were churning and whose meaning was never completely understood or agreed upon. The economy was going through both high inflation and high unemployment, and there was uncertainty about which was the more urgent problem at any moment and about what was coming next. The role of macroeconomic policy—fiscal and monetary policy—in dealing with this situation was unclear. Although no one was any longer for "price and wage controls," there were some economists and policymakers who believed that "some kind of incomes policy" could be helpful in restraining inflation while allowing macroeconomic policy to concentrate on fighting unemployment. Others disagreed. Even insofar as the role of macroeconomic policy was accepted, opinions differed sharply about the reliance that could be placed on monetary policy, relieving the burden on fiscal policy. There was, moreover, declining confidence in an ability to describe or implement the fiscal policy that would play its assigned role.

The attempt to fine-tune fiscal policy in order to counter short-run changes in the economy had to be adapted to and constrained by extremely difficult and uncertain longer-run concerns. A slowdown in the long-run growth of productivity became more and more apparent, and the need to deal with that became an increasingly dominant consideration. The short-run adaptations had to be made with an eye to not foreclosing the ability to deal with the long-term problem.

The reasons for the slowdown of productivity growth were not then, and are not now, clear.[55] But the idea developed that the principal cause, or the one about which something could be done, was inadequacy of private investment. "Capital shortage" became the new hot subject of economic discussion. This view was especially congenial to the business community and was actively promoted by it. The implication of shortage for the business community was that taxes on income from capital needed to be reduced in order to increase the incentives of business to invest. This argument had been made continuously by business leaders since at least the New Deal, but it seemed more compelling after the slowdown in economic growth became apparent in the Ford and Carter years. Where the additional savings would come from to finance the

---

[55]See Edward F. Denison, *Accounting for Slower Economic Growth: The United States in the 1970s* (Washington, D.C.: Brookings Institution, 1979).

additional investment was never made clear. There was a Keynesian answer—that additional investment would raise the national income, which would raise savings—but the business advocates of cutting taxes on capital income did not make that argument. Anyway, the argument would not have been good for the long run but applied only to a situation in which total output was below its potential level.

Others, mainly economists outside the business community, felt that although tax incentives for investment might be necessary, these would have to be accompanied by measures to increase saving. The most available way to do that seemed to be to reduce the budget deficit or generate a surplus. So, a logical fiscal program for accelerating long-run growth was a combination of reduction of taxes on capital and reduction of the budget deficit. Measures to stimulate the economy in recession would have to be limited in size and duration in order to make later achievement of a balanced budget possible. But to reduce capital taxation without a reduction of taxation for the great mass of taxpayers seemed politically impossible. In any case, the political attractiveness of offering relief to the middle-income taxpayer had become enormous. Inflation had pushed many middle-income people into tax brackets they had never contemplated before, and they were ripe to be sold tax reduction. So there could not be a small tax reduction targeted on the promotion of investment. Any tax reduction would have to be a big one, which would threaten the desired future reduction of the deficit. This dilemma could be resolved if expenditures were curtailed, and that was to be the theme of the Ford administration and, to a surprising degree, of the administration of Jimmy Carter in its later years. But this was also a period of rising awareness that the nondefense expenditures were being driven by commitments to social security and health programs and that the world situation did not permit big defense cuts. Moreover, both President Ford and President Carter were uncomfortable with large budget deficits and believed that the public shared this attitude. This served as a curb on the tax reduction that economic or political considerations might have produced.

It was during the Ford and Carter years that the new congressional budget procedure, established by the Budget Reform Act of 1974, came into effect. This was the latest of a series of attempts to impose some higher-level limits on the decisions that emerged from the several committees of the two houses. A new Budget Committee was established in each house. The Budget Committees would make recommendations for limits on expenditures by major categories and for revenue targets; when approved by the two houses, these recommendations would constrain the final outcomes. The two Budget Committees and Congress as a whole would have the assistance of an expert staff, the Congressional Budget Office (CBO).

Just what effect the new procedures had on what I call fiscal policy—the aggregates of expenditure, revenue, and deficit—is hard to say. The new procedure was not created because of dissatisfaction with fiscal policy in that sense or because of any strongly held views about what fiscal policy should be. In fact, at the time the procedures were created, fiscal policy was in what most people would have thought a satisfactory state. The deficit for fiscal 1974 had been the lowest in many years, and the federal debt was smaller relative to GNP than at any other time before or since in the period after World War II. Congress established the new procedures because it disliked the president's assertion of authority to impound funds that Congress had appropriated. It wanted to recapture its authority over expenditures—not because it thought the total expenditures were too great but because it wanted to impose its own priorities. If it was going to do that, and remove the president's ability to cut expenditures unilaterally, it felt it would have to demonstrate its own capacity to deal responsibly with the big aggregates. But it had no theory or principle for deciding how the big aggregates should behave. The 1974 Budget Reform Act was later described as a failure because deficits continued to rise. But the restraint of deficits had not been one of the original objectives of the act.

Living with the new responsibility to have a fiscal policy did not generate in Congress any more or different policy than before. If Congress had any general rule during this period, it was that the deficit should be a little larger than what the president proposed. It rationalized this, insofar as it felt the need to do so, by the desire to further reduce unemployment. The Congressional Budget Office abetted Congress in taking this position. The underlying approach of the CBO at this time could be described as early Kennedy-Heller. That is, it was always estimating how much deficit was needed to get to high employment, and its answer almost always was "more."[56]

And so fiscal policy lurched from side to side, trying to respond to an

---

[56]In later years the CBO would establish a reputation for producing objective and highly competent estimates of the costs of proposed expenditure programs, estimates on which Congress would rely. This reduced the opportunity or the temptation to rationalize pro-

uncertain and ambiguous short-run situation while retaining the possibility of dealing with an increasingly demanding long-run situation. In October 1974 President Ford, believing inflation to be the overwhelming national problem, proposed a small tax increase but coupled that with an increase in unemployment compensation and a jobs program to come into effect if unemployment should rise. But three months later, then believing recession and the energy crisis to be the overwhelming problems, he proposed a big increase in energy taxes, coupled with equal increases in expenditures, and a $16 billion stimulus program consisting mainly of tax rebates to be paid in the first half of 1975. The idea was to get the stimulus over so that the budget could return to a long-run path toward smaller deficits.

In a similar experience, in January 1977 President Carter proposed a one-time tax cut to get the economy moving again and reduce unemployment. Two months later he withdrew the proposal because the economy was rising faster than had been expected. Also, Congress had not been enthusiastic about the idea of temporary tax cuts. The main advocates of tax reduction are generally after a permanent cut, not a temporary one.

A year later, in January 1978, Carter again proposed a tax reduction, on the ground that the pace of the economic recovery was inadequate. Three months later, because of mounting inflation, Carter reduced the size of the tax cut he was proposing and postponed its effective date.

In January 1980, Carter proposed an "austere" budget because of the continuing high inflation rate. The deficit for fiscal 1981 would be only $15 billion. In March he revised the budget, cutting expenditures further, because of surging inflation and complaints from the financial community that the deficit was still too large. In July he reversed course, proposing additional expenditures and some tax cuts, because the economy seemed to be falling into recession.

Thus, the stage was set for Reaganism, or perhaps one should say that a vacuum was left for Reaganism to fill. Inflation had raised taxes to a level, relative to GDP, not previously experienced since World War II except for two years when the Vietnam War tax surcharge was in effect. Everyone recognized that there was a popular demand, if not an economic necessity, for tax reduction. In fact, almost every budget since

posed expenditure programs by fictitious estimates of their costs and also reduced the amount of wrangling over what the costs would be.

Ford's of January 1975 had proposed some tax reduction. At the same time the expenditures looked extremely hard to cut. What we now call mandatory programs, mainly for social security and health, plus interest and defense, accounted for about 80 percent of the budget. Even if all other expenditures had been cut by 50 percent, there would still have been a deficit.

The demand for tax relief and the intractability of expenditures created an obvious pressure for large budget deficits. And there was little reason to resist that pressure. The idea that there was some precise, knowable size of deficit that was consistent with the stability of the economy had been dissipated by the experience with fine-tuning. The idea of balancing the budget as a normal rule of policy had come to seem a fantasy. There had been only one balanced budget in the previous twenty years, despite politicians' ritual obeisance to the idea. The CEA continued to calculate the full-employment deficit and use it as a shorthand measure of the degree of fiscal stimulus or restraint. But there was no implication that the full-employment budget should be balanced or that the full-employment deficit should be stable.

In the circumstances, and given the obvious attractiveness of cutting taxes and raising expenditures, the question was not why the deficits were so large but why they were not much larger. Even more clearly than at the end of the Nixon administration, what remained of restraint was the fear of going "too far," of driving the deficit into unknown territory. For the politician policymakers, this was a fear of economic consequences and of public reaction. But "too far" meant farther than we had already been, which by 1980 was farther than by 1974. The budget deficits of the Ford-Carter period averaged about $40 billion a year. (That is how the figures looked then; present calculations show larger deficits.) There was a deficit of $66 billion in FY1976. Carter faced deficits in the range of $50 billion. Somewhere in that neighborhood of $40 billion to $60 billion was a range of deficits that were acceptable, even if worrisome.

Moreover, although no one any longer expected to see a balanced budget, there seemed to be a need to demonstrate a yearning and intention to get there. This, of course, did not have to be demonstrated by actually getting there. The intention was apparently enough for all political purposes. In a peculiar way the practice of submitting a five-year budget, originally a favorite proposal of economists seeking rationality in budget policy, made this hypocrisy easier to practice. Until 1981 one could always show a balanced budget five years away without having to take any real steps to get there. After 1981 the net was lowered, so that one could still promise success in achieving budget "responsibility" five years away, without having any immediate obligations.

The fiscal rule of 1980 was to try to avoid exceeding the deficits previously experienced and to show a desire to get to balance—but not yet. This was, obviously, an unstable situation. When—through inadvertence, neglect, or intention—the actual deficit exceeded the previous limit for a year or two, a new higher figure would become the tolerable figure beyond which deficits should not be allowed to go. The size of deficit that the public would find shocking would rise. The rule of policy would become to stay below a new deficit ceiling—not $50 billion but $100 billion or $200 billion—and fiscal chastity would consist of promising to get down from there, in time.

The absence of an "expert" consensus on fiscal policy, a consensus that might have guided policymakers, was revealed in a paper I delivered in March 1976, in which I identified what I thought were the main schools of thought about fiscal policy at that time:

1. The pure old-fashioned Keynesian functional financers.
2. The fiscal monetarists: They believed that aggregate demand is governed by monetary policy but that monetary policy is governed by fiscal policy, which left them in much the same position as the old-fashioned Keynesians.
3. The monetarist-Parkinsonians: They believed that aggregate demand is governed by monetary policy and that the amount of government expenditures is governed by the amount of taxes. The object of policy is to hold expenditures down by holding taxes down.
4. The monetarist-neutrals: They believed that money determines aggregate demand and that the effect of fiscal policy is on the long-run rate of economic growth through the effect of the deficit or surplus on the availability of saving for investment. The size of the surplus or deficit should be determined by a political decision about the desirable rate of economic growth.
5. The supply-side fiscalists.[57] They also believed that aggregate demand is determined by money. However, aggregate supply is determined by taxation, including negative taxation, or transfer payments. Both

[57]My use of the term "supply-side" in 1976 was the origin of the use of that term as applied to economic policy in the years that followed.

inflation and unemployment can be reduced by reducing taxes and transfer payments, and this should be the objective of policy. It may be implied that surpluses are better than deficits, but probably only because they are the route to tax reductions.

6. Conventional eclectics: They believed that both fiscal policy and monetary policy affect aggregate demand, but they had not figured out the best combination.

7. Growth-oriented eclectics: They believed that a combination of long-run budget surpluses and of a complementary monetary policy would get both stability and growth but that this was not yet the time to get to the budget surpluses.[58]

The existence of an "expert" consensus might not have constrained the decisions of politicians who were making fiscal policy. But the absence of a consensus and the existence of so many "respectable" options increased the freedom of politicians to choose the policy that was most attractive to them. This turned out to be the "supply-side" policy, which legitimized tax reduction—what everyone wanted anyway.

The next step would be taken by the Reagan administration.

REAGAN AND AFTER

The year 1981 was the year of the Big Budget Bang. The combination of a large tax cut and a large increase in the defense program ballooned the deficit up to levels never seen before. Fiscal policy in all the years since, at least up to this writing in 1994, was dominated by efforts to deal with the consequences of that event. These efforts succeeded in curbing the growth of the deficit, but they did not succeed in eliminating the deficit or even in reducing it to a size that was not regarded as a major problem. The experience of living with the deficit, of trying to cope with it, and of thinking about it has probably taught us some things. What has been learned has been mainly negative—ideas that looked plausible in 1980 look less plausible today. There has been some coalescence among experts on what constitute the general criteria of a sound fiscal policy. Whether these criteria are more valid than those we have now discarded, whether we can translate the general criteria into

---

[58]Herbert Stein, "The Decline of the Budget-Balancing Doctrine; or, How the Good Guys Finally Lost," in *Fiscal Responsibility in Constitutional Democracy*, ed. James M. Buchanan and Richard E. Wagner (Boston: Martinus Nijhoff, Social Science Division), 1978.

specific, quantitative guides to action, and whether policymakers will come to follow those guides—these all remain open questions in 1994.

Even now, thirteen years later, there are people who argue about whether the tax cut of 1981 caused the subsequent deficits. Some say that the tax cut simply held revenues at about the same fraction of GDP that they had been in the 1970s, keeping the fraction from rising sharply, as it would have done as a result of inflation and real growth. In this version of the story, it was the continued growth of expenditures relative to GDP that caused the deficits. As arithmetic, this is unassailable and insignificant. We can say that the deficits occurred because expenditures rose more than revenues or because revenues rose less than expenditures. These statements are the same.

But if one asks what happened that had not happened before, and that produced deficits that had not been experienced before, the answer is clear. Candidate Reagan promised and President Reagan delivered a tax cut so large that it would yield a large deficit unless some improbable conditions occurred, without any feasible way out of the deficits if the conditions did not occur. President Ford and President Carter had both promised and delivered tax cuts. Inflation was generating a large revenue increase that left room for tax cuts. But the size of the tax cuts had been limited so that under probable conditions the deficits would not be larger than we had been accustomed to and might be hoped to decline in the future.

Candidate Reagan broke out of that pattern. He was not a leader in doing so. The congressional Republicans had led the way when, in 1978, they had raised the banner of a 30 percent across-the-board cut of individual income-tax rates. Their position is understandable. At that point the Republicans had not controlled the House of Representatives for twenty-four years. They were more desperate than the presidential wing of the party, which had been in the White House for more than half of the same period. Moreover, as members of Congress, they did not have the same budgetary responsibility that presidents have.

Reagan did not become a supporter of the big tax cut until 1979. The attractiveness for a candidate of promising a big tax cut is obvious. What is not obvious is how Reagan and his team reconciled that, for themselves and for the public, with other objectives, including traditional Republican totems of fiscal prudence. The general answer is that there was a willing suspension of disbelief, a willing acceptance of the improbable that would be so nice to believe. There needs, however, to be a more specific catalogue of the arguments used at the time, in the Reagan camp, because the same arguments would be made and tested in subsequent years.

The most distinctive argument was that a reduction of the tax rates would increase the revenue. There has been some disagreement about whether Reagan actually believed this. Perhaps he did not believe this all the time, and he probably would not have given the same answer to the question in all contexts. But it seems quite clear that he did believe it some of the time.

My own most direct experience with Reagan's attitude came some time around 1984 at a meeting of the President's Economic Policy Advisory Board.[59] I said that I hoped he would not rule out a tax increase for ideological reasons. He replied that his reasoning was not ideological but that he remembered the Muslim philosopher who reported that the king came into office with high taxes and left with low revenues.

Certainly some of the people associated with Reagan in the early years, such as Congressman Jack Kemp, did believe that cutting taxes would raise the revenue, and other people who supported the big tax cut accepted that proposition as making the tax cut legitimate. The idea is persuasive to people who know a little economics, who know that supply curves slope up and that if you pay more for a thing you will get more for it. But the critical question is whether, if you raise the return to work and saving by cutting the tax rates, you will get *so much more* that the revenue will be higher despite the lower tax rate. This was never plausible when applied to the generality of taxes, although it may be true of some particular taxes. In fact, when the Reagan administration was in office his budget projections never did assume that cutting taxes

---

[59]PEPAB, as it was called, was established at the time Reagan came into office. It consisted of about twelve people, all Republicans, almost all of whom had served in the Nixon or Ford administrations and almost all of whom had been advisers to Reagan during the campaign. George Shultz was the first chairman, and after he became secretary of state he was succeeded by Walter Wriston, chairman of Citicorp. The group met for a day at a time, about four times a year at first and with diminished frequency thereafter until it expired near the end of Reagan's second term. At each meeting the president would appear for about an hour; the remainder of the day was spent in discussions with officials from the Treasury, the OMB, and the CEA. What purpose PEPAB was intended to serve is unclear. The board received too little publicity to serve any public relations purpose for the White House, and no one inside the administration seemed eager to hear the board's advice. The meetings with the president consisted mainly of compliments to him from the board and Hollywood stories from him. The only subject, as far as I remember, of disagreement with the president was the voluntary import restraints on automobiles, which the board opposed.

would raise the revenue. That was not the same, as critics complained, as assuming that there were no "feedback" effects—meaning no tendency for a cut of tax rates to raise the tax base. It meant only that the feedback effect would not be so large as to offset the primary, revenue-reducing effect of the rate cut.

Another proposition used by the Reagan team during the 1980 campaign was that even without a big boost from the proposed tax reduction, the probable course of the economy was to yield a big surplus that would permit substantial revenue loss and still leave the budget in balance. Forecasts like that were in circulation in 1980, but they all assumed the continuation of a very high rate of inflation, which Reagan was devoted to curtailing and which actually was curtailed.

Some members of the Reagan team took comfort in the idea that there were enormous amounts of expenditures in the federal budget that were of no value and that could easily be eliminated by a president who was determined to do so. That was a delusion. There may have been large amounts of expenditures that were of no value from some "social" or Olympian standpoint, but there was little that did not seem valuable to sectors of the population that all politicians, including Republicans, thought important. When the Reagan administration came into office, it would find the amount of expenditure cuts it was willing to specify and fight for disappointingly small. The net effect on the expenditure side of the budget would be especially small because the budget had to accommodate an increase in defense expenditures above previous plans.

Parkinsonian thinking probably also influenced the Reaganite attitude toward the budget. This was the idea that expenditures would accommodate themselves to, and equal, the available revenues. So some thought that if the revenues were cut, the expenditures would inevitably follow. But if this relation were valid, the actual $50 billion deficits of the Carter period would be hard to explain. There was probably some point to the notion that a reduction of the revenues would tend to restrain expenditures, but nothing in past experience suggested that the amount of the expenditure restraint would equal the amount of the expenditure reduction, and subsequent experience would confirm that.

The most realistic expectation was that the tax and defense program of candidate Reagan would be inconsistent with the forecast or goal of a balanced budget by fiscal 1984.[60] The only surprise was how big the

[60]William Niskanen, *Reaganomics: An Insider's Account of the Politics and the People*

gap would be. There were several reasons for that. The tax reduction enacted by Congress and accepted by the administration was larger than Reagan's proposal. Conservative folklore had it that congressional Democrats loved taxes and hated to cut them. That was a mistake, as all history shows.[61] When the president declared open season for tax reduction, everyone was willing to join in. Also, the size of the defense program, decided by Reagan and Caspar Weinberger, secretary of defense, outside the budget process, exceeded what had been contemplated during the campaign. And the inflation rate declined faster than had been foreseen, which substantially reduced the expected revenues.

By the time President Reagan signed the 1981 tax reduction act, on August 13, 1981, the budget was clearly far off the projected path, although even then no one knew how big the deficits were going to be. From that time up to the present writing, the history of fiscal policy followed two tracks. One was the track of action—the continuous and never satisfying effort to deal with the deficits that were alleged by everyone to be a major national problem. The other track was the track of ideas—the effort to decide whether deficits mattered, in what way they mattered, and how much they mattered.

I shall not follow either of these tracks in great detail but will try only to indicate the general nature of what was going on and where the tracks had led by 1994.[62] The story may be summed up in two sentences.

(New York: Oxford University Press, 1988), distinguishes between the forecast of a balanced budget made during the campaign and the goal of a balanced budget made explicit in the early days of 1981, after Reagan's inauguration. This may not be a significant difference, in the sense that the campaign program was constrained by a goal of balancing the budget even if that goal was not explicit. The difference may mean, however, that although the balanced budget was forecast during the campaign, this was not the determinant of the policy chosen and that the policy would not be changed if the forecast did not come true. In any case, when in office, the Reagan administration did act as if the balanced budget was a goal.

[61]As James Reston said of Kennedy's tax proposal in 1963, "No doubt the President will get his tax cut in the end, for conservatives and liberals tend to like money more than they like theories." *New York Times,* January 23, 1963.

[62]Various aspects of the story of fiscal policy in the 1980s, told from various standpoints, may be found in the following: Martin Anderson, *Revolution* (Palo Alto, Calif.: Hoover Institution Press, 1988); Michael Boskin, *Reagan and the Economy: The Successes, Failures, and Unfinished Agenda* (San Francisco: ICS Press, Institute for Contemporary Studies, 1987); Martin Feldstein, ed., *American Economic Policy in the 1980s* (Chicago: University of Chicago Press, 1994); Niskanen, *Reaganomics;* Stein, *Presidential Economics;* C. Eugene Steuerle, *The Tax Decade: How Taxes Came to Dominate the Public Agenda* (Washington, D.C.: Urban Institute Press, 1992); David A. Stockman, *The Triumph of Politics: How the Reagan Revolution Failed* (New York: Harper and Row, 1986).

Although Reagan came into office with the goal of balancing the budget, since his first year in office the deficit has never been below $150 billion and is now over $200 billion (a little more than 3 percent of GDP). Consensus about the consequences of large budget deficits has settled on the negative effect on future economic growth, but the size of this effect is quite uncertain.

In the month after the big tax cut was signed, the stock market fell by 14 percent. This precipitated the first effort to cope with the consequences of the Reagan budget policy, whose success had just been triumphantly hailed. The coping would take the form of Phase II of the Reagan program—an attempt to cut expenditures by $10 billion and enact "revenue enhancements" (called tax increases by some) to yield $3 billion. Why anyone thought that this minimal step was coping with the causes of the stock market decline is unclear. It looked more like a symbolic measure to propitiate the gods of Wall Street. It also looked like Carter's action in March 1980, after a similar reversal in the financial markets.

Congress did not accept Reagan's Phase II but decided to wait until 1982, when it would deal with the new budget. At that time Congress, especially the Republican leaders in the Senate, became the driving force in trying to deal with the budget deficit, which for the first time looked as if it would exceed $100 billion—a number that looked terrible in the White House. The congressional plan included several measures to raise the revenue, mainly from business, without raising income-tax rates. Only the first step of the three-step tax cut adopted in 1981 had taken effect, so that the revenue increase proposed was not an increase over what was already in force but was a withdrawal of some cuts scheduled for the future.

President Reagan was reluctant to accept the congressional proposal, but he was persuaded to go along, partly because what was being done could be described as "loophole closing" rather than "tax-raising."[63] The president also apparently believed that the tax increase was part of a deal with Congress under which expenditures would be cut three dol-

[63]On August 9, 1982, when President Reagan's reluctance to agree to the tax increase was reported in the press, I wrote him a letter explaining that even if the tax increase was accepted, the ratio of federal revenue to GNP would be lower than he had proposed during the campaign. He called me up to thank me and say that he had not been aware of that fact. He used that argument in a subsequent speech to the nation explaining his decision to go along with the congressional plan.

lars for every dollar of additional revenue. This expenditure cut did not occur. Whether there ever was such a deal is still in dispute.[64] But the incident remained for a long time Exhibit One in the argument that no expenditure cuts could be obtained from Congress as a quid pro quo for agreeing to a tax increase.

The legislation of 1982 added a substantial amount to future revenue. At the beginning of 1983, however, the administration was facing a deficit of around $200 billion. That was partly a result of the recession of 1981–82, but calculations at the time suggested that even when high employment had been regained, the deficit would exceed $100 billion. The administration was reluctant to present such a picture, and some members, especially in the Treasury, were reluctant to believe that growth of the economy would not reduce the long-run deficit substantially. Most of all, they were reluctant to propose a tax increase. This problem was resolved by the proposal of a "contingent" tax increase— a tax increase that would go into effect only if the deficit did not fall below a specified level. Another condition was added to the proposal. The tax increase would not go into effect unless Congress agreed to a bundle of expenditure cuts the president recommended.[65] Congress did not agree, and the package did not go into effect.

Some contribution to reducing the deficit came through the back door, without administration initiative, in 1983. Because the social security trust fund looked to be in weak condition, a bipartisan commission, chaired by Alan Greenspan, had been created to recommend corrective measures. The recommendations included an increase in the social security payroll tax and the exposure of some social security benefits to individual income taxation. President Reagan did not like these "tax increases" but accepted them when he learned that the proposals only advanced the effective date of some proposals made earlier by President Carter, so that he—Reagan—was not really responsible for raising taxes.

[64]See Stockman, *The Triumph of Politics.*
[65]Niskanen, in *Reaganomics,* comments that the plan was illogical because cutting the expenditures would have made the tax increase less, not more, appropriate. The proposal can, however, be rationalized in either of two ways. One is that the Treasury did not want a tax increase anyway, regardless of the deficit, and insisted on the expenditure cut as a condition for the tax increase in the expectation, which turned out to be correct, that Congress would not accept the expenditure cut, thus relieving the administration of responsibility for the deficit. The other explanation is that since the administration disliked raising taxes and since Congress disliked cutting expenditures, no package would be acceptable that did not include some of each.

The Greenspan Commission proposal and subsequent legislation were notable as the first social security bills ever to reduce benefits significantly, even though the reduction would come only long in the future by an increase in the retirement age.

Nevertheless, despite this assistance from the social security side, when the administration faced the budget problem again at the beginning of 1984 the deficit was still forecast as in the neighborhood of $180 billion in each of the fiscal years 1984 to 1987. Just a year earlier the administration had forecast a deficit below $150 billion for FY1986. But 1984 was the year of a presidential election, not a year for a major attack on the deficit. Congress did pass "The Deficit Reduction Act of 1984," which, it was estimated at the time, would yield almost $100 billion of additional revenue in the next five years; but that was accomplished entirely by "loophole" closing, without rate increases, so it did not count as a tax increase. The most important fiscal event of the year was the statement by the Democratic candidate, Walter Mondale, that if elected, he would raise taxes. After his overwhelming defeat, the idea that to raise taxes, or at least to say that one would raise taxes, was politically suicidal became more firmly established than ever.

The most drastic move to reduce the budget deficit came in 1985, with the passage of the Gramm-Rudman-Hollings Act. This act specified a path of annual deficit ceilings for the next five years, reaching a balanced budget in the fifth year. Its unusual feature was the provision that if the ordinary budgeting process yielded deficits in excess of the ceiling, there was to be an across-the-board cut in expenditures, with some specified exceptions, such as expenditures for social security. Probably no one expected or wanted the across-the-board cut to take place; the rationale for the plan was that the president and Congress would be so afraid of the across-the-board cut that they would manage to conform to the deficit ceiling in a more reasonable way.

But by 1987 Congress and the president discovered that they did not have to conform to the ceiling or to endure the "train wreck" of the across-the-board cut. They could amend the act, now to be called Gramm-Rudman with the defection of Senator Fritz Hollings, to postpone the date at which the balanced budget would be achieved. And so they did.

Also, in 1987, after a sharp decline of the stock market, the administration proposed a small deficit-reduction package. This was another effort to propitiate the gods of Wall Street, a replay of the effort that had been made in 1980 by Carter and in 1981 by Reagan. It also had some echo of Hoover's proposal of a tax increase in 1932.

As more evidence of seriousness in dealing with the deficit, as part of the Omnibus Budget Reconciliation Act of December 22, 1987, a *very* high level bipartisan commission was established to "recommend ways of reducing the Federal budget deficit of the United States government that would encourage economic growth but without disproportionately undermining any particular group in society or region of the country." The commission reported on March 1, 1989. All members agreed that reducing the deficit was important, but neither the Democratic side nor the Republican side presented a specific plan for doing that.

In 1988, presidential candidate George Bush presented his plan by which he would bring the budget into balance in five years if he was elected. The plan included no tax increase but promised a "flexible freeze" on expenditures. That meant that total spending would be frozen but no specific expenditure would be restrained.

By the spring of 1990 the deficits in prospect were clearly far above the Gramm-Rudman path and also far above the Bush flexible-freeze path. The discrepancy was too great to be credibly remedied by another revision of the Gramm-Rudman targets. Also, the Democrats had been wounded by Bush's campaign pledge: "Read my lips! No new taxes!" They were not about to enter into a new budget deal unless Bush co-operated by agreeing to a tax increase. So a new package was constructed, including a tax increase. The new package was "the biggest deficit reduction program in history." It did not include any specific deficit targets, but it did imply very large deficit reductions.

By the beginning of 1993 it was clear that the deficit was far outrunning the expectations of the 1990 budget agreement.[66] Moreover, in the 1992 campaign, partly because of the insistence of Ross Perot, the size of the deficit had come to be regarded as the primary symbol of the ineptitude of government and of the fragility of the American economy. So the new president, Clinton, proposed and, after some struggle, obtained another budget package that was "the biggest in history."

---

[66]This did not mean that the 1990 agreement had been a failure. That agreement, as noted above, did not set any deficit targets. It only required the government to behave in a certain way. The government did, in fact, observe those rules, but nevertheless the deficit turned out to be much bigger than expected, primarily because the forecasts of expenditures under existing programs turned out to be incorrect.

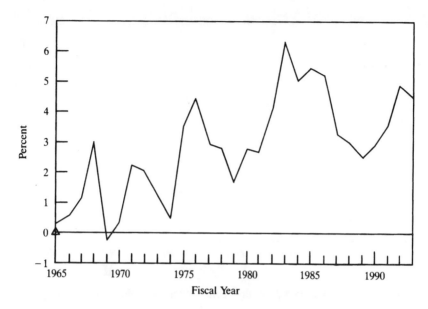

Figure 5.1. Budget deficit (percent of GDP)

Figures 5.1 through 5.4 show where the country stood after thirteen years of trying to cope with big budget deficits. In absolute terms the deficit was bigger than ever, whether or not standardized to remove the effects of variations in the unemployment rate. Even in relation to the size of GDP, the deficits were extraordinarily high. The most common forecast was that unless radical action was taken, the deficits would soon begin to rise again, absolutely and as a fraction of GDP, because of the trend of expenditures for social security and health care.

No politicians and few other commentators—in fact, hardly anyone except a few economists—were prepared to say that the existing deficits were not among the biggest problems for the country. In early 1994 the situation was thought to be so extreme that 63 senators and 271 representatives voted for a resolution to incorporate in the Constitution an amendment requiring the budget to be balanced. This was less than the two-thirds majority required for such a resolution, and some who voted in favor might not have done so if they had expected the resolution to pass. But still, the vote at least indicates how many members thought their constituents wanted a show of determination to balance the budget.

Why did this problem, which the public and governmental decision-

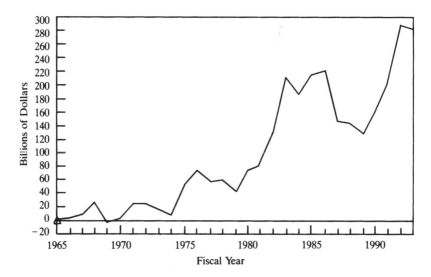

Figure 5.2. Budget deficit (billions of dollars)

makers apparently thought was terribly serious, persist after so long a struggle? One part of the answer may be that reducing the deficit was unusually difficult. Because economic growth was slow the annual increase of revenues generated by growth was small. The annual increase of revenues from inflation was also small because the inflation rate was lower than in the 1970s and because after 1985 the individual income tax was indexed for inflation. At the same time, the built-in expenditures for numerous entitlement programs—social security, Medicare, and Medicaid, primarily—were rising rapidly. And the deficits themselves caused a cumulative increase in interest costs.

But still, these were only difficulties. Eliminating the deficit was always mathematically possible. It was always possible to put together a package of measures to eliminate the deficit, measures that could be plausibly defended as not impairing economic growth or other important national objectives.[67]

A common explanation of the failure to reduce the deficit further is

---

[67]I described such a package myself in *Governing the $5 Trillion Economy*, 104. The package relied mainly on reducing subsidies for health care, taxing part of social security benefits, broadening the base of the income tax, and raising taxes on cigarettes, gasoline, and alcoholic beverages.

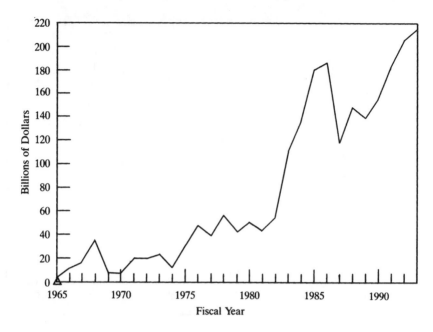

Figure 5.3. High-employment budget deficit (billions of dollars)

"gridlock." This implies that the responsible actors, Democrats or Republicans, liberals or conservatives, have plans for reducing the deficit but that they cannot implement these plans because they cannot agree enough to get a majority behind any effective program. There was undoubtedly some of that. In general, for example, Republicans resisted cuts of defense, and Democrats resisted cuts of social programs.

But probably what the parties agreed on was even more important than their disagreements. They agreed not to impose any large costs on the middle class, either by raising taxes or by cutting programs of chief benefit to this class. This ruled out a large part of the area in which significant deficit reduction would have to be found. And the presidents and members of Congress who took that position represented the wishes of the American people or, at least, thought they were doing so.

To say that the deficits were not reduced further because the American people and their representatives, despite their talk, did not think it sufficiently important to do so is a truism. But the truism raises important questions. It raises the issue of the costs of deficits. What are the costs

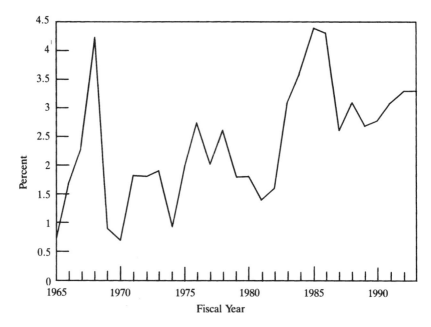

Figure 5.4. High-employment budget deficit (percent of GDP)

of deficits? Are there costs that decision-makers fail to appreciate? Has there been a reasonable decision that the costs of deficits, realistically evaluated, are less than the costs of the steps that would be needed to reduce the deficits?

During the Nixon administration, as we have seen, the main cost attributed to large deficits was inflation, and this worry continued until well into the Reagan administration. Because of the rise of the monetarist idea that "inflation is always and everywhere a monetary phenomenon," the argument had to be given a monetary cast. Large deficits, it was said, caused inflation by causing the monetary authority—in our case, the Federal Reserve—to expand the money supply too much. But this argument did not have a strong basis. There was no reason for the Federal Reserve to behave in that way. And as we proceeded through the Reagan administration, with amazingly large deficits, the inflation rate actually declined. The Federal Reserve did not have to expand the money supply at a rate that would cause inflation. And the anti-inflationary argument faded out of the case against deficits.

At various times in the past twenty years large deficits have been said to endanger the achievement of high employment, and deficit reduction has been claimed to contribute to short-run economic expansion. Some such reasoning was reflected in the efforts at deficit reduction after financial market declines in 1980, 1981, and 1987. Worry that the deficit would abort the recovery was prominent in 1982. But when the Reagan Council of Economic Advisers, chaired by Martin Feldstein, analyzed that proposition in the 1983 economic report, it did not claim that the deficit would abort the recovery. It said only that because of the deficit, the recovery would be "lopsided." That is, some industries would rise less, and other industries would rise more, than if there had been no deficit. But the report never explained why this recovery would be anything other than an equilibrium, sustainable response to the actual state of affairs. As the recovery continued into 1990, the "lopsided" argument disappeared.

In fact, the case in economic theory for saying that deficits depress the economy in the short run is weak. In the Keynesian model, an increase of the deficit stimulates the economy. The monetarist model denies that but does not say the reverse; it says only that an increase of the deficit has neither a stimulating nor a depressing effect. One can, of course, make up models in which an increase of the deficit depresses the economy, but there is no evidence that such models conform to the actual world.

The experience of the Clinton administration in 1993 illustrates the recent state of thinking about deficits and the short-run behavior of the economy. At the beginning of the year the administration proposed a deficit-increasing budget package that it claimed was important to stimulate the economy. That claim did not impress many people, and Congress rejected it. Congress then passed Clinton's deficit-reducing package, which the administration then claimed caused the economic recovery of that year. But that claim did not impress many people either. The current state of thinking about deficits and recoveries is that if there is an effect, we do not know what it is.

By the late 1980s, explanations of the consequences of large budget deficits concentrated on the long-run effects of long-continued deficits. These explanations came in several different versions. Some people were impressed by the simple arithmetic of deficits and debt: the federal debt will rise as long as the federal government runs a deficit, and increase of the debt cannot go on forever. But that is incorrect in a growing economy. If the deficit does not exceed a certain size, relative to the national income, the ratio of the debt to the national income will not rise. For example, if the debt is initially 50 percent of the national income, and the national income (in nominal terms) rises by 6 percent a year, the debt will remain at 50 percent of the national income if the deficit is 3 percent of the national income. There is some size of deficit that can go on forever. But even if concern is with deficits larger than that, ones that presumably cannot go on forever, we still do not know how long they can go on. Knowing that a deficit of, for example, 6 percent of the national income cannot go on forever tells us nothing about what must be done in this year or even in this decade.

A more substantive argument concerns the tax effects of continuing deficits. As the debt rises, the interest costs of the debt will also rise. If these rising costs are not met by rising revenues, the deficit will also rise, and that will accelerate the rise of the debt and speed up the arrival of the day when things can no longer go on. If the debt is rising relative to the national income, providing the revenue to pay the interest cost will require higher tax *rates*, which will have adverse effects on work and saving. To avoid that, it is said, deficits must at least not exceed the size that would hold the ratio of debt to national income constant.

This principle, however, immediately runs into the trade-off problem. Suppose that the interest rate on the debt is 6 percent. A permanent increase of the debt by, say, $100 billion will require $6 billion a year of additional taxes forever to pay the interest costs. But to avoid the increase of the deficit will require $100 billion of additional taxes this year. Will the adverse incentive effects of raising $100 billion of taxes this year be greater than the adverse incentive effects of raising $6 billion a year forever? No one knows, and this issue has not been prominent in consideration of budget policy, even among economists.

Most recent discussion of the adverse effect of budget deficits has run through the saving and investment chain of events. This is also the traditional way of looking at the problem and is what I called "grandfather economics" when I wrote about the Eisenhower administration in *The Fiscal Revolution in America*. The basic economic argument is that a budget deficit has to be financed out of private saving. The larger the budget deficit, the smaller will be the amount of private saving available for private investment, the smaller will be the amount of private investment, the smaller will be the rate of growth of total output, and, therefore, the smaller will be the incomes of our children and grandchildren.

This argument, apparently so clear and simple, unfortunately runs into infinite complications. At the outset, it must be recognized that some government expenditures do, or at least may, go for public investments that contribute to economic growth. One cannot, therefore, say that an increase of the deficit will slow down economic growth without knowing what public expenditures are being financed by the deficit. Thus, the common suggestion is that the size of the relevant deficit is the size of the conventionally measured deficit less the "capital" or "growth-promoting" expenditures of government. But which expenditures fit into that category is far from clear—especially once one gets beyond roads and bridges. Neither is it clear whether each dollar of government capital expenditure is worth as much, in promoting growth, as each dollar of private investment.

There is a special difficulty in applying the "grandfather" argument to the Reagan period, when deficits were at their biggest. This was also a period of unusually high expenditures for defense. Was the benefit to our children and grandchildren of relieving them of the danger of nuclear war—if that was the consequence of the defense expenditure—not more valuable than the higher private investment that might have resulted from smaller deficits? Such questions make it hard to look on deficits simply as burdens handed down to our grandchildren.

Another aspect of the Reagan experience muddies the saving-investment approach to the consequences of budget deficits. Domestic investment is not equal to private domestic saving minus the budget deficit. There is another variable in the equation: the inflow of foreign capital. When the large size of the Reagan deficits began to appear, at the end of 1981, there were a few people, most notably William Nis-kanen, who suggested that the adverse effects of those deficits on investment in the United States would be significantly offset by foreign capital.[68] This idea was commonly rejected at the time because it implied a capital inflow on a scale such as had never been seen before. But in fact the capital inflow in the eight years from 1981 to 1988 equaled more than half the size of the federal deficit. So one cannot assume that private domestic investment will be reduced dollar-for-dollar by the budget deficit. There may be such a reduction for the world as a whole, but it will not all be in the United States.

[68]Niskanen was then a member of the Council of Economic Advisers. For a report on this issue and others as viewed at the time, see Herbert Stein, "Why Deficits Matter," *AEI Economist,* January 1982.

Moreover, the saving-investment analysis assumes that private domestic saving is a given amount, so that the amount of such saving available for investment will be reduced by the amount of the deficit. As deficits increased in the 1980s, more attention was paid to a theory that denied all that, a theory associated with the name of the economist Robert Barro. This theory held that private people would be aware that the government deficit was absorbing savings, depressing private investment, and thus lowering the incomes of their grandchildren. Being aware of that fact, private people would increase their saving and, in fact, increase it enough so that the incomes of their grandchildren would not be harmed.

This private response seemed not to have happened in the United States in the 1980s, although there are claims that the theory has been validated in other times and places. In the United States, private saving, relative to income, declined while the deficit was rising. That fact raises another question. Why did families reduce their saving rates in spite of the fact that the deficits were presumably harming the economic prospects of their descendants? One possibility is that both the rising deficits and the declining private saving rate reflected a change in attitudes about the future. That is, both the deficits and the low private saving rate may have reflected a decline in concern for and obligation to the future, a decline that might be seen in other aspects of behavior. In that case, the Barro critique of the deficit-saving-investment analysis may still be valid. That is, despite the political decision about the size of the deficit, private decisions about the amount of private saving may adjust to yield the amount of net total saving—private less deficit—that corresponds to private valuations of future income.

But even if one returns to the simple idea that a deficit reduces investment by an equal amount, the significance of a deficit is unclear. That is because of uncertainty about *how much* a reduction of investment reduces future income. This "how much" is very important. Telling a policymaker that running a deficit will reduce the income of grandchildren does not help him to make a decision. To avoid the deficit, he has to do something unpleasant, like raising taxes or cutting expenditures. He has to know whether the loss of future income as a result of the deficit will be so great as to justify the measures that would reduce the deficit. And economists are unable to tell how big the loss of future income would be. In 1989 the Congressional Budget Office presented estimates of the magnitude of the effect of deficit reduction on future consumption. The CBO calculated that according to one economic model, reducing the deficit by 2 percent of GDP would make total consumption after fifty years 2 percent higher than it would otherwise have been. But according to another model, total consumption would have been 14 percent higher. In its 1994 report the Council of Economic Advisers presented an estimate that the effect of the 1993 deficit-reduction package would be to make consumption "eventually"—say, after fifty years—2.5 percent higher than it would otherwise have been. But it recognized that this estimate depended on a number of assumptions that might not be realized and that the gain might be quite different.

The net of all this is that as of 1994, estimates of the real consequences of deficits are too remote, complicated, and uncertain to serve as much constraint or guidance for policymakers. Presidents and members of Congress are left with the feeling that deficits are bad—but how bad, as well as how many good things should be given up to avoid them, is terribly uncertain.

A feeling persists in the country that budgets should be balanced. So politicians find it desirable to show that they are on the side of balancing the budget. But the country does not demand that budgets be balanced. No one gets thrown out of office because there is a deficit. All that is required from politicians is a show of desire to balance the budget. This can be done by submitting a five-year budget plan, however unrealistic, that reaches balance in the fifth year. It can also be done by voting for a balanced-budget amendment or for a plan like Gramm-Rudman.

A kind of aggregate restraint on deficits remains in the form of a reluctance to exceed a deficit of the size that we have already experienced. Thus, in the early 1990s, concern mounts and has more influence on decisions when the deficit exceeds $200 billion or is likely to do so. That is not because anyone has figured out that $200 billion is the optimum size for a deficit or that it is the maximum desirable size of deficit. It is simply that we have lived with a deficit of $200 billion and have not seen any adverse consequences, but we do not know what would happen if it were larger. Moreover, politicians probably find it more difficult to claim that they are on the side of balancing the budget if they are generating deficits bigger than have ever been experienced before. But this is an unstable situation. If accident or a lapse of policy should generate deficits of, say, $300 billion for a while, that could then become the sticking point beyond which policymakers would be loath to go.

There is still a feeling that deficits impose a cost and that this cost lies somewhere in the area of the burdens placed on grandchildren. But there is no longer a feeling that this cost is qualitatively different from the cost of raising today's taxes or cutting today's expenditures, as would be required to avoid the deficit. Once upon a time, such decisions seemed to be qualitatively different. Running deficits was a sin, whereas spending or taxing might or might not be an error. That difference no longer exists.

Aside from the need to show concern for a balanced budget and the reluctance to exceed previously experienced deficit levels, decisions are being made that reflect a balancing of the costs of deficits against the costs of cutting expenditures or raising taxes. This is just like the balancing that goes on between the benefits of spending $10 billion on fighter aircraft and the benefits of spending $10 billion on Head Start. This balancing is not very explicit and not very systematic. We have no way of reducing the benefits of these various budget decisions to a common denominator. As we have seen, we are unable to estimate very reliably the benefits of reducing the deficit. But neither are we able to estimate very reliably the benefits of the fighter aircraft or of Head Start. We have only a process in which duly elected people, using whatever hunches they have and responding to whatever interests they represent, make whatever decisions they make. That applies to the decision about the deficit as well as to all the other decisions about the budget. The idea that there is some dominating rule about the deficit—the traditional rule of balancing the budget, or the economists' rule of the deficit that yields high employment, or the attempted synthesis of these rules in the notion of balancing the high-employment budget—has disappeared.

In the preface to *The Fiscal Revolution in America*, I said that the book "describes how the evolution of conditions, goals and ideas influenced the responses of policy-makers to their problems and how the responses in turn influenced subsequent conditions, goals and ideas." Looking back at that book, I am impressed by the degree to which the story as I told it was dominated by a single condition, a single goal, and a single idea. The condition was the Great Depression, the goal was the avoidance of another such depression, and the idea was the Keynesian idea—that there was a knowable and manageable fiscal policy that would achieve the goal.

Looking at the period covered by the present essay, I am struck by the contrast—by the absence of any such unifying themes. There has been no dominating condition like the Great Depression. Whereas the stability problem had seemed to mean mainly the unemployment problem, experience showed that it had a serious inflation aspect as well. Twenty years of slower economic growth after 1973 reminded us that stability was not everything, or even the main thing. And the upsurge of worry about poverty, crime, racial antagonism, and family disintegration showed us that economic growth was not everything either.

As a result of experience after 1964, fiscal policy acquired a much more diverse, and partially conflicting, set of goals. At the same time, economists acquired a more diverse set of theories, or one much more eclectic theory, of how fiscal policy worked. In 1965 Milton Friedman had said, "We are all Keynesians now, and no one is any longer a Keynesian." In 1994 one might say, "We are all Keynesian-monetarist-supply-side-traditionalists now, and no one any longer knows what that means." We know that deficits and surpluses, tax rates and subsidy programs, and the money supply all matter—but we don't know, within considerable limits, how much they matter. We don't know, for example, by how much an increase of the budget deficit by $100 billion will change the national income—or even whether the change will be positive or negative. We are similarly ignorant about the size and, in some cases, even the direction of the effects of other policy variables.

The net of all this is that decision-makers, ultimately the public, must select policies to achieve a variety of different, at least partially inconsistent, goals, not reducible to any common denominator, and that economics can tell them little with confidence about the connection between specific policies and specific goals. Policy is not disciplined by national agreement on goals or by common understanding of the mechanism for reaching the goals. Policy becomes the outcome of a political struggle of factions trying, in the ways they believe in, to achieve private goals, which does not necessarily mean "selfish" goals but may include traditional or totemic goals, such as balancing the budget.

I do not want to exaggerate this proposition. There are points at which certain goals are recognized as of overriding importance. A clearly perceived national security threat is an obvious example. But probably there is also some unemployment rate—say, over 10 percent lasting for a year—that would make the reduction of unemployment the dominant goal. Probably there are similar points concerning the rate of inflation, the rate of economic growth, and the degree and persistence of poverty. Also there are probably points at which, despite the uncertainty of all economic calculations, most economists would agree that the deficit, or the rate of growth of the money supply, or the top marginal tax rate, or some expenditure variable was "too high"—or at least dangerous because we had no experience living with it.

Still, this leaves a large space within which political forces can play. That is nothing new. What was probably new was the belief, which reached its peak in the early 1960s, that economic science had provided commands that politics would and should obey. That belief has now disappeared.

III

Tax reform and the political process

6

Learning the ways and means:
Wilbur Mills and a fiscal community,
1954–1964

JULIAN E. ZELIZER

When Wilbur Mills arrived in Washington in 1938, he encountered an American state that had grown significantly during the previous six years. The Roosevelt administration and Congress had created many administrative agencies, welfare programs, and regulatory commissions in response to the Great Depression. In the process, they had increased the power of the executive branch. But there were limits to these changes. The federal government remained structurally fragmented. New Deal programs, moreover, were generally administered at the state and local levels. As a result, politicians still managed the government through policy-making processes that had existed since the turn of the century.[1]

[1] I am indebted to the following individuals for their assistance with this project: Louis Galambos, W. Elliot Brownlee, Viviana Zelizer, Nora K. Moran, Brian Balogh, James Kloppenberg, Stanford Ross, Dorothy Ross, John Manley, Raymond Smock, Robert Frizzel, William Davis, and all the participants in the Woodrow Wilson International Center workshop. I am also grateful to the Johns Hopkins University, the Everett Dirksen Center for Congressional Research, the John F. Kennedy Library, and the Lyndon B. Johnson Library for supporting this research.

The following abbreviations are used in these notes: WMPC, Wilbur Mills Papers Collections, Conway, Arkansas; NA, National Archives, Washington, D.C.; LBJL, Lyndon B. Johnson Library, Austin, Texas; JFKL, John F. Kennedy Library, Boston; SSP, Stanley S. Surrey Papers, Harvard University Law Library, Cambridge; JMIC, John Manley Interview Collection (in the author's possession). The John Manley interviews were conducted during the mid-1960s. These extensive interviews include thirty-one members of the Ways and Means Committee, two officials of the Treasury, two social security officials, and four congressional attorneys. Since I cannot name the sources of my quotations for publication due to an agreement between Manley and his subjects, I refer to a source as "one Republican" or "a Treasury official."

On the limits of the New Deal, see Barry D. Karl, *The Uneasy State: The United States From 1915 to 1945* (Chicago: University of Chicago Press, 1983); Ellis W. Hawley, *The*

During Mills's legislative career, the state was transformed: It became so vast in size, so complex in structure, and so dense in its membership that it turned substantive policy-making into a new type of task. The institutional complexity of the state was compounded by decision-making hierarchies that were tenuous and constantly shifting. There were thus few individuals or organizations capable of singlehandedly pushing through a policy. In short, it was difficult for policymakers such as Mills—as it is for scholars who are now interested in their history—to understand what, if anything, constituted the American "state."

This essay, which examines the relations between fiscal policy and the American state in the postwar period, begins to answer that question. I contend that between 1946 and 1974 a particular political culture within the state provided considerable coherence to policy-making. This culture included a distinct language with its own vocabulary and conceptions of the political economy, certain types of social interactions between members of government, and established ways of learning the political process.[2] To analyze this dynamic state culture and its changing institutional base, this essay looks at its influence on one powerful member of the state, Wilbur Mills, former chairman of the House Ways and Means Committee. Given Mills's important role in U.S. fiscal politics, his career provides an excellent vantage point from which to view the evolution of the American state culture.

Between 1954 and 1964 that culture was an important element in a new fiscal policy community of which Mills was a part; this community engaged in deliberations that culminated in the Revenue Acts of 1962 and 1964. Mills had a significant role in these deliberations. The legislation enacted the largest postwar tax reductions until 1981 and, for the first time, openly endorsed deficits. The revenue bills were attempts to

New Deal and the Problem of Monopoly: A Study in Economic Ambivalence (Princeton: Princeton University Press, 1966); Brian Balogh, *Chain Reaction: Expert Debate and Public Participation in American Nuclear Power, 1945–1975* (Cambridge: Cambridge University Press, 1991), 11–13; Alan Brinkley, *The End of Reform: New Deal Liberalism in Recession and War* (New York: Knopf, 1995).

[2]My understanding of the term "political culture" comes from the following works: Robert Kelley, "The Interplay of American Political Culture and Public Policy: The Sacramento River as a Case Study," *Journal of Policy History* 1, no. 1 (1989): 19; Jean H. Baker, *Affairs of Party: The Political Culture of Northern Democrats in the Mid-Nineteenth Century* (Ithaca, N.Y.: Cornell University Press, 1983); Daniel Walker Howe, *The Political Culture of the American Whigs* (Chicago: University of Chicago Press, 1979). For a good discussion of the fragmented nature of America's fiscal policy-making institutions, see Sven Steinmo, *Taxation and Democracy: Swedish, British, and American Approaches to Financing the Modern State* (New Haven: Yale University Press, 1993).

promote full employment and to enhance economic productivity. Despite having a few objections to both pieces of legislation, Mills advocated the measures and considered them a major success. In 1965, he praised the revenue acts as a watershed in public policy; together, he said, the new laws had increased the nation's economic growth, lowered unemployment, and raised the chances of achieving a balanced budget.[3] By that time, Mills loomed large in the fiscal community—a community that had a dramatic impact on the finances of the federal government and thus was a powerful force in the state.

Most scholars who have discussed Mills have taken his power for granted or have focused on the process through which he maintained this power.[4] They have not historically analyzed how Mills learned to exercise his power or how he expanded his influence beyond the official duties of the chairmanship. As a result, scholarly accounts of the period present Mills and his committee as "obstacles" to modern fiscal policy-making. They suggest that Mills derived his power exclusively from his ability to block presidential initiatives and to remain outside the policy-making processes of the state.[5]

This essay examines how Mills obtained his influence by working *within* the state culture—and not *against* it. By learning the skills of

[3]Wilbur Mills, "Remarks to the Kiwanis Club, Little Rock, Arkansas" (December 14, 1965), File 17, Box 658, WMPC.

[4]In this essay, my approach differs from John F. Manley's in his classic study of Mills and the Ways and Means Committee: *The Politics of Finance: The House Committee on Ways and Means* (Boston: Little, Brown, and Company, 1970). Manley's work adopted a Parsonian model to explain how Mills achieved such power during the 1960s. Mills did so, according to Manley, through a consensus-building approach to issues, through his actual expertise, and through the value system of the committee. But Manley was interested primarily in timeless processes, and his study largely picked up after 1964, once Mills had achieved his power. By developing a more comprehensive historical interpretation of Mills and viewing the 1960s in the context of the 1950s, I hope to show that Mills's success was anything but inevitable or consensual: Mills had to learn how to be influential as chairman. His growing influence during this period stemmed from two important factors that Manley neglects: first, he developed a close relationship to the policy-making community outside of Congress; and second, he mastered the discourse that shaped that community. My concept of Mills's mastery of the "discourse" encompasses, but is broader than, Mills's "actual expertise," which Manley stressed. Unlike Manley, I critically examine the notion of "expertise" as a construct within a larger political culture and as a part of an ongoing discourse about the nature of politics in the postwar era. Finally, I focus much of my analysis on the Mills policies that passed, rather than just the process through which he devised them.

[5]For books that tend to present Mills in this light, see Cathie J. Martin, *Shifting the Burden: The Struggle over Growth and Corporate Taxation* (Chicago: University of Chicago Press, 1991); Steinmo, *Taxation and Democracy*; Howard A. Winant, *Stalemate: Political Economic Origins of Supply-Side Policy* (New York: Praeger Publishers, 1988); Herbert Stein, *The Fiscal Revolution in America* (Chicago: University of Chicago Press, 1969).

modern congressional politics and by learning to work with the policy communities that had emerged during this period, Mills helped shape fiscal policies from their conception to their enactment.[6] To show how he mastered this process, the essay divides the first 25 years of his career into three stages. It first examines Mills's career between 1939 and 1953, years when he was first learning about the state's fiscal policy-making processes. Between 1954 and 1957, he joined the emerging fiscal policy community and adapted to significant changes in the state's institutions and culture. Mills came to power with the new fiscal community between 1958 and 1964, a period culminating with the passage of the Revenue Act of 1964.[7]

DEMOCRATS AND LOBBYISTS, 1939–1953

Mills grew up in a world far removed from the complicated policy-making networks of Washington, D.C. On May 24, 1909, Wilbur Mills was born in Kensett, Arkansas, to Ardra Pickens Mills, a bank president, and to Abbie Lois Daigh, the manager of a family grocery store. In his late teens, Wilbur enrolled in a Methodist liberal arts college in Conway, Arkansas, where he graduated at the top of his class in 1930. His record was good enough to get him into Harvard Law School, where he continued to excel. At Harvard, Mills took courses in constitutional law and state and local taxation. At this time, there still were no courses offered in federal tax law.[8] In Cambridge, Mills's classmates included Leon Keyserling, Fred Scribner, and Gerald Morgan, all of whom be-

---

[6]The process of "social learning" within the state has been explored by two important volumes from the Woodrow Wilson International Center: Michael J. Lacey and Mary O. Furner, eds., *The State and Social Investigation in Britain and the United States* (Cambridge: Cambridge University Press and Washington, D.C.: Woodrow Wilson Center Press, 1993), and Mary O. Furner and Barry E. Supple, eds., *The State and Economic Knowledge: The American and British Experiences* (Cambridge: Cambridge University Press and Washington, D.C.: Woodrow Wilson International Center for Scholars, 1990). There has been little discussion, however, of what role Congress played in the process of state-building. On the general failure of scholars to integrate congressional studies into a broader synthesis about the state, see Joel H. Silbey, "The Historiography of the American Legislative System," in *Encyclopedia of the American Legislative System: Studies of the Principal Structures, Processes, and Policies of Congress and the State Legislatures since the Colonial Era*, ed. Joel H. Silbey (New York: Charles Scribner's Sons, 1994), 281–99.
[7]The fourth stage of his career (1965–74) is beyond the purview of this essay.
[8]"Interview with Erwin N. Griswold, Former Dean and Langdell Professor of Law Emeritus, Harvard University Law School," *ABA Section of Taxation Newsletter*, Spring 1992, 57.

came top-level government officials. Mills recalled that he went to Harvard to "learn how to talk to President Roosevelt."[9] He achieved that goal, but by doing so, he built a major source of tension into his life. As a prominent colleague once said: "Mills comes from a little town of 2,500, which is a small rural town, but he nevertheless is a Harvard Law School graduate who has got an incisive mind. Now, you can't work with these men [congressional representatives] unless you understand those 'inconsistent' factors."[10] At graduation in 1933, Mills opted for a career that would bring these "inconsistent factors" to the surface; he returned to Arkansas and began his political career as a probate judge. He won congressional election in 1938 with a platform of fiscal responsibility.[11] During the next decade, Mills remained too low on the seniority ladder to exercise much power, but he was able to advance his education in politics. He concentrated on mastering the policy-making processes of the state.

By 1950, Mills had already learned a great deal about the two main fiscal policy-making channels of the federal government: political parties and interest-group politics. Political parties helped politicians secure office, achieve electoral stability, and get important government positions. Each party maintained a Committee on Committees, which assigned newly elected members to committees and reassigned members who wanted to transfer. Leadership positions within committees, moreover, were parceled out according to seniority. Party officials thus influenced which types of legislation representatives would support.[12]

The Democratic Party eased Mills's way into the federal government through the congressional committee system. In 1939, Mills earned a seat on the House Banking and Currency Committee, and in 1942 he was placed by the Democrats on Robert Doughton's (D-N.C.) Ways and Means Committee. The powerful Speaker of the House, Democrat Sam Rayburn (D-Tex.), helped Mills obtain this prestigious position. Ray-

---

[9] Wilbur D. Mills Memorial Foundation, "Wilbur D. Mills: A Public Life and Historic Career," pamphlet at the Wilbur D. Mills Archives in Conway, Arkansas.

[10] Wilbur Cohen, interview with David McComb, December 8, 1968, 18, Tape 1, Oral History Interview Collection, LBJL. See also Lawrence O'Brien, interview with Michael Gillette, July 24, 1986, 49–50, Interview XI, Oral History Interview Collection, LBJL.

[11] "Judge Wilbur D. Mills of Searcy Makes Announcement for Congress," *Melbourne Times,* June 10, 1938; C. P. Lee, Jr., "White County Judge Says 'No' Successfully," *Arkansas Gazette,* April 26, 1936.

[12] Gary W. Cox and Mathew D. McCubbins, *Legislative Leviathan: Party Government in the House* (Berkeley: University of California Press, 1993).

burn took a keen interest in Mills from the start; during Mills's first years in Congress, Rayburn even assigned one senior House member, Edward Cox (D-Ga.), and the Roosevelt-appointed comptroller of the General Accounting Office, Lindsey Warren, to teach him the "norms" of the House.[13] While working with Rayburn, Mills learned the importance of tailoring bills so that they would be likely to receive a solid House majority. Assuring a majority required constant interaction with party leaders and committee chairs.

Interest-group politics, a second federal policy-making channel, consisted of alliances between congressional committees and interest groups.[14] Interest groups were most active whenever their particular tax matters were in question. Due to the large numbers of organizations interested in tax policy, lobbyists were either directly or indirectly a constant presence in the deliberations. One of the most important roles of lobbyists was to push tax loopholes through the committees, since these loopholes were extremely difficult to eliminate once they had been established. The mineral-depletion allowance, for example, was a loophole that had saved the oil industry billions of dollars since 1926 by compensating companies for the high cost of exploratory drilling. Since its enactment, powerful organizations such as the American Petroleum Institute had guarded this provisi on. Immediately on arrival at Ways and Means, Mills encountered the power of these interest groups and their intimate relations with the committee. Rayburn allowed only Democrats who supported the oil lobby's depletion loopholes to be placed on Ways and Means, and Mills was no exception to that rule.[15]

Rayburn taught Mills the parliamentary skills needed to balance the demands of interest groups, tax-collecting agencies, and the Democratic Party; meanwhile Colin Stam, who headed the staff of the Joint Committee on Internal Revenue Taxation (JCIRT), was helping Mills learn how to use expertise in his new job. He provided Mills with the analytical skills needed to propose policies that administrators could enforce and that interest groups would accept. To help him in this task, Stam

---

[13]Wilbur Mills, interview with Anthony Champagne, March 13, 1986, 17–19, Sam Rayburn Library, Bonham, Texas.
[14]Political scientists call these relationships "iron triangles" by stressing the interdependence of interest groups, congressional committees, and agencies. But the interest that the IRS had in loopholes was not the same as the interest that the Department of Agriculture, for example, had in price supports. Although "iron triangle" is a useful term to describe many federal policies, it fails to explain the politics of taxation.
[15]JMIC.

served as a conduit of political information between interest groups, committee members, and Mills.[16]

THE WAYS AND MEANS AND JOINT ECONOMIC COMMITTEE STUDIES, 1954–1957

From 1954 to 1957, Mills used his political skills and new capabilities to become deeply involved with the fiscal policy community taking shape in Washington, D.C. By the final years of the Truman presidency, Mills had reached a position high enough on the seniority ladder to have a significant influence on committee policy. Between 1954 and 1957, Mills chaired the subcommittees on fiscal policy for the Ways and Means Committee and the Joint Economic Committee. Responding to the Internal Revenue Code of 1954, which included high statutory rates and an unprecedented number of loopholes, these subcommittees conducted several major studies on fiscal policy and economic growth. The studies served as an educational forum for a new generation of policymakers and helped to define a fiscal community. During these studies, Mills and his classmates identified the "leading experts" on fiscal issues while discovering new approaches to funding the state.

On the Ways and Means, Mills conducted a series of comprehensive hearings and investigations into the possibilities of "base-broadening" tax reforms. These were reforms designed to eliminate loopholes and to tax new types of income. Beginning in 1954, Mills and Thomas Curtis (R-Mo.) participated in this project through the Special Subcommittee on the Taxation of Life Insurance Companies. The subcommittee met with staff from the Joint Economic Committee and the Treasury Department, state insurance commissioners, insurance industry representatives, and selected experts. The subcommittee staff then helped Mills and Curtis to write a quantitative position paper that led to a major reform in 1959. Besides life insurance, Mills headed the Subcommittee on Internal Revenue Taxation, which conducted studies to correct "technical errors" in the revenue code, errors that were costing the government millions of dollars and hurting private investment. Mills formed

[16]For a discussion of central issues facing policymakers during the 1940s, see Robert M. Collins, "The Emergence of Economic Growthmanship in the United States: Federal Policy and Economic Knowledge in the Truman Years," in Furner and Supple, *The State and Economic Knowledge*, 138–70; Alan Brinkley, "The New Deal and the Idea of the State," in *The Rise and Fall of the New Deal Order 1930–1980*, ed. Steve Fraser and Gary Gerstle (Princeton: Princeton University Press, 1989), 85–121.

specialized advisory groups, consisting of selected experts and business leaders, who studied particular sections of the tax code under the guidance of the committee staff.[17] These accomplishments earned Mills a reputation within Congress as the "brain" behind the Ways and Means.[18]

Meanwhile, Mills's bipartisan subcommittee on fiscal policy for the Joint Economic Committee (JEC) conducted two major studies on economic policy. The first, which began in December 1955, examined the criteria for evaluating tax policies designed to stimulate economic growth. That winter, Mills's subcommittee arranged several panels that heard testimony on this issue. One panel focused on tax policy and its relation to short-run economic stabilization and long-run economic growth. Another panel investigated the possibilities of tax reform, including the potential impact that a rate reduction would have on consumption and investment. Other panels discussed the effect of recent fluctuations in the federal tax base.[19] A second study in 1957 examined the role of expenditure policies in economic growth and inflation. Tax and spending, the subcommittee concluded, must be considered together. To help do this, the subcommittee formed several panels with topics that included efficiency in government expenditures, procedures for determining the value of federal spending programs, the problem of "auto-

[17]"Rep. Mills Outlines Plans for Technical Revision of Code: Opposes Tax Cuts Now," *Journal of Taxation*, February 1957, 112–15; U.S. House of Representatives, Committee on Ways and Means, *Technical Amendments to Internal Revenue Code: Hearings*, 84th Cong., 2d sess., 1956; Charles MacLean, Jr., "Problems of Reincorporation and Related Proposals of the Subchapter C Advisory Group," *Tax Law Review* 13, no. 4 (May 1958): 407–37. See in WMPC, Unprocessed: Leo Irwin to Wilbur Mills (February 1, 1954); Irwin to Mills (October 12, 1956); Mills to George Humphrey (November 16, 1956); Staff, U.S. House of Representatives, Ways and Means Committee, Subcommittee on Internal Revenue Taxation, "Staff Data: Suggested Problems for Advisory Group on Subchapter C" (December 3, 1956); Norris Darrell to Mills (December 28, 1956); U.S. Department of Treasury, "Technical Information Release" (January 2, 1957); Colin Stam to Mills (January 8, 1957); Irwin to Jere Cooper and Mills (February 8, 1957); Fred Scribner to John Moss (February 21, 1957); Mills to James Casner (n.d.); Stam to Mills (August 14, 1957). And see James Riddell to Stanley Surrey (October 24, 1956), Surrey to Sherwin Kamin (December 12, 1956), and Surrey to Riddell (October 30, 1956), all in File 4, Box 20, SSP.
[18]JMIC; Thomas Curtis, "The House Committee on Ways and Means: Congress Seen through a Key Committee," *Wisconsin Law Review*, no. 1 (Winter 1966): 138.
[19]U.S. Congress, Joint Economic Committee, "Report to the Congress" (August 25, 1955), File 11, Box 700, WMPC; Paul Douglas to Wilbur Mills (September 13, 1955), File 1, Box 701, WMPC; John Morris, "Democrats Map New Tax Survey," *New York Times*, May 5, 1955; U.S. Congress, Joint Economic Committee, Subcommittee on Tax Policy, "Tax Policy for Economic Growth and Stability," 1955, WMPC, Unprocessed.

matic" expenditures, and improved methods for calculating what impact expenditures have on economic growth.[20]

These two JEC studies helped to bring into the federal government a new generation of individuals and organizations from the sort of policy-making channels that the political scientist Hugh Heclo has called "issue networks."[21] Issue networks consisted of relationships between staff members of the executive and congressional branches, university academics, specialists, activists, publishers and editors of professional journals, and participants in professional think tanks—all of whom had some expertise in tax policy. Although parts of these networks had existed before World War II, their numbers increased significantly in the postwar era, and they achieved a new level of cohesion.[22] By the mid-1950s, the involved issue networks were starting to negotiate with political parties and interest groups over formulating fiscal policy. Aware of this development, Mills helped mediate between the issue networks and congressional politics.

[20]U.S. Congress, Joint Economic Committee, Subcommittee on Fiscal Policy, "Hearings on Federal Expenditure Policy for Economic Growth and Stability" (November 8, 1957), File 702, Box 9, WMPC; Norman Ture to Wilbur Mills, "Draft of Subcommittee's Report" (June 18, 1957), File 1, Box 703, WMPC; Mills to the Members of Congress (June 28, 1957), WMPC, Unprocessed; Mills, "Introduction by Wilbur D. Mills, Chairman Subcommittee on Fiscal Policy" (n.d.), File 9, Box 702, WMPC; "No Time for Nodding," *Christian Science Monitor,* March 2, 1957; "Toward a Fuller Economy," *Washington Post,* March 3, 1957.

[21]Hugh Heclo, "Issue Networks and the Executive Establishment," in *The New American Political System,* ed. Anthony King (Washington, D.C.: American Enterprise Institute, 1978), 90–121.

[22]The following works discuss the massive proliferation of professional experts, staff, bureaucrats, and think tanks throughout the state after World War II: Herbert Stein, "The Washington Economics Industry," *American Economic Review* 76, no. 2 (May 1986): 1–10; Michael A. Bernstein, "American Economics and the American Economy in the American Century: Doctrinal Legacies and Contemporary Policy Problems," in *Understanding American Economic Decline,* ed. Michael A. Bernstein and David E. Adler (Cambridge: Cambridge University Press, 1994), 361–93; Donald R. Kennon and Rebecca M. Rogers, *The Committee on Ways and Means: A Bicentennial History, 1789–1989* (Washington, D.C.: Government Printing Office, 1989), 215–357; David M. Ricci, *The Transformation of American Politics: The New Washington and the Rise of Think Tanks* (New Haven: Yale University Press, 1993); James A. Smith, *The Idea Brokers: Think Tanks and the Rise of the New Policy Elite* (New York: Free Press, 1991); Thomas J. Reese, *The Politics of Taxation* (New York: Quorum Books, 1980); Balogh, *Chain Reaction,* 21–59; Matthew A. Crenson and Francis E. Rourke, "By Way of Conclusion," in *The New American State: Bureaucracies and Policies since World War II,* ed. Louis Galambos (Baltimore: Johns Hopkins University Press, 1987), 137–77; Jeffrey H. Birnbaum, *The Lobbyists: How Influence Peddlers Get Their Way in Washington* (New York: Random House, 1992); and Henry J. Aaron, *Politics and the Professors: The Great Society Perspective* (Washington, D.C.: Brookings Institution, 1978), chapter 5.

The Mills Subcommittee did this by soliciting oral testimonies and scholarly papers by the leading experts in several of the fiscal networks that took shape during these years.[23] Panels were set up with particular issue networks in mind. One network—the one that included Walter Heller, an economist at the University of Minnesota; Herbert Stein, director of research for the Committee for Economic Development; and Paul Samuelson, an economist at MIT—focused on Keynesian macroeconomic policies to promote economic growth. Stanley Surrey, Harvey Brazer, Thomas Atkeson, Randolph Paul, Richard Musgrave, and Joseph Pechman were prominent professors of law and economics who formed a second network around revenue-raising tax reforms on the depletion allowance, business expense deductions, cooperatives, and foreign income. Another network scrutinized proposals to stimulate private investment, ranging from liberalized depreciation to lower capital gains taxes to investment credits. This network included the university professors E. Cary Brown and Paul McCracken, the government and think-tank economists Arthur Burns, Dan Throop Smith, Gerhard Colm, and Raymond Saulnier, the interest-group experts George Terborgh and Emerson Schmidt, and the accountant Maurice Peloubet. A fourth network—which included Otto Eckstein and Arnold Soloway—analyzed the relationship between expenditures and economic growth, while Wilbur Cohen and Robert Myers led a fifth network on the taxation of the elderly.

As he tried to incorporate these networks into the policy process, Mills worked extensively with a group of federally employed economic experts. Grover Ensley, executive director of the JEC, and Norman Ture, the JEC economist, helped with the studies and provided him with in-depth analyses of current research on taxation and spending.[24] During the studies, Ensley acted as a liaison to the economics departments of several major universities while building close ties to interest groups and research organizations such as the Tax Foundation. After meeting with

[23]U.S. Congress, Joint Economic Committee, Subcommittee on Fiscal Policy, "Press Release" (April 25, May 9, and June 24, 1955), File 10–11, Box 700, WMPC; U.S. Congress, Joint Committee on the Economic Report, Subcommittee on Tax Policy, "Minutes of Meeting of the Subcommittee on Tax Policy" (May 5, 1955), File 10, Box 700, WMPC.

[24]Norman Ture to Wilbur Mills (October 7, 1957), File 9, Box 702, WMPC; Ture to Mills (September 11, 1957), File 1, Box 703, WMPC; Ture to Mills (September 13, 1957), File 4, Box 703, WMPC; Ture to Mills (December 20, 1956), WMPC, Unprocessed; Grovner Ensley to Mills (May 16, 1956), File 2, Box 701, WMPC; Ensley to Mills (May 23, 1957), File 8, Box 701, WMPC.

these organizations, Ensley would brief JEC members on economic conditions to help them define their policy options.[25]

Ture worked even more closely with the subcommittee. At age thirty-two, with a master's degree in economics and four years of experience on the Treasury staff, Ture had been recruited by Ensley to join the Joint Committee in 1955.[26] At the JEC, Ture was instrumental in setting up the studies and determining which experts were the most qualified to participate.[27] Ture also wrote background reports on the proposals submitted to the committee, providing Mills with "factbooks" and questions to use at the hearings. Mills learned how to benefit from Ture's expertise without becoming dependent on him; Ture recalled, "He [Mills] could glance at two or three questions [provided to him for the hearings] and immediately pick up on the train of thought." Once Mills had read the questions, "he would take them over himself and would never have to look down at the paper again." Ture added: "And it also did not come out as a committee member dutifully and sometimes with great difficulty reading the prose of some other staff member. It was Wilbur Mills asking the questions, and twisting them and using them to bring out what he wanted to see brought out."[28] When the hearings were done, Ture wrote the subcommittee reports by synthesizing the materials from the studies with other data that he had gathered from executive departments and research institutions.[29]

The hearings helped Mills to understand the delicate process of cre-

[25]Grover Ensley, interview with Richard Allan Baker, November 1, 1985, 60–75, Oral History Interview Collection, JFKL; Ensley to Wilbur Mills (November 14, 1956), File 1, Box 701, WMPC; Ensley, "A General Preview of the Tax Outlook for 1957: Address to the Fourth Annual Conference on the Economic Outlook, University of Michigan, Ann Arbor" (November 15 1956), File 1, Box 701, WMPC; Ensley to Paul Douglas (March 22, 1955), File 2, Box 701, WMPC; Ensley to Mills (June 2, 1955), File 10, Box 700, WMPC; Ensley to Mills (October 14, 1955), File 11, Box 700, WMPC.
[26]Paul Douglas to Wilbur Mills (January 22, 1955), and Grover Ensley to Douglas (March 22, 1955), both in File 2, Box 701, WMPC.
[27]Norman Ture to Wilbur Mills (October 22, 1955) and Mills to Ture (October 28, 1955), both in File 10, Box 700, WMPC; U.S. Congress, Joint Committee on the Economic Report, Subcommittee on Tax Policy, "Minutes of Meeting of the Subcommittee on Tax Policy" (May 5, 1955), File 10, Box 700, WMPC.
[28]Norman Ture, interview with Julian Zelizer, Washington, D.C., December 13, 1993.
[29]Norman Ture to Wilbur Mills, "Draft of Subcommittee's Report" (June 18, 1957), File 1, Box 703, WMPC. See also Ture to John Hoghland II, acting assistant secretary for congressional relations, Department of State (September 24, 1957), File 13, Box 705, WMPC; Ture to Mills (September 13, 1957), File 4, Box 703, WMPC; Mills to Ture (August 31, 1956), File 10, Box 700, WMPC. Ture, for example, corresponded with Treasury officials—through Mills's name—about a statistical study on taxation on personal holding companies. See File 9, Box 700, WMPC: Dan Throop Smith to Mills (July 5, 1956); Ture to Mills (September 17, 1956); Mills to Throop Smith (September 18,

ating the impression of an "objective" forum for congressional policy-making. In August 1955, for example, Senator Paul Douglas (D-Ill.) complained that the experts for the Joint Economic Committee hearings were weighted on the side of business. Mills and Ture denied this charge. Nonetheless, Mills told Douglas and Ture that, in the future, they should "avoid as much as possible the implication or charge" that they were weighting the panels. Mills noted, "I want all segments of our economy to be permitted to voice their opinions, as I am sure you do." Ture solved this problem by inviting more economists to represent the "public interest."[30] Stressing his commitment to "objectivity," Mills frequently urged that policy decisions "be based on careful economic analysis, rather than on the popular catch phrases" that were "frequently and indiscriminately attached to legislative proposals."[31]

Reactions to the JEC hearings were mixed. Some party leaders seemed troubled. One reporter observed, "Recent studies by the two subcommittees have been conducted on such a lofty nonpolitical plane that some of Mr. Mills' Democratic friends have privately accused him of catering to the economic intellectuals of the business and educational world to the detriment of his own party's interests."[32] But others were more impressed with Mills's innovative "panel of experts" approach to congressional politics. One journal commented that the JEC hearings "were so scholarly in tone and so completely lacking in partisan strife that reporters soon quit covering them."[33] Politicians and academics also praised Mills. Heller said: "The tax hearings a couple of years ago broke new ground in the organization and procedure of Congressional inquiries into fiscal policies. . . . Thanks to your leadership, and Norman Ture's skillful planning and follow-through, a significant advance in American fiscal thinking has been scored."[34] Even Harvard's Stanley Surrey, in an article that criticized the legislative tax-process, cited Mills's

1956); Throop Smith to Mills (October 1, 1956); Ture to Mills (October 18, 1956); E. J. Engquist, Jr., to Mills (October 25, 1956); Engquist, Jr., to Mills (January 4, 1957).
[30]Mentioned in Wilbur Mills to Paul Douglas (August 8, 1955), Douglas to Mills and Norman Ture (August 1, 1955), and John Lehman to Mills (August 3, 1955), all in File 10, Box 700, WMPC. For a similar dispute, see Wright Patman to Mills (December 6, 1955) and Mills to Patman (December 7, 1955), File 11, Box 700, WMPC.
[31]"Congressional Group Urges Budget Surplus Be Used to Cut Debt Instead of Taxes, If Business Boom Holds," *Wall Street Journal*, December 30, 1955. See also Wilbur Mills to the Congress (June 28, 1957), File 1, Box 703, WMPC.
[32]"Economic Statesman: Wilbur Daigh Mills," *New York Times*, December 20, 1957.
[33]Louis Cassels, "This Man Shapes Your Tax Bill," *Nation's Business*, March 1956, 66. See also Grover Ensley, interview with Richard Allan Baker, November 1, 1985, 73.
[34]Walter Heller to Wilbur Mills (December 16, 1957), File 5, Box 775, WMPC. These

subcommittee as an "excellent illustration of what can be done to increase understanding of tax issues."[35] Reactions were so favorable that the JEC could not satisfy the demand, from academic and government officials, for the subcommittee's compendium of papers.[36] Such success encouraged Mills to maintain close relationships with individuals who were crucial to the new fiscal community. Surrey, for instance, corresponded very often with Mills during these three years, discussing primarily the issue of foreign income.[37]

By introducing him to new policymakers and to new policy ideas, these hearings pushed Mills to define his legislative agenda. By 1958, Mills argued that the state should use moderate tax adjustments, rather than higher expenditures, to ensure economic growth and a full-employment balanced budget; his reliance on taxation instead of public spending reflected a general trend among policymakers during these years.[38] Mills said that a permanent rate reduction tied to expenditure control and revenue-raising reforms would eliminate the "drag" of high taxes on investment and demand.[39] Lower rates and fewer loopholes would also bring a degree of "fairness" to the tax code.[40] Mills's lan-

boxes are filled with letters of praise from people ranging from professors to representatives.

[35]Stanley S. Surrey, "The Congress and the Tax Lobbyist: How Special Tax Provisions Get Enacted," *Harvard Law Review* 70, no. 7 (May 1957): 1172. See also Surrey to Wilbur Mills (December 13, 1955), File 11, Box 700, WMPC.

[36]U.S. Congress, Joint Economic Committee, "Minutes from Meeting of Joint Economic Committee" (January 13, 1958), File 1–3, Box 701, WMPC.

[37]Stanley Surrey to Wilbur Mills (December 13, 1955), File 11, Box 700, WMPC. See WMPC, Unprocessed: Mills to Surrey (May 4, 1956); Surrey to Mills (May 14, 1956); Mills to Surrey (May 21, 1956); Surrey to Mills (November 19, 1956); Surrey to Mills (February 1, 1957); Mills to Surrey (February 4, 1957); Surrey to Mills (February 7, 1957); Mills to Surrey (February 11, 1957); Surrey to Mills (March 25, 1957).

[38]Robert M. Collins, *The Business Response to Keynes, 1929–1964* (New York: Columbia University Press, 1981), 142–209.

[39]See, for example, Allen Drury, "Capital Expects Economic Review to Be Optimistic," *New York Times*, January 20, 1958; "Recession Is a Fighting Word," *Business Week*, January 25, 1958, 28.

[40]These views were later summarized in Wilbur Mills, "Are You a Pet or a Patsy?" *Life*, November 23, 1959, 62. For a good look at Mills's discussion of taxation, see Wilbur Mills, "Preface," *Virginia Law Review* 44, no. 6 (October 1958): 835–38; "Rep. Mills Outlines Plans for Technical Revision of Code: Opposes Tax Cuts Now," *Journal of Taxation*, February 1957, 112–15; "Keep the Income Tax but Make It Fair," *U.S. News and World Report*, July 27, 1956, 68–80; Wilbur Mills, "The Relation of Taxes to Our Economy: Speech" (n.d.), File 2, Box 218, WMPC; Wilbur Mills, "Remarks of Mr. Mills before the Arkansas Association of Public Accountants Concerning the Internal Revenue Code of 1954" (1955), File 13, Box 783, WMPC; Wilbur Mills, "Federal Tax Policy for Economic Growth: Speech" (May 1, 1956), File 20, Box 783, WMPC; Wilbur Mills, "Remarks of Wilbur Mills to the Section of Taxation of the American Bar Association" (August 25, 1956), File 11, Box 780, WMPC; Wilbur Mills, "Remarks of the Honorable

guage of reform closely resembled that of Surrey or even Joseph Pechman; it included specific proposals for eliminating foreign tax havens,
tightening the definition of capital gains, reducing the oil-depletion allowance, and even tightening restrictions on travel and entertainment
deductions.

Besides his views on taxation, Mills wanted to expand the "insurance"
component of social security (OASDI) to include higher benefits, increased taxes, and more recipients. He firmly believed that the program
should remain self-supporting and that annual insurance benefits and
payroll tax revenue should be tied together. In sharp contrast, he hoped
to curtail nondefense expenditures that encouraged "dependency" and
"government centralization" while destroying the family. Although Mills
shared a traditional conservative aversion to deficit spending, he specifically targeted *welfare* expenditures; like others in the fiscal community,
Mills's rhetoric against deficits displayed much more flexibility toward
"uncontrollable" military and social "insurance" programs.

The Ways and Means and Joint Economic Committee studies of the
mid-1950s helped a young generation, including Mills, gain a sense of
themselves as a policy-making community. The studies offered a forum
for its members to engage colleagues with their ideas. With the help of
the JEC, policymakers from these specialized networks gradually began
to coalesce and to interact on a regular basis with the members of the
political parties and interest groups. These efforts were complemented
by the community-building work of the Treasury Department, presidential task forces, and cabinet committees. From this process emerged a
distinct, self-contained policy community, which included a new generation of policymakers and a new type of policymaker. Most of its members had acquired their first jobs in the expanding apparatuses of the
state between 1932 and 1945, where they helped consummate the marriage between the professions and the federal government.[41] Mean-

Wilbur D. Mills before the National Automobile Dealers' Association" (November 14,
1956), File 2, Box 781, WMPC; Wilbur Mills, "The Challenge of Federal Tax Policy in
1957: Address before the Seventeenth Annual Federal Tax Dinner of the Federal Tax
Forum" (December 6, 1956), File 1, Box 781, WMPC; Wilbur Mills, "Let's Strengthen
the Income Tax: Speech" (1956), File 16, Box 408, WMPC; Wilbur Mills, "Federal Tax
Policy and the Economic Challenges of 1957: Address to the Tax Executives Institute,
Inc." (February 18, 1957), File 12, Box 780, WMPC; Wilbur Mills, "Factors in Tax
Reduction and Revision: Address to the American Tax Foundation" (December 2, 1957),
File 5, Box 775, WMPC; Wilbur Mills, "Remarks of the Honorable Wilbur D. Mills
before the Society of Public Accountants" (September 1958), File 9, Box 775, WMPC.
[41]Balogh, *Chain Reaction*.

while, they interacted with a new generation of congressional leaders, including Russell Long (D-LA) and Lyndon Johnson (D-TX).[42]

Although there were varying degrees of involvement and different levels of power within this community and although serious ideological divisions existed among its members, they operated within a circumscribed policy-making arena and they shared a common political language. They would be collectively responsible for the tax and spending legislation of the 1960s. Between 1958 and 1964, Mills continued to learn how to use the resources of this community. But first, he had to master the difficult art of modern congressional politics.

WORKING CONGRESS AND BECOMING AN "EXPERT,"
1958–1961

Mills entered the inner circle of fiscal policy-making in 1958. Following the death of Jere Cooper (D-Tenn.), he became chairman of the House Ways and Means Committee. The chairmanship empowered Mills through the large jurisdiction of this committee and its status within the state.

Ways and Means had maintained an influential role in national politics throughout the twentieth century due to its constitutional power to write tax legislation. The Constitution (Article I, Section 7) ensured that this sort of revenue legislation would always emanate from the House, and as one representative noted, Ways and Means was the "fountainhead of the economic structure."[43] Whereas the Senate Finance Committee was also powerful, its role was to amend and modify the basic proposals put forth by the House. Since 1910, the Ways and Means had also been the Democratic Committee on Committees, making all committee appointments for the party.

Given the centrality of social insurance and public assistance to do-

---

[42]This statement is drawn from my analysis of the material in "Vital Statistics—House," a column that appeared in the *Congressional Quarterly Almanac*. For the 1950s and 1960s, this column included extensive personal and professional data about each member of the House. In addition, I used the following oral histories: John McCormack, interview with Sheldon Stern, March 30, 1977, Oral History Interview Collection, JFKL; Mike Mansfield, interview with Seth Tillman, June 23, 1964, Oral History Interview Collection, JFKL; Oren Harris, interview with Ronald Grele, November 3, 1965, Oral History Interview Collection, JFKL; Hale Boggs, interview with T. H. Baker, March 13, 1969, and March 27, 1969, Oral History Interview Collection, LBJL; Russell B. Long, interview with Michael Gillette, February 22, 1977, Oral History Interview Collection, LBJL.

[43]JMIC. See also, Catherine E. Rudder, "The House Committee on Ways and Means," in Silbey, *Encyclopedia of the American Legislative System*, 1033–48.

mestic policy, Ways and Means exercised a great deal of control over federal expenditures. The committee had also developed its own expenditure program based on tax exemptions, deductions, and exceptions. The Internal Revenue Code of 1954 had strengthened this system by creating an unprecedented number of loopholes, including liberalized definitions of exemptions, a new tax credit for retirement income, higher deductions on charitable donations, and a credit and an exclusion for dividend income.[44] Allowing the committee to forgive individuals and corporations of their responsibilities, these provisions functioned as a hidden system of government expenditures that remained under the tight control of the tax-writing committees.[45]

To help him preside over this complex system, the chairman relied on a talented group of staff experts. Leo Irwin was the chief counsel; John Martin, Jr., served as assistant chief counsel; and Gerard Brannon, James Riddell, and Raymond Conkling led the professional staff. Ways and Means had at its disposal several additional sources of expertise, including the House Legislative Counsel, the Library of Congress, and the staff of the JCIRT. As chair, Mills discovered that the bipartisan staff of the JCIRT, which included skilled economists, lawyers, and tax accountants, was very influential in the tax-writing process.

The JCIRT staff helped Mills forge compromises between the House, the Senate, and the executive branch during the deliberative process. Because of its influence, the staff attracted some of the most respected tax experts in the nation: Colin Stam led this group from 1938 until 1964; Laurence Woodworth took over in 1964, having served on the staff since 1944.[46] Starting in his first year as chair, Mills drew heavily on their analytical skills. Stam and Woodworth published several important studies on revenue-raising reforms, they interpreted proposals from the executive branch, and they provided important analyses on the budget.[47] Furthermore, they wrote the "guff" of committee reports,

[44]John F. Witte, *The Politics and Development of the Federal Income Tax* (Madison: University of Wisconsin Press, 1985), 146–50.

[45]The concept of "tax expenditures" was developed by Stanley S. Surrey in *Pathways To Tax Reform* (Cambridge, Mass.: Harvard University Press, 1973). See also William F. Hellmuth and Oliver Oldman, *Tax Policy and Tax Reform, 1961–1969: Selected Speeches and Testimony of Stanley S. Surrey* (Chicago: Commerce Clearing House, 1973).

[46]JMIC; Joseph Barr to Claude Desautels (February 25, 1963), File 2, Box 177, SSP; Reese, *The Politics of Taxation*, 61–88; Manley, *The Politics of Finance*, 307–19.

[47]Colin Stam to Wilbur Mills (January 28, 1957), File 1, Box 701, WMPC; Staff, JCIRT,

which included a general explanation, a history, and a summary of each particular bill.[48] Through these projects, Stam and Woodworth mediated between the policymakers who proposed legislation and the "technicians" from the Tax Legislative Counsel who drafted committee bills. Ed Craft and Ward Hussey, Mills's tax technicians, also maintained extensive files of "Limbo Drafts," bills that were kept on file until an opportunity emerged to propose them. Eugene Keogh's (D-N.Y.) plan to provide self-employed persons with tax-deductible retirement plans, for example, remained in limbo for almost three decades.[49]

When Mills became chair of this committee and its staff, he clearly stepped into an important position. As chair, Mills could accept or reject presidential tax proposals; he supervised an elaborate expenditure sys-

"Staff Study I: Simplification of the Individual Income Tax Return" (January 28, 1957), WMPC, Unprocessed; Stam to Mills (May 13, 1957), WMPC, Unprocessed; Eugene Thore to Mills (October 31, 1957), WMPC, Unprocessed; Leo Irwin to Members of the Committee on Ways and Means (January 11, 1958), File: Budget-1961, Box 6337, 87th Cong., RG 233 (Papers of the House Committee on Ways and Means), NA; Stam to Mills (February 19, 1958), WMPC, Unprocessed; Staff, JCIRT (February 25, 1958), 85th Cong., File: Income Rates, Box 6342, RG 233, NA; Irwin to Members of the Committee on Ways and Means (February 26, 1958), 86th Cong., File: Income Rates, Box 6342, RG 233, NA; Stam to Mills (January 23, 1959), File: Budget 1959, Box 460, RG 128 (Papers of the Joint Committee on Internal Revenue Taxation), NA; Gerard Brannon to Leo Irwin (May 10, 1958), File: Taxation of Co-ops, Box 6345, 87th Cong., RG 233, NA; Norman Ture to Irwin (May 6, 1959) and Ture to Harry Kahn and Danny Holland (May 11, 1959), 86th Cong., File: Income Rates, Box 6342, RG 233, NA; Herbert Miller to Congressional Members (December 15, 1959), File: Income Tax—Rates, Box 6342, 87th Cong., RG 233, NA; Brannon to Mills (December 8, 1960), File: Economy, Box 6338, 87th Cong., RG 233, NA; Irwin to Members of the Committee on Ways and Means (January 23, 1961), File: Budget-1961, Box 6337, 87th Cong., RG 233, NA; Irwin to Members of the Ways and Means Committee (March 8, 1961), File: Economy, Box 6338, 87th Cong., RG 233, NA; Gerard Brannon to Irwin (June 28, 1961), File: Budget-1961, Box 6337, 87th Cong., RG 233, NA; Irwin to Democratic Members of the Committee on Ways and Means (August 30, 1961), File: Budget-1961, Box 6337, 87th Cong., RG 233, NA; Staff, JCIRT, "Treatment of Costs in Excess of Mineral Income" (1962), File: Sec. 611 1956–64, Box 337, RG 128, NA; Mortimer Caplin to Irwin (April 5, 1962), File: Exemptions—Income Tax, Box 6339, 87th Cong., RG 233, NA; Donald Lubick, interview with Julian Zelizer, Washington, D.C., May 16, 1994; Ward Hussey, interview with Julian Zelizer, May 19, 1994; JMIC.
[48]David J. Stern, "Congress, Politics, and Taxes: A Case Study of the Revenue Act of 1962" (Ph.D. diss., Claremont Graduate School, 1965), 218–19.
[49]Ward Hussey, interview with Julian Zelizer, May 19, 1994. For theoretical discussions of the congressional staff, see the following: Michael J. Malbin, *Unelected Representatives: Congressional Staff and the Future of Representative Government* (New York: Basic Books, 1979); Susan Webb Hammond, "Congressional Staffs," in Silbey, *Encyclopedia of the American Legislative System*, 785–800; Harrison W. Fox, Jr., and Susan Webb Hammond, *Congressional Staffs: The Invisible Force in American Lawmaking* (New York: Free Press, 1977).

tem; and he had access to one of the most talented staffs in Congress. He could depend on a committee whose membership was relatively consensual. The twenty-five-member tax-writing committee consisted of stable, political moderates who had worked for years through the committee system and came from relatively "safe" districts.[50] When considering legislation, according to congressional folklore, the committee focused on how much money the government could raise before it decided on how much the government would spend. Through a reputation of "fiscal responsibility," the members and their leader gained a considerable amount of political capital within a culture that valued technical expertise and incremental change.[51]

But as Mills learned immediately on taking over the Ways and Means, his political success depended on more than just holding a powerful position. He learned that to shape—rather than simply to reject or to accept—fiscal policies, he needed to master the complex institutions and culture of the postwar state. He began by sharpening his skills in the old-fashioned art of congressional politics, an art that had changed in recent years.

His effort to increase his effectiveness in Congress lasted four years. He had some success. He passed, for instance, the Technical Amendments and Small Business Tax Revision Act (1958) and the Life Insurance Taxation Reform Act (1959). But during 1958 and 1959, he learned that as the American state had expanded, congressional politics had become more complex and difficult to control. Congressional leaders had to tailor legislation that would allow representatives to support the bills in spite of an unprecedented number of demands. Mills at first failed to do this. In 1958, the first bill he proposed as chairman provided for a sixteen-week extension of unemployment compensation for workers whose benefits had run out, with compensation to be paid to many noncovered workers as an outright federal grant. Mills had not packaged the measure properly, leaving it open to charges of being a "dole" that threatened to "destroy the insurance principle underlying unemployment insurance."[52] The House soundly rejected the committee bill, and a

[50] Manley, *The Politics of Finance*, 45–63; Richard F. Fenno, Jr., *Congressmen in Committees* (Boston: Little, Brown, and Company, 1973).

[51] JMIC.

[52] U.S. House of Representatives, Committee on Ways and Means, *Temporary Unemployment Compensation Act of 1958*, April 23, 1958, H1656 (Committee—Print); Daniel Reed, Press Release (April 18, 1958), 85th Cong., File: HR 12065 1 of 9, Box 638, RG

coalition of southern Democrats and Republicans substituted a pale version of the proposal.[53] In other legislative battles—over highway construction and Treasury bond interest rates, for example—Mills again proved incapable of pushing a bill through swiftly or even of maintaining control of his committee.[54] Some Washington pundits began to label the Ways and Means as the "No-Ways & By No-Means" committee. Others said that Mills simply lacked the qualities needed for strong leadership. In 1959, *Time* magazine described Mills's performance during his first year as chairman as "inept."[55]

Confronting professional disaster, Mills quickly learned how to "read" the needs of his fellow postwar congressional representatives and to "sell" them his proposed policies. He developed a keen awareness of the multiple policy pressures that influenced them. Success depended on the ability to exchange benefits skillfully in return for support, without sacrificing the integrity of complex fiscal legislation. After the unemployment compensation fiasco, Mills never again allowed a bill out of his committee until he was certain that it would pass the House; the chairman once said: "There's no point in bringing out a bill just for show, knowing it will be beaten on the floor. . . . Our job is to work

233, NA; John McCormack and Wilbur Mills, Press Release (March 11, 1958), WMPC, Unprocessed; Robert Albright, "Democratic Jobless Aid Bill Cleared," *Washington Post*, March 30, 1958.

[53] Mills later claimed that he did not really lose the bill, since the House rejected the part of the legislation—funding benefits for uncovered workers through general revenue—that he had known they would reject. Mills claimed to have added that section of the measure to distract attention from the more moderate sections—which he and the Eisenhower administration had sought all along. Ultimately, the moderate sections passed. This statement, however, seems at best a rationalization for the devastating loss: Mills had always been aware that major defeats dealt a severe blow to a committee chairman, and it thus seems highly unlikely that he would set himself up for a loss at such an early stage of his career. Regardless of his intentions, the defeat raised many questions among policymakers and the media about his abilities, thus tarnishing his reputation.

[54] John Morris, "Democrats Study a New Bond Plan," *New York Times*, January 18, 1960; "Democrats Stall Mills' Compromise on Rate Ceiling," *Wall Street Journal*, February 17, 1960; "House Unit Votes Compromise Bill on Bid to End Bond Rate Ceiling," *Wall Street Journal*, February 24, 1960; Editorial, "No Compromise with Reason," *Wall Street Journal*, February 29, 1960; "House Unit Urges Approval of Compromise Bill to Revoke 4¼% Ceiling on Some Bonds," *Wall Street Journal*, March 2, 1960; Editorial, "Frozen in Politics," *Wall Street Journal*, April 26, 1960; *Congressional Quarterly Almanac*, 86th Cong., 1st sess., 1959, 273–75.

[55] "Decline and Fall," *Time*, September 7, 1959, 11; "Tax Overhaul Plan," *Wall Street Journal*, June 29, 1959; Charles Sieb, "Steering Wheel of the House," *New York Times*, Sunday, March 18, 1962, Section 6; Robert Novak, "Ways and Means Woe," *Wall Street Journal*, January 12, 1962; "Wilbur Mills . . . 'Mr. Taxes' in the Congress," *Newsweek*, January 14, 1963, 14–18.

over a bill until our technical staff tells us it is ready and until I have reason to believe that it is going to get enough support to pass."[56] As the political scientist John Manley argued, Mills learned to nurture the votes of southern conservatives and to tailor bills to ensure majorities in the House. Mills also made extensive use of "Member's Bills." Every year, time was allotted to allow committee members to propose minor, "technical" provisions that benefited one of the specific interest groups that supported them. These bills usually passed unanimously and with little opposition.[57]

To ensure passage of more comprehensive legislation, Mills consciously avoided the partisanship of previous chairmen, particularly Robert Doughton, who had chaired the committee between 1933 and 1953.[58] Instead, Mills developed a bipartisan norm that Manley called "restrained partisanship," which stressed that "partisanship should not interfere with a thorough study and complete understanding of the technical complexities of the bills under consideration."[59] The chairman achieved this difficult task by working closely with committee Republicans, especially John Byrnes (R-Wisc.). He even refused to meet privately with Sam Rayburn or with a Democratic caucus to devise legislation.[60]

As he became an effective leader, Mills earned the trust of numerous representatives and consolidated his position on the Ways and Means. In 1961, for example, he centralized control by eliminating the various subcommittees of the Ways and Means. He always obtained a closed rule from the Rules Committee; the closed rule meant that the House could only accept or reject, not modify, committee legislation. Mills argued that the "technical complexity" of fiscal legislation and the danger of chaotic horse-trading in the House called for a closed rule. After his first few years as chair, members of Congress knew that Mills would craft legislation to accommodate as many interests as possible, and thus they granted him this power. They were willing to delegate this much responsibility only to a leader they knew was competent and politically safe. As the chairman once said: "A conscientious congressman knows he can't make an adequate personal study of all the complicated bills he's required to vote on. So when something comes up that's outside his

[56]Sieb, "Steering Wheel of the House." See also Douglas Cater, "The Ways and Means of Wilbur Mills," *Reporter*, March 29, 1962, 26.
[57]Manley, *The Politics of Finance*, 79–81.
[58]JMIC.
[59]Manley, *The Politics of Finance*, 64–68.
[60]JMIC.

field, he tries to find somebody he can rely upon to give him straight facts and intelligent judgments." He concluded: "After you've been here for a while, you're tabbed as either knowing your subject or not knowing it. I've sought to know my subject."[61] As a result, when Mills took a measure to the Rules Committee, "it was a *fait accompli*."[62]

By the early 1960s, Mills thoroughly understood the parliamentary process. In 1960, for example, he pushed through a major bill that provided the states with federal support for medical programs for the "medically indigent" (the Kerr-Mills Act); in 1961, moreover, he passed social security amendments that included a 20 percent increase in the minimum OASDI benefit and an increase in widows' benefits. From 1962 on, Mills's legislative record was very positive. "There was no one," the congressional liaison Lawrence O'Brien said, "more effective in handling legislation than Wilbur Mills."[63] Members from both parties praised Mills's "legislative expertise" in getting bills through Congress.[64]

But to succeed in postwar congressional politics, the legislator also had to keep pace with an expanding number of policy arenas. Given the vast size of the federal government, changes were taking place constantly as specialized policy communities moved in different and often contradictory directions. Congressional representatives frequently had great difficulty in adjusting to these changes without alienating their districts. Like their colleagues, members of the tax-writing committees had to monitor these developments carefully.

While mastering the parliamentary process, Mills encountered a serious threat to his influence. This happened between 1958 and 1962 when the national government, including many members of the fiscal community, began to shift to a more liberal position on civil rights.[65] The

[61]Cassels, "This Man Shapes Your Tax Bill," 35; Joseph Alsop, "The Legislator," *Washington Post,* January 8, 1962.
[62]Lawrence O'Brien, interview with Michael Gillette, December 17, 1986, 19, Interview XVII. On Mills's use of the closed rule, see also the following: Bernard J. Lammers, "The Role of Congressional Tax Committees" (Ph.D. diss., Columbia University, 1967); Randall Strahan, *New Ways and Means: Reform and Change in a Congressional Committee* (Chapel Hill: University of North Carolina Press, 1990); Linda Katherine Kowalcky, "The House Committee on Ways and Means: Maintenance and Evolution in the Post-Reform House of Representatives" (Ph.D. diss., Johns Hopkins University, 1991).
[63]Lawrence O'Brien, interview with Michael Gillette, July 24, 1986, 36, Interview XI.
[64]JMIC. One survey of House members and the Washington Press Corps in 1964 voted him the single most effective U.S. representative: "Who Is Best? Who Is Worst?," *Pageant,* November 1964.
[65]Hugh Davis Graham, *The Civil Rights Era: The Origins and Development of National Policy* (Oxford: Oxford University Press, 1990), chapters 1–5; James L. Sundquist, *Pol-*

powerful civil rights movement temporarily threatened Mills's political standing back in the district, thus causing him to hesitate before taking action on any innovative fiscal policies that might be considered too liberal in Arkansas; these included investment incentives, loophole-closing reforms, and deficit financing. One Washington associate astutely noted, "Wilbur may look very conservative up here, but in his district people call him up and say, 'Wilbur, don't you go too far along with that crowd, now.' "[66] Indeed, the chairman had a difficult time adapting to this particular transition because his constituency had little sympathy for federal intervention in racial matters, particularly after the Little Rock incident.[67] Since World War II, Mills had consistently opposed federal involvement in racial issues. In 1956, for instance, he signed the "Southern Manifesto," which denounced *Brown v. Board of Education*. The Little Rock crisis put him and his Arkansas colleagues on the national hot seat. As pressures intensified, Mills remained adamant. In 1960, Mills opposed the Civil Rights Act as unnecessary and unconstitutional.[68]

The congressional redistricting of Arkansas in 1960 compounded Mills's problems. Due to the 1960 census, Arkansas lost two congressional seats, and the ensuing redistricting threatened to derail Mills's career. Once preparations for the census had begun in 1958, he found himself obliged to defend strongly the outspoken segregationist Arkansas representative Dale Alford (D-Ark.), a close friend of Governor Orval Faubus's; otherwise, Faubus would have been able to use his power over the state legislature to redistrict Mills out of office.[69] Mills was successful, but he paid a price for this effort. Supporting Alford cost Mills status

---

itics and Policy: The Eisenhower, Kennedy, and Johnson Years (Washington, D.C.: Brookings Institution, 1968), chapter 6.

[66]Edmond Le Breton, "Mills Holds Ground on Principle," cited in U.S. Congress, House of Representatives, *Congressional Record*, 87th Cong., Appendix, March 26, 1962, A2316–17.

[67]The intensity of the resistance of Mills's constituents to virtually every civil rights measure cannot be overstated. For examples, see Boxes 323 and 684, WMPC.

[68]Wilbur Mills, "Extension of Remarks of Honorable Wilbur D. Mills of Arkansas in the House of Representatives" (April 4, 1960), File 9, Box 784, WMPC; U.S. Congress, House of Representatives, *Congressional Record*, 86th Cong., 2d sess., March 23, 1960, 6398–6400; Mills to J. K. Hale (January 14, 1960), WMPC, Unprocessed. See also Mills to Marion Thomas (February 22, 1960), File 2, Box 684, WMPC; Mills to Martha Humphreys (October 9, 1962), File 14, Box 323, WMPC; Mills to J. K. Hale (March 22, 1960), WMPC, Unprocessed.

[69]Wilbur Mills to John McCormack (November 24, 1958), and Mills to Henry Bailey (December 22, 1958), both in File 7, Box 637, WMPC.

in Washington circles: Mills felt "besieged" by the accusation that he was a "captive of Southern discrimination tradition."[70] After the redistricting, the pressures continued. Alford, who was now in Mills's district, threatened to challenge him in an election. The chairman was thus forced to act conservatively on all issues that might be considered too "liberal" back in the district, issues ranging from civil rights to tax reform.[71] Many of his colleagues and the press believed that civil rights and redistricting had cost Mills the speakership of the House after Rayburn's death in 1961.[72] Unable to win the speakership, Mills used the chairmanship of the Ways and Means to establish his power in Washington.

Even that approach was made difficult after redistricting added Little Rock and its labor unions to Mills's constituency. This brought a new interest group into his formerly rural constituency and forced Mills to change course again. In one incident, Mills seemed to have delayed hearings on an insurance-taxation bill because of union opposition. Preoccupied with redistricting and the unions, Mills made a couple of uncharacteristic "slip-ups." The unions continued to pressure Mills, particularly on health care.[73] An AFL-CIO representative later warned President John Kennedy that the redistricting issue might paralyze Mills politically.[74] Mills himself conveyed a strong sense of being cross-pressured. He told George Ellison, of the United Steelworkers of America, that he would allow discussion of the Medicare proposal only if the union people promised "to cease stirring up grass roots complaints in his district."[75]

Mills was resilient, however, and he withstood the pressures of civil rights and redistricting. Several developments helped ease him to success. First, in 1962, Alford unsuccessfully ran against Faubus for governor. This loss ended Alford's congressional career. Without Alford's electoral threat, Mills could concentrate more of his attention on federal policy-

---

[70]Norman Ture, interview with Julian Zelizer; Editorial, "Mr. Sam's Chair," *New Republic,* December 30, 1957, 5.

[71]Richard Lyons, "Redistricting Can Give 4 Arkansans Trouble," *Washington Post,* February 9, 1961; Cassels, "This Man Shapes Your Tax Bill," 66.

[72]John McMillan to Wilbur Mills (December 11, 1961) and Mills to McMillan (December 14, 1961), both in WMPC, Unprocessed; Mills to Emerson Schmidt (September 4, 1959), File 6, Box 691, WMPC; "Decline and Fall," *Time,* September 7, 1959, 11.

[73]JMIC.

[74]Henry H. Wilson, Jr., to Lawrence O'Brien (April 13, 1961), File: Memorandum 3/1/ 62–3/5/62, Box 3, White House Staff Files, Henry Hall Wilson, JFKL.

[75]James O'Brien to Lawrence O'Brien (April 2, 1962), File: House File, Wilbur Mills, Arkansas, Folder 1, Box 10, White House Staff Files, JFKL.

making and less on the district. Second, Mills and his staff worked with well-situated government administrators at the local and national levels to satisfy the demands of crucial constituents and their interest groups.[76]

Mills's success was also related to his achievements with the fiscal community and his growing reputation as a "fiscal expert." The chairman's highly praised work with the community diverted attention from his regional ties, even though he continued to oppose most civil rights measures. He was able to walk the fine line between alienating the South and losing support in Congress. It was not always easy to stay on this line. Some southern colleagues expressed deep concern over his new identification. As one journalist commented, "Southern conservatives accuse him of trying to be an economic statesman—of being too greatly impressed by economists and other Northern eggheads."[77]

But Mills stayed on the line and strengthened his reputation. In January 1958 and November 1959, Mills brought together the various people, most of whom were drawn from the same pool of experts that he had used in previous years, who were working on tax reform.[78] Behind the scenes, Ture and Surrey gathered participants and collected information in an "objective" fashion to avoid any "political" opposition.[79] While conducting these hearings, the committee introduced several new

[76]Mills, for example, worked with Mortimer Caplin's staff in the IRS and with Robert Goodwin in the Department of Labor to help Arkansas fish farmers with their tax problems. See Mortimer Caplin to Wilbur Mills (June 6, 1962, and March 6, 1963), File: Govt Dept. of Treasury, Internal Revenue Service #1 Fish Farming 1962–67/2, Box 155, WMPC; Charles Donahue to Mills (February 25, 1963), File: Dept. of Treasury, Internal Revenue Service #1, Fish Farming, 1962–67/3, Box 155, WMPC; Robert Goodwin to Mills (March 19, 1962), File: 12, Box 319, WMPC. See also Leo Irwin to K. C. Harbour (June 22, 1961), File: Accounting Method J., Box 6337, 87th Cong., RG 233, NA. Back in the district, he worked with several key administrators. See Jack Calvert to Wilbur Mills (March 11, 1961), File: Government Social Security Administration "XYZ's" 1961–62, Box 21, WMPC; Mills to Roxie Jennings (April 1, 1958), File 1, Box 589, WMPC; Mills to June Key (February 3, 1961), File: Government Social Security Administration, "K's" 1961–62, Box 21, WMPC. See Boxes 21–26 for correspondence about social security. For example, Louise Miles to Mills (December 9, 1962), Mills to Frederick Gray, (December 13, 1962), and Gray to Mills (December 17, 1962), all in File: Government Social Security Administration: "M's" 1961–62, Box 21, WMPC; Mills to Doris Miller (July 26, 1963), File: Govt #2-Dept. of Treasury, Internal Revenue Service, 1963–64/1, Box 232, WMPC.
[77]"The Man Who Steers Tax Policy," *Business Week*, March 22, 1958, 62.
[78]Wilbur Mills to Stanley Surrey (March 3, 1958), File 1, Box 28, SSP; Surrey to Mills (November 7, 1958) and Mills to Surrey (November 14, 1958), both in WMPC, Unprocessed; Surrey to Mills (January 22, 1958), Surrey to Mills (July 30, 1959), Surrey to Mills (July 8, 1959), and Surrey to Mills (August 26, 1959), all in File 1, Box 28, SSP.
[79]Stanley Surrey to Wilbur Mills (December 24, 1958), File 5, Box 40, SSP. See also Surrey to Mills (November 17, 1959), File 1, Box 28, SSP.

actors into the policy community, including Mortimer Caplin, a leading scholar on tax reform from the University of Virginia.[80] Mills, Surrey, and Gerard Brannon produced a highly praised 2,382-page compendium on loophole-closing tax reform and rate reduction, with lead articles by Surrey, Heller, and Pechman. There were also specialized articles and hearings on reforming the taxation of the aged, the taxation of interest on state and local bonds, the taxation of foreign income, and the taxation of capital gains. To complete the research, Woodworth wrote several analyses of the feasibility of specific base-broadening reforms.[81] The compendium became a "tax law bible" for the next generation of policymakers.[82]

The studies made political headlines by effectively articulating the idea of tax reform. "Tax reform," according to the committee, should reduce tax rates "without sacrificing revenues required for responsible financing of government." This would create a more favorable climate for economic growth, stable prices, greater compliance, and "horizontal equity"—the notion that equal incomes should pay equal taxes and that

[80]Mortimer Caplin, interview with Shelley Davis and Kecia McDonald, November 18–25, 1991, 5–6, Internal Revenue Service, Oral History Interview; U.S. House of Representatives, Committee on Ways and Means, *Tax Revision Compendium: Compendium of Papers on Broadening the Tax Base,* 86th Cong., 1959; U.S. House of Representatives, Committee on Ways and Means, *General Revenue Revision: Hearings before the Committee on Ways and Means,* 85th Cong., 2nd sess., 1958. Regarding Mills's use of a common pool of experts, see Norman Ture to Wilbur Mills (May 11, 1959), File: Income Tax—Rates, Box 6342, 87th Cong., RG 233, NA; Norman Ture to Mills (October 29, 1959), Mills to Ture (November 2, 1959), and Ture to Mills (November 5, 1959), all in File 7, Box 784, WMPC; "Tax Reform Panel to Discuss Wide Range of Topics," *Wall Street Journal,* June 5, 1959; Editorial, "Studying the Obvious," *Wall Street Journal,* May 20, 1959. The Ways and Means also held some smaller, less publicized hearings on particular tax code issues that needed reform. See U.S. House of Representatives, Committee on Ways and Means, *Taxation of Mutual Savings Banks and Savings and Loans Associations: Hearings,* 87th Cong., 1st sess., 1961; U.S. House of Representatives, Committee on Ways and Means, *"Gross Up" in Connection with Foreign Tax Credit Allowed Domestic Corporations on Dividends from a Foreign Subsidiary: Hearings,* April 11, 1960, 86th Cong., 2nd sess., 1960.

[81]Joint Staff, JCIRT and the Treasury Department, *The Technical Amendments Bill of 1960 H.R. 9625 and H.R. 9626,* January 14, 1960, H4790 (Committee—Print); Joint Staff, JCIRT and the Treasury Department, *Staff Data: Notes on Background of Existing Provisions of the Federal Income and Employment Tax Laws,* August 25, 1960, H11261 (Committee—Print); Staff, JCIRT, File: Sec. 521, Box 336, RG 128, NA; Staff, JCIRT, *Internal Revenue Code of 1954 as Amended and in Force on January 3, 1961,* January 3, 1961, J0535 (Committee—Print); Staff, JCIRT, *General Explanation of Committee Discussion Draft of Revenue Bill of 1961,* August 24, 1961, H3129 (Committee—Print). See also footnote 47.

[82]Mortimer Caplin, interview with Shelley Davis and Kecia McDonald, November 18–25, 1991, 5.

there should thus be fewer distinctions between different types of income. Until such reforms were completed, citizens would continue to convert most of their wealth into nontaxable income; lower rates, combined with loophole-closing reforms, could thus raise more revenue than under the existing system. Ultimately, reform would create a tax system that operated with minimum interference in the "operation of the free market mechanism in directing resources into their most productive uses."[83] The studies filled out these broad principles with concrete suggestions for reform, such as Surrey's proposal for withholding on interest and dividends.

Although these ideas were not new to the tax field, this was the first time that they had been synthesized so effectively and given so much attention in Washington. More important, they were completed under the aegis of a tax-writing committee that was known more for its work with oil lobbies than for its ties to Harvard economists. Certainly, there were problems with the studies; in 1959, for example, the House Republican leader, Charles Halleck of Indiana, publicly attacked the liberal Senator Douglas (D-Ill.) for infiltrating the studies by placing his expert, Norman Ture, on the staff of the Ways and Means Committee.[84] These sorts of struggles were understandable because on many occasions, committee members delegated authority to the experts to evaluate the demands of other policymakers.

But Mills handled these problems effectively, and they were overshadowed by his success during these hearings at creating new levels of "expertise" in the tax-writing process. In doing so, he became the first modern chairman of the Ways and Means whose professional reputation within Washington rested in large part on his fiscal "expertise" rather than on his partisanship or his ability to broker congressional deals.[85]

---

[83]U.S. House of Representatives, Committee on Ways and Means, *Tax Revision Compendium: Compendium of Papers on Broadening the Tax Base,* 86th Cong., ix. See also Leo Irwin to Stanley Surrey (October 29, 1957), File 1, Box 28, SSP.

[84]"Tom," from McGraw Hill, to Wilbur Mills (November 7, 1959), WMPC, Unprocessed.

[85]The reputations of previous chairmen had been based on one of three principal characteristics: their devotion to a particular political ideology, their partisanship, or their success at brokering congressional deals. For a good discussion of Claude Kitchin, see W. Elliot Brownlee, "Social Investigation and Political Learning in the Financing of World War I," in Lacey and Furner, *The State and Social Investigation,* 323–64, and W. Elliot Brownlee, "Economists and the Formation of the Modern Tax System in the United States: The World War I Crisis," in Furner and Supple, *The State and Economic Knowledge,* 401–35. For descriptions of Mills's other predecessors, see Kennon and Rogers, *The Committee on Ways and Means.* Nor have the chairmen who followed Mills developed reputations within Washington as "experts." Al Ullman was known more for

The chairman, said colleagues, knew "the tax system just inside and out, backwards and forwards," and could "run circles around anybody in the country on the tax law and its problems."[86] Members of the Ways and Means were convinced of the accuracy of such statements; as one representative said: "We have a chairman who is so thoroughly knowledgeable in his field. There isn't anything in taxes he fails to understand or fails to relate to what has gone before and tie it into today."[87] His knowledge was so thorough that government officials began to say he did not even depend on the experts. "He understands tax legislation better than any person I know," commented one lawyer. "He reads every bill and report as thoroughly as the staff. He can hold his own in a technical discussion with any tax attorney, or with any of the Treasury's experts."[88]

In practice, however, Mills carefully used experts to enhance this image. He relied on them to persuade other legislators to grant him authority over complex policies. One staff member recalled that during committee markups, "Woodworth would go over the staff pamphlet with Mills the night before. As a result, Mills and Woodworth had the material down cold. At the markup Mills would say things like, 'Larry, didn't we try something like this back in 1954?' Woodworth had told him about that the night before." After that, "The rest of the members would just sit there dumbfounded, dazzled by the knowledge of Mills and Woodworth."[89] A prominent committee member remembered a similar encounter with Stam. "He and Stam would go back and forth on the bill section by section: what happened in '36, '37, '38. It was quite a performance."[90] To improve his knowledge, the chairman also depended on experts to pass information between himself and the fiscal

---

his partisanship and his "liberalism," whereas Dan Rostenkowski's reputation focused on his ability to broker congressional "deals." Mortimer Caplin, for example, extensively discussed the contrast between Mills and Rostenkowski in Caplin, interview with Julian Zelizer, June 13, 1994.

[86] Gardner Ackley, interview with Joe Franz, April 13, 1973, 4, Oral History Interview Collection, LBJL.

[87] JMIC. Almost all of the people whom Manley interviewed mentioned two factors— beyond Mills's official position—that accounted for his influence: his congressional skills and his fiscal expertise. Literally hundreds of private and public statements were made in praise of his expertise.

[88] John Cauley, "Mills of Arkansas: Powerful Voice In Congress," *Kansas City Times,* August 22, 1961. For similar comments by other Washington pundits, see Lawrence O'Brien, interview with Michael Gillette, December 5, 1985, 42–43, Interview V; Statement by Hale Boggs, May 24, 1962, File 11, Box 411, WMPC.

[89] Cited in Reese, *The Politics of Taxation*, 69.

[90] JMIC.

community and to analyze a flow of data that was admittedly "cryptic and technical."[91]

By 1961, Mills had overcome some of his most difficult challenges by acquiring two important assets. First, his congressional acumen ensured the passage of most of the bills that he supported. Second, his reputation as an expert and his analytic skills provided him access into the complex, technocratic world of the fiscal community. As one close colleague astutely noted: "I had some misgivings when Mills took over as chairman from Cooper because I thought it might be better to have two men in the two roles. The two roles are the procedural chairman, and the technical. I thought it was better to have these separate, Cooper as chairman, Mills for technical matters. But it's worked out perfectly, beyond all my hopes. Mills is both, procedural and technical, and he does both beautifully."[92]

Mills's position was such that he could move on, becoming even more influential in the fiscal community. Sam Rayburn's death, his replacement by a politically timid John McCormack (D-Mass.), and the reform of Howard Smith's (D-Va.) powerful Rules Committee created a congressional power vacuum. Mills stepped in. In 1962, several major pieces of legislation were on the floor under the jurisdiction of the Ways and Means Committee, including the revenue act, social security amendments, the trade expansion act, and public welfare reform. One journalist noted: "This year, he [Mills] is somewhat reluctantly destined for an unprecedented apotheosis. For the first time in living memory, all four of the session's biggest, toughest bills must be handled by a single congressional committee, the Ways and Means Committee, headed by Mills."[93] He soundly met this challenge, passing all four bills.

THE REVENUE ACT OF 1962

When John Kennedy arrived at the White House in January 1961, he brought into the executive branch several members of the new fiscal community. Following Kennedy's election, Theodore Sorenson, special counsel to the president-elect, put together the pre-presidential Taxation Task Force and Economic Policy Task Force by recruiting people directly from the community who had helped with the congressional studies. Just

[91]Joseph Pechman to Wilbur Mills (September 17, 1959), WMPC, Unprocessed.
[92]JMIC.
[93]Alsop, "The Legislator."

as the hearings had functioned in Congress, the task forces promoted the ideas and personnel of the community within the executive branch. The Taxation Task Force, for example, included Surrey, Caplin, Ture, Adrian de Wind, and Richard Musgrave, with Cary Brown assisting on an informal basis. Building on the studies of the Ways and Means Committee, the task forces developed three proposals that became crucial to the administration: a targeted, 15 percent investment credit to increase private capital formation; an across-the-board rate reduction to stimulate investment and demand; and loophole-closing reform, such as restricting business expense deductions and tightening the definition of capital gains, to raise more revenue.[94]

Once in office, Kennedy placed several of these policymakers in important positions. Surrey became assistant secretary to the treasury, Henry Fowler was named under secretary of the treasury, and Joseph Barr served as a legislative liaison; Walter Heller, Kermit Gordon, and James Tobin formed the Council of Economic Advisers (CEA); Robert Ball became commissioner of the Social Security Administration; Wilbur Cohen was made assistant secretary of health, education, and welfare (HEW); and Mortimer Caplin became commissioner of the Internal Revenue Service (IRS). Within the administration, the academic triumvirate who ultimately pushed hardest for tax reduction and reform—Surrey, Heller, and Caplin—had all been involved in the early Joint Economic Committee and/or Ways and Means hearings between 1955 and 1960. Surrey, the Office of Tax Analysis, and the IRS, for instance, completed a study of 1959 federal tax returns; their report provided shocking statistical documentation about unreported income, such as the $500 million lost as capital gains and the $834 million as dividends. The study concluded, "Although our statutory marginal tax rates go up to 91 percent, the average tax rates actually paid at high income levels are relatively low."[95] Surrey also conducted monthly meetings on tax reform

[94]Taxation Task Force, "Tax Policy for 1961: Contents, Listing of Matters Covered, Brief Summary of Recommendations, Detailed Discussion of Recommendations" (December 31, 1960), File: Taxation Task Force, Box 1072, Task Force Reports, Pre-presidential Papers, JFKL; Edward S. Flash, Jr., *Economic Advice and Presidential Leadership: The Council of Economic Advisers* (New York: Columbia University Press, 1965), chapter 6; "Tax Policy Report for Kennedy Outlines Ways to Spur Economy, Cut Income Taxes," *Wall Street Journal*, January 10, 1961; Stern, "Congress, Politics, and Taxes," 8–12; Mortimer Caplin, interview with Shelley Davis and Kecia McDonald, 5–9; Theodore Sorensen, interview with Carl Kaysen, May 20, 1964, 145–47, Oral History Interview Collection, JFKL.
[95]Stanley Surrey to Wilbur Mills (September 22, 1961), File 1, Box 163, SSP; Surrey to Douglas Dillon (July 30, 1962), File 6, Box 177, SSP; Harvey Brazer to Surrey (October

with Treasury consultants who were handpicked from the fiscal community.[96]

After 1961, Mills thus encountered an aggressive executive branch armed with its own expertise. Under Presidents Kennedy and Johnson, the executive branch repeatedly attempted to encroach on the fiscal powers of Congress. In many respects, this confrontation was merely another battle in a long-standing war between the executive branch and the legislature over control of the American state.[97] But it was an important battle, both to the presidents and to Mills. Kennedy, for instance, expanded the role of the CEA.[98]

The administration charged that the Ways and Means Committee was failing to respond to pressing national needs. Powerful interest groups, the White House said, controlled its members. Moreover, Ways and Means members were charged with holding outdated economic ideas.[99] Only the executive branch had the expertise and the "freedom" from interest-group pressure that was needed to carry out effective fiscal policies, the administration said. The White House engaged in aggressive lobbying. According to Wilbur Cohen, officials like Ivan Nestingen (under secretary of the HEW), felt that "all you had to do was chop Mills up, grind him up, put the pressure on him, and the thing would fall into Kennedy's hands."[100] The administration even organized a powerful in-

26, 1961), File 5, Box 176, SSP. The Treasury also conducted an important study on depreciation; see Dillon to Mills (November 7, 1961), File 1, Box 170, SSP.

[96]Stanley Surrey to Seymour Harris (October 23, 1962), File 1, Box 178, SSP; Surrey, Handwritten Notes (October 23, 1962), File 4, Box 175, SSP; Michael McGreevy to Surrey (September 24, 1963), File 1, Box 126, SSP; Harvey Brazer to Cary Brown (October 17, 1961), File 1, Box 170, SSP; Brazer to Surrey (October 24, 1962), File 1, Box 781, SSP.

[97]Stephen Skowronek, *Building a New American State: The Expansion of National Administrative Capacities, 1877–1920* (Cambridge: Cambridge University Press, 1982); Sidney M. Milkis, *The President and the Parties: The Transformation of the American Party System since the New Deal* (New York: Oxford University Press, 1993); David L. Porter, *Congress and the Waning of the New Deal* (Port Washington: National University Publications, 1980).

[98]Flash, *Economic Advice and Presidential Leadership*; Erwin C. Hargrove and Samuel A. Morley, eds. *The President and the Council of Economic Advisers: Interviews with CEA Chairmen* (Boulder: Westview Press, 1984), chapter 4; Walter Heller to Lyndon Johnson (December 1, 1963), File: The Heller Council 7/63–12/63, Box 4, Kennedy-Johnson Files, Walter Heller Papers, JFKL.

[99]Merriman Smith, "Progress Robs President of Traditional Weapon," *Nation's Business,* July 1963, 23–24; Seymour Harris, "The Gap between Economist and Politician," *New York Times,* Sunday, April 14, 1963, Section 6.

[100]Wilbur Cohen, interview with William Moss, July 20, 1972, 86–88, Oral History Interview Collection, JFKL. See also Wilbur Cohen, interview with William Moss, May 24, 1971, 73.

terest group, the Business Committee for Tax Reduction, to lobby its proposals.[101] Although there were constitutional limits to the power the president could achieve, Kennedy attempted to expand executive power as much as possible.

In response to Kennedy's aggressive approach, Mills protected his position by working closely with the fiscal community to shape policies at every stage of the tax-writing process. He was in a position to do so because as chair of Ways and Means, he stood at the crossroads of the various networks in the community—the parties, the interest groups, and the issue networks—and they all depended on him to sell their proposals to Congress. Rather than passively accepting what these networks offered, Mills expanded his own influence by participating actively throughout the policy-making process. This required exhaustive efforts; one colleague acknowledged of Mills at this point in his career: "[He is] so single minded, never goes out, no social life or cocktail parties. He's thoroughly absorbed, goes home and thinks about the legislation."[102]

While devising the Revenue Acts of 1962 and 1964, Mills and the fiscal community interacted through staff studies, letters, memoranda, informal brunches, formal breakfasts and dinners, confidential meetings, and "stag dinners."[103] Congressional hearings and studies served as an important meeting ground. The Treasury consulted Mills at all times; as one official said privately, "Mills is kept informed the most and, obviously, influences our pre-message deliberation."[104] Throughout the deliberations, many of Mills's most important contacts were with key executive staffers, administrators, and experts. For instance, Fowler, un-

[101]Martin, *Shifting the Burden*, 52–80.
[102]JMIC.
[103]Invitations, File 3, Box 676, WMPC; Lawrence O'Brien, interview with Michael Gillette, December 5, 1985, 36, Interview V; Walter Heller, interview with David McComb, December 21, 1971, 22, Interview II, Oral History Interview Collection, LBJL; Robert Solow to Walter Heller, Kermit Gordon, and James Tobin (April 24, 1961), File: Tax Cut 4/61–11/61, Box 6, Kennedy-Johnson Files, Walter Heller Papers, JFKL. For correspondence between Wilbur Mills and the Treasury, see Mills to Douglas Dillon (August 26, 1961), File: Insurance Company Act, Box 6343, 87th Cong., RG 233, NA; Mills to Dillon (October 24, 1961), File 2, Box 734, WMPC; Mills to Dillon (January 10, 1962), File 2, Box 734, WMPC; Stanley Surrey to Mills (June 26, 1962), File: Unmarked, Box 6348, 87th Cong., RG 233, NA; Dillon to Mills (July 11, 1962), File: Depreciation, Box 6341, 87th Cong., RG 233, NA; Mills to Dillon (November 26, 1962), File 14, Box 19, WMPC; Mortimer Caplin to Mills (March 29, 1963), 88th Cong., File: Gross Income—Business Expenses, Box 38, RG 233, NA; Dillon to Mills (January 8, 1964), 88th Cong., File: Public Debt 1963–64, Box 48, RG 233, NA; Mills, interview with Joe Franz, November 2, 1971, 15, Oral History Interview Collection, LBJL; Mortimer Caplin, interview with Julian Zelizer.
[104]JMIC.

der secretary of the treasury, earned the title of "Ambassador to Arkansas" due to his frequent visits with the chairman. Lawrence O'Brien, Kennedy's legislative liaison, also mediated between the chairman and the President on most policy matters. Mills even had the unprecedented privilege, for a representative, of participating in Kennedy's policymaking Troika and Quadriad. These top-secret meetings included the secretary of the Treasury, the director of the Bureau of the Budget, the chairman of the CEA and occasionally, the chairman of the Federal Reserve. Moreover, all of the leading interest groups and think tanks bombarded Mills with technical information and position papers. The oil industry, the insurance industry, commercial banks, and the stock market were particularly aggressive in this respect.[105] Laurence Woodworth played an important role during these encounters; he emerged as Mills's chief confidant, serving as the key link between Mills and the fiscal community. Every Saturday, for example, Woodworth met at his home with the Treasury's Tax Legislative Counsel to formulate compromises among the committee, the administration, and interested organizations.

The Kennedy administration began its push for a more aggressive compensatory fiscal policy on April 20, 1961, with its proposal to stimulate economic productivity and growth. The main components of the bill—the investment credit and loophole-closing reforms—had originated from Surrey's Task Force on Taxation and from the Ways and Means hearings of 1958–59.[106] Those who proposed the investment credit hoped to encourage businesses to invest in new assets by allowing them to deduct part of the cost of these purchases from their income

[105]See, for example, Jerry Voorhis to Wilbur Mills (August 4, 1961), File: Taxation of Co-ops, Box 6345, 87th Cong., RG 233, NA; Dan Jones to Wilbur Mills (May 16, 1962), File: Foreign Trade and Tariffs, Box 6340, 87th Cong., RG 233, NA; William Hogan, *Depreciation Reform and Capital Replacement* (Washington, 1964), and The Research Institute of America, *Making the Most of Depreciation and Investment Credit* (Washington, 1964), both in 88th Cong., File: Gross Income 1963–64, Box 39, RG 233, NA.
[106]In its public statements, the Kennedy administration repeatedly acknowledged the influence of the studies of Mills's committees. See U.S. House of Representatives, Committee on Ways and Means, *Our Federal Tax System: Message from the President of the United States Relative to Our Federal Tax System*, 87th Cong., 1st sess., 1961; U.S. House of Representatives, Committee on Ways and Means, *President's 1963 Tax Message along with Principal Statement, Technical Explanation, and Supporting Exhibits and Documents*, 88th Cong., 1st sess., 1963, 28–30; Curtis, "The House Committee on Ways and Means," 121–47; Douglas Dillon to Wilbur Mills (August 2, 1961), File: Treasury 7/61–8/61, Departments and Agencies, Box 89, Presidential Office Files, JFKL; Robert Solow to Walter Heller, Kermit Gordon, and James Tobin (April 24, 1961), File: Tax Cut 4/61–11/61, Box 6, Kennedy-Johnson Files, Walter Heller Papers, JFKL. For a good discussion of reforms, see Caplin, interview with Shelley Davis and Kecia McDonald.

liability. Many income-tax experts actively supported this proposal. But at the Ways and Means hearings in April 1961, the majority of corporate interest groups rejected it because they feared that the credit would cost them liberalized depreciation rates, a tax benefit that business had grown accustomed to since 1954. Moreover, they were angered that the proposed credit would cover only some sectors of business.[107]

Mills too feared that a targeted credit would distort market-oriented economic decisions and lose excessive amounts of revenue. He wanted a smaller, broader credit, and in the end, he forged a compromise assisted by George Terborgh, research director of the Machinery and Allied Products Institute, and Maurice Peloubet, a prominent tax accountant. The Mills compromise transformed the 15 percent, targeted credit into a 7 percent, flat-rate credit, which capital-intensive industries found very attractive. Corporate interests were even more enticed by the liberalized depreciation allowances announced by the Treasury in July 1961. Treasury officials also helped ensure legislative success by adjusting their "semantics" to convince business that the investment credit was "not a subsidy but a broadly applicable yet somewhat selective reduction in the effective rate of the corporate income tax."[108] Together, the credit and the liberalized depreciation provided the biggest reduction in corporate taxes since 1954.

The sections of the proposal that spurred the most intense conflict were the revenue-raising reforms. These included limitations on foreign tax havens, higher capital gains taxes, and the withholding of income on dividends and interest—three major tax-escape routes for corporations. The reforms angered powerful interest groups whose privileges seemed to be threatened. For the first time in decades, substantive tax reform seemed possible, and in the hearings and in private correspondences, organizations such as the U.S. Chamber of Commerce and the National Association of Manufacturers vigorously attacked the plans. As the struggle indicated, this issue was driven largely from "inside the beltway." The chairman recalled: "You have so much pressure to preserve preferences within the law and so little pressure on the part of those who contend generally that they want tax reform and equality of

---

[107]For a more nuanced discussion of the corporate reaction to these proposals, see Martin, *Shifting the Burden,* and Collins, *The Business Response to Keynes.*

[108]Harvey Brazer to Stanley Surrey (November 28, 1961), File 1, Box 92, SSP. See also Surrey, handwritten notes (March 31, 1961), File 3, Box 91, SSP; Surrey to Myer Feldman (January 5, 1962), File: Tax Proposals, 1/62–1/63, White House Staff Files, Myer Feldman Files, JFKL.

taxation. They have no lobby."[109] Mills realized that reformers needed
to stir demand for reform inside and outside of the fiscal community.
When the Ways and Means Committee was ready to bring the bill to
the House floor, for instance, he told administration officials to "gear
friendly pressure groups into motion."[110]

But this time Mills was unable to organize his forces for the attack.
A strong tax-reform lobby did not materialize. In the end, the chairman
was forced to give ground on many of the reforms in exchange for the
investment credit and for the retention of some of the reforms. But before he did, he demonstrated his willingness to confront entrenched interests. Mills staunchly defended the loophole-closing provisions, such
as the withholding of income on dividend and interests and reforms on
mutual savings banks. When Mills saw that he did not have the support
he needed for his other reforms, he crafted the best compromise he could
get in a measure he knew would pass. Determined not to repeat the
mistakes of his first year as the chair, he negotiated yet another round
of compromises among the various members of the fiscal community.

As usual, his calculation of the opposing forces was correct. After
Mills maneuvered to cut the investment credit from 15 to 7 percent and
to change it from a targeted provision to a flat-rate credit for all capital-
intensive industries, the Rules Committee granted the Ways and Means
a closed rule. Several important reforms were passed: a crackdown on
foreign tax havens; new limits on benefits for cooperatives; a more rigorous system for reporting income on interest and dividends; and tighter
restrictions on travel and entertainment deductions.

By mid-March, the Revenue Act of 1962 passed the Ways and Means.
On March 22, Kennedy sent the chairman a highly congratulatory letter
thanking him for its passage, and soon after the Senate approved the
legislation.[111] Mills was forced to drop the withholding provision after
the Senate Finance Committee soundly defeated it. At the urging of the
administration, Mills decided not to pursue that reform in conference.[112]

In the Conference Committee, staff experts collected and filtered the

[109]Wilbur Mills, interview with Joe Frantz, November 2, 1971, 19. See also Mills, "Remarks of the Honorable Wilbur D. Mills, Chairman, Committee on Ways and Means,
before the Society of Public Accountants" (September 1958), File 9, Box 775, WMPC.
[110]Henry Wilson, Jr., to Lawrence O'Brien (March 1, 1962), File: Wilbur Mills, Arkansas,
Folder 1, Box 10, White House Staff Files, Lawrence O'Brien, JFKL.
[111]John F. Kennedy to Wilbur Mills (March 22, 1962), File: 3/21–31/62, Box 50, Presidential Office Files, Departments and Agencies, JFKL.
[112]Stern, "Congress, Politics, and Taxes," 397.

mountains of data gathered from the fiscal community. In the final meetings of the committee, five representatives from Ways and Means and five representatives from the Senate Finance Committee met with legislative staff members and Treasury experts to formulate the specific language of the tax law. Each day focused on a specific set of technical provisions.[113] The staff forged compromises between the competing interests, leaving to Woodworth and the Tax Legislative Counsel the bulk of the work of writing the actual text. When the tax-revision battle heated up, Mills turned primarily to Woodworth for advice because Stam opposed the major loophole-closing reforms. In 1964, Woodworth would officially replace Stam as the chief of staff of the JCIRT.[114]

Even though Mills closely monitored the staff, they were very influential at this stage. This was particularly true under Kennedy, since his administration's proposals were written vaguely, leaving the staff with considerable room to shape the substance of legislation.[115] While the committee met, individual experts actively pursued provisions of their choice. Gerard Brannon, for example, pushed hard for the liberalization of depreciation rates because he thought they were "horribly out-of-date"; he also urged the reform of foreign taxation laws and generally supported the investment credit.[116] In the Senate, said one lawyer: "If

[113]"Notes of John Martin on Conference Committees on H.R. 10650 in May and September of 1962," in File: H.R. 10650, Box 15, 87th Cong., RG 233, NA; Stern, "Congress, Politics, and Taxes," 217–21. My understanding of this stage of the tax-writing process during these years also comes from my oral histories with Donald Lubick and Ward Hussey and from the JMIC.

[114]Until his retirement, Colin Stam remained very influential in the Senate. Stern, "Congress, Politics, and Taxes," 70; Stanley S. Surrey, "Tribute to Dr. Laurence N. Woodworth: Two Decades of Federal Tax History Viewed from This Perspective," *National Tax Journal* 32, no. 3 (September 1979): 226–28.

[115]JMIC.

[116]Brannon's activities and positions can be traced through the following documents: Gerard Brannon to Wilbur Mills (November 5, 1958), WMPC, Unprocessed; Brannon to Mills (January 27, 1959), WMPC, Unprocessed; Brannon to Mills (March 1, 1960), File: Depreciation, Box 6341, 87th Cong., RG 233, NA; Brannon to Leo Irwin (March 1, 1960), File: Gross Income—Exclusions, Box 41, 88th Cong., RG 233, NA; Brannon to Mills (September 1, 1960), File: Legislative File, Box 13, 87th Cong., RG 233, NA; Brannon to John Byrnes (January 4, 1961), File: Gross Income—Business Expense, Box 39, 88th Cong., RG 233, NA; Brannon to Mills (June 20, 1961), File: Leg. File Co-ops, Box 13, 87th Cong., RG 233, NA; Brannon to Mills (June 23, 1961), File: Foreign Income Tax Treatment, Box 6339, 87th Cong., RG 233, NA; Brannon to Stanley Surrey (November 7, 1961), File: H.R. 10650, Box 13, 87th Cong., RG 233, NA; Brannon, "Commentary on Committee Decisions on Revenue Act of 1961," File: H.R. 87A-D14, H.R. 10650, Box 13, 87th Cong., RG 233, NA; Brannon to Mills (January 17, 1962), File: H.R. 10650, Box 14, 87th Cong., RG 233, NA; Brannon to Mills (January 17, 1962), File: Withholding, Box 13, 87th Cong., RG 233, NA; Brannon to Mills (February 17, 1962), File: Leg. File Co-ops, Box 13, 87th Cong., RG 233, NA; Brannon to Mills

Stam thinks there is no merit in the idea, the Congressman will usually drop it. If Stam thinks there is merit, the Congressman is likely to sponsor it."[117] Since the staff played such an important role, lobbyists occasionally bypassed representatives to work directly with the experts.[118]

The staff also helped determine how effective the reforms would be once enacted. One member of Ways and Means relied on experts to find out if a bill was "a giveaway for someone"; the experts helped "W + M decide the *merits* of bills."[119] Capitalizing on this knowledge, the staff sometimes limited the choices of legislators. Several senators at the Conference Committee, for example, were angered with Mills's decision to tighten restrictions on travel and entertainment deductions.[120] But Mills's provision was saved by the two men who drafted the legislation, Woodworth and Donald Lubick. When Woodworth and Lubick met with the senator who threatened to kill the reform, by prearrangement they brought three different versions of the bill to the meeting. The first two drafts they presented to the senator were clearly too strict for him to accept. After the senator emphatically rejected the first draft, Woodworth "convinced" Lubick that he should show a more lenient provision, but the senator again said "no!" Finally, Woodworth urged Lubick to show the senator an even more "generous" bill, which they had drafted just that morning. Lubick shook his head and responded, "Look, look Larry this is absolutely out, the administration won't take it!" This draft, of course, was the one they and Mills had wanted all along; after

(March 21, 1962), File: Income Tax Credit, Box 14, 87th Cong., RG 233, NA; Brannon to Mills (March 26, 1963), File: Gross Income—Deductions and Depletion, Box 39, 88th Cong., RG 233, NA. For examples of Leo Irwin's work, see Irwin to Mills (February 8, 1957), WMPC, Unprocessed; Irwin to Mills (June 27, 1961), File: Gross Income—Depletion, Box 39, 88th Cong., RG 233, NA; Irwin to Hale Boggs (February 27, 1963), File: Gross Income—Depletion Oil, Box 39, 88th Cong., RG 233, NA.

[117]E. W. Kenworthy, "Special-Interest Tax Legislation: A Washington Mystery Unfolds," *New York Times*, November 11, 1963. See also E. W. Kenworthy, "Colin Stam: A Study in Anonymous Power," in *Adventures in Public Service: The Careers of Eight Honored Men in the United States Government*, ed. Delia Kuhn and Ferdinand Kuhn (New York: Vanguard Press, 1963), 107–36.

[118]C. F. Hotchkiss to Leo Irwin (February 15, 1960), File: Small Business, Box 6345, 87th Cong., RG 233, NA; Gerard Brannon to Wilbur Mills (February 15, 1960), File: Taxation of Co-ops, Box 6345, 87th Cong., RG 233, NA; James Carr to Mills (March 3, 1962), File: Accounting Method, Box 6337, 87th Cong., RG 233, NA; Irwin to Mills (April 19, 1960), File: Gross Income, Business Expenses, Box 39, 88th Cong., RG 233, NA; Peter Heller to Irwin (March 12, 1963), File: Stock Options 1963–64, Box 48, 88th Cong., RG 233, NA.

[119]JMIC.

[120]Stanley Surrey to the Files (March 9, 1962), File 2, Box 92, SSP; Surrey to the Files (March 23, 1962), File 1, Box 167, SSP.

some prodding, Lubick changed his mind. The senator took the bait and insisted on that version of the bill.[121]

In the end, the base-broadening reforms and the investment credit were important achievements. The new investment incentives of the revenue act lowered corporate taxes from 4.2 percent of GNP in 1960 to 3.6 percent in 1962. They saved corporations almost $90 billion in taxes between 1962 and 1981.[122] Meanwhile, the Treasury had also liberalized depreciation allowance schedules in 1962. The successful reforms closed some major loopholes, marking a significant break from the loophole-oriented path of the previous decade. Although these reforms did not overhaul the system, they were well appreciated by policymakers who understood the difficulties of eliminating *any* loophole from the code.

THE REVENUE ACT OF 1964

The next important step in Mills's career was the Revenue Act of 1964, which involved a push by the policy community for a massive, across-the-board tax reduction, paired again with a drive for loophole-closing reform. The reduction was a measure that the community had sought now for almost a decade. This time, the proposed reduction was tied to reforms that included repealing the interest and dividend income credit and exclusion, taxing capital gains accrued at death, lowering the capital gains rate, and limiting the mineral-depletion allowance.

Within the fiscal community, Mills faced two difficult challenges. First, corporate interests once again opposed the proposal to close loopholes. Now, the chairman openly acknowledged his limits; regarding the proposed reform of an oil industry loophole, he privately told Kennedy "You know that reform's going to have tough sledding, it's scratch double-ended depletion or one of those things and it's never going to, uh, never happen."[123] Mills dealt with the administration primarily on the rate reduction, since this was so central to his agenda. The reduction

---

[121]Donald Lubick, interview with Julian Zelizer.

[122]Martin, *Shifting the Burden*, 12.

[123]Off-the-record meeting with Wilbur Mills (August 6, 1962), Presidential Recordings Transcripts: Tax Cut Proposals Volume I, Audiotape 7, Item 1, 7, Presidential Office Files, JFKL. See also Off-the-Record Meeting with Wilbur Mills, Lawrence O'Brien, C. Douglas Dillon (July 29, 1963), Presidential Recording Transcripts: Tax Cut Proposals Volume II, Audiotape 101, Item 4, 6, Presidential Office Files, JFKL; Lawrence O'Brien, interview with Michael Gillette, December 5, 1985, 34–37, Interview V.

would perhaps allow for future loophole-closing reforms, and it would, Mills thought, stimulate economic growth and full employment.

While concentrating on the reduction, Mills left the Treasury with the difficult task of devising base-broadening reforms.[124] Treasury officials responded to the challenge with a program designed to stimulate economic growth and full employment, to reduce nontaxable income, and to simplify the tax system. Regarding wealth redistribution, Surrey wrote, "The reform program should . . . leave the issue of vertical equity more or less undisturbed—that is, tax liabilities after the reform program has been enacted should be so distributed among income brackets that each income pays roughly the same proportion of the total tax bill as it does now."[125] For his part, Mills still insisted on reforms to offset some of the cost of the rate reduction; he considered the reduction as a sweetener to interest groups who otherwise would oppose reforms.[126] Throughout the hearings, Mills tried to "drive home to the Committee the fact that the repeal of the dividend credit" could result in "substantially lower rates in upper brackets."[127]

Mills's second challenge stemmed from disagreements with the Kennedy administration over how to structure the tax reduction and what its timing should be. The administration's first move against Mills was a failed proposal in January 1962 for presidential authority to reduce tax rates.[128] In April, Mills warned Surrey that he "should not [again] be put in the position of 'ceding' jurisdiction of his committee."[129] Beginning in the summer of 1962, Mills and Kennedy squared off in a heated battle over tax reform. Since its early days in office, the administration had called for a massive tax reduction to end the problem of fiscal drag and to avoid future recessions. In the summer of 1962, the call for a quick and temporary tax reduction emanated from the CEA and other Kennedy experts who predicted a recession after the stock market crashed in May.

[124]JMIC.
[125]Stanley Surrey to Douglas Dillon (July 19, 1962), Box 177, File 5, SSP.
[126]JMIC; Stanley Surrey to the Files (December 10, 1962), File 4, Box 179, SSP.
[127]Joseph Barr to Claude Desautels (July 1, 1963), File: 2 July 1963, Folder 1, Legislative Leaders Breakfast Material, Box 26, White House Staff Files, Lawrence O'Brien, JFKL. See also Lawrence F. O'Brien to John F. Kennedy (July 2, 1963), File: Legislative Files 7/63, Box 53, Presidential Office Files, JFKL.
[128]Stanley Surrey to Walter Heller (January 24, 1962), File: Stand-By Tax Authority 1/62–6/64, Box 21, Kennedy-Johnson Files, Walter Heller Papers, JFKL. For an excellent discussion of the administration's aggressive promotion of its fiscal policies, see Martin, *Shifting the Burden,* chapter 3.
[129]Stanley Surrey to the Files (April 24, 1962), File 1, Box 182, SSP.

In July and August, the administration and key policymakers held a series of meetings about the possibilities of a temporary reduction to spur investment and demand. After Heller suggested that a reduction would avert an upcoming recession, the Mills committee held private hearings with members of the fiscal community, beginning on July 26. One reporter noted: "On the tax issue, Mills is the man to watch. Pres. Kennedy is relying on Mills' advice on whether to ask for a quick tax cut or to hold off until early next year."[130]

As these hearings proceeded, several respected interest groups and experts in the community challenged Heller's analysis that a recession was imminent. Mills then developed a "coolness" toward the proposed cut and used select quantitative data from the hearings to combat the administration; the best statistical indicators, Mills argued, did not show that a recession was just around the corner. The proposed reduction, according to "privy information" from government officials, would also aggravate the nation's balance-of-payments situation.[131] Congress, said the chairman, would certainly reject a quick, deficit-inducing temporary cut without clear indications of a recession, and the proposal would only damage the possibilities for a more comprehensive bill.

Instead, Mills insisted on the program that the fiscal community had developed since the mid-1950s: a permanent tax reduction tied to some tax reform to combat the problem of "fiscal drag." Relying heavily on Woodworth's data, Mills suggested that a revenue loss of roughly $11 billion to $12 billion might be acceptable if there were "firm" presidential assurances of expenditure control.[132] Kennedy responded to this last request by writing the chairman a widely publicized letter that promised "an even tighter rein" on federal spending and that assured him, "Our long-range goal remains a balanced budget in a balanced, full-employment economy."[133] Despite this promise, Mills referred to the

---

[130]"Hopes for Tax Cut Take Setback," *Business Week,* August 4, 1962, 27–28.

[131]Wilbur Mills, interview with Joseph O'Connor, April 14, 1967, 9–11, Oral History Interview Collection, JFKL; Lee Preston to Walter Heller (August 7, 1962), File: Tax Cut 8/62, Box 6, Kennedy-Johnson Files, Walter Heller Papers, JFKL. For the best look inside these hearings, see memorandums from Walter Heller to Kennedy in Files: Council of Economic Advisors Summaries of Ways and Means Testimony 7/62 and CEA 8/1/62–8/7/62, Boxes 74 and 75, Presidential Office Files, Departments and Agencies, JFKL; "Ways and Means," *New York Times,* July 29, 1962, Section 4.

[132]Stanley Surrey to the Files (August 27, 1963), File 4, Box 48, SSP; Off-the-record meeting with Wilbur Mills (August 6, 1962), Audiotape 7, 10–15, Presidential Recordings Transcripts: Tax Cut Proposals, Volume I, JFKL; Surrey to the Files (August 16, 1963), File 2, Box 185, SSP; Curtis, "The House Committee on Ways and Means," 128–32.

[133]John Kennedy to Wilbur Mills (August 21, 1963), File: Tax Message to the Nation (TV)

economic indicators and steadfastly resisted the temporary reduction. By August he had forced Kennedy to back down.

Discussion of a temporary reduction had receded by November. According to one administration official, "Wilbur Mills really put the kibosh on the idea."[134] Determined nevertheless to push through an economic stimulus, the president now sought a permanent, across-the-board tax reduction that would start in January 1963. Conflict quickly began over the issue of timing. Mills did not want the cut to begin until January 1964, and he insisted on tying tax reform and expenditure control to the package.[135] During a three-and-a-half-hour meeting in November, Mills told Fowler that he was keeping in "very close touch" with the economic situation. "Current indicators," said the chairman, showed economic improvement, making an immediate cut unnecessary. Mills added that he fully supported a permanent reduction tied to revenue-raising reforms and nondefense expenditure limitations, even if it meant large budget deficits; existing rates, he told Fowler, were a major drag on economic growth, and they prevented higher levels of employment. Following this meeting, the executive budget director told Kennedy, "We can probably make a very strong case of the kind that Mills is after . . . at the expense of deferring a number of things that really are needed."[136] On November 26, Stam and Surrey established joint staff subcommittees to draft each section of the proposal.[137] By December, all sides agreed on the need for a permanent rate reduction with some expenditure control and loophole-closing reform, as long as the deficit did not exceed

9/18/63, Box 76, JFK Speech Files 1961–63, Theodore Sorenson Papers, JFKL; "Tighter Spending Rein Promised by President," *Washington Post,* August 22, 1963.

[134] Gardner Ackley, interview with Joe Franz, April 13, 1973, 3, Oral History Interview Collection, LBJL.

[135] Joseph Barr to Claude Desautels (May 13, 1963), File: 13 May 1963, Folder 1, Box 25, Legislative Leaders Breakfast Material, White House Staff Files, Lawrence O'Brien, JFKL; Wilbur Mills, interview with Joe Franz, November 2, 1971, 10–12; Henry Fowler, interview with David McComb, January 10, 1969, 21–30, Oral History Interview Collection, Tape I, LBJL.

[136] Off-the-record meeting with Douglas Dillon, Henry Fowler, David Bell, Willard Wirtz, Walter Heller, Kermit Gordon, Edward Gudeman, Charles Schultze, Paul Samuelson, Robert Solow, James Tobin, Gardner Ackley (November 16, 1962), Presidential Recordings Transcripts: Tax Cut Proposals, Volume II, Audiotape 58, Item 2, 12, Presidential Office Files, JFKL. See also Henry Fowler to Douglas Dillon (November 1962), File: Treasury 11/11–12/62, Box 90, Presidential Office Files, Departments and Agencies, JFKL; Douglas Dillon to Wilbur Mills (November 15, 1962), File 14, Box 19, WMPC.

[137] Stanley Surrey to Douglas Dillon (November 30, 1962), File 1, Box 178, SSP.

$12 billion.[138] The only issue that was not settled was the question of timing.

The president and Mills struggled over that dimension of the problem while Kennedy was drafting his December speech to the Economic Club. Kennedy planned to call for an immediate, permanent rate cut. But Mills still rejected an immediate cut. On December 5 he told O'Brien that tax cuts should not be effective until January 1964. He urged Kennedy not to focus on the reduction during his upcoming speech. Mills warned that since the economy was improving, Congress would have an "extremely adverse" reaction to an immediate, deficit-inducing reduction. To make matters worse, the CEA's faulty prediction of an economic downturn had raised serious questions within Congress about the quality of the administration's expertise.[139] Privately, even administration officials felt uneasy about their economic analysis; only a few days earlier, the Troika staff had given two predictions of the effect the reduction would have on GNP, predictions that were almost $10 billion apart.[140]

Chairman Mills also sent a message to the White House in the form of an interview with *U.S. News and World Report,* in which he declared his opposition to an immediate cut. Mills cited the experts of the fiscal community; both "business and Government sources," he said, indicated that there had "not been a deterioration" in the economy.[141] As the *Washington Post* headline commented, "Blow Dealt 1963 Tax Cut Plan."[142] On December 12, Mills and Kennedy met privately in the White House in an effort to resolve their differences. Following that meeting, Kennedy remarked: "Well, I think that Mr. Mills' interview should be read in entirety. If you read the entire article, it does not suggest that the Administration, under some circumstances, and Mr. Mills, may be far apart." He added, "Quite obviously, Mr. Mills will have a very decisive voice in the final decision, but we hope to adjust our viewpoints so that we can get some action on this program next year."[143] Some administration officials were less conciliatory; they were angry

[138]Stanley Surrey to the Files (December 28, 1962), File 4, Box 179, SSP.
[139]Lawrence O'Brien to John F. Kennedy (December 5, 1962), File: O'Brien, Lawrence 9/62–11/63, Box 64, Presidential Office Files, JFKL.
[140]Robert Wallace to Douglas Dillon (December 4, 1963), File 4, Box 179, SSP.
[141]"Why a Tax Cut Is Unlikely in '63," *U.S. News and World Report,* December 17, 1962, 42–45.
[142]"Blow Dealt 1963 Tax Cut Plan," *Washington Post,* December 11, 1962; Editorial, "Mills Says No," *Washington Post,* December 12, 1962.
[143]"Tax Cut in '63? Here's the Argument," *U.S. News and World Report,* December 24, 1962, 23–24. See also Frank Porter, "President Still Resolved to Seek Tax Cut in '63,"

with Mills, whose remarks were "not within the spirit of his commitment last summer and within the spirit of his relations with the President."[144]

On December 13, the Committee for Economic Development announced its support for the president's plan, but when Kennedy delivered his famous speech to the Economic Club on December 14, he backed off on the issue of an immediate reduction. For the time being, at least, Mills had won the battle. At this point, the administration was not inclined to continue the struggle with the powerful chair of the Ways and Means Committee. As Kennedy told Sorenson: "Wilbur Mills . . . knows that he was chairman of Ways and Means before I got here and that he'll still be chairman after I've gone—and he knows I know it. I don't have any hold on him."[145]

During these heated debates, Mills continued to rely on his experts to help him stay involved in the deliberations. Experts, Mills understood, were the glue that held the large and growing fiscal community together. They provided him with access to vital information about the reduction and proposed reforms, and they ensured the dissemination of his ideas. He relied on their analyses during his meetings with the administration. Experts also kept him informed on the positions of other policymakers and interest groups, both inside and outside of committee hearings.[146] Mills made certain that his experts were well situated in key meetings, hearings, and studies. He insisted, for example, that two Ways and Means staffers be included in the interstaff meetings between the Treasury and the JCIRT, despite Stam's attempt to exclude them.[147]

By January 1963, Mills had secured a permanent rate reduction, with

Washington Post, December 13, 1962; Richard Mooney, "President Says Tax Plan Offers Cuts Next Year," *New York Times,* December 13, 1962.

[144]Frank Porter, "Tax Cut Plan Heading for Major 'Hill' Fight," *Washington Post,* December 12, 1962; Frank Porter, "$11 Billion Cut in Taxes Urged by CED: Experts See Slash Aiding U.S. Growth," *Washington Post,* December 14, 1962.

[145]Theodore C. Sorenson, *Kennedy* (New York: Harper and Row, 1965), 426.

[146]Staff, U.S. House of Representatives, Committee on Ways and Means, *"The Revenue Act of 1962": Comparative Analysis of Prior Law and Provisions of Public Law 87–884 (H.R. 10650),* April 19, 1962, H2128 (Committee—Print); Colin Stam to Wilbur Mills (January 15, 1963), File: Gross Income 1963–64, Box 39, 88th Cong., RG 233, NA; Staff, JCIRT, *Tax Tables and Charts Print No. 8,* September 9, 1963, H4789 (Committee—Print); Staff, JCIRT, *Summary of the President's 1963 Tax Message as Presented to the Committee on Ways and Means,* April 1963, J0510 (Committee—Print); Staff, JCIRT, *Staff Data: Listing of Certain Primary Items of Allowable Deductions Available to Individuals under the Revenue Acts from 1913 through 1962,* June 6, 1963, H8832 (Committee—Print); Staff, JCIRT, *Digest of Testimony Presented and Statements Submitted to the Committee on Ways and Means with Respect to the President's 1963 Tax Message,* June 12, 1963, J0280 (Committee—Print).

[147]Wilbur Mills to Henry Fowler, Stanley Surrey, and Colin Stam (December 4, 1962), File

some loophole-closing reforms, to be implemented the following year. Within the committee, Mills obtained the appointments of Pat Jennings (D-Va.) and Ron Bass (D-Tenn.), two advocates of tax reduction. According to Lyndon Johnson's notes at a cabinet meeting, moreover, "Nothing here [in the Revenue Act] won't receive approval of Mills."[148] On the week of January 11, Mills's power was discussed in cover stories in both *Time* and *Newsweek* magazines. *Time* reported that Mills's special authority derived "from the sheer weight of his expertise." The magazine added, "He is beyond dispute Congress' leading authority on taxation."[149] That power was there for all to see later in the year when Kennedy spoke at the Little Rock fairgrounds and participated in the dedication of the Greer's Ferry Dam on the Little Red River at Mills's request. One White House aide half-joked, "If Wilbur wanted us to go down to Heber Springs and sing 'Down by the Old Mill Stream,' we'd be glad to do it."[150] By this time, most administration officials had accepted Mills's argument that the reduction should be permanent, that it should begin in 1964, and that it should be tied to some reforms and expenditure limits.[151] On January 9, Mills urged that the tax program include $4 billion to $5 billion in reform to offset part of the deficit or else it would be "wrong to reduce rates." Surrey convinced Mills that these figures were too high.[152]

The president announced his final plan in the State of the Union address on January 14, 1963. Individual tax rates were to be cut by $11 billion and corporate taxes by $2.6 billion. Revenue-raising reforms, including changes in the dividend credit and exclusion and in the mineral-depletion allowance, were to produce $3.4 billion.[153] During the Ways and Means hearings, which began on February 6 and lasted until

2, Box 18, WMPC; Surrey to Fowler (November 13, 1962), File 2, Box 178, SSP; Surrey to Douglas Dillon (November 30, 1962), File 1, Box 178, SSP.

[148]Lyndon Johnson, Handwritten Notes (January 10, 1963, 10:00 A.M.), Box 2, Handwriting Files, LBJL. Comments by administration and congressional members in the JMIC, as well as oral history interviews from the presidential libraries, support the assertion that Mills had a formidable role in shaping the proposed legislation. This is also evident by examining how the structure and content of the legislation, particularly concerning the tax reduction, met Mills's specifications. See also Wilbur Mills, interview with Joseph O'Connor, April 14, 1967, 10–11.

[149]"An Idea on the March," *Time,* January 11, 1963, and "Wilbur Mills . . . 'Mr. Taxes' in the Congress," *Newsweek,* January 11, 1963, 14–18.

[150]Tom Wicker, "President Visits Arkansas Today," *New York Times,* October 3, 1963.

[151]Stanley Surrey to George Porter (April 4, 1963), File: FI 11-4-1-63-5-10-63, Box 225, White House Central Subject Files, JFKL.

[152]Stanley Surrey to the Files (January 12, 1963), File 4, Box 58, SSP.

[153]Martin, *Shifting the Burden,* 72.

September 10, a number of interest groups opposed the revenue-raising reforms. The oil companies, for example, campaigned aggressively against a change in the depletion allowance and even purchased advertisements on Arkansas radio stations to protest the measures.[154] Despite these threats, Mills felt confident that his seat was secure. The chairman privately told Kennedy about a constituent who had said to him: "It doesn't make a bit of difference to me or to anybody in Arkansas what you do about taxes. We think you know what oughta be done. Now, if you were against the tax bill, we're not gonna argue with you about it." After such encounters, Mills told Kennedy, "I feel pretty good that they've got that degree of confidence and they are *not* twisting my arm."[155] This allowed Mills to continue defending controversial reforms, such as limiting capital gains, and to push hard to bring individual tax rates down to 15–65 percent.[156]

In July 1963, Mills promised the administration that he could pass the bill within a few months but only if the president stressed his commitment to expenditure control.[157] In mid-September, before the House vote, Mills worked extensively with the Democratic whip, the administration, and John Byrnes to ensure that both parties would support the legislation.[158] Later that month the House passed the measure by a vote of 271 to 155. The president was pleased with Mills's work; as the secretary of the Treasury noted, the chairman's statement on the legislation generally followed "the Administration line" and was "an excellent description of the economics of tax reduction."[159]

The Revenue Act of 1964 emphasized demand, not investment (as had

[154]Off-the-record meeting with Wilbur Mills, Lawrence O'Brien, C. Douglas Dillon (July 29, 1963), Presidential Recording Transcripts: Tax Cut Proposals, Volume II, Audiotape 101, Item 4, 6, Presidential Office Files, JFKL.

[155]Ibid., 32. For the views of colleagues who realized this independence, see Wilbur Cohen, interview with William Moss, July 20, 1972, 113; Lawrence O'Brien, interview with Michael Gillette, July 24, 1986, 50, Interview XI.

[156]Stanley Surrey to the Files (May 10, 1963), File 1, Box 176, SSP; Surrey to the Files (May 13, 1963), File 1, Box 176, SSP; Surrey to the Files (May 14, 1963), File 1, Box 176, SSP. See also Surrey to the Files (May 13, 1963), File 4, Box 58, SSP; Surrey to the Files (May 24, 1963), File 1, Box 187, SSP; Surrey to Douglas Dillon (May 13, 1963), File 1, Box 176, SSP.

[157]Off-the-record meeting with Wilbur Mills, Lawrence O'Brien, C. Douglas Dillon (July 29, 1963), Presidential Recordings Transcripts: Tax Cut Proposals, Volume II, Audiotape 101, Item 4, 3–46, Presidential Office Files, JFKL.

[158]Ibid., 7; Randall B. Ripley, *Majority Party Leadership In Congress* (Boston: Little, Brown, and Company, 1969), 46–48; JMIC.

[159]Douglas Dillon to John F. Kennedy (September 16, 1963), File: Treasury 9/63, Box 90, Presidential Office Files, Departments and Agencies, JFKL.

been the case in 1962). This new legislation resulted in across-the-board tax reductions of approximately $10 billion, including corporate rate cuts from 52 percent to 48 percent; it also reduced personal income-tax rates from a range of 20 to 91 percent to a range of 14 to 70 percent. The legislation contained a handful of important revenue-raising reforms. John Watts (D-Ky.) and Hale Boggs (D-La.), for example, had negotiated a deal that reformed taxation on corporate dividend income by repealing the 4 percent dividend credit. The legislation also rescinded the privilege of grouping oil and gas properties to get extra benefits from the depletion allowance.[160]

In the Conference Committee, Mills had of course traded away many reforms to placate representatives and their interest groups in return for the rate reduction.[161] Whereas the 4 percent dividend credit was repealed, for example, the fifty-dollar exclusion was doubled. John Martin's technical analyses, moreover, helped derail several major reform proposals on capital gains taxation.[162] The committee also rejected a provision to increase the deduction for child care; the Ways and Means Committee, Surrey wrote, was "simply not interested in encouraging women to work."[163]

In the end, Mills had used the proposed higher tax on capital gains, the oil-depletion allowance, and the effort to curtail foreign tax havens as bargaining chips to ensure passage of the rate reduction, a central item on his larger agenda for reform. Interest groups were clearly more secure with the permanent tax reductions provided by their loopholes

[160]Joseph Barr to Claude Desautels (June 24, 1963), File: 25 June 1963, Folder 1, Box 26, Legislative Leaders Breakfast Material, Lawrence O'Brien Papers, White House Staff Files, JFKL; Stanley Surrey to the Files (August 16, 1963), File 4, Box 194, SSP; Stanley Surrey to the Files (May 8, 1963), File 4, Box 58, SSP; Martin, *Shifting the Burden,* 56.
[161]Stanley Surrey to the Files (March 4, 1964), File 5, Box 193, SSP; Walter Heller to Theodore Sorenson (July 8, 1963), File: Legislative Leaders 1963 (Meetings) 12/18/62–3/26/63, Box 59, Legislative Leaders Files 1961–64, Theodore Sorenson Papers, JFKL; Heller to John F. Kennedy (June 7, 1963), File: Tax Reduction and Reform Message to Congress 1/24/63, Box 76, JFK Speech Files 1961–63, Theodore Sorenson Papers, JFKL; Joseph Barr to Claude Desautels (June 3, 1963), File: 4 June 1963, Folder 1, Box 29, Legislative Leaders Breakfast Material, White House Staff Files, Lawrence O'Brien, JFKL; Arlen Large, "House Unit Votes to Drop 4% Dividend Credit over Two Years; Sum Excludable Is Doubled," *Wall Street Journal,* August 16, 1963; "Observer," *New York Times,* January 15, 1963; John Morris, "Tax Reform: Outlook Dim," *New York Times,* June 16, 1963; John Morris, "Tax Adjustments Kennedy Seeks Face Rocky Road in Congress," *New York Times,* January 8, 1962.
[162]Reese, *The Politics of Taxation,* 62; Joseph Bowman to Claude Desautels (June 10, 1963), File: 11 June 1963, Folder 1, Box 26, Legislative Leaders Breakfast Material, White House Staff Files, Lawrence O'Brien, JFKL.
[163]Stanley Surrey to the Files (June 10, 1963), File 1, Box 175, SSP.

than with the promised relief of future rate reductions. But in the end, most interest groups received both.[164] Once President Johnson assured Congress that nondefense spending would be controlled, the new measure glided through the Senate. The Finance Committee approved the legislation following Johnson's assurance of budget cuts in January 1964, and then the tax experts drafted the final legislation. The Revenue Act of 1964, with its permanent rate reductions, its expenditure controls, and its limited reforms, passed Congress in February 1964.

Mills was pleased with this measure, particularly because it promised to stimulate economic growth and create full employment through moderate tax adjustments. Regarding public spending, moreover, the Revenue Act of 1964 marked an important break for Mills and his community. This act turned to reduced taxation instead of increased public spending to spur growth. On the House floor, Mills called this legislation a "turning point" for just this reason:

I am convinced that there are two roads the Government can follow toward the achievement of this larger and more prosperous economy. I believe we are at the fork of those two roads today. One of these is the tax reduction road. The other is the road of Government expenditure increases. . . . Although it is possible to achieve the prosperity we desire by either of the two routes I have outlined to you, nevertheless, there is a big difference—a vital difference—between them. The route of Government expenditure increases achieves this higher level of economic activity with larger and larger shares of that activity initiating in the Government. . . . This road leads to big Government, especially big Central Government.

Mills told Congress, "The route I prefer is the tax reduction road which gives us a higher level of economic activity and a bigger and more prosperous and more efficient economy with a larger and larger share of the enlarged activity initiating in the private sector of the economy."[165]

By this time, Mills's influence was openly discussed by many policymakers within the fiscal community. He was no longer dependent on even the president to obtain services for his district; O'Brien commented: "Anything the White House could do to accommodate Wilbur Mills was done. Wilbur Mills didn't need the White House."[166] Kennedy privately

---

[164]Albert Gore, Sr., to John F. Kennedy (November 15, 1962), File: Treasury 11/11–12/62, Box 90, Presidential Office Files, JFKL. See also Claude Desautels to Joseph Barr (March 4, 1963), File: 5 March 1963, Folder 1, Box 23, Legislative Leaders Breakfast Material, White House Staff Files, Lawrence O'Brien, JFKL.

[165]U.S. Congress, House of Representatives, Congressional Record, 88th Cong., 2nd sess., September 24, 1963, 17908–9.

[166]Lawrence O'Brien, interview with Michael Gillette, July 24, 1986, 38, Interview XI.

acknowledged this, using the term "to Wilbur Mills" a tax bill, meaning to pass a bill that no one wants in an election year.[167] During the legislative deliberations, Mills had received increased funding for military installations and public works programs in Arkansas; he was in that regard immune from the limitations he proposed for others.[168] At this point in his career, Mills's power could be exercised in a variety of realms; one administration official recalled about health care reform, "I think that at no time, right up to the end of the road on Medicare, did we feel we could take on Wilbur Mills and try to override him . . . ; there was nobody in that conference [committee] who was going to buck Wilbur Mills on the House side and probably there was little appetite to buck him on the Senate side either."[169]

Mills's status in this central policy-making community also gave him power that extended beyond fiscal affairs. In international relations, for instance, Mills overrode the demands of Ambassador George Kennan, who strongly requested favorable trade status for Poland and Yugoslavia. Mills single-handedly defeated this request with a provision in the Trade Expansion Act of 1962. When Kennan called the president to tell him how disastrous this action would be, Kennedy simply transferred Kennan on the telephone directly to Mills, who said there was nothing he could do.[170] O'Brien recalled: "Wilbur Mills was a key player. . . . You were always aware of the absolute need for us to keep in total and constant communication with him, and probably more than that—keep him apprised of what you were doing."[171] As policymakers from interest groups to experts to congressional representatives explained, if Mills opposed a bill it "would be dead."[172] In 1963, one reporter commented,

[167]Joseph Barr to John F. Kennedy (April 2, 1962), File: LE FI 11 9-26-61-4-10-62, Box 476, White House Central Subject Files, JFKL.
[168]Staff notes (1963), File: Mills, Wilbur D., Box 24, Congressional Favors File, LBJL; Boxes 141–42, WMPC; Claude Desautels to Lawrence O'Brien (December 5, 1961), House File: Wilbur Mills, Arkansas, Folder 1, and Desautels to O'Brien (December 20, 1962), House File: Wilbur Mills, Arkansas, Folder 2, both in Box 10, White House Staff Files, Lawrence O'Brien, JFKL.
[169]Lawrence O'Brien, interview with Michael Gillette, July 24, 1986, 45, Interview XI. For media discussions on Mills's power in the health care debate, see Editorial, "Movement on Medicare?" *New York Times,* November 13, 1964; Editorial, "One-Man Veto on Medicare," *New York Times,* June 26, 1964; Marjorie Hunter, "Major Fight Is Due over Medical Care," *New York Times,* Sunday, February 16, 1964, Section IV; John A. Grimes, "Care for the Aged," *Wall Street Journal,* August 31, 1961.
[170]George Kennan, interview with Louis Fischer, March 23, 1965, 70–90, Oral History Interview Collection, JFKL. See also "A Measure of Doubt," *Washington Post,* October 7, 1962; *Congressional Quarterly Almanac,* 88th Cong., 1st sess., 1963, 260–61.
[171]Lawrence O'Brien, interview with Michael Gillette, December 4, 1985, 9, Interview IV.
[172]John Manley's Personal Notes (February 4, 1964), John Manley Papers, LBJL; Henry Wilson to Lawrence O'Brien (November 7, 1961), File: Memoranda 11/1/61–11/9/61,

"Not since the halcyon days of the late Speaker Sam Rayburn, has any one man so dominated a Congress as Wilbur Mills, by the sheer power of his office and his knowledge of tax matters, dominate[s] the 88th Congress."[173] By the time the Revenue Act of 1964 had passed, some were calling Mills the "Third House of Congress." One journal argued that he was "actually one of the three or four most powerful men in Washington." It added, "Indeed, one poll has ranked him only second to the President."[174]

THE POSTWAR FISCAL DISCOURSE

As we have seen, Mills had strengthened his power by helping the fiscal community achieve its legislative victories in 1962 and 1964. But the process through which these bills were formulated had clearly been full of conflict, contest, and uncertainty. There were moments when Mills and his colleagues could not have been farther apart on important issues. Despite these differences, the policymakers had acted as a community: they had recognized themselves as the legitimate figures in policy-making who shared certain approaches to politics.

Between 1954 and 1964, the ties between policymakers had been strengthened by a shared political language, which included its own vocabulary and certain conceptions of the political economy.[175] As Mills's colleagues came to express their ideas in this language, they communicated with each other more effectively and at the same time limited access to their debates. They were, as one former Treasury official noted, a "community of like-minded people."[176] What they were like-minded about was the postwar fiscal discourse—a discourse about what role fiscal policy should play in the economy and about how fiscal policies should be decided. Since this discourse combined several important, and

---

Box 3, White House Staff Files, Henry Hall Wilson, JFKL; "Shifts in the Odds," *Business Week,* January 5, 1963, 15–18.

[173]"Man in the News," *Insurance News Week,* January 12, 1963, 57.

[174]"Key Man in the Medicare Battle," *Medical World News,* February 26, 1965, 33. Similar comments can be found throughout the JMIC, media accounts of the period, and oral history interviews.

[175]In discussing political language, I draw on the following works: Dorothy Ross, *The Origins of American Social Science* (Cambridge: Cambridge University Press, 1991); J. G. A. Pocock, *Virtue, Commerce, and History: Essays on Political Thought and History, Chiefly in the Eighteenth Century* (Cambridge: Cambridge University Press, 1985), 1–34.

[176]Stanford Ross coined this useful phrase during a workshop at the Woodrow Wilson International Center for Scholars.

often contradictory, intellectual traditions, policymakers selected the parts of the language that they wanted to use. But these choices were always constrained by the central characteristics of the discourse that defined their community.

This discourse included a domesticated Keynesianism that was framed in terms of moderate government intervention to ensure the health and stability of the corporate capitalist economy.[177] The goal of "economic growth," rather than the threat of "stagnation," was a central feature of the language: growth, the policymakers argued, promised a larger piece of the pie for every citizen.[178] To reach the full potential of the market, they said, the government should accelerate both investment and demand, thus combining the ideas of Andrew Mellon and John Maynard Keynes.

In the 1960s version of Keynesianism, the federal government was called to intervene regularly while avoiding direct management of economic institutions, leaving corporate managerial prerogative untouched. Government policymakers could strengthen the economy through expansive fiscal policies in three ways: by spurring capital investment through government incentives such as tax breaks; by stimulating demand through monetary adjustments and tax reductions; and by increasing defense or automatic expenditures. Taxation, not spending, should serve as the central instrument for promoting investment and increasing demand. The fiscal discourse looked on moderate budget deficits as useful, even in nonrecessionary times, since they could spur growth, generate more revenue, and create full employment. Although policymakers thus openly accepted deficits by the early 1960s, the ghosts of the traditional balanced-budget rhetoric and the importance of "fiscal responsibility" lurked in the rhetoric of the day. Even President Kennedy made this point, proclaiming: "Our choice today is not between a tax cut and

---

[177]Stein, *The Fiscal Revolution in America*; Collins, *The Business Response to Keynes*; Brinkley, "The New Deal and the Idea of the State"; Margaret Weir and Theda Skocpol, "State Structures and the Possibilities for 'Keynesian' Responses to the Great Depression in Sweden, Britain, and the United States," in *Bringing the State Back In*, ed. Peter B. Evans, Dietrich Rueschemeyer, and Theda Skocpol (Cambridge: Cambridge University Press, 1985), 107–63; Margaret Weir, *Politics and Jobs: The Boundaries of Employment Policy in the United States* (Princeton: Princeton University Press, 1992); Brinkley, *The End of Reform*.

[178]For the best analyses of growthmanship, see Robert M. Collins, "The Emergence of Economic Growthmanship in the United States: Federal Policy and Economic Knowledge in the Truman Years," in Furner and Supple, *The State and Economic Knowledge*, 138–70; Ronald F. King, *Money, Time, and Politics: Investment Tax Subsidies and American Democracy* (New Haven: Yale University Press, 1993).

a balanced budget. Our choice is between chronic deficits resulting from chronic slack, on the one hand, and *transitional deficits* temporarily enlarged by tax revision designed to promote full employment and thus make possible an ultimately balanced budget."[179]

In seeking faster growth, Kennedy, Mills, and the community articulated the acceptance of a particular type of state. Given the "chronic and growing" economic problems of the post–World War II era, Mills noted that the income tax, social security, unemployment, and workmen's compensation had "become basic to the health and vigorous functioning of our free, competitive, private enterprise."[180] Mills often reminded audiences, "We live in a complex and dangerous age and there is no use pretending that on some happy day very soon we can cut government expenditures to the point where we will no longer need large tax revenues."[181] In his language and voting record, Mills proved an ardent defender of expansive military programs and contributory, family-centered social welfare; regarding social security, Mills argued: "How can it be said that we are doing something for that individual [benefit recipient] for nothing? Certainly he is at least entitled to say he is buying and paying for that security against need in his old age."[182] Mills spoke of financing welfare programs that maintained the "traditional family

---

[179]Emphasis added. John F. Kennedy, Press Release, "The White House: Special Message on Tax Reduction and Tax Reform" (January 24, 1963), File: 1/24/63 Special Message on Tax Reduction and Reform, Box 52, Presidential Office Files, JFKL. See also Theodore Sorenson, interview with Carl Kaysen, March 26, 1964, 50–57; Henry Fowler, interview with David McComb, January 10, 1969, 19–24; Walter Heller, interview with David McComb, February 20, 1970, 24, Interview 3.

[180]Wilbur Mills, "Let's Strengthen the Income Tax: Speech" (n.d.), File 16, Box 408, WMPC. See also Wilbur Mills, "Remarks of the Honorable Wilbur D. Mills before the Little Rock Rotary Club" (November 29, 1962), File: Mills Speeches, Box 591, WMPC; Wilbur Mills, "Fiscal Policy and the Economy: Speech" (November 4, 1965), File 6, Box 658, WMPC; Wilbur Mills, "The Role of Employment Security in a Changing Economy: Address to the Institute of the IAPES, Little Rock, Arkansas" (October 27, 1960), File 5, Box 781, WMPC.

[181]Mills, "Are You a Pet or a Patsy?" 62.

[182]Cited in Martha Derthick, *Policymaking for Social Security* (Washington, D.C.: Brookings Institution, 1979), 248–49. See also Wilbur Mills, "Improvements in Social Security Programs Made by the 86th Congress: Address to Meeting of State Welfare Department Employees of the State of Arkansas" (1960), File 11, Box 784, WMPC; "Social Security Benefit Lift of 5% Voted by Panel," *Wall Street Journal*, June 25, 1964; Joseph Loftus, "Tax Rise Is Asked in Social Security," *New York Times*, May 31, 1963. For the best analysis of Mills's voting record on these issues, see the annual columns "House Party Unity" and "House Support for Larger or Smaller 'Federal Role,'" in the *Congressional Quarterly Almanac*. On Mills's support for programs for the developmentally disabled, see Stafford Warren, interview with Ronald Grele, June 7, 1966, and David B. Ray, Jr., interview with John Stewart, March 5, 1968, both in Oral History Interview Collection, JFKL.

structure" and that avoided interfering, as much as possible, with the market. Welfare programs, he argued, should enable people to become "self-sufficient," and they should avoid causing "dependency" on the government.[183]

Mills argued that the American state helped create social stability in a pluralistic society. In his language, the federal government helped maintain a social equilibrium by forging compromises among competing interest groups that, according to Mills, embodied the desires of the entire populace. Throughout his career, Mills spoke of the nation in functional, pluralistic terms. "American citizens," said Mills, consisted of "business, agriculture, labor, and so on."[184] Mills even claimed that the largely white, male, wealthy members of Ways and Means represented a "cross-section of the people of the United States."[185] In discussing the state, the chairman thus drew on a comforting pluralistic discourse that described a nation consisting of multiple groups that were harmonized through the proper intervention of the government.

For Mills, one of the most important elements in a proper intervention was growth-oriented fiscal policy. Most scholars have characterized Mills as steadfastly opposing the use of fiscal policy to affect the economy.[186] In doing so, they often quote Mills's statement: "I believe that the function of taxation is to raise revenue. . . . I don't go along with economists who think of taxation primarily as an instrument for stimulating, braking or otherwise manipulating the economy." Mills, however, was more flexible than these studies suggest. Although he was indeed cautious in advocating active fiscal policies, he talked about the

---

[183]Wilbur Mills, "The Congress and the Demands for Service: Remarks before the Arkansas Conference of Social Welfare" (November 6, 1964), File 7, Box 590, WMPC; Wilbur Mills, "A New Charter for Public Welfare: Address to the Public Welfare Employees of the State of Arkansas" (December 13, 1962), File: Mills Speech, Box 591, WMPC; Wilbur Mills, "Improvements in Social Security Programs Made by the 86th Congress: Address to Meeting of State Welfare Department Employees of the State of Arkansas" (1960), File 11, Box 784, WMPC. For a good discussion of the centrality of the word "dependency" and the gendered component of American welfare policies, see Nancy Fraser and Linda Gordon, " 'Dependency' Demystified: Inscriptions of Power in a Keyword of the Welfare State," *Social Politics* 1, no. 1 (Spring 1994): 4–31. This rhetoric was most evident in Mills's discussion of the Public Welfare Amendments of 1962, which he hoped would curb dependency on welfare and stimulate incentives for people to work.

[184]Wilbur Mills, interview with Joseph O'Connor, April 14, 1967, 10.

[185]Cited in Winant, *Stalemate*, 109–10; Stephen Horn interview of Congressman Wilbur Mills for Operation Government, Sponsored by Westinghouse Broadcasting Company, October 11, 1967, JMIC.

[186]See Martin, *Shifting the Burden*, and Stein, *The Fiscal Revolution in America*.

need to do so to spur economic growth and to reach full employment. Revealingly, those who cite the previous quotation usually cut off the rest of his statement: "But I do believe that, when tax rates are as high as they are now, we must take into account the fact that any changes we make inevitably will have far-reaching economic effects."[187]

The chairman acknowledged that, after the expansion of the tax system since the 1940s, there was "not a single economic activity" that was "not affected and conditioned by our Federal tax laws." He added, "Without losing sight of the basic purpose of Federal taxation—raising revenue to defray the expense of Government—there is an ever-widening awareness of the significance of the Federal tax structure in shaping the complexion of our economic growth."[188] American economic performance since World War II, said Mills, confirmed "the importance of sound public policy in providing the setting in which this spirit" could "impel our private economy to new achievements."[189] Once he began to focus on taxation and its relation to growth, Mills grew more insistent on limiting public expenditures on nondefense items. Economic growth should be achieved, he said, by the adjustment of tax policies rather than increased government spending on welfare programs. More than any other point in the postwar fiscal discourse, the question of public welfare spending created conflict within the state and fiscal community.[190]

Increasingly, Mills acknowledged the necessity of temporary deficits. By the late 1950s, chronic deficits had become a subject of considerable discussion.[191] Mills once told a reporter: "I am not one of those who believe that the budget must necessarily be balanced over each *12-month period.* Nevertheless, I do firmly believe in a balanced budget over *a period of years,* or over a business cycle."[192] Similarly, at a private meet-

[187]Cassels, "This Man Shapes Your Tax Bill," 66. See also Wilbur Mills, "Remarks of Honorable Wilbur Mills before Chamber of Commerce Banquet" (December 4, 1964), File 15, Box 660, WMPC; "The Man Who Steers Tax Policy," *Business Week,* March 22, 1958, 62; "How Taxes Will Be Cut," *Nation's Business,* October 1957, 60–64.

[188]Wilbur Mills, "The Challenge of Federal Tax Policy in 1957: Address to the Seventeenth Annual Federal Tax Dinner of the Federal Tax Forum" (December 6, 1956), File 1, Box 781, WMPC.

[189]Wilbur Mills, "Federal Tax Policy for Economic Growth: Speech" (May 1, 1956), File 20, Box 783, WMPC.

[190]Jill Quadagno, *The Color of Welfare: How Racism Undermined the War on Poverty* (New York: Oxford University Press, 1994); Linda Gordon, *Pitied but Not Entitled: Single Mothers and the History of Welfare* (New York: Free Press, 1994).

[191]Stein, *The Fiscal Revolution in America,* chapters 11–14.

[192]"The Top Man on Taxes Tells What to Expect," *U.S. News and World Report,* December 12, 1958, 109–13; Allen Drury, "Capital Expects Economic Review to Be Optimistic," *New York Times,* January 20, 1958.

ing with Kennedy in 1962, Mills commented: "I don't see anything wrong with having a deficit. . . . It's much better to have employment and the economy going, even if you have some deficits, providing it's not excessive and inflationary."[193] Like Kennedy, Mills argued, quoting Andrew Mellon, that tax reduction would spur enough growth to generate budget-balancing revenues in the future. As he explained to his congressional colleagues, "Our long-range goal remains a balanced budget in the balanced full employment economy."[194] The term "balanced full employment economy" blended neoclassical and Keynesian discourse in a manner typical of Mills.

For Mills and others in the fiscal community, these were issues that should be debated and settled in a technocratic manner.[195] Previous politicians and reformers had often discussed taxation as an issue of "social class" and "wealth distribution."[196] The postwar fiscal discourse, however, downplayed those issues. Instead, that discourse portrayed taxation as a technocratic problem: professional experts should determine fiscal policy using quantitative and legalistic analyses in an "objective," nonpartisan process. When the discussion became "emotional" or "partisan," for example, Thomas Curtis urged his colleagues to "get it off the demagoguery and back to economics."[197]

---

[193]Off-the-record meeting with Wilbur Mills (August 6, 1962), Presidential Recordings Transcripts: Tax Cut Proposals Volume I, Audiotape 7, Items OB-1, 7, Presidential Office Files, JFKL.

[194]U.S. Congress, House of Representatives, *Congressional Record*, 88th Cong., 2nd sess., September 24, 1963, 17907. See also U.S. Congress, House of Representatives, *Congressional Record*, 88th Cong., 1st sess., February 25, 1964, 3556, and Wilbur Mills, interview with Joe Frantz, November 2, 1971, 11–14. For a good discussion of how "domesticated Keynesianism" continued to employ the rhetoric of a balanced budget, see Stein, *The Fiscal Revolution in America*.

[195]This component of the fiscal discourse did not have its roots in any particular economic theory. Evolving during the Progressive Era, it was a general approach to policy-making. For the origins of this discourse, see the following: Ross, *Origins of American Social Science*; Guy Alchon, *The Invisible Hand of Planning: Capitalism, Social Science, and the State in the 1920s* (Princeton: Princeton University Press, 1985); and JoAnne Brown, *The Definition of a Profession: The Authority of Metaphor in the History of Intelligence Testing, 1890–1930* (Princeton: Princeton University Press, 1992). For a good discussion of the technical nature of the discussions of social security matters, see Derthick, *Policymaking for Social Security*, 58–61.

[196]Several works discuss the radical tone that political discourse on taxation often took during earlier periods: Brownlee, "Economists and the Formation of the Modern Tax System"; Brownlee, "Social Investigation and Political Learning in the Financing of World War I," 323; Mark H. Leff, *The Limits of Symbolic Reform: The New Deal and Taxation, 1933–1939* (Cambridge: Cambridge University Press, 1984); and Alan Brinkley, *Voices of Protest: Huey Long, Father Coughlin, and the Great Depression* (New York: Vintage Books, 1982).

[197]U.S. House of Representatives, Committee on Ways and Means, *President's 1961 Tax Recommendations: Hearings*, 87th Cong., 1st sess., 1961, 369.

Mills insisted that fiscal policy be handled by a small number of "experts" who knew the technocratic language and functioned in an insulated environment. To a considerable extent, the Revenue Acts of 1962 and 1964 were handled in this manner. Although Mills often questioned whose experts were correct, he rarely contested the importance of experts themselves. "Political bravery," said Mills, was the "skillful and objective analysis of the facts without prejudice, to recommend action on the basis of those conclusions." As an example of "political bravery," he lauded President Johnson for having shown a "deep understanding of hard economic analysis" in 1964.[198] Mills tried to do the same in his meetings with administration officials and lobbyists, relying heavily on expert data for evidence to bolster his position. The chairman reified the importance of expertise by using medical metaphors that linked his committee to a highly respected profession. Mills often asked hearing participants, "Is the medicine that you are suggesting we use here on the patient the proper medicine?"[199] This metaphor suggested that economic problems, like "diseases," were curable if expert "doctors," such as the Ways and Means Committee, could apply the proper fiscal remedies.[200]

Technocratic policy-making involved a ritual of deference to expertise. Members of the fiscal community normally prefaced their remarks with an assertion or denial of their expertise. The refrain of "I am not an expert" became commonplace during the Ways and Means hearings. In one telling exchange, Bruce Alger (R-Tex.) asked Secretary of Commerce Luther Hodges: "On page 11 you mention the business cycle. How would you define the 'business cycle'?" Hodges responded: "I will have to ask one of my experts on that. It will probably get you confused too, as it does me."[201] In the 1961 hearings for the investment credit, John Byrnes commented to Douglas Dillon: "Because . . . I just have not had a chance to absorb all the details, I am going to limit myself today in my questioning. I feel in a way somewhat like Congressman Barden who expressed his frustration one time when he said he wished he was smart

---

[198]Wilbur Mills, Unmarked Speech (1965), File 9, Box 590, WMPC.

[199]This astute observation was made in Julia Duscha, "The Most Important Man on Capitol Hill Today," *New York Times,* Sunday, February 25, 1968, Section 6.

[200]For an interesting analysis of the use of medical metaphors during the Progressive Era, see Brown, *The Definition of a Profession.*

[201]U.S. House of Representatives, Committee on Ways and Means, *President's 1963 Tax Message: Hearings before the Committee on Ways and Means,* 88th Cong., 1st sess., 1963, 572.

enough to understand what some people were driving at or dumb enough that it did not bother him."[202]

In this context, policymakers attacked each other on the basis of their expertise; to discredit someone's expertise was to discredit their position. Mills and other committee members challenged the administration in these terms. One year Mills had reportedly embarrassed the Treasury experts by finding seventy errors in one of President Dwight Eisenhower's tax proposals. He played that card again in the 1960s, publicly revealing one hundred technical flaws in Kennedy's 1961 tax proposal. He used similar tactics against the early medical care proposals, questioning their numbers regarding future hospital costs and funding. Other Ways and Means colleagues joined Mills in these challenges. Curtis, for instance, accused the administration of "juggling statistics."[203]

Quantitative data, economic theory and analysis, and technical legal jargon were the principal mediums of communication for these experts. Since this generation made far more extensive use of this rhetoric than did older generations of policymakers, one had to master this language in order to participate fully in the community. The language thus limited who could participate and dictated how they should participate. Mills was a master of the new technical rhetoric. As one colleague commented, "Wilbur just doesn't like to get up there and talk unless he has all of his people right there behind him with charts and tables of figures."[204] In closed executive committee sessions, Mills went law-for-law and number-for-number with the interest groups and administration experts on the most detailed provisions of legislative packages.[205] Regarding social security, Wilbur Cohen said: "[Mills] is probably the only man out of the five hundred and thirty five people in Congress who completely understands the actuarial basis of Social Security. He is completely conversant with the basis for making the actuarial estimates and all of the factors that enter into it."[206] Statistics, tables, economic rhetoric, and

[202]U.S. House of Representatives, Committee on Ways and Means, *President's 1961 Tax Recommendations: Hearings,* 87th Cong., 1st sess., 1961, 337.

[203]U.S. House of Representatives, Committee on Ways and Means, *President's 1963 Tax Message: Hearings,* 88th Cong., 1st sess., 1963, 620, 634–35, 796. For another good example, see U.S. House of Representatives, Committee on Ways and Means, *President's 1961 Tax Recommendations: Hearings,* 1961, 87th Cong., 1st sess., 1961, 3028.

[204]"Wilbur Mills: What's His Tax Strategy?" *Nation's Business,* February 1968, 51.

[205]The transcript of the executive sessions on Medicare-Medicaid offers the best illustration of Mills's work in closed session. Portions of the transcript are in the John Manley Papers, LBJL.

[206]Wilbur Cohen, interview with David McComb, December 8, 1968, Tape 2, 7–8, Tape 1, 27.

legislative laws were the texts that policymakers such as Mills read. Days before the passage of the Revenue Act of 1964, the staff of the JCIRT published crucial revenue estimates relating to each version of the legislation. The text included thirty-one pages of tables and statistics on the revenue effect of each reform; it contained virtually no nonquantitative narrative.[207] In this and other ways, Mills emphasized the importance of mastering the technical details, driving this idea into the heads of new members to the committee.[208]

One can glean a sense of the complexity of this discourse through private correspondence. Surrey, for instance, explained a tax provision in the following terms: "Because of the 85 percent dividends received deduction, an intercorporate dividend is subject to tax to the recipient only to the extent of 15 percent of the amount of the distribution. Under existing law, the amount of the intercorporate dividend is limited to the basis of the property in the hands of the distributing corporation."[209] Staff experts communicated with other experts in even more technical jargon.[210] Owing to its importance to the postwar fiscal discourse, technocratic information became a key commodity of political exchange.[211]

---

[207]Staff, JCIRT, *Revenue Estimates Relating to the House, Senate, and Conference Versions of H.R. 8363, the Revenue Bill of 1964*, February 21, 1964, J1046 (Committee—Print). See also Colin Stam to Wilbur Mills (September 27, 1962), File: H.R. 10650, Box 15, 87th Cong., RG 233, NA; Staff, JCIRT, *Staff Data* (June 6, 1963), and Staff, JCIRT, *Summary of the President's 1963 Tax Message* (1963), both in File: Taxes-General, Box 31, 88th Cong., RG 233, NA.

[208]JMIC.

[209]Stanley Surrey to Wilbur Mills (June 26, 1962), File: Unmarked, Box 6348, 87th Cong., RG 233, NA. See also Surrey to Mills (September 12, 1962), File: H.R. 10650, Box 15, 87th Cong., RG 233, NA; Surrey to Mills (September 22, 1961), File: Tax Revision 1961 Dividends and Interest, Box 13, 87th Cong., RG 233, NA; Surrey to Mills (September 12, 1962), File: H.R. 10650, Box 13, 87th Cong., RG 233, NA; Surrey to Leo Irwin (March 8, 1962), File: H.R. 10650, Box 15, 87th Cong., RG 233, NA; Douglas Dillon to Mills (January 8, 1964), File: Public Debt 1963–64, Box 48, 88th Cong., RG 233, NA; Mortimer Caplin to Mills (March 29, 1963), File: Gross Income—Business Expenses, Box 38, 88th Cong., RG 233, NA.

[210]For examples of Mills's correspondence with other state actors and of experts' correspondence with each other, see the following: Leo Irwin to Jim Wright (November 15, 1961), File: Credit Against Tax, Box 6338, 87th Cong., RG 233, NA; Gerard Brannon to Harvey Brazer (January 31, 1962), File: H.R. 10650, Box 13, 87th Cong., RG 233, NA; Irwin to Martha Griffiths (July 30, 1962), File: Exemptions—Income Tax, Box 6339, 87th Cong., RG 233, NA; E. J. Enquist, Jr., to Irwin (December 10, 1962), File: Tax-Income, Box 31, 88th Cong., RG 233, NA; Wilbur Mills to Peter Rodino, Jr. (February 6, 1963), File: Gross Income—Business Expenses, Box 38, 88th Cong., RG 233, NA; Mills to Frances Bolton (April 28, 1964), File: Gross Income—Interest, Box 40, 88th Cong., RG 233, NA.

[211]See, for example, Keith Funston to Wilbur Mills (February 16, 1960), File: Sec. 34, Box

Not all of the legislators were comfortable with this jargon. One committee member remarked: "When I first went on the Committee I used to leave the meetings with a headache, truly a headache! The stuff was just over my head. . . . The things we deal with are so complex! Detail and technical, oh there's so much detail and it's so technical!"[212] Another recalled his first hearing: "I was sitting there one day not knowing what . . . was going on. Title 19, Title 18. You sit there trying to look smart and I really felt phony. I remarked to the Chairman that this was calculus and I hadn't had arithmetic yet."[213]

Mills was well aware of the complexity of this discourse. On occasion, he used his mastery of its vocabulary and its syntax to his political advantage. Politicians less comfortable with the rhetoric deferred to the chairman, since he could engage the experts on their own linguistic terrain.[214] Regarding Medicare, O'Brien's assistant told him in 1964, "[Cohen] expects that before Mills starts his executive sessions he'll call in Cohen to brief him for half a day and then in the executive sessions he'll keep Cohen on the stand all week going over all the combinations till the committee is so groggy it'll throw up its hands and let Mills write the bill."[215] Mills occasionally warned that because of what Surrey once called a "technical curtain," the tax system had become "increasingly remote to most Americans and . . . the exclusive province of a technically trained elite."[216] But he nevertheless used that elite and the fiscal discourse to his own political advantage.

322, RG 128, NA; American Bar Association, "Report on the Problem of Underreporting of Income from Dividends and Interest" (1961), File: Withholding (ABA), Box 207, RG 128, NA; Keith Funston to Colin Stam (November 10, 1961), File: Sec. 1201–2, Box 359, 87th Cong., RG 233, NA; Charles Stewart to Mills (January 16, 1962), File: Sec. 38, Box 322, RG 128, NA; J. W. Fulbright to Mills (September 6, 1962), File: H.R. 10650, Box 13, 87th Cong., RG 233, NA; Thomas Power to Mills (September 11, 1962), File: H.R. 10650, Box 13, 87th Cong., RG 233, NA; Robert Higgins to Mills (September 17, 1962), File: H.R. 10650, Box 12, 87th Cong., RG 233, NA; Douglas Dillon to Mills (October 5, 1962), File: H.R. 10650, Box 15, 87th Cong., RG 233, NA; William Keller to Mills (February 18, 1963), File: Tax Suggestions 1963–64, Box 33, 88th Cong., RG 233, NA; George Lee to Mills (June 3, 1963), File: Tax Correspondence—Capital Gains, Box 28, 88th Cong., RG 233, NA; William Goeckel to Mills (August 16, 1963), Unfiled, Box 56, 88th Cong., RG 233, NA.
[212]JMIC.
[213]Ibid.
[214]Ibid.
[215]Henry H. Wilson, Jr., to Lawrence O'Brien (March 2, 1964), Folder: M, Box 19, White House Office Aides Files, LBJL.
[216]Wilbur Mills, "How Your Income Taxes Can Be Cut," *Nation's Business,* November 1959, 76; Surrey, "The Congress and the Tax Lobbyist," 1175.

This discourse was dense, difficult to understand, and highly conservative. Its definition of "tax reform" blended the concepts of Henry Simons, who argued that equal income should be treated equally, of Andrew Mellon, who claimed that lower tax rates would increase economic productivity, and of John Maynard Keynes, who promised that rate reductions could stimulate consumer demand and bring full employment.[217] Successful tax reform should achieve all three of these objectives simultaneously. Gone from the public rhetoric were terms such as "redistribution of wealth," "social class," and "economic justice." The new language of tax reform downplayed the discussion of income redistribution and social justice while focusing on economic "efficiency" and "growth." Policymakers such as Mills disliked the fact that taxpayers in identical circumstances and with identical incomes sometimes paid different amounts of income tax. Relationships between different income levels, however, attracted less of Mills's attention. One journalist noted that the goal of the reforms of the early 1960s was to rid the internal revenue code of the "ghosts of the Depression," with its "the soak-the-rich tone."[218]

Now, tax reform was merely a means to achieve tax reduction. As Joel Barlow of the U.S. Chamber of Commerce said, "Rate reduction—rate revision—is really the greatest reform."[219] In this rhetoric, tax reform would free up money for "investment" and "consumption," while compensating for part of the loss from tax reduction. Reform would also eliminate the inefficient investments prompted by tax shelters. Mills told one journal: "We should seek a tax climate favorable to economic growth, income taxes under which people with the same income should pay like amounts of tax, an income tax that interferes as little as possible with decisions of the market place. We seek a system . . . which will respond quickly to changes in economic conditions to restrain inflation and recession."[220]

The primary goal of reform, according to Mills, was to "bring greater

[217]Henry Simons, *Personal Income Taxation: The Definition of Income as a Problem of Fiscal Policy* (Chicago: University of Chicago Press, 1938); Andrew W. Mellon, *Taxation: The People's Business* (New York: Macmillan, 1924); John Maynard Keynes, *The General Theory of Employment, Interest, and Money* (London: Macmillan, 1936). For an excellent analysis of Simons, see Witte, *Development of the Federal Income Tax,* chapter 3.
[218]"An Idea on the March," *Time,* January 11, 1963, 20.
[219]U.S. House of Representatives, Committee on Ways and Means, *President's 1963 Tax Message: Hearings,* 88th Cong., 1st sess., 1963, 2369.
[220]"Wilbur Mills Talks on Taxes," *Nation's Business,* August 1964, 81.

fairness and equity to it [the tax code] in the interest of greater economic growth."[221] The existing high tax rates, said Mills, directed too much money away from investment and consumption and toward an excessive federal establishment. This "fiscal drag" clearly retarded economic growth. Reformers such as Mills and Surrey also argued that existing high tax rates (which had been better suited to the World War II economy) caused individuals and organizations in the higher brackets to avoid taxes by creating loopholes or by cheating. In 1959, Mills branded the tax code a "House of Horrors," filled with provisions that allowed individuals and corporations to escape their responsibilities.[222] He lamented: "These high rates are part of the vicious cycle in which the income tax has been ensnared. When we have rates so high, taxpayers make determined efforts to obtain preferential treatment for various types of income and expenses. To the extent that they succeed, the tax base shrinks, thereby reinforcing the need for high tax rates."[223]

Ironically, excessive progressivity had thus become a "problem" that reformers hoped to solve. As Mortimer Caplin told a group of business leaders: "As we review the fiscal history of the 1960s, it is clear that our tax policy has moved far beyond the tax philosophy of the 1930s. Our income tax is no longer the prime tool to redistribute the wealth of our citizenry. Even an ardent tax reformer has said: 'After more than 20 years of rates reaching beyond 80 and 90 percent, a rate schedule that stops at 70 percent is welcome respite.' "[224] To promote growth and prevent tax avoidance, policymakers had to *reduce* the progressivity of the statutory income tax rates. In an interview, Mills recalled, "The basic reform that we sought all the way through was not just the reform of a section of the law or a dozen sections of the law . . . but also reform of the tax rate structure."[225] The existing high tax rates were described by policymakers as "confiscatory," "unrealistic," and "excessive." Of course, said reformers, few individuals would pay the top rate of 91

[221]Wilbur Mills to Harlow Sander (July 25, 1959), File 4, Box 694, WMPC. See also Mills, "How Your Income Taxes Can Be Cut," 70–76; "Outlook for a New Tax System," *Nation's Business*, March 1959, 70–77.
[222]Mills, "Are You a Pet or a Patsy?" 51; Mills, "Preface," 835–38.
[223]Wilbur Mills, "Federal Tax Policy for Economic Growth: Speech" (May 1, 1956), File 20, Box 783, WMPC. See also Wilbur Mills, "Remarks before the Annual Meeting of the Arkansas Savings and Loan League" (October 15, 1960), File 10, Box 781, WMPC; Mills, "Are You a Pet or a Patsy?" 62.
[224]Mortimer Caplin, "Address to the National Conference on Tax Reform of the Chamber of Commerce," in U.S. Chamber of Commerce Press Release (February 14, 1968), File 3, Box 183, SSP.
[225]Wilbur Mills, interview with Joseph O'Connor, April 14, 1967, 13.

percent; taxpayers were practically "forced" to find avenues for tax avoidance. But if the statutory rates were lower, compliance—and thus the "effective" rates, the amount of revenue actually collected by the government—would be higher. The reformers assumed that the wealthy would comply with lower tax rates.

Unlike some tax reformers of the 1920s and 1930s, who had called for higher taxes on the wealthy and on corporations, Mills insisted that the proposed reforms did not entail "the imposition of a new tax but, rather, a vehicle for the purpose of collecting taxes . . . due under the Internal Revenue Code similar to the vehicle . . . in operation with respect to salaries and wages."[226] By raising more revenue, reform would allow for less progressive rates and economic growth. The conservative foundations of this version of reform resolved the paradox of "a conservative Congressman such as Chairman Mills strongly supporting the concept of tax reform."[227]

Actually, the words "progressive" and "reform" had become increasingly difficult to define. Even among policymakers, the meaning of those terms was unclear; for those outside the beltway, the terms were virtually impossible to understand. To be a "tax reformer," argued the policymakers, one needed the "technical" sophistication to comprehend the differences between "statutory" and "effective" rates, to grasp the rationale behind "base broadening," and to know the relation between "horizontal" and "vertical" equity. Given the complexity of these issues, the "experts" said that they needed to "educate" and "lead" the public. "It is the duty of tax men," insisted Mills, "to inform the American people of the consequences of continuing to deal with the federal tax structure and the demands for particular relief which it engenders on a case by case basis."[228] As Mills's statement indicates, even the once-explosive rhetoric of "tax reform" had been absorbed into the technocratic discourse of the postwar era.

This version of reform gained widespread currency among policymakers and activists. The "liberal" tax reformer Senator Albert Gore

[226]Wilbur Mills to B. L. Goad (August 8, 1961), File 4, Box 735, WMPC; U.S. Congress, House of Representatives, *Congressional Record*, 87th Cong., 2nd sess., March 28, 1962, 5305–6.

[227]Joseph Barr to Claude Desautels (March 4, 1963), File: 5 March 1963, Folder 1, Box 23, Legislative Leaders Breakfast Material, White House Staff File, Lawrence O'Brien, JFKL.

[228]Wilbur Mills, "Remarks of the Honorable Wilbur D. Mills before the Society of Public Accountants" (September 1958), File 9, Box 775, WMPC.

(D-Tenn.), for instance, once wrote to the "conservative" Mills, "Frankly, I had no idea our views of existing inequities were so parallel."[229] While criticizing the Revenue Act of 1964, *The Nation* praised Mills for injecting sanity into the deliberations. He was scarcely a popular figure in liberal circles, but the editorial noted: "Nobody—except Mr. Mills—seems prepared to brave the anger of those whose tax privileges are to be taken away. . . . It will be well to consider Mr. Mills' proposals when he is ready to put them before Congress. He is an extremely diligent legislator and he has another virtue which is rare in both the executive and legislative branch: he puts the horse before the cart."[230] Even Surrey wrote: "Very high rates of individual income taxation have come to be recognized as bad, even by those who in the past have favored virtually confiscatory tax rates on ethical grounds. . . . Tax reform involving rate reduction and loophole closing will give a law that is in many respects simpler, and in all respects, fairer and more conducive to sound economic development."[231]

The postwar fiscal discourse served Mills well. It articulated his desire to finance an American state that would maintain the stability of a pluralistic society. The state could help maintain stability through contributory, universal welfare programs that avoided "dependency." This discourse emphasized the use of taxation policies, rather than spending policies, to spur growth and achieve full employment without abandoning the balanced-budget rhetoric. Most important, the language took an appealing technocratic approach to taxation; its version of "reform" helped rid the fiscal discourse of the "ghosts" of class conflict. Although there were clearly bitter debates among policymakers, these usually occurred within the boundaries of the discourse.

CONCLUSION

Mills's experiences help us discern three major characteristics of the political culture of the state—a culture that influenced congressional tax-writing committees—in the post–World War II period. It was important that in devising the tax reductions of the early 1960s, Mills worked

[229]Albert Gore, Sr., to Wilbur Mills (December 21, 1959), WMPC, unprocessed.
[230]Editorial, "Tax Reform First," *The Nation*, January 19, 1963, 48–49; Editorial, "Shelve It!" *The Nation*, March 16, 1963, 217–18.
[231]Stanley Surrey to Henry Fowler (September 27, 1961), File 3, Box 176, SSP. See also Donald Lubick, interview with Julian Zelizer.

primarily through a specialized policy community. This community included several policy-making networks, including political parties, interest groups, and issue networks. Scholars have tended to isolate these—stressing the importance of one over the other—yet in fact, in Mills's career, each was an important part of the whole. Although these several networks were never fully integrated and although conflict periodically disrupted their relationship, they interacted to such an extent that they can be understood only as a larger policy community. Mills identified with, and operated through, this larger community. By balancing the competing needs of its members, he built and maintained his power.

By the 1950s, specialized policy communities of this sort had become the core of the state and its political culture. Historians have gathered considerable evidence on the emergence of similar communities around other issues, such as civil rights, environmentalism, defense, energy, social welfare, and deregulation.[232] Like the political parties of the nineteenth century, these dynamic communities perpetuated shared values among policymakers, provided professional networks of communication, and offered a means of uniting dispersed officials, their staffs, and their clients. Even though tensions regularly occurred among the members, the participants maintained a sense of themselves as a community through regular exchanges of information, through a shared political language, and through their constant involvement with a common issue.[233]

A patterned political discourse was an important aspect of the state culture. The postwar fiscal discourse helped Mills and other policymakers to communicate and to devise substantive policies. This style of discourse also shaped the ways in which Mills and his colleagues perceived

[232]For the best evidence of other policy communities during this era, see the following: Graham, *The Civil Rights Era*; Samuel P. Hayes, *Beauty, Health, and Permanence: Environmental Politics in the United States, 1955–1985* (Cambridge: Cambridge University Press, 1987); David Halberstam, *The Best and the Brightest*, 4th ed. (New York: Ballantine Books, 1992); Balogh, *Chain Reaction*; Allen J. Matusow, *The Unraveling of America: A History of Liberalism in the 1960s* (New York: Harper Torchbooks, 1984); Martha Derthick and Paul J. Quirk, *The Politics of Deregulation* (Washington, D.C.: Brookings Institution, 1985).

[233]For the best theoretical discussions about "policy communities," see the following: Jack L. Walker, "The Diffusion of Knowledge, Policy Communities, and Agenda Setting: The Relationship of Knowledge and Power," in *New Strategic Perspectives on Social Policy*, ed. John E. Tropman, Milan J. Dluhy, and Roger M. Lind (New York: Pergamon Press, 1981), 75–97; John W. Kingdon, *Agendas, Alternatives, and Public Policies* (Boston: Little, Brown, 1984); Paul Burstein, "Policy Domains: Organization, Culture, and Policy Outcomes," *Annual Review of Sociology* 17 (1991): 327–50.

their political world; discourse, as the historian Dorothy Ross has argued, develops "over time, centering around certain problems, setting the terms of discussion for those who enter into it, and at the same time responding to the different intentions of participants."[234] This fiscal discourse led Mills to conceive of himself as involved in a common intellectual and political project with other policymakers; in this case, their project was the achievement of economic growth and stability through the careful manipulation of the nation's fiscal policies.[235]

As Mills found, the new state culture and its distinctive communities were crucial to expanding one's influence among policymakers within the state, even if one was the chair of the Ways and Means. By the mid-1960s Mills had, through fierce struggles, become highly influential on all levels of the fiscal community and the state. As Mills reportedly said about his rejection of a presidential bid, "You don't need the title to run things in Washington."[236] What Mills did need, however, was to work closely with a policy community that had come to power alongside him. He understood that those who operated most successfully in these networks, those who drew most effectively on the language of their community, and those who adapted most quickly to change joined a small elite that exercised a substantial degree of control over the polity by deciding the key issue of national politics: who would pay for the federal government and which programs they would pay for. Cultural factors were a crucial element in the achievement of power within that fragmented complex.

Power acquired in this state could be maintained over long periods of time, but it was tenuous. During the second half of the 1960s, Mills continued to push forward his legislative agenda: he supported moderate adjustments in taxation—when his experts said they were needed and when he felt that the measures could pass Congress—coupled with expenditure control to help the economy; he continued to advocate base-broadening tax reform; he helped expand the social security system to unprecedented levels; and he mounted devastating attacks on the public welfare system. But in the early 1970s, Mills discovered the extent to which his power depended on the state culture and the support of his

---

[234]Ross, *Origins of American Social Science*, xviii–xix.
[235]This type of discourse touched on other issues, including the cold war and poverty. But these interactions are beyond the scope of this chapter. I do, however, extensively discuss these issues in my dissertation "Taxing America: Wilbur Mills and the Culture of Fiscal Policy, 1949–1969."
[236]Kennon and Rogers, *The Committee on Ways and Means*, 324.

community. Of course, the most visible factor behind his decline involved a highly publicized relationship with a stripper and their disgraceful display of drunkenness in the tidal basin. The incident was particularly damaging to an individual who had built his professional reputation on technocratic expertise and a hard-work ethic.

Nonetheless, as one scholar has argued, "The political climate in the House was such that Mills's centralized, consensus-oriented leadership regime and the committee's autonomy and extensive authority would likely have come under attack even if the Arkansas Democrat had spent all of his evenings in 1974 home studying the tax code."[237] During the era of Vietnam and Watergate, political reformers attacked the federal government and its culture. Indeed, the Ways and Means and the fiscal community had been partially responsible for many of the problems that reformers targeted, including the failures of social security, the loophole-ridden tax code, the failure of countercyclical tax policies, the influence of experts in the policy-making process, and the secretive culture of federal politics.

This reform movement had a significant impact on the state. Most important, it ultimately forced many leading officials, including Mills, out of office. Furthermore, the reformers obtained some moderate changes in the structure of federal institutions and programs, such as decentralizing the committee system and indexing social security. They also fostered an intense cynicism toward several aspects of the state culture that had previously been sacrosanct. But until these reforms took place, Mills's influence was sustained by a distinctive post–World War II culture grounded in a policy community and its shared fiscal discourse.

[237]Strahan, *New Ways and Means*, 38.

7

◦◗▬◦◗▬◦◗▬◦◗▬◦◗▬◦◗▬◦◗▬◦◗▬◦◗▬◦◗▬◦◗▬◦◗▬◦◗▬◦◗▬◦◗▬◦◗▬◦◗▬◦◗▬◦

American business and the taxing state:
Alliances for growth in the postwar period

CATHIE JO MARTIN

INTRODUCTION: PRIVATE INTERESTS AND STATE GOALS

If I had it to do all over again, I might have become a tax lawyer. Major tax acts shake up the system every couple of years, confusing everyone and keeping people like Walter Mitty and me in business. For a dry topic, second only to death in certainty and dreariness, the politics of taxation is full of upheavals and revolutionary reversals. One might call it the Eastern Bloc of public policy.

The Sturm und Drang in tax policy-making is especially vivid on the corporate side. Take the investment tax credit. Created in 1962, it was suspended in 1966, reinstated in 1967, revoked in 1969, reinstated in 1971, expanded in 1981, cut back in 1982, and revoked in 1986. President Bill Clinton tried to resurrect the old dog in 1993, but corporate America cried, "Enough already!"

In the go-go 1980s, tax policy turned truly wild and crazy. Although the corporate share of total federal budget receipts declined throughout the postwar period, the Economic Recovery Tax Act of 1981 brought the corporate tax share down to a postwar low of 6.2 percent in 1983. In 1986, tax reform brought the corporate share back up to 12.4 percent of total receipts.[1]

Where were our leaders of industry when all this was going on? If the state is a tool of the capitalist system, as we learn in Marxism 101, or even if business is the most powerful interest group among many in a pluralist system, these dramatic changes in the corporate code would not

---

[1]Joseph Pechman, *Federal Tax Policy* (Washington, D.C.: Brookings Institution, 1983), 353.

353

be allowed to happen. There are two possible explanations for these shifts. First, business *power* may vary across time: Corporate power may have declined between 1981 and 1986. The budget deficit could have reduced our collective willingness to give business tax breaks. Second, business *preferences* for tax policy may vary over time so that corporate leaders themselves changed their minds about taxes. The first possibility suggests a shift in the context of business; the second suggests a shift within the business community. Although the first possibility may be true, I focus here on the second.

The central argument of this essay is that economic ideas, important to policy experts in developing tax proposals, also profoundly shape the expression of private interests. Even businesspeople, supposedly the most material of economic actors, are guided in their deliberations of their interests by ideas about the determinants of economic growth and stability. Economic ideas not only offer technical prescriptions for growth and stability but also contain assumptions about market functionings, the appropriate role of government in the economy, and state-society relations.

The state is central to private preference formation in two ways. First, the state has considerable control over the production of economic ideas, the dissemination of information about the economy, and the framing of the tax debates.[2] Ideas and information about economic conditions influence business managers' perceptions of their interests. The state's technical expertise thereby influences private support for public policies.

Second, the state is critical to private preference formation in an even more active sense through the leadership of presidential administrations. Presidential aides help business managers to endorse a growth strategy by organizing coalitions of private interests in support of the administration's legislative agendas. Because divided government and weak parties frustrate executive leadership in policy-making, presidents often turn to outside power sources to help push their initiatives through Congress. Naturally, political leaders begin with private sectors whose interests are potentially most compatible with those of their administrations. But the process of focusing on broad themes, negotiating between difficult trade-

[2]W. Elliot Brownlee, "Economists and the Formation of the Modern Tax System in the United States: The World War I Crisis," in *The State and Economic Knowledge: The American and British Experiences*, ed. Mary O. Furner and Barry Supple (Cambridge: Cambridge University Press and Washington, D.C.: Woodrow Wilson Center Press, 1990), 401.

offs, and expanding the coalitions to bring in a wider spectrum of the business community transforms corporate preferences. Participants view their interests within the context of the larger growth agenda and become willing to consider policies that would be rejected in another context.

These broad coalitions, organized around changing growth strategies, are responsible for the remarkable shifts in corporate taxation. The history of postwar fiscal policy must be thought of as a series of subregimes, each with its own central organizing economic idea and with disciples of this idea from the public and private sectors.[3]

To support my argument, I present selected cases in which the corporate tax code underwent important transitions. Evidence is offered that changing economic ideas helped to alter corporate preferences in each case and that government efforts to build private sector coalitions around the tax initiatives helped to convert business managers to the shifting economic strategies. These coalitions enhanced the immediate influence of business: corporate participants were instrumental both in securing the passage of the legislation and in leaving their indelible marks on the final products. These coalitions also contributed to the long-term expansion of business political capacity. Thus presidential coalitions spurred the remarkable increase of corporate mobilization in the 1970s, and that mobilization in turn encouraged the continuing reliance by presidential administrations on private sector allies.

PRIVATE INTERESTS AND STATE GOALS
IN POLICY FORMATION

Explanations for the development, expansion, and contraction of the tax system tend to fall into two broad categories: those tying the impetus for change to private sector interests and those tying it to public sector ideas and institutions.

The interest approach suggests that private sector groups use their resources to secure tax advantages.[4] Although scholars debate the relative weight of various private interests in the tax sphere, they adhere to

---

[3]A discussion of growth or accumulation subregimes is found in the work of Michel Aglietta, *A Theory of Capitalist Regulation* (New York: Verso, 1987), and Alain Lipietz, *Mirages and Miracles* (New York: Verso, 1987), 14.

[4]Joseph Schumpeter, "The Crisis of the Tax State," *International Economic Papers: Translations Prepared for the International Economic Association*, no. 4 (London: Macmillan, 1954).

the fundamental assumption that power relations are more important than goals and that the impetus comes from society rather than the state.[5] This view portrays interests as fixed and immediately perceptible.[6] Yet, much of the recent work on corporate strategies emphasizes the fluidity of preference and the indeterminacy of behavior.[7] If business preferences are indeterminate, what factors contribute to the choice of position? Unfortunately, the interest-based approach usually limits its analysis to economic conditions, neglecting the important ideas and institutions that shape the emergence of preference.

The other broad category of explanation relates tax changes to the goals of government. The goal of raising revenue for military needs during major wars expanded the tax system and motivated structural changes in the tax code. The goal of equity prompted debates about how to expropriate wealth in a just and equitable fashion. The goal of revenue collection spurred government to stimulate economic growth in order to protect its revenue base.[8]

Accepting the premise that taxation is goal-directed does not, however, automatically inform us about outcomes. First, goals may come into conflict, and government decision-makers must determine which goal to emphasize. Capitalist-state theorists argue that the goals of growth and equity are fundamentally incompatible.[9] The political scientist Ronald King suggests that the postwar period saw a shifting from

[5]Benjamin Page, *Who Gets What from Government?* (Berkeley: University of California Press, 1983); Randall Bartlett, *Economic Foundations of Political Power* (New York: Free Press, 1973); John Witte, *The Politics and Development of the Federal Income Tax* (Madison: University of Wisconsin Press, 1985). See also Robert Collins, *The Business Response to Keynes, 1929–1964* (New York: Columbia University Press, 1981); Kevin Phillips, *The Politics of Rich and Poor* (New York: Random House, 1990); David Calleo, *Beyond American Hegemony: The Future of the Western Alliance* (New York: Basic Books, 1987).

[6]Those studying tax revolts represent an exception; they recognize that ideas and normative assessments of the state influence public demands for legislative change.

[7]Thompson points out that the firm has multiple objectives and should be viewed as a "nonunitary actor" with conflicting and ambiguous interests. Graham Thompson, "The Firm as a 'Dispersed' Social Agency," *Economy and Society* 11, no. 3 (August 1982): 233. David Plotke, "The Political Mobilization of Business, 1974–1980," in *The Politics of Interest*, ed. Mark Petracca (Boulder, Colo.: Westview Press, 1992); Neil Fligstein, *The Transformation of Corporate Control* (Cambridge, Mass.: Harvard University Press, 1990).

[8]Paul Kennedy, *The Rise and Fall of the Great Powers* (New York: Random House, 1988); W. Elliot Brownlee, chapter 2, this volume; Charles Lindblom, *Politics and Markets* (New York: Basic Books, 1977).

[9]Adam Przeworski and Michael Wallerstein, "Democratic Capitalism at the Crossroads," *Democracy*, July 1982. Also see Roger Benjamin and Stephen Elkin, *The Democratic State*

the goal of equity to one of economic growth as decision-makers (persuaded in part by business elites) determined that distributional conflict was less important than an expanding economic pie.[10]

Second, diverse economic ideas offer competing prescriptions for tax intervention. Thus, whereas King's characterization of postwar tax politics is partially true, it misses the conflict over the means to achieve the goal of growth. Despite the general shift from equity to growth as the central goal of taxation, conflict continued to plague tax politics even within the business community.

Third, there are a number of ways to combine resources for production and many types of national economies.[11] The goal of stimulating domestic manufacturing may suggest a policy package different from that necessary for the goal of stabilizing the currency and protecting the interests of the international banking industry.[12] Policy choices usually reflect both the explanatory power of economic ideas and the realpolitik of political struggle.

It is not enough to simply assert that fiscal policies reflect state goals. We must explain the political and economic conditions under which an economic idea gains adherents. What are the microfoundations—the public and private constituents, their ideas and interests—for growth-oriented policies?

Institutional analyses of government policy-making recognize the necessity of placing state goals in an ideological and institutional context.[13]

(Lawrence: University Press of Kansas, 1985), and James O'Connor, *The Fiscal Crisis of the State* (New York: St. Martin's Press, 1973).

[10]Ronald F. King, *Money, Time, and Politics: Investment Tax Subsidies and American Democracy* (New Haven: Yale University Press, 1993).

[11]Aglietta, *Theory of Capitalist Regulation;* Lipietz, *Mirages and Miracles,* 14; Jill Quadagno, *The Transformation of Old Age Security* (Chicago: University of Chicago Press, 1988), 6.

[12]Lance LeLoup, "Congress and the Dilemma of Economic Policy," in *Making Economic Policy in Congress,* ed. Allen Shick (Washington, D.C.: American Enterprise Institute, 1983), 9.

[13]Hugh Heclo, *Modern Social Politics in Britain and Sweden* (New Haven: Yale University Press, 1974); Theda Skocpol, "Bringing the State Back In: Strategies of Analysis in Current Research," in *Bringing the State Back In,* ed. Peter Evans, Dietrich Rueschemeyer, and Theda Skocpol (Cambridge: Cambridge University Press, 1985), 3–43; Margaret Weir, *Politics and Jobs: The Boundaries of Employment Policies in the United States* (Princeton: Princeton University Press, 1992); Walter Salant, "The Spread of Keynesian Doctrines and Practices in the United States," in *The Political Power of Economic Ideas,* ed. Peter Hall (Princeton: Princeton University Press, 1989), 37; Thomas Reese, "The Politics of Tax Reform," in Laurence N. Woodworth Memorial Symposium, *National Tax Journal* 32, no. 3 (September 1979): 249–50; Randy Strahan, "Members Goals and

But these analyses largely neglect business.[14] Indeed, many assume that in order for ideas to play a causal role, government officials must enjoy a degree of separateness from public interests.[15] Otherwise pluralist pressures would simply overwhelm public decision-making and reduce goals and ideas to residuals.

Moreover, private interests find guidance in economic ideas and broad growth strategies. The state is critical to the joining together of ideas and interests in private preference formation. First, the state is a key location for the production of economic knowledge and thereby greatly influences the framing of the debates in which private parties deliberate. New knowledge becomes especially influential during crises that attack the validity of the existing paradigms.[16] State institutions are the battleground for competing ideas and the crucible for social learning.[17]

Second, presidents often seek outside allies to build political support for their primary growth projects. Divided government frustrates presidential efforts to quickly enact tax policy. Stymied by political enemies in other branches and parties, presidents look for sympathetic interests beyond the bounds of government and often find convergence with parts of the business community. Government leaders can augment their power against their own political enemies by mobilizing interest groups that will support their policy positions.[18]

Presidents have periodically used business mobilization since the development of the modern trade association. Historians have described the 1920s as an era of private-interest government.[19] And the more recent decline of party leadership and organized labor has enhanced the corporate role as political partner. Presidents John Kennedy and Lyndon Johnson actively promoted corporate involvement as a way to offset the power of congressional conservatives. This government courtship of business served to enhance corporate institutional capacity. By the

---

Coalition-building Strategies in the U.S. House," *Journal of Politics* 51, no. 2 (1989): 373–84.

[14]Hall argues that ideas are important in organizing both realms. Peter Hall, "Policy Paradigms, Social Learning, and the State," *Comparative Politics* 25, no. 3 (April 1993).

[15]See, for example, Skocpol, "Bringing the State Back In."

[16]Mary O. Furner and Barry Supple, "Ideas, Institutions, and State in the United States and Britain: An Introduction," in Furner and Supple, *The State and Economic Knowledge*, 4, 19.

[17]Heclo, *Modern Social Politics in Britain and Sweden.*

[18]Cathie Jo Martin, "Business Influence and State Power: The Case of U.S. Corporate Tax Policy," *Politics and Society* 17 (1989).

[19]See, for example, Ellis W. Hawley, ed., *Herbert Hoover as Secretary of Commerce: Studies in New Era Thought and Practice* (Iowa City: University of Iowa Press, 1981).

1980s, business managers were full-fledged members of the tax policy community.

This does not mean that business reacts in passive fashion to government puppeteers. Business visionaries have joined with government leaders in using the state to organize the wider corporate community around new approaches to economic growth. Nor do I want to suggest that ideas are the only motivating factor. Business and/or government may be attracted to the coalition for self-interested reasons, but ideas are the organizing principles.

We should think of each of the subregimes of the postwar tax regime as shaped by a fundamental growth strategy. In each subregime, presidents tried to build governing coalitions around each of these growth strategies by mobilizing business constituents and other relevant interests from private society.[20] Kennedy, for example, sought to construct a subregime around a domesticated Keynesian growth strategy. President Ronald Reagan moved to another subregime with his supply-side revolution and then shifted course again with a postindustrial growth strategy.

TRUMAN AND FULL EMPLOYMENT

The postwar economy was organized around a Fordist production strategy: goods were made with capital-intensive mass production, and growth occurred by increasing productivity. High levels of mass consumption were needed to guarantee a market for the enormous output created by this production mode. The system also required government regulation of the economy to coordinate production and consumption.[21]

A "domesticated Keynesian" fiscal philosophy supported this system of production. This peculiarly American brand of Keynesian theory had a conservative tint compared with Western European versions.[22] The stabilization mechanism in domesticated Keynesianism would be automatic rather than subject to fine-tuning. Policymakers would set tax rates so that the budget would be balanced at high employment: when the

[20]For two very different views of this, see Bob Jessop, ed., *Accumulation, Regulation, and the State* (London: Century-Hutchinson, 1988), and Heclo, *Modern Social Politics in Britain and Sweden.*

[21]David Calleo, *The Imperious Economy* (Cambridge, Mass.: Harvard University Press, 1982); Ed Greenberg, *Capitalism and the American Political Ideal* (Armonk, N.Y.: M. E. Sharpe, 1985).

[22]Collins, *The Business Response to Keynes.*

economy dropped below this level, the budget would go into deficit. The process was to work free from human meddling. Domesticated Keynesian theory also put greater emphasis on investment incentives than did more radical Keynesian perspectives. In this way it presented a balance between accumulation and consumption. To address investment, the policy delivered selective tax breaks to stimulate investment and savings and guarantee adequate capital for the supply side.

Keynesian policy in America, even in its domesticated form, also took longer to become established. Although the United States experimented early with Keynesian policy in the 1938 tax cut, the nation showed considerable reluctance to embrace Keynesian economic interventions in subsequent years. The 1938 cut was a somewhat pragmatic and ad hoc effort, without much reliance on Keynesian theory. The political scientist Margaret Weir attributes this paradox of early experimentation combined with delayed endorsement to three historical legacies. First, Americans associated public spending with party patronage; therefore, they were reluctant to endorse a comprehensive strategy for economic growth that rested on public works. Second, since Keynesian intervention required expanded capacity in the executive branch, the politics of public spending became tied to the politics of executive branch expansion. Third, Keynesian policies were linked to the most radical aspects of the New Deal; therefore, this packaging constrained its acceptance among the congressional conservative coalition.[23] Selling the new fiscal philosophy to business was also a very slow process and further removed domesticated Keynesianism from its European counterparts.

The battle to adopt the new growth strategy began during the administration of Harry Truman. There were essentially two sides to Truman's fiscal policy. On the one hand, the Employment Act of 1946 previewed a business-government partnership in support of domesticated Keynesianism. On the other hand, the battle over tax reduction in 1948 reflected the class conflict of the New Deal era. Truman's failures in legislating Keynes are important because they represent the "starting points for his successors."[24]

The Truman administration's original proposal for "full employment" legislation sought to establish a right of all Americans to full employ-

[23]Weir, *Politics and Jobs*, 31–49.
[24]Michael Lacey, "Introduction and Summary," in *The Truman Presidency,* ed. Michael Lacey (Cambridge: Cambridge University Press and Washington, D.C.: Woodrow Wilson Center Press, 1989).

ment, to commit the government to taking action during economic downturns, and to give responsibilities to the president for monitoring the economy and to Congress for legislating the program.[25] The act encountered considerable opposition from many in the business community, but a core group of businessmen, often described as corporate liberals, were willing to accord government greater responsibility over the economy in order to further the long-term interests of the system. The Committee for Economic Development (CED) was a center for such thinking. (Groups with a contrary point of view included the National Association of Manufacturers, the U.S. Chamber of Commerce, the Committee for Constitutional Government, and the American Farm Bureau Federation.)[26] CED Chairman Paul Hoffman dismissed conservative complaints that the bill would make government into a gigantic employer, arguing that it would merely set government up "to establish conditions under which the free enterprise system" could operate "most effectively and to counteract the tendencies in the system toward booms and depressions."[27]

The CED, however, had held major reservations about the original bill, and it leveraged changes in the final legislation. As a consequence, the final legislation favored macroeconomic management through fiscal policy over more interventionist programs of public spending or price controls. Also, the act favored automatic stabilizers—a potentially more technocratic approach than one involving presidential discretion. Finally, the act abandoned a commitment to full employment as a right. Beardsley Ruml of the CED had testified that the language of rights was too strong and excessive for the goal of full employment and that the operational definition of full employment was apt to vary over time as the structure of the economy changed.[28]

Despite the moderate consensus that emerged in support of the Employment Act of 1946, there was little common ground between Truman and business on specific tax issues. Truman and business generally replayed the old progressivity versus laissez-faire arguments of the early twentieth century. The liberal wing of the business community had not yet developed a position distinct from that of its conservative counter-

[25] Steven Bailey, *Congress Makes a Law* (New York: Columbia University Press, 1950), 13–14.
[26] Ibid., 129.
[27] Cited in Karl Schriftgiesser, *Business Comes of Age* (New York: Harper and Brothers, 1960), 97.
[28] Ibid., 96.

parts, and the Democrats had not yet moved away from the progressive stance of the New Deal.[29]

The major fiscal conflict concerned the tax-reduction bill that eventually passed in 1948. Conservative congressional Republicans wanted lower rates and a variety of reductions in corporate taxes. Truman wanted a redistributive forty-dollar tax credit that would be paid for by an increase in the corporate rate.

Truman did not do much to mobilize business in the manner of his Democratic successors. During the war mobilization effort, government had enjoyed close relations with business: "There was everywhere a yearning for 'cooperation' rather than conflict among the institutions and sectors of American society."[30] But after the war, this cooperation disappeared, and business engaged in a major campaign to resist all efforts at pushing the policy and institutional gains of the New Deal forward and to scale back the role of government. Truman's seizure of the steel mills also increased hostility between the president and the business community. Truman initially hoped that business would engage in voluntary cooperation to support his various policy goals. But when business mobilized to attack his initiatives, he instead began a populist attack on corporate America. A fundamental ideological disagreement over the role of politics thus divided Truman from most of the business community. The corporate mobilization against Truman limited the achievements of the administration and set the stage for the emerging postwar order.[31]

KENNEDY AND THE DOMESTICATED KEYNESIANS

The administration of Dwight D. Eisenhower did little to advance activist countercyclical policies. His administration did expand corporate incentives for growth by creating accelerated depreciation allowances in 1954. But Eisenhower focused on promoting price stability and protecting the dollar as an effective medium of international exchange. Consequently, he resisted fiscal stimulants and accepted relatively high rates of unemployment.[32] Eisenhower paid a political price for this policy by opening the way for John F. Kennedy to campaign on a promise "to get

[29]Robert Griffith, "Forging America's Postwar Order, Domestic Politics, and Political Economy in the Age of Truman," in Lacey, *The Truman Presidency*, 72.
[30]Crauford Goodwin, "Attitudes toward Industry in the Truman Administration: The Macroeconomic Origins of Microeconomic Policy," in Lacey, *The Truman Presidency*, 97.
[31]Griffith, "Forging America's Postwar Order," 63–65.
[32]Stephen Weatherford and Lorraine McDonnell, "Macroeconomic Policy Making beyond

American business and the taxing state   363

the country moving again." Kennedy came into office convinced that he had a mandate for vigorous economic stimulation.

Tax legislation during the Kennedy administration and shortly thereafter greatly accelerated the tendency to use tax policy as an agent of economic stimulation. The Kennedy tax strategy depended on the domesticated Keynesian hybrid. Keynesians within the administration sought to increase demand with countercyclical adjustments in tax levels to offset booms and busts and with tax cuts for lower-income individuals, who were most likely to consume rather than to save the additional dollars. Those more sympathetic to a neoclassical orientation made economic incentive arguments. Ensuring an adequate supply of capital was necessary to investment and growth; therefore, selective investment incentives were a more appropriate vehicle for fiscal expansion.

The two prongs of the domesticated Keynesian growth strategy were represented in Kennedy's two major tax initiatives. To address investment, the Revenue Act of 1962 created the investment tax credit and shortened depreciation asset lives. These tax incentives were to become major growth stimulants in the postwar era. The Revenue Act of 1964, originally designed to combine tax reform with across-the-board rate reductions, dropped most of the reforms but lowered tax rates in order to stimulate consumption and to reduce the so-called fiscal drag caused by excessively high taxation.

The macroeconomic context. The Kennedy tax legislation must be viewed within the framework of the conflict between the goals of domestic growth and those of international monetary stability. Domestic growth was very much a problem when Kennedy took office in 1961. The Council of Economic Advisers (CEA) estimated in the spring that less than 80 percent of industrial capacity was currently being utilized; 5.5 million people were unemployed.[33] At the same time, deficits in the international balance of payments rose, and the U.S. share of the monetary stock of the "Free World" declined from 43 percent to 26 percent by 1962.[34]

Unfortunately, the policy prescriptions for the problems of domestic

the Electoral Constraint," in *The President and Public Policy Making*, ed. C. Edwards III (Pittsburgh: University of Pittsburgh Press, 1985).
[33]Council of Economic Advisers to JFK, "Memorandum: A Second Look at Economic Policy in 1961" (March 17, 1961), CEA 1/61–3/61, Box 73, Presidential Office Files, Kennedy Library, Boston.
[34]E. Ray Canterbury, *Economics on a New Frontier* (Belmont, Calif.: Wadsworth Publishing Company, 1968), 90.

growth and payment deficits were rather different; this tension in goals and between the advisers behind the goals undoubtedly contributed to the vacillating nature of the administration's economic policy. Tax cuts to stimulate demand can cause inflation and exacerbate currency problems. Balance-of-payments deficits dictate high interest rates to keep investment at home and to curb the trend in foreign portfolio investment. High interest rates, however, hurt domestic expansion. Walter Heller, chairman of the CEA, described the mutually exclusive goals as a "cruel dilemma of economic policy."[35]

Ideas and interests within government. Both neoclassical and Keynesian economists were influential in the Kennedy administration, and they differed on three fundamental issues: the appropriate role of government in the economy; the engine of economic growth; and the legitimacy of budget deficits. The Keynesian economists viewed government intervention as essential and proper, identified both consumption and investment as necessary for growth, and portrayed budget deficits as an appropriate tool for macroeconomic intervention. Neoclassical economists rejected government intervention, emphasized investment as the source of growth, and renounced budget deficits.

The conflict between macroeconomic ideas and policies materialized in a deep division between the CEA and the Treasury. Walter Heller endorsed an explicitly Keynesian policy package. To stimulate demand, Heller advocated tax cuts (and public works), believing that budget deficits were necessary to close the gap between actual and potential GNP. Heller also worried that the domestic economy would be sacrificed to international monetary concerns, and he argued that a healthy, growing economy was the best solution to long-term balance-of-payments problems. Therefore, Heller believed, the administration should pursue growth strategies aimed at the modernization and expansion of industry, which would encourage productivity and competitiveness.[36]

Douglas Dillon and the Treasury Department based their policy prescriptions on neoclassical economics. Although Dillon shared Heller's urge to cut taxes, he wanted to cut taxes for the neoclassical rationale that progressive taxation interfered with savings, risk, and investment.[37]

---

[35] Heller to JFK, "Memorandum: The Balance-of-Payments Dilemma" (November 28, 1961), CEA 11/61, Box 73, Presidential Office Files, Kennedy Library.
[36] Ibid.
[37] "To Bring Two Deficits under Control," *Business Week,* March 4, 1962, 30–32.

At the same time, Dillon wanted spending cuts to offset tax reduction. He rejected budget deficits, which he viewed as both inherently illegitimate and threatening to the balance-of-payments problem.[38] Dillon was also primarily concerned with balance-of-payments deficits and urged that solutions to domestic stagnation not interfere with this goal.

Another source of influence in the policy debate was Wilbur Mills (D-Ark.) and his fellow congressional fiscal conservatives. Mills's orientation was largely neoclassical in that he viewed progressive taxation as interfering with savings and investment, sought base-broadening reforms, resisted budget deficits, and opposed manipulation of tax levels for short-term stabilization purposes. As head of the House Ways and Means Committee, Mills could choose how and when to report bills out of committee and, thereby, could control fiscal legislation.

The Kennedy administration adopted a compromise fiscal program of domesticated Keynesianism linked with growth-oriented tax incentives. Domesticated Keynesianism avoided the threats of inflation and of the international monetary instability associated with vigorous Keynesianism but, at the same time, offered some stimulation of demand. Selective growth incentives promised to stimulate the growth of productive capacity, as well as to provide a moderate stimulus to total demand, and would thus relieve the inflationary pressure that resulted from excess demand.

Pattern of business interests. The 1960s found the business community in transition. Much of it remained skeptical of budget deficits and Keynesian tricks. But a small group of corporate leaders, mainly multinational manufacturers and bankers, were frustrated with the seemingly unnecessary recessions under Eisenhower, were enamored with high European growth rates, and were willing to believe that the business cycle could be tamed. In 1958 a committee set up by the Rockefeller Brothers Fund recommended a variety of growth stimulants including a 5 percent across-the-board tax reduction.[39] As a measure to dampen the swings of the business cycle, the Commission on Money and Credit (CMC) suggested that flexible standby authority be given to the president to increase or decrease individual income taxes by as much as 5 percent for

---

[38]Douglas Dillon to JFK, Memorandum (September 5, 1961), Treasury 9/61, Box 89, Presidential Office Files, Kennedy Library.
[39]Herbert Stein, *The Fiscal Revolution in America* (Chicago: University of Chicago Press, 1969), 335.

up to six months. Heller noted, "It's doubtful that we will get such blue-blooded launching facilities as the CMC Report."[40]

Industry divided largely along sectoral lines. Financial interests wanted all domestic economic policy to be tailored to the management of balance-of-payments deficits over domestic growth. The large New York banks stood to lose $2 billion in foreign official deposits if the role of the dollar as reserve currency was lost.[41] Within this constraint, private bankers were eager that the government take a more active part in formulating economic policy, one that was targeted toward investment and carried out within a balanced budget. Thus in 1962, banking was generally favorable to the investment tax credit as a mechanism to increase domestic growth without incurring deficits. The industry not surprisingly fought withholding on interest and dividends, wanted the 1964 cuts to be viewed as an investment stimulant, pushed for greater reductions in the top brackets, and supported spending cuts and reforms to balance the budget.[42] When the administration discussed a "quickie" tax cut in the summer of 1962, the industry cautioned against hasty tax reduction.[43]

Prominent financiers evidently pressured their Western European peers to steer the Kennedy administration away from policies that could damage the balance of payments. Thus Heller reported that President Karl Blessing of the West German central bank had been asked to convert some dollars into gold "to put pressure on the Kennedy Administration to pursue more conservative policies."[44] New York bankers sought to scare European counterparts with stories about Kennedy's inflationary fiscal policy and thereby to alter the president's economic program.[45]

Export-oriented manufacturers showed more movement toward the new domesticated Keynesian growth strategy; they were more concerned about the expansion of the domestic economy. Manufacturers accepted a government role in stimulating both supply and demand and were

[40]Walter Heller to JFK, "Memorandum: The Case for Flexible Tax Authority" (December 23, 1961), CEA 12/61, Box 73, Presidential Office Files, Kennedy Library.

[41]"Report of the Bank for International Settlement in Basle," Treasury 6/62, Box 89, Presidential Office Files, Kennedy Library.

[42]"House Votes $11.2 Billion Tax Cut," *Congressional Quarterly Almanac* (Washington, D.C.: Congressional Quarterly Service, 1963), 481.

[43]Douglas Dillon to JFK, "Memorandum: Visit with New York Bankers" (July 27, 1962), Treasury 7/16/62–7/31/62, Box 89A, Presidential Office Files, Kennedy Library.

[44]Walter Heller to JFK, "Memorandum: Highlights of Paris—Bonn—Frankfurt Consultations" (n.d.), CEA 6/16/62–6/30/62, Box 73, Presidential Office Files, Kennedy Library.

[45]"Memorandum: Protecting the Dollar from the New York (and Swiss) Bankers" (October 16, 1961), CEA 10/61, Box 73, Presidential Office Files, Kennedy Library.

more tolerant of budget deficits. For example, in a November 1962 meeting with forty business economists, Heller found that 80 percent of the group favored a substantial tax cut, even with a large deficit and increased expenditures.[46]

Despite the manufacturing sector's concern about growth and its ultimate support for the domesticated Keynesian stimulants, in 1961 many manufacturers opposed the investment tax credit, which they viewed as entailing excessive government interference into investment decisions. Donald Hardenbrook, president of the National Association of Manufacturers, called the investment credit a "subsidy" for some businesses, one that would place heavier burdens on all business.[47] Later, manufacturers would come to be the strongest supporters of the measure.[48] Their initial opposition caused the *New York Times* to note: "Seldom has a measure caused a deeper split among its friends. And seldom have designated beneficiaries of tax legislation joined in opposition with those whose taxes were to be raised."[49]

The difference between manufacturers and bankers is clear in their attitudes toward the 1964 tax cuts. Manufacturing sectors supported tax reduction earlier, demanded fewer qualifications, and were more willing to consider deficits.[50] When the quickie tax cut was considered in the summer of 1962, many manufacturers, unlike their counterparts in finance, supported the move. In part this reflected less concern about budget deficits. In his 1962 meeting with forty business economists, Heller found that all but one present wanted a two-stage bill, with the tax rate reductions to be followed by reforms.[51] The Advisory Committee on Labor-Management Policy, led by Henry Ford II of Ford Motor and Thomas Watson of IBM, warned that tax reform should not be allowed to delay the cuts.[52]

---

[46]Walter Heller to JFK, "Memorandum: Business Views on the Economic Outlook and Tax Cuts" (November 10, 1962), CEA 11/7/62–11/14/62, Box 75, Presidential Office Files, Kennedy Library.

[47]Robert Metz, "Tax Aid for Expansion," *New York Times*, April 2, 1962, 39.

[48]"Congress Enacts Major Tax Law Provision," *Congressional Quarterly Almanac* (Washington, D.C.: Congressional Quarterly Service, 1962), 484.

[49]Arthur Krock, "In the Nation an Unexpected Variation of Divide and Conquer," *New York Times*, April 5, 1962, 32.

[50]"What for Taxes?" *New York Times*, December 17, 1962, 10.

[51]Walter Heller to JFK, "Memorandum: Business Views on the Economic Outlook and Tax Cuts" (November 10, 1962), CEA 11/7/62–11/14/62, Box 75, Presidential Office Files, Kennedy Library.

[52]Richard Mooney, "10-Billion Tax Cut Urged by Labor-Business Panel," *New York Times*, November 20, 1962, A1, 22.

Small business was a limited force in fiscal politics during the early 1960s. The U.S. Chamber of Commerce was the only association that could claim to speak for the little guys. The chamber opposed the investment tax credit, fearing that it would favor larger concerns and discriminate against "small or money-losing companies."[53]

Thus Kennedy faced a business community that had some fledgling interest in his economic agenda. Even those willing to consider more activist economic intervention, however, were divided about the appropriate goal of this intervention. It remained to the administration to unify these disparate views and expand the enthusiasm for the new growth strategy across the business community.

Legislating the Revenue Act of 1962. Although the 1964 tax cut was in many ways the fiscal highlight of the Kennedy-Johnson administrations, the 1962 tax act was more significant for corporate taxation. First, the act created the investment tax credit, one of the major corporate growth incentives. Second, the initiative was initially met with considerable suspicion by the business community; the lessons of 1962 motivated the administration to develop its business-mobilization strategy.

The centerpiece of the act, first proposed in 1961, was a 15 percent investment tax credit on capital outlays exceeding a firm's depreciation allowance. To offset the revenue loss from the credit, the administration proposed a change in the treatment of capital gains on depreciable property, a withholding provision on interest and dividend income, and the repeal of the fifty-dollar exclusion and the 4 percent credit on dividend income. The administration also sought changes in business entertainment deductions, in the tax preferences of mutual savings and loans, and in the treatment of U.S. foreign subsidiary income.[54]

Despite their concerns about growth, many businesspeople were initially quite skeptical about the investment tax credit. They feared that it would give government excessive control over private investment decisions, and they preferred accelerated depreciation as a policy vehicle for government subsidization of capital investment. Leaders of industry—the Chamber of Commerce, the Committee for Economic Development, American Telephone and Telegraph, and fifty other firms and organi-

---

[53]Richard Mooney, "Two Business Groups Oppose Tax Program at Senate Hearing," *New York Times*, April 4, 1962, A1.

[54]John Morris, "Test of President's Message and Budget Analysis," *New York Times*, January 19, 1962, 14.

zations—testified in full force. George Terborgh, of the Machinery and Allied Products Institute, pronounced the credit "as complicated as it is novel."[55] Many financial groups, by comparison, supported the measure as a means of stimulating growth and offsetting the balance-of-payments deficits. Charls Walker, vice-president of the American Bankers Association, believed that the investment incentive would increase American productivity and curb the dollar outflow.[56] Influenced by ideas, the ones with the most to gain testified against the measure, whereas the ones with the least to gain supported it.

As the chair of the House Ways and Means Committee, Wilbur Mills had the power to decide how and when to report bills out of committee, and he used this power to control fiscal legislation. Mills was not impressed with the credit but agreed to report out the bill if the administration could get the AFL-CIO to "promise to cease stirring up grass roots complaints in his district."[57] Mills also requested a Titan II missile base for Arkansas and asked the president to dedicate a combination watershed and recreation project, saying, "No one else will be acceptable."[58]

In January 1962 the administration returned to Ways and Means with a new, more palatable proposal: an across-the-board 8 percent tax credit. The administration estimated that the new credit would add $1.8 billion to 1962 corporate profits.[59] In the Senate an unusual coalition of conservatives, led by Harry Byrd (D-Va.), and liberals, led by Albert Gore, Sr. (D-Tenn.), formed to oppose the capital spending incentive.[60] It looked as if even the new, improved tax credit was dead on arrival.

But the administration decided not to take business opposition at face value. Instead it set out to court the intended beneficiaries of the measure and to convince them that both their short-term interests and the long-term interests of the country would be served by their endorsement of the tax credit. Ironically, this turning point dates from shortly after the nadir of Kennedy's relations with the business community: the confrontation with Roger Blough of U.S. Steel. The administration had worked

[55]"Tax Plan Draws More Brickbats," *Business Week,* May 20, 1961, 36.
[56]"ABA Backs Plan on Plant Outlays," *New York Times,* May 9, 1962, 69.
[57]George Ellison to James O'Brien, Letter (April 2, 1962), Wilbur D. Mills, Arkansas, Folder 1, White House Staff Files, O'Brien, Kennedy Library.
[58]Larry O'Brien to Ken O'Donnell, Memorandum (April 6, 1962), and Claude Desautels to Larry O'Brien, Memorandum (September 17, 1962), both in Wilbur D. Mills, Arkansas, Folder 1, White House Staff Files, O'Brien, Kennedy Library.
[59]"Tax Credit a Spur to Capital Outlays," *Outlook,* February 26, 1962, 920.
[60]"Senate Coalition to Fight Kennedy on Tax Proposal," *New York Times,* April 1, 1962.

hard with U.S. Steel and the United Steelworkers of America to negotiate a noninflationary contract. When the steel company reneged on the deal, the president took it personally and publicly charged that all steelmen were "sons of bitches."[61]

Kennedy's charge did much to strengthen the president's antibusiness image. But a less-publicized tactic was much more successful and served as a harbinger of things to come. The administration persuaded Joseph Block, chairman of Inland Steel and a member of Kennedy's Labor-Management Advisory Council, to reject the price increase. Block worked with Edward Gudeman, the under secretary of commerce, to persuade four other small companies to hold the line.[62] The lesson for Kennedy was that publicly chastising business was counterproductive but that using business allies to win over their deviant peers promised success.

After the steel crisis, the administration began to court business more fervently with meetings to solicit industry's input on the tax bill and a range of economic issues.[63] At Dillon's urging, the administration announced a commitment to depreciation reform at a May meeting of the Business Council; this seemed to help the investment credit.[64] Henry Fowler, under secretary of the Treasury, observed, "In the press conference that followed, Roger Blough went out of his way to exude goodwill and approbation of this announcement as an important step toward the restoration of business confidence and the betterment of government-business relations."[65] During the earlier Ways and Means hearings, the administration had been unable to get any businessmen to testify in favor of the credit.[66] Yet, in August a Research Institute of America survey of six thousand executives found 65 percent in favor of the credit.[67] By the time the bill reached the Senate floor, the administration had persuaded trade associations from a number of sectors—including coal, railroads,

---

[61]Hobart Rowen, *The Free Enterprisers* (New York: G. P. Putnam's Sons, 1964), 90–104.
[62]Ibid., 101.
[63]"Memorandum of Discussion at President Kennedy's Luncheon of July 12, 1962" (July 17, 1962), Treasury 7/16/62–7/31/62, Box 89A, Presidential Office Files, Kennedy Library.
[64]Walter Heller to JFK, "Memorandum: Douglas Dillon on Depreciation Revision Speed-up" (April 18, 1962), CEA 4/62, Box 74, Presidential Office Files, Kennedy Library.
[65]Fowler to JFK, "Memorandum: Business Council Meeting" (May 15, 1962), Treasury 5/62, Box 89, Presidential Office Files, Kennedy Library.
[66]"Acid Test in the Senate," *Business Week*, March 3, 1962, 25.
[67]"Congress Enacts Major Tax Law Provisions," *Congressional Quarterly Almanac* (Washington, D.C.: Congressional Quarterly Service, 1962), 484.

aerospace, cotton, petroleum, chemicals, electronics, small business, utilities, and machinery and allied products—to contact legislators.[68]

The administration's ultimate success in passing the investment tax credit (albeit in a scaled-back form) did not extend to the revenue-enhancing reform measures in the bill. Here traditional interest-group politics intervened. Withholding on interest and dividends passed in the House with a minimum of debate but encountered a firestorm of controversy in the Senate. The Investor's League said of the proposal: "[It] smacks of police state methods. . . . It is in a sense burning down the house to catch the mouse."[69] When a lone banker testified in favor of the requirement, Senator Robert Kerr jokingly asked him if he needed police protection to exit the building safely.[70] The U.S. Savings and Loan League engineered a massive letter-writing campaign; one institution's letter to stockholders stated that about 60 percent of all individuals would lose one-fifth of their receipts of dividends and interest.[71] Although the president attacked the savings industry for "misinforming many millions of people" and shamed it into calling off the campaign, the damage had been done, and the withholding provision was dropped.[72] A similar industry offensive gutted the proposal to reduce the bad-debt deduction for savings and loans institutions.

The administration ran into trouble with export-oriented manufacturers (important potential allies for its economic activism) with a reform proposal to increase taxes on the foreign income of U.S. corporations. The administration hoped to curb tax havens, to decrease capital outflows by 10 percent, and to alleviate the balance-of-payments problems.[73] The big export-oriented manufacturers testified in droves and so praised their overseas ventures that Senator Gore jokingly concluded, "If one assumes these 19 companies are typical, then the best way to solve our balance-of-payments problem, the best way to solve our unemploy-

[68]"Industry Support of H.R. 10650," Treasury 8/1/62–8/20/62, Box 89A, Presidential Office Files, Kennedy Library. See also Richard Mooney, "Two Liberals Voice Tax Plan Qualms," *New York Times,* April 5, 1962, 54.

[69]Senate Finance Committee, William Jackson's Testimony, *Hearings on the Revenue Act of 1962,* H.R. 10650, 87th Cong., 2d sess., Item 1038 (Washington, D.C.: Government Printing Office, 1962), 2181.

[70]Senate Finance Committee, John Sadlik's Testimony, in ibid., 2248.

[71]Gene Smith, "Mutual Funds: Drive against Tax Bill of U.S.," *New York Times,* May 7, 1962, 42.

[72]"President Charges Deceit by Withholding-Tax Foes," *New York Times,* May 10, 1962.

[73]"Why the Tax Bill Scares Businessmen," *Business Week,* May 5, 1962, 92.

ment problem, is to move all of our factories and our industry and our business abroad."[74] Ultimately the administration accepted a significant reduction of the proposed tax increase.

Legislating the Revenue Act of 1964. The 1962 effort to lower corporate taxes by increasing subsidies for capital investment was surprising in that it received as little business support as it did. The 1964 experience was surprising in its own way. Of course, business might have been expected to go along with lower tax rates (especially for upper-income payers). But many corporate leaders also accepted the proposition that budget deficits and fiscal stimulation by government were appropriate tools for macroeconomic management.

The 1964 tax cut started out meaning different things to different people. In fact, this was partly a result of administration tactics. Kennedy encouraged discordant views in order to bring as many people in under the umbrella as possible.

During the formation of the proposal, one debate concerned the timing of the tax reduction. The administration ultimately resolved this issue by delaying the cut until just before the election. The CEA wanted a quickie tax cut during the summer of 1962 to ward off the threatening recession and to protect the Democrats' reputation as a party of recession fighters.[75] The Treasury, however, wanted to tie tax reduction to later revenue-raising reforms and to package reduction as a long-term measure rather than as a short-term, macroeconomic stabilization tool.[76]

Treasury and the CEA took different positions on the political economy of political business cycle dynamics. Treasury suggested a medium-length recovery, followed by a short downturn and then a brisk recovery immediately before the election; this precluded a quickie tax cut. Fowler argued: "Your Administration should be inextricably associated with 'good times' in the minds of the people. . . . Can that rare political asset—Kennedy prosperity—be preserved until November 1964?"[77] The CEA preferred a long expansion, fearing that Fowler's short recession

[74]Senate Finance Committee, *Hearings on the Revenue Act of 1962*, 5242.

[75]Council of Economic Advisers to JFK, "Memorandum: What It Takes to Get to Full Employment," CEA 3/3/62–3/15/62, Box 74, Presidential Office Files, Kennedy Library; Arthur Schlesinger, Jr., to JFK, "Memorandum: Tax Cut" (July 17, 1962), Treasury 7/16/62–7/31/62, Box 89A, Presidential Office Files, Kennedy Library.

[76]Seymour Harris to JFK, Memorandum (June 7, 1962), Treasury 6/62, Box 89, Presidential Office Files, Kennedy Library.

[77]Fowler to JFK, Letter (November 31, 1961), Treasury 10/61–12/61, Box 89, Presidential Office Files, Kennedy Library.

would be hard to control and that a strong recovery before the election would be hard to achieve.[78]

Within the administration, the opposing camps on early tax reduction actively solicited business views to bolster their positions. Dillon canvassed the Treasury's Advisory Committee (drawn from the American Bankers Association and the Investment Bankers Association) and found only one investment banker in favor.[79] G. Keith Funston, president of the New York Stock Exchange, even went on television to caution against hasty tax reduction without spending controls.[80] Heller corresponded with Murry Shields, the head of a Wall Street consulting firm, who reported finding widespread panic over the state of the economy in his canvass of manufacturers. Heller reported, "More and more often, the anti-government business community is looking to the President to exercise his powers under the mandate of the Employment Act of 1946." Shields, Heller reported, said that "the impression of 'indecision and impotence' coming out of Washington" was "more damaging than any of the alleged anti-business moves."[81]

Another debate occurred over whether the administration should embrace deficits as appropriate policy tools and acknowledge them as likely side effects of the cuts. Heller and the CEA strongly wanted to bring budget deficits out of the closet. By 1963 parts of the business community found deficits tolerable; these segments believed that lost revenue would be made up through increased entrepreneurial activity. The Committee for Economic Development was, of course, an early convert; the Chamber of Commerce changed course in the summer of 1962, and in November the Advisory Committee on Labor-Management Policy endorsed tax reduction even with a budget deficit.[82] But the Treasury and the financial community opposed budget deficits as policy. They worried about the impact of deficits on the dollar. Charls Walker argued that the stakes were "the prospects for the free world itself."[83]

---

[78]Arthur Okun to Walter Heller, "Memorandum: Another Myth for Our List" (June 31, 1962), CEA 6/16/62–6/30/62, Box 74, Presidential Office Files, Kennedy Library.

[79]Douglas Dillon to JFK, "Memorandum: Visit with New York Bankers" (July 27, 1962), Treasury 7/16/62–7/31/62, Box 89A, Presidential Office Files, Kennedy Library.

[80]Cabell Phillips, "Senate Test Near on Tax Measure, Reforms Deleted," *New York Times,* July 23, 1962, A1.

[81]Walter Heller to JFK, "Memorandum: Report from Scattered Sectors—Economic and Tax Front" (June 20, 1962), CEA 7/16/62–7/25/62, Box 74, Presidential Office Files, Kennedy Library.

[82]"Juggling Deficit and Tax Cuts," *Business Week,* November 17, 1962, 44.

[83]Charls Walker, "A Federal Tax Cut This Summer: Some Neglected Considerations," *Commercial and Financial Chronicle* 196, no. 6178 (July 19, 1962): 1, 20.

President Kennedy's own position on the budget deficit was somewhat inconsistent. During his famous Yale speech, the president publicly rejected the idea that deficits cause inflation or that a balanced budget is automatically a good thing.[84] Yet on other occasions the administration tried to avoid saying that the tax cuts were geared to produce growth-stimulating budget deficits. Kennedy told the Economic Club of New York that this was not "a mere shot in the arm to ease some temporary complaint" but was an effort to increase "the financial incentives for personal effort, investment and risk-taking."[85] The economist John Kenneth Galbraith described the speech as the most Republican since Hoover.

Another debate concerned whether to make tax reduction contingent on reform. Fiscal conservatives such as Dillon and Mills considered reform vital to offset revenue losses. They were joined by liberal tax reformers such as Stanley Surrey, assistant secretary of the Treasury, and Albert Gore. Financial interests also wanted to tie the cuts to reforms. The CEA, however, supported postponing the reforms, placing them in a second bill after the enactment of the cuts. Most manufacturing interests joined in this stance either because they felt that immediate stimulus was necessary or because they had a lot to lose. Heller agreed, at least tactically. He explained, "Vested interests, just because we feed them a high-protein diet of tax cuts, [won't] be any less venal or voracious when we kick them in their private parts."[86]

The president presented the broad outlines of his tax program in January 1963: the top rate was to be cut from 91 to 65 percent, and reforms would partially offset the revenue reduction. At the time the tax program was announced, the administration chose to emphasize long-term growth, fiscal responsibility, and reform instead of stabilization and deficit stimulation. The president's neoclassical packaging was largely intended to appease Mills and other fiscal conservatives in both parties. Dillon reminded Kennedy, "Any suspicion that the Administration considers that a deficit is good per se tremendously increases the pressures in Congress favoring drastic expenditure reductions."[87]

---

[84]"Washington Outlook," *Business Week,* June 16, 1962, 43–44.

[85]Richard Mooney, "Tax Cut Debate: How Much, For Whom?" *New York Times,* November 25, 1962, E10.

[86]Walter Heller to JFK, Memorandum (June 7, 1962), CEA 6/1/63–6/13/63, Box 76, Presidential Office Files, Kennedy Library.

[87]Douglas Dillon to JFK, Memorandum (March 5, 1963), Treasury 3/63, Box 90, Presidential Office Files, Kennedy Library.

Under Secretary of the Treasury Fowler met with Mills on November 14, 1962, to work out what was necessary to obtain Mills's support for the legislation. Mills made it clear that although he believed "the present tax rate structure" was "a drag on the economy," tax reduction necessitated both reform and expenditure control. He suggested a ratio of $11 billion of revenue loss to $5 billion of reform. He also asked that the president portray the bill as a mechanism for long-term growth in the State of the Union address. Finally, he urged that the administration also negotiate an early agreement with Chairman Harry Byrd of the Senate Finance Committee.[88] To accommodate Mills, the president drastically revised his tax proposal. Kennedy abandoned the two-stage concept of reductions followed by reform and gave up the retroactive date of January 1, 1963.[89] Because many of the reform proposals were later gutted during the Ways and Means markup, Chairman Mills continued to press for spending cuts.

The administration expected considerable difficulty in getting the bill through the Senate Finance Committee because Chairman Byrd opposed the bill on budgetary grounds. Fowler warned that the Republicans would try to "put a Republican trade-mark on this tax bill in the form of specific expenditure limits." He warned that opponents would "wish to divide the Administration from its allies in the business and financial community and ride the acknowledged thrust of public and editorial opinion for expenditure control as an accompaniment to a tax cut."[90]

Ultimately the Senate moved quite quickly. Undoubtedly President Kennedy's untimely death made enactment easier. But the administration's business mobilization strategy was another important factor in the ultimate success of the 1964 tax legislation.

The business mobilization strategy. Disappointments over the 1962 revenue act and the considerable hostility within Congress to the president's new growth agenda led the Kennedy administration to adopt a systematic program of cultivating business supporters. But why did the administration turn to business?

One possibility is that the Kennedy administration, just like Keynesian

---

[88]Fowler to Files, "Memorandum: Conference with Chairman Wilbur Mills re Tax Program" (n.d.), Treasury 11/62–12/62, Box 90, Presidential Office Files, Kennedy Library.
[89]"An Idea on the March," *Time*, January 11, 1963, 19–21.
[90]Henry Fowler to JFK, "Memorandum: Tax Bill Strategy and Tactics" (n.d.), Treasury 9/63, Box 90, Presidential Office Files, Kennedy Library.

governments everywhere, had to mobilize interests in society to assist with its expanded projects of economic and social management.[91] Andrew Shonfield suggests that countries with very different histories of business-government relations demonstrated a similar impulse toward greater state reliance on public interests.[92] But the unique challenge of divided government in the United States had much to do with the desire of the Kennedy administration to mobilize business. Responsibility for managing the macroeconomy fell to the president, yet the executive branch received no additional power to accomplish its new task, and congressional conservatives from both parties opposed increased governmental intervention into the economy.[93]

Fowler led the way in implementing a business mobilization strategy. He proposed that the administration organize "a private, independent, non-partisan organization" of businesspeople to support the tax bill. He suggested a list of names to be considered for a Temporary Executive Committee to organize the group, and he recommended that the membership in the larger organization be as broad and representative as possible, drawing from diverse industries, regions, and groups. Fowler advised that the executive committee should convene a general meeting by May with membership in the hundreds. The administration (Treasury, Commerce, and the Office of the President) could contribute to this membership by compiling a list of five hundred names. Fowler also laid out an agenda for an initial meeting: President Kennedy should discuss the tax proposal and preside over a discussion of organizing methods and tactics. Fowler emphasized that the resulting group, however, should not be publicly linked with the administration but should appear to have arisen spontaneously from the private sector. Fowler and Larry O'Brien would continue to serve as liaisons with the group.[94]

[91]Joel Krieger, *Reagan, Thatcher, and the Politics of Decline* (New York: Oxford University Press, 1986), 22–23
[92]See, for example, Andrew Shonfield, *Modern Capitalism* (New York: Oxford University Press, 1965), 231, and John Goldthorpe, *Order and Conflict in Contemporary Capitalism* (Oxford: Clarendon Press, 1984), 325. For Wolfgang Streeck and Phillip Schmitter, private interest government made policy more practical, realistic, and legitimate. Wolfgang Streeck and Phillip Schmitter, "Community, Market, State, and Associations?," in *Private Interest Government,* ed. Streeck and Schmitter (Beverly Hills, Calif.: Sage Publications, 1985), 22.
[93]Weatherford and McDonnell, "Macroeconomic Policy Making beyond the Electoral Constraint"; William Keech, "Elections and Macroeconomic Policy," in *The President and Economic Policy,* ed. James Pfiffner (Philadelphia: Institute for the Study of Human Issues, 1986).
[94]Henry Fowler to JFK, "Memorandum: Organizing Procedure for the Business and Fi-

Kennedy accepted Fowler's idea and began by meeting with thirty-five business leaders on April 25. They formed a committee along the lines proposed by Fowler. The group, named the Business Committee for Tax Reduction agreed to recruit three hundred members by June. Henry Ford II (Ford Motor Co.) and Stuart Saunders (Norfolk and Western Railway) were the co-chairmen. Vice-chairmen included Mark Cresap, Jr. (Westinghouse), Sam Fleming (Third National Bank of Nashville), and Frazer Wilde (Connecticut General Life Insurance Co.). Other executive committee members included Frederick Kapel (AT&T), David Rockefeller (Chase Manhattan Bank), and J. Harris Ward (Commonwealth Edison of Chicago).[95] The large export-oriented manufacturing sector was heavily represented among the membership. Despite the administration's key role in its origins, the committee denied any link to the administration. "The organization itself and its program," the committee declared, "were developed by a bipartisan group of businessmen who wrote their own ticket."[96]

The business mobilization strategy had three important results. First, corporate mobilization helped to get the bill passed. In the final weeks of the Ways and Means deliberation, the group began a grass-roots campaign to pressure hesitant members of Congress to support the legislation. The goals of the grass-roots campaign were twofold: "approval of the House bill and a call for its early enactment by the Senate."[97] The administration encouraged those organizations favoring the bill to convey "a concrete expression of sentiment of constituents to individual Congressmen and Senators." In response, the business groups sent out mass mailings, such as the chamber's "Tax Alert Bulletin," in support of the bill. Fowler found these activities especially helpful with the Republican and southern Democratic legislators. Fourteen out of fifteen southern governors supported the bill, largely through the intervention of the business groups.

Second, the business mobilization strategy shaped the final legislation. The administration followed policy consistent with the business position in the areas in which finance and manufacturing interests were in agree-

nance Committee for Tax Reduction in 1963" (n.d.), Treasury 4/63, Box 90, Presidential Office Files, Kennedy Library.
[95]"Tax Cut Committee Picks Co-Chairmen," *New York Times,* May 4, 1963, 34.
[96]"National Conference on Tax Reduction" (September 1963), 3, Treasury Tax Reduction Business Committee 9/63, Box 90, Presidential Office Files, Kennedy Library.
[97]Henry Fowler to JFK, Memorandum (September 23, 1961), Treasury 9/63, Box 90, Presidential Office Files, Kennedy Library.

ment. The administration agreed to concentrate the reductions in the top brackets and tie the reductions to spending cuts. The administration dropped many of the original reform measures, including reducing the depletion allowance, repealing the fifty-dollar exclusion on interest and dividend income (Congress doubled it instead), and increasing the holding period for long-term capital gains (Congress ended up creating two categories). Fowler convinced the administration that reintroducing the reforms in the Senate would divide the business community and alienate many of the supporters in the committee. To advance the bill through the Senate, he urged that Dillon state clearly to the press that the president was willing to forgo further consideration of reform.[98]

Finally, the business mobilization strategy altered the economic preferences of the business participants. The Businessmen's Committee helped spread the Keynesian word, convincing other business groups that the president's plan was a legitimate economic exercise. Fowler noted that the Businessmen's Committee had been "of immeasurable assistance in marshaling support among the various established trade organizations and avoiding the 'knee jerk' type of opposition that normally characterizes response to any initiative from a Democratic President."[99]

The Kennedy administration's efforts helped domesticated Keynesian tax policy capture the imagination of corporate America. Business leaders closely connected to the administration worked to change the minds of their corporate peers. In a speech to the National Retail Merchants Association, Henry Ford urged business to try to understand why government intervention was growing in business areas and to stop opposing this growth reflexively. Businesspeople should "support rather than oppose well-considered Government programs to accomplish what Government can do and business can't do." He added, "Both Government and business must expand their responsibilities and activities."[100] In like fashion Theodore Levitt observed that the top CEOs in America had embraced the interventionist state, "completing what may turn out to be the most remarkable ideological transformation of the century, perhaps since the beginning of the corporate economy." President Kennedy's honeymoon with business had become a marriage.[101]

[98] Ibid.
[99] Ibid.
[100] "Henry Ford Asks Government and Business to Redefine Their Roles to Avoid Conflict," *Wall Street Journal,* January 13, 1967.
[101] Theodore Levitt, "The Johnson Treatment," in U.S. Congress, House of Representatives, *Congressional Record* 113, 20, February 9, 1967, H1211.

REAGAN AND THE SUPPLY-SIDE REVOLUTION

In 1981, Ronald Reagan ushered in another subregime in tax policy with a supply-side platform aimed at ending the Keynesian hegemony. Reagan's gains reflected the disintegration during the mid-1970s of the consensus behind domesticated Keynesianism. Declining rates of productivity led a new generation of economists to emphasize macroeconomic policy based on investment-oriented incentives. Critics such as Norman Ture claimed that the existing incentives were insufficient. They argued that economic salvation lay in expanding tax incentives to save and invest and in shifting the tax burden off upper-income payers.[102]

The major manifestation of the new fiscal philosophy was the Economic Recovery Tax Act of 1981. The act legislated the largest tax decrease in the history of the United States and reduced the taxation of capital in an effort to increase investment and to resuscitate the economy. To stimulate savings, investment, and work effort, the tax favored upper-income individuals and corporations. Individual rates were cut across the board by 23 percent, with the greatest savings concentrated in the upper brackets. The act drastically reduced estate taxes and created a number of exclusions to the windfall profits tax. It also radically expanded tax incentives for investment by greatly shortening the depreciation periods for capital with the Accelerated Cost Recovery System (ACRS) and by enlarging the investment tax credit. The economist George Kopits calculated the U.S. tax subsidy rate on manufacturing investment to be 1.3 percent of the asset price in 1973; after the 1981 act, the rate jumped to 12.8 percent.[103]

The macroeconomic context. This sea change in economic thinking was grounded in substantially altered economic conditions that can be traced to the 1973 oil crisis or before.[104] Especially problematic to Keynesian analysis was the emergence of stagflation.[105] The Keynesian Phillips

[102]Martin Feldstein, "Fiscal Policy for the 1980's," in *New Directions in Federal Tax Policy for the 1980's,* ed. Charls Walker and Mark Bloomfield (Cambridge, Mass.: Ballinger, 1983); Norman Ture and Kenneth Sanden, *The Effects of Tax Policy on Capital Formation* (New York: Financial Executives Research Foundation, 1977).

[103]George Kopits at the International Monetary Fund, cited by Michael Barker and Michael Kieschnick, "Taxes and Growth," *Tax Notes,* special report, May 7, 1984, 635.

[104]Samuel Bowles, David Gordon, and Thomas Weisskopf, *Beyond the Waste Land* (Garden City, N.Y.: Anchor Press, 1983).

[105]Barry Bosworth, *Tax Incentives and Economic Growth* (Washington, D.C.: Brookings Institution, 1984), 7.

curve suggests a reciprocal relationship between unemployment and inflation: an increase in one produces a decline in the other. Yet the 1970s saw the onset of stagflation, in which the economy experiences high unemployment and high inflation simultaneously. The year before Reagan's election, the growth rate of real income was almost zero, unemployment was up to 7.5 percent, and inflation was almost 10 percent.[106] Contributing to inflationary pressures was a startling decline in the growth of productivity. From 1948 to 1966, U.S. productivity grew at an annual rate of 3.3 percent; from 1966 to 1973, 2.1 percent; and from 1973 to 1978, 1.2 percent.[107]

Inflation was pernicious. It pushed individuals and families into higher marginal tax brackets (bracket creep), thereby raising tax revenues without legislative authority. Inflation decreased the value of the personal exemption; thus, middle-class families found themselves increasingly squeezed by the tax state. Inflation also hurt corporate payers by eroding the value of depreciation allowances over time. Indirectly, inflation encouraged increased interest rates, which cut the rates of return to capital and corporate profits.[108] The average net after-tax rate of profit of domestic nonfinancial corporations dropped from nearly 10 percent in 1965 to less than 6 percent by the second half of the 1970s.[109]

Ideas and interests within government. Three strands of economic thought offered solutions to the economic malaise. Monetarists blamed inflation on the excessive growth rate of the money supply. The only way to cure the confusing stagflation of the 1970s was first to achieve price stability through restricted growth in the money supply and then to implement a responsible, predictable monetary policy. Monetarists feared that the proposed cuts would enlarge deficits, crowd out private borrowing, increase interest rates, and further fuel inflation.[110]

Supply-side advocates, such as Paul Craig Roberts, placed low taxes

---

[106]Gerald Epstein, "Domestic Stagflation and Monetary Policy," in *The Hidden Election,* ed. Thomas Ferguson and Joel Rogers (New York: Pantheon, 1981), 141–95.

[107]Edward Wolff, "The Magnitude and Causes of the Recent Productivity Slowdown in the United States," in *Productivity Growth and U.S. Competitiveness,* ed. William Baumol and Kenneth McLennan (Oxford: Oxford University Press, 1985), 32.

[108]C. Eugene Steuerle, *The Tax Decade: How Taxes Came to Dominate the Public Agenda* (Washington, D.C.: Urban Institute Press, 1992), 18–22, 28–30.

[109]Bennet Harrison and Barry Bluestone, *The Great U-Turn* (New York: Basic Books, 1988), 115–17.

[110]Stephen Rattner, "Top Officials Clash on Tax Cut Timing," *New York Times,* January 28, 1981, D1, 4.

at the center of their economic program. Supply-siders stressed that taxes constrain incentives to work, save, and invest, stifling entrepreneurial spirit and preventing capital formation. Tax reductions were needed, they believed, to increase personal incentives for work, savings, and investment. Further, drawing on the "Laffer curve," supply-siders believed that such reductions stimulated productive gains, which would, in turn, actually increase tax revenues.[111]

Traditional neoclassical economists, who included the monetarists among their numbers, disagreed with this approach. They agreed that taxes could damage incentives, but they believed that any fiscal adjustments should be carried out in the context of a balanced budget. Deficits withdrew resources from the pool of savings available to private borrowers and raised interest rates, thereby limiting investment. In this vein, Alan Greenspan informed the Ways and Means Committee that the tax cuts should be accompanied by budget cuts.[112] Paul Volcker agreed. Financial markets, he told the Ways and Means Committee, would act adversely if tax cuts were made before spending cuts.[113]

As a candidate, Reagan differentiated himself from his fellow candidates by endorsing supply-side economics early in the prenomination period. Supply-side economics was a way for him to reconcile the conflicting economic pressures on him, since it promised that everything could be attended to at once. This "economics of joy" offered a bright counterpoint to President Jimmy Carter's many policy reversals, which had failed to bring inflation under control and had thrown the country into recession.[114] Reagan's no-sacrifice solution to the double bind of inflation and unemployment consisted of 30 percent tax cuts to generate growth and a consistent, restrictive control of the money supply to control inflation.[115]

The president may also have seen the enormous tax cuts as a mechanism for reducing the revenue base of the state and, thereby, generally

[111]Paul Craig Roberts, *The Supply-Side Revolution* (Cambridge: Harvard University Press, 1984).

[112]Alan Greenspan, "Statement," *Hearings before the Committee on Ways and Means: Tax Aspects of the President's Economic Program*, Serial 97–100 (Washington, D.C.: Government Printing Office, 1981), 496–500.

[113]Rattner, "Top Officials Clash on Tax Cut Timing."

[114]This delightful term is Stein's. Herbert Stein, *Presidential Economics: The Making of Economic Policy from Roosevelt to Reagan and Beyond* (New York: Simon and Schuster, 1984), 255–56.

[115]James Fallow, "The Reagan Variety Show," *New York Review of Books*, April 12, 1984, 10.

curbing governmental power. Director of the Office of Management and Budget David Stockman's remarkable confession that no one understood the numbers and that few within the administration believed in the supply-side miracle gives weight to the view that Reagan intended the tax cut to derail the engine of government.[116]

Once in office, Reagan relied on economists from competing schools, including supply-siders, monetarists, and traditional neoclassical economists. The tensions between competing economic concerns were played out in institutional conflicts within the administration. Monetarists were located in the Federal Reserve under Volcker. Among the Treasury staff were a large number of supply-side economists who caught the ear of Secretary Don Regan. Neoclassical economists concentrated in the CEA under Murray Weidenbaum and then Alan Greenspan. The administration resolved these ideological and institutional tensions with a bizarre division of labor between policy spheres. The monetarists commanded control of monetary policy, and the supply-siders were allowed free rein with the tax code. Reagan's campaign promises to lower taxes radically and at the same time to stop inflation reinforced this division of labor.

A final political factor significant to the tax legislation in 1981 was the role of the Democrats. The Democrats were badly beaten in the budget battle, and early evidence suggested that Reagan would approach taxes with a similar take-no-hostages attitude.[117] Therefore, they decided to fight the president on the individual cuts, which they attacked as inequitable and inflationary, and to outbid the Republicans on the corporate provisions. Why did the Democrats decide to battle the president on the individual taxes and to sign on to cuts in the corporate code so readily? To some extent this had to do with the enormous cost of the individual cuts and the much lower price tag of the corporate reductions. Democrats correctly perceived that the individual tax reductions would limit the scope of government and inhibit future spending initiatives. Democratic acceptance also represented the degree to which an accumulation-oriented fiscal philosophy had captured converts across the political spectrum.

Politics also played a part in the Democratic decision. Dan Rostenkowski and the other leaders of the party believed Americans to be ambivalent about the supply-side measures and knew that the southern

---

[116]David A. Stockman, *The Triumph of Politics: How the Reagan Revolution Failed* (New York: Harper and Row, 1986).
[117]"Democrats Draw a Battle Line over Tax Cuts," *Business Week*, April 13, 1981, 135.

Democrats most likely to break rank with the party were ill-disposed to budget deficits.[118] Rostenkowski's leadership of the Ways and Means Committee offered the hope that the party could control the battleground of taxation. In a larger sense the decision reflects the "right turn" of the Democratic Party as it determined that its future lay with the interests of the middle class.[119] Finally the Democrats wanted to reconstruct an identity. Allegedly, Carter even called Rostenkowski and said, "Do what you have to do, but win." One staff person recalled that the lobbyists held cheerleading sessions to ready themselves for the budget battle. The pressure on the Democrats was enormous.[120]

Pattern of business interests. Reagan's endorsement of supply-side economics—and of the Accelerated Cost Recovery System as the cornerstone of corporate tax reform—also reflected the political dynamics within the business community. The economics of joy attracted business because it promised to transfer wealth to corporate interests and because it masked differences between corporate sectors.

The organization of business had flourished during the 1970s.[121] Consequently, by the 1980s, presidents had no choice but to recognize business as a powerful institutional presence in the policy domain. Interest groups had become increasingly important both in financing campaigns (with the advent of PACs) and in constructing governing coalitions. Meanwhile, political parties and organized labor had declined. Continuing decentralization in Congress expanded the number of decision-making points and limited the authority of congressional leaders.[122] All of these factors made it more difficult for political elites to control tax policy and required those elites to seek out business allies.

Although firms and trade associations offered considerable corporate support to the Reagan program, they had a diverse and potentially contradictory wish list of reforms. Capital-intensive manufacturing groups

[118]"Conservative Southerners Are Enjoying Their Wooing as Key to Tax Bill Success," *Congressional Quarterly,* June 13, 1981, 1023–24.
[119]Thomas Ferguson and Joel Rogers, *Right Turn* (New York: Hill and Wang, 1986); Thomas Edsall, *The New Politics of Inequality* (New York: W. W. Norton, 1984).
[120]Interviews with Ways and Means Committee staff (fall 1994 and spring 1995).
[121]The Business Round Table emerged as the lobbying arm of big business. The American Council for Capital Formation, founded in 1973 by Charls Walker, focused on economic policy. Membership in the Chamber of Commerce grew from 50,000 in 1970 to 215,000 in 1983. David Vogel, *Fluctuating Fortunes* (New York: Basic Books, 1989); Edsall, *Politics of Inequality.*
[122]James Sundquist, *The Decline and Resurgence of Congress* (Washington, D.C.: Brookings Institution, 1981).

put a priority on depreciation reform to solve the capital shortage. In addition, these firms wanted credit and deduction refundability. This was a technique that would allow unprofitable firms paying no taxes to receive reimbursement for the incentives they could otherwise have deducted. They argued that the tax code discriminated against "poor" companies. These firms also sought the repeal of the corporate minimum tax on tax preference items.[123]

Financial sectors argued that the economy required savings incentives, such as individual retirement accounts, to augment capital formation. The U.S. Savings and Loan League proposed an "all-savers provision," which would make savings certificates worth under $1,000 tax-exempt.[124] High-technology firms wanted a 10 percent research-and-development tax credit and a restricted employee stock option. The Treasury opposed this measure on the ground that the credit would fail to increase research activity.[125] Small business groups wanted graduated income tax rates, expensing of capital outlays in the first year (rather than accelerated depreciation over a period of years), and simplified accounting systems.[126]

Business leaders were convinced that they needed to reach consensus on corporate tax measures, in part because of the intervention of Jim Jones (D-Okla.) and Barber Conable (R-N.Y.). Manufacturing firms led the way by building support in the business community for a faster depreciation schedule. They formed the Carlton Group, a forum to bring together representatives from a wide range of the business community. The group included the Chamber of Commerce and the National Association of Manufacturers. Small-business involvement was considered critical for political appeal. Therefore, the group invited the National Federation of Independent Business and the National Association of Wholesaler-Distributors. The Carlton Group included as well the American Business Conference, which presented itself as the voice for high-tech, fast-growing firms.[127]

The Carlton Group decided to concentrate on speeding up depreciation allowances for fixed assets, and it began working on a compromise

---

[123]Interviews with industry representatives (fall 1994 and spring 1995).

[124]" 'All Savers' Plan: Some Second Thoughts," *Congressional Quarterly*, July 11, 1981, 1214.

[125]American Electronics Association, "Not by Accident: Heroes of the 1981 Tax Bill," internal document.

[126]Michael Thoryn, "It's Taxes' Turn," *Nation's Business*, December 1980, 38.

[127]A. F. Ehrbar, "The Battle over Taxes," *Fortune*, April 19, 1982, 62.

tax position in early 1979. Under the prior depreciation system, each capital asset had an estimated useful life; a corporation would take a depreciation deduction gradually, over the course of the life. The new Accelerated Cost Recovery System, or "10-5-3," replaced these asset lives with three general categories. Business could write off real estate in ten years, most equipment in five, and trucks in three. The shape of the bill represented an effort to incorporate something for everyone. The "5" in "10-5-3" greatly benefited manufacturers of products such as steel, airplanes, and paper products, since previous asset lives in these categories were ten or fifteen years. The ten-year depreciation of commercial buildings made real estate investments extremely attractive. Small business liked the compromise because the new depreciation system was extremely simple, and they could depreciate trucks more quickly. Also, wholesalers and retailers could depreciate their warehouses more rapidly. Finally, small businesses agreed to support "10-5-3" if the new system of depreciation changes was linked with substantial cuts in the individual rates, which applied to the vast majority of small businesses.[128]

With such widespread endorsement from the business community, it is not surprising that the Reagan administration picked accelerated cost recovery (a version of "10-5-3") as the centerpiece of its corporate tax cut. As a high-ranking official in the administration later explained: "It was a ready-made lobby with a ready-made plan. Eighty percent of the business lobbyists would go along."[129]

Nonetheless, significant business groups were dissatisfied with accelerated cost recovery as the basis for a corporate compromise. Some small business representatives complained that the compromise failed to recognize their specific concerns. The National Small Business Association broke with the National Federation of Independent Business and rejected "10-5-3," which held very little for its constituents.[130] Independent oil companies doubted that accelerated depreciation would have much benefit for them, since depreciation would fail to account for intangible drilling costs.[131] Some high-technology business managers doubted that

---

[128]Edward Knight, *The Reagan Strategy: Implications for Small Business* (Washington, D.C.: Congressional Research Service, 1981), 1137.
[129]Interview with high-ranking administration official.
[130]Small Business National Unity Council Testimony, *House Ways and Means Committee Hearings: Tax Aspects of the President's Economic Program,* part 2 (Washington, D.C.: Government Printing Office, 1981), 1137.
[131]Interview with oil trade representative.

the decrease in asset depreciation lives from seven years to five would really help their industries.[132] Finally, although financial interests supported savings incentives, they had nothing to gain from changes in the depreciation schedules and worried that Reagan's cuts in the personal income tax would give up too much revenue.[133]

Presidential leadership was a less important force in corporate taxation in 1981 than it had been in 1964. The task for the president was to preserve the fragile business unity established through corporate efforts: to keep corporate supporters focused on accelerated cost recovery and to keep other items reserved for a promised second-stage bill. The president also needed to keep corporate allies supportive of the individual tax cuts, regardless of whether spending cuts were made to balance the budget. Reagan's task was similar to Kennedy's before him, albeit on a much grander scale. Still, the cognitive leap for business in 1981 was not as great. Business was asked to sign onto a tax act that transferred resources to upper-class individuals and to corporations. Although business priorities varied and the deficits were threatening, the basic thrust of the legislation was consistent with prevailing corporate attitudes toward taxation.

Legislating the Economic Recovery Tax Act. President Reagan's proposed bill combined 30 percent across-the-board individual tax cuts with the "10-5-3" proposal. In April 1981 Rostenkowski, chair of the Ways and Means Committee, offered a Democratic alternative: a one-year tax cut with the individual reduction concentrated in the $20,000-to-$50,000 income bracket. Rostenkowski rejected "10-5-3" as discriminatory toward small, labor-intensive industries. Instead, he proposed a modest accelerated depreciation schedule coupled with research-and-development credits, individual retirement accounts, graduated income tax rates, and special tax credits on historic buildings.[134]

For a brief period of time, bipartisan compromise seemed possible.

[132]Ann Reilly, "What Business Wants from Reagan," *Dun's Review,* March 1981, 47.
[133]A group of trade associations—including the American Bankers Association, the Mortgage Bankers Association of America, the National Association of Mutual Savings Banks, and the U.S. League of Savings Institutions—wrote to the president urging caution in cutting personal taxes and reminding the president that exacerbated budget deficits could lead to higher interest rates and inflation. They were joined by two housing groups: the National Association of Realtors and the National Association of Home Builders. *Tax Aspects of the President's Economic Program,* 699–700.
[134]Dale Tate, "Reagan and Rostenkowski Modify Tax Cut Proposals to Woo Conservative Votes," *Congressional Quarterly,* June 6, 1981, 979.

The White House asked Conable to approach Rostenkowski with a deal: the Democrats would propose "10-5-3" and a two-year personal tax cut that would lower the top rate from 70 to 50 percent. In return, the president would let Congress handle the second-stage bill. But the effort failed. Democratic insiders say the problem was that the Democrats were forced to negotiate with Don Regan but that Regan was not authorized to make deals. The White House expected Rostenkowski to state his bottom line to Regan and then wait until Regan reported back to Jim Baker and the president. Republicans claim that the problem lay with a split Democratic leadership.[135]

After the hopes of compromise evaporated, a bidding war began. On June 4, Reagan offered a new proposal: curbing the ACRS, liberalizing estate and gift taxes, extending the exemption from the windfall profits tax for small royalty owners, and making permanent the exclusion on dividends and interest. These were concessions to the southern Democrats, whose constituents were mainly in farming and the oil industry.[136]

The corporate lobbyists who had worked so hard to bring about the ACRS went ballistic. Richard Rahn accused the administration of a "breach of faith." Members of the Carlton Group met with Jim Baker, Elizabeth Dole, and Don Regan to demand a policy reversal. After the emotionally charged meeting, the Treasury agreed to a compromise: a staged implementation of the full ACRS benefits. The press reported that CEOs descended on Washington to demand that the president reinstate the cuts, but corporate lobbyists remember things differently. The White House spent the weekend contacting CEOs of major corporations to gain support for the altered version; the CEOs, in turn, instructed their Washington representatives to support the president. One lobbyist remarked, "If the CEOs had been brought in earlier by the president, we wouldn't have gotten anything back at all."[137]

June saw a series of rapid concessions to special interests on both sides. Rostenkowski agreed to include the all-savers provision to satisfy the National Association of Home Builders. Although the proposal ultimately made it into the Republican version as well, the home builders was one of the few trade associations to remain loyal to the Democrats.[138]

---

[135]Interviews with members of Congress and staff.
[136]Tate, "Reagan and Rostenkowski Modify Tax Cut Proposals."
[137]Interviews with various administration and industry participants.
[138]Interview.

The lobby for high-tech industries persuaded Senate Finance Committee Republicans to provide a research-and-development tax credit. The Democrats in the House Ways and Means Committee soon followed suit. One hundred and sixty members of the American Electronics Association came to Washington and met with eighty-three individuals in the two branches of government, and the administration subsequently allowed stock options to be included in the Senate Finance Committee bill. The journalist Jack Robertson observed, "Elated electronic industry officials last week watched as rival Democratic and Republican tax bills vied to offer the most research and development tax incentives, accelerated depreciation, and lowest corporate income tax rates."[139] Politicians on both sides offered refundability schemes to the "sick six" of basic industry: steel, autos, railroads, paper, airlines, and mining.

Meanwhile, independent oil producers, who had originally supported the president's two-stage process, began to lobby for the repeal of the windfall profits act. They decided that if others were getting provisions originally designated for the second bill, the oil industry should press harder as well. At a June 25 strategy meeting of the Independent Petroleum Association of America (IPAA), participants expressed the fear that their previous "attitude of cooperation" had been "purposely misinterpreted as acceptance of the status quo." They decided that a "geographically representative group of independents" should meet with the Senate Finance Committee to increase the visibility of the industry. But that meeting failed to satisfy them, and they then met with the president himself on July 9. Reagan made a strong case for loyalty: "You're used to having me ask for money, but this time I want blood."[140] Ultimately, however, the Ways and Means Committee adopted a set of oil provisions designed to woo southern Democrats away from the president. The administration later caved in as well. The lobbyists were surprised that they got so much of what they had demanded.[141]

In a final desperate move to cover all the bases, the administration contacted the Securities Industry Association (SIA) during the last week of the legislative battle. Members of the industry had been quite wary of the individual cuts and felt that the corporate cuts offered little of value for them. They won a deal. The industry promised to go out and

[139]Jack Robertson, "Industry Applauds Both Democratic and GOP Tax Cut Bills," *Electronic News*, July 27, 1981, 8.
[140]Interviews; *Petroleum Independent*, October 1981, 10–15.
[141]Interview with industry representative.

"burn the telephone wires" generating support for the administration in return for the lowering of the holding period on capital gains from one year to six months. The *Wall Street Journal* reported that in five days, the industry made twenty thousand calls to members of Congress.[142]

The Republicans won the bidding war, passing the bill with 48 Democratic defections in the House and 37 in the Senate.[143] The final legislation scaled back the accelerated cost recovery provision slightly to pay for all the new provisions. But this adjustment was grossly inadequate; the bill promised to lose more revenue than ever.

The business mobilization strategy. The Reagan administration carried out a highly sophisticated corporate-mobilization effort that went beyond simply offering concessions to individual trade associations. The administration developed a business tax steering committee to lead in generating support for the president's bill. The committee had computerized records of sympathetic business managers and their ties to swing members of Congress.

The Reagan strategy of business mobilization had several effects. First, it expedited the passage of the bill. The core of corporate supporters helped to engineer the Republican victory. On July 27 the president appeared on television to request support for the cuts. At the end of the speech he called on the American people to contact members of Congress and demand the Republican version. During the next forty-eight hours, key congressional offices were flooded with telephone calls favoring the president's program. The administration claimed that this represented mass support for its agenda. But individuals involved on the corporate side report that there was a concerted effort by the business community, led by the administration, to "tie up the lines" of targeted congressional offices, preventing the expression of opposing views.[144]

Second, business mobilization influenced the content of the bill. The partisan bidding war for corporate support gave business an inordinate amount of influence. The initial high point in corporate unity enabled business to forge a class agenda in support of the "10-5-3" proposal and thus set the agenda for corporate taxation. As the partisan compe-

[142]Interviews; Tim Carrigton, "Sold Short? Many Wall Streeters Regret They Helped Reagan Pass Tax Bill," *Wall Street Journal,* September 11, 1981, 1, 20.

[143]"Reagan Economic Plan Nears Enactment," *Congressional Quarterly,* August 1, 1981, 1371.

[144]Interviews with industry representatives and members of the administration.

tition for business support increased, business unity began to disintegrate, and business groups competed to reap the rewards of political conflict. As the broad consensus gave way to interbusiness bickering, the corporate actors succeeded both in continuing to dominate the broad outlines of the debate and in winning their own particular concessions. Thus, Reagan had tried, like Kennedy and Johnson before him, to aggregate corporate interests around his proposal and to use this societal pressure to discipline Congress. But where Kennedy and Johnson had succeeded, Reagan failed because both Democrats and Republicans in Congress courted business, and this conflict erased the earlier business unity.

Third, the business mobilization strategy influenced corporate preferences. In a way, the impact was less in 1981 than it had been earlier. Businesses did not have to stretch too far to support the corporate provisions in the Economic Recovery Tax Act of 1981 because they shared the assumptions of neoclassical economics. Business was naturally predisposed to back the version of the Republican Party, since most sectors of business had supported Reagan during the 1980 election. One oil lobbyist explained, "You dance with him that brung ya."[145] But Reagan had persuaded business to accept the rationale for the radical supply-side individual cuts. The willingness to countenance huge budget deficits deviated sharply from the balanced-budget mentality of an earlier age. Even though years of Keynesian fiscal theory had eroded this balanced-budget mentality, the Reagan cuts were of an entirely different order of magnitude. The corporate and public acceptance of supply-side theory was a remarkable leap of faith.

TAX REFORM AND THE POSTINDUSTRIAL ORDER

Despite the overwhelming triumph of laissez-faire values in the Economic Recovery Tax Act of 1981 (ERTA), by the mid-1980s a new growth strategy guided public and private policymakers in the writing of tax reform. Almost as soon as Congress passed ERTA, critics began to attack its accumulation-oriented measures as ineffective and inequitable. The Tax Equity and Fiscal Responsibility Act (TEFRA) partially repudiated ERTA by enacting the largest peacetime revenue increase in

---

[145]Interview with industry lobbyist.

the postwar period and scaling back the corporate provisions considerably.[146] But the Tax Reform Act of 1986 transformed "partial repudiation" into "paradigm shift." It rejected the capital-intensive investment measures developed under both the domesticated Keynesian and the supply-side growth strategies. Instead, it embraced tax neutrality and a growth strategy that emphasized investment in human resources and knowledge-intensive sectors.

The Tax Reform Act of 1986 both reduced vertical progressivity in the nominal rates and greatly increased horizontal equity. On the one hand, profound cuts in the individual rates greatly scaled back nominal progressivity. Before tax reform, there were eleven rates, ranging from 11 to 50 percent; the tax act condensed the bracket into two and lowered the top rate to 28 percent (with a 33 percent surtax on some income). The act increased the standard deduction and personal exemption, which removed some six million individuals at the lower end from the tax system altogether. The act also lowered the corporate rate from 46 to 34 percent.[147]

On the other hand, the act eliminated or scaled back many of the selective tax incentives that had upset horizontal equity for many years. The major corporate provisions were the investment tax credit, accelerated depreciation allowances, passive loss deductions, and the differential treatment of capital gains.[148] The bill significantly shifted the balance between the individual and the corporate burden. Some estimates held that the measure would transfer about $120 billion to firms and return the corporate share to pre-1980 levels.[149] Thus wealthy individuals might benefit as "heads of household," but they would suffer as "leaders of industry."

The macroeconomic context. A confluence of macroeconomic conditions provides the backdrop for the repudiation of both the supply-side tax cuts and the investment incentives. First, as Eugene Steuerle points out

[146]*Ways and Means Committee Hearings: Administration's Fiscal Year 1983 Economic Program,* part 1 (Washington, D.C.: Government Printing Office, 1982).

[147]David Rosenbaum, "Sweeping Tax Bill Is Voted by House, Senate Acts Next," *New York Times,* September 26, 1986, D1, 17.

[148]David Rosenbaum, "Senate, 74–23, Votes Tax Bill, Widest Revisions in Forty Years Cut Rates, Curb Deductions," *New York Times,* September 28, 1986, 1, 34.

[149]Andrew B. Lyon, "Tax Reform and Economic Productivity: An Overview of the Goals and Results of the Tax Reform Act of 1986," *National Productivity Review,* Autumn 1987, 360.

in this volume, there was a significant change in the general fiscal climate. Since World War II, fiscal slack in an easy financing era had permitted a non–zero-sum attitude toward tax decisions.[150] The budget deficits created by ERTA made policymakers much more cognizant of the costs to their revenue-losing provisions. In a time of retrenchment, tax expenditures are much harder to justify.[151] The indexing of tax brackets to inflation in 1981 also meant that hidden tax increases, achieved as individuals were pushed into higher brackets, were no longer possible.[152]

Second, the investment incentives themselves seemed to perform less well than they had earlier. The remarkable tax transfers to the business community as a consequence of ERTA had not restored economic prosperity. Evidence also suggested that the investment incentives changed the composition of, rather than increased the total amount of, capital.[153] Indeed, tax breaks redistributed the tax burden among industrial sectors in a way that disproportionately benefited large corporations.[154] Firms with capital-intensive production processes, growing markets, and large-scale operations were major beneficiaries of tax incentives. Using 1975 data, Michael Lugar found the "receipt of new tax credits per dollar of net income" to be as low as $.0004 in the food and food-processing industry and as high as $0.71 in the lumber and wood products industry.[155]

The fact that a firm's tax burden was affected by its ability to use the selective tax incentives meant that ERTA had produced a significant change in the distribution of the corporate income tax. By 1980 capital-intensive manufacturers were paying much lower effective tax rates than labor-intensive manufacturing and service sectors. *Tax Notes* surveyed the 1980 tax burden of major corporations in different industrial sectors and found the following: metal manufacturing had an effective tax rate of 11.8 percent; paper and wood products, 11.1 percent; transportation, 11.9 percent; utilities, 8.5 percent; and chemical firms, 8.3 percent. By

[150]C. Eugene Steuerle, chapter 8, this volume.

[151]R..Kent Weaver, *Automatic Government: The Politics of Indexation* (Washington, D.C.: Brookings Institution, 1988).

[152]Steuerle, *The Tax Decade.*

[153]Michael Lugar, "Tax Incentives and Tax Inequities," *Journal of Contemporary Studies,* Spring 1982, 33–47; Robert Eisner and M. I. Nadiri, "Investment Behavior and Neoclassical Theory," *Review of Economics and Statistics* 50 (1986): 369–83.

[154]Alan Feld, *Tax Policy and Corporate Concentration* (Lexington, Mass.: Lexington, 1982).

[155]Lugar, "Tax Incentives and Tax Inequities," 36–37.

comparison, labor-intensive sectors were much higher: publishing and printing, 38.2 percent; food processing, 36.3 percent; food retailers, 31.5 percent; and nonfood retail, 27.2 percent. High-technology firms, also labor-intensive, paid high effective tax rates as well: electronic and appliance firms, 33.5 percent; instrument companies, 39.7 percent; and office equipment, 23.0 percent.[156] Critics worried that the investment incentives created a tendency toward overinvestment (inappropriately replacing individuals with capital) and overinnovation (the excessively rapid introduction of new technology).[157]

Third, the capital-intensive manufacturing sectors that had benefited the most from the old order were now faltering. Imports as a percentage of the GNP originating in the U.S. manufacturing sector increased from 13.9 percent in 1969 to 37.8 percent in 1979 and to 44.7 percent in 1986.[158] Between 1979 and 1984, steel companies laid off 45 percent of their work force. Exports of construction equipment dropped 63 percent from 1981 to 1983; machine tools dropped 60 percent in this period.[159] Postindustrial prophets claimed that new jobs in the future would come from rapidly growing, sunrise industries and questioned the special incentives for basic manufacturing.[160]

Ideas and interests within government. The combination of the end of easy financing, budget deficits, faulty performance of growth incentives, and problems with international competition made the investment-oriented credits and deductions harder to justify. Growing middle-class criticism of the inequity of these and other "tax expenditures" made

---

[156]Tax Analysts, "Effective Corporate Tax Rates in 1980," *Tax Notes,* special supplement (Arlington, Va.: Tax Analysts, 1981).

[157]Bowles, Gordon, and Weisskopf, *Beyond the Waste Land;* Keith Schneider, "Services Hurt by Technology," *New York Times,* June 29, 1987, D1, 6; Stephen Roach, "America's Technology Dilemma: A Profile of the Information Economy," *Morgan Stanley Special Economic Study,* April 22, 1987, 1–2; Robert Brenner, "The International Crisis and U.S. Decline" (paper presented at "Seminar on State and Capitalism since 1800," Cambridge, Massachusetts, October 2, 1990), 2–3. Even the *Harvard Business Review* began to worry about the human climate in which equipment is introduced. See Wickham Skinner, "The Focused Factory," *Harvard Business Review* 52 (1974): 113–14; Steven Wheelwright and Robert Hayes, "Competing through Manufacturing," *Harvard Business Review* 63 (1985): 99–109; Robert Hayes and William Abernathy, "Managing Our Way to Economic Decline," *Harvard Business Review* 58 (1980): 76–77.

[158]Harrison and Bluestone, *The Great U-Turn,* 9.

[159]Charles Alexander, "That Threatening Trade Gap," *Time* 9 (July 1984): 63.

[160]George Silvestri and John Likasiewicz, *Monthly Labor Review: U.S. Department of Labor Statistics,* September 1987, 49–50.

them attractive targets for tax reform. But new ideas about economic growth also stoked the fires of tax reform.

Two strands of economic thought lay behind the tax reform act. First, neoclassical admonitions against government micromanagement of the economy resurfaced. Treasury staff, for example, worried that the investment incentives distorted capital spending decisions. Accelerated cost recovery applied the same rate of depreciation to assets with very different useful lives. "This created incentives to buy different types of equipment for tax rather than economic reasons."[161] Tax reform sought to achieve neutrality, or a "level playing field," for investment capital. The supply-side economist Richard Darman wrote, "A depreciation system that is nearly neutral across classes of investment will lead to a more efficient allocation of capital."[162]

Changes within government accelerated the movement toward reduced micromanagement and greater tax neutrality. The proliferation of units responsible for economic policy had greatly increased the level of technical expertise within the state. But at the same time, multiple jurisdictional units made it much harder to exert leadership and to make the tough judgment calls necessary when using selective incentives to direct economic growth.[163] Automatic decision-making mechanisms and reduced discretionary power seemed appropriate to an era of declining political leadership.[164] Steuerle suggests that the broad principles of taxation used in 1986 reflected this changed political climate.[165]

Second, a shift in thinking about national investment strategy also furthered tax reform. An emerging "postindustrial" growth strategy attacked the fundamental emphasis on capital-intensive manufacturing, suggested that investment in human resources was also important to growth, and recognized the importance of services and knowledge-intensive sectors in the future economy.[166] To postindustrial strategists, tax reform could promote a more efficient use of capital stock. Although

[161]Steuerle, *The Tax Decade,* 111.
[162]"What Tax Reform Really Means," *Business Week,* June 17, 1985, 129.
[163]Sundquist, *The Decline and Resurgence of Congress.*
[164]Weaver, *Automatic Government.*
[165]C. Eugene Steuerle, chapter 8, this volume.
[166]Piore and Sabel describe this postindustrial growth strategy. This strategy would shift production processes from Fordist mass production to "flexible specialization" producing small-batch specialty products. Investment strategies would, therefore, also change from an emphasis on capital-intensive investment to investment in human resources and knowledge-intensive industries. Michael Piore and Charles Sabel, *The Second Industrial Divide* (New York: Basic Books, 1984).

traditional avenues to growth rested on increasing the capital stock of the economy, an alternative route would be to use the stock more effectively and revive investment in human resources.[167]

To these ends, the President's Commission on Industrial Competitiveness recommended restructuring the tax code to equalize investment in physical and human capital.[168] The commission proposed keeping one major tax incentive, the research-and-development credit, to help shift investment into new sectors. Darman wrote, "With the elimination of most other credits, the research and development tax credit will be more attractive, and increased R & D will improve productivity."[169]

Administration supply-siders also favored tax reform. They saw in it an opportunity to continue cutting taxes. Regan and others did not like the reduction of investment incentives for business, but they were very supportive of the reformers' attack on progressivity in the individual rates. "Tax reform became a code word among conservatives for tax reduction. This gave the thing enormous impetus."[170]

Politics, as well as ideas, guided the administration toward tax reform. Over a period of time, loopholes in the tax code had allowed individuals and companies with similar incomes to pay vastly different taxes. The journalists Jeffrey Birnbaum and Alan Murray write, "In part, the deterioration of the tax code had gone so far that something had to be done. The American people were disgusted with the system, and that disgust represented a latent political force waiting to be tapped."[171] The economist Robert Kuttner suggests that the Republicans sought to harness this discontent and achieve a critical realignment, shifting mass allegiance to the Republican Party and cementing the Reagan legacy.[172] The political scientists Martin Shefter and Benjamin Ginsberg agree that "yuppies" were a critical swing vote: tax reform benefiting middle-class professionals was an attempt to establish a durable link between these groups and the Republican Party.[173] A January 1985 poll showed 75

[167]Lyon, "Tax Reform and Economic Productivity," 360.
[168]President's Commission on Industrial Competitiveness, *Global Competition: The New Reality* (Washington, D.C.: Government Printing Office, 1985), 28, 35.
[169]"What Tax Reform Really Means," *Business Week,* June 17, 1985, 129.
[170]Interview with participant (November 1989).
[171]Jeffrey H. Birnbaum and Alan S. Murray, *Showdown at Gucci Gulch: Lawmakers, Lobbyists, and the Unlikely Triumph of Tax Reform* (New York: Random House, 1987), 17–22.
[172]Robert Kuttner, *The Economic Illusion: False Choices between Prosperity and Social Justice* (Boston: Houghton Mifflin, 1984).
[173]Martin Shefter and Benjamin Ginsberg, "Institutionalizing the Reagan Regime," in *Do*

percent agreeing that the "present tax system benefits the rich and is unfair to the ordinary working man or woman."[174]

The postindustrial growth strategy associated with tax reform also appealed to the Reagan administration as a way to compete with Democratic ideas. When ERTA failed to revive the economy, the Democrats sought an idea to recapture the economic agenda and came up with economic restructuring through industrial policy.[175] The Republicans saw that this Democratic concept addressed the transformation of the American economy and realized that they needed a parallel idea to appeal to their constituents in high-tech and service sectors.[176] Republicans rejected industrial policy as entailing excessive government intervention and distorting markets.[177] Tax reform, however, might solve the problem equally well by terminating skewed investment incentives and redistributing resources toward rapidly growing sectors while minimizing state intervention and the targeting problems of industrial policy.[178]

Many Democrats preferred deficit reduction and industrial policy to tax reform, but they also signed on to the tax agenda. They liked loophole closing and the economic critique of investment incentives. Also, when the Republicans made tax reform a major policy issue, the Democrats wanted to retain a partisan claim to a potentially realigning issue.[179] To some extent the Democrats lost control of the tax agenda when Democratic presidential candidate Walter Mondale made his famous prediction in 1984 that both parties would raise taxes, but the party worked to regain its status as a player on tax reform.

Pattern of business interests. The kind of tax reform proposed in 1986 would increase the aggregate corporate tax burden, but some business

---

Elections Matter?, ed. Benjamin Ginsberg and Alan Stone (Armonk, N.Y.: M. E. Sharpe, 1986), 193.

[174]Survey by ABC News and *Washington Post* (January 11–16, 1985), *Public Opinion*, February–March 1985, 23.

[175]Felix Rohatyn, *The Twenty-Year Century* (New York: Random, 1983), 129–33. Advocates of industrial policy also recommended tax reform; however, this was a sideshow to the main program. I am indebted to Jim Shoch for clarifying the connection between the Democrats' industrial policy agenda and tax reform.

[176]Bruce Stokes, "Conservatives Eying Tax Reform as Step to Pro-Business Federal Economic Role," *National Review*, December 1, 1985, 2298–2301.

[177]Kenneth McLennan, "The Case for a Non-targeted Approach to Industrial Strategy," in *Revitalizing the U.S. Economy*, ed. F. Stevens Redburn, Terry Buss, and Larry Ledebur (New York: Praeger, 1986), 52–54.

[178]Ibid., 46–47.

[179]Interview (November 1989).

sectors endorsed the new system of taxation and its underlying growth strategy. This support, not surprisingly, came from the parts of the business community most discriminated against by the old investment incentives. High-technology, small business, and service sectors believed that they would benefit from the tax act through the corporate rate cuts. The high-technology industry's interest stemmed from its belief that the ACRS discriminated in favor of heavy machinery. Products and equipment become obsolete more quickly in high technology; the ACRS only marginally quickened the write-off period. This sector of business was a primary supporter of the research-and-development incentives.[180]

Small business and service firms hoped that a more neutral tax system would increase investment in their firms and would generate more disposable income for consumers.[181] This bill was "pro-consumption and anti-capital investment," a bill "destined to accelerate the nation's already powerful shift from a manufacturing to a service economy."[182] A study found that 60 percent of the small business firms sampled thought that tax reform would *not* lead to higher taxes. Of the small manufacturing and construction firms in the sample, 54 percent feared a tax increase, as opposed to only 25 percent of the service companies.[183] Hardwich Simmons, vice-chair of Shearson Lehman Brothers, said of the Senate Finance Committee bill, "If the bill becomes law as it is, we're in fat city."[184]

Although these sectors eventually decided that a more neutral tax system would serve them well, they came to this position only gradually. One participant explained that accepting an increase in corporate taxation required a "paradigm shift."[185] This shift in thinking began in 1982 during the legislation of TEFRA to make up for some of the deficit losses of ERTA. Low taxpayers from aging industrial sectors proposed a surtax to gather revenue on the corporate side. High taxpayers responded by supporting a minimum tax and by forming the Coalition to Reduce High Effective Tax Rates. The administration pushed the coa-

[180]American Electronics Association, "A Perspective on the 1986 Tax Reform Act," October 10, 1986, internal document.
[181]American Retail Federation, "President Reagan Unveils Tax Reform, Retailing Supports Major Features," *Federation Report* 12, no. 21 (June 3, 1985): 1.
[182]Ann Reilly, "A Tax Bill That Hits Investment," *Fortune*, December 23, 1985, 106.
[183]Bill Liebtag, "Capital Formation by Small Business," *Journal of Accountancy*, June 1987, 91.
[184]Anna Gifelli Isgro, "The Tax Upheaval: What It Means for Business," *Fortune*, June 9, 1986, 18.
[185]Interview with small business lobbyist.

lition either to support or at least to remain neutral on the revenue-raising tax increase. Participants recall that this was the first time they had actively tried to raise someone else's taxes.[186] Although the coalition became dominant between 1982 and 1986, the members had formed a new identity as a group of high taxpayers.

Capital-intensive manufacturing sectors and real estate sectors had the most to lose from the new approach to growth, since they had been the biggest beneficiaries under the old subregime. Lobbyists for capital-intensive industries attacked the new assumptions about growth under-lying tax reform and warned that competitiveness would suffer. Groups such as the Basic Industry Association, the American Council for Capital Formation, and the Coalition for Jobs, Growth, and International Com-petitiveness worked to build support for policies to foster capital-intensive investment. For example, CEOs of fifteen large capital-intensive companies paid $40,000 to belong to the Coalition for Jobs, organized by Charls Walker.[187] Real estate interests also had much to lose from two aspects of reform: the second-home interest deduction and passive loss rules. The National Realty Committee organized three hundred large developers and syndicators to fight reform.

The task for presidential leadership in 1986 was to persuade those most discriminated by the old order to support a tax increase on their fellow business managers. In addition, the administration hoped to sell the much lower rates as an attractive substitute for the threatened in-vestment incentives.

Legislating the tax reform act. In 1981 both political parties had en-dorsed the broad outlines of a growth strategy and had then engaged in a bidding war to take credit for its implementation. In 1986 the old enemies were eager to avoid making the same mistake, and so they en-gaged in an impressive feat of bipartisan cooperation. A significant por-tion of the business community joined the effort. But this spirit of bipartisan cooperation emerged only gradually.

The first reform proposal produced by the Treasury Department was largely a product of experts. Secretary Regan had a limited understand-ing of tax issues and left most decisions up to his staff. The staff knew that the proposal might end up as a study but welcomed the chance to

[186]Interview.
[187]Isgro, "The Tax Upheaval," 20.

"fill the hopper with good ideas."[188] Before the proposal was unveiled, Treasury officials met with industry representatives to urge their support; but the result was very different from what the Treasury wanted. The American Electronics Association, for example, told the *Wall Street Journal* that the plan would sap "the very lifeblood of America's high risk, high-technology companies."[189] President Reagan immediately distanced himself from the proposal, saying that he would "listen to the comments and suggestions of all Americans" before offering his own plan.[190]

At this point a fortunate and fortuitous occurrence changed the course of tax reform. Chief of Staff Jim Baker and Secretary of the Treasury Don Regan traded jobs. Baker wanted to become a principal in an important substantive area within the administration. His lateral move to the Treasury was critical to tax reform because Baker understood the distribution of power in Washington and would make the political compromises necessary for the proposal to work. Indeed, Baker spent his early months at the Treasury meeting with potential business allies to garner support for a new version of reform. The Treasury reinstated the capital gains differential for high-tech firms, took out the passive loss provisions to appeal to real estate interests, and reestablished the graduated corporate income tax for small business. One person explained that Treasury I was a trial balloon; Treasury II was a working proposal.[191]

Rostenkowski then enthusiastically took up tax reform. He was hardly anyone's idea of a reformer, but the Democrats wanted to stay on top of a potentially realigning issue, and Rostenkowski looked at the measure as a way to build his career.[192] An important Ways and Means staff member also credited Chairman Rostenkowski's participation with the Republicans to his experience:

Rostenkowski's political record was that when he did stuff with the president, he won; but when he fought, he lost. He likes to be at the center of things, likes

---

[188]Timothy J. Conlan, Margaret T. Wrightson, and David R. Beam, *Taxing Choices; The Politics of Tax Reform* (Washington, D.C.: Congressional Quarterly Press, 1990), 57–58.

[189]Laurie McGinley and Alan Murray, "High-Tech Firms Cool on Tax Plan," *Wall Street Journal,* December 6, 1984, 64.

[190]Pamela Fessler, "Treasury Tax Overhaul Excites Little Interest," *Congressional Quarterly,* December 1, 1984, 3016.

[191]Interviews with representatives in industry and government.

[192]Conlan, Wrightson, and Beam, *Taxing Choices,* 91.

to win. So Rostenkowski had a choice to either say "no" which would take him out of the action, or to be the guy that did tax reform. [He believed he could] get the president into the pit, and figured that Reagan was so dumb that he could get Reagan to do what he wanted.[193]

The administration and House leadership differed on the best strategy for passage. Baker wanted Rostenkowski to take a blitzkrieg approach (like that used to garner support for the Omnibus Budget Reconciliation Act of 1981) and to construct a precooked deal similar to the bipartisan strategy used in legislating the 1982 tax act. Baker began secret meetings with the tax reformers in Congress to explore possibilities for compromise.[194]

Rostenkowski resisted. He wanted to draft a bill more favorable to the middle class and to explore more carefully the interests of his committee.[195] He tried to get the committee to make all changes revenue neutral and to work from the staff option instead of from existing law (both strategies later used by Senator Bob Packwood), but he could not get acquiescence. Business groups that opposed reform began assaulting each of the reform proposals. Both the Chamber of Commerce and the National Association of Manufacturers lobbied vigorously against the Ways and Means version. President Reagan remained noticeably silent, although his support could have bolstered the Ways and Means effort; the House Republicans threatened to revolt.[196] Only after the business supporters of the proposal began a major grass-roots campaign did the president begin pushing House Republicans to support the bill at least until the Senate took it up.

Senate Finance Committee Chair Bob Packwood (D-Oreg.) was also no tax reformer. Known as "Mr. Packman," the chairman had received over $6 million in campaign contributions between 1981 and 1986.[197] Packwood began reviewing the proposal by making deals with precisely those interests most threatened by the measure: timber, oil and gas, and basic manufacturing. Packwood admitted that his plan set out to reverse the "favorable treatment" accorded wholesalers and retailers in the pres-

---

[193]Interview with Ways and Means Committee staff (November 1989).
[194]Conlan, Wrightson, and Beam, *Taxing Choices*, 92.
[195]Interview with Ways and Means Committee staff.
[196]American Retail Federation, "Reagan's Efforts Result in House Tax Action," *Federation Report* 12, no. 58 (December 23, 1985): 2.
[197]Birnbaum and Murray, *Showdown at Gucci Gulch*, 182.

ident's and the Ways and Means bills.[198] To raise revenue, Packwood suggested an entirely new tax constructed around denying deductions for federal excise taxes and tariffs. The Basic Industry Association testified in favor. But representatives of the wholesalers and retailers hit the ceiling. Some believed that Packwood was "deliberately out to get them."[199]

Packwood's patchwork strategy failed to produce committee support for the markup legislation. A Senate Finance Committee aide remarked, "Senator Packwood tried to get rewarded business groups to help keep the bill on track, but they just weren't there for him."[200]

On April 18, 1986, Packwood adjourned the markup session indefinitely and went out for a now famous, beery "two-pitcher" lunch with his chief aide, Bill Diefenderfer. In a moment of daring, the two decided to go the radical route. If they set rates low enough, they might conquer the political constraints that plagued them. Packwood asked Dave Brockway, chief of the Joint Tax Committee, to develop a proposal.[201] The chairman reconvened the Finance Committee and presented the new, revised version as "Brockway's plan," in part to distance himself from the radical measure and in part to give the proposal the credibility accorded to joint committee documents. The Finance Committee members cautiously warmed to the low-rate idea. Senator Malcolm Wallop (R-Wyo.) remarked, "This is closer to real reform; maybe I can do this."[202]

Packwood put together a core group of bipartisan Finance Committee senators who supported reform. To belong to the core group, a senator had to promise not to offer amendments on the Senate floor. The group was used to lobby other senators; Packwood coordinated its activities with those of the business coalition.

The business mobilization strategy. Scholars have made much of the relative state autonomy in the legislation of the tax reform act. Timothy Conlan and his collaborators emphasized the role of Treasury Depart-

---

[198]American Retail Federation, "Packwood Takes Aim at Tax Provisions Impacting Retailers," *Federation Report* 13, no. 12 (March 31, 1986): 1.

[199]Interviews with Senate Finance Committee aides, Joint Committees staff, and business representatives.

[200]Interview.

[201]Interview with staff person.

[202]Interview with congressional staff.

ment professionals in setting the agenda for tax reform.[203] Steuerle (the economic coordinator of the Treasury's effort and, later, deputy assistant secretary of the Treasury for tax analysis) argued that this early staff dominance allowed for a more consistent plan.[204] Indeed, the Treasury staff may well account for the broad vision of the act.

At the same time, it is important to remember that both Democrats and Republicans worked closely with business allies to secure passage of the act and that business support for the reform package proved to be significant. A Senate Finance Committee staff member subsequently reflected, "Tax reform in 1986 was an oddball thing: it shifted the tax burden back onto business, but business was a core support for the '86 act."[205]

The primary business group was the Tax Reform Action Coalition (TRAC), composed of firms and associations from high-technology, wholesale, retail, food-processing, and other small business sectors. The group, an offspring of the Coalition to Reduce High Effective Tax Rates, formed at the behest of the administration, which wanted to cultivate private sector support. TRAC announced its existence shortly after the announcement of the Treasury II proposal and eventually had seven hundred groups from business and consumer causes.

The goal of the group was to keep the legislative eye focused on the prize of the corporate rate cuts. To belong to TRAC, members had to offer public support for lower tax rates. The group did not interfere in its members' negotiations over special favors, but it encouraged its members to restrain their demands for specific provisions. It warned that creating new loopholes might eventually lead to a restoration of high tax rates.[206]

The business coalition was extremely useful to the administration in getting the legislation passed. TRAC had an elaborate vote-counting operation. TRAC continuously tabulated congressional votes on a five-point scale that expressed degrees of support for the administration bill. The business group also lobbied for the bill at critical points. When the early silence by President Reagan inspired a House Republican revolt against the Ways and Means version of the bill, TRAC mobilized a

[203]Conlan, Wrightson, and Beam, *Taxing Choices*.
[204]Steuerle, *The Tax Decade*, 103.
[205]Interview (November 1989).
[206]Interview with participant (November 1989).

grass-roots campaign, encouraging every member of the group to contact legislators and create "a barrage of pressure from home."[207]

When the battle reached the Senate, TRAC joined a coalition called "15/27/33." Mary McAuliffe from the Commerce Department had organized this coalition, which consisted of business groups and "do-gooders" such as the League of Women Voters. The coalition required its members to make a commitment: if they lobbied against the bill, they had to leave the group. McAuliffe held daily briefings on the progress of the committee and gave participants assignments to contact senators. Usually she sent a "do-gooder" citizens group and a business representative to lobby together.[208]

Business allies also used the media and the press to build support for the legislation. TRAC staged events to try to influence public opinion. For example, just before the final vote, TRAC met with Rostenkowski and presented him with a sledgehammer "gavel." This gesture alluded to a session in which Rostenkowski had broken his gavel while calling the committee to order. TRAC's Lee Williams said that he hoped the gavel would help Rostenkowski "hammer out a fair and equitable tax reform bill."[209] TRAC organizers contacted the press during the House revolt to complain that the real problem with tax reform was not the president but rather Don Regan. One participant called Mrs. Reagan and urged her to intervene, arguing that Regan's influence was threatening her husband's most important second-term initiative as well as his place in history.[210]

The business coalition influenced the legislative outcome. Owing to the zero-sum nature of the tax legislation in 1986, fewer benefits were given to special interests. Policymakers and business allies alike sought to prevent the emergence of pork barrel politics that characterizes other tax acts. Yet business tax reformers won in a larger sense, in seeing the tax code redrawn to reflect the changing nature of the economy.

Finally, business mobilization in both 1982 and 1986 had an important influence on corporate preferences. One lobbyist remarked, "Tax reform represented a realignment of power in the business community."[211]

---

[207]Ibid.
[208]Interview with Senate aide (November 1989).
[209]American Retail Federation, "TRAC to Support Ways and Means Tax Reform Bill," *Federation Report* 12, no. 48 (December 9, 1985): 1–2.
[210]Interviews with industry participants (November 1989).
[211]Interview with industry representative (November 1989).

Business allies of tax reform joined the cause in part because they realized that the old system of growth incentives did not meet their needs. At the same time, a fundamentally different set of economic ideas helped them see their interests and the general interest in a new way. Because tax reform was linked to a more profound transformation of the economic system, the effort took on aspects of a mass social movement for participants in both government and business. One lobbyist recalled, "Tax reform was all consuming for many of us." Another high-technology industry representative expressed his view that tax reform was necessary to growth in a very different world:

Tax reform represented a big reset button: clearing the decks of political deals made by previous generations of lawmakers and allowing them to enter into new political deals with the new powers that be. The economy is changing and it is appropriate that there be adjustments in the fiscal system to reflect changes in the economy. . . . We got rid of a lot of preferences that were no longer justifiable and improved the overall legitimacy of the tax code.[212]

CONCLUSION

I have argued in this essay that economic ideas and broad growth strategies influence the expression of corporate interests. All too often we neglect the role of ideas in shaping business preferences. But ideas and macro-level growth projects matter to business strategies, just as they influence state actions. In the 1960s business managers came to support fiscal adjustments, even though the changes violated the balanced budget. In the 1980s corporate leaders became convinced that selective corporate tax incentives were both inequitable and bad for growth. Arguably, these policy positions were in the self-interest of their corporate supporters; nonetheless, they represented important deviations from past business positions. Corporate taxation reflects the distribution of power in society, but the battle over taxes is a battle of words and ideas as well as a battle of power.

Government policy entrepreneurs, especially within the presidency, have played a major role in shaping corporate preferences by reaching out to potential business allies. In their efforts to construct broad policy coalitions, government actors exposed an ever larger part of the business

---

[212]Interviews with industry representatives (November 1989).

community to the ideas that lent legitimacy to their policy initiatives. Thereby, policy entrepreneurs brought corporate representatives into the community of experts who define tax legislation. Scholars have often noted that with the decline of parties, the fragmentation of authority in Congress, and the increasing importance of corporate money in electoral politics, business interests have become an increasingly powerful force in the American political economy. But, in the tax sphere, business managers have contributed not only as agents of power but also as participants in tax policy networks. Corporate participants in these policy coalitions contribute ideas as well as money.

The organization of public-private coalitions around broad growth strategies helps explain dramatic shifts in corporate positions on taxation. Corporate actors have shifted their fiscal preferences as they have adapted to changing economic conditions and changing strategies of growth.

Does business sensitivity to economic ideas mean that we can stop worrying about the abuses of corporate power? Probably not. The good news about the role of ideas in organizing business coalitions is that corporate preferences seem more flexible than many assume. Activist presidents have used corporate allies to influence less flexible congressional opponents.

But there is also bad news about governance through business coalitions. First, although business groups endorse broad economic ideas, they usually extract a policy price. Coalition members demand concessions to their self-interests in exchange for their support of the big picture. The long-term decline in the corporate tax burden reflects this high cost.

Also, economic ideas often win support largely for political reasons. Political leaders may endorse economic ideas because the ideas give them a way to differentiate themselves from their electoral competitors. Corporate figures may embrace ideas because these ideas justify redistributing the tax burden in ways that benefit them. When politics determines growth strategies, a dysfunctional economic system can result.

Second, political leadership has become excessively dependent on corporate allies. Private sector groups have assumed many state functions such as drafting legislation, acting as legislative liaisons, and generating legitimation. Just as an artificial limb becomes almost a part of the living organism, business coalitions have become almost a part of the state apparatus. As private groups take on more state tasks, it may become increasingly difficult for normal channels to function without them.

Thus, the relationship between the public and the private spheres is complex. Explaining policy in terms of either state action or private interests misses the mutuality of interests between the two domains. Influence is reciprocal as actors on both sides struggle to construct the public agenda. In the struggle to determine our economic future, pockets of knowledge and power blur the boundaries between the public and the private.

Finally, business mobilization strategies have contributed to the widely reported increase in institutional capacity within the business community. Corporate America has responded to presidential outreach with an enormous investment in political resources. But although business may help government legislate, it cannot help the state govern. Business mobilization strategies have accelerated the appropriation of state power for private ambitions and aggravated the lopsided balance of class power.

IV

The next revenue regime

8

Financing the American state
at the turn of the century

C. EUGENE STEUERLE

OVERVIEW

As the next century approaches, how will the American state be financed? Will the American people be able to direct the resources of the state to the most pressing needs of society? Will the state be able to overcome long-standing fiscal problems, projected despite recent reform efforts to grow well into the next century? Although today's social environment and level of government activity differ greatly from the environments and activities of previous eras, fiscal crises and financing dilemmas are hardly new. The difficulty of making fiscal choices—of paying for what we want—is as old as the American state itself. One of the fundamental problems facing the new American government in 1789, for example, was the chaotic state of public debt; the prior government and various states under the Articles of Confederation had defaulted on their debts and were unable to make interest payments to lenders. The new government was severely constrained in trying to raise funds and to meet the demands placed on it.

Fiscal crises, however, are also times of opportunity.[1] In dealing with fiscal problems and dilemmas, government often adopts new standards, methods, and processes that guide the direction not just of fiscal policy but of government policy-making itself. Here I am referring to those broader directional reforms that transcend particular choices regarding levels and types of expenditures and taxes. Few directional changes were as defining as the law-making processes determined under the new con-

[1]W. Elliot Brownlee, chapter 2, this volume.

409

stitution or as determining for future fiscal and monetary policy as the new American government's simple standard that it would always pay its debts. For farsighted individuals like Alexander Hamilton, the fiscal problems of the American state became opportunities to set a new fiscal course for the nation and, in the process, to build a government with the flexibility and ability to meet future needs.[2] This essay is centered historically on the financing of the federal government during approximately the last half of the twentieth century. Its orientation, however, is toward the future; it is an attempt to discern, mainly through this recent history, some of the ways in which the nation might deal with, and perhaps move beyond, the current fiscal problems. Given the failure of economic prognosticators to "predict" or describe well even the recent past, a futuristic orientation runs the risk of lapsing into weakly informed speculation. I believe, however, that for those who listen well, a brief examination of how the American state was financed in recent decades provides many telling clues about its future. Sometimes these clues are fairly clear in indicating what the nation must do—or do differently than in the past—even if they are vague about the specifics of how this will be achieved.

The twentieth century as precedent. A common method of projecting from the past is to take historic trend lines and assume that these linear time paths will continue forever. Though useful at times, such an approach is naive at best and misleading if the slope of the lines, relative to such factors as size of the economy, cannot be maintained. Contrariwise, carrying forward trend lines can be more informative about what will *not* happen. That is, using a form of reductio ad absurdum, it is often possible to conclude how the future will differ from the past. If taxes have grown faster than the economy, they will not continue forever to do so. Health care will not absorb more than 100 percent of expenditures no matter what its past growth rate. And so forth. To paraphrase Herb Stein, my colleague in these studies, "What can't continue won't!"

As this nation and other industrial nations approach the twenty-first century, it is becoming increasingly obvious that the growth in domestic

---

[2]For a review of Hamilton's use of the debt-funding crisis as both an economic and a political opportunity, see Bruce F. Davie, "Monetizing the Post-Revolutionary American Economy: A Bicentennial View of Hamilton's Reports to the First Congress," *Proceedings of the Eighty-fourth Annual Conference, National Tax Association* (Salt Lake City: National Tax Association, 1992).

government efforts and the financing of those efforts were twentieth-century phenomena without precedence. Although century dividing lines are arbitrary—the latter part of the nineteenth century certainly provided a great deal of impetus for what was to follow—the twentieth century was by far the most expansionist ever for domestic policy within industrialized countries. The numbers, of course, force the conclusion. Within the United States, for instance, federal, state, and local expenditures as a percent of GNP equaled 7.7 percent in 1902; near the end of the century they equaled 41.8 percent. Revenues, in turn, were 7.8 percent of GNP in 1902; in the mid-1990s, they equaled 37.4 percent.[3]

For other parts of the industrialized world, government growth in the twentieth century was even more profound. By international standards, the United States was a laggard, partly because it nationalized and regulated fewer of its industries. Some Communist countries attempted at times to regulate, tax, or expend almost all aspects of their economies. Among European members of the Organization for Economic Cooperation and Development (OECD), spending and taxes average almost 11 percentage points of GDP higher than in the United States, with much of their growth coming in the last two or three decades.[4]

These numbers also suggest that the twentieth century will stand out prominently relative to future centuries, not just the past. Repeating twentieth-century growth rates for long is extraordinarily unlikely, and repeating them continually requires impossible scenarios such as govern-

---

[3]Although most numbers reported in this essay are reported as a percent of gross domestic product (GDP), the 1991 figures here were converted from GDP to gross national product (GNP) for comparison with available 1902 figures. All figures for 1991 are by fiscal year, but state and local fiscal years may not match precisely with the federal fiscal year. GNP figures for 1902 are by calendar year. Sources: U.S. Bureau of the Census (1975); U.S. Bureau of the Census (1993), vols. 1 and 2. The 1991 fiscal GNP was estimated by taking 1991 fiscal GDP and multiplying by the ratio of 1991 (quarter II) GNP to 1991 (quarter II) GNP. See *Economic Report of the President, 1994* (Washington, D.C.: Government Printing Office, 1994), 294.

[4]Total government outlays rose from 31.3 percent of GDP in 1960 to 47.6 percent in 1989 for OECD-Europe, as compared with 27 percent in 1960 and 36.1 percent in 1989 for the United States. Similarly, taxes for OECD-Europe rose from 24.2 percent of GDP in 1955 to 40.6 percent in 1992, as compared with 23.6 percent in 1955 and 29.4 percent in 1992 for the United States. Sources: Organization of Economic Cooperation and Development (OECD), *Revenue Statistics of OECD Member Countries, 1965–1993* (Paris: OECD, 1994), and OECD, *Historical Statistics, 1960–1990* (Paris: OECD, 1992).

Note that figures reported here are lower than earlier ones for total expenditures and revenues. Expenditures are higher than outlays because they include those expenditures that might be covered by fees, premiums, and other nontax sources of revenues used to reduce the measure of government outlays. Revenues, in turn, are higher than taxes primarily because the former include nontax sources and fees.

ment absorbing all of the economy and continuing to increase that share. Indeed, those countries that became the most socialized or Communist in this century are now moving in reverse fashion and attempting to privatize whole segments of their economies.

The uniqueness associated with the growth in government financing of domestic programs in the twentieth century has profound implications for how we think about and how we organize the financing of the American state. New initiatives in domestic policy cannot continually be financed through the type of growth available in the past. At the same time, government must be able to undertake initiatives that respond to the evolving needs and demands of its people.

Government shares and a growing economy. The issue of financing the American state is often confused by the related, but more political, debate over the size of government relative to the economy or, in shorthand, "government shares." This study can be understood only by placing that debate in perspective. Political philosophies or historical treatises that define themselves around perpetual trend lines usually run into the same reductio ad absurdum problem already noted. The extreme Communist-Socialist argument that history demanded 100 percent public ownership, for instance, made clear its own doom by its failure to answer the simple question, "Then what?" A similar objection can be made to a liberalism that defines itself naively by an ever growing government share of the economy, which is about as realistic as a conservatism that requires a never growing or always declining share.[5]

Although the debate over the government's share of the economy is an intense one, the new resources available to government over the long run will be determined primarily by economic growth, not by changes in the government's share of the economic pie. This can be seen most easily in the following example. Suppose a government's share of the national pie was either to increase from 40 percent to 50 percent or to decrease from 40 percent to 30 percent. Then the real resources available for it to spend per person would either increase or decrease by one-quarter. Now suppose that the economy maintains its long-term per

---

[5]Advocates of a higher share at the end of the twentieth century point out that industrialized countries in Europe have sustained larger governments and lower poverty rates, whereas opponents point to the much higher employment growth in the United States and its greater ability to innovate and to adapt to changing economic conditions.

capita growth rate of 1.75 percent and that the government's share of the total remains constant.[6] Then the real resources available for the government to spend per capita would grow by approximately one-quarter within thirteen years, would increase by one-half within twenty-three years, and would double within forty years.

A balanced and sustainable view about shares—one more supportable than perpetual trend lines both in theory and by historical evidence—is that size of government is related largely to influences on demand and supply of public goods and services relative to private goods and services. Demand for public goods and services in a growing economy, for instance, may be affected by levels of satiation obtained for the existing types of private goods and services or by lack of satiation for newer types. No citizen, of course, desires taxes for their own sake any more than a private purchaser seeks higher prices for a particular set of private goods and services. Taxes and prices represent the cost, not benefit, side of the calculation.

The actual amount of goods and services eventually supplied, in turn, is related to the ability of different providers, including government, to meet demands both efficiently and equitably. Interestingly enough, compared with developed countries, most developing countries have greater individual needs yet less capability to collect revenues. Tax systems depend on sophisticated private accounting systems and broad public acceptance of a rule of law.

Many factors go into these societal calculations of the benefits and costs of government activity. Taxes often have efficiency costs that distort behavior in ways less likely to occur with private purchases. Economists also argue that distortions increase exponentially as tax rates increase arithmetically. For example, raising an income tax rate from 0 percent to 1 percent takes away only 1 percent of a taxpayer's current income, whereas raising the rate from 99 percent to 100 percent takes away 100 percent of any remaining incentive to earn income.

On the other hand, I would argue that equity itself, especially in terms of equal justice under the law and some greater equality of opportunity, is more than just a matter of taste: it is a government service that indi-

[6]Robert J. Barro cites 1.75 percent as the per capita growth rate in the United States from 1870 to 1990 and 1.8 percent as the average growth rate for 114 countries between 1960 and 1990. See Barro, "Recent Research on Economic Growth," *NBER Reporter*, Summer 1994.

viduals are willing to purchase if the price is right. This willingness to pay, in turn, means that the efficiency of government action cannot be determined without relating it to both the demand of individuals and the costs that government, as supplier, incurs in attempting to meet it.[7] In my view, there is no sound historical or philosophical basis for knowing the balance level at which the state should be financed at a point in time without giving attention to the demands of individuals and the relative supply capabilities of organizations within each historic period. In the late nineteenth and twentieth centuries, for example, the growth in the efficiency of the large organization—including its ability to combine large groups of individuals in common purpose and to develop increasingly sophisticated accounting systems—made possible the pooling and allocation of resources in ways never before achievable. Thus, the establishment and growth of the income tax was largely dependent on the ability of the corporation or large employee organization to keep an accurate accounting of earnings. Even today, the IRS has trouble enforcing an income tax on farmers and small businesses, which are estimated, in aggregate, to underreport their net income by about one-third or more.

Government growth in many areas was a natural complement to private growth at least in the sense of being led by many of the same, rather than opposing, forces.[8] For instance, the demand and supply of public and of private insurance—both requiring large pools of insured individuals and administrative capabilities to handle them—grew hand in hand. The demand for private pensions may even have grown as the availability of social security led to earlier retirement and vice versa.

By way of contrast, in a period when an economy finds more efficient ways to produce by breaking up large private organizations and provid-

---

[7] In economic theory, this statement implies that individuals' perceptions of equity must be treated independently as among those goods and services that add to their well-being and utility.

[8] As an example of how public and private services may act as complements and respond to the same forces, Gregory Acs and I have found a large, significant correlation between the growth in the private provision of pensions and health insurance and the growth in the public provision of the same items. Part of the correlation, of course, can be attributed to the government's simultaneous increase of public insurance and provision of tax incentives for private insurance. Both public insurance and private insurance, however, were responding to the rising individual demands and the development of institutional capabilities to pool insurance risks and to rely on good earnings records kept by large employer-based organizations. See Gregory Acs and C. Eugene Steuerle, *Trends in the Distribution of Non-Wage Benefits and Total Compensation* (Washington, D.C.: Urban Institute, 1993).

ing greater diversity, large public institutions are also likely to decline in importance. Recently, governments worldwide have attempted to move away from monopoly ownership of such activities as postal services and electricity production, to deregulate airlines and other industries, and to find ways to allow greater flexibility in public services such as education.

From growth financing to reallocative financing. In a period of growth for any set of institutions, the great debates are likely to center on the growth itself. Perhaps this is one reason why liberalism and conservatism came to define themselves so much in the twentieth century around the naive issue of "shares." The issues of how to create new products, new programs, new agencies, and new committees are crucial and usually appropriate focal points. At least in relative terms, new demands in a growth period can be met more easily through increases in resources than through their reallocation. After maturity is reached, however, the debate begins to center more on how well programs are running with what they have and on how resources must be divided, then redivided, among them. It is not surprising that the search for the best practices in the private industrial sector[9] or the effort to create the learning organization in private manufacturing[10] runs in parallel with the attempt to reinvent government.

There are never enough resources available to do all that an individual or society would like to do. Needs, however, change over time, and opportunities expand with a growing economy. Financing mechanisms, therefore, must be designed to reconcile shifts in relative demands and needs with changes in both government and private capabilities of meeting those demands.

When a successful business or government discovers there are fewer new funds available to it, current uses of money become less protected and more inviting targets for financing change. In a period of maturity, restraining some uses of resources to grow at a slower rate becomes relatively more important as a means to finance new uses. Dedicated sources of funds similarly become subject to greater examination. Note, however, that constraints on existing programs do not necessarily have to force the programs into decline. If existing government programs are

---

[9]Michael L. Dertouzos et al., *Made in America: Regaining the Productive Edge* (Cambridge, Mass.: MIT Press, 1990).
[10]Robert H. Hayes et al., *Dynamic Manufacturing: Creating the Learning Organization* (New York: Free Press, 1988).

merely held constant in real terms, for instance, the government's tax share of a growing economic pie—shown above to be the dominant long-run source of financing for domestic programs—becomes increasingly available to finance new efforts and meet new demands.

In the body of this essay, I will briefly examine the recent history of the financing of the American state. This history will support the observation, derived partially from this overview, that domestic programs in the United States and throughout the industrialized world are in a transition period from growth financing to reallocative financing within the domestic programs themselves and that much angst over government and its capabilities reflects this shift in fiscal environments. The shift is in relative, not absolute, terms; that is, as domestic programs as a whole move toward a more stable or cyclical (but not perpetually growing) share of national income, new domestic needs can be financed only through a reallocation within that share. In absolute terms, however, new needs can be financed through economic growth if the revenues available from that growth have not already been spent in ways that prevent such reallocation.

FROM EASY FINANCING TO FISCAL STRAITJACKET: A BRIEF HISTORY

Recent U.S. fiscal history quite starkly reflects a shift in fiscal environments, but it hardly follows a straight-line course. In the United States, the growth financing for domestic programs can be viewed as coming largely from the reallocation of taxes first raised to pay for defense costs in wartime. This section of the essay tells the story, in its simplest form, of how the nation has confronted financing issues over approximately the last half of the twentieth century, as well as the implications at the turn of the century.

In the United States, taxes rose mainly in wartime and stabilized at a fairly constant percent of GDP throughout the post–World War II period. This postwar period can be divided into two parts, the first of which can be labeled the "Easy Financing Era." In this era, government could expand domestic expenditures in ways that seldom required current legislative recognition of who would pay. Defense cuts, little-noticed social security tax increases, and inflationary taxes on holders of government bonds and on income taxpayers each provided the equivalent of hundreds of billions of dollars for Congress and presidents to reallocate. Legislatively, elected government officials appeared magically capable of raising domestic expenditures and cutting taxes without ever appearing to balance the ledger. The payers were hidden or little noticed.

The Easy Financing Era was itself an unusual historical occurrence and began to wane by the mid- to late-1970s. The year 1981 was a watershed year, but mainly in signaling the last legislation adopted under the rules of the old era, not the one to follow. Legislative recognition of the shift in financing regimes occurred in 1982. In that year Congress abandoned the enactment of bills that were primarily deficit-increasing and shifted to bills that almost always were deficit-reducing or at least deficit-neutral.

In the succeeding part of the postwar period, the "Fiscal Straitjacket Era," the mechanisms of easy financing, such as cutbacks in the defense budget, were not so much abandoned as deemphasized. Meanwhile, however, presidents and legislators had become more successful at pre-committing future resources, as reflected in higher percentages of the budget for "mandatory expenditures" and "entitlements" and in increasing portions of the budget financed through dedicated taxes. The combination of prior commitments and waning sources of hidden or automatic funding eventually eliminated fiscal slack and created a situation in which even future budgets, measured at full employment, were significantly in deficit. Legislation in this latter period began to require more explicit recognition of who would pay additional amounts—the "losers" in the political equation. Many of the major pieces of legislation were aimed almost solely at deficit reduction, but other reforms also required more explicit recognition of losers and more elaborate trade-offs among programs.

Two sources of financing began to be used in unprecedented amounts: deficit financing, which was unsustainable and simply forestalled the day of judgment; and, in much of the 1980s, significant cutbacks in those particular forms of expenditures that are hidden in the tax code. Tax reform in 1986 represented perhaps the high point of the latter effort, although the reduction in tax expenditures—sometimes called base-broadening—was used primarily to reduce tax rates.

Although base-broadening was based on such principles as equal treatment of equals and economic efficiency, tax changes in the early 1990s for the most part moved away from this source of financing and involved a more eclectic set of provisions. Many of the easier tax reforms had been achieved, and Congress and Presidents George Bush and Bill Clinton returned to a style of deficit reduction that primarily involved bargaining, mainly within Congress, over items on laundry lists. In the early 1990s no overriding philosophy or principles guided the financing of the American state, either in terms of how much should be financed or in terms of what the financing mechanisms should be. Nor have the most recent presidents sought to find out the implications of such principles through internal means such as the Treasury Department study that led to tax reform in 1986.

In the mid-1990s the nation remained in the era of fiscal straitjackets, helping explain the many recent budget reform efforts of both major political parties. The continued growth of many existing expenditures was promised in earlier decades, thus explaining the politicians' lament that they have no control over how to spend taxes that are collected currently.

Throughout the industrialized world, this "yoke of prior commitments" falls mainly in the area of health benefits and retirement income, which, together with disability, now occupy about half of the U.S. federal expenditures and are projected to occupy an increasing share. Social security and Medicare benefits for an average-income couple retiring today, for instance, now approach $500,000 in value—up from about $100,000 in 1960.[11]

Again following a simple reductio ad absurdum reasoning, the vast expansion in the share of the government budget devoted to health care and retirement—benefits financed mainly by transfers from the young and middle-aged to the near-elderly and elderly—can be shown to be a unique twentieth-century phenomenon that itself must inevitably level out, giving way to using resources for other purposes. Given the level of prior commitments made, the aging of the population, and the middle-class nature of these entitlements, however, this financing dilemma will not be resolved easily.

Although taxes may be raised to help fill the present and future deficit gaps, they are unlikely to be sufficient as long as expenditures shares of national income grow automatically—eventually overwhelming onetime shifts in tax shares. More important, *merely reducing the deficit to manageable size is inadequate to finance the needs of the American state in the future.* Whether accomplished through tax increases or expenditure

[11]C. Eugene Steuerle and Jon M. Bakija, *Retooling Social Security to the Twenty-First Century: Right and Wrong Approaches to Reform* (Washington, D.C.: Urban Institute Press, 1994).

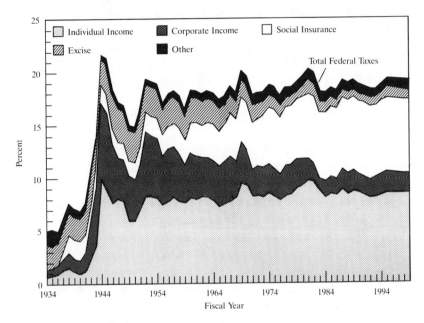

Figure 8.1. Federal tax receipts as percentages of GDP, 1934–99 (C. Eugene Steuerle and Deborah Chien, Urban Institute, 1994; calculations based on Office of Management and Budget, *Budget of the U.S. Government, Historical Tables, Fiscal Year 1995* [Washington, D.C.: Government Printing Office, 1994])

cuts, deficit-cutting meets only one important objective: increasing federal saving (or reducing federal dissaving). It does not free up resources from prior growing commitments to be put toward other needs, such as children, central cities, foreign affairs, or whatever else society deems to be most important. It does not create the necessary fiscal slack.

The Easy Financing Era and its demise. The expansion of the U.S. federal tax system can be traced directly to wartime financing.[12] Figure 8.1 displays federal taxes from 1929 onward and vividly reveals how taxes as a percentage of GDP rose in World War II, fell only moderately after that war was over, rose back up in the Korean conflict, and have fluctuated only modestly ever since. When viewed over this longer horizon, many of the outcomes of the great tax debates that preoccupied the

[12]See W. Elliot Brownlee, chapter 2, this volume, for several historical examples, and Carolyn C. Jones, chapter 3, this volume, on the establishment of the income tax on a mass scale beginning in World War II.

nation are fairly hard to detect, involving only small changes in the average tax rate in the economy.

A constant tax rate in a growing economy, of course, produces enormous amounts of additional revenues. Above we demonstrated the point theoretically. We find that as total real output in the economy quadrupled over the postwar era, so also did federal receipts. Real federal spending on domestic programs, however, multiplied nineteenfold over the same period.[13]

The relative constancy in average tax rates at first belies this occurrence. For our purposes here, we define financing to include almost any way that monies are found to change course or direction. For example, public financing of new programs is achieved not only through taxation but also through reductions in the size of existing programs. Under this broader definition of financing, there were four major means, beyond economic growth, by which various Congresses and presidents were able to fund much legislative activity in the decades after World War II. Each of these financing mechanisms would provide the equivalent of hundreds of billions of dollars annually.

First, there were relative cuts in the size of the defense budget. At the height of the Korean War buildup in 1953, for instance, defense expenditures approximated 14.5 percent of GDP. Although there were various cyclical exceptions such as during the Vietnam War and a modest buildup in the early 1980s, defense spending fell to a level of about 4.2 percent of GDP by 1994. Each percentage point of GDP translated at the end of 1994 to about $70 billion annually that could be spent elsewhere without raising average tax rates.

Second, social security tax increases were large, steady, continual, and little noticed.[14] In 1950, the combined employer-employee tax rate was equal to 3.0 percent; 1960, 6.0 percent; 1970, 9.6 percent; 1980, 12.23 percent; and 1990, 15.3 percent. The rate expansion was so regular, through Republican and Democratic administrations alike, that it can be traced with a simple rule of thumb: 3 percentage points per decade.

[13] Real GDP increased from $1.6 trillion in 1946 to $6.3 trillion in 1993; real receipts increased from $292 billion to $1,154 billion; and real federal domestic outlays grew from $48 billion to $901 billion. Domestic outlays are estimated as total outlays less defense, international affairs, and interest on the debt. Office of Management and Budget, *Budget of the U.S. Government, Historical Tables, Fiscal Year 1995* (Washington, D.C.: Government Printing Office, 1994).

[14] See Edward D. Berkowitz, chapter 4, this volume, for a further examination of the forces behind this expansion.

At 1994 levels of income and the social security tax base in that year, each percentage point translated to about $28 billion annually.[15]

The third and fourth sources were attributable mainly to inflation, which interacted with both monetary policy and tax policy. First, there was the adjustment to a world of more permanent inflation. In the period following World War II, many feared that the country might return to its historic cycles of both deflation and inflation—rather than a world of more permanent inflation. Accordingly, they were willing to buy bonds at fairly low interest rates. After much fluctuation at the end of World War II and during the Korean conflict, the rate of price increase began to rise. As measured by the consumer price index (CPI), the index most observed by the public, inflation reached a high of 13.3 percent in 1979.[16] In contrast, the inflation rate had been less than 2 percent between the end of the Korean conflict and 1966.

Those who bought long-term bonds at low interest rates often found themselves facing inflation rates even higher than the interest rate; for example, those buying at 6 percent interest rates received real interest rates of −2 percent when inflation rose to 8 percent. Rising inflation rates effectively exerted a very large tax on existing bondholders, and the real value of their bonds fell. From the government's perspective, rising inflation rates for a while meant that government could run significant deficits and still find that its ratio of debt to national income would decline. An unexpected increase in inflation of 1 percentage point translated into an initial annual tax at a rate of about ½ of 1 percent of GDP ($35 billion currently) on outstanding debt when that debt was about one-half the level of GDP.[17] For most of the postwar period, public debt held by the private sector exceeded one-half of GDP.

Inflation and real growth in the economy also raised the level of income in the economy and tended to push individuals into higher tax brackets for individual income-tax purposes. In an unindexed, progressive, individual income tax, each 1 percent increase in income raises average individual income-tax rates by more than 1 percent. It was not until after 1984 that income-tax brackets were indexed for inflation (but

---

[15]Net revenues are actually a bit lower, since the income-tax base is eroded by the expansion in the social security tax.

[16]*Economic Report of the President, 1994,* 340.

[17]The gains from a onetime increase are reduced as soon as new instruments begin to replace old ones. That is, the tax applies to interest on government obligations outstanding at the time. New short-term bills, then longer-term notes and bonds, will be sold at higher interest rates to replace those sold at lower inflation rates.

not real growth), thus keeping average tax rates constant for those whose income grew only with inflation. Bracket creep over many years eventually succeeded in raising annual tax collections by hundreds of billions of dollars over and above the additional taxes that would have been available if the average individual income-tax rate had been kept constant with respect to inflation.[18]

Almost all these sources of funds involved little explicit recognition of losers—of who was going to pay. Inflation was indirect and presumably unsought; the taxes it raised required no new legislation. Social security tax increases were little noticed, partly because the system started fairly small, and the increases were often deferred until years after the legislation actually passed. Social security benefits, moreover, were so generous to everyone that until the 1990s, all social security beneficiaries— rich and poor alike—received far more in benefits than they put into the system in the way of taxes and of interest they could have earned on those taxes.[19] Despite modest opposition by defense contractors, defense cuts were largely acceptable to the population because the defense buildups themselves had originally been justified as responses to temporary emergencies.

The four major sources of easy financing were available in such quantities that much of the budget, expenditure, and tax legislation in the first decades following World War II appeared to involve only winners. Winners included those individuals who were identified in legislation to receive such expenditures as expanded welfare or social security benefits, and state and local government officials whose jobs were made easier through increases in revenue sharing. Less recognized were those who paid, such as those who might have had their taxes lowered, instead of being shifted to domestic expenditures, as defense expenditures fell.

On the tax side, total federal taxes remained relatively steady as a percent of GDP as Congress and presidents legislated "winners" through new tax reductions, especially in income taxes, to offset the mor , automatic growth in taxes. Individual income taxes, it turned out, also

---

[18]According to the U.S. Treasury Department, indexing the individual income tax for inflation in the years after 1984 reduced government receipts by $57 billion by fiscal year 1990. Office of Management and Budget, *Budget of the U.S. Government, Fiscal Year 1990* (Washington, D.C.: Government Printing Office, 1989), 4–18. Inflation between 1984 and 1989 equaled 19.2 percent; between 1960 and 1984 alone, it equaled 250 percent. Inflation calculations are based on implicit price deflators for GDP as reported in *Economic Report of the President, 1994*.
[19]Steuerle and Bakija, *Retooling Social Security*.

remained remarkably steady as a percent of GDP, with many legislated tax cuts, particularly in the 1960s, 1970s, and 1981, essentially offset by bracket creep or vice versa. Of course, those who benefited from the legislated tax cuts were not always the same as those who paid more through bracket creep. For example, bracket creep generally reduced the value of the personal exemption, which was very important to families with children, whereas the tax cuts were usually made without regard to family size. The net impact was to shift greater relative burdens onto families with dependents.

Bracket creep and social security tax increases were able to support not only legislated individual income-tax cuts but also a decline in two other federal revenue sources: corporate taxes and excise taxes. Although some of the decline was due to legislation creating new investment incentives or cutting excise taxes, large portions were due to relative declines in corporate profits as a percent of GDP and to excise tax assessments that did not keep pace with inflation and did not extend to many growing parts of the economy, particularly in the service sector.

Still another reflection of the healthy nature of the budget, at least in terms of deficits, was in the measure of the full-employment budget. Throughout the Easy Financing Era, this budget was scheduled to move into surplus in future years. In effect, as long as unemployment rates did not rise too high and the economy was not in recession, maintenance of current law would eventually result in future budgets with receipts in excess of expenditures. Even when new expenditures or cuts in taxes were enacted, they only delayed the coming of projected surpluses. These legislated deficit increases were generally offset within a few years by increases in the easy financing sources of funds. In effect, the future always contained some fiscal slack: growing revenues would provide new opportunities for Congresses to shift resources toward some new or perceived need.

First signs of a turnaround. In the early 1970s, domestic programs continued to expand rapidly. Programs grew partly in fulfillment of the promises enacted under the earlier "War on Poverty." Meanwhile, Vietnam-era defense expenditures were being cut, thus renewing the use of this stalwart source of funding for domestic programs. In 1971 President Richard Nixon even decided to make an expanded "General Revenue Sharing Program" the centerpiece of his "New Federalism." Total federal grants to state and local governments in 1972 dollars rose from $23 billion in 1969 to $37 billion by 1973.[20]

The ratio of the nation's debt to GDP hit its low point in 1974 at the end of the presidency of Richard Nixon—slightly less than three decades after World War II ended.[21] The turnaround in the direction of the debt-to-GDP ratio, which began to head upward after 1974, provided one of the first indicators of a change in financing regimes. The inflation tax on bondholders acts as a tax collector for the government only to the extent of the size of outstanding government debt. As an extreme example, if the debt is zero, rising inflation cannot place any indirect tax on existing government bondholders; by the same token, starting at zero debt, any deficit at all must increase the debt-to-GDP ratio. Thus, with a smaller debt-to-GDP ratio, the government had made itself less dependent on higher inflation rates as a source of financing—even while those rates were continuing to rise.

There were some other signs of change reflected in enactments at the time. Congress, partly in reaction to the impoundment of funds during the Nixon administration, established new budget committees within Congress and also the Congressional Budget Office. Whatever the merits of the battle between the two branches, we can now see both sides as attempting to establish processes and methods for gaining greater control over a budget that was starting to yield fewer future surpluses. By the mid-1970s, federal grants-in-aid to state and local governments also began moving from a growth industry to a cyclical industry. These grants actually fell in real-dollar terms between 1973 and 1974, resumed a more temperate and temporary growth between 1975 and 1981, and then fell again in the early 1980s when general revenue sharing (as opposed to specified grants) was dropped entirely.[22]

By the late 1970s, the monetary authorities began an attack on inflation; their efforts would bear fruit in a period of declining inflation rates throughout the 1980s and early 1990s. These declining inflation rates would turn out to have important implications on the financing of the American state, although it is not clear that much attention was given to these fiscal impacts at the time. Just as rising inflation rates often

[20]U.S. Department of the Treasury, Office of State and Local Finance, *Federal-State-Local Fiscal Relations: Report to the President and the Congress* (Washington, D.C.: Government Printing Office, 1985), 385, 65.
[21]*Economic Report of the President, 1994*, 362; see discussion by Herbert Stein in chapter 5, this volume.
[22]U.S. Department of the Treasury, *Federal-State-Local Fiscal Relations*, 65.

imposed an unexpected tax on holders of old bonds, declining inflation rates would provide them with a windfall. Debt-to-GDP ratios would rise along with effective real government interest payments. Thus, past purchasers of government bonds paying 12 percent interest rates would find themselves with very high rates of return as inflation and interest rates on new bonds fell.

The last gasp of the Easy Financing Era. Although the Federal Reserve had already begun its concerted attack on inflation at the end of the administration of Jimmy Carter—the inflation rate peaked in 1979—Ronald Reagan was elected president partly as a reaction to inflation. Rising inflation rates had been a primary factor in two tax revolts: the first against state and local property taxes in the late 1970s and the second against large increases in individual income taxes, which were rising quite rapidly, especially when inflation hit double digits in 1974, 1979, and 1980. In the individual income tax, a family of four with income at about twice the median income had seen its marginal tax rate—the rate paid on any additional dollar of earnings—double in only thirteen years, from about 22 percent in 1967 to 43 percent in 1980.[23]

President Reagan immediately proceeded to push for a cut in individual tax rates and succeeded in getting those rates reduced by about 23 percent,[24] although some of this cut was offset by bracket creep during the years it was being phased in. Although the net cut was large, it really did no more than offset several years of inflationary tax increases. By 1985, when the cuts were fully phased in, for instance, individual income taxes equaled 8.4 percent of GDP, exactly the same level that had prevailed in 1978, although below the postwar peak of 9.6 percent in 1981.[25]

Among the most important congressional provisions added to the Reagan tax proposals was the indexing of individual income taxes for infla-

[23]Allen H. Lerman, *Average and Marginal Federal Income Tax, Social Security Tax, and Medicare Tax Rates for Four Person Families at the Same Relative Positions in the Income Distribution, 1955–1994* (Washington, D.C.: Office of Tax Analysis, Department of the Treasury, 1993).

[24]Reagan's original proposal would have cut rates by 10 percent over three years. Congress enacted cuts of 10 percent, 10 percent, and 5 percent. Because each succeeding cut was taken against a smaller base, the net cut was equal to 23 percent (90 percent times 90 percent times 95 percent leaves remaining tax rates equal to 77 percent of their original size).

[25]Congressional Budget Office, "What Happened to Deficit Reduction in 1990 and 1993," *Reducing the Deficit: Spending and Revenue Options* (Washington, D.C.: Government Printing Office, 1994), 25.

tion for years after 1984—thus substantially diluting bracket creep as a future source of funds. Real bracket creep, however, would be allowed to remain; few even recognized its existence. Nonetheless, the individual tax cuts in each year up to 1984 and indexing for inflation thereafter combined to remove automatic increases in income taxes as a significant source of financing for other legislation.

Partly because of the exaggerated claims of some supply-siders as to the ability of tax cuts of only a tiny fraction of GDP to produce a booming economy, many have attributed deficits since 1981 to the Reagan tax cuts in 1981. This, I believe, fails to put the tax cuts into a broader historical perspective.

If one examines the tax proposals in 1981 in detail, they turn out largely to resemble, in both size and form, those proposed by President John Kennedy and enacted in the early 1960s. President Kennedy's proposals centered on large reductions in individual tax rates, including a drop in the top rate from 90 percent to 70 percent, and an investment tax credit. He also had included some moderate tax-reform proposals, but they were not at the heart of his Keynesian attempt to boost the economy, and they were later dropped.[26] President Reagan's cuts also centered on rate reductions and an investment incentive, the latter in the form of the Accelerated Cost Recovery System, that is, an accelerated use of deductions for writing off the cost of purchases of physical assets. In a bidding war, Congress later added a number of other provisions, but Reagan's original proposal was confined to the very same two types of proposals that had dominated the Kennedy round.

Neither individual tax reductions nor investment incentives, therefore, were all that original by 1981. In the years after the initial Kennedy round, moreover, the nation witnessed several further individual tax reductions, though of more modest size. Although there was a very temporary surtax to help finance the Vietnam conflict in 1969 through 1970, individuals also received net tax reductions in 1969, 1971, 1975, 1977, and 1978.[27] Similarly, depreciation allowances had been accelerated

[26]See Julian Zelizer, chapter 6, this volume, for a discussion of the efforts of the chairman of the House Ways and Means Committee, Wilbur Mills, to confine the extent of the bill.
[27]The Tax Reform Act of 1969, interestingly enough, billed itself as a long-term tax reduction (mainly for individuals), even though it temporarily extended a 5 percent individual surtax and repealed the investment credit to deal with Vietnam financing. U.S. Congress, Joint Committee on Internal Revenue Taxation, *General Explanation of the Tax Reform Act of 1969* (Washington, D.C.: Government Printing Office, 1970), 13.

three other times, in 1954, 1962, and 1971, and the investment credit had become a permanent part of the law by 1981.[28] Both individual tax cuts and investment incentives could be justified partly as inexact offsets to tax increases due to inflation—the bracket creep discussed above and, for business, the declining value of depreciation allowances at higher rates of inflation.[29] If anything, 1981 represented the culmination, the final act, in that play.

Despite the similarity in form, the justification for the cuts had changed fairly radically: the Kennedy cuts were argued from a Keynesian or demand-side perspective of stimulating the economy; the Reagan cuts were supported from a supply-side perspective of providing greater work and saving incentives. The temporary adoption of supply-side language might be viewed as filling a void that had been left by the gradual aban-donment of Keynesian-style language. Herbert Stein, in this volume, ar-gues that this turn against Keynesian-style language was occurring at almost the same time that the language peaked in bipartisan political acceptance with Nixon's attack on "mechanically balanced budgets" and his later statement, "Now I am a Keynesian in economics."[30] De-spite the change in language, it is clear that President Reagan and some of the supply-siders in his administration looked back on the tax cuts of the early 1960s with nostalgia.

There was one exception to the similarity. In the early 1960s, the long-term deficit would not rise, regardless of whether the Keynesian argu-ment on the stimulative impact of tax cuts was right or wrong. Within a few years, the automatic sources of funds—such as expected declines in the relative size of the defense budget and bracket creep in the indi-vidual income tax—were available in such quantity that the debt-to-GDP ratio would inevitably go down. This was no longer the case by the early 1980s. Put another way, in the 1960s the full-employment budget was always in surplus in the out years. By the 1980s the full-employment budget was always in deficit in the out years. There was no fiscal slack to allocate to future needs; the slack had become negative.

---

[28]C. Eugene Steuerle, *The Tax Decade: How Taxes Came to Dominate the Public Agenda* (Washington, D.C.: Urban Institute Press, 1992), 29. See also Herbert Stein, chapter 5, this volume, for discussion of attempts during the first Nixon administration to tinker with the investment credit.

[29]The cost of the purchase of a depreciable asset is not indexed for inflation, so that depreciation of that cost in future years is worth less as the amount deducted falls in real value.

[30]See Herbert Stein, chapter 5, this volume.

Of the four major sources of funds available in the Easy Financing Era, only social security tax increases remained in any large quantity throughout most of the 1980s—and even those increases were largely due to legislation passed in the late 1970s. Falling inflation rates had made real interest rates on old debt relatively high, and there was a windfall, not a tax, for holders of government debt. The indexing of individual income taxes for inflation (along with lower rates) left little or no bracket creep in the economy. (Technically, real growth in per-household income would cause a modest amount of bracket creep, but limited real growth in taxable wages per worker constrained this effect.) Finally, following on some of President Carter's efforts to raise the defense budget late in his administration, President Reagan temporarily removed the last of the four major sources of funding for domestic programs: declines in the relative size of the defense budget. Whereas the defense budget had declined from a temporary peak of 9.7 percent of GDP in 1968 to 4.8 percent in 1978 and 1979, it rose to another cyclical peak of 6.5 percent of GDP by 1986.[31]

The yoke of prior commitments. Here 1981 represents a watershed year mainly because it hosted the last of the large expenditure increases and tax cuts enacted under the procedures, but not the economic circumstances, of the Easy Financing Era. The gradual elimination of the funding sources, however, was not the only factor that increasingly made such enactments fiscally difficult. On the expenditure side of the ledger, presidents and various Congresses had become more and more adept at enacting programs in such a way that they would grow over time—and in many cases grow faster than the economy—without any further legislation. At the same time, various tax expenditures—such as home mortgage interest deductions, state and local tax deductions, and exclusion of many employee benefits from taxation—would also grow in size without any further legislation.[32]

Some associate this automatic growth with the indexing of programs for inflation. Indexing for inflation, however, is not a factor in the au-

---

[31]Office of Management and Budget, *Budget of the U.S. Government . . . 1995,* 85–87; C. Eugene Steuerle and Susan Wiener, *Spending the Peace Dividend: Lessons from History* (Washington, D.C.: Urban Institute, 1990).

[32]Kent Weaver speaks to some of the issues of automatic government, although he principally dwells on the indexing of programs for inflation. See R. Kent Weaver, *Automatic Government: The Politics of Indexation* (Washington, D.C.: Brookings Institution, 1988).

tomatic *real* growth in program and tax expenditures. Indexing does nothing more than ensure that programs will not be affected by the whims of inflation. Before the modern era of inflation, no one counted on inflation to put programs into decline; this limited type of indexing merely restored to programs the status they had held throughout most of U.S. history, when deflation was expected as much as inflation. The automatic growth in real government payments—due to such factors as increased coverage of new health care services subsidized under both Medicare and the tax exclusion for employer-provided health care—is what eats up the federal revenues growth that accompanies a growing economy. Although in recent years this problem has come to be discussed mainly under the banner of "entitlements," in fact prior commitments can be established in almost any type of program. The newer terminology is due partly to the significant expansion in social transfer payments within the budget. Social welfare types of payments to individuals came to be associated with "rights" or "entitlements"; such language had been applied less frequently to obligations to businesses, whether in the form of contracts or tax subsidies.

Regardless of banner, perhaps the most crucial distinction for fiscal policy is whether a program somehow or other is scheduled to grow over time and, in particular, grow faster than the economy. Two primary examples dominate. Medical care programs of the government fall in the fast-growth category, largely because what is bought and how much is spent are decided by individual clients and their doctors while the payments are made by other individuals through their taxes. That is, at a zero price for the individual, patient demand for new types of health care is unlimited. Social security cash payments, in turn, have grown faster than the economy largely because improvements in health and longevity have meant that a larger share of the population is living to retirement and that people are receiving more years of support in retirement as long as the retirement age is fixed. These cost increases are added to a program already designed to grow as fast as the economy, even in absence of longer lives, through a benefit formula that indexes new awards of annual benefits to grow as fast as individual earnings.[33] At the same time, revenue sources increasingly came to be dedicated, so that the discretionary revenues to the government declined in line with discretionary expenditures.

[33]Steuerle and Bakija, *Retooling Social Security*, chapters 3 and 4.

Trends in discretionary versus entitlement spending reflect these patterns. In 1962, discretionary spending was 13.5 percent of GDP, whereas entitlements and other mandatory spending were less than half that amount, only 5.8 percent of GDP; by 1981, the two groups were of about equal size, with discretionary spending at 10.4 percent of GDP and entitlements and mandatory spending at 11.5 percent of GDP.[34]

Whatever the merits of different programs, locking in growth rates determines in advance how tomorrow's revenues will be spent. It gives to past policymakers the power to allocate increases in revenues made possible by economic growth. When a new real or perceived need of society arises, revenues from a growing economy become less available, are not available at all, or as in the 1980s and 1990s, have already been spent more than once.

Although the yoke of prior commitments was becoming increasingly burdensome throughout the Easy Financing Era, it was largely ignored as long as the defense budget was large and social security, Medicare, and other health outlays were relatively modest in size. To understand why the 1981 enactments added to growing future deficits, therefore, one must consider both the elimination of the prior easy financing sources and the extent to which prior commitments increasingly locked in future expenditures. Some discretionary expenditure cuts also enacted in 1981 were too small and had too little of an impact on these prior commitments to resolve the dilemma.

The Fiscal Straitjacket Era. Whereas 1981 witnessed the last budget enacted under the rules of the Easy Financing Era, the year 1982 legislatively represented year one of the succeeding era, here dubbed the "Fiscal Straitjacket Era." In 1982 Congress passed and the president signed the first of what was to be many deficit-reduction bills. Relative to the size of the GDP, the major deficit-reduction efforts of the following years can be ordered as follows: 1982, 1990, 1993, 1984, and 1987, with a number of lesser enactments in between.[35]

The major deficit-reduction efforts of the 1980s concentrated in large

[34]Congressional Budget Office, *The Economic and Budget Outlook: Fiscal Years 1995–1999* (Washington, D.C.: Government Printing Office, 1994), 93. For a discussion of the evolution of the yoke of prior commitments, see also Joseph Cordes, "The Yoke of Prior Commitments: How Yesterday's Decisions Affect Today's Budget and Fiscal Options," in *The New World Fiscal Order,* ed. C. Eugene Steuerle and Masahiro Kawai (Washington, D.C.: Urban Institute, forthcoming).

[35]This simple ranking may exaggerate the importance of the 1982 bill, since many of its deficit reductions were achieved by disallowing some of the provisions that had been passed in 1981 but that had not yet been phased in.

measure on tax increases, with base-broadening in the income tax as an important component. Both the 1982 and the 1984 bills, especially the former, rescinded or reduced in value some of the business incentives enacted in 1981. These bills also included a number of enforcement provisions, such as expansion in the number of information reports to the government, in areas like capital gains. Much of the base-broadening in the 1982, 1984, and 1987 bills was in the area of business income taxation. The focus on compliance and business income taxation, of course, also helped exclude the broad middle class from paying much directly toward deficit reduction.

The deficit-reduction efforts in the 1990s contrasted with the bills of the 1980s. Most funding in 1990 and 1993 came from three sources: tax increases on the top 1 percent of all taxpayers, defense cuts, and reductions in the rate of growth of Medicare. The Congressional Budget Office estimated that the top 1 percent of the income distribution contributed a large share of all revenue increases in both acts: 37 percent in 1990 and 76 percent in 1993. Defense spending was cut from 5.4 percent of GDP in 1990 to 3.9 percent in 1994 and, to keep within the bounds set by the 1993 agreement, would be reduced to about 3.0 percent by 1999. Of cuts in mandatory spending, 57 percent in 1990 and 73 percent in 1993 were cuts in Medicare.[36] Both bills also contained an assortment of excise taxes and fees and significant increases in an earned income tax credit (EITC) for lower-income workers. There were efforts in 1995, in turn, to avoid most tax increases and focus on non–social security expenditure reduction, including means-tested and welfare programs.

Legislatively and politically, Congress and presidents found themselves in just the opposite situation from the Easy Financing Era. In the earlier period, legislation appeared to identify only the winners, with the losers or payers hidden. In a time of fiscal straitjackets, legislation appears mainly to identify losers, whereas the winners—such as those who receive the higher federal payments to individuals—remain largely hidden because their gains were already scheduled. These winners, indeed, seldom recognize themselves as such. New social security retirees, for instance, hardly ever note that they have higher annual benefits and more years of benefits than older social security retirees, whereas the rapid

---

[36]For a further discussion of this issue, see C. Eugene Steuerle, "Will the Middle Class Pay for the Next Deficit Reduction: Economic Perspective," *Tax Notes*, April 18, 1994, 363–64; Congressional Budget Office, "What Happened to Deficit Reduction in 1990 and 1993?" *Reducing the Deficit*.

growth in real health benefits is viewed simply as part of a health insurance package that was already provided by the government.

It is mainly in new legislation, not existing legislation, that the political calculus of winners and losers is made. In the new era, initiatives had to be financed up front. That is, any type of tax cut or expenditure increase usually had to be paid for fairly immediately by an offsetting tax increase or expenditure cut. At first, these requirements were imposed implicitly, since members of Congress refused to consider or pass bills that added largely to the deficit. Later, the requirements became imbedded in explicit rules such as deficit targets, ceilings, and rules of order on deficit-increasing bills. Perhaps the most famous set of rules with explicit deficit targets was known as Gramm-Rudman-Hollings (GRH), as set in the Balanced Budget and Emergency Deficit Control Act of 1985. The GRH set targets of achieving zero deficits by fiscal year 1991 and required the president to "sequester" or withhold funds if those targets were not met. The targets, indeed, were not met, but Congress then overrode its own GRH requirements. Later rules amended the Balanced Budget Act to make targets more politically attainable and less subject to the whims of fluctuations in the economy.[37] Given a baseline estimate, targets for deficit reduction or total spending by major category (such as discretionary or mandatory) were then set. New discretionary programs and tax reductions had to be paid for on a "pay as you go" (PAYGO) basis, although spending increases under mandatory or entitlement spending were not subject to similar rules. These later amendments came out of other budget agreements, such as those enacted in 1990 and 1993.[38]

---

[37]The Reaffirmation Act of 1987 made GRH deficit targets less stringent and pushed the fiscal year in which the budget had to be balanced from 1991 to 1993. The Budget Enforcement Act (BEA) of 1990 again raised GRH deficit targets and no longer mandated a balanced budget, since it required only a reduction in the deficit by 1995. The BEA also required deficit targets to be adjusted periodically for changes in economic assumptions and budgetary concepts and definitions. For further details, see Office of Management and Budget, "The Evolution of Budgeting in the United States" (unpublished paper, 1994), and Allen Schick, Robert Keith, and Edward Davis, *Manual on the Federal Budget Process* (Washington, D.C.: Congressional Research Service, 1991).

[38]The BEA of 1990 created discretionary spending caps that are adjusted for changes in inflation, budget concepts and definitions, and estimates of credit subsidy costs. The BEA also created the PAYGO process, which requires that any legislation increasing mandatory spending or decreasing revenues be offset by spending cuts or increased revenues. PAYGO does not require offsets when increased spending or reduced revenues are due to existing law, such as an increase in the number of participants in the Medicare program. Most mandatory spending programs are established under permanent law; thus PAYGO does affect their growth. The Omnibus Reconciliation Act of 1993 extended

In "deficit-neutral" types of bills, note that there were as many "losses" created as "winnings." Now add to these bills the many deficit-reduction efforts—which identified only "losses," or at least more "losses" than "winnings." Using crude arithmetic, we can see that the combination of these two types of enactments meant that legislation as a whole in this era recognized more losses than winnings. The job of elected officials was the reverse of that required in the Easy Financing Era: now they had to decide legislatively who was going to pay more taxes or receive fewer expenditures.

New and old sources of financing. The fiscal pressures of the new era cried for some relief. Higher deficits—more borrowing at home and abroad—can be viewed as one means that was adopted to fund expenditures. Not only was this source of relief temporary, of course, but the higher levels of interest payments on the debt would inevitably lead to reduced expenditures, higher taxes, or both.

A second source was perhaps less expected. Tax expenditures—those expenditures hidden in the tax code—came under attack. As noted above, a significant portion of the financing achieved in all of the deficit-reduction efforts of the 1980s came from a cutback in the size of these expenditures. In addition, as will be discussed in further detail below, two of the major reforms of the era—social security reform in 1983 and tax reform in 1986—also relied on reductions in tax expenditures.

Most tax expenditures are similar to direct entitlements in that both are made permanent, both dodge the annual appropriations process, and both grow in value over time. Given the difficulty that Congress has in dealing with direct entitlements, what explains its greater ability to reduce tax entitlements in the 1980s? At least three related factors probably combined to bring cutbacks in tax expenditures to the fore as a major source of funding in the 1980s.

First, there was a simple reaction to the excesses of the 1970s and 1981. In particular, the growth in the tax shelter market led to concerns over the fairness of the tax system, the efficiency of economic investment, and the ability of the IRS to administer the tax system.

Second, given the fiscal pressures, tax expenditure cuts may initially have been more acceptable politically than the other principal options,

the BEA provisions, which would previously have expired in 1995 to 1998. For further details, see Office of Management and Budget, "Evolution of Budgeting," and Schick, Keith, and Davis, *Manual on the Federal Budget Process.*

which were mainly (but not entirely) dodged: tax rate increases and cuts in other entitlements. Tax rate increases were also opposed by Presidents Reagan, Bush, and Clinton, with an exception in the last case for the very highest income taxpayers. Perhaps no other governmental change so obviously affects the middle class as an across-the-board increase in tax rates. Direct entitlements are also middle-class intensive, since they are dominated by various forms of old age, health, and disability insurance. Many of the tax expenditure cutbacks in the 1980s, on the other hand, concentrated on business income taxation. Cathie Jo Martin, in this volume, stresses that business is often a weaker constituency.[39]

This second explanation, however, can be given only so much weight. A number of tax expenditure cuts did affect the middle class. Fees and excise taxes were raised in most deficit-reduction bills. Discretionary spending cuts would also take place during this period. Some broader tax and social security reforms did reduce tax expenditures available to the middle class.

In considering what Congress might have found to be the most palatable among many poor-tasting options, we must also note a third factor: the unique status of the tax-writing committees and of the Treasury Department. Throughout the Fiscal Straitjacket Era, all major budget, tax, and expenditure legislation has been dominated by the tax-writing committees of Congress. The jurisdiction of these committees is widespread: they are in charge of all taxes, those one-third to one-fourth of expenditures hidden in the tax code, and what may be surprising, more direct expenditures than the appropriations committees.[40]

Charged with bearing some share in reducing the deficit, the committees may have given greater weight to reduction of tax expenditures simply because of the ammunition provided them by the Treasury Department and the Joint Committee on Taxation. The problems of many tax expenditures had been aired for years and were viewed as making the tax system unduly complex. In contrast, direct expenditures were often broadly supported by other departments of government. In the case of tax reform, of course, nontax options were off the table for a Treasury

---

[39]See Cathie Jo Martin, chapter 7, this volume.
[40]One estimate put total tax expenditures in 1988 at $315 billion even after the many reforms of that decade. See Thomas Neubig and David Joulfaian, "The Tax Expenditure Budget before and after the Tax Reform Act of 1986," *Office of Tax Analysis Paper 60* (Washington, D.C.: U.S. Department of the Treasury, 1988).

Department examining only programs under its own jurisdiction: Tax rates could be cut only with reductions in tax expenditures.

The complexity of some direct entitlement issues may also have contributed to the emphasis first on tax entitlements. Congress tried several times to confront the direct entitlement that has the largest growth rate—health—but with only limited success. Indeed, the pattern was the same on both the direct and the tax expenditure sides of the budget. The main tax expenditure for health—the exclusion from taxation for employer-provided health benefits—stayed even more immune to reform than many direct health expenditures. The inability to enact significant or well-designed health reform—a fiscally sound Medicare system, catastrophic health care for the elderly in 1987–88, or major health reform for the nonelderly in 1993–94—may also be a function of the complex multicommittee jurisdiction that surrounded those bills.

By the end of the 1980s, both Congress and the succeeding presidents largely turned away from cutbacks in tax expenditures. No longer were "base-broadening," "simplifying the tax code," or "equal taxes for taxpayers with equal incomes" goals to be achieved. Cleaning up the tax code became increasingly uninteresting partly because politically easier targets had already been hit and partly because Presidents Bush and Clinton were lukewarm to traditional tax-reform principles and wanted to add their own breaks to the code. With the end of the cold war, the renewed availability of cutbacks in the defense budget also temporarily reduced the pressure to find alternative sources of funds. Except for fees, gasoline tax increases, further taxation of some social security benefits, and a paring of Medicare growth rates, most of the middle class would again be unaffected by the deficit-reduction efforts of the 1990s, just as they had usually been exempted in the 1980s.

This section on sources of financing in the Fiscal Straitjacket Era would be incomplete if it did not return again to economic growth. Although many "apparent losers" were created during the many efforts at deficit reduction in this era, one must distinguish between economic and political measures of winners and losers. The economy grew modestly throughout this period, even if the lower economic growth rates of the late twentieth century reduced the corresponding rate of growth in new revenues available to the government. On average, people became richer even while some became poorer and even though some measures, such as cash wages per full-time worker, stagnated at times. On average, people also received more in the way of government benefits and transfers. Adjusted for inflation, for instance, real federal payments per individual rose from $1,828 in 1981 to $2,370 in 1993, or by close to 30 percent over those twelve years.[41]

Making trade-offs: Further examination of three reform efforts of the Fiscal Straitjacket Era. As noted, legislation changed dramatically in content and form in this era of fiscal stringency. Government, however, did not come to a standstill. The deficit-reduction efforts, however incomplete, represented one reaction. Three reform efforts of this period also reveal a good deal about how policymakers reacted to the new fiscal pressures.

First, social security reform in 1983 demonstrated that "entitlements" were never entirely off the table. For perhaps the first time ever, Congress and the president in 1983 agreed to a significant paring in the rate of growth of social security cash benefits for the elderly. The political justification for immediate action was important: the trust funds had insufficient revenues to pay out promised expenditures within the next few years. Since many people wanted to receive their checks, they had less problem accepting reform.

The 1983 enactment, however, went far beyond the short-term goal of paying benefits for the next few years. It attempted to restore financial solvency over the long term as well. It increased the normal retirement age (the age at which full benefits are available) from sixty-five to sixty-seven over a period of approximately two decades beginning at the start of the next century. A significant middle-income tax expenditure was also reduced: social security benefits of some recipients were made subject to taxation for the first time. In effect, this reduced the after-tax value of benefits.

Although tax rate increases on workers were also enacted, they mainly involved an acceleration of increases already scheduled. As a consequence, the decade from 1990 to 2000 eventually came to be the first in over a half-century in which there were no scheduled increases in the social security tax rate. Congress did turn, in both 1990 and 1993, to social security base expansion, primarily by increasing the level of earn-

[41]Adjusted for inflation, real payments to individuals rose from $420.5 billion in 1981 to $611.9 billion in 1993, whereas the population grew from 230.0 million to 258.2 million. See Office of Management and Budget, *Budget of the U.S. Government . . . 1995*, 86–87, and *Economic Report of the President, 1994*, 307.

ings subject to Medicare tax. These changes, however, were quite modest when compared with the tax rate increases of the past.

Tax reform in 1986 presented a second model for the types of reforms that would be required not simply during this new era but during any era in which the easy sources of financing were not so readily, or even automatically, available. Tax reform was really the first major reform to set a constraint of "deficit-neutrality": the requirement that tax reductions or expenditure increases be offset by tax increases or expenditure cuts so that the bill would not increase the deficit. Such a constraint technically was not required by the budget rules in 1984, when a Treasury study on reform was first released, but some of the architects of proposals, including myself, strenuously argued that this was the only way that tax reform stood a chance of being considered. This standard would be followed and eventually required under budgetary rules for most succeeding legislation.

In the tax reform bill, cutbacks in tax shelters, the elimination of several credits and deductions, and the paring in value of several types of deductions and exclusions provided the sources of funds necessary to pay for rate reduction, increases in personal exemptions, elimination of income taxation for most of the poor, and expansion of an earned income tax credit (EITC).[42] Although many of the reforms were incomplete and much simplification was abandoned by the time the process ended, this effort still resulted in the reduction from $509 billion to $315 billion, or almost $200 billion annually, in the value of various tax expenditures.[43] According to John Witte, seventy-two provisions tightened tax expenditures, and fourteen tax expenditures were repealed, "a figure approximately equal to the total that had been repealed from 1913 to 1985."[44]

The health-reform effort of 1994 represented the third area in which new fiscal realities tended to dictate what could and would be proposed. Despite the eventual failure of the effort as a comprehensive measure, almost all of the proposals put forward by both political parties attempted to achieve deficit-neutrality in the first years by taking expen-

---

[42]Further details on many of the enactments of the 1980s, especially tax reform, can be found in Steuerle, *The Tax Decade.*

[43]Much of that reduction was due to the lesser value of these tax expenditures at lower tax rates rather than to their outright elimination. See Neubig and Joulfaian, "The Tax Expenditure Budget."

[44]John F. Witte, "The 1986 Tax Reform: A New Era in Politics?" *American Politics Quarterly,* October 1991.

ditures made available through large projected growth rates in existing health programs and then transferring those gains to other purposes, such as subsidies for low-income purchasers of insurance. The health debate itself was engaged in no small part because of the requirement to bring government health expenditures under control. By the same token, many believe that its failure lay in still giving inadequate attention to the cost issues. The initial administration proposals attempted mainly to promise that almost everyone—the uninsured, the partially insured, small businesses, large businesses bearing health-cost shifts, the elderly— would win without paying. In a fiscally constrained world, this required that budgetary problems be handled through the back door of mandates and cost controls.

In all three reform efforts, estimates became a dominating factor. The power of the estimator—the person who made point estimates of proposed changes in revenues and expenditures—was enhanced, often in ways undesired by both the legislator and the estimator. If a member of Congress could not get provisions to add up in a way that met the deficit constraints and budget rules of the era, his or her proposals would not be considered.

Social security reform relied heavily on estimates of whether there would be a seventy-five year balance in the trust funds. Commitment to this standard meant that income to the trust funds, plus interest on the money in those funds, had to be sufficient to pay out benefits for seventy-five years. This standard, more than any other factor, forced attention to longer-run issues. Even the incompleteness of the 1983 reform effort is often measured by the same seventy-five-year standard. Among the reasons for the incompleteness were that economic assumptions underlying the estimates were too optimistic and that inadequate attention was paid to years beyond seventy-five—large deficit years that would fall into the calculation as time passed.

Tax reform, in turn, depended on estimates of both revenues and distribution. The goals of revenue and distributional neutrality meant that revenue increases and decreases in each income class had to be of approximately the same size. This often implied that one amendment to a package required several others, to restore the revenue and distributional goals. Here there was also a long-term standard, but of a different type: the standard that lower rates and a broader tax base would promote equity and long-term efficiency in the economy.

The health reform effort stretched estimation to its limits and greatly constrained what Congress could enact. Congressional and executive branch estimators could only guess at the efficacy of price controls on private sector health premiums or at the cost-effectiveness of attempts to establish market incentives. Yet such reforms were at the heart of the debate. Congressional Budget Office (CBO) statements often forced would-be reformers back to the drawing boards. The CBO's analyses, for instance, frequently indicated that certain expenditure or revenue options might not be administrable; another influential decision was that mandated payments by employers would be treated as receipts of the government. All of these analyses had strong effects on the final outcome.

Regardless of one's assessment of the success or value of these efforts, they clearly indicate a different type of policy-making than that of the Easy Financing Era. Reallocative financing had become far more important than growth financing, whether to move toward greater system balance (as in social security), to reduce tax rates and taxes on the poor (as in tax reform), or to make new expenditure initiatives (as in health reform). Thus, all three of these reform efforts tried to rely heavily on some form of domestic expenditure or tax expenditure reduction to help finance the changes being sought. In addition, changes had to be financed more directly within each reform bill itself. Concerns over financing had forced policymakers to develop much more comprehensive packages, to tie financing and expenditure issues together in the same bills, to make trade-offs across a fairly broad spectrum, and to depend heavily on estimators to indicate whether proposals fit within budgetary rules.

TOWARD THE TWENTY-FIRST CENTURY

Today the nation remains in a fiscal straitjacket, one that will not be removed simply by achieving temporary deficit reduction targets. The absence of fiscal slack—or future full-employment budget surpluses, even in the presence of real revenue growth—denies future legislators the power to choose how to allocate new revenues as they deem most appropriate.

Fiscal crises, however, are also times of opportunity. Government, after all, will adapt, one way or another. One type of response is centered narrowly on legislative changes in expenditures, taxes, or both for the next few years. Government can also adapt through directional changes, that is, changes in the processes, methods, and standards by which choices are made. The adoption of assorted budgetary rules, expenditure caps, and limits on the introduction of legislation, as well as the creation of a Congressional Budget Office—represent important but fledgling attempts at such directional change.

Ignoring prior commitments, the temporary economic pressures on the budget actually are relatively light at the end of the century. No world threat, depression, or other major crisis demands large fiscal resources. As documented by Elliot Brownlee in this volume, the creation of distinct tax regimes was often the consequence of a crisis imposed from the outside.[45] The current fiscal crisis, however, is almost entirely self-imposed. Demographically, the last decade of the twentieth century and the first decade of the twenty-first century represent a period of calm. A large group of baby boomers now occupies the labor force and provides financing for the relatively small group of baby busters—those born in the Great Depression and World War II—who are now filling the ranks of the elderly. The country still benefits from the end of the cold war, providing probably the last use of the defense budget to finance expanding domestic programs.

Soon this economic reprieve will end. The country will no longer be able to rely on defense cuts. Meanwhile, the elderly population will swell in the next century as the baby boomers become older while a declining share of the population will occupy the labor force as another group of baby busters begins to displace the baby boomers. The ratio of working-age individuals to elderly will fall dramatically.

The problems can be seen in the nation's programs for retirement, health, and disability. From 1950 to the mid-1990s, these programs climbed from about 10 percent of federal expenditures to over 50 percent. (See Figure 8.2.) That ratio is scheduled to continue climbing mainly because of current large growth rates in health expenditures and the need in the next century to cover both retirement and Medicare expenses for the baby boomers as they age. As a percentage of the population, persons aged sixty-five and over will remain between 12 percent and 13 percent between 1990 and 2010, then jump to 20 percent or more in the years after 2030. The United States, however, is hardly alone; many industrialized countries face the same or worse demographic pressures. They too are constrained by prior commitments that

---

[45]W. Elliot Brownlee, chapter 2, this volume.

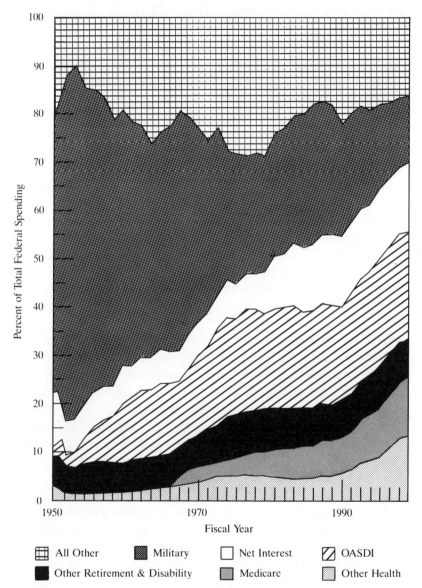

Figure 8.2. Change in the composition of the federal budget, 1950–99 (C. Eugene Steuerle and Deborah Chien, Urban Institute, 1994; data based on Office of Management and Budget, *Budget of the U.S. Government, Historical Tables, Fiscal Year 1995* [Washington, D.C.: Government Printing Office, 1994] and President Bill Clinton FY1995 budget proposal)

preclude much governmental action toward dealing with new issues and problems.

In parallel with the twentieth-century growth in domestic expenditures, the phenomenal growth in the share of the budget devoted to retirement and health represents another trend that can never again be replicated, in spite of looming demands. These expenditures are not going to rise to over 90 percent or 100 percent of the federal budget. From a broader perspective, the vast expansion in share of national resources devoted to retirement and health is also likely to represent a unique twentieth-century phenomenon.

Despite the favorable economic conditions affecting the budget at the end of the twentieth century, the self-imposed fiscal straitjacket politically ties up the nation's policy-making. The yoke of prior commitments leaves no room for handling emergencies or for dealing with important social problems. Again, this can be seen in projections of mandatory versus discretionary spending. Although mandatory spending and discretionary spending were of about equal size around 1980, by 1993 mandatory spending had grown to 12.1 percent of GDP while discretionary spending had fallen to 8.6 percent.[46] By 2004, current projections show mandatory spending climbing to 14.1 percent of GDP and discretionary spending falling yet farther to 6.0 percent.

These numbers will become even worse when the upcoming demographic shift adds to the retirement, health, and disability demands that accompany an aging population. So far, however, many of the issues are being ignored. The health reform proposals of 1994, for instance, dodged the intermediate- and long-term problem of trying to restore balance to the Medicare trust funds; even social security was ignored in 1995 budget efforts.

Certainly taxes may be increased to deal with some of these needs. As long as expenditure growth rates continue to rise inexorably faster than economic growth rates, however, tax increases can never fully close the deficit gap. Even if they could, merely reducing the deficit to manageable size is inadequate to finance the needs of the American state in the future. Deficit cuts, in turn, are aimed primarily at saving objectives. By restricting the flows of public debt, they make saving more available for other purposes such as private investment, and they reduce the impact of interest payments on future budgets. Lower deficits, by themselves, do not

[46]Congressional Budget Office, *Economic and Budget Outlook . . . 1995–1999*, 93.

provide the financing necessary to meet any of the nation's new crises and needs. That is, if deficits under current law are merely made manageable, there would still be no fiscal slack. If children, central cities, a foreign crisis, or any other need is to take precedence, the yoke of prior commitments must be broken.

Conclusion: Toward the creation of fiscal slack. From easy financing to fiscal straitjacket has been the course of the last half of the twentieth century. Both eras have led to misleading perceptions of how government is financed, with the first era hinting that government actions required no new resources and the second suggesting that no new resources were available.

The primary source of additional government financing over the long term is an expanding economic pie, whether the government's tax share is increasing or decreasing. In one year, the fiscal benefits of economic growth may seem modest, but over the course of decades, it means that revenues will multiply. In economic terms, then, money has always been made available in increasing quantities to policymakers—although not necessarily in the profusion of the Easy Financing Era.

The major fiscal and budgetary issue at the end of the century is whether past or current policymakers control the use of those additional resources. The nation's fiscal straitjacket will remain until there is some fiscal slack—the allowance of some leeway to policymakers in each period to rank which current needs are most important.

How might this be achieved? Since this chapter focuses primarily on recent fiscal history and its broad implications for the future, I have been reluctant so far to speculate on exactly what new mechanisms might be involved. At the same time, I have argued that the near future may see important directional shifts beyond simple changes in expenditures and taxes in various budget bills. For the sake of clarification, therefore, let me point to some directional shifts that could have a profound influence in moving the nation out of its fiscal straitjacket. All of them really do nothing more than limit the yoke of prior commitments through implicit or explicit budget rules. Among the possibilities are the following:

1. Adoption of processes and rules that would limit the ability of policymakers to build real growth into programs in the long run, for

example, rules that no bill can contain significant deficit increases after five years

2. Restrictions on the built-in real growth rate of existing programs, for example, requirements that programs not grow faster than inflation, or at least the economy, over the long run without future legislative action

3. Automatic review of most direct entitlements and tax entitlements on a periodic basis, with new legislation required to renew or reestablish them

4. Enforcement of balance in all trust funds (e.g., through a guaranteed presidential veto or a floor rule forbidding the adoption of a budget for any program imbalanced in the long run)

5. A line-item veto, which gives a president power not simply to reduce a deficit but to threaten veto if certain shifts in expenditures do not occur

These process changes may at first appear esoteric, but they are capable of working the nation out of its current fiscal straitjacket within a few years. Indeed, through the creation of fiscal slack, they would provide much greater flexibility for future fiscal policy to respond to current needs. When Alexander Hamilton helped convince a reluctant nation that it must set a standard of paying off its debt, he set in motion a process that similarly enhanced the fiscal capabilities of the government—yet without complete knowledge as to what would be done with those capabilities.

A final warning is in order: The creation of fiscal slack makes the reallocations required in the twenty-first century easier to accomplish politically; it provides no guarantee that they will be done well. Future policymakers will still need to decide how to divide and use the resources made available to government by economic growth. Uncommitted resources may provide greater freedom to choose, but greater freedom in fiscal policy-making does not guarantee greater responsibility. The requirement for diligence is not bound by eras.

Funding for this chapter was provided in part by the Ford Foundation. Opinions expressed are those of the author and should not be attributed to the Urban Institute, its officers, or its sponsors.

About the authors

EDWARD D. BERKOWITZ is Professor of History at George Washington University. He is the author of *Mr. Social Security: The Life of Wilbur J. Cohen* (1995), *America's Welfare State: From Roosevelt to Reagan* (1991), and *Disabled Policy: America's Programs for the Handicapped* (1987), and coauthor of *Social Security and Medicare: A Policy Primer* (1993), *Group Health Association* (1988), and *Creating the Welfare State* (1980).

W. ELLIOT BROWNLEE is Professor of History at the University of California, Santa Barbara, and a former Fellow of the Woodrow Wilson International Center for Scholars. He is currently writing a history of the financing of World War I in the United States.

CAROLYN C. JONES is Professor of Law at the University of Connecticut School of Law. She has written articles on the legal history of taxation in the United States on topics ranging from taxation arguments in the woman suffrage movement to the use of public relations in the selling of the mass federal income tax.

CATHIE JO MARTIN is Assistant Professor of Political Science at Boston University. She is the author of *Shifting the Burden: The Struggle over Growth and Corporate Taxation* (1991) and a forthcoming book on business and the politics of social innovation.

HERBERT STEIN is a Senior Fellow of the American Enterprise Institute for Policy Research. He was a member of the president's Council of Economic Advisers, 1969–71, and its chairman, 1972–74. He is the author of *Presidential Economics,* rev. ed. (1994), *The Fiscal Revolution in America,* rev. ed. (1990), *Governing the $5 Trillion Dollar Economy* (1989), and, with Murray Foss, *The New Illustrated Guide to the American Economy* (1995).

C. EUGENE STEUERLE, Senior Fellow of the Urban Institute, is the author of a weekly column for *Tax Notes* magazine, a former Deputy Assistant Secretary of the Treasury, and the original organizer and economic coordinator of the Treasury Department's 1984–86 tax-reform effort. His books include *Retooling Social Security for the Twenty-first Century* (1994, coauthored with John Bakija) and *The Tax Decade* (1991).

JULIAN E. ZELIZER is a Research Fellow of the Brookings Institution. He is completing his dissertation, "Taxing America: Wilbur Mills and the Culture of Fiscal Policy, 1949–1969," in the Department of History at Johns Hopkins University.

Index

447